Sino-Foreign Cultural Exchange

Understanding culture as a whole way of life, this book touches on various aspects of Sino-foreign interactions, tracing cultural exchanges depicted in Chinese and foreign sources, with particular attention to events or anecdotes in the Tang and Qing periods.

In addition to a discussion of the Sogdians and Turks in medieval China, an investigation of the localization process of pugs and lions through different Chinese dynasties, an analysis of the incorporation of Manichaeism into Chinese culture, and the depiction of the "Kunlun slaves" in Chinese Buddhist texts, this book also examines the "caravan tea" trade between Russia and China, the Russian-American company's attempt to do business in Canton, the translation of the *Three Character Classic* in Russia, the "Russian case" in the Tianjin missionary incident, as well as the Dutch factory in Canton and the Dutch mission in Beijing. This book concludes with a discussion of Chinese workers in Southeast Asia in the late nineteenth and early twentieth centuries. From Central Asia to the South China Sea to the northern border with Russia, this book reveals its great diversity, yet with an intense focus on China's interactions with the outside world.

This book will be essential reading for students and scholars of Chinese studies, medieval Central Asian studies, and those interested in world history.

Cai Hongsheng was Professor of History at Sun Yat-sen University, China. He specialized in the history of Sino-foreign relations, particularly the research about ancient Turks and Buddhism in the Tang period, and the Canton trade in the Qing dynasty.

China Perspectives

The *China Perspectives* series focuses on translating and publishing works by leading Chinese scholars, writing about both global topics and China-related themes. It covers Humanities & Social Sciences, Education, Media and Psychology, as well as many interdisciplinary themes.

This is the first time any of these books have been published in English for international readers. The series aims to put forward a Chinese perspective, give insights into cutting-edge academic thinking in China, and inspire researchers globally.

To submit proposals, please contact the Taylor & Francis Publisher for China Publishing Programme, Lian Sun (Lian.Sun@informa.com).

Titles in history currently include:

The History of Chinese Presence in Nigeria (1950s-2010s)
Factories, Commodities, and Entrepreneurs
Shaonan Liu

The Indigenization of Christianity in China I
1807–1922
Qi Duan

A Cultural History of the Chinese Character "Ta (她, She)"
Invention and Adoption of a New Feminine Pronoun
Huang Xingtao

A Concise History of China's Population
Jianxiong Ge

Sino-Foreign Cultural Exchange
A Historical Perspective
Cai Hongsheng

For more information, please visit https://www.routledge.com/China-Perspectives/book-series/CPH

Sino-Foreign Cultural Exchange
A Historical Perspective

Cai Hongsheng

LONDON AND NEW YORK

This work has been generously supported by the Chinese Fund for the Humanities and Social Sciences in 2021 (21WGJB003).

First published 2024
by Routledge
4 Park Square, Milton Park, Abingdon, Oxon OX14 4RN

and by Routledge
605 Third Avenue, New York, NY 10158

Routledge is an imprint of the Taylor & Francis Group, an informa business

© 2024 Cai Hongsheng

Translated by Wu Lanxiang and Yu Aixia

The right of Cai Hongsheng to be identified as author of this work has been asserted in accordance with sections 77 and 78 of the Copyright, Designs and Patents Act 1988.

All rights reserved. No part of this book may be reprinted or reproduced or utilised in any form or by any electronic, mechanical, or other means, now known or hereafter invented, including photocopying and recording, or in any information storage or retrieval system, without permission in writing from the publishers.

English Version by permission of Elephant Press Ltd.

Trademark notice: Product or corporate names may be trademarks or registered trademarks, and are used only for identification and explanation without intent to infringe.

British Library Cataloguing-in-Publication Data
A catalogue record for this book is available from the British Library

Library of Congress Cataloging-in-Publication Data
Names: Cai, Hongsheng, 1933–2021, author.
Title: Sino-foreign cultural exchange : a historical perspective / Cai Hongsheng.
Other titles: Zhong wai jiao liu shi shi kao shu. English
Description: New York : Routledge, 2024. |
Series: China perspectives | Includes bibliographical references and index. |
Identifiers: LCCN 2023028181 (print) | LCCN 2023028182 (ebook) | ISBN 9781032611860 (hardcover) | ISBN 9781032616384 (paperback) | ISBN 9781032616353 (ebook)
Subjects: LCSH: China—Foreign relations.
Classification: LCC DS740.4 .C22313 2024 (print) | LCC DS740.4 (ebook) DDC 327.51—dc23/eng/20230825
LC record available at https://lccn.loc.gov/2023028181
LC ebook record available at https://lccn.loc.gov/2023028182

ISBN: 978-1-032-61186-0 (hbk)
ISBN: 978-1-032-61638-4 (pbk)
ISBN: 978-1-032-61635-3 (ebk)

DOI: 10.4324/9781032616353

Typeset in Times New Roman
by codeMantra

Contents

Foreword   vii
Acknowledgments   xiii

1 Tributes from the Nine Surnames of the Sogdians in the Tang Period   1

2 Rituals and Customs of the Nine Surnames of the Sogdians in the Tang Period   32

3 "Seven" as a Venerated Number among the Nine Surnames of the Sogdians in the Tang Period   63

4 The Mu Sogdians in the Tang Period   74

5 Worship of Fire and Sky among the Ancient Turks   90

6 Legal Practice in the Turkic Khaganate   104

7 Local Products of the Turks   134

8 Tracing the History of Pugs   144

9 Lions in China   156

10 Variation of Manichaeism in the Coastal Areas during the Tang and Song Periods   176

11 The Kunlun Slaves in Buddhist Books of the Tang and Song Periods   185

12	"Caravan Tea"	198
13	Russian-American Company and the Canton Port	228
14	"Qin Huan" from the Russian Hotel	254
15	The *Three Character Classic* in Russia	259
16	The "Russian Case" in the Tianjin Missionary Incident	262
17	The Dutch Factory in Canton during the Qing Period	270
18	Wang Wengao's Historical Poems about the Dutch Tribute	290
19	Chinese Workers in Southeast Asia Before 1912	308
	Index	*339*

Foreword

When Professor Wu Lanxiang approached me to join this translation project in 2021, I was very pleased to accept the invitation. I met Professor Cai Hongsheng more than 20 years ago, when he invited me to give a lecture in his graduate class. Since then, I have been involved in many lectures and conferences in which Cai participated and helped to organize. I have come to appreciate his devotion to detail and his uncanny ability to extract historical data from a wide range of disparate sources, in various languages. His knowledge of China's long history of interactions with outside peoples is far reaching and spans several centuries.

In the chapters that follow, Cai takes us on a geographical journey through space and time. He begins in the Tang dynasty with a discussion of the "Nine Surnames of the Sogdians." The Sogdians were tribal people who traded with China under the so-called tribute system. By extracting minute details from tribute letters and other available records, we learn a great deal about these individuals. He discusses the routes they traveled, the structure of their families and tribes, religious practices, and the various animals that they raised, including horses, lions, and dogs. The Sogdians brought a variety of items to China including peaches, tulips, indigo, brass, salt, agates, carpets, textiles, utensils, and food such as honey and wine.

In Chapters 2–10, Cai goes into greater depth about all aspects of the lives of the tribal people in Central Asia and their interactions with China. We learn that the Sogdians "have no marriage rituals" and that the wives have the final say within the family. Funerals were accompanied by the sacrificial slaying of livestock and the cutting of one's face, hair, and ears. Black was the appropriate attire for a funeral, while white is reserved for auspicious occasions.

Cai shows us that there were three types of nuptial arrangements, namely, legal marriage, concubines, and cohabitation. Under certain circumstances, the wife and husband were allowed to divorce each other and remarry. Sogdians learned how to trade at a very early age, with training beginning at five years old. When men reached the age of 20, they were well prepared to begin their travels to other countries. A man's status within society and his reputation were closely connected to his skill in trading and accumulating wealth.

In society and religion, auspicious numbers were important. Various Zoroastrian rituals were conducted over "seven" days, and exorcising might take place in the "seventh" month. Creation had "seven" stages and meditative devotion to the founder of Zoroastrianism, and the "seven" holy immortals might be performed over "seven" years. Other auspicious numbers were 10, 12, and 72.

Surnames were important to tribal people, because they were a direct connection back to their ancestral lineages. The Sogdians originated from one of the "Nine Surnames of Zhaowu." Cai points out, however, that it is not always easy to identify the different tribes from the Chinese records. Over time, different characters might be used to transliterate Sogdian names making it difficult to identify their lineages.

Cai retraces the origin of Zoroastrian fire worship and sorcery back to the middle of the sixth century. Various Buddhist texts, as well as Chinese dynastic records from Zhou, Sui, and Tang, discuss the early religion of the Turkish people. Cai pieces together the Shaman doctrine that includes the heavenly realm of stars, sun, moon, and planets; the human world which is the sorcerers' domain; and an underworld with various spirits and goblins. Sorcerers and sorceresses were the mediators between the different realms utilizing various instruments, spells, and rituals to correct imbalances in cosmology.

The Turks of Central Asia had an established set of legal traditions as well. The practice referred to as "delimited land" restricted certain grazing areas to specific tribes. This was very important because livestock needed daily access to water and pasture, and any interruption in that access could be devastating to their entire community. Each tribe had their own "livestock mark" that identified which animals belonged to them. And one of the societal classifications was that of "slave," which actually had two very different meanings. One meaning was synonymous with courtier or a royal attendant. The other meaning was more traditional and referred to a person who was the property of another person and could be bought or sold as desired.

The Turks were renowned for their livestock, which were often sent to China as tribute. In one tribute mission, the tribal chieftains "arranged to have about ten thousand horses, twenty thousand sheep, five hundred camels, and five hundred cows" sent to China, which shows the vastness of their livestock herds. The Turkish horses were especially prized by the Chinese as they were known for their ability to traverse long distances, and they were good at hunting. The Turks exchanged animals for the famed Chinese silk. They also brought birds, wine, medicine, and other items to China, all of which were incorporated into Chinese society.

Another favored Turkish import was the pug. This animal became very popular among the well-to-do and elite in China. Some of the emperors also had pugs as pets. Many Chinese artistic objects and poems depicted animals, which Cai illustrates in great detail. The dogs went by several different names in Chinese.

The Turks sometimes brought lions to China and offered them as tribute gifts. These animals, however, could pose problems to the emperor as they were of no practical use and of no personal enjoyment like dogs were. The lions could be trained, of course, but it was expensive and problematic maintaining them, and they provided no equivalent satisfaction in return. Lions were thus sometimes rejected as tribute gifts, but Cai shows that they nonetheless became important symbols within Chinese society, even though they were not native to China. They were honored in Chinese art, prose, and verse as the king of beasts, but in religion and mythology, lions were always placed under the awe-inspiring dragon. One popular celebration in China that continues to the present day is the famed "Lion Dance."

Manichaeism was brought to China by the Turks. Cai retraces different aspects of Manichaeism that were incorporated into Chinese culture. It was a belief that adopted elements from various religious systems, including Christianity, but with an emphasis on the conflict between light and darkness. Chinese emperors banned the practices and persecuted the practitioners, from time to time, but Cai shows that various elements of the belief survived within Chinese Buddhism and folk religions.

In Chapter 11, Prof. Cai turns to a discussion of the "Kunlun slaves." The Kunluns were seafaring people who were from a vaguely defined area stretching from Vietnam to Java on its eastern border to the east coast of Africa on its western border. They show up in many Chinese texts as Kunlun slaves. They appear in Zen Buddhist texts as well and were renowned for their skills in swimming and taming wild animals. In China, they often became slaves to officials or wealthy private individuals. Cai found many descriptions of the Kunlun people who became a sort of curiosity in China with their strange physical characteristics. They show up in the visual arts as well, as terra-cotta figures or in murals.

Chapter 12 turns to the trade with Russia at Kiachta in the Qing dynasty and the "caravan tea." Tea was introduced to Europe during the Ming dynasty, and shortly thereafter, it became a popular drink in Russia. Cai shows that by 1674, there were a number of shops in Moscow offering tea for sale. Unlike the tea trade at Guangzhou which was always tea leaves, the Russians consumed brick tea as well. Cai also discusses the "Shanxi tea merchants" and the camels and oxen carts that carried the tea from Zhangjiakou to Kiachta, a distance of 4,300 *li*. The carts were nicknamed "One Room" because during their long trip the merchants lived in them. There were three basic routes, and the caravans often consisted of thousands of carts and animals. In 1817, for example, 2,500 camels and 1,420 carts arrived in Kiachta from China loaded mostly with tea. In 1829, 9,670 camels and 2,705 oxen carts arrived there, which shows the growth of the trade over time.

Chapter 13 discusses the "Russian-American Company and the Canton Port." The Russians had a separate treaty with China that allowed them to trade only in Kiachta. Thus, when a Russian ship showed up in the Pearl River Delta in 1805 and was eventually permitted to go up to Whampoa, there was a lot of backlash from the emperor. An investigation was launched to determine how and why this was allowed, and the emperor put a stop to it so that no Russian vessels would again be allowed to trade in Canton.

Cai then turns to a discussion of Sino-Russian relations and the Russian doctor known in China as "Qin Huan." The Russians kept an office in Beijing, and Qin Huan became widely renowned for his unique medical skills. Cai retraces the references to Qin Huan in Chinese texts and unravels the mysteries behind his legacy in the 1820s and 1830s.

The Russians kept a translation office in Beijing, and documents were translated into both languages. Cai retraces the lives of some of the translators in the eighteenth and early nineteenth centuries. Of course, the men went through a lot of training before actually being employed as translators. The Chinese document known as the *Three Character Classic* was translated into Russian and became very popular in the early nineteenth century so the cultural interchanges were clearly disseminated in both directions.

On 21 June 1870, an incident occurred in Tianjin which came to be known as the "Russian Case." Rumors circulated that three French missionaries had abused some Chinese officials. Upon hearing this, several Chinese individuals took it upon themselves to avenge the officials. They spotted two foreign men and one woman and viciously attacked them. The Chinese attackers had mistaken the three persons to be the French abusers, but in reality, they were Russians. All three of them were stabbed to death. It took 16 months to finally settle the case. The Russian Consul Skachkov was eager to restore relations so that their trade with China would not be interrupted; so, he pleaded for leniency with the attackers, despite three of his citizens having been brutally murdered.

In Chapter 17, Cai turns to a discussion of the Dutch who were known as the "red-haired foreigners" in China. Having had many communications with China via their colony in Java, the Dutch were well known to Chinese traders and officials. Cai briefly retraces the beginning and progression of the Dutch trade in Guangzhou in the eighteenth century and the representation of the Dutch people in Chinese texts.

In Chapter 18, Cai gives an account of the Dutch mission to China in 1794–1795, under the leadership of Ambassador Titsingh. Unlike other accounts of the mission, however, which use Dutch texts, Cai pieces most of the discussion together from what he could find in Chinese texts. There were of course many Chinese involved in the mission who escorted the Dutch from Canton to Beijing. There were also many Chinese involved in the initial meeting with Titsingh in Canton in 1794. The Chinese traveler Wang Wengao also wrote a number of poems about the Dutch mission, which provide insights into the particulars of the embassy that are not expressed in other texts.

Cai returns to his focus on Southeast Asia in Chapter 19, with a discussion of the Chinese laborers who migrated there in the late nineteenth and early twentieth centuries. This was the so-called coolie trade when thousands of Chinese left China every year to seek work abroad. These Chinese migrants were colloquially known as "pigs" and were often coerced or fooled into signing long contracts that were not always in their best interests. When they arrived at their destinations, they were housed in "pig houses" that were controlled by heads of Chinese secret societies. Cai shows that in essence, these migrations were just another form of slave labor.

As can be seen, these chapters cover a wide variety of topics. However, despite their great diversity, one thing that comes across clearly is that Cai was intensely focused on China's interactions with the outside world. From Central Asia, to the South China Sea, to the Northern border with Russia, Cai recounts the many exchanges China had with other people. Cai's acute interest in all peoples and cultures, his skill at exploring many documents in various languages, and his uncanny ability to extract real meaning from obscure and often illusive texts such as prose, poetry, and religious doctrine provide us with a very lively, objective, and unbiased look at these exchanges, from a uniquely Chinese perspective.

Credit must also be given to Professor Wu Lanxiang who appreciated the value of Cai's work and had the insight and initiative to put together this translation project. Many of these texts were very difficult to translate as they are filled with historical terms and names that are no longer in use. In some cases, the flow of the narrative might seem somewhat cumbersome. I know that all persons involved in this project, including myself, have tried to keep the translation true to the original Chinese text, while at the same time make it flow smoothly in English. In many paragraphs, this objective was very difficult to accomplish owing to the many archaic names, titles, and terms.

Nevertheless, these translated chapters will undoubtedly be of great benefit to anyone who appreciates exploring other cultures and especially to persons who have an interest in Chinese interactions with the outside world. I heartily welcome this new English language publication, which I am sure will be much appreciated by scholars from a variety of disciplines.

Paul A. Van Dyke, retired professor of history,
Sun Yat-sen University, Guangzhou, April 2023

Acknowledgments

The translators of this book first acknowledge the financial support provided by the Chinese Fund for the Humanities and Social Sciences and the translation permission granted by the Elephant Press, both of which were essential for this translation project. We are also gratefully indebted to Paul A. Van Dyke for his invaluable suggestions and support throughout the entire translation process. He read every chapter of this book and tried to improve the readability of some sentences. It is through Paul A. Van Dyke that we understood the necessity of converting the dates from those in the lunar calendar to the solar calendar. We also owe our thanks to him for the "Foreword," which offers a concise introduction to the contents of this book.

The other team members were wonderfully supportive. Xie Guoquan assisted us with the interpretation of archaic expressions, the conversion between the lunar and solar calendars, and the preparation of chapter abstracts in Chinese. Jiang Yinghe proofread the translation and shared with us his knowledge about the Canton trade in the Qing period, which was truly helpful. Kanika Batra edited some chapters, and reminded us of the importance of adding "translators' notes." The joint efforts of all these scholars have made possible the successful completion of the book.

Thanks also go to David A. Porter for his timely editing suggestions, to Dr. Song Xiumei who searched everywhere for Russian sources and helped tremendously with the bibliography, and to our students in the School of Foreign Languages, Southeast University, for their support in one way or another. They are Chen Wenting, Feng Yuan, Feng Yusheng, Jiang Haoxuan, Kai Wei, Liu Wen, Li Yaxuan, Lv Wenbo, Xia Zixin, Xin Yiheng, Yang Ying, Yang Yue, Ying Qingyuan, Zeng Yuxi, Zhang Rongzhi, Zhou Yi, and Zhu Zhilan.

Also worthy of mention are the editors who contributed to this book. Ms. Sun Lian, Ms. Gao Yan, and Ms. Li Yanan coordinated the translation project, and Ms. Luo Jingran patiently answered all our questions about the book publication. Finally, we must show our gratitude to Swetha K from codeMantra, who carefully read the whole manuscript and facilitated the publication of this translated book. It was truly a pleasure to work with all these wonderful professionals.

1 Tributes from the Nine Surnames of the Sogdians in the Tang Period

The Nine Surnames of the Sogdians (also called the Nine Tribes of Zhaowu)[1] were well known for being "good at conducting business." Inheriting the tradition of ancient Sogdian businessmen who traded "in the name of paying tribute,"[2] these "Phoenicians of Inner Asia" trudged across deserts on camels or horses through Central, West, and East Asia, traveling to the East for business. From the early to the middle Tang period, they continued paying tribute for over 100 years. Their diverse and abundant tributes deserve a careful interpretation. First, it was a commonly accepted practice during the Han and Tang dynasties that Sogdian merchants were also tribute envoys, and naturally, the contact between the Nine Surnames and the Tang empire was primarily realized through "paying tribute" and "receiving gifts from an emperor." As business was carried out under the cover of "paying tribute," the goods they offered took on a dual nature as both a special trade commodity and a gift. Thus, by examining the tribute commodities, we can gain an indirect and rich economic understanding of the structure of the trade. Second, tributes from the Nine Surnames included both locally made products and resaleable goods, with the latter forming a greater proportion. These glamorous and diversely "exotic treasures" not only reflected the link between Sogdian states in Central Asia and countries such as Fulin,[3] Persia, and India, but also showed the scale and characteristics of commodities in circulation in the interior part of Asia in the early Middle Ages. Finally, tributes flowing into the Tang empire also spread from the imperial palace to the outer court, some of which were imitated and became products for daily use (such as wine and stone honey), enriching life in the Tang period. In essence, the history of tribute was the history of material and cultural exchange. This is a challenging field, demanding a wide range of knowledge.

Tribute Route and Tribute Frequency

Bao Fang, an imperial scholar (*jinshi*)[4] in the later years of the Tianbao reign (742–756), presented a magnificent picture of a tribute offering in his poem "Random Thoughts" ("Zagan"):

> The Han empire has enjoyed peace for a long time,
>   bringing kings from numerous vassal states to the court to bow down to an emperor in or past his prime.

>Royal horses constantly chew on alfalfa imported from abroad,
>Sogdian merchants annually pay tribute with wines the taste of which is sublime.[5]

Although brief, these lines contain information about route, frequency, and tributes. I start with a discussion of the first two before moving on to the latter.

In the Tang period, the tributary route of the Nine Surnames started from Transoxiana in Central Asia; passed through the Suyab River, the Issyk-Kul, the large desert, and the Hexi Corridor; and finally arrived at Chang'an. Diverse mountains and rivers formed a complicated geographical barrier on this route, and one can get a rough idea about it through Jia Dan's article "Entering the Western Territories through Anxi Protectorate" in the *New Book of Tang* (*Xin Tang shu*), volume 43. Besides the harsh natural conditions, there were also robbers who frequented part of this tribute road, so the Nine Surnames had to synchronize their tributary schedules and organize themselves into a caravan to ensure a safe travel. In terms of trading locations, from the west to the east, the three cities, Suyab[6], Gaochang (now in Turfan), and Liangzhou, had the closest connection with tribute delivery.

Suyab was located in Ake-Besim, Kyrgyzstan.[7] It was a trade city where "merchants from foreign countries mix,"[8] and it was also the capital of the "shixing kehan" [Western Turkic Khaganate]. In 679, Pei Xingjian, a famous general of the Tang court, defeated one of the tribes led by Ashina Duzhi, and his deputy general Wang Fangyi remodeled the city of Suyab. As stated in "A Biography of Wang Fangyi" ("Wang Fangyi zhuan") in the *New Book of Tang*:

>It took fifty days to complete the project. There are three gates on each side. The city is so meandering and circuitous that it confuses those who come and go. Foreigners from the Western Regions studied the city carefully, yet they could not understand his intention, so they all came to offer their treasures.

With a mixed residence of foreign merchants and accumulated treasures, Suyab enjoyed a special position on the tribute route from the Western Regions. Its importance can also be revealed by the fact that the Tang court appointed a defense commissioner (*zhenshou shi*) to be stationed there. At that time, rich families and eminent officials even hired maids or servants from Suyab. In Rong Yu's five ballads under the title of "How Bitter!" ("Kuzaixing"), the third one gives this line: "In the previous years, I bought servants who came from Suyab." This was probably because of the chaotic political situation in Suyab. As is described in "Records of Samarkand" ("Kangguo zhuan") of the *New Book of Tang*, volume 221, "Along the thousand miles of the Suyab River, there are tens of thousands of Turkic soldiers bearing different surnames. Now the farmers are all clad in armor, looting each other and turning other people into their slave servants."

Another important stronghold on the tribute route was Gaochang, 4,300 *li*[9] away from Chang'an. As a border city, both Chinese and the local language were used here. According to "Records of Yanqi" ("Yanqi zhuan") in the *Old Book of Tang* (*Jiu Tang shu*), volume 198, "Since social upheaval started in the later years of the Sui dynasty, the entrance to the large desert was closed, so all the tributary officials from the Western Regions had to detour through Gaochang." It is no wonder that when Xuanzang went west for Buddhist scriptures, the king of Gaochang could write 24 diplomatic letters for him, facilitating his travel through 24 states in the Western Regions. As a hub city, Gaochang was important not only because of its position on the tribute route but also because of its convenience for tax collection. Moreover, its special location enabled it to become a "monitoring post" for the Tang empire so that royal members of Gaochang could "report all the movements of the states in the Western Regions in a memorial without any delay."[10] Later, King Qu Wentai rebelled against the Tang suzerainty. He ordered his men to "plunder Sogdian merchants and block tribute."[11] Then in 640, Emperor Taizong of the Tang dynasty sent an army to conquer Gaochang and turned it into Xizhou commandery (Xizhou *dudu fu*). Among the documents unearthed in Turpan in recent years, there were two files that indicate that Xizhou in the Tang dynasty functioned as a connecting city on the tribute route, just like Gaochang under the rule of the Qu family, witnessing an endless stream of merchants and traders. One of these is a camel-selling contract in 673 signed in Xizhou by "a Sogdian merchant conducting business (*xingsheng hu*), someone named Kang Wupoyan from the state of Kang [Samarkand]."And the other is a file case in which sojourning merchants like Gecha and others "are moving their households to the Tang capital" and asked the officials of Xizhou for a "travel pass" (*guosuo*).[12]

Liangzhou, alternatively called Wuwei or Guzang, was an important city in the Hexi Corridor, a place where officials from the Nine Surnames had to pass on their way to pay tribute. The word "Guzang" is the transcription of "Kc'n" in the ancient Sogdian documents.[13] According to "Sogdiana" ("Sute") in the *Book of Wei: Records of the Western Regions* (*Wei shu: Xiyu zhuan*), as early as the midfifth century, "merchants of this country went to Liangzhou to trade." At the beginning of the Tang dynasty, when Xuanzang was passing this place before heading out of the border pass, he was deeply impressed: "As the regional capital city of the Hexi Corridor, Liangzhou borders the Western Regions and links the countries west of the Congling [Pamirs] and there is an endless stream of merchants coming and going."[14] The traveling traders from the Nine Surnames lived in the form of clans in Liangzhou, forming intertwined groups, among which the An clan was particularly famous. It is stated in the *Comprehensive Mirror in Aid of Governance* (*Zizhi tongjian*), volume 219, in the year 757,

> After Gai Tinglun, the military commander (*bingmashi*) of Hexi, united with An Menwu, a merchant from the Nine Surnames in Wuwei [Liangzhou] and some other people, they killed Zhou Mi, the military commissioner (*jiedushi*), and gathered a crowd of 60,000 people. Within the city of Wuwei, there are seven small towns, and Sogdians occupied five of them.

This record is sufficient to show that the Nine Surnames played a critical role in Liangzhou.

In the Tang period, the Nine Surnames did not pay tribute on a regular basis, and there was no fixed custom to decide tribute frequency, but the total number of tribute is quite impressive. Based on the related information from the *Prime Tortoise of*

4 *Tributes from the Nine Surnames of the Sogdians*

the Record Bureau (*Cefu yuangui*), Table 1.1 gives a list of tributary states, tribute time, name of tributary envoys, and their tribute. (Note: Those marked with an asterisk (*) are entries added from the *New Book of Tang*.)

Table 1.1 A List of Tributes from the Nine Surnames of the Sogdians in the Tang Period

State[15]	Time	Envoy	Tribute
Kang康(Samarkand)	6th month of 624		
Kang (Samarkand)	7th month of 624	Luoshenzhi	
Cao曹(Kabudhan)	7th month of 624		
Kang (Samarkand)	12th month of 626		Famous horses [no quantity given in the original document unless specified]
He何(Kushaniyah)	5th month of 627		
Kang (Samarkand)	5th month of 627		
Shi石(Chach)	12th month of 634		
Kang (Samarkand)	635(no month given)		Lion(s)
Kang (Samarkand)	637(no month given)		Golden peaches; silver peaches
An安(Bukhara)	11th month of 638		
Kang (Samarkand)	2nd month of 639		
Kang (Samarkand)	1st month of 642		
Cao (Kabudhan)	1st month of 642		
Shi史(Kesh)	1st month of 642		
Kang (Samarkand)	1st month of 643		
Kang (Samarkand)	1st month of 644		
Kang (Samarkand)	1st month of 645		
Shi (Chach)	1st month of 646		
Shi (Chach)	1st month of 647		
Kang (Samarkand)	1st month of 647		
Kang (Samarkand)	1st month of 648		
Shi (Chach)	1st month of 648		
An (Bukhara)	2nd month of 649		
Cao (Kabudhan)	10th month of 652		
Cao (Kabudhan)	11th month of 653		
Cao (Kabudhan)	4th month of 654		
Kang (Samarkand)	4th month of 654		
An (Bukhara)	4th month of 654		
Kang (Samarkand)	3rd month of 671		
Kang (Samarkand)	10th month of 679		
Shi (Chach)	9th month of 682		
An (Bukhara)	4th month of 697		Two-headed dog(s)
Kang (Samarkand)	6th month of 707		
An (Bukhara)	3rd month of 717		
Kang (Samarkand)	3rd month of 717		Brocade; indigo
Mi米(Maimurgh)	2nd month of 718		
Shi (Chach)	2nd month of 718		
Mi (Maimurgh)	4th month of 718		*Tabi* dance rug(s); chalcopyrite

(*Continued*)

Table 1.1 (Continued)

State	Time	Envoy	Tribute
Kang (Samarkand)	718 (no month given)		Chainmail armor(s); crystal glass(es); agate bottle(s); ostrich egg(s); *yuenuo* fabric
An (Bukhara)	2nd month of 719		Two Persian horses (*lou*); one Fulin embroidered *qushu* 氍毹; 30 *jin*[16] of tulips; 100 *jin* of raw stone honey; two large *tabi qushu*; one embroidered *qushu*
Kang (Samarkand)	2nd month of 719		One good horse; one Persian camel; two Persian horses (*lou*)
Shi (Chach)	12th month of 720		
Shi (Chach)	2nd month of 721		
Kang (Samarkand)	4th month of 724		One dwarf; two horses two dogs
An (Bukhara)	2nd month of 726		One male cheetah; one female cheetah
An (Bukhara)	5th month of 726	King's younger brother Kexilan Dagan Fudanfali 可悉烂达干拂耽发黎	Horse(s); cheetah(s)
Kang (Samarkand)	11th month of 726		Cheetah(s)
Kang (Samarkand)	5th month of 727		Sogdian dancing girl(s); cheetah(s)
Shi (Kesh)	5th month of 727		Sogdian dancing girl(s); wine
An (Bukhara)	5th month of 727		Horse(s)
Shi (Kesh)	7th month of 727		Sogdian dancing girl(s); cheetah(s)
Mi (Maimurgh)	11th month of 727		Lion(s)
Mi (Maimurgh)	4th month of 728	* Grand Chieftain (*da shouling*) Mi Huhan 米忽汗	
Mi (Maimurgh)	1st month of 729		Three Sogdian dancing girls; one cheetah; one lion
Mi (Maimurgh)	4th month of 730	* Grand Chieftain Moyemen 末野门	
Shi (Chach)	4th month of 730		
An (Bukhara)	10th month of 740		Jewel encrusted bed(s); ostrich egg(s); cup(s)

(Continued)

Table 1.1 (Continued)

State	Time	Envoy	Tribute
Kang (Samarkand)	10th month of 740		Jewel encrusted incense burner(s); white jade cup(s); agate(s); crystal eyedrop bottle(s)
Shi (Kesh)	3rd month of 741	Chieftain Bodimishi勃帝米施	
Cao (Kabudhan)	3rd month of 742		Horse(s)
Shi (Chach)	3rd month of 742		
Shi (Chach)	12th month of 743	King's son-in-law Kang Randian 康染颠	
An (Bukhara)	3rd month of 744		From here until the second "7th month of 745", the tribute is recorded as "horse(s); jewelry."
Kang (Samarkand)	7th month of 744		
Shi (Kesh)	7th month of 744		
Xica西曹 (Western Cao, in Ishitikhan)	7th month of 744		
Mi (Maimurgh)	7th month of 744		
Shi (Chach)	7th month of 744		
Shi (Chach)	7th month of 745		
An (Bukhara)	7th month of 745		15 horses
Shi (Chach)	3rd month of 746		
Shi (Chach)	10th leap month of 746		Dance rug(s); *tadeng* 毾㲪; red salt; black salt; *zhihan*质汗[17]; stephania tetrandra root; glazed tile; gold; silver
Shi (Kesh)	10th leap month of 746		
Mi (Maimurgh)	10th leap month of 746		
Shi (Chach)	5th month of 747		Horse(s)
Shi (Chach)	8th month of 749	Prince Yuan'en	
Kang (Samarkand)	1st month of 750	Grand Chieftain Moyemen	10 horses
An (Bukhara)	1st month of 750		100 horses
Huoxun (Khwarazm)	9th month of 751		
Kang (Samarkand)	9th month of 751		
An (Bukhara)	9th month of 751		
Kang (Samarkand)	12th month of 752		
Huoxun火寻 (Khwarazm)	5th month of 753		Purple roe deer hides; white jade; stone honey; black salt
An (Bukhara)	7th month of 753		
Shi (Chach)	12th month of 753		
Mi (Maimurgh)	4th month of 754		
Kang (Samarkand)	9th month of 754		
Kang (Samarkand)	3rd month of 755		
Huoxun (Khwarazm)	3rd month of 755		
Cao (Kabudhan)	3rd month of 755		
Kang (Samarkand)	6th month of 758	Senior Officer (*zhangshi*) Kang Zhongyi	

(Continued)

Table 1.1 (Continued)

State	Time	Envoy	Tribute
An (Bukhara)	3rd month of 759	An Mochunse 安莫纯瑟	
Shi (Chach)	12th month of 762		
Kang (Samarkand)	12th month of 772		
Mi (Maimurgh)	12th month of 772		

As Table 1.1 shows, the Nine Surnames started to pay tribute in 624 and stopped in 772, totaling 94 tributes over 150 years. In terms of tributary states, the order is as follows: Kang (Samarkand) 32 tributes, Shi (Chach) 19 tributes, An (Bukhara) 16 tributes, Mi (Maimurgh) 10 tributes, Cao (Kabudhan and Ishitikhan) 8 tributes, Shi (Kesh) 5 tributes, Huoxun (Khwarazm) 3 tributes, and He (Kushaniyah) 1 tribute. Of the Sogdian states, only Wudi[18] was not recorded. In the preceding list, Samarkand ranks first among the Nine Surnames, accounting for about one-third of the tributes. There are two reasons for this. First, Samarkand was a core city-state. As explained in the *Great Tang Records on the Western Regions* (*Da Tang xiyu ji*), "of all the Sogdian states, this one sits in the center, and all the other states from near or far imitate its manner and style." Second, Samarkand prioritized commercial activity. According to the *Comprehensive Institutions* (*Tongdian*):

> People in Samarkand are good at conducting business. When a boy is about five years old, he is sent away to learn. After obtaining the basics, he is sent back to study how to manage business. Whether a person performs well is judged by the profits he has earned.

That explains why this large commercial city-state was at the forefront of tribute commerce and contact with the Tang court.

In terms of tribute time, the highest frequency can be found in the reign of Emperor Xuanzong of the Tang dynasty from 717 to 755, totaling 56 trips, accounting for about 60% of the total visitations. This noticeable phenomenon is assumed to bear a connection with the "Prosperous Period of Kaiyuan and Tianbao"[19] and its influence on foreign countries, illustrated by the aforementioned poetic lines – "The Han empire has enjoyed peace for a long time, / bringing kings from numerous vassal states to the court and bow down to the emperor in or past his prime." Similarly, in his book *Authentic Records Transmitted from the Kaiyuan and Tianbao Eras* (*Kaitian chuanxin ji*), Zheng Qi also viewed the repeated visits by the vassal states as a sign of the peaceful world where "the Yellow River is clear and the sea is calm." But as a matter of fact, there is another motivation that explains why the Nine Surnames frequently paid tribute in the first half of the eighth century. It is related to the encroaching invasion of the Arabs into Transoxiana in Central Asia. If we take a look at the tribute letters sent by Sogdian kings to the Tang court, we can know about their troubles.

8 *Tributes from the Nine Surnames of the Sogdians*

An Analysis of the Tribute Letters

In the documents kept by the Tang government, the tribute letters all date from the Xuanzong reign (712–755) and were sent, respectively, by the states of An (Bukhara), Kang (Samarkand), Shi (Chach), and Cao (Kabudhan). I present the contents of these letters in chronological order before briefly analyzing each.

The first is the tribute letter from Tughshada笃萨波提, the king of Bukhara, in the second month of 719:

> From Tughshada, one of the millions of grass-like slaves on the steppe, to Your Majesty, the heavenly lord who governs the entire world, an emperor of virtue and sage. On my bended knees, I offer my blessings in a faraway place in the same way that I pay homage to the gods. Since the founding of Bukhara, there have been endless fights for the kingship, but both soldiers and civilians in our country have been wholeheartedly loyal to Your Majesty. Now disturbed by the Arab robbers, there is no peace on this land. I fall on my knees today and beg Your Majesty the Emperor to show mercy and liberate us from our sufferings. Please order the Turgesh to come to our rescue. Upon their arrival, I will immediately take command of my troops, and we will surely defeat the Arabs. I sincerely ask Your Majesty to grant me this request. Hereby I present two Persian horses (*lou*), one Fulin embroidered *qushu*, 30 *jin* of tulips and 100 *jin* of raw stone honey. Moreover, since I have already been qualified to wear an official purple attire, I humbly ask Your Majesty to grant me a title of the third rank (*san pin*)[20]. Also, my wife, the khatun (*kedun*) of Bukhara, is sending two large *tabi qushu* and one embroidered *qushu* to the Empress. If I can receive a kind favor from Your Majesty, please reward me with saddles, bridles, reins, royal regalia, robes and belts, and give my wife some clothes and make-up.[21]

This request for assistance was sent out at the end of the reign of King Tughshada I (Тукаспада I, 700–720), who was later executed by Arab conquerors in 727. It expresses an urgent wish to use the influence of the Tang court to organize troops, a joint military force of the Turgesh and Bukhara, to fight against the Arabs. In this letter, King Tughshada called himself "one of the millions of grass-like slaves on the steppe," which is a very humble way of addressing oneself in the Sogdian language. The same can be found in the following letter where the king of Samarkand addresses himself as "one of the millions of grass-like slaves under the horses' hooves," which, in the original Sogdian language, literally means "an insignificant slave."[22]

The second is the tribute letter from Gurak乌勒伽, the king of Samarkand, in the second month of 719:

> From Gurak, one of the millions of grass-like slaves under the horses' hooves, to Your Majesty, the heavenly lord who governs the entire world. My country and other Sogdian states have been wholeheartedly loyal to Your Majesty,

doing what is good for the Tang empire, never rebelling, or encroaching on your border. For the past 35 years, whenever the Arab robbers started a war against us, we would assemble military forces to fight, never troubling Your Majesty to send soldiers to our aid. Six years ago, the Arab supreme commander Qutayba Ibn Muslim led his troops here. We resisted the invasion bravely, but many of my soldiers were hurt and killed. Since the Arabs disproportionately outnumbered us, we saw no prospect of winning the war. We retreated into the city for self-defense, but they surrounded the city with 300 stone-throwing carts, and they even passed through our defensive pits three times, attempting to break into the city. I implore Your Majesty the Emperor, after discerning these circumstances, to send some of your troops to lift us from our misery. This Arab empire has had only a hundred years to become strong, and it will be the 100th this year. If the Tang troops come to assist us, we would definitely be able to defeat the Arabs. Hereby I present one good horse, one Persian camel and two Persian horses to Your Majesty. If I can receive a kind favor from Your Majesty, please leave the rewards for me with my envoys. I wish there will be no invasion against my country in the future.[23]

Apparently, this tribute letter reviews the fighting history of the Nine Surnames against the Arabs. By referring to some western documents and unearthed cultural relics, I give a brief interpretation here.

First, the time phrase "for the past 35 years" alludes to the campaign in 683 when the governor of the Khurasan, Salm ibn Ziyad (known in Arabic documents as Salm), invaded Bukhara. To save her country, the khatun of Bukhara proposed a marriage to Tarkhun, the king of Samarkand, to "become his wife" in exchange for his assistance.[24] Since then, the fire of war had extended from the west of Sogdiana to the east.

Second, the aforementioned Qutayba Ibn Muslim (also known as Emir Qutaiba) was also a famous commander in the Arab conquest of Transoxiana. "Six years ago" alludes to the fall of the capital of Samarkand in 712, six years before this tribute letter was written. Here Gurak is vague about his surrender to Qutayba. In fact, the terms of the peace treaty he was forced to sign with Qutayba were clearly recorded in a Persian document found in Turkey in 1936. In this treaty, it was stipulated that Samarkand should pay two million silver coins and an equivalent price of 3,000 slaves (each worth 200 silver coins) and politically accept Qutayba's protection.[25] Unwilling to be humiliated, Gurak soon led his followers out of his country and sought refuge in Kabudhan. During his exile, he sent a tribute letter to borrow "the Tang troops," which was actually part of his restoration plan.

Third, more details about "stone-throwing carts" used by the Arabs in the war can be seen in one of the fresco fragments unearthed in 1970 at the ruins of Panjikent in Central Asia, about 60 kilometers east of today's Samarkand. Depicting a launching scene of a "stone-throwing cart," this fresco clearly shows its structure – a support frame, an ejection rod, and five tow ropes pulled by five shooters. In terms of structure, this is a Chinese-style trebuchet, similar to the single-tipped cannon (*danshao pao*) in the *Complete Essentials for the Military Classics* (*Wujing zongyao*). As for the ethnic identity of the five shooters, judged from their dressing style and appearance, they are not Chinese, neither Arabs nor Sogdians. It is likely that they are indigenous inhabitants of West Asia who surrendered to the Arabs.[26]

Fourth, as for the statement "This Arab empire has had only a hundred years to become strong, and it will be the 100th this year," the duration of years is probably counted according to the Hijri calendar which started on 16 July 622, when Muhammad and his followers migrated from Mecca to Medina. When the tribute letter was written, only 97 years had passed, but in the letter, it is written as "one hundred years." This can be explained by the fact that the Islamic calendar does not include leap years, and for every 30 years, there is a one-year difference, thus the saying of "one hundred years." From this, it can be speculated that in the anti-conquest movement of the Nine Surnames in the early eighth century, there was in circulation a prophetic remark that "The Arab empire ends in 100 years," expressing their hope for restoring their countries. This political prophecy was probably disseminated by Zoroastrian priests who were good at "cursing over fire."

The third tribute letter came from Yina Tudun Qule 伊吐屯屈勒, the king of Chach, in 741:

> For thousands of generations, we have been loyal to the Tang court, just like the Turgesh khan who is now sincere to Your Majesty. Now all principalities are subservient. Once Your Majesty - Tengri Qaghan (*tian kehan*), was betrayed by the Turgesh and they became a burning problem under Your Majesty's feet. Now that the Turks have surrendered to Tengri Qaghan, so the only threat is the Arabs in the west, yet their power has not yet surpassed that of the Turks. Thus, I beg Your Majesty not to leave the Turks aside. [United,] we can defeat the Arabs, and then all the vassal states will naturally submit and resign in peace.[27]

Faced with threat from the Arab empire, similar to the king of Bukhara, the king of Chach also proposed to unite with the Turks. For the Nine Surnames in the mid-eighth century, this seemed to be the only strategy for achieving a "peaceful submission and resignation of all the vassal states."

The fourth tribute letter came from Geluopulu 哥罗仆禄, the king of Kabudhan, in 745:

> Since the time of our ancestors, we have been loyal to Tengri Qaghan. Having the history of being subjugated, we implore Your Majesty to take our land as one of the small prefectures of the Tang empire. If Your Majesty needs us to be of service, we will be wholeheartedly loyal and fight for the empire.[28]

In Arabian history books, Geluopulu is known as "Хара – Бугра." He was first the king of Eastern Kabudhan (720–740) and then the king of Western Kabudhan (740–760). When he pleaded for his country to be treated as "one of the small prefectures of the Tang empire," he was actually hoping to break free from the Arabian threat. What he meant by "fight[ing] for the empire" is actually an anti-conquest wish.

Through the analysis of the above tribute letters, it can be seen that the Nine Surnames placed their hope of defending and restoring their countries on the Tang court. Whether to unite with the Turks or borrow troops from the Tang empire, they must obtain the approval of Chinese emperors. Therefore, different from the regular commercial trade "in the name of paying tribute," the tribute climax during the reign of Xuanzong (712–755) was the result of the political upheaval in Central Asia at that time. As history shows, it was in the first half of the eighth century that the Arabs gradually established their domination over Transoxiana in Central Asia: they conquered Bukhara in 706–709, and Khwarazm and Samarkand in 710–712. Then in 751, Chach also lost its independence.[29] In a sense, this wave of "Holy War" swept across the city-states of Sogdiana and pushed Sogdian envoys/merchants from the Western Regions onto the tribute road to seek attachment to the Tang empire. Some of them ended up being "Sogdian guests" (*hu ke*) who lived in Chang'an and needed provisions from the Court of State Ceremonial (*Honglusi*) for their living.[30]

The list of tribute envoys from the Nine Surnames is noticeably incomplete. For example, from 731 to 739, no record of any tribute is evident, so something is definitely missing. As only the names of ten envoys can be seen in the above table, it is difficult to make any precise analysis. But a brief pattern can be identified here. First, in terms of the rank of tribute envoys, one king's younger brother and another king's son-in-law stand out as the top two. Second, tribute envoys of Samarkand, Bukhara, Kesh, and Maimurgh came to the Tang court after their countries had been destroyed, so it is likely that they represented their government in exile or the forces that wished to restore their country. Third, although it is hard to know how many people were included in one delegation, it can be inferred that it was about the size of a caravan. As revealed in the *Prime Tortoise of the Record Bureau*, volume 971, in the year 753, "the third tribe of the Karluks sent envoys to pay tribute. There were 130 people in total. They were divided into four teams, entering the imperial court one after another." For a delegation from the Western Regions, their "leader" was also a "merchant," showing a vague yet decipherable integration of two identities into one. As Édouard Chavannes pointed out in the fourth volume of *Documents on the Western Turks*, "if the envoys who came to China to pay tribute at that time did not say clearly which king sent them, it is possible that they were caravan merchants rather than envoys."

Tributes from the envoys needed to be inspected and appraised by official institutions. There is a clear record about specific regulations in the "Treatise on Officialdom" ("Baiguan zhi") of the *New Book of Tang*, volume 48:

> The tribute horses are inspected by the Palace Administration (*dianzhong sheng*) and the Court of the Imperial Stud (*taipu shi*). The good ones are sent to the former, and the old and sick ones go to the latter. The tribute medicine, after being inspected by the Court of State Ceremonial, is priced by the Directorate for Imperial Manufactories (*shaofu jian*). As eagles, falcons, dogs and cheetahs cannot be appraised, they are left to the Court of State Ceremonial to decide whether they are valuable or not. All portable tributes are shown by [Sogdian] guests to the emperor. For camels and horses, they

are led to the imperial court for a display. Tributes that are not good enough to be offered to the emperor go to prefectures or counties.

Tribute Categories and Interpretations

Since the Han and Wei dynasties, there had been some noticeable differences between foreign tribute and domestic tribute. Although the former functioned as a commercial exchange, what was offered was not dress, food, or utensils for daily use, but rather "special antiques," "famous treasures," "exotic products," or "stunning skills" from distant places. Tributes from the Nine Surnames in the Tang period did not venture beyond this classification. As dwarfs and Sogdian dancing girls in the category of "stunning skills" were tribute artists, they should not be put side by side with tribute objects, here I limit my discussion to the other six categories, namely, animals, plants, minerals, textiles, utensils, and food, and selectively explain the sound and meaning, properties, and uses of these tributes.

Animals

1 **Lions.** The word "lion" is spelled as "Srrw" in Sogdian texts. Samarkand was known for being home to Central Asian lions. As revealed in the *Book of Wei: Records of the Western Regions* (*Wei shu: Xiyu zhuan*):

> The state of *Xiwanjin*[31] [Samarkand], with its capital in *Xiwanjin* city [Samarkand], is located west of Mimi [Maimurgh], about 12,700 *li* away from the state of Dai. To the south of Samarkand are Ghazna mountains, where many lions are found. Every year, lions are offered as a tribute to the imperial court.

This shows that when Samarkand offered tribute lions to the Tang court, they were actually following the accepted practice. Tribute lions must be tamed before they were offered. Concerning lion-taming skills in ancient Central Asia, Chen Cheng provided a description in his report "A Record of the Foreign Countries in the Western Regions" ("Xiyu fanguo zhi"):

> A lion is usually born in the reeds of the Amu Darya River. It is said that after birth, it does not open its eyes until seven days later. For those who want to capture and domesticate it, it is best to get it when its eyes are still closed. When a lion grows up, it will be hard to tame, as it becomes ferocious and brutal.

Because a tribute lion was trained and its wild nature was somewhat constrained, it was possible that "in the late Kaiyuan period, a tribute lion from the Western Regions" could be "tied to a tree in front of a horse station when it reached the west road of Chang'an."[32] Yet, lions are carnivorous animals. It is said that "[f]or a single day, a lion eats two live sheep. It also drinks two bottles of each of these: vinegar, bitter wine, honeyed cheese."[33] So, even if a tribute lion had been domesticated, it was still an exhausting job to feed it along an extremely long journey. In 635, when Samarkand offered its first tribute lion to the Tang court, "Emperor Taizong treasured this gift from afar so much that he ordered Yu Shinan, the Director of the Palace Library (*mishu jian*), to compose a rhapsody."[34] But for later tribute lions, court ministers started to show their objections. For example, in the third month of 696, Yao Shu, in his memorial "Please decline the tribute lions offered by the state of Shi [Chach]," stated why it was not suitable to receive the tribute: "Lions are ferocious carnivores. It is too costly to move them from Suiye [Suyab] to our capital and to feed them here."[35] Although the proposal was accepted by Empress Wu Zetian, her grandson Emperor Xuanzong did not follow her practice. On two occasions, he accepted tribute lions from the Nine Surnames, respectively, in 727 and 729. More information about lions in China is given in the chapter entitled "Lions in China" of this book.

2 **Horses.** On ten occasions, horses were offered to the Tang court by the Nine Surnames, topping the tribute list. As stated in the *New Book of Tang: Records of Samarkand*, the Western Regions was the place where "good horses come from." This is also indicated by the aforementioned poetic line "Royal horses constantly chew on alfalfa imported from abroad" where Bao Fang alluded to what was happening in the Tang period by referring to the situation in the Han dynasty. There are also descriptions of tribute horses in other Tang poems, such as Qiao Zhizhi's "Songs for an Exhausted Stallion" ("Leijun pian"):

> Spewing snow-white spittle, and emitting a long hissing sound, you came all the way from the northwest to be on display,
>   undoubtedly you are a forerunner of the dragon (*longmei*) of today.
>   As a tribute, you traveled ten thousand *li* to reach the gate of the Forbidden City,
>   where the nine-tiered imperial palace is open for you in every way.[36]

Here the "forerunner of the dragon" refers to the thoroughbred from Samarkand. As explained in the entry entitled "Marks for Horses from Foreign States" ("Zhufan mayin") in the *Institutional History of Tang* (*Tang huiyao*), volume 72, "Horses from Samarkand in Sogdiana are Ferghana horses. They are huge in size. During the Wude era (618–626), Samarkand brought in 4,000 tribute horses. The official horses used today are mostly descendants of this breed."[37] Here, it needs to be pointed out that, although the "outstanding horses" tributed by Samarkand in 626 may have been used as stallions, there is no such record about these "four thousand horses" in any other documents, so there might be an error in recording "forty" 四十 as "four thousand" 四千. As a matter of fact, tribute horses from the Nine Surnames always came in small batches, ranging from two to several hundred. These limited tribute horses from Samarkand were not used for postal services, nor were they employed in military marches. Rather, they were harnessed by the Bureau of the Imperial Saddlery (*shangcheng ju*) in the Palace Administration to serve an emperor or trained as either "ball-playing horses" or "dancing horses."[38] The two imperial horses of Emperor Xuanzong – "Jade-Flower Piebald Horse 玉花驄" and "Night-Shining White 照夜白" – were both of unknown origin, but it can be inferred from Du Fu's poem "Ballad of a Piebald Horse" ("Congma xing") that piebald horses came from Central Asia, as the poem mentions "piebald horses of Ferghana breed." About how to train tribute horses to dance, Zheng Chuhui's "Miscellaneous Records of Emperor Ming: Additions" ("Minghuang zalu: Buyi") provides a detailed account:

> Emperor Xuanzong once had people train dancing horses, with 400 hooves [100 horses] standing to the left and right, divided into different sections and group-named "Somebody's Favorite" or "Somebody's Pride." At that time, there were also good tribute horses coming from regions beyond the Great Wall. His Majesty asked people to train them, and all of the horses danced out the wonder of music. Then it was decreed that these horses should be clothed in embroidery, accessorized with gold and silver jewelry, and their manes should be decoratively interspersed with pearls and jade. Dancing to the tune entitled "Pleasure of Pouring from a Cup" ("Qingbeile") which has about 10 turns, the horses shook their heads and wagged their tails, moving up and down, left and right, echoing the rhythm. Sometimes, a three-tiered wood-plank platform was set up, then a horse was driven up atop and spun around as if in flight. At other times, a very strong man was ordered to lift up a couch where a horse could dance. Around these were musicians, who were all young and beautiful lads, each dressed in a pale-yellow robe with a jade belt on the waist. On the "Thousand-Autumn Festival" [the emperor's birthday], the horses were taken out to dance outside of the Hall of Zealous Administration (*Qinzheng dian*). Later, His Majesty moved to Shu 蜀 and honored this place with his presence, and all these horses were then scattered to different areas of the country.

A recently unearthed silver jug in the shape of a leather bag from the Tang period, engraved with the image of a dancing horse wearing fluttering ribbons on its mane and holding a cup in its mouth, with its knees bent, proves that what is recorded about dancing horses whose "manes should be decoratively interspersed with pearls and jade" is true. The same can be said for Zhang Shuo's description in the third poem of "Songs of Dancing Horses" ("Wuma ci,"), a collection of six poems about horses – "Each bending knees, and holding a cup in its mouth, horses celebrate the emperor's birthday in a devoted manner."

3 **Pugs from Samarkand.** In the Tang era, tribute dogs from Samarkand were called "Kangguo wozi" [pugs from Samarkand], and they were a plaything for court officials and noble ladies. For example, on one summer day in the late

Tianbao period [Tianbao reign: 742–756], Emperor Xuanzong played chess with one of his kings, and:

> Imperial Consort Yang stood aside and watched the game. When the emperor was about to lose, the Imperial Consort put a *wozi* by his side. The dog jumped onto the chessboard and the game was ruined, which made the emperor very happy.[39]

This precious breed of dog from the Western Regions had been highly valued from the Tang and Song periods until the Ming and Qing eras. They were addressed by slightly different names on account of the different shipping routes to China, either across the land or through the sea. More details about them are given in another chapter of this book "Tracing the History of Pugs." Also, a "two-headed dog" offered by Bukhara should be briefly mentioned here. As volume 970 of the *Prime Tortoise of the Record Bureau* records, "In the fourth month of 697, Bukhara offered a two-headed dog." Here the quantifier is placed before the noun, so what is called "a two-headed dog" is actually a conjoined freak. No wonder it was taken as an ominous omen of Empress Wu Zetian's approaching reign in which there would be two leaders in one country. As the old saying goes, "because of an extra head, the top becomes different."[40]

Plants

1 Golden peaches and silver peaches. Samarkand was home to flowers and fruits in Central Asia. Chinese Buddhist monk Xuanzang had a description of the local botanical landscape in his book *Great Tang Records on the Western Regions*: "Trees are luxuriant and lush, and flowers and fruits flourish." Yelv Chucai from the Yuan period also repeatedly chanted in his poems about the Hezhongfu [Samarkand], "White plum blossoms and pink peach flowers create a bright world in front of my eyes."[41] These helped to explain why peaches produced in Samarkand were also found among the tributes from the Nine Surnames. According to the *Prime Tortoise of the Record Bureau*, volume 970, in the year 637, "Samarkand offered golden and silver peaches, and the emperor issued an edict that the seeds should be planted in the palace garden." Then in 647, a court official followed the emperor's decree to list the golden peach as a "precious fruit" in the tribute catalog, recording that "Samarkand presented yellow peaches, each as big as a goose egg. As they are golden in color, they are also called golden peaches." In "Records of Sogdiana" ("Kangju zhuan") of the *Comprehensive Institutions*, volume 193, the year of recording the golden peach into the tribute catalog was mistakenly written as the year of receiving the tribute, so this record cannot be taken as evidence. Considering the fact that peach trees had long been planted in China, and before the Tang period they had been introduced to India where they were called "Charvi" in Sanskrit,[42] one might ask: why were these yellow and white peaches from Samarkand treated so favorably by the Tang court, seeded in the imperial garden as well as recorded into the tribute catalog? While this could be related to their shapes and colors, the more likely explanation is that they appealed to the national psyche of the ancient Chinese, as the peach ["tao" in Pinyin] was believed to "promise longevity," as shown by "fresh or confectionery peaches offered as a birthday gift" (*shoutao*); to "ward off evil spirits," as revealed by "peach wood charms" (*taofu*); or even to make one "become an immortal," as indicated by "peaches of immortality" (*xiantao*).

2 **Tulips.** Tribute tulips from Bukhara were a genus of saffron. According to "Notes to Flowers" ("Zhong xiang pian") in the *Collection of Translated Buddhist Terms* (*Fanyi mingyi ji*), volume three:

> What is called *chajumo* is actually tulips. In the *Rites of Zhou* (*Zhouli*), it is written that Yuren, the official of rituals in the Ministry of Spring (*chunguan*),[43] used tulips to make a tasty wine. In the book *Explaining Unit Characters and Analyzing Compound Characters* (*Shuowen jiezi*), it is elucidated that tulips are herbaceous flowers, a species tributed from afar, the juice of which is extracted by the Yunren to add to wine, which then will be used to invite the spirits or pay homage to ancestors.

This kind of fragrant flower is native to Kapisa.[44] Its properties and uses are well documented in Chinese literature. For instance, volume 14 of the *Compendium of Materia Medica* (*Bencao gangmu*) cites the *Record of the Peculiar Products of the Nanzhou* (*Nanzhou yiwu zhi*) as saying:

> Tulips come from Kapisa where they are planted. They are used as an offering for the Buddha. After they wither in a few days, they can be used. At this time the flowers are just yellow in color, similar to the young and tender lotus in water hibiscus. They can make wine more fragrant.

Also, volume 970 of the *Prime Tortoise of the Record Bureau* describes tulips' flowering season and planting method by referring to the tribute category recorded in 647:

> The leaves are like those of ophiopogon root. Blooming in September, they look like water hibiscus, with a purple or blue color and a fragrance that can be smelled ten paces away. Tulips do not bear fruit although they bloom, thus those who want to plant them should dig out the root.

In terms of their usage in the daily life of the Tang people, apart from being an offering to the Buddha, tulips had two secular functions. First, they were used in wine brewing. This can be proved by Li Bai's poem "Writing as a Guest" ("Kezhong xing"): "Lanling wine with tulip juice is intoxicating and fragrant, / in a jade bowl it is as clear as amber light." Second, they were used to make one's clothes smell good. Duan Chengshi had a collection of poems entitled

"Presenting a Playful Interpretation of an Ancient Text to Feiqing" ("Rouqing jieji xi cheng Feiqing"), the third one of which reads: "Tulips grow to have thin flower spikes, / fragrance emanates from the collar when they are dried and placed in a kid's robe." A similar description can be found in "Palace Lyrics" ("Gongci") written by Madame Huarui which reads "Red tapestries on the walls, cyan brocade carpets on the floor, / the whole room was covered with valuable spices of dipterocarps and tulips." Here "covering the room with valuable incense of dipterocarps and tulips"[45] was a required arrangement when an emperor of the Tang court chose to sleep with one of his consorts. It should be noted that, when Bukhara offered tribute tulips in 719, four pieces of *qushu* were also included in this batch; thus, it can be seen that incenses came together with tapestries and rugs.

3 **Indigo.** It was commonly used as makeup for women in ancient Central Asia. From the Ferghana Valley to the Caspian Sea coast, "women did not use powder, but simply painted their eyes with indigo."[46] Indigo is a dye extracted from indigo plants. In China, women had an early history of painting their eyebrows with indigo. For example, in the *Verses of Chu* (*Chuci*), there is a description of "black-painted eyebrows and white-powdered cheeks, and sweet balm on faces." The tribute indigo from Samarkand would not have been an "exotic product" if it was not the famous "Persian Indigo." But as the harem beauties of the Kaiyuan and Tianbao periods had a beauty trend of "painting eyebrows long and thin with indigo,"[47] this Western cosmetic was still a timely product.

Minerals

1 **Chalcopyrite.** Chalcopyrite (*tou*) is a shortened transliteration of the Persian word tūtiya, referring to brass made from zinc and copper.[48] The earliest appearance of the character 鍮 can be found in the eighteenth chapter of an ancient Chinese document called *Jade Chapters* (*Yupian*) where a list of words with the radical "金" (metal) is given: "The word 鍮 is pronounced as 'tou.' It is similar to gold."[49] The tribute chalcopyrite from Maimurgh was probably re-sold from Persia, as both *Book of Wei* (*Wei shu*) and *Book of Sui* (*Sui shu*) list chalcopyrite as a native product there. Volume 11 of the *Great Tang Records on the Western Regions* also mentions that Persia "produces gold, silver, and chalcopyrite." In the *Essential Criteria of Antiques* (*Gegu yaolun*) written by Cao Zhao in the Ming period, it is stated that "Real chalcopyrite comes from Persia, and it does not fade when burned, just like gold." In its heyday, Persia extended its border to the Caucasus on the eastern shore of the Black Sea. That is why chalcopyrite relics unearthed in the Caucasus in recent years can help to verify Chinese documents. In 1967, the burial site of Moshtcevaya Balka was excavated in the northwestern Caucasus mountains, dating from the eighth to ninth centuries. Of the 47 unearthed artifacts, there were 33 chalcopyrite products, accounting for 70% of the total. Based on their chemical compositions, chalcopyrite can be divided into two types: the low-zinc product containing less than 14% zinc and the high-zinc product with a zinc content as high as 15%–50%. These unearthed

artifacts can be cross-referenced with what is given in Shi Xilin's *Supplement to "Sound and Meaning of All Sutras"* (*Xu yiqiejing yinyi*), volume five:

> In the Western Regions, herbs are added to refine copper, and then chalcopyrite of two different qualities would be produced. One is called *huizhe* [literally 'gray fold'], which is somewhat whiter in color and low in quality, while the other is called *jinzhe* [literally 'golden fold'], more golden in color and good in quality. The latter one is also termed as 'real chalcopyrite' or commonly known as '*bubojin*' [literally 'nonexchangeable gold'].

As a type of mineral similar to gold, *jinzhe* was prevalent in the Caucasus along the Silk Road.[50] Thus seen, in the commodity structure of inland trade in Asia in the early Middle Ages, "real chalcopyrite" was highly valued and that explains why it was chosen as the tribute by the Nine Surnames. About the usage of chalcopyrite in the Tang period, there are two points to be mentioned. First, it was used in the casting of Buddhist statues. As indicated in the sequel to the *Miscellaneous Writings from Youyang* (*Youyang zazu*), volume five, in Chang'an, "the six-foot-high chalcopyrite statue of Vairochana Buddha in the Huayan Temple is a fine example of the ancient style." During the Tang period, the use of chalcopyrite to cast statues was so common that when Emperor Wuzong banned Buddhism, he gave the imperial order to "melt gold, silver and chalcopyrite statues [for precious metals] to cover national expenses."[51] Second, it was used to decorate official attires. In "A Treatise on Official Chariots and Attires" ("Che fu zhi") of the *New Book of Tang*, volume 24, it is stipulated that "official attires for the eighth and ninth *pin* were greenish blue, decorated with chalcopyrite." Probably because the "gold-like" chalcopyrite was rare, common people were sometimes fooled by vulgar profit-seekers. In "A Merchant's Pleasure" ("Gu ke le"), a poem by Yuan Zhen, a fraudulent use of chalcopyrite as gold is revealed:

> Once you understand the street language,
> there is no love for your hometown.
> An armlet made of chalcopyrite,
> and a necklace made of glutinous rice will surely let you down.
> When brought back and sold in the village,
> these armlets can be hit lightly as if they were gold to produce a crisp sound.

2 **Red salt and black salt.** Both are "halite," the properties of which cannot be found in the related literature and are difficult to ascertain. According to the *Book of Sui* and the *New book of Tang: Records of the Western Regions*, black salt was produced in Zabulistan[52] and southern India. Red salt seems to be "chiyan" in the *Book of Wei: Records of the Western Regions* where we read an entry entitled "Jiaseni guo" ["The Country of Ghazni"]: "Red salt was produced on this land." As "Jiaseni" is the mistaken transcription of Zabulistan's capital Ghazna, it is clear that both types of salt were local products of this state.

Zabulistan was located to the south of the Iron Gate Pass and thus quite far from the states north of the Pass such as Khwarazm, Kesh, and Chach; therefore, tribute salts from the other Nine Surnames countries were probably bought from Zabulistan. In terms of their usage, both these salts can be used as medicine. In the *Compendium of Materia Medica*, volume 11, under the entry "Rongyan" [halite], black salt is "mainly used to cure flatulence," while red salt is "strong enough to keep a man energetic."

3 **Agate.** Agate was one of the "seven treasures" of the Western Regions and was renowned in ancient and medieval times.[53] In the Northern Wei dynasty, Yuanchen, the king of Hejian, had some "treasures" from the Western Regions, and one of them was an agate bowl.[54] According to "Notes to Seven Treasures" ("Qibao pian") in the *Collection of Translated Buddhist Terms*, volume three, "What is mentioned as *moluojiali* in the Buddhist texts is actually agate. This treasure looks like horse brain, hence the name." Red agate was more valued. As declared by the *Essential Criteria of Antiques*, "The ancient saying goes: if your agates are not red, you are going to be poor for the rest of your life." Also, a line in Du Fu's poem "Appreciating General Cao's Horse Painting at the Residence of Secretary Wei Feng" ("Wei Feng lushi zhai guan Caojiangjun huama tu") – "a dark red agate bowl was sent from the Department of Imperial Household" – indicates that a rare and precious agate product is undoubtedly dark red. The tribute from the Nine Surnames must have been agates of such top quality. On An Lushan's birthday, Emperor Xuanzong bestowed upon him two small agate plates and one large agate plate flattened with gold.[55] This proves that an emperor's reward was a major means for the tribute to spread from the inner palace to the outer court. In terms of size, agates from the Western Regions in the Tang period were not the small ornaments familiar to future generations. They could be amazingly large. In 677, when Pei Xingjian defeated the "shixing kehan" [Western Turkic Khaganate], he received some spoils of war, among which was an "agate plate, with a diameter more than two *chi*[56], spectacularly eye-catching in its pattern and color." No wonder that Tang officials and soldiers regarded it as a "treasure."[57]

Textiles

1 *Tadeng* **and** *Qushu*. *Tadeng* 毾㲪 was a famous woolen carpet in the ancient Western Regions. It appears in Li He's poem "Song of the Palace Maids" ("Gongwa ge") where a description of the palace maids' loneliness is provided: "Fragrance spurts from the elephant mouth of the incense burner, and one feels warm on a *tadeng* carpet, / the Big Dipper hangs over the city, and the time funnel announces a deep night." Wang Qi, in his book *Annotations of Li Changji's Poems* (*Li Changji geshi huijie*), offered a rather detailed explanation:

> 毾㲪[Tàdēng](*tadeng*) sounds the way 榻登[Tàdēng] (footrest in front of a bed) is pronounced. *Picang* 埤苍 [a dictionary] explains it as a kind of woolen carpet. *Excerpts from Books in the Northern Hall* (*Beitang*

shuchao) contends that a finer *qushu* 氍毹 is called *tadeng*. The *Abridged Collection of Rhymes of the Ancient and Modern* (*Gujin yunhui juyao*) suggests that *qushu* is a kind of woolen mattress, and it might also be called *tadeng*. Finally, the *Comprehensive Elegances* (*Tongya*) [a major encyclopedic text] claims that *tadeng*, called 氆氇 [*pulu*, a woolen fabric] today, is produced in central India.

Roughly speaking, the difference between *tadeng* and *qushu* lies not in raw materials but in the craft. According to Fujita Toyohachi, "*Tadeng* is a finer woolen carpet while *qushu* is coarser."[58] In the tales from the Northern Qi dynasty, *tadeng* is depicted as a token of extravagant life for wealthy Sogdian merchants: "Zhi Facun, a Sogdian by birth, grew up in Guangzhou. He was highly skilled in medicine and soon became very rich. His family had eight or nine *chi* of *tadeng* patterned with various figures, spectacular and magnificent."[59] As for *qushu*, apart from its function to keep the room warm, it could also be used for house decoration. In Cen Shen's poem "Song of General Gai at Yumen Pass" ("Yumenguan Gaijiangjun ge"), there is a line that reads "In a warm room of embroidered curtains and red braziers, / there are patterned *qushu* as wall hangings." This indicates that *qushu* could be used as a wall tapestry when woven into a certain pattern. Although *tadeng* and *qushu* could be produced in Sogdiana during the Tang period,[60] the craftsmanship was far below those made in the Byzantine empire.[61] The royal weaving workshop of Constantinople had a high reputation in the ancient Near East. In the *Records of the Three Kingdoms* (*Sanguo zhi*), volume 30, there is a quote from *A Brief History of Wei* (*Wei lue*) about the Byzantine empire which writes: "Products like *zhicheng* [woven carpets], *qushu*, *tadeng*, and *jizhang* 罽帐 [woven tents] are all good in quality, and they are more colorful than textiles produced in the kingdoms east of the Sea." Therefore, when Bukhara paid tribute in 719, specific mention was made about the "Fulin embroidered *qushu*" in the tribute letter to emphasize that it was a famous Byzantine product and not a native one of Bukhara.

2 **Yuenuo** 越诺. In the *Book of Sui*, volume 93, it is stated that "yuenuo fabric" was produced in Persia, which means that it was a local product of Iran rather than Sogdiana. About the origin of this term, there are two suggested explanations. Berthold Laufer traced it back to the Persian word Var-nax, a compound made of "silk fabric" and "brocade."[62] But Paul Pelliot believed that it is a transcription of the Sanskrit colloquial word "Varnakā," the root of which is "varṇā" (color or flower).[63] In the time of the Arab caliphate, this Persian damask seemed to have a change, and only the white ones were considered to be of top quality. For instance, in both the *Representative Answers from the Region beyond the Mountains* (*Lingwai daida*), volume three, and the *Records of Foreign People* (*Zhufan zhi*), volume one, there are references to "white yuenuo fabric" that was produced in Baghdad. In the early years of the Northern Song period, "white yuenuo fabric" was offered by the Arabs twice: one was in 993 with "two pieces of white yuenuo fabric" and the other was in 995 with "three pieces of white yuenuo fabric."[64]

3 **Dancing rugs.** In the Tang period, when the imperial court or wealthy households held banquets, dancers and musicians were invited to perform. The covering over the stage was called a dancing rug (*wuyan*).[65] From Dunhuang frescos, we can see two forms of dancing rugs: one is rectangular, as revealed by a face-to-face dance on the north wall of Cave 172 (around the golden age of the Tang dynasty); the second is circular, as shown by the solo dance in Cave 180 (also around the golden age of Tang). There are abundant descriptions about dancing rugs in Tang poems, which can fill the gap left by historical texts. For instance, Bai Juyi's poem "Twenty Rhymes for Green Felt Tents" ("Qingzhanzhang ershi yun") mentions about "set[ting] a low seat for singers on the side and spread[ing] a small dancing rug on the floor." Liu Yuxi's poem "An Improvisational Outpouring of Emotions upon the Visit by Mr. Linghu from Bianzhou" ("He Bianzhou Linghu xianggong daozhen gaiyue oushu suohuai") has a line that reads "On the high platform are performers holding white silk fans, and on the dancing rug are girls in gold-threaded shirts." In Li Shangyin's poem "Willow" ("Liu"), we can read "Once pursuing the east wind, just like girls performing on various dancing rugs, / at a time when people were having fun in the Garden of Pleasure in a blossoming spring." It is also mentioned in the 84th poem of Wang Jian's 100 poems of "Palace Lyrics" ("Gongci"): "As the jade flute changes the tune, and the zither is relocated, / performers are urged to put on costumes of red gauze and step onto a new embroidered dancing rug." The above examples indicate that a dancing rug was an embroidered fabric that could be spread on a platform, or put on a bare floor, and could be changed during the performance to enhance the stage effect. Undoubtedly, the tribute dancing rug was meant for the use of court dancers. In the Tang period, two exceedingly gorgeous dancing rugs came from Persia in 750, one was an "embroidered dancing rug with flame-colored edges" and the other was an "embroidered dancing rug with long tassels on the four edges."[66] As the Sassanid dynasty had ended by this time, those who claimed to be tribute envoys must have been Sogdian merchants from Persia rather than real tributary officials. As for the "*tabi* dancing rug" they offered, it might not be a good one, as "*tabi*" (written as tàbì "拓壁" or tàbì "拓必")[67] is nothing more than a coarse woolen material, which is explained as a "woolen mat" by Shi Huilin in the *Sound and Meaning of All Sutras* (*Yiqiejing yinyi*).

Utensils

1 **Crystal eyedrop bottles.** Among the tributes from the Nine Surnames, this tribute had a certain cultural background. In the Tang period, famous ophthalmologists of the Western Regions were not Sogdians but monks from India and the Byzantine empire. For the Indian doctor, we can refer to Liu Yuxi's poem "For my Ophthalmologist – A Brahman Monk" ("Zeng yanyi poluomen seng"): "Gradually seeing red as green, / my eyes fear strong sunlight and wind. / With your excellent surgical skills, can you treat my cataract to restore my eyesight to normal?" As for the doctor from the Byzantine empire, Du Huan's *Record of Travels* (*Jingxing ji*) provides a clue: "Doctors in Daqin [Byzantine empire] are

particularly good at treating eye diseases and dysentery. They can detect disease before the onset, or cut open a skull to pick out worms." The medical skills of the Nestorian monks from the Byzantine empire had long been known along the eastern shore of the Mediterranean. There were also traces of their presence in China during the Tang period. In the ninth century, in Chengdu, there was "a monk ophthalmologist from Daqin" recorded in the *Collected Works of Li Wenrao* (*Li Wenrao wenji*), volume 12. Qin Minghe, the palace physician who pierced the two acupuncture points of Baihui and Naohu for Emperor Gaozong to make his eyes "bright," [68] may have been a Daqin [Byzantine] ophthalmologist, in consideration of the common practice of "taking the country name as one's surname" prevalent among the Sogdians who came to China. In addition, it should be taken into account that Byzantium was famous for producing "crystals," though what was called "crystal" in the Tang period was not necessarily real "crystal" in the modern sense but a kind of glass with high luminosity. This is evidenced by Wei Yingwu's "Ode to Crystal" ("Yong shuijing"), which is actually a poem about glass: "Taking the color of the object it reflects, / the crystal is empty of surface and essence. / Held towards the bright moon, the shiny object turns into the color of sad water." Based on the above analysis, it may be inferred that "crystal eyedrop bottle(s)" tributed by Samarkand in 740 were actually glass bottles bought from Byzantium.

2 **Treasure beds.** A "*huchuang*" [literally "Sogdian bed"] was an easy-to-carry stool popular during the Wei and Jin, Sui and Tang periods. It could be folded, hung, or carried around. Yu Jianwu of the Liang period, in his poem "Ode to the Sogdian Bed: A Reply Poem" ("Yong huchuang yingjiao"), made a good point:

> Enjoying a good fame in the Western Regions,
> the stool is accepted and trusted in the Central Plains.
> Even though one is crippled, his upper body straightens up;
> even though one's handwriting is twisted, as a person he
> still naturally sits up.

Also, in Cave 402 of Dunhuang, a fresco from the Sui period depicts warriors sitting on this kind of stool. A western sinologist has published a monograph about the "Sogdian bed," which can be a good source for reference.[69] In the Tang period, states in the Western Regions continued to offer "Sogdian beds" as a tribute. In 747, Persian envoys came to "offer agate bed(s)."[70] As mentioned above, agate was one of the "seven treasures," so the "treasure bed" offered by the Nine Surnames was probably a stool inlaid with agates.

Food

1 **Stone honey.** In ancient Asia, there were three types of stone honey. The first was rock honey, that is, natural stone honey. What Li Changji mentioned in the line "putting on rattan shoes to collect stone honey" in his poem "The South

Garden" ("Nanyuan") refers to this kind of food. Tao Hongjing, in his book *Notes to Herbal Medicine* (*Caoben zhu*), gave more explanations:

> Also known as rock honey, stone honey can be collected on rocks in high mountains. It is greenish in color, slightly sour in taste, and brings about a feeling of vexation in one's heart after one eats it, and the bees that produce stone honey are black in color like gadflies.

As this food comes with an adverse reaction – "a feeling of vexation in one's heart," it is definitely unsuitable for an offering as tribute. The second was malt sugar. The entry entitled "Sugarcane" ("Ganzhe") in the *Encyclopedia of Arts and Letters* (*Yiwen leiju*), volume 87, gives an explanation by quoting from the *Records of the Eight Counties in Nanzhong Region* (*Nanzhong bajun zhi*):

> Jiaozhi [Now northern Vietnam] is the place where sugarcane grows. Much like bamboo, sugarcane is several *cun* in diameter and more than one *zhang*[71] in length. If you break it in halves and chew it, you find it rather sweet. Expose the juice squeezed from the sugarcane to the sun for a few hours, you will get malt sugar. Put it inside your mouth, it immediately melts away. Local people call it stone honey.

As this stone honey is "rather sweet," it could be a fitting tribute. However, stone honey produced in West Asia was very different from malt sugar in terms of properties. As Du Huan pointed out in the *Record of Travels*, local people "carve stone honey into *lushe* [a delicacy] which is similar to a Chinese imperial carriage in shape, and present it to an eminent person on festivals." If it can be carved, stone honey must be solid rather than gelatinous, nothing like malt sugar. The third type was called "shageling," a transcription of the Sanskrit word Sarkarā. Its making method originated from India. It was produced by boiling sugarcane pulp with milk and oil and then solidifying it into a lump.[72] Since the first two possibilities have been ruled out, it can only be assumed that the tribute stone honey from the Nine Surnames was Sarkarā. Here a few words about the local custom of Samarkand should be added. In "Records of Samarkand" of the *New Book of Tang*, it is written:

> When giving birth, a woman keeps the stone honey in her mouth and gelatin in her palm, hoping that this coming child will speak pleasant words when he grows up, and the treasure he has accumulated will stay with him like glue on hand.

It is clear that stone honey was considered auspicious by the Sogdians in Central Asia, and as a result, it could be offered as a tribute. Stone honey can be black or white depending on ingredients. As the tribute from Bukhara was only labeled as "raw stone honey," and no specification was given, we do not know what type it was.

2 **Wine.** The Nine Surnames were not only good at conducting business but also known for being "wine-loving" people, whose traditional product, wine, had gained fame in China as early as the Han and Jin dynasties. In the *Book of the Later Han- Records of the Western Regions* (*Hou Hanshu: Xiyu zhuan*), it is written: "Having a fertile soil, Sogdiana is a land of abundant fruits, and that is why wine in this place is particularly famous." There is a more detailed account in Zhang Hua's *Records of Diverse Matters* (*Bowuzhi*), volume five:

> Wine in the Western Regions can be preserved for many years without going bad. There is a local saying that goes: Drinking the wine after it is kept for ten years gets one so drunk that he will not get sober until the end of the next day.

Thus seen, paying tribute with wine was fully in line with the Sogdian practice both in terms of natural condition and cultural feature. As other scholars have done a fairly detailed study about the history of introducing wine from the Western Regions to China,[73] I only add two points here about the production of wine based on some archaeological data.

The first concerns the wine tally. The Sogdian document No. 69 unearthed at Mount Mugh is a wine tally of eight lines carved on a wooden strip, recording the quantity of wine taken from the cellar by 11 Sogdians, varying from three, four, or five Sogdian Kpc (about 10 liters) each.[74]

The second is related to wineries. The ruins of wineries from the seventh to eighth centuries have been found in Panjikent, Khwarazm, and Tashkent successively, indicating that Transoxiana in Central Asia was indeed the production base of wine. In 1979, another winery was excavated from the ruins of the Sutrushana in the Tang period. This winery was located on a hill, with pipes connecting wine tanks. Also unearthed were pottery containers.[75] It needs to be pointed out that, after Emperor Taizong of Tang "defeated Gaochang, brought back the seeds of mare's milk grapes, planted them in the royal garden, and obtained the winemaking method from the Gaochang people,"[76] the Nine Surnames continued to offer wine as a tribute during the Kaiyuan period. Also at a royal garden party, Imperial Consort Yang still sipped at "wine from the Western Liangzhou."[77] These accounts indicate that, after 70 or 80 years of imitative brewing, the quality of wine produced by the Han Chinese still could not compete with that of the tribute wine.

On the whole, tribute from the Western Regions had a clear commercial orientation. As Samarkand, Bukhara, Turgesh, and other states were "mostly offering rare and exotic treasures," then in 719, Emperor Xuanzong set the rule of "rewarding by value and paying with generosity,"[78] thus revealing a distinct feature of the international contact in the medieval times. As a special commodity, tribute was complex in its composition, reflecting the diversity of its origins. The following is a tentative explanation about this.

Tributes and the Nine Surnames' Contact with the Outside World

During the Tang period, the city-states of the Nine Surnames constituted the key points along the east-west transportation route. This region was the converging place for the four ancient civilizations – China, India, Persia, and Byzantium, thus occupying an important position in the world.

Among the Nine Surnames, Samarkand topped the tribute list in terms of frequency. This is due to the fact that its capital was the trade center of Central Asia in the medieval times, where "treasures from foreign countries are mostly gathered here."[79] This intermediary role lasted until the beginning of the Ming dynasty. As is written in "A Record of the Foreign Countries in the Western Regions": "Although there are many goods, none of them are locally produced. They are mostly brought over from other countries." Such a commodity structure would naturally leave a mark on the tribute. Based on the above analysis, we know for certain that local products of Transoxiana in Central Asia included lions, horses, golden peaches, silver peaches, indigo, and wine. The rest of the tributes were mostly of foreign origin. For example, Fulin embroidered *qushu* and Fulin dogs came from Byzantium; chalcopyrite and *yuenuo* were bought from Persia, and tulips and raw stone honey were probably introduced from India. These three sources of tribute goods have varying degrees of historical provenance. First, in the ancient times, the province of Syria in the Byzantine empire was the center of the gem trade.[80] This is clearly stated in "Records of Fulin" ("Fulin zhuan") of the *Old Book of Tang*, volume 198, "the majority of precious treasures in the Western Regions come from this country." In the mid-sixth century, Mani Achi, who traveled to Istanbul by the order of the Turkic khan, was a Sogdian merchant who aimed to trade silk for gems.[81] This helps to explain why the tribute from the Nine Surnames contained treasure from the Byzantine empire. Second, the Sogdian city-states bordered Eastern Iran, and there had been a long history of mutual interaction. For one evidence, the Behistun inscription, authored by the Persian king Darius I in the sixth century BC, mentions Khwarazm and Sogdiana, both of which were part of the 16th taxation district of the Achaemenian dynasty. For another, Persia was home to Zoroastrianism. As is stated in "Records of Persia" ("Bosi zhuan") in the *Old Book of Tang*, volume 198, "All the Sogdian states in the Western Regions practiced Zoroastrianism and many Sogdians went to Persia for religious instruction." As a region where Zoroastrianism was prevalent, the Nine Surnames not only embraced Persian culture but also revealed a distinct Persian feature in the physical dimension, for example, in their style of architecture and clothing, so it was a natural choice for them to buy Persian products as tributes. Third, there was also a long-standing contact between India and Sogdiana. By the middle of the third century BC, Emperor Ashoka had already spread Buddhism to the Amu Darya River basin. The influence of the Indian civilization on the Nine Surnames is clearly shown on one of the murals excavated in Panjikent, which uses the story of a prince playing chess in the fourth section of the *Mahabharata* as a theme.[82]

Finally, there is an important historical text that deserves to be explored. According to the *New Book of Tang: Records of Samarkand* (*Xin Tang shu – kangguo zhuan*), volume 221, section 3:

> The state of He [Kushaniyah], also called Qushuangnijia [Kushanika] or Guishuangni [Kushan], is located on the site of a former city-state called Fumocheng. There is a tower on the left side of the capital city. On the northern wall of this tower are paintings of emperors from ancient China, on the east are the king of Turkic Khanate, and the Brahman [of India], and on the west are the kings of Persia and Fulin [Byzantium]. The king of this state comes every morning to perform the ritual bow and then leaves.

Located between Samarkand and Bukhara, the state of He was known as the "heart of Sogdiana." The paintings of emperors or kings in this tower are reminiscent of the famous saying about the "Four Sons of Heaven." Also known as the "Four Lords," ruling the east, south, west, and north, respectively, they were the "lord of men" in China, the "lord of elephants" in India, the "lord of treasures" in Persia, and the "lord of horses" in the state of the Yuezhi or Turks.[83] It should be noted that the paintings in the above-mentioned tower were meant for the king to bow from the south, that is, it is unlikely for the paintings to be positioned in four directions, and thus, they could only be found in the left, center, and right. This may cause the orientation of the "Four Lords" to be different from the legendary one, but the idea is roughly the same. Obviously, this group of paintings worshiped by the king of He is not only a manifestation of the deterrent power of the "Four Lords" but also a microcosm of the international connection between the Nine Surnames. When viewed through this lens, the diversity of tributes from the Nine Surnames in the Tang period becomes fully understandable.

Notes

1. During the Sui and Tang dynasties, most of the Sogdians living in China assumed one of the Nine Surnames in accordance with the land of their origin. In Chinese sources, they were called *jiuxinghu* 九姓胡. There are different English translations for *jiuxinghu*, such as "Nine Surnames of the Sogdians," "Nine Sogdian Surnames," "Nine Tribes of Zhaowu," "Nine Barbarian Clans," or "Nine Barbarian Families." Here the first one is used and simplified as the "Nine Surnames" hereafter. —Trans.
2. "Records of the Western Region" ("Xiyu zhuan") in the *Book of Han* (*Hanshu*), vol. 96.
3. In the Tang dynasty, the Eastern Roman Empire, namely, the Byzantine empire, was called "Fulin" 拂菻, "Folin" 佛菻, or "Daqin" 大秦. —Trans.
4. *Jinshi* 进士 was the highest and final degree in the examination system in ancient China. Only those who passed the examination held in the imperial capital were called *jinshi*. Started in the Sui dynasty, this practice continued until the Qing dynasty. —Trans.
5. *Complete Tang Poems* (*Quan Tangshi*), case 5, book 6, scroll (juan) 307.
6. In Chinese history, Suiye was also called "Suyecheng 素叶城" or "Suyeshuicheng 素叶水城," literally meaning "a city by the Suyab River." —Trans.
7. Clauson, 1961: 1–13.
8. Xuanzang, vol. 1.
9. The *li* 里 is a Chinese unit of distance. In the Tang period, one *li* was approximately 323 meters. —Trans.

10 "Records of Gaochang" ("Gaochang zhuan") in the *Book of Old Tang*, vol. 198.
11 See "Records of Gaochang" in the *New Book of Tang*, vol. 221. In the *Book of Old Tang*, it is written as "In the following months, the tribute from the Sogdian merchants was restrained and stopped 自后数月，商胡被其遏绝贡献." Feng Chengjun assumed that "there might be some words missing here." See *Collected Works of Translation for the Study on the History and Geography of the Western Regions and South China Sea* (*Xiyu nanhai shidi kaozheng lunzhu huiji*), 80. According to the *Essentials of the Government of the Zhenguan Era* (*Zhenguan Zhengyao*), volume nine, this sentence should be "Since then, several merchants have claimed that their tribute had been restrained and stopped 自后数有商胡称其遏绝贡献."
12 "Documents Unearthed in Turpan," vol. 7, 88–94, 389–390.
13 Henning, 1948: 609.
14 Huili and Yancong, vol. 1.
15 Kang 康 (Samarkand) was in modern Samarkand; Mi 米(Maimurgh) was located either southeast of the Zerafshan River or Panjikent; Shi 史(Kesh) in modern Shahrisabz; Shi 石 (Chach) in modern Tashkent. For the English translation of some state names, the translators have referred to a published essay by Valerie Hansen, Professor of History at Yale University. See "The Impact of the Silk Road Trade on a Local Community: The Turfan Oasis, 500–800," in *Les Sogdiens en Chine*, edited by Vaissière and Trombert (Paris: École française d'Extrême-Orient, 2005): 283–310. —Trans.
16 The *jin* 斤 [catty] is a traditional Chinese unit of mass. In the Tang period, one *jin* was approximately 596 grams. —Trans.
17 *Zhihan* 质汗 is a herbal medicine originating from the Western Regions. It is mainly used to treat injuries by metal objects. It also helps to stop bleeding and grow new muscles. —Trans.
18 It was located near modern Türkmenabat in modern Turkmenistan. —Trans.
19 Kaiyuan era (713–741) and Tianbao era (742–756) are two era names used by Emperor Xuanzong of the Tang dynasty. —Trans.
20 In the "official rank" system (*pin*) of the Tang dynasty, there were nine ranks, with detailed divisions within each one. —Trans
21 Wang Qinruo et al., vol. 999.
22 Livshits, *Sogdian Documents from Mount Mugh: Legal Documents and Letters*, 78, 81.
23 Wang Qinruo et al., vol. 999.
24 Narshakhi, 40–41.
25 Smirnova, "A Brief History of the Arab Conquests in Central Asia," 119–133; "On the History of the Samarkand Agreement of 712," 69–79.
26 Belenizki and Marshak, 215–221.
27 Su Mian et al., vol. 99.
28 Wang Qinruo et al., vol. 977.
29 Hitti, 1979: 241–243; Wang Zhilai, 244–252.
30 See the entry dated "The Third Year of Zhenyuan in the Reign of Dezong" ("Dezongji zhenyuan sannian") in the *Comprehensive Mirror in Aid of Governance* (*Zizhi tongjian*).
31 The state of Kang or Xiwanjin referred to the same country. It was called Xiwanjin in the *Book of Wei* and Kang in the *Book of Sui*. —Trans.
32 Li Zhao, vol. 1.
33 Zhang Tingyu, *History of Ming: Records of the Western Regions* (Mingshi: xiyu zhuan), vol. 332.
34 *New Book of Tang: Records of Samarkand* (*Xin Tang shu - kangguo zhuan*). The word "rhapsody" (fu 赋) in this quote is a form of Chinese rhymed prose which was the dominant literary form in China during the Han dynasty (206 BC-AD 220). As an intermediary form between poetry and prose, a rhapsody allows a writer to describe in detail and from many perspectives. —Trans.
35 Dong Gao et al., vol. 169.
36 *Complete Tang Poems*, case 2, book 3, scroll 81.

37 Zuev, 110.
38 Kroll, 240–269.
39 Duan Chengshi, vol. 1. See also Wang Renyu, vol. 2.
40 "Treatise on the Five Agents" ("Wuxing zhi") in the *New Book of Tang*, vol. 35.
41 Yelv Chucai, vol. 5.
42 In the Tang period, the Indian peach which originally came from China was called "han chilai" 汉持来 in Chinese. See Xuanzang, *Great Tang Records on the Western Regions*, vol. 4.
43 The *Rites of Zhou* (*Zhouli*) is a description of the putative organization of the government during the Western Zhou period (11th–770 BC). In the *Rites of Zhou*, the Ministry of Spring oversees the school system, ceremonies, rituals and festivals and is part of the Six Ministries. It is also known as the Ministry of Rights and the Ministry of Rites. —Trans.
44 In Chinese sources, Kapisa is known as Jibin 罽宾, Jiapi 伽毗 or Jiabishi 迦毕试.
45 See Pang Yuanying, *Miscellaneous Records of Wenchang* (*Wenchang zalu*), vol. 3, in the *Complete Library in Four Sections*.
46 See Du You, *Comprehensive Institutions* (*Tongdian*), vol. 193 where it quotes from *Record of Travels* (*Jingxing ji*).
47 See Bai Juyi's poem "The Gray-Haired Maiden of Shangyang" ("Shangyang baifa ren").
48 Laufer, 1964: 340–343.
49 Rao Zongyi, 627–630. See also Zhang Hongzhao, 343–355.
50 Jerusalemskaya, 1986: 100–109.
51 *Old Book of Tang: Annals of the Wuzong Emperor* (*Jiu Tang shu: Wuzong ji*).
52 Zabulistan is also known as caoguo 漕国, Caojuzha 漕矩吒, or Xieyu 谢颭 in different Chinese sources.
53 See Markovin, 270–274.
54 Yang Xuanzhi, vol. 4.
55 Yao Runeng, vol. 1.
56 The *chi* 尺 is a traditional Chinese unit of length equal to 10 *cun* 寸. In the Tang period, one *chi* was approximately 30.7 centimeters. —Trans.
57 *Old Book of Tang* (*Jiu Tang shu*), vol. 84.
58 See Fujita Toyohachi, *Collected Essays on the Ancient Maritime Traffic in the South China Sea* (Shanghai: The Commercial Press, 1936), in particular, the chapter entitled "Ta, Tadeng and Qushu." See also Ma Yong, 50–55.
59 See Li Fang et al., *Extensive Records of the Taiping Era* (*Taiping guangji*), vol. 119, where it quotes from *Stories of Retribution* (*Huanyan ji*).
60 "Records of Sogdiana" in the *Comprehensive Institutions*, vol. 193.
61 See Belenizki and Bentovich. "A Brief History of the Silk Weaving Industry in Central Asia," 66–78. See also Belenizki et al., "Brocade Unearthed from Mount Mugh," 108–119.
62 Laufer, 1964: 323–325.
63 See Schafer, 201. See also Pelliot, *Notes on Marco Polo*, 483–484.
64 "Records of the Arab Empire" ("Dayi zhuan") in the *History of Song* (*Song shi*), vol. 490.
65 Ren Bantang claims that "what is called wuyan 舞筵 should be a stage rug." See Ren Bantang, *A Study of Tang Opera* (*Tangxi nong*), 976.
66 "Records of Persia" ("Bosi zhuan") in the *Old Book of Tang*, vol. 198.
67 Laufer traced this word back to an ancient Persian word "tābix."
68 See the entry entitled "The First Year of Hongdao" ("Hongdao yuannian") in the *Comprehensive Mirror in Aid of Governance*, vol. 203.
69 Fitzgerald, 1–88.
70 Wang Qinruo et al., vol. 971.
71 The *zhang* 丈 is a customary Chinese unit of length equal to 10 *chi* 尺. In the Tang period, one *zhang* was approximately 3.07 meters. —Trans.

72　Ji Xianlin, 1982: 124–136; 1984: 25–42.
73　Laufer, 1964: 43–70; Schafer, 141–145.
74　Bogolyubov and Smirnova, 32–33.
75　Berdimuradov, 210–214.
76　Wang Qinruo et al., vol. 970.
77　See Yue Shi, vol. 1.
78　Wang Qinruo et al., vol. 168.
79　Xuanzang, vol. 1.
80　Hirth, 98–106.
81　Jerusalemskaya, 1967: 119–126.
82　Semenov, 216–228.
83　Pelliot, 1962: 84–103.

Bibliography

Ban Gu. *Hanshu (Book of Han)*. Beijing: Zhonghua shuju, 1962.
Belenizki, Alexander Markovich, and Ilona Borisovna Bentovich. "A Brief History of the Silk Weaving Industry in Central Asia." [In Russian.] *Soviet Archeology*, no. 2 (1961): 66–78.
Belenizki, Alexander Markovich, and Boris Ilyich Marshak. "The Most Ancient Image of Lithobolos in Central Asia," in *Ancient and Early Medieval Oriental Culture*. [In Russian.] Edited by Vladimir Grigoryevich Lukonin. Leningrad: Aurora Art Publishers, 1978. 215–221.
Belenizki, Alexander Markovich, et al. "Brocade Unearthed from Mount Mugh." [In Russian.] *Soviet Ethnology*, no. 4 (1963): 108–119.
Berdimuradov, Amridin Ergashovich. "Wineries in Northwestern Sutrushana." [In Russian.] *Soviet Archaeology*, no. 4 (1986): 210–214.
Bogolyubov, Mikhail Nikolaevich, and Olga Ivanovna Smirnova. *Sogdian Documents from Mount Mugh: Business Documents*. [In Russian.] Moscow: Oriental Literature Publishing House, 1963.
Cao Zhao. *Gegu yaolun (Essential Criteria of Antiques)*. Beijing: Zhongguo shudian, 1987.
Chen Cheng. "Xiyu fanguo zhi (A Record of the Foreign Countries in the Western Regions)," in *Xiyu xingchengji xiyu fanguo zhi xianbinlu (A Record of the Journey to the Western Regions/A Record of the Foreign Countries in the Western Regions/A Record of All Guests)*. Beijing: Zhonghua shuju, 1991. 65–116.
Clauson, Gerard. "Ak-Beshim-Suyab." *Journal of the Royal Asiatic Society of Great Britain and Ireland* 93, no. 1/2 (1961): 1–13.
Fa Yun, ed. *Fanyi mingyi ji (Collection of Translated Buddhist Terms)*. Nanjing: Jiangsu guangling keyinshe, 1990.
Feng Chengjun. *Xiyu nanhai shidi kaozheng lunzhu huiji (Collected Works of Translation for the Study on the History and Geography of the Western Regions and South China Sea)*. Beijing: Zhonghua shuju, 1963.
Fitzgerald, Charles Patrick. *Barbarian Beds: The Origin of the Chair in China*. London: The Cresset Press, 1965.
Fujita, Toyohachi. *Collected Essays on the Ancient Traffic in the South China Sea*. Translated by He Jianmin. Shanghai: Shangwu yinshuguan, 1936.
Gu Yewang, ed. *Yupian (Jade Chapters)*. Beijing: Zhonghua shuju, 1987.
Henning, Walter Bruno. "The Date of the Sogdian Ancient Letters." *Bulletin of the School of Oriental and African Studies* 12 (1948): 601–615.

Hirth, Friedrich. *China and the Roman Orient: Researches into their Ancient and Mediaeval Relations as Represented in Old Chinese Records*. [In Chinese.] Translated by Zhu Jieqin. Beijing: Shangwu yinshuguan, 1964.

Hitti, Philip K. *History of the Arabs*, vol. 1. [In Chinese.] Translated by Ma Jian. Beijing: Shangwu yinshuguan, 1979.

Ji Xianlin. "Gudai yindu shatang de zhizao he shiyong (The Production and Use of Granulated Sugar in Ancient India)." *Lishi yanjiu*, no. 1 (1984): 25–42.

Ji Xianlin. "Yizhang youguan yindu zhitangfa chuanru zhongguo de Dunhuang canjuan (A Fragmented Dunhuang manuscript Revealing how the Sugar Producing Method in India was Introduced to China.)" *Lishi yanjiu*, no. 1 (1982): 124–136.

Jerusalemskaya, Anna Alexandrovna. "Ancient Chalcopyrite on the Trade Route of Caucasus." [In Russian.] *Soviet Archaeology*, no. 4 (1986): 100–111.

Jerusalemskaya, Anna Alexandrovna. "Sogdian Relations with Byzantium and Egypt." [In Russian.] *People of Asia and Africa*, no. 3 (1967): 119–126.

Kroll, Paul. "The Dancing Horses of Tang." *Toung Pao* 67 (1981): 240–269.

Laufer, Berthold. *Sino-Iranica*. [In Chinese.] Translated by Lin Yunyin. Beijing: Shangwu yinshuguan, 1964.

Li Zhao. *Guoshi bu* (*Supplement to the History of the State*). Shanghai: Shanghai guji chubanshe, 1979.

Livshits, Vladimir Aronovich. *Sogdian Documents from Mount Mugh: Legal Documents and Letters*. [In Russian.] Moscow: Oriental Literature Publishing House, 1962.

Ma Yong. "Xinjiang qulu wenshu zhi Ko'sava ji qushu kao (Qushu and Ko'sava in Qulu Documents in Xinjiang)," in *Zhongguo minzu guwenzi yanjiu* (*Research on Chinese Ethnic Paleography*). Edited by Chinese Association for the Study of Ethnic Paleography. Beijing: Minzu chubanshe, 1983. 50–55.

Markovin, Vladimir Ivanovich. "Carnelian: 'Stone of Happiness.'" [In Russian.] *Journal of Archaeological Materials and Research in the USSR* 130 (1965): 270–274.

Narshakhi, Abu Bakr Muhammad ibn Jafar. *The History of Bukhara*. Translated by Richard N. Frye. Cambridge, MA: The Mediaeval Academy of America, 1954.

Pelliot, Paul. "Four Sons of Heaven." [In Chinese.] Translated by Feng Chengyun and collected in *Xiyu nanhai shidi kaozheng yicong sanbian* (*The Third Collection of Translated Works for the Study on History and Geography of the Western Regions and South China Sea*). Edited by Feng Chengyun. Beijing: Shangwu yinshuguan, 1962. 84–103.

Pelliot, Paul. *Notes on Marco Polo*. Paris: Imprnationale, 1959.

Quan Tangshi (*Complete Tang Poems*). Collected by Peng Dingqiu et al., and edited by Cao Yin. Shanghai: Shanghai guji chubanshe, 1986.

Rao Zongyi. "Shuo toushi (On Chalcopyrite)," in *Dunhuang tulufan wenxian yanjiu lunji* (*A Collection of Papers on Dunhuang and Turfan Documents*), vol. 2. Beijing: Beijing daxue chubanshe, 1983. 627–630.

Ren Bantang. *Tangxi nong* (*A Study of Tang Opera*). Shanghai: Shanghai guji chubanshe, 1984.

Schafer, Edward Hetzel. *The Golden Peaches of Samarkand: A Study of T'ang Exotics*. Berkeley: University of California Press, 1963.

Semenov, Grigory Lvovich. "The Mahabharata in the Katajikent Murals," in *The Cultural Heritage of the East*. [In Russian.] Edited by Julian Vladimirovich Bromley. Leningrad: Nauka, 1958. 216–228.

Shi Xilin. *Xu yiqiejing yinyi* (*Supplement to "Sound and Meaning of All Sutras."*) Shanghai: Zhonghua shuju, 1949.

Sima Guang, et al. *Zizhi tongjian* (*Comprehensive Mirror in Aid of Governance*). Beijing: Zhonghua shuju, 1976.

Smirnova, Olga Ivanovna. "A Brief History of the Arab Conquests in Central Asia." [In Russian.] *Soviet Oriental Studies*, no. 2 (1957): 119–133.

Smirnova, Olga Ivanovna. "On the History of the Samarkand Agreement of 712." [In Russian.] *Bulletin of the Institute of Oriental Studies of the USSR Academy of Sciences* 28 (1960): 69–79.

Tuotuo and Alutu, eds. *Song shi* (*History of Song*). Shanghai: Shangwu yinshuguan, 1937.

Wang Qi, ed. *Li Changji geshi huijie* (*Annotations of Li Changji's Poems*). Shanghai: Zhonghua shuju, 1936.

Wang Renyu, ed. *Kaiyuan Tianbao yishi* (*Anecdotes of the Kaiyuan and Tianbao Periods*). Taipei: Taiwan shangwu yinshuguan, 1983.

Wang Zhilai. *Zhongya shigang* (*History of Central Asia*). Changsha: Hu'nan jiaoyu chubanshe, 1986.

Yao Runeng. *An Lushan shiji* (*Biographical Accounts of An Lushan*). Shanghai: Shanghai guji chubanshe, 1983.

Yelv Chucai. *Zhanran jushi wenji* (*Collected Works of Yelv Chucai*). Beijing: Zhonghua shuju, 1986.

Yue Shi. *Yang Taizhen waizhuan* (*An Unofficial Account of Yang Taizhen*). Taipei: Taiwan shangwu yinshuguan, 1986.

Zhang Hongzhao. *Shiya: Baoshishuo* (*Lapidarium Sinicum: On Precious Stones*). Shanghai: Shanghai guji chubanshe, 1993.

Zhang Hua. *Bowuzhi* (*Records of Diverse Matters*). Beijing: Zhonghua shuju, 1980.

Zhang Tingyu, et al., eds. *Ming shi* (*History of Ming*). Beijing: Zhonghua shuju, 1974.

Zheng Chuhui, ed. *Minghuang zalu* (*Miscellaneous Records of Emperor Ming*). Beijing: Zhonghua shuju, 1994.

Zhou Qufei. *Lingwai daida* (*Representative Answers from the Region beyond the Mountains*). Annotated by Yang Wuquan. Beijing: Zhonghua shuju, 1999.

Zuev, Yuri Alexeyevich. "Horse Tamgas from Vassal Princedoms," in *New Materials on Ancient and Medieval History of Kazakhstan*. [In Russian.] Edited by Viktor Fedorovich Shakhmatov. Almaty: National Academy of Sciences of the Republic of Kazakhstan, 1960. 93–140.

2 Rituals and Customs of the Nine Surnames of the Sogdians in the Tang Period

In his preface to the *Great Tang Records on the Western Regions* (*Da Tang xiyu ji*), Xuanzang summarized the customs of the Nine Surnames of the Sogdians (shortened as the Nine Surnames hereafter) as follows:

> Beyond the Black Mountains[1], you see Sogdian customs everywhere. Although these ethnic minorities inhabit the same land, there are clear cultural divisions between them. Between well-defined boundaries, local customs vary significantly. They build walled towns, cultivate the land, and raise livestock. They value wealth and disregard benevolence and righteousness. They have no marriage rituals, and there is no distinction between seniors and juniors. In a family, the wife has the say while the husband takes an inferior position. If someone dies, this person is cremated, but there is no fixed period of mourning. [To pay homage to the deceased,] they cut their faces, rip their ears, chop their hair, tear their garments, and slay livestock, to offer sacrifice to the spirit that is about to depart from them. For auspicious occasions, they wear white clothes; when in mourning, they are dressed in black.

In the same volume, Xuanzang gave further descriptions of Sogdian customs when he returned to the subject:

> They wear clothes made of felt and dress themselves in animal furs, which are often close-fitting and tight. They keep their hair cut short and their heads uncovered. Some of them have their hair trimmed or their heads shaved in a certain way so that they can ornament their heads or have net-like objects hanging down the foreheads. They are tall in height, but timid in temperament. Probably on account of local custom, they are superficial and treacherous, and behave in a perfidious way. Mostly avaricious and greedy, they are even calculating and profit-oriented in father-son relationship. The wealthy are honored and esteemed, regardless of whether their social status is well-born or low-born. A person can be a millionaire, but he still lives a simple life of taking rough meals. Half of the population are farmers and the other half traders.

Based on the above quotes, I examine the Sogdian customs by dividing them into ten categories: family, marriage, funeral and burial, dwelling, dress, diet, calendar, festivals, business, and nomenclature. Following the principle of mutual confirmation between Chinese sources and Sogdian artifacts, I explore the customs of the Nine Surnames during the Tang dynasty in a systematical and structured way, with the hope that it can provide reference for further research on Sogdian society and culture in the Middle Ages.

Family

In Xuanzang's descriptions of Sogdian customs, two elemental family relationships are mentioned. Between husband and wife, "the wife has the say while the husband takes an inferior position"; and between father and son, "[m]ostly avaricious and greedy, they are even calculating and profit-oriented in father-son relationship." Following these two quotations, I try to delineate the Sogdian family structure with the help of limited historical documents available.

As early as the Han dynasty, from the west of Ferghana Valley to Parthia, Sogdian families followed the practice that "women are honored and respected. Whatever a wife says will be resolutely obeyed by her husband."[2] This custom was still in fashion among the Nine Surnames in the Tang dynasty. According to the first volume of the *Biographical Account of An Lushan* (*An Lushan shiji*), as Imperial Consort Yang's adopted son, An Lushan "for each audience, kneeled down and kowtowed to Taizhen [Imperial Consort Yang] first. When Emperor Xuanzong asked him why, he replied that ethnic minorities all show respect to mother first and then to father! This made Xuanzong very happy."[3] Apparently, what emboldened An Lushan to behave this way was the long-standing Sogdian custom of "show[ing] respect to mother first and then to father." Although this custom was contradictory to the ethics of the Han Chinese, it happened to win the favor of Xuanzong and his wife. What was mentioned in a joking manner in ancient history about this particular feature of matriarchy was also reflected in the political life of the Nine Surnames. We can cite three examples as evidence. First, according to the *Book of Sui* (*Sui shu*), volume 83, the king of Bukhara, "after receiving reports, sits together with his wife and his minister to have a discussion about national affairs." Second, as recorded in the *Prime Tortoise of the Record Bureau* (*Cefu yuangui*), volume 999, in the second month of 719, Tughshada笃萨波提, the king of Bukhara, sent an envoy to pay tribute, and his wife khatun offered her share in her own name. Third, on the two Sogdian bronze coins, numbered 1482 and 1484, the obverse of each coin is engraved with the head images of the king and khatun side by side.[4]

Within a Sogdian family in the Tang dynasty, "the wife has the say" and one "show[s] respect to mother first and then to father," revealing traces of matriarchy. But in essence, it was still a patriarchal family structure dominated by male lineage, most strongly evidenced by the naming style of legal documents. For example, in a document unearthed from Mount Mugh numbered B-8, which is a land purchase contract signed in 707 or 708, the signatures of the buyer and the seller and four witnesses were all given as "somebody is the son of somebody":

Seller:	Šinvaγcˇ and Satafsarak are the sons of Farnxund-a.
Buyer:	Mxcˇ and Xšùmvandak are the sons of Asmancˇ-a.
Witness:	Wrk'n is the son of Bγtwrz.
	nny – prn is the son of Bγw'rz.
	Š'(w)c is the son of prny-'n.
	tws'γ is the son of zym.[5]

The other two documents numbered Nov. 3 and Nov. 4 are two pieces of the famous marriage contract signed in the tenth year (710) of Tarkhun, the king of Samarkand, wherein the bride, groom, witness, and recorder each had their father's name written before his or her own name.[6] Such a unique naming style was also reflected in Sogdian epitaphs of the early Tang dynasty. For example, Kang A'da from Samarkand who lived during the Zhenguan period gave his name as "A'da, the son of the deceased grand commandant-equivalent (*shangyitong*) of the Great Tang, Kang Moliang."[7] This naming style is consistent with the signing format on legal documents. The fact that Sogdian legal documents attached such importance to the paternal lineage of the concerned parties is strong evidence that Sogdian families were essentially patriarchal. The so-called inferior position of men was just a formality, an etiquette to "show respect to mother first and then to father." It is not indicative of female superiority over the male.

Another important aspect of a Sogdian family concerns a person's rites of passage. Leaving aside the discussion of marriage and funeral customs to a separate section, here I mainly examine the three stages from one's birth to adulthood. First, there was a ritual for blessing a child's birth. As narrated in the *New Book of Tang* (*Xin Tang shu*), volume 221, book three:

> When giving birth, a woman keeps the stone honey in her mouth and gelatin in her palm, hoping that this coming child will speak pleasant words when he grows up, and the treasure he has accumulated will stay with him like glue on hand.

Second, learning started in childhood. In the *Comprehensive Institutions* (*Tongdian*), volume 193, there is a quote from the *Record of the Western Minorities* (*Xifan ji*), which reads:

> When a boy is about five years old, he is sent away to learn. After obtaining the basics, he is sent back to study how to manage business. Whether a person performs well is judged by the profits he has earned.

Third, one started to conduct business in adulthood. In the *New Book of Tang*, volume 221, book three, it is written that "When a man reaches the age of 20, he travels to neighboring countries. Wherever he can make money, he will go." From the above-mentioned characteristics of the three age groups, it can be seen that instilling business awareness in children allowed them to inherit business traditions. After the initial ability of "being good at conducting business" was developed, Sogdian teenagers could move from family to society, and from Central Asia to China, strongly motivated by their "greedy pursuits."

In the Tang dynasty, it was common to see a Sogdian father taking his son(s) to "the neighboring countries" to conduct business. A batch of archives unearthed in Turpan demonstrates that, in 685, among the Sogdian merchants conducting business (*xingsheng hu*) who applied to the Office of the Commander-Governor (*dudu fu*) of the prefecture of Xizhou for a "travel pass" (*guosuo*), there was a 55-year-old Kang Gecha who brought his two sons "Shebi" and "Funile" to the Tang capital to "conduct business."[8] Since Sogdian men went wherever they could make money, and often spent many years traveling to other countries or lived there for long periods, the cohesiveness of Sogdian families would be weakened, and gender relations would be looser than those of agricultural states. That is why their family relationship was branded as "superficial." Meanwhile, with the penetration of commodity and monetary values into families, brothers fought over profits and disregarded moral values. On the back of a Dunhuang manuscript numbered Pelliot 3813, there is a fragment of the *Collected Verdicts of Tang Cases* (*Tang pan ji*), which records the case of a Sogdian merchant named Shi Potuo, stating that:

> Shi Potuo, a native of Chang'an county, became extremely rich by conducting business, winning an honorary official title of commandant of courageous guards (*xiaoqiwei*). His wealth is comparable to that of noblemen, having everything such as gardens, houses, clothes, artifacts, servants, and concubines. He has a younger brother called Jieli who lives separately. Jieli is poverty-stricken, but his older brother does not offer him any help. Shi Potuo has a neighbor named Kang Mobi. Kang wanted to borrow clothes from him but was refused, so Kang sued Shi Potuo for his violation of the law.

Although the case sounds fictitious without supporting evidence, the antagonistic relations between Shi Potuo and his brother and between Shi Potuo and his neighbor share something in common, revealing the characteristics of the Nine Surnames as a commerce-oriented ethnic group. The verdict ends with a conclusive statement:

> Although Jieli lives separately, he is still tied to Potuo through kindred. Legally it is not appropriate to expropriate one person's wealth to help the other, but we express deep sympathy for him. For the older brother, giving away a tiny portion of his wealth to relieve the poverty of his younger brother is a well-praised act. Yet he only thinks about his wealth, how much that hurts! This verdict is also sent to the county magistrate to arrange for a sympathizing relief.

Clearly, the case of Shi Potuo shows that different cultural backgrounds lead to different ethical understandings. In terms of family relations, there were huge differences between the practices of Sogdians and Han Chinese. The family is the cell of society. Taking family as the basis, we might find it easier to understand other customs of the Nine Surnames.

Marriage

In the documents and tablet inscriptions of the Sui and Tang dynasties, we can find many records about Sogdian marriages. They can be divided into two types: royal marriage and civil marriage.

Royal marriages can again be divided into two types. The first is royal marriages within the Nine Surnames. There are two known cases: (1) King Siavash of Bukhara married the daughter of the king of Samarkand. In the *Book of Sui* (*Sui shu*), volume 83, it is recorded as "Shelideng [Siavash], the king of one of the Nine Surnames of Zhaowu, belongs to the same ethnic group as the king of Kangguo [Samarkand]. His wife is the daughter of the king of Kangguo." (2) The daughter of the king of Chach married the Grand Chieftain of Samarkand. In the *Prime Tortoise of the Record Bureau* (*Cefu yuangui*), volume 971, it is recorded as "In the 12th month of 743, Tigin, the king of Shiguo [Chach] sent his son-in-law Kang Randian, the Grand Chieftain of Kangguo [Samarkand], to present gifts." The second type is marriages between royal families of the Nine Surnames and the Turkic Khaganate. There are also two cases: (1) Shishpin, the king of Samarkand, married the daughter of Tardu Qaghan. In the *Book of Sui*, volume 83, it is recorded as "King Shi Shibi [Shishpin][9] is tolerant and generous, respected by all. His wife is the daughter of Tardu, the Turkic qaghan."[10] (2) Qushuzhi, the king of Samarkand, married the daughter of Tong Yabghu Qaghan. In the *Old Book of Tang* (*Jiu Tang shu*), volume 198, it is recorded as "In the reign of Emperor Yang of the Sui dynasty (605–616), Qushuzhi took the daughter of Yehu kehan [Tong Yabghu Qaghan] as his wife, thus [this state was] subjugated to the Western Turkic Khaganate." Royal marriages in the Middle Ages served a political purpose. The Nine Surnames were no exception. Besides Qu Shuzhi's marriage that reflects how a royal marriage accompanied the vassal relationship, in 683, the khatun of Bukhara also proposed a marriage to Tarkhun, the king of Samarkand, to "become his wife" in exchange for his assistance to resist against the invasion of the Arab empire.[11] This exposed the political essence of royal marriage to the utmost.

As for civil marriages, we know from the tablet inscriptions about the great number of marriages within the descendants of the Nine Surnames who lived within the Han Chinese.[12] (1) Marriage between Kang and Cao [Kabudhan] as seen in Kang Xian's wife from a Cao family;[13] (2) Marriage between Kang and Shi [Chach] as evidenced by Kang Ayiqu marrying "a woman from a Shi family in Jiaohe";[14] (3) Marriage between An [Bukhara] and He [Kushaniyah] as seen in An Pu's wife from a He family;[15] (4) Marriage between An and Kang as seen in An Shi's wife from a Kang family;[16] (5) Marriage between He and Kang as seen in He Wenzhe's wife from a Kang family;[17] (6) Marriage between He and An as seen in He Hongjing's wife from an An family in Weiwu;[18] and (7) Marriage between Shi [Chach] and Kang as seen in Shi Mochuo's wife from a Kang family.[19] In addition, there are two special cases. The first one is an epitaph which records that He

Junzheng, the owner of the grave, married a woman from an An family and that he had three daughters-in-law, respectively, from An, Kang, and Kang families.[20] That is, two generations of He married women from three Sogdian surnames. The second one provides an example of marriage within the same surname. In Wu Bolun's book *A Brief History of Xi'an* (*Xi'an lishi shulue*), it is mentioned that Mi Jifen, "whose ancestors came from the state of Mi [Maimurgh] in the Western Regions," had "a woman from a Mi family" as his spouse. Of the nine cases listed above, the surname of Kang accounted for seven, which may not be a coincidence. As the leading surname among the Nine Surnames, Kang [Samarkand] enjoyed a prominent position. Although descendants of Samarkand resided in different areas of the Tang empire, just as other people from the Nine Surnames, in terms of marital life, Kang as a prestige surname seemed to have a lasting influence among the Sogdians.

Besides the aforementioned intermarriage examples, some specific norms can be found in Sogdian marriages during the Tang period. The Sogdian documents Nov. 3 and Nov. 4 unearthed in Mount Mugh are a marriage contract signed in 710, the text and annex of which were written on both sides of two separate leather sheets, with a total of 90 lines. Signed in the "Hall of Law," in the presence of five witnesses, the contract was made in duplicate, and the unearthed document was the copy held by the bride, Ctth, the daughter of the king of Nujakath. Ctth's groom was 'WTTkyn, a Turkic aristocrat. In this contract, in addition to stipulating the responsibilities that the husband and wife should bear, the text also established two noticeable clauses. On the back of Nov. 3, lines 16–18 stipulate that without the consent of the first wife, the husband is not allowed to take a concubine or illicitly cohabit with a lover. Line 22 on the front and lines 2–9 on the back concern the occasion of divorce, distinguishing clearly between the liabilities of "wife divorcing her husband" and "husband divorcing his wife" and recognizing the legality of "husband remarrying" and "wife remarrying" after the agreed compensation. The annex stipulates the groom's obligation for the bride's guardian, his father-in-law. According to Vladimir Aronovich Livshits, the translator and interpreter of this marriage contract, "This Sogdian marriage contract shows that polygamy existed in Sogdiana before the Arab conquest, and there were at least three forms of relationships: formal marriage (legal wife), concubine, and cohabitation."[21]

This contract signed in 710 indicates that the marital life of the upper class in Samarkand already had a fairly complete legal form. Thus, later accounts of consanguineous marriages in Huichao's *Memoir of the Pilgrimage to the Five Kingdoms of India* (*Wang wu tianzhuguo zhuan*), and Du Huan's *Record of Travels* (*Jingxing ji*),[22] revealing "an extremely evil custom of promiscuity, [evidenced by a man's] taking his mother and sisters as his wives," and "fornication with one's mother or younger relatives prevalent among the foreigners," can only be seen as a reflection of the unbalanced development of the marriage system in Transoxiana in Central Asia depicted in the Tang travelogues. They should not be taken as presenting the overall picture of the marriage customs of the Nine Surnames in the Tang dynasty, as it is known that there were different marriage customs at that time, including those among the Zoroastrian, the Turkic, the aristocratic, and plebeian.

Funeral and Burial

The death-related rituals and customs of the Nine Surnames can be divided into two categories: funeral and burial.

At a funeral, people "cut their faces, rip their ears剺面截耳." This practice was prevalent among the northern and western ethnic groups for a long time and became a major feature of funeral culture in ancient inland Asia. Regarding the pronunciation and meaning of the word "剺(li)," Huilin explained that:

> Its pronunciation is the combination of the initial sound of "理" (li) and the final sound of "之" (zhi). In the *Examination of Sounds* (*Kao sheng*), 剺 means to cut and scratch. The *Forest of Words* (*Zilin*) has the word '豾,' saying that it is written as '㓨' in scriptures. A check through all the dictionaries fails to reveal such a word. Judging from the word form and meaning, one can be sure that it should be剺, with its component part "刀" as its radical, and the other half deciding its pronunciation.[23]

Cutting one's face and ripping one's ears so that both blood and tears flow downward was originally a mourning ritual among the nomads north of the Gobi Desert. Its wide use across space and time indicates that this custom had a strong vitality. The following are more examples. (1) Among the Xiongnu: in 91, "hearing about the death of Geng Bing, everyone in Xiongnu cried, and some of them cut their faces and bled."[24] (2) Among the Turks: "After someone dies, the corpse is kept inside the tent. His offspring and relatives pile sheep or horses they have killed in front of the tent. They cut their faces with knives and weep, causing both blood and tears to flow downward. They do this seven times before they stop."[25] (3) Among the Uyghurs: in 759, Bilge Qaghan died. His wife, Princess of Ningguo, "followed the Uyghur custom to cut her face and cry."[26] (4) Among the Mongols: in the *Comprehensive Records on the Mongol Tartars* (*Meng Da beilu*), there is an account that goes: "What is described as White Tartars[27] are those who look comparatively handsome in appearance. They are polite, prudent and filial. Over their parent's death, they cut their faces and cry." (5) Among the Jurchens[28]: "After the death of one's friend or relative, this person cut his forehead with a knife, causing his blood and tears mixed together, which is called bidding farewell to the deceased with blood and tears."[29] As for the spread of this custom among the ethnic minorities in the Western Regions, there are repeated records from the Three Kingdoms to the Sui and Tang dynasties. In 227–233, Cang Ci, the governor (*taishou*) of Dunhuang, died in his tenure:

> Hearing about the death of Cang Ci, the ethnic groups in the Western Regions gathered at the offices of the temporary commandery (*wuji xiaowei*) and the administrator (*zhangshi*) to mourn for him, and some of them cut their faces with knives to show their sworn loyalty.[30]

In 519, Song Yun, a native of Dunhuang, traveled through the state of Khotan, and he saw "a mourner chop his hair and cut his face to show his sadness. Normally, the hair is cut to be four *cun* long."[31] In the fifth month of 649, when Emperor Taizong of the Tang dynasty passed away:

> People of ethnic origins who held officialdom in the imperial court or who came to pay tribute, several hundred of them in number, all cried bitterly. They chopped their hair, cut their faces and ripped their ears, and blood was spilled all over the floor.[32]

Thus seen, Xuanzang's account that "they cut their faces, rip their ears, chop their hair, tear their garments" sums up the Sogdian funeral ceremony in the Tang period, covering both the past and present. These historical records are also confirmed by cultural relics unearthed in Sogdiana. At the No. 2 ruin site of Panjikent, there is a main hall. On the south wall of this hall, there is a large-scale mural, painting six Sogdians and five Turks ripping their ears and cutting their faces in front of a tent in which the deceased is laid.

In Sogdian cultural history, "cutting one's face and ripping one's ears" was not only used as a mourning ceremony but also employed for other occasions relating to interpersonal relations. The first was to bid farewell. In the "Biography of Guo Yuanzhen" ("Guo Yuanzhen zhuan") of the *New Book of Tang* (*Xin Tang shu*), volume 122, we read:

> When Emperor Ruizong of the Tang dynasty succeeded the throne, Guo Yuanzhen was appointed as the minister of the Imperial Stud (*taipu qing*). Before his departure, some chiefs of Anxi bid farewell to him by cutting their faces and weeping bitter tears.

Farewell usually implies one's reluctance to let someone go. That is what happened to An Sishun in 751. When Gao Xianzhi was ordered to replace An Sishun as the military commissioner of Hexi, "Sishun suggested to many Sogdians that they urge him to stay by ripping their ears and cutting their faces. Later it was decreed that Sishun should stay in Hexi."[33] The second is to complain of injustice. This case happened in 696:

> Ashina Huselo, one of the Sogdian chieftains had a servant girl who was good at singing and dancing. Junchen wanted this girl, so he instigated his followers to fabricate a false accusation, suing Huselo for conspiracy against the government. Many chieftains went to the capital, complaining of injustice on his behalf by ripping their ears and cutting their faces. In the end, the Ashina were exempted from the clan execution.[34]

The above cases indicate that "cutting one's face and ripping one's ears" not only expressed the grief of mourning, the sadness of farewell, but also conveyed the indignation of injustice, revealing a diversified Sogdian culture.

Regarding the burial custom of the Nine Surnames, we can take the practice in Samarkand as an example. In the *Comprehensive Institutions* (*Tongdian*), volume 193, there is a quote from Wei Jie's *Records of the Western Minorities* (*Xifan ji*), which reads:

> There were over 200 households outside the city, specializing in burial business. Each of them had built a separate yard and kept their dogs there. Whenever someone died, they would fetch the corpse and placed it in the yard for dogs to eat. When human flesh was eaten up, they would collect bones and bury them. No coffin was used.

This practice looks like "wild burial" or "forest burial" (*shilin*) in India. The entry entitled "Śitavana" ("Shituolin") in the *Sound and Meaning of All Sutras* (*Yiqiejing yinyi*), volume 73, provides this information:

> The correct expression is 'Shiduopona.' It is called 'Cold Forest' in this place, for it is dark, deep and cold. Around the royal city, it is the place where most of the deceased are sent. Now this expression is used to indicate the burial ground for the corpses. Shituolin [Śitavana] is just another way of saying this.

Before the Arab conquest, Zoroastrianism was prevalent among the Nine Surnames in the Tang period, so it was impossible for them to have a burial custom in accordance with the "Buddhist Dharma." According to the *New Book of Tang: Records of Persia* (*Xin Tang shu: Bosi zhuan*), "Sogdians in the Western Regions are subject to their law and practice Zoroastrianism." Thus seen, the custom of leaving the corpses to dogs and collecting bones for burial in Samarkand might have originated from Persia. In the *Histories*, volume one, section 140, Herodotus wrote, "It is said that the body of a male Persian is never buried, until it has been torn either by a dog or a bird of prey." According to a Chinese source, the origin of Samarkand burial custom could be found in the land of Zoroastrianism. In "Records of Persia" ("Bosi zhuan") of the *Comprehensive Institutions*, volume 193, it is narrated that:

> Most of the deceased are left in the mountains. The mourning lasts for a month. There are people who live outside the city, specializing in burials. They are called 'unclean persons' (*bujing ren*). When they enter the city, they ring a bell to show who they are.

Apparently, burial specialists in Samarkand were the counterpart of "unclean persons" in Persia. Also two points should be noted here. First, the aforementioned yard dogs were by no means "pugs of Samarkand" (*kangguo wozi*). Rather, they were Persian dogs known as "spirited dogs" (*junquan*). As explained in "Records of Persia" in the *Old Book of Tang*, volume 198, "A Persian dog is a variegated dog with a dominant golden coat (*bojin quan*) that can travel seven hundred *li* on a scorching summer day." This type of dog liked to eat human flesh. The early record of this can be seen in an account of the despotic rule of Gao Chuo, the king of Nanyang, in 564:

> A woman was walking along the road with her child in her arms. [Seeing Gao Chuo] approaching, she stepped aside to the bushes nearby. When Gao Chuo snatched her child to feed his Persian dog, the woman wailed loudly. Gao Chuo was irritated, and he ordered the dog to eat the woman. [Seeing that] the dog did not respond, he smeared the child's blood on the woman, and then the dog ate her up.[35]

Second, among the Sogdians, although "no coffin was used" after a person's death, there was a utensil to "collect bones and bury." It was a special container: an ossuary. The one used in the royal family was made of gold. As stated in "Records of Chach" ("Shiguo zhuan") of the *Book of Sui*, volume 83:

> On the sixth day of the first lunar month and the 15th day of the seventh lunar month, a gold ossuary which contains the after-cremation bones of the king's deceased parents is placed on a throne. A ritual circuit of the throne is performed, and fragrant flowers and various fruits are offered. Then the king starts to present his sacrificial offering, followed by his ministers.

For the ordinary people, ceramic urns were used, as evidenced by the frequently unearthed ossuaries in the area of Khwarazm. Among them, ossuaries excavated in Tokugar have images engraved on their surface, and these images depict precisely what the Sogdians did at a mourning ceremony, cutting their faces and ripping their ears.[36] As a unique burial device, the ossuary had important cultural significance. According to Vasily Vladimirovich Bartold, what characterized Zoroastrianism in Russian Turkestan with a local color and made it different from Persian Zoroastrianism is the wide use of ossuaries for burial.[37]

Finally, there is also a relevant historical account that needs to be examined. According to "A Biography of Li Hao" ("Li Hao zhuan") of the *Old Book of Tang*, volume 112, during the Kaiyuan era in the Tang dynasty, the burial custom of leaving corpses to dogs was prohibited in Taiyuan:

> There was an old custom in Taiyuan. For those monks who practiced Zen Buddhism as a career, after their death, they were not buried. Instead, their corpses were sent to the suburbs to feed birds and animals. After many years like this, a place called 'Yellow Pit' (*huang keng*) by the locals was formed. About a thousand of hungry dogs gathered nearby, feeding themselves with the human flesh of the deceased. As these dogs harmed and hurt the young and the weak, people far and near regarded them as a scourge, yet many officials before and after Li Hao could not stop this from happening. After Li took office, he seriously explained the decree to the monks, and expressed his hope that such a disaster would never happen again. Then he sent troops to hunt down the dogs. Later this custom was changed.

Cen Zhongmian opined that "this was a Zoroastrian custom, and the 'Yellow Pit' mentioned here was what is called Silence Tower by the Westerners."[38] This assertion was probably deduced from the above-mentioned burial custom of Samarkand described in the *Record of the Western Minorities*, but it might not be tenable. I believe that the custom of sending corpses "to the suburbs to feed birds and animals" was a "wild burial" of Indian style, a practice of "leaving corpses in forests for animals" which Xuanzang wrote about in the *Great Tang Records on the Western Regions*, volume two. This practice was carried out by the Zen monks[39] in Taiyuan, which is a manifestation of their adhering to the ancient Indian law. As for why it was called "Yellow Pit," it is probably because of the discoloration of bones over years. It was actually what Buddhists called a burial ground (called "Śitavana" in ancient India). This cannot be likened to the "dog yard" in Samarkand or the Zoroastrian "throne," either in form or in practice. Taking the geography of religion into consideration, we can presumably trace the local custom of "wild burial" in Taiyuan back to India, as it was located in Hedong where Buddhism flourished, but it is not appropriate to build up a far-fetching relationship with Sogdian customs in Central Asia.

Dwelling

The Nine Surnames inhabited the oasis of inland Asia, which, generally speaking, were warm and comfortable. But the overall natural environment here was characterized by an arid climate of scarce rainfall. According to Du Huan's *Record of Travels*, from Talas to the Western Sea, "from the third to the ninth month, there is no rainfall, thus farmers in all states can only rely on water from snow-capped mountains to work the land." Corresponding to such kind of climate was the architectural style of their dwellings, the features of which are as follows:

First, they were flat-roofed. Volume 83 of the *Book of Sui* clearly records that, in Bukhara, "all palaces are flat-roofed." The ruins of Penjikent and other sites also prove that flat-roofed buildings were popular in Sogdiana. The roof structure with one side slope or herringbone shape for easy drainage is certainly not as practical as a flat-roofed house in places where there is "no rainfall" for most of the year.

Second, they were built with clay bricks. In the *Record of Travels*, Du Huan wrote, "From Ferghana to the Western Sea, people all live inside earthen houses [houses made with clay bricks]." Although called an "earthen house," this kind of dwelling had wooden pillars and lintels. So, in practice, it was a clay-wood structure. This is how Du Huan described the houses in the state of Mulu (i.e., the state of Mu): "The city walls are high and thick, and the houses are square and flat, with wood carvings or soil paintings." Murals were the most distinctive inner decoration of Sogdian "earthen houses." For ordinary houses, they were fairly simple and plain, but those in the palaces and monasteries were spectacular, resembling a gallery in scale.

Dwellings 3 and 4 of the ruins of Penjikent reveal that a more spacious house usually had a drawing room to entertain guests. In this room, the wall opposite the door was decorated with paintings, and a three-legged stone table was placed underneath. It was the most honorable place in the room. Stoves were also important in a Sogdian house. There were three types: fire pit, ground stove, and fireplace.[40] It seems that the kitchen as an outbuilding had not appeared in the Sogdian dwellings in the early Middle Ages.

As far as indoor etiquette is concerned, besides sitting cross-legged, there were also two kneeling postures. The first one was explained by Shi Huilin like this: "The right knee is on the ground, the left knee is upright, and [this person's] back is straightened. It is also called mutual kneeling."[41] This posture can be seen in an artifact of the Bezeklik Thousand Buddha Caves which Albert von Le Coq carved and sawed away at, the kneeling statue of a Sogdian donor. The second posture is mentioned in the *Records after the Guests Have Left* (*Bintui lu*), volume seven, authored by Zhao Yushi, a scholar in the Song dynasty: "With both knees on the ground, people in the past sat on their toes which were turned backward, just like a Sogdian man kneeling today." On a mural painted on the wall of the east chamber at the ruin site of Penjikent old city, there are five donors who sit with their knees on the ground and their toes turned backward, which seems to be the basic "Sogdian kneeling" posture.

Dress

As for the dress of the Nine Surnames in the Tang period, Liu Zhengyan offered a featured description in his poem "A Night View of Sogdian Dancers Jumping and Leaping at the Residence of Vice Censor-in-chief Wang" ("Wangzhongchen zhai ye guan wu hu teng"):

Chach lads are rare to see,
squat dancing at the banquet, they are as swift as a bird can be.
Their Sogdian caps made of *zhicheng* have a pointed top,
their garments of refined cotton are narrow in sleeves.
Juggling with wine cups,
they look westward, suddenly thinking of the distant road to their hometown.
As they turned and jumped like a rolling wheel, their ornamented belts tinkled,
their stomping reveals soft embroidered boots in different colors. [42]

The dance costume of "Chach lads" was different from regular clothes as the former tended to be more gorgeous, yet the description here reveals a general picture of Sogdian dress: hat, garment, belt, and boots. Following this top-to-bottom order, I examine them one by one here.

1 **Hat.** Apart from "the king's felt hat decorated with gold and jewelry,"[43] there were two kinds of hat for common people: one is the pointed cap described in the above poem, and the other is the "rolled brim hat."[44] Although both types were common, they had different functions. The pointed cap helped to protect one against wind and snow, while the rolled brim hat was suitable for shading. Both were indispensable headdresses for Sogdian merchants who traveled

around to conduct business. The painted clay figurines unearthed from a tomb of the Tang period at Astana, Turpan, confirmed that these two types of hats did coexist.

2 **Garment.** The line "Their garments [...] are narrow in sleeves" corresponds to what Xuanzang commented as "close-fitting and tight."[45] In other words, it was characterized by tight-fitting clothes with narrow sleeves. This kind of garment, which was very different from the loose-fitting clothes with wide sleeves, made its wearer look vigorous and flexible. It may have evolved from ancient hunting garb.

3 **Belt.** There were two types of belts: a soft girdle and a hard plaque. Common people wore a soft girdle knotted at the waist to keep them warm. It also made it easier for them to move or jump. This is probably the type of belt worn by "Chach lads." As for the hard plaque, it was of high quality, made of either gold or silver, serving as a sign of nobility. As shown on the murals in Panjikent, there is a leather pouch attached to the "ornamented belt" for carrying weapons such as swords, knives, or daggers. In addition to gold or silver buckles, the "ornamented belt" could also be decorated with gemstones.[46] In 627, a Sogdian gold belt was tributed by the Western Turkic Khaganate. It is called "a golden belt perforated and decorated with numerous jewels" ("wan ding baodian jindai")[47] in Chinese sources.

4 **Boots.** The soft boots worn by "Chach lads" were a common style, matching their regular clothes. Sogdian figures on the murals also wear a kind of straight leather boots that reach up to the knees, like a military uniform.[48]

To provide a more comprehensive picture of Sogdian dress, I will now discuss several issues in a more general sense.

The first concerns the color of clothes. Huilin wrote in the *Sound and Meaning of All Sutras*, volume 21, "Common people in the Western Regions are all dressed in white," while Xuanzang in the *Great Tang Records on the Western Regions*, volume one, clearly pointed out the taboos and rules concerning the color of clothes: "For auspicious occasions, they wear white clothes; when in mourning, they are dressed in black." In Samarkand, during the festival of "begging for the bones of the divine scion" which was held in the seventh month every year, people were all "dressed in black," which indicates that they changed their regular clothes for black mourning dress in accordance with the dressing taboo.

The second concerns the hairstyle. The *Book of Wei: Records of the Western Regions* (*Wei shu: Xiyu zhuan*) records that "Adult men in Samarkand have their hair cut short." Similarly, Huichao's *Memoir of the Pilgrimage to the Five Kingdoms of India* notes that "here Sogdians all have their beards and hair cut." It can be seen that Sogdians followed the old Persian custom of "having one's hair cut" instead of taking the Turkic style of "wearing one's hair long." As for the females, in addition to the account that "women do their hair into buns" as recorded in the *New Book of Tang: Records of Samarkand* (*Xin Tang shu: Kangguo zhuan*), the murals at Panjikent proved that female Sogdians braided their hair. The hair was combed into five plaits on a girl's head, two at each side and one behind, each reaching to the waist.

A cross-reference with Tajik and Uzbek folk customs indicates that this was the hairstyle for maidens.[49] Finally, as recorded in Du Huan's *Record of Travels*, Sogdians living around the Western Sea "coated their hair with oil" extracted from "Yeximi," which is actually Royal jasmine, a species of jasmine with smaller leaves. In the *Miscellaneous Writings from Youyang* (*Youyang zazu*), volume 18, we read a similar message: "People from the Western Regions often pick these flowers and turn them into oleoresin by extraction, which smells fragrant and feels smooth."

The third pertains to apparel fabrics. It is needless to say that fabrics for Sogdian clothes fell into different types: wool, leather, cotton, and brocade, in accordance with their social status. Among them, there is one type called "zhicheng" which might cause confusion. Ren Dachun, a scholar in the Qing dynasty, once gave a brief definition in the *Explanations of Silks* (*Shi zeng*): "Without relying on other materials, one weaves with this fabric, then a fantastic product comes out, that is why it is called zhicheng." In the Tang dynasty, "zhicheng" was a precious fabric. In his poem "The Heir-Apparent's Secretary Zhang Sent Me a Piece of Embroidered Zhicheng Mat" ("Taizi Zhang sheren yi zhicheng ruduan"), Du Fu explained why he did not dare to accept such a lavish gift:

> A traveler came from the northwest, presenting me
> with a turquoise zhicheng embroidery
> [...]
> I acknowledged his good intention,
> but I am not a high-ranking official.
> Keeping it could bring me misfortune,
> but using it would make it a mat for my
> kindling firewood.

This kind of "turquoise zhicheng embroidery" probably came from the Western Regions. "Zhicheng" was used by "Chach lads" to make hats. We also read "a zhicheng cover over the Buddha umbrella" in the *Records of Mysterious Manifestations* (*Mingxiang ji*) and "a zhicheng garment train" awarded to Zhao Feiyan on the day she was crowned empress in the *Miscellaneous Records of the Western Capital* (*Xijing zaji*).[50] For the Nine Surnames in the Tang period, using "zhicheng" to make garments and hats revealed a Persian influence, because in the *Book of Sui: Records of Persia* (*Suishu: Bosi zhuan*), among the list of local products in Persia, there had already been a "gold-threaded zhicheng." Regarding this Persian brocade, the *Old Book of Tang: Records of Persia* clearly states that "headdresses and shawls are mostly bluish-white, trimmed with zhicheng brocade around the edges." In the *New Book of Tang*, the word "zhicheng" is deleted and the original sentence is abbreviated to "headdresses and shawls were trimmed with brocade," which turns the proper noun "zhicheng brocade" into a more general term. This is really a bad omission. As a decorative fabric in Sogdian dresses, "zhicheng" was sewn along the collar or on cuffs, or attached to the garment yokes or the lower hems of a skirt. This is the "Sassanian" ornamentation commonly seen in the Panjikent murals.[51] The pointed caps that "Chach lads" wore might not have been made entirely with "zhicheng." Probably they were only decorated with this kind of fabric along the rim. At the "Moshtcevaya Balka" burial site located in the mountainous area of the northwestern Caucasus, which could be dated back to the eighth to ninth centuries, a lady's robe was unearthed.[52] This robe was trimmed with a beaded brocade, which can be regarded as physical evidence for the recorded dress "trimmed with zhicheng brocade around the edges."

Diet

When Xuanzang remarked that of Sogdiana residents, "[a] person can be a millionaire, but he still lives a simple life of taking rough meals," he had in his mind a comparison with the living standard of the Han people in the early Tang dynasty. The fact is that Sogdian diet had its own unique features. Otherwise, it would not have been possible that "noble or royal people all go for Sogdian food"[53] since the Kaiyuan era of the Tang period.

Wine, a traditional product of the Nine Surnames, was very popular in China during the Han and Tang periods. There were two wine-making methods in Central Asia. One was to brew grapes with fruit juice, and the other was to boil grape juice. As the national beverage of the Nine Surnames, wine served as an offering to thank gods and as a tribute in their contact with the Tang court. For the latter, Bao Fang's poetic line "Sogdian merchants annually pay tribute with wines the taste of which is sublime" proved to be one indication of the prospering Tang empire. Written as "patrōδ" in Sogdian, "poluo"[54] was a famous Sogdian wine vessel, a bowl-shaped wine cup frequently mentioned in Tang poems. It appears in Li Bai's poetic line "Wine, in gold poluo, and a 15-year-old beauty from Wu on a dwarf horse," and it is also cited in Cen Shen's poem "Jiaohe wine and gold poluo." Next in quality were silver and bronze poluos.[55] At the banquet scenes shown on the murals of Penjikent, a wide-mouthed wine vessel frequently appears, which could be the famous poluo in ancient China.

Food bills from the early eighth century unearthed in Mount Mugh show that Sogdians mostly took sheep as their meat source. Of the unearthed bills, B11R is a bill for meat consumption. There are only 11 lines left, and there is no information regarding the year. This bill records that from the 13th day of the ninth month to the eighth day of the tenth month, a Sogdian resident in Penjikent fetched sheep six times and slew 12 ewes and two rams in total.[56]

Sogdiana had a warm climate, suitable for the growth of grains. As barley and wheat were their main crops, the Sogdians relied heavily on flour for their staple food. In the *Sound and Meaning of All Sutras*, volume 37, Shi Huilin wrote: "What Sogdians eat is mostly pilaw, baked cake, naan, *dana* 搭纳, etc." With regard to all the baked flatbread, Xiang Da has made detailed textual research about them.[57] What I want to point out here is that the popularity of Sogdian food extended further than the Tang period. In the Southern Song dynasty, the state banquet in the Hall of Gathering Talents (*jiying dian*) was a combination of Sogdian food and Han food, as shown in Lu You's *Jottings from the Life-Long Learning Hut* (*Laoxue an biji*):

> A banquet was held in the Hall of Gathering Talents to treat the envoys from the Jin State. Nine courses were served. The first course was roasted pork

with processed black beans, the second was stir-fried mutton with double-cooked pork and fried dumplings with butter, the third was lotus-shaped pancakes with stir-fried meat and sauced bones in the middle, the fourth was plain boiled pork inside naan, the fifth was grilled meat platter with pilaw, the sixth was fake fish meatballs,[58] the seventh was jasmine petals sprinkled on vermicelli soup, the eighth was shark-shaped meat,[59] the ninth was cold cooked rice, pickled black beans, freshly pickled cucumbers, and pickled gingers.

After 600 years of localization and improvement, when it came to Lu You's time, some of the "rough meals" in Xuanzang's time, such as "naan" and "pilaw," had already gone into a state banquet and become two of the "nine courses," helping to form the "Hu-Han imperial feast."

Calendar

The *Prime Tortoise of the Record Bureau* (*Cefu yuangui*) and the *Institutional History of Tang* (*Tang huiyao*) list the following tribute letters from the Western Regions: the tribute letter from Tughshada, the king of Bukhara in 719; from Gurak, the king of Samarkand in 719; from Yina Tudun Qule, the king of Chach in 741; and from Geluopulu, the king of Kabudhan in 745. As these four tribute letters were dated by the reign titles of the Tang dynasty, there is no way to discern the Sogdian calendar from these sources. But cultural relics unearthed in Mount Mugh tell us that documents at that time were dated by the reign of their king or the lord of the city. For example, the aforementioned marriage contract was signed in the tenth year of the king of Tarkhun, and the contract of land purchase was legalized "in the 15th year of King Chikin Chur Bilge, Lord of Panjikent." In light of the dating style of Sogdian documents, we can assume that the original letters must have been dated in their own calendar time, but when they were translated into Chinese, the dating method was changed.

Before the Arab conquest, the Persian "Zoroastrian calendar" was used in the Nine Surnames, but with a slight variation. In this calendar, there were 365 days in a year, divided into 12 months, 30 days in each month, plus 5 days for intercalation. However, because the calendrical degrees of the Zoroastrian calendar could not be fully synchronized with the movement time of celestial bodies, which resulted in six hours less in a year, and a total of one day less in four years, the beginning of each year in the Sogdian calendar had to be advanced by one day every four years to make up for this deficiency.[60] For example, in 710–713, the beginning day of each year was the first day of the sixth month; in 714–717, the beginning day was the 31st day of the fifth month; in 718–721, it was the 30th day of the fifth month; in 722–725, it was the 29th day of the fifth month.[61] This changing calendar time led to divergent records about the beginning day of a Sogdian new year in Chinese sources. For example, in Wei Jie's *Record of the Western Minorities*, "The year begins on the first day of the sixth month"; in Du Huan's *Record of Travels*, "According to the local custom, the year begins in the fifth month"; and when the *New Book of Tang: Records of Samarkand* came out, it became this: "The year begins in the 12th month."

Similar to the Zoroastrian calendar, each of the 12 months in the Sogdian calendar was named after a god [or a goddess]. For example, the eighth month was named after the god of water, the ninth month the god of fire, and the 12th month the goddess of land. Thirty days also had their own names, most of which were after gods. Only the eighth, 15th, and 23rd days were not specifically named. They were generally called "Creator's Day." With one month divided into four periods, the system of a four-week calendar was faintly visible.[62]

Weeks were an important part of the Sogdian calendar. There were seven days in a week, named after the Sun, the Moon, and the five stars (Mars, Mercury, Jupiter, Venus, and Saturn). In the *Sutra of Lunar Mansions and Planets* (*Jixiong shiri shan'e xiuyao jing*) translated by Amoghavajra[63] in 759, the name transcription of the Sogdian seven days in one week roughly matches those in the Sogdian Almanac found at the site A12 of Mount Mugh in 1933, as shown in the following pairs: mi/myγš, mo /m'γ, yunhan/wrγ 'n), die/tyr), huwu/wrmšt, naxie/nryδ. Yet for "zhuyuan" or "jihuan," which is supposed to match the Sogdian word Kaivān,[64] neither is close in pronunciation. As for the spread of the seven-day calendar in China and its relationship with divination, some scholars have already discussed it in detail,[65] so I will not repeat it here.

Festivals

In the existing Chinese sources, there were four recorded Sogdian festivals to celebrate the new year, offer sacrifices to ancestors, implore for the bones of the divine scion, and pray for frost by splashing water over each other. Featured with sports, entertainment, and temple fairs, these festivals were held regularly in chronological order every year, forming a cycle of life rhythm.

First, the festival for celebrating a new year. In Wei Jie's *Record of the Western Minorities*, it is written that:

> The year begins on the first day of the sixth month. On this day, both the king and common people wear new clothes, and have their hair cut and beards trimmed. In the woods east of the town, horse racing and archery go on for seven days. When it comes to the final day, a coin is glued to the target, and the person who hits it can act as a king for one day.

The fact that both "the king and common people" dressed up to join this festive ceremony indicates that this seven-day annual holiday was a national activity. The coin-shooting competition on the seventh day constituted the climax of this festival in Samarkand, and the ritual of making the winner a temporary one-day king is reminiscent of the old practice of "electing the able man as the king" prevalent in the era of military democracy. It is no wonder that James Frazer, in his book *The Golden Bough*, cites it as a historical example of the ancient custom that featured this "temporary king" tradition.[66]

Second, the festival for offering sacrifices to ancestors. In Samarkand, it was held in the sixth month of every year at the national ancestral temple. Except a brief mention of its time and place in the *Book of Sui*, volume 83, stating that "[it is held] at the national ancestral temple in the sixth month, and all the other states sent envoys to assist with the offering ceremony," no further details are available.

Third, the festival for imploring for the bones of the divine scion. It was a religious festival held in the seventh month. According to the *Comprehensive Institutions*, volume 193:

> It is a local custom to worship the divine scion. Legend has it that this divine scion died in the seventh month, and upon his death, his bones were lost. So, every year at about that time, three to five hundred worshipers, dressed in black and barefoot, are scattered in the field, bawling and beating their breasts in grief. They do this to beg for the return of his bones. It lasts for seven days.[67]

The "divine scion" whose bones were lost was Adonis-Tammūz.[68] The reverence for him originated in Babylonian times, reflecting the hope for the revival of crops.[69] After many years of dissemination, the Semitic word for "divine scion" has undergone many variations, but the original festive nature has been passed on to various ethnic groups in West and Central Asia. In Sogdiana, the myth about the "divine scion" evolved into the legend of Siyavush, a hero who crossed the Amu Darya River to build a city in the state of Bukhara where he was brutally killed, and then his burial place was consecrated by later generations. Every year, early in the morning of the New Year's Day, inhabitants of Sogdiana went out into the field to hold a memorial ceremony for him. They offered roosters and sang dirges.[70] As a ceremonious festival, the Sogdian custom of gathering "in the field" and imploring for the bones of the "divine scion" is not much different from the reverence for Adonis, an occasion to pray for the rejuvenation of the earth.

Fourth, the festival for praying for frost by splashing water over each other. In the *New Book of Tang: Records of Samarkand*, it is narrated that "in the 11th month, people beat drums, pray for frost, and splash water over each other for amusement." The *Comprehensive Examination of Literature: Ceremonial Music* (*Wenxian tongkao: Yuekao*), volume 21, provides more details about this ceremonial festival:

> Praying for frost was an amusement popular in the state of Kang [Samarkand]. The musical instruments included bass drums, snare drums, pipa [Chinese lutes,] pentachords, Konghou [Chinese harps], and flutes. Held roughly in the 11th month, [it was the occasion when] people went naked, gathered at thoroughfares and main streets, and splashed water over each other. They beat drums, and danced to beseech for frost.

Playing music and dancing added to the fun, so did the water-splashing. There is no doubt about that. But as a festival particular to a nation state, in addition to entertainment, it should also have social significance. It should be noted that the Sogdian water-splashing festival on the 30th day of the tenth month is related to a legend.

According to this legend, during the reign of Peroz in the Persian Sassanid dynasty (459–483), there was a severe drought, but fortunately, the king saved his subjects. Later, to commemorate this particular day, people splashed water over each other for fun.[71] In volume 40 of the *Sound and Meaning of All Sutras*, when Shi Huilin gave an explanation to *sumozhemao*, he offered a similar idea: "According to a local legend, this play is meant to exorcise the evil, drive away demons and ghosts that might devour and plague people." Thus seen, the festival to pray for frost in the 11th month of every year was a folk activity to exorcise evil spirits and avoid calamities. Regarding their gratitude to the king's kindness, it was expressed in the title of a play called "Praying for Frost by Splashing Water over the Sogdian King."[72] As for their "go[ing] naked," "beat[ing] drums, and danc[ing]" when they were splashing water, these were just traces of ancient witchcraft.

Surely, for the Nine Surnames in the Tang period, there must have been more than the above-mentioned four festivals. As a Muslim writer in the Middle Ages declared that the Sogdians, like the Persians, had many festivals and memorial days in one year. According to Al Biruni (973–1048), there were festive celebrations and trading fairs on the second and 15th days of June, "the merchants of all countries gather and hold a fair of seven days duration."[73] As mentioned earlier, the festivals to celebrate a new year and to implore for the bones of the divine scion also lasted for seven days, which indicates that these festivals were probably held at the same time as the temple fair. Moreover, it can be clearly seen that some Sogdian festivals were celebrated during the grape harvest season. As Al Biruni noted, the 18th of May was "Bāba-Khwāra," also called "Bāmi-Khwāra" which means "drinking the good, pure must," and the 26th of May was "Karm-Khwāra," which means "tasting grapes." This festive period lasted for a long time in the second half of the year, from 16 July to 9 August.[74] It is quite a pity that such an agricultural festive period is not recorded in Chinese sources. However, one piece of fragment of the *Geographic Writings of Shazhou and Yizhou* (*Shazhou yizhou dizhi*) mentions that, during the Zhenguan reign of the Tang dynasty, "Kang Yandian, the Grand Chieftain of the state of Kang [Samarkand]" led the Sogdians to a place four *li* south of the Shicheng garrison and planted grapes there and that is how the "Grape Town" got its name. Given this account, it is quite possible that festivals like "Bāba-Khwāra" were also brought into Puchang Hai [now Lop Nur] where the Sogdians settled in the Tang period.

Business

The Sogdians were "good at conducting business," selling goods as far as they could travel. Although from the Wei and Jin to the Sui and Tang dynasties, there had been ceaseless records about Sogdian merchants' commercial activities, yet with regard to the habits or customs directly related to their business behavior, few complete records can be found. With some clues sorted out from different sources, the following presents my current understanding about this topic.

The first is related to the caravan. In 703, Cui Rong submitted a memorial to the emperor, saying: "There are many bandits along state borders, so all these years Sogdian merchants have traveled in the form of a caravan."[75] When faced with the risk along the border and the threat from "bandits," these Sogdian merchants formed a caravan, because only by traveling together could they undertake a safe journey. Anyone who left the caravan to travel alone was likely to encounter danger. In the early years of the Zhenguan period, when Xuanzang went west for Buddhist scriptures, he witnessed a tragedy in Karasahr (also called Yanqi):

> Among the merchants who traveled together, about a dozen Sogdians set off secretly in the middle of the night, because they wanted to do business before others. After walking for over ten *li*, they were robbed and killed by bandits. No one escaped.[76]

In Cave 45 of Dunhuang, there is a mural from the Tang period which confirms this narration. Based on "The Lotus Sutra's Universal Gate Chapter" ("Guanshiyin pusa pumen pin"), this painting shows a bandit blocking the way with a machete and a Sogdian merchant begging for mercy on his knees. The caravan had two characteristics, and one salient feature was the synchronized routines. According to the Dunhuang manuscript *A Guide to Shazhou Commandery* (*Shazhou dudufu tujing*) numbered "Pelliot No. 2005," Xinghu Lake[77] outside the Yumen Pass got its name on account of the Sogdian merchants:

> About 110 *li* northwest of Shazhou, the lake has salty and bitter water. People can only drink from the nearby springs. Sogdian merchants have to pass through this place when they travel to and from the Yumen Pass. That is how the lake got its name.

Another characteristic was the selection of a temporary leader. This leader did not have to be a merchant. The *Continued Biographies of Eminent Monks: A Biography of Xuanzang* (*Xu gaoseng zhuan: Xuanzang zhuan*) provides an account of how Master Xuanzang who enjoyed higher prestige than common people became a leader, "all of the five hundred travelers unanimously selected Xuanzang as their leader, and let him camp in the middle while the others defended on all sides." From this quote, it can be inferred that the Sogdian caravan in the Tang period took the form of circular camping like that of the caravan in modern Central Asia. In the Sogdian caravan, besides merchants, there were also a considerable number of laborers such as slaves, maidservants, craftsmen, and horse doctors, as revealed by the documents unearthed in Turpan.

The second concerns Sogdian merchants' custom of praying for blessings. This activity was held at a Zoroastrian temple. Zhang Zhuo, in volume three of the *Record of the Imperial Court and Beyond* (*Chaoye qianzai*), gave a detailed description of this ceremony.

> Both in Lidefang of Henan prefecture, and Xifang of southern Luoyang, there are Zoroastrian temples that serve Sogdians. Every year when Sogdian merchants pray for blessings, they offer cooked pork and mutton. They play

pipa, beat drums, blow into flutes, sing and dance to their hearts' content. After they offer sacrifices to gods, they search and find a Sogdian to be the Zoroastrian priest, and the others give him money. This priest takes out a horizontal knife (*heng dao*), the blade of which is so sharp that a feather cannot pass it without being cut into halves, and the surface of which gives off a cold light like that of frost and snow. The priest stabs himself in the abdomen with this knife until the end comes out of his back. Then he grabs the handle and stirs his intestines haphazardly, making blood flow all over the place. Shortly after that (about the time for a meal,) he chants a magic spell on the bloody body, then his abdomen becomes as intact as before. This is probably an illusory trick in the Western Regions.

According to one fragmentary Dunhuang manuscript – *the Geographic Writings of Shazhou and Yizhou* (*Shazhou Yizhou dizhi*), this is called "performing a Zoroastrian god-inviting ritual." In a state of frenzy, the ritual-performing priest declared that "all of the things going on in the empire were in line with the will of Heaven and had god's blessing." These two quotes indicate that Sogdian merchants' praying for blessings included three parts: offering sacrifices and playing music, performing a Zoroastrian god-inviting ritual, and a Zoroastrian priest speaking words of blessing.

The third pertains to wealth competition. Sogdians judged a person by the wealth he earned, so there emerged the custom of wealth competition:

> It is the custom of the Sogdians to hold an assembly once a year, and participants bring out their treasures for everyone to see. The person with most treasures sits down with a hat over his head, and the others stand aside, taking their places according to how much treasure they have.[78]

This custom of arranging seats according to wealth can be seen as a footnote to what Xuanzang commented as "they value wealth," revealing the penetration of commerce into the Sogdian concept of hierarchy. Yan Liben in the Tang dynasty had a painting called "Exotic Countries Compete in Treasure" ("Yiguo doubao tu"), according to volume one of the *Catalog of Paintings of the Xuanhe Era* (*Xuanhe huapu*). But it was lost, so there is no way to know the details.

Finally, let us take An Lushan as an example to see how the above-mentioned rituals were practiced on specific occasions. Before his rebellion, An Lushan was in Fanyang to inspect treasures. As written in the *Biographical Account of An Lushan* (*An Lushan shiji*):

> Sogdian merchants who lurked in various places sent him [An Lushan] exotic treasures every year, amounting to millions in number. When merchants came to visit him, Lushan would sit on a Sogdian chair in his Sogdian dress. Incense was burned, and various treasures were on display. He then ordered over a hundred Sogdian men to stand around him, and the other Sogdians to kneel around below, [to start the ritual of] begging for blessings from heaven. Lushan presented sumptuous meals of livestock meat, and shamans played drums, sang and danced until night.

On this occasion, An Lushan obviously regarded himself as a treasure lord and acted in accordance with the Sogdian custom. If we compare his behavior with the aforementioned rituals, we can see a striking similarity: sitting "on a Sogdian chair in his Sogdian dress"/"sit[ting] down with a hat over his head"; "presented rich meals of livestock meat"/"offered cooked pork and mutton"; "played drums, sang and danced"/"play pipa, beat drums, blow into flutes, sing and dance to their hearts' content"; and shamans' performance/a Zoroastrian priest's illusory trick. It seems that An Lushan's treasure inspection ceremony was the reproduction of the above-mentioned ritual. This is not surprising, as An Lushan came from "a mixed Sogdian origin in Yingzhou," and he once worked as a "broker of mutual trade" (*hushi yalang*), so he was quite familiar with Sogdian customs. Through "praying for blessings" and "treasure competition," he gained the support of Sogdian merchants and prepared for his rebellion in the last few years of the Tianbao reign.

Sogdian Nomenclature

Of the nine surnames of the Sogdians in the Tang period, seven commonly recorded ones were Kang康, An安, Cao曹, Shi石, Mi米, He何, and Shi史. In "A Biography of Ge Shuhan" of the *Old Book of Tang*, volume 104, we read this sentence: "Ethnic minorities often use their tribal names as their surname."[79] Thus, in the Chinese translation of Sogdian names, it became a common practice to use a country's name as an individual's surname. Just as what Deng Mingshi explained in volume 24 of the *Differentiation of Ancient and Modern Family Names* (*Gujin xingshi shu bianzheng*): "People who are surnamed Mi get this family name after their Sogdian ancestors' arrival in China from Mi [Maimurgh] in the Western Regions." Regarding this practice of "taking their country name as their surname," many historical records, inscriptions, and excavated documents provide a large number of examples, which need not be listed here one by one.

If the research on Sogdian surnames has already borne fruitful results through the hard work of previous scholars such as Kuwabara Jitsuzo, Xiang Da, Feng Chengjun, and Yao Weiyuan, then the study about Sogdian personal names remains a new terrain to be explored. As Chen Yinke pointed out in sincerity: "Apart from the research on Sogdian surnames, Sogdian personal names also need immediate attention in our historical studies."[80] But for half a century, very few scholars have undertaken research in this area. Up to now, the international academic community has made great progress in the study of Sogdian names, and there are a number of methods we can learn and many research results we can use. In particular, the comparison of Sogdian personal names between Sogdian documents unearthed in Mount Mugh, and Chinese documents unearthed in Dunhuang and Turpan shows a promising research prospect. In this section, I examine and interpret Sogdian personal names in some historical materials. This is done not to fill in the research gap left by preceding scholars. Rather, it is an attempt with a new research method.

With regard to Sogdian names in the Tang dynasty, there are two well-known ones: An Lushan, the culprit of the An Lushan Rebellion (known as the An-Shi Rebellion in China), and Shi Pantuo, who showed Xuanzan the way out of the national border. As these two Sogdian names are frequently mentioned, they should not be left out.

The following is a list of Sogdian names that contain "Lushan" as the personal name: "An Lushan" in the *Biographical Account of An Lushan*; "Cao Lushan" on page 470 of the *Documents Unearthed in Turpan* (*Tulufan chutu wenshu*), volume six; "Kang Lushan" on page 470 of the *Documents Unearthed in Turpan*, volume 7; and "Mi Lushan" on a purchase ticket (*shiquan*) issued in the 19th year of Kaiyuan in Xizhou. An Lushan was a "shepherd of lowly origin," and the other three also came from the bottom of society. This shows that "Lushan" as a personal name was quite popular among the families surnamed An, Cao, Kang, and Mi. If variant forms such as "Shi Alushan" in the *Labor Service Register* (*Chaike bu*) unearthed in Dunhuang, and "An Alushan" in the Lease Contract (*dianren wenshu*) contained in the *Otani Document* No. 2368 are added, it can be seen that this Sogdian personal name enjoyed an even wider popularity. According to Henning's research, "Lushan" is the transcription of a Persian word Roxšan, meaning "light" or "brightness." In the early fourth century BC, Roxana, the Bactrian princess who married Alexander the Great, once used this name.[81] From Persians to Sogdians, from noblemen to the common people, "Lushan" as an auspicious word enjoyed a long history. No wonder this personal name appeared again and again in historical sources.

In the early years of Zhenguan reign of the Tang dynasty, when Xuanzang was about to cross the national border at Guazhou, he found a young Sogdian who was willing to show him the way: "When asked about his name, he answered he was called Shi Pantuo."[82] "Pantuo" was also a common Sogdian personal name, as seen in Cao Pantuo recorded on page 351 of the *Documents Unearthed in Turpan*, volume seven; He Pantuo on page 319 of the *Documents Unearthed in Turpan*, volume three; and two persons with the name of An Pantuo, one on page 365 of the *Documents Unearthed in Turpan*, volume six, and the other on the *Labor Service Register* unearthed in Dunhuang. "Pantuo" was the transcription of a Sogdian word "bntk," meaning "slave" or "servant."[83] But if we take into consideration the name of Zhai Pantuo on one fragment of the *Geographic Writings of Shazhou and Yizhou* (in the first year of the Guangqi reign of the Tang dynasty), who was a "Zoroastrian priest" in Yizhou, it seems that we should not take Xuanzang's guide as a "slave" or "servant." Perhaps it is more appropriate to interpret it as a child's pet name like Anu,[84] which might better suit his identity as a young Sogdian. The earlier record of Sogdian names containing "Pantuo" can be seen in the documents prior to the Tang period. According to the *Book of Zhou: Records of the Turks* (*Zhou shu: Tujue zhuan*), Emperor Wen of the Western Wei dynasty sent an envoy to the Turks in 545 and that envoy was "An Nuopantuo, a Sogdian from Jiuquan." Here "Nuo" in this name "An Nuopantuo" is a shortened translation for the word "Nāhid" which is a god's name, and "pantuo" means "the servant of Goddess Nanâ." Its Sogdian spelling NanēBandak can be found in ancient Sogdian letters.[85]

After an illustrative explanation of what they mean, the following section goes further to study the pattern and structure of Sogdian personal names. In particular, the following points are worthy of special attention.

Commonly Used Last Word in Sogdian Personal Names

According to Vladimir Aronovich Livshits, a famous scholar of Sogdian Studies, "The names with the suffix -y'n[86] and -prn[87] are the most popular male names in the documents of Mount Mugh."[88] A comparison with translated texts from the Tang period shows that they were translated into "yan" and "fen." Bernhard Karlgren's list of pronunciations of ancient Chinese words reveals "yan" to be pronounced as "ian" and "fen" as "piugn,"[89] which match the Sogdian words in the documents of Mount Mugh. In the sources related to the Tang period and also in the unearthed documents, there are many Sogdian names containing these two words, so it is not easy to give a complete list. Here, only two groups of personal names are used as evidence:

First, names ending with "yan." In the *Documents Unearthed in Turpan*, volume three, there are Cao Alanyan on page 120 and Cao Poyan and He Poyan on pages 319–321; in volume six, there are Cao Yanyan and Shi Wupoyan on page 479; and in volume seven, there are An Moyan on page 94, Kang Wupoyan on page 389, and Kang Tuoyan on page 470. In the *Labor Service Register*, names such as Cao Fudiyan, Shi Liaoyan, and An Liaoyan are mentioned.

Second, names ending with "fen." In the *New Book of Tang*, volume 193, the name Shi Yanfen is mentioned; in the epitaph of Shi Chongjun of the Tang period, the name Shi Ningfen is found; in the epitaph of Mi Jifen of the Tang period, the name Mi Jifen ends with "fen"; in the *Labor Service Register*, there are names such as Shi Shifen, An Hushufen, Kang Jieshifen, He Fudifen, and Shi Bodifen; and in the *Documents Unearthed in Turpan*, volume seven, there is the name Cao Mopen.

In the Sogdian language, "yan" is interpreted as "gift," which also means "honor, blessing," and the word "fen" means "honor, luck."[90] Understanding common endings of Sogdian personal names and knowing their meanings can help to identify Sogdians' family lineages, which is of great importance to historical textual research. For example, the Dunhuang manuscript *A Guide to Shazhou Commandery* includes an account of Kang Fudanyan, the general of the Shicheng garrison, and his younger brother Dishebo. Haneda Toru made a mistake by taking the name "Fudanyan" to be "Furs-todan" (meaning "the person knowing the doctrine"), a Persian who wrote a book about the doctrines of Mani in the Tang dynasty.[91] This mistake arose because he was not aware that the word "yan" is irreplaceable. Recent Sogdian research has shown that "Fudanyan" can be traced back to Pərtam – yân, meaning "the first gift."[92] Thus, it is more logical that the name "Fudanyan" implies "firstborn" because Fudanyan was Dishebo's older brother.

Religious Colors with Sogdian Personal Names

The area inhabited by the Nine Surnames during the Tang period can be described as a religious exposition in the Middle Ages. Religious beliefs here were complex. Not only did Zoroastrianism and Buddhism coexist, Nestorianism and Manichaeism also held a place, not to mention that native deities attracted a large number of worshipers. Thus, it is not surprising that Sogdian personal names were religiously colored. Aside from the connection between the name "Mi Sabao" and Zoroastrianism, as pointed out by previous authors, there are also several other examples:

The name Fudiyan (pwty'n) was a Sogdian personal name commonly seen in the Dunhuang and Turpan documents. As the word "Fudi" (pwt) in this name is derived from the loan word "Buddha," this personal name can be interpreted as "Buddha-given" or "Buddha-blessed." The name "Fudifen" (pwtypnn) is also colored with the Buddhist belief, as it means "protected by the Buddha."[93]

The Sogdian name "Ningningfen" (nnyprn) or "Ningfen," containing the name of Goddess Nana (written in Sogdian as nny),[94] clearly bears the imprint of Sogdian local faith.

In addition, regarding the relationship between Sogdian personal names and names of gods, there is one more thing that should be brought up for discussion. In the unearthed documents, we often see names such as "Cao Alanyan," "Kang Alanyan," and "Cao Alanpen." The middle part "Alan" seems to be related to a divinity called "Alan" who was worshiped in a temple in Rouyuan town, Yizhou in the Tang dynasty, a border prefecture deeply influenced by the Sogdian culture. "Alan" seemed to be a Sogdian deity. As the Sogdian word "r'm" means "tranquility, peace,"[95] Sogdian names containing Alanyan (r'my'n) probably imply a prayer for god's blessings for safety.

Turkic Elements in Sogdian Personal Names

At the beginning of the seventh century, Tong Yabghu Qaghan of the Western Turks "occupied the Western Regions, took over the land where the Wusun[96] used to inhabit, and moved the royal court to Qianquan north of the state of Shi [Chach]. All the kings in the Western Regions were granted the title of Xielifa.[97] Put under the supervision of a tudun (*tutun*),[98] they were responsible for tax collection."[99] Under this supervisory system, the Sogdian regions were gradually Turkified. With the spread of Turkic culture from the nobles to the folk, the way Sogdians named their children was also colored by Turkic elements. In the documents unearthed in Dunhuang and Turpan, there are many such Turkified Sogdian names. Here are some examples. The name An Jiasha (q'š'ns in Sogdian) is the transcription of the Turkic word "iron." This is explained in volume 199 of the *Universal Geography of the Taiping Era* (*Taiping huanyu ji*), "it is said that this place is rich in good iron, which is called Jiasha." The name He Moheduo should be the transcription of the Turkic word Bāγatur, which means "brave" and "strong." And personal names in An Dahan, Luo Teqin, He Tutun, and Kang Yijin are all derived from the 28 ranks of Turkish official titles, respectively, Tarqan, Tigin, Tudun, and Irkin. As for the name Cao Fulei,[100] it is the transcription of Orkhon Turkic word "Bars," which means "tiger."[101]

The above exploration is not an exegetical interpretation of Sogdian names, but a brief investigation of the relationship between Sogdian customs and Sogdian names, indicating that names are also part of the culture of the Nine Surnames. As "a name is dependent on reality," so we cannot value historical research but ignore the interpretation of names.

Notes

1 *Heiling* 黑岭 is the name of an ancient mountain. It refers to the mountainous area south of the Hindu Kush in eastern Afghanistan. —Trans.
2 "Account of Ferghana" ("Dayuan liezhuan") of the *Records of the Grand Historian* (*Shiji*), vol. 123.
3 In the *Comprehensive Mirror in Aid of Governance* (*Zizhi tongjian*), vol. 215, the sentence "ethnic minorities all show respect to mother first and then to father!" is changed to be "Sogdians show respect to mother first and then father!" The changed sentence is more in line with the ethnic group An Lushan belonged to.
4 Smirnova, 1981: 359–361.
5 Livshits, 1962: 47.
6 Livshits, 1962: 23–26.
7 Zhang Wei, vol. 2. The original sentence reads 大唐上仪同故康莫量息阿达. Here, the word "xi" 息 means somebody's son, or offspring.
8 *Documents Unearthed in Turpan* (*Tulufan chutu wenshu*), vol. 7: 94.
9 In the Tang dynasty, the word "世 (shi)" was changed into "代 (dai)" to avoid using the same Chinese character that appeared in Emperor Taizong's name – Li Shimin 李世民.
10 Wei Zheng et al., vol. 83.
11 Narshakhi, 40–41.
12 Lu Zhaomeng, 844–845.
13 See *Inscriptions from the Tombstones of Luoyang* (*Mangluo zhongmu yiwen*), series 4, vol. 3, for the epitaph of Kang Xian in the Tang dynasty.
14 See the *Collected Works of Yan Zhenqing* (*Yanlugong ji*), vol. 9, where the inscriptions on the stone tablets along the sacred ways of Kang Ayiqu Tarkhan are provided.
15 For "Epitaph for An Po in the Tang Dynasty, the Grand Chieftain of Six Sogdian Prefectures," see Zhao Zhenhua and Zhu Liang, "A Preliminary Study of An Po's Epitaph" ("An Po muzhi chu tan"), *Zhongyuan wenwu*, no. 3 (1982): 37–40.
16 "Epitaph for An Shi, an Commander Unequaled in Honor, a Senior General-in-chief in the Tang Dynasty," in *Inscriptions from the Tombstones of Luoyang*, series 4, vol. 3.
17 For "Epitaph for He Wenzhe," see Lu Zhaomeng, "Textual Research and Interpretation of He Wenzhe's Epitaph" ("He Wenzhe muzhi kaoshi"), *Kaogu*, no. 9 (1986): 841–848.
18 For "Epitaph for He Hongjing, the Weibo Military Commissioner in the Tang Dynasty," see Handan Cultural Relics Office, "The Epitaph for He Hongjing Found in Daming County, Hebei Province" ("Hebei Daming xian faxian He Hongjing muzhi"), *Kaogu*, no. 8 (1984): 721–725.
19 "Epitaph for Shi Mochuo," in Duan Fang, *The Collected Records of Stone Inscriptions by Taozhai* (*Taozhai cangshi ji*), vol. 30.
20 "The epitaph of He Junzheng, the Aid of Tribal Affairs under the Supervision of the Regional Inspector of the Jitian Prefecture in the Later Jin Dynasty of the Five Dynasties" collected by Shanxi Museum. It is briefly mentioned in a newsletter in *Taiyuan wenwu*, no. 1 (1982): 58–58.
21 Livshits, 1962: 30.
22 Huichao set out for India in 723, and he ended his travel account in 729. Du Huan wrote his travel book after he returned to China in 762. —Trans.
23 Shi Xuanying and Shi Huilin, vol. 14.
24 *A Biography of Geng Bing* (*Geng Bing zhuan*) in the *Book of the Later Han* (*Hou Hanshu*), vol. 49.
25 Volume one of "Records of the Turks" ("Tujue zhuan") in the *Comprehensive Institutions*, vol. 197.
26 "Records of the Uyghurs" ("Huihe zhuan") in the *Old Book of Tang*, vol. 195.
27 Tatars is the Chinese designation for the Mongols especially after the end of the Yuan period (1279–1368). In Chinese sources, there is a distinction between the Black Tatars (the Tatars proper), the White Tatars (Önggüd), and the "raw" Tatars, tribes living most far away from the Jin empire. —Trans.

28 The Jurchens were a federation of tribes living in the northeast of China. The Jurchens conquered northern China and founded the Jin dynasty (1115–1234). —Trans.
29 See Yuwen Maozhao (the Song period), *Record of the Great Jin Dynasty* (*Dajin guozhi*), vol. 39.
30 *A Biography of Cangci* (*Cangci zhuan*) in the *Records of the Three Kingdoms* (*Sanguo zhi*), vol. 16.
31 Yang Xuanzhi, vol. 5.
32 Sima Guang, vol. 199.
33 Sima Guang, vol. 216.
34 "A Biography of Lai Junchen" ("Lai Junchen zhuan") in the *Old Book of Tang*, vol. 186, book 1.
35 "A Biography of Gao Chuo, King of Nanyang (Nanyangwang chuo zhuan)" in the *Book of Northern Qi,* vol. 12.
36 Shukurov, 104–109, and Figure 22.
37 Bartold, 1962: 9–10.
38 Cen Zhongmian, 1982: 319.
39 In the *New Book of Tang*, vol. 78, "Zen monks in Taiyuan" is written as "those who practice Buddhist Dharma."
40 Voronina, 87–95. See also Belenitski et al., 1973: 25–38.
41 Shi Xuanying and Shi Huilin, vol. 36.
42 *Complete Tang Poems* (*Quan Tangshi*), case 7, book 9.
43 *New Book of Tang*, vol. 221.
44 "General Li of the House Guard's 'Zhe Branch'" ("Jinwu lijiangjun zhezhi") in *The Collected Works of Zhang Chengji* (*Zhang Chengji wenji*), vol. 8.
45 Xuanzang, vol. 1.
46 Belenitski et al., "Sogdian 'Gold Belts'," 1980: 213–217. See also Raspopova, 78–91.
47 *Old Book of Tang*, vol. 194.
48 Bentovich, 203.
49 Bentovich, 208. See also Belenitski, *Central Asia: Art of the Sogdians* (*Mittelasien: Kunst der Sogden*), 1980: 57, 74–75. Regarding the hairstyles of Sogdians, see also Li Sichun, "Hairstyles of Different Ethnic Groups" ("Shuo minzu fashi") in *Ten Essays by Li Sichun* 江村十论 (Shanghai: Shanghai renmin chubanshe, 1957): 58–59.
50 See Li Fang, vol. 116, vol. 236.
51 Bentovich, 200–201. Belenitski, *Central Asia: Art of the Sogdians*, 1980: 85–87.
52 Jerusalemskaya, 1978: 159.
53 "Treatise on Carriages and Robes" ("Yufu zhi") in the *Old Book of Tang*, vol. 45.
54 In some Chinese sources, "polou" 叵罗 is also written as "polou" 破罗. For details about polou, see Cai Hongsheng, 1986: 106–107.
55 See an entry entitled "Wang Ya" in the *Extensive Records of the Taiping Era*, vol. 144.
56 Bogolyubov and Smirnova, 36.
57 Xiang Da, 48–50.
58 This dish was made with pork, mutton, etc. After being cooked with various seasonings and broth, it tasted like fish. —Trans.
59 This dish was actually made with pork, lamb, chicken, duck, fish, etc. —Trans.
60 Livshits, 1975: 321.
61 Livshits, 1962: 58.
62 Freiman, 33. See also Henning, "A Sogdian Calendar," in *Selected Papers*, vol. 1, 1977: 629–635.
63 Amoghavajra whose Chinese name was Bu Kong 不空 (705–774), was a well-known Buddhist monk in the Tang dynasty. —Trans.
64 Freiman, 60.
65 See Ye Delu, 137–157; and Wang Chongmin, 116–133.
66 Frazer, 420.

67 Du You, *Comprehensive Institutions* (*Tongdian*), vol. 193.
68 Henning, 1965: 252.
69 Frazer, 474.
70 Narshakhi, 23.
71 Lobacheva, 24–25.
72 See "Annal of Emperor Zhongzong of Tang" in the *Old Book of Tang*, vol. 7.
73 Al-Biruni, 234.
74 Al-Biruni, 234–235. See also Lobacheva, 27.
75 "A Biography of Cui Rong" in the *Old Book of Tang*, vol. 94.
76 Huili and Yancong, vol. 2.
77 A lake that has dried up and has been buried under the sand in the northwest of Dunhuang city, Gansu province. —Trans.
78 See the entry entitled "Wei Sheng" in the *Extensive Records of the Taiping Era*, vol. 403, where it quotes from *Records of Original Transformations* (*Yuanhua ji*), a collection of legendary stories of ancient China.
79 For the study about Sogdian surnames, see Yao Weiyuan, *Textual Research of Sogdian Surnames in the Northern Dynastie* 北朝胡姓考 (Beijing: Science Press, 1958); and Nikolai Alexandrovich Baskakov, *Russian Surnames of Turkic Origin* (Moscow: Nauka, 1979).
80 Chen Yinke, 1980: 242.
81 Pulleyblank, 1952: 333.
82 Huili and Yancong, vol. 1.
83 Livshits, 1962: 197.
84 Anu 阿奴 was a name used by the elders to express intimacy with the younger. —Trans.
85 Harmatta, 18.
86 In the *Avesta*, the suffix is written as yana-, yāna-; in Ancient Persian, it is written as yāna-.)
87 In the Median language, it is written as farnah-.
88 Livshits, 1962: 58.
89 Karlgren, 43, 95.
90 Henning, 1940: 6.
91 Haneda, 401–402.
92 Pulleyblank, 1952: 333.
93 Weber, 199–201. See also Ikeda On, "A Sogdian Colony in Dunhuang in the Mid-eighth Century," translated into Chinese by Xin Deyong, in Liu Junwen, ed., *Selected Translations of Japanese Scholars' Works on Chinese History* 日本学者研究中国史论著选译, vol. 9 (Beijing: Zhonghua shuju, 1993): 156–171.
94 Weber, 98. See also Livshits, 1962: 53.
95 Weber, 202. There is one proposed idea to trace "Alan 阿揽" back to "Alan 阿兰," the evidence of which sounds too circuitous to be trusted and adopted here. But in the *Collected Works of Zhang Chengji* (*Zhang Chengji wenji*), volume four, there are a set of poems under the title of "Four Poems about the Huaqing Palace" ("Huaqinggong sishou") and the third one contains a line that reads "Villagers are still playing the tune of Alandui on their flutes." Based on this sentence, Wang Shizhen in his book *Goblet Words in the Realm of Art* (*Yiyuan zhi yan*) doubted whether the tune of "Alandui 阿滥堆" "originated from the Qiang and Hu" or maybe it was related to "Alan 阿览."
96 The Wusun were a nomad people living in the southeast of Lake Balkhash and the Ili River basin. The state of Wusun was established during the Western Han period. —Trans.
97 Xielifa 颉利发 was a Turkic official title, referring to the chief of a clan or an official below the minister in the Tang dynasty. —Trans.
98 *Tutun* 吐屯 was a Turkic official title. A *tutun* was usually held by a royal member, and his job was to act as a supervisor in various ministries. —Trans.

99　*Records of the Turks* in the *Old Book of Tang*, vol. 194.
100　Cao fulei 曹浮类 is the Chinese translation of a Sogdian name. In some other sources, it is translated as Cao Pulei 曹蒲类. —Trans.
101　Radlov, 1911: 1487.

Bibliography

Al-Biruni. *The Chronology of Ancient Nations*. London: William H. Allen and Co, 1879.
Amoghavajra, trans. *Jixiong shiri shan'e xiuyao jing (Sutra of Lunar Mansions and Planets)*, in *Zhonghua dazang jing (Chinese Tripitaka)*, vol. 2. Beijing: Zhonghua shuju, 1984.
Bartold, Vasily Vladimirovich. *Four Studies on the History of Central Asia: A Short History of Turkestan*. Leiden: E. J. Brill, 1962.
Belenitski, Alexandre Markovitch. *Central Asia: Art of the Sogdians (Mittelasien: Kunst der Sogden)*. [In German.] Leipzig: Seemann, 1980.
Belenitski, Alexandre Markovitch, et al. *Medieval Cities of Central Asia*. [In Russian.] Leningrad: Nauka, 1973.
Belenitski, Alexandre Markovitch, et al. "Sogdian 'Gold Belt'," in *Eastern Countries and People*. [In Russian.] Edited by Vadim Alexandrovich Romodin. Moscow: Nauka, 1980. 213–217.
Bentovich, Ilona Borisovna. "Costume of Early Medieval Central Asian as Inferred from the Murals between the Sixth to Eighth Centuries," in *Eastern Countries and People*. [In Russian.] Edited by Vadim Alexandrovich Romodin. Moscow: Nauka, 1980. 196–212.
Bogolyubov, Mikhail Nikolaevich, and Olga Ivanovna Smirnova. *Sogdian Documents from Mount Mugh: Business Documents*. [In Russian.] Moscow: Oriental Literature Publishing House, 1963.
Cai Hongsheng. "Suishu kangguo zhuan tanwei (*An Explorative Study of the Record of Samarkand in the 'Book of Sui'*)." *Wenshi* 26 (1986): 103–108.
Cen Zhongmian. *Suitang shi (History of the Sui and Tang Dynasties)*, vol. 1. Beijing: Zhonghua shuju, 1982.
Chen Shou. *Sanguo zhi (Records of the Three Kingdoms)*. Beijing: Zhonghua shuju, 2006.
Chen Yinke. *Jinming guan cong gao (Collected Writings of Jinmingguan)*, vol. 2. Shanghai: Shanghai guji chubanshe, 1980.
Deng Mingshi, ed. *Gujin xingshi shu bianzheng (Differentiation of Ancient and Modern Family Names)*. Shanghai: Shangwu yinshuguan, 1936.
Du Huan. *Jingxing ji (Record of Travels)*. Beijing: Zhonghua shuju, 1963.
Du You, ed. *Tongdian (Comprehensive Institutions)*. Beijing: Zhonghua shuju, 1988.
Duan Chengshi. *Youyang zazu (Miscellaneous Writings from Youyang)*. Beijing: Zhonghua shuju, 1981.
Duan Fang. *Taozhai cangshi ji (The Collected Records of Stone Inscriptions by Taozhai)*. Shanghai: Shanghai guji chubanshe, 1996.
Fan Ye, ed. *Hou Hanshu (Book of the Later Han)*. Zhengzhou: Zhongzhou guji chubanshe, 1996.
Fraser, James George. *Golden Bough*. [In Chinese.] Translated by Xu Yuxin, Wang Peiji, et al. Beijing: Dazhong wenyi chubanshe, 1988.
Freiman, Alexander Arnoldovich. *Catalogue and Interpretation of Records in Mount Mugh*. [In Russian.] Moscow: Oriental Literature Publishing House, 1962.
Haneda, Toru. *Collected Essays on History by Dr. Haneda Toru*, vol. 1. [In Japanese.] Kyoto: Toyoshi Kenkyukai, 1957.
Harmatta, János. "Iran-Turcica." *Acta Orientalia Academiae Scientiarum Hungaricae* 25 (1972): 263–272.

Henning, Walter Bruno. "A Sogdian God." *Bulletin of the School of Oriental and African Studies* 28, no. 2 (1965): 242–254.
Henning, Walter Bruno. *Selected Papers*, vol. 1. Leiden: E.J. Brill, 1977.
Henning, Walter Bruno. *Sogdica.* London: Royal Asiatic Society, 1940.
Huichao. *Wang wu tianzhuguo zhuan* (*Memoir of the Pilgrimage to the Five Kingdoms of India*). Lanzhou: Lanzhou guji shudian, 1990.
Huili and Yancong, eds. *Da Tang Da Ci'en si sanzang fashi zhuan* (*A Biography of the Tripitaka Master of the Great Ci'en Monastery of the Great Tang Dynasty*). Annotated by Sun Yutang and Xie Fang. Beijing: Zhonghua shuju, 1983.
Jerusalemskaya, Anna Alexandrovna. "The Alanian World on the Silk Road," in *Eastern Culture in the Ancient and Early Middle Ages*. [In Russian.] Edited by Vladimir Grigoryevich Lukonin. Leningrad: Aurora Art Publishers, 1978. 151–162.
Karlgren, Bernhard. *Analytic Dictionary of Chinese and Sino-Japanese*. Taipei: Cheng-wen Publishing Company, 1973.
Li Fang, et al., eds. *Taiping guangji* (*Extensive Records of the Taiping Era*). Beijing: Zhonghua shuju, 1961.
Linghu Defen, et al., eds. *Zhou shu* (*Book of Zhou*). Beijing: Zhonghua shuju, 1971.
Liu Xu, et al., eds. *Jiu Tang shu* (*Old Book of Tang*). Beijing: Zhonghua shuju, 1975.
Livshits, Vladimir Aronovich. *Sogdian Documents from Mount Mugh: Legal Documents and Letters*. [In Russian.] Moscow: Oriental Literature Publishing House, 1962.
Livshits, Vladimir Aronovich. "Zoroastrian Calendar," in *Chronology of the Ancient World*. [In Russian.] Edited by Elias Bickerman. Moscow: Nauka, 1975. 320–332.
Lobacheva, Nina Petrovna. "A History of Calendar-based Festive Rituals among the Peasants of Central Asia," in *Ancient Customs and Sacrificial Ceremonies of Central Asian People*. [In Russian.] Edited by Vladimir Nikolaevich Basilov. Moscow: Nauka, 1986. 6–30.
Lu You. *Laoxue an biji* (*Jottings from the Life-Long Learning Hut*). Beijing: Zhonghua shuju, 1979.
Ma Duanlin. *Wenxian tongkao* (*Comprehensive Examination of Literature*). Block-printed edition from the Ming dynasty.
Mangluo Zhongmu yiwen (*Inscriptions from the Tombstones of Luoyang*). Collated and recorded by Luo Zhenyu. Block-printed edition of 1914–1917.
Narshakhi, Abu Bakr Muhammad ibn Jafar. *The History of Bukhara*. Translated by Richard N. Frye. Cambridge, MA: The Mediaeval Academy of America, 1954.
Ouyang Xiu, et al., eds. *Xin Tang shu* (*New Book of Tang*). Beijing: Zhonghua shuju, 1975.
Pulleyblank, Edwin G. "A Sogdian Colony in Inner Mongolia." *T'oung Pao* 41 (1952): 317–356.
Quan Tangshi (*Complete Tang Poems*). Collected by Peng Dingqiu et al., and edited by Cao Yin. Shanghai: Shanghai guji chubanshe, 1986.
Radlov, Vasily Vasilievich (also known as Friedrich Wilhelm Radloff). *Experimental Dictionary of Turkic Dialects*, vol. 4, second Fascicule. Saint Petersburg: Imperial Academy of Sciences, 1911.
Raspopova, Valentina Ivanovna. "Sogdian Belts in the Seventh and Eighth Centuries." [In Russian.] *Soviet Archaeology*, no. 4 (1965): 78–91.
Shi Daoxuan. *Xu Gaoseng zhuan* (*Continued Biographies of Eminent Monks*). Beijing: Zhonghua shuju, 1970.
Shi Xuanying, and Shi Huilin, eds. *Yiqiejing yinyi* (*Sound and Meaning of All Sutras*). Shanghai: Shanghai guji chubanshe, 1986.
Shukurov, Sharif Mukhammadovich. "Fundamentals of Portrait Drawing in the Plastic Art of Central Asia," in *Ancient and Medieval Central Asia* [In Russian.] Edited by Bobojan Gafurovich Gafurov and Boris Anatolyevich Litvinsky. Moscow: Nauka, 1977. 103–111.

Sima Guang, et al. *Zizhi tongjian* (*Comprehensive Mirror in Aid of Governance*). Beijing: Zhonghua shuju, 1976.

Sima Qian. *Shiji* (*Records of the Grand Historian*). Beijing: Zhonghua Shuju, 1982.

Smirnova, Olga Ivanovna. *Summary Catalog of the Sogdian Coins: Bronze.* [In Russian.] Moscow: Nauka, 1981.

Su Mian, et al., eds. *Tang huiyao* (*Institutional History of Tang*). Shanghai: Shangwu yinshuguan, 1936.

Uncertain authorship. *Xuanhe huapu* (*Catalog of Paintings of the Xuanhe Era*). Shanghai: Shanghai shuhua chubanshe, 1984.

Voronina, Veronika Leonidovna. "Features of the Early Medieval Dwelling of Central Asia." [In Russian.] *Soviet Ethnology*, no. 6 (1963): 84–96.

Wang Chongmin. *Dunhuang yishu lunwen ji* (*Collected Essays on the Dunhuang Manuscripts*). Beijing: Zhonghua shuju, 1984.

Wang Qinruo, et al. *Cefu yuangui* (*Prime Tortoise of the Record Bureau*). Beijing: Zhonghua shuju, 2003.

Wang Yan. *Mingxiang ji* (*Records of Mysterious Manifestations*). The book is no longer extant, but some fragments are included in *Gu xiaoshao gouchen* (*Selected Collection of Chinese Classical Fiction*). Edited by Lu Xun. Jinan: Qilu shushe, 1997.

Weber, Dieter. "On the Sogdian Personal Names." (Zur sogdischen Personennamengebung). [In German.] *Indogermanische Forschungen* 77, nos. 2–3 (1972): 191–208.

Wei Jie. *Xifan ji* (*Record of the Western Minorities*). The book is no longer extant, but some fragments are included in the *Tongdian* (*Comprehensive Institutions*). Edited by Du You. Beijing: Zhonghua shuju, 1988.

Wei Shou. *Wei shu* (*Book of Wei*). Changchun: Jilin renmin chubanshe, 1995.

Wei Zheng, et al. *Sui shu* (*Book of Sui*). Beijing: Zhonghua shuju, 1973.

Wu Bolun. *Xi'an lishi shulue* (*A Brief History of Xi'an*). Xi'an: Shaanxi Renmin chubanshe, 1979.

Wuhan daxue lishi xi, et al., eds. *Tulufan chutu wenshu* (*Documents Unearthed in Turfan*), vol. 7. Beijing: Wenwu chubanshe, 1986.

Xiang Da. *Tangdai Chang'an yu xiyu wenming* (*Tang Dynasty Chang'an and the Culture of the Western Regions*). Beijing: Sanlian shudian, 1957.

Xuanzang, dictated. *Da Tang xiyu ji* (*Great Tang Records on the Western Regions*). Transcribed by Bian Ji. Beijing: Wenxue guji kanxingshe, 1955.

Yan Zhenqing. *Yan Lugong ji* (*The Collected Works of Yan Zhenqing*). Shanghai: Shanghai guji chubanshe, 1992.

Yang Xuanzhi. *Luoyang qielan ji* (*A Record of Buddhist Monasteries in Luoyang*). Annotated by Liu Weidong. Beijing: yanshan chubanshe, 1998.

Yao Runeng. *An Lushan shiji* (*Biographical Accounts of An Lushan*). Shanghai: Shanghai guji chubanshe, 1983.

Ye Delu. "Qiyaoli ru Zhongguo kao (Introduction of the Seven-day Calendar to China)." *Furen xuezhi* 11, nos. 1–2 (1942): 137–157.

Yue Shi. *Taiping huanyuji* (*Universal Geography of the Taiping Era*). Taipei: Wenhai chubanshe, 1963.

Yuwen Maozhao, ed. *Dajin guozhi* (*Records of the Great Jin Dynasty*). Shanghai: Guangwen shuju, 1968.

Zhang Wei. *Longyou jinshi lu* (*Inscriptions of Longyou*). Lanzhou: Lanzhou junhua yinshuguan, 1944.

Zhang Zhuo. *Chaoye qian zai* (*Record of the Imperial Court and Beyond*). Beijing: Zhonghua shuju, 1979.

3 "Seven" as a Venerated Number among the Nine Surnames of the Sogdians in the Tang Period

From a barbarian state to a civilized society, people of ancient nations came up with mysterious numbers, such as seven, ten, twelve, or seventy-two. Taken as a unique cultural category, these numbers penetrated their religious and social lives and were often considered a symbol of primitive culture.[1] In the Tang period, foreigners in the north (*beifan*) who lived in the felt tents of the northern grassland, and foreigners in the west (*xihu*) who inhabited the oasis city-state of Central Asia, inherited their ancestral beliefs and also idolized mysterious numbers. This legacy of primitive mentality is worth exploring. One rough study has shown that the Turks (*Tujue*) regarded "ten" as a holy number. The situation is as follows:

> As the legend of ancient Turks has it, almost everything is connected to the number "ten." The forefather of the Turks had a "ten-year-old" son who in his adulthood had "ten males" by a she-wolf. Neduliu had "ten wives." When the Turkic state was founded, "there were ten levels of official titles, from high or low rank." The Turkic law stipulated: "The thief will pay ten times the worth of stolen goods." The military and administrative system of the Western Turks also had a trace of "ten": "Each group, under the title of 'ten sets,' was commanded by one person. Because each set was bestowed with an honorary arrow, they were also known as the 'ten arrows.'" It is evident that, with the total number of human fingers as its origin, the number ten was applied to the social structure and military organization of the Turkic clans. Even for the famous khan "Tumen," his name is nothing more than the fourth level of the decimal system. Undoubtedly, in the ancient Turkic belief, "ten" was believed to be the mysterious number that generated everything in the world.[2]

The mysterious numbers revered by the Nine Surnames of the Sogdians (*Jiuxinghu*) in the Tang dynasty are more difficult to decipher than those of the Turks. As the information available is incomplete, it is hard to construct an overall picture, but some historical traces have emerged after my research. In my opinion, for the Nine Surnames, "seven" was their mysterious number. This veneration was related to the "Seven Holy Immortals" of Zoroastrianism, which, by way of localization, found its way into a play called the "Team of Seven Holy Immortals" during the Northern Song dynasty.

My research on the Turks is far from being conclusive, but it is based on historical evidence and thus cannot be that inaccurate. However, the following origin-tracing effort may involve making personal conjectures; it should therefore only function as a reference for further study into the cultural exchange between the Hu people and the Han Chinese in the Middle Ages. I hope that this disclaimer helps to avoid possible confusion on the part of readers.

Historical Evidence of the Nine Surnames' Veneration for "Seven"

Records concerning the Nine Surnames of the Tang period are rather detailed in terms of their tributary role, development, and their rise and fall, with more attention to political history than cultural interaction. Occasionally, out of historical texts, we can glean some information relevant to their reverence of the number "seven". There are also some fragmentary pieces available in Arabic history books as well as unearthed documents in Central Asia. I have assembled below whatever I could find and put them down in a classified order, with some comments to illustrate the occasions when "seven" is mentioned and what it means.

Seeking the Divine Scion in the Wilderness

In volume 193 of the *Comprehensive Institutions* (*Tongdian*), there is a quote from Wei Jie's *Record of the Western Minorities* (*Xifan ji*):

> [In Samarkand,] it is a local custom to worship the divine scion. Legend has it that the divine scion died in the seventh month, and upon his death, his bones were lost. So, every year at about that time, three to five hundred worshipers, dressed in black and barefoot, are scattered in the field, bawling and beating their breasts in grief. They do this to beg for the return of his bones. It lasts for seven days.

Regarding the worship of "the divine scion" at the festival held in the seventh month in Samarkand and its mythological function, I have given my interpretation in another publication.[3] As my focus here is on mysterious numbers, the two occasions where "seven" is mentioned need to be emphasized: "the divine scion died in the seventh month" and "It lasts seven days." Here, "seven" is used as a time concept and is connected to their worship of the "divine scion." With this observation as the starting point, it will be easier for us to understand how the Sogdians venerated the number "seven."

Archery Match in the Woods

Here is another quote from Wei Jie's *Record of the Western Minorities*:

> [In Samarkand,] the year begins on the first day of the sixth month. On this day, both the king and common people wear new clothes, and have their hair cut and beards trimmed. In the woods east of the town, horse racing and

archery go on for seven days. When it comes to the final day, a coin is glued to the target, and the person who hits it can act as a king for one day.

In this ancient custom of selecting a "temporary king,"[4] the mysterious number of "seven" appears twice: the match lasts for "seven days," and "the last day" is the "seventh" day. Similar to the religious rite of "seeking the divine scion," this secular festival of "archery match" also highlights the number "seven."

Zoroastrian God-inviting Ritual

In one fragmentary piece of the Dunhuang manuscripts – *Geographic Writings of Shazhou and Yizhou* (*Shazhou Yizhou dizhi*), there is the following record:

> At a Zoroastrian Temple in Yiwu, there were numerous sketches, telling different stories. Before the state of Gaochang had been conquered, a priest named Zhai Pantuo came to the imperial capital to pay homage to the emperor and he performed a Zoroastrian ritual there. First, he stabbed himself with a sharp knife at his left waist until the blade emerged out of the right side. Then he pulled the knife out of his body, cut off the blade, wrapped his hair on the central part of the knife, grasped the ends, and turned the knife up and down. When he did this, he declared that all of the things going on in the empire were in line with the will of Heaven and had god's blessing, and that all could be verified. After the divine force withdrew, he fell down stiffly. For seven days, he could barely breathe. But then he recovered and was as healthy as before.[5]

It is not surprising to see a Zoroastrian priest performing an illusory trick from the Western Regions. What is worth noting is that it took seven days for him to recover after "the divine force withdrew," pointing to the same mysterious number "seven" in the "Zoroastrian ritual." With regard to how long it took a performer to recover, there are other different stories from the Tang period. For example, a Zoroastrian priest in Henan prefecture seemed to have more magical power: "A moment later, when someone sprayed water on his face and chanted a spell over him, he immediately recovered and was as good as before." Compared to this priest, the one in Liangzhou was comparatively weaker, as he "recovered and restored his health after resting for more than ten days."[6] Obviously, the time required for recovery after the ritual varied. But generally speaking, "seven days" seemed to be more typical.

Exorcising Evil Spirits

In volume 40 of the *Sound and Meaning of All Sutras* (*Yiqiejing yinyi*), Shi Huilin gave an explanation of *sumozhemao*:

> 苏莫遮 (*sumozhe*), also called 飒磨遮 (*samozhe*) in a local language of the Western Regions, originated from the state of Qiuzi, and has been on stage till today. In Qiuci, this play involves dance and song performances like

huntuo 浑脱, *da'mian* 大面, *botou* 拨头, and the like. Sometimes performers pretend to be animals, or ghosts, wearing all sorts of costumes and masks; sometimes they sprinkle muddy water over audiences; or they take hooks and ropes, catching passers-by for fun. Every year in the beginning of the seventh month, this play is publicly on show, and lasts for seven days. According to a local legend, this play is meant to exorcise evil spirits, drive away demons and ghosts that might devour and plague people.

As a play from the Western Regions, *sumozhe* was a performance prevalent in Samarkand. Also, Qiuci was not the state of its origin. Rather, it was the place from which the play spread out. That can be evidenced by one of Zhang Shuo's five poems about *sumozhe*: "*Sumozhe* originated from the Western Regions, where people have blue eyes and blonde beards. /Aware that the mercy of the emperor is all over the world, they come to visit and bring more fun with songs and dances." As a way to exorcise evil spirits, *sumozhe* was performed in "the seventh month," and lasted for "seven days," revealing a clear veneration for the number "seven." As for why water splashing was involved in the play to make this festival different, that is a different story.

Lion Taming

Chen Cheng recorded the following in "A Record of the Foreign Countries in the Western Regions" ("Xiyu fanguo zhi"):

> A lion is usually born in the reeds of the Amu Darya River. It is said that after birth, it does not open its eyes until seven days later. For those who want to capture and domesticate it, it is best to get it when its eyes are still closed. When a lion grows up, it will be hard to tame, as it becomes ferocious and brutal.

Samarkand was famous for being home to Central Asian lions, as revealed in the *Book of Wei: Records of the Western Regions* (*Wei shu: Xiyu zhuan*):

> The state of Xiwanjin[7], with its capital in Xiwanjin city, is located west of Mimi, about 12,700 *li* away from the state of Dai. There is a mountain called Mount Jiasena in the south of this country, and this is where many lions are found. Every year, lions are offered as a tribute to the empire.

It is understandable that the people of Samarkand tended to tame a lion when it was newly born. As for the saying that a lion "does not open its eyes until seven days later," this is too magical to be believable, only to reveal a superstitious mentality and their veneration for the number "seven."

Folk Calendar

In the Tang period, a seven-day calendar was widely used among the Nine Surnames, as evidenced by the "Almanac" discovered in Cave A12 of Mount

Mugh in 1933. Each of the seven days was named after the Sun, the Moon, and the five stars (Mars, Mercury, Jupiter, Venus, and Saturn). The Sogdian name for each day was the same as that in the translated scriptures in the Tang period.[8]

Cycle of the Temple Fair

According to Al Biruni (973–1048), the Sogdians in the Middle Ages had a clear time cycle: "Merchants of different countries gathered here for the temple fair for seven days."[9] As mentioned earlier, for the Nine Surnames, both the New Year's celebration and the "archery match" in the seventh month lasted for seven days, and this probably means that the festivals and the temple fair were held at about the same time. This "double seven" phenomenon again reveals the age-long tradition of revering the number "seven."

The Spell of a Witch Doctor

For the modern Turkmen who lived on the same land as the Nine Surnames in the Tang period, some ancient customs of venerating "seven" were retained. A local witch doctor, for example, when he treated a patient who had a fever, would cast a spell in this manner:

> The witch doctor was weaving some camel hair into a strong thread, muttering a mantra as he did so. Then he tied seven knots on this thread, blew on each one, and pulled them tight. After that, the patient wore the knotted thread on his wrist like a bracelet, and untied one knot each day. When the seventh knot was untied, he crumpled up the thread and threw it into the river, indicating that his fever drifted away with the water.[10]

To cure the disease by untying the knots, the witch doctor was simply acting on the principle of homeopathic witchcraft. But the number "seven" in this practice – seven knots for seven consecutive days – shows the deep-rooted reverence for this number. That is, "seven" was not only applicable to the occasion of the Zoroastrian ritual and used in the play to exorcise evil spirits but also provided a measurable therapy for a witch doctor: seven knots on a seven-day treatment. In the custom of the Nine Surnames, the divine power of "seven" cannot be underestimated.

As shown above, the mysterious number "seven" was widely found in the social and cultural life of the Nine Surnames and became an important part of their custom. Is it possible that this reverence might be traced back to the Persian civilization? After all, besides linguistic and ethnological connections, there is some historical literature to support the claim that the Nine Surnames were a branch of the Persian population. First, the Behistun inscription of the Persian empire in the sixth century BC listed Khwarazm and Sogdiana as the 16th and 18th provinces of Achaemenian Persia (539–331 BC), which, under the rule of Darius I, had 23 satrapies.[11] Second, political reliance leads to religious dependence. As the *New Book of Tang: Records of Persia* (*Xin Tang shu: Bosi zhuan*) states: "The Hu people in the Western Regions accepted their belief and embraced Zoroastrianism."

The same can be said of the Nine Surnames in the Tang period: "According to the legend, Zoroastrianism originated in Persia, and by the divine power of Heaven, it worked magic here and thus a Zoroastrian Temple was set up."[12] Third, the theocratic politics of ancient Persia was epitomized by a famous saying by King Darius: "Ahura Mazda is mine and I am Ahura Mazda's."[13] As a state religion, Zoroastrianism endowed the Persian law with sanctity, and it also became a major feature of politics for the Nine Surnames: "The legal documents are placed in the Zoroastrian Temple. When a verdict is needed, they will be taken out for reference."[14]

With such a deep-rooted historical and cultural Persian origin, the Nine Surnames' veneration of "seven" was unlikely to go beyond this source of influence. The following section further examines why the number "seven" became the shared religious symbol for the Nine Surnames and the Persians.

"Seven" in the Cosmological Structure of Zoroastrianism

In the Persian Zoroastrian theological system, "seven" as a mysterious number was not only related to the founding legend but also directly affected the structure of theogony.

"Seven" Years of Meditation

The founder of Zoroastrianism, whose Persian name was Zarathustra, meaning "he who can manage camels," was born in the Iranian plateau of West Asia. There was a fascinating story about how he founded this religion. It is said that at age 20, he left his parents and started traveling around, seeking people of virtue. At first, he was known for his acts of kindness such as setting off haystacks for lighting and purifying water with juice from herbs such as Haoma. Then he lived a reclusive life in a cave, meditating on the world. After "seven" years of prayerful meditation, he came to a thorough revelation. After that, he followed the "teachings" of Ahura Mazda and preached in eastern Iran for a long time until he was killed at 77 years old by an anti-religious Turanian.[15]

"Seven" Stages of Creation

For Zoroastrians, the creation of the world went through "seven" stages. According to Mary Boyce, its prototype could be found among the early Indo-Iranians:

> The creation of the world can be divided into seven stages: first, the creation of the stone sky, which enclosed the world like the shell of an egg; second, the creation of water by filling the lower half of the "egg"; third, the creation of the earth which was shaped like a flat disk, floating on the primeval waters; fourth, the creation of a single plant in the middle of the earth; fifth, the creation of a bull next to the plant; sixth, the creation of a man next to the bull, called Gayōmard, which means a "mortal life"; and the seventh creation was fire, visible or invisible, which was said to provide warmth and life to

the universe. The sun, as part of the fire created by Ahura Mazda, stood still in the middle of the sky, motionless.[16]

In this myth, fire was the final product of the seven stages of creation, capable of permeating and generating all things in the world. It is no wonder that it was revered as the "holy fire."

Seven Holy Immortals

The cosmological world of Zoroastrianism is ruled by seven holy immortals, forming a distinct sevenfold structure. The first is Ahura Mazda, the One Lord who is everywhere; the second is Vohu Manah who is associated with the animal kingdom; the third is Asha Vahishta who governs the element of fire; the fourth is Khshathra Vairya who rules the mineral kingdom; the fifth is Spenta Armaiti who is related to the earth; the sixth is Haurvatat who regulates the water, and the seventh is Ameretat who is associated with the plants.[17]

This Persian-style theological structure shows, as Friedrich Engels has pointed out, "in order to become a religion, monotheism has ever had to make concessions to polytheism - since the time of Zend-Avesta."[18] For Ahura Mazda, his divinity is shown through the other six mighty intelligences, and all of the seven constitute a sevenfold expression of the divine reality. From one lord to seven gods, this seems to be the result of "concession."

The above discussion has revealed the connection between the Nine Surnames' reverence for "seven" and the Persian theology. What follows is an exploration of a more perplexing issue. By examining the folk activities during the Song period, I look for possible traces of veneration for the number "seven" left by the Nine Surnames after their settlement in China during the Tang period.

"Team of Seven Holy Immortals": A Play Reminiscent of Zoroastrianism

As early as the Tang period, "Seven Holy Immortals" had been mentioned in relation to a miracle in a Buddhist temple in Chang'an. According to the "Record of the Xuan Chamber (Xuanshi zhi)":

There was a Hall of Holy Paintings at Yunguang Temple, Chang'an, and local residents believed that those were the paintings drawn by seven holy immortals. When the temple was first built, a young man came to the temple and said, "I and my six brothers are good at painting, and we would like to paint the walls free of charge." The monks agreed. Then these seven men arrived at the temple with color pigments. Before they started, they said to the monks: "Don't push open the door during the following seven days." The monks agreed. For the following six days, there was no sound inside the hall. Puzzled, the monks ripped the seal and pushed open the door. From within the hall, seven pigeons were flying away. What was left were the colorful paintings on the walls, with the northwest top unfinished. Later, when a painter was invited to examine the paintings, he was astonished, lauding "magical!"[19]

Although this anecdote touches upon the number "seven" as in "seven men" and "seven days," it has a heavier color of Buddhism than Zoroastrianism, and hence, it cannot be used as good evidence here.

In the Northern Song dynasty, in Bianjing, there was an acrobatic play called "Seven Sacred Knives," and the performers started their show amid smoke:

> Seven men emerged out of smoke, tattooed, wearing long hair, and dressed themselves in thin, dark short jackets, with splendid embroidered belts wrapped around their waists. One of them wore a small, golden, flowery hat and held a white flag in one hand, and the rest wore headbands. With real knives in hand, they were fighting and stabbing each other, pretending to gash the opponent's face and cut open his belly. This is called Seven Sacred Knives.[20]

Regarding this description, Ma Mingda, an expert in the history of martial arts, proposed a new explanation, arguing that "the play of Seven Sacred Knives was neither acrobatics nor martial arts. It was a kind of ritual or magic of ancient Zoroastrianism."[21] He also quoted two stories from Hong Mai's *Records of Yijian* (*Yijian zhi*) from the Southern Song dynasty as evidence, one of which is the story entitled "A Spearhead Ghost at Geshan" ("Geshan paijun") in the eighth volume:

> Zhu San, a resident of Raozhou, was a bully who had tattoos on his thighs, arms, chest and back. He was good at cooking animal offal, but this could only earn him a meager living. Every year, when it was the time to welcome the gods, Zhu volunteered to be the leader of the "Team of Seven Holy Immortals." In the 16th year of the Chunxi reign of the Song dynasty [1189], Zhu was going to buy some sesame at Geshan. Before his departure, his wife said to him, "I heard people say that there are ghosts in that place. You worship a different god, how dare you go there?" Zhu replied, "I have spells to protect myself from whatever demons or ghosts out there. They cannot hurt me!" Many acquaintances also advised him not to go.

The "spells" mentioned by Zhu San were "Spells of Seven Holy Immortals." Ma Mingda quoted from the *Record of Prosperity and Splendor by the Old Man of the West Lake* (*Xihu laoren fansheng lu*) to prove this: "Street performers presented their show of 'Spells of Seven Holy Immortals' inside the ring. They cut off one performer's head, cast a spell on that, and after a while put it back over the body." Here, Ma connected the "Spells of Seven Holy Immortals" of the street performance with Zoroastrianism, which was an inspiring effort, providing important evidence for the localization of Zoroastrian ritual. As for the questions he posed: "For the play of the Seven Sacred Knives, why did it have to be performed by seven people, and what could be the connection between the number 'seven' and Zoroastrianism?" I might, following the ancient motto – "when baffled by a difficult question, we should share our understandings," summarize my discussion and provide an answer which might not be that perfect but could be used as a reference for further study.

First, veneration for the number "seven" was a deep-rooted custom among the Nine Surnames in the Tang period, the origin of which can be traced back to the Persian civilization.

Second, seven holy immortals constitute the core of the cosmological structure in the Persian theology, and the creation spirit Ahura Mazda occupies a supreme position in the theogony. It is no wonder that performers in the Song period let this character lead the "Team of Seven Holy Immortals," followed and supported by the figures of the other six mighty intelligences.

Third, both the "Spells of Seven Holy Immortals" and the "Zoroastrian Practice" used a knife to conduct a dazzling performance. The show of "cutting open one's belly with a sharp knife" was an "illusory trick from the Western Regions," showing the long-standing pagan style of Zoroastrianism.

Fourth, the flag bearer in the team of "Seven Sacred Knives" wore a "small, golden, flowery hat," which could be a symbol of crown in the Nine Surnames, if we refer to the *Book of Sui* (*Sui shu*), volume 83, "wearing a crown with the design of a golden flower made of seven treasures (*qibao jinhua*)." As for the dressing manner of seven performers – "with splendid embroidered belts wrapped around their waists," it was also similar to the kind of "Hu garment" (*hu fu*) with a brocade tie.

In general, the play "Team of Seven Holy Immortals" in the Song period bore distinctive features of Zoroastrianism, whether in terms of character arrangement, props, actions, or costumes. Its significance for the cultural exchange between the Hu and the Han deserves further exploration and elaboration.

Notes

1 Levy-Bruhl, 213–214. Also see two essays by Yang Ximei, "The Mysterious Numbers in Ancient China" and "A Mysterious Number – 72," in *The Cultural History of the Pre-Qin Period* (Beijing: Zhongguo shehui kexue chubanshe, 1995): 616–716.
2 Cai Hongsheng, 1998: 174.
3 Cai Hongsheng, 1998: 34.
4 Frazer, 420.
5 Wang Zhongluo, 204.
6 Zhang Zhuo, 64–65.
7 *Kangguo* or *Xiwanjin* referred to the same country. It was called *Xiwanjin* in the *Book of Wei* and *Kangguo* in the *Book of Sui*. —Trans.
8 Freiman, 60; Ye Delu, 137–157.
9 Al-Biruni, 234.
10 Frazer, 360.
11 Rak, 419.
12 Duan Chengshi, vol. 1.
13 Yarshater, 424.
14 *Book of Sui: Records of Samarkand* (*Sui shu: Kangguo zhuan*).
15 Lv Kai, et al., 454–455.

16 Lin Wushu, 1995: 52.
17 Gong Fangzhen and Yan Kejia, 101–102; Yuan Wenqi, 138–139. For the discussion of Zoroastrianism in Dunhuang manuscripts, see Jiang Boqin, *The Religion of Art and the Civilization of Ritual and Music in Dunhuang* (*Dunhuang yishi zongjiao yu liyue wenming*) (Beijing: Zhongguo shehui kexue chubanshe, 1996): 489–494. Also see Rong Xinjiang, *Medieval China and Foreign Civilizations* (*Zhonggu zhongguo yu wailai wenming*) (Beijing: Sanlian shudian, 2001): 334–342.
18 *Engels*, 2001: 43.
19 Zeng Zao, 256–262. This tale is included in the 23rd volume of the *Categorized Tales* (*Lei shuo*) where Zeng quotes from the *Record of the Xuan Chamber* (*Xuanshi zhi*).
20 Meng Yuanlao, vol. 7.
21 Ma Mingda, 256–262.

Bibliography

Al-Biruni. *Chronology of the Ancient Nations*. London: William H. Allen & Co, 1879.
Cai Hongsheng. *Tangdai jiuxinghu yu tujue wenhua* (*Nine Surnames of the Sogdians in the Tang Dynasty and the Turkic Culture*). Beijing: Zhonghua shuju, 1998.
Du You, ed. *Tongdian* (*Comprehensive Institutions*). Beijing: Zhonghua shuju, 1988.
Duan Chengshi. *Youyang zazu* (*Miscellaneous Writings from Youyang*). Beijing: Zhonghua shuju, 1981.
Engels, Friedrich. *Engels on Religion.* [In Chinese.] Translated by Compilation and Translation Bureau of Works of Marx, Engels, Lenin and Stalin of the CPC Central Committee. Beijing: Renmin chubanshe, 2001.
Frazer, James George. *The Golden Bough.* [In Chinese.] Translated by Xu Yuxin, et al. Beijing: Dazhong wenyi chubanshe, 1988.
Freiman, Alexander Arnoldovich. *Catalogue and Interpretation of Records in Mount Mugh.* [In Russian.] Moscow: Oriental Literature Publishing House, 1962.
Gong Fangzhen, and Yan Kejia. *Xianjiao shi* (*The History of Zoroastrianism*). Shanghai: Shanghai shehui kexueyuan chubanshe, 1998.
Hong Mai, ed. *Yijian zhi* (*Records of Yijian*). Beijing: Zhonghua shuju, 1981.
Levy-Bruhl, Lucien. *Primitive Mentality.* [In Chinese.] Translated by Ding You. Beijing: Shangwu yinshuguan, 1997.
Lin Wushu. *Bosi baihuojiao yu gudai zhongguo* (*Zoroastrianism and Ancient China*). Taipei: Xinwenfeng chubanshe, 1995.
Lv Kai, et al., eds. *Shijie shenhua baike quanshu* (*Encyclopedia of World Mythology*). Shanghai: Shanghai wenyi chubanshe, 1992.
Ma Mingda. *Shuo jian conggao* (*Draft Essays on the Sword*). Lanzhou: Lanzhou daxue chubanshe, 2000.
Meng Yuanlao. *Dongjing menghua lu* (*The Eastern Capital: A Dream of Splendor*). Beijing: Zhongguo shangye chubanshe, 1993.
Ouyang Xiu, et al., eds. *Xin Tang shu* (*New Book of Tang*). Beijing: Zhonghua shuju, 1975.
Rak, Ivan Vadimovich. *Myths of Ancient and Early Medieval Iran Zoroastrianism.* [In Russian.] St. Peterburg: Zhurnal "Neva," 1998.
Wang Zhongluo. *Dunhuang shishi dizhi canjuan kaoshi* (*Examination of the Dunhuang Fragments about Stone Chambers and Geographical Writings*). Shanghai: Shanghai guji chubanshe, 1993.

Wei Jie. *Xifan ji* (*A Record of the Western Minorities*). The book is no longer extant, but some fragments are included in the *Tongdian* (*Comprehensive Institutions*). Edited by Du You. Beijing: Zhonghua shuju, 1988.
Wei Zheng, et al., eds. *Sui shu* (*Book of Sui*). Beijing: Zhonghua shuju, 1973.
Xihu Laoren. *Xihu Laoren fansheng lu* (*Record of Prosperity and Splendor by the Old Man of the West Lake*). Beijing: Shangwu yinshuguan, 1982.
Yarshater, Ehsan, ed. *Encyclopedia Iranica*, vol. 1, fascicle 4. London: Routledge & Kegan Paul, 1983.
Ye Delu. "Qiyaoli ru Zhongguo kao (Introduction of the Seven-day Calendar to China)." *Furen xuezhi* 11, nos. 1–2 (1942): 137–157.
Yuan Wenqi. *Er'yuan shen lun* (*Dualism in Theology*). Beijing: Zhongguo shehui kexue chubanshe, 1997.
Zeng Zao. *Lei shuo* (*Categorized Tales*). Fuzhou: Fujian renmin chubanshe, 2000.
Zhang Zhuo. *Chaoye qian zai* (*Record of the Imperial Court and Beyond*). Beijing: Zhonghua shuju, 1979.

4 The Mu Sogdians in the Tang Period

In ancient Central Asia, unlike the coastal areas, the land along the Amu Darya River was densely populated by the inland city-states. Connected to Persian, Indian, and Byzantine civilizations to varying degrees, the states here played an intermediary role in the economic exchange and cultural dissemination between the Western Regions and China. On the western side of the Amu Darya River was the state of Mulu,[1] which is called Mouru in *Khordeh Avesta* (also known as *Little Avesta*). In the *Book of the Later Han: Records of the Western Regions* (*Hou Hanshu: Xiyu zhuan*), it is recorded that "Mulu, with a state title as Xiao Anxi [eastern Parthian Empire],[2] is 20,000 *li* away from Luoyang."[3] In the Sui and Tang dynasties, due to differences in transcription, Mulu 木鹿 was called "Mu" 穆 or "Molu" 末禄 and genealogically became a member of the "Nine Surnames of Zhaowu." According to the "Records of the Western Regions" ("Xiyu zhuan") in the *Book of Sui* (*Sui shu*), volume 83:

> The state of Mu, whose capital lies west of the Oxus River,[4] is located in what used to be Anxi. Like the king of Kang [Samarkand], the king of Mu also took the tribal surname Zhaowu, but his personal name is Alanmi. The capital is about three *li* in radius, with an armed force of 2,000 soldiers. This country neighbors Wunahe[5] on the east, about 200 *li* away, and in the northeast is the state of An [Bukhara], about 500 *li* away. In the west is the Persian Empire, about 4,000 *li* away, and it is about 7,700 *li* away from Guazhou[6] in the east.

In the inland transportation network of medieval Asia, the state of Mu was on the middle route for the "Three Roads of the Western Regions." As explained in "A Biography of Peiju" ("Peiju zhuan") in the *Book of Sui*, volume 67: "The middle route starts from Gaochang. It passes through Yanqi, Qiuzi, Shule, then it goes up over Chongling [Pamirs], and continues through Bohan, Suduishana, the state of Kang, the state of Cao, the state of He, the state of An, the state of Lesser An, the state of Mu, before it ends in Persia where it contacts the Western Sea."[7] As "Sogdian merchants were busy running back and forth to the frontier towns to trade,"[8] it is not surprising to find traces of the Mu people among them.

As Xiang Da has accurately pointed out: For those who came to China from the Western Regions, most of them bore the surname of either Shi 石, Cao 曹, Mi 米, Shi 史, He 何, Kang 康, An 安, or Mu 穆, and they were probably the descendants of the Nine Surnames of Zhaowu.[9] Of the extant literature, records about the Mu Sogdians are rather sparse and that has partially led to an unbalanced research in the field of Sogdian studies. To make up for what I have not touched upon in my book *Nine Surnames of the Sogdians in the Tang dynasty and the Turkic Culture* (*Tangdai Jiuxinghu yu Tujue wenhua*), I hope that what is provided below will help in compiling sources for later research.

Old Records and New Evidence about the State of Mu

Among the descriptions about the state of Mu in the Tang dynasty, Du Huan's *Record of Travels* (*Jingxing ji*) is the most complete. The following is a quote from "Border Defense" ("Bianfang dian") in the *Comprehensive Institutions* (*Tongdian*), volume 193:

> The state of Mulu[10] is about seven hundred *li* southwest of the state of Yamei. The Sogdians here bear the surname of Mu, and they are mostly local residents. Their capital city is about 15 *li* in radius, with an iron gate, a salt pond and two Buddhist temples. The country covers an area of 140 *li* from east to west, and 180 *li* from north to south. It is densely populated, with verdant trees and connected villages. Within the territory, moving sand can always be seen. In the south, there is a big river flowing through the this place, which is then divided into hundreds of canals, irrigating the farmlands of the whole country. The land is fertile, and the residents over this land look clean and tidy. The city walls are high and thick, and the houses are square and flat, with wood carvings or soil paintings. There are also fine soft laminated fabric and lamb furs, the best of which might be worth hundreds of silver coins. As for fruits, there are red peaches, white apricots, brown plums, yellow plums and white plums. The largest kind of melon is called Xunzhi, and one can feed ten people. A snake melon can be more than four *chi* long. As for vegetables, there are spinach, turnips, scallions, onions, brassicas, cucumbers, eggplants, beets, dill, chives and bottle gourds. It is particularly rich in grapes here. There are also cattle, wild horses, ducks, and chukars. In terms of social customs, May is taken as the beginning of a new year, and for the celebration of each new year, painted jars are offered. During public festivities, people play balls and swings. As the commissioner from the Arab empire[11] is officially positioned here, Arabs and Persians live together in peace, extending from this place until the Western Sea. Local residents worship gods. They do not eat the meat of animals that have died naturally or the meat that has been left overnight. They like to use sesame oil on their hair.

76   *The Mu Sogdians in the Tang Period*

The account quoted above involves geography, produce, customs, and political arrangements, almost like a miniature national record of the state of Mu. Among the literature about this country, Ding Qian's textual criticism and Zhang Yichun's annotation are of great value.[12] But if we take into consideration unearthed cultural relics in Turkmenistan during the past decade and related books written by Russian scholars, we can see that there are still gaps to be filled. Following the order of description in Du Huan's book, I provide my interpretation from four aspects to contribute to this field of research.

Temples

In Du Huan's book, it is clearly stated that there were "two Buddhist temples" in the city-state of Mu. Regarding these temples, Cen Zhongmian concluded that "the two Buddhist temples should be Nestorian temples,"[13] as there were Nestorian monks preaching here in the fifth century. However, such an explanation seems debatable. In the mid-eighth century, Du Huan lived in Central Asia for more than ten years, and he knew the difference between the religious beliefs of the Arabs, the Byzantines, and the Zoroastrians, so it is unlikely that he would mistake "Nestorianism" for "Buddhism." Archaeological excavation in Central Asia has also produced some evidence. At the ruins of Gyaur-Kala – an ancient city constructed at the location of the state of Mu, in the southeast corner, there was a pagoda with a square base (12.5 m × 13 m). Opposite this pagoda was a clay statue of Buddha. But what remained was only a painted Buddha head, about 75 cm high, with blue eyes and ushnisha [crown of hair]. Not far away, fragments of Buddhist scriptures written on birch bark in Brahmi were also found. Outside the city, there was another Buddhist temple, with an area of about 140 square meters.[14] Here, a clay tablet of a Buddhist painting was unearthed. On the left side of the painting was a pagoda with banners hanging down on all sides. On the right side was a devout believer who contributed to this temple, and in the middle was the Buddha who sat cross-legged, holding a bird in his arms. And there was light over the Buddha's head.[15] This bird could be a pigeon, and the painting was probably meant to narrate the famous legendary story in the *Nirvana Sutra*: Hidden in the shadow of the Buddha, the pigeon is quiet; out of his shadow, it looks scared. These Buddhist buildings may have been destroyed in the early sixth century, during the reign of Khosro I of the Sassanid Empire (531–579). By the time Du Huan traveled around the state of Mu, the "two Buddhist temples" had been abandoned, and there were no monks inside, confirming what Xuanzang, a famous Buddhist monk, saw in Samarkand: "there are two temples but no monks live inside."[16]

Canals

Located in an oasis, the state of Mu had a well-developed irrigation system. The river that Du Huan mentioned in his book was the Murghab River which "was divided into hundreds of canals, irrigating the farmland of the whole country." There were two types of canals: natural and man-made. The man-made ones were mostly well-canals, underground ditches, similar to the karez well. In his book *On the History of Irrigation in Turkestan*, Bartold devoted one chapter to the irrigation projects along the Murghab River. According to him, at the ruins of Gyaur-Kala, there should have been four water canals flowing from the west to the east. The third one on the west "Raji Canal" was the main canal, supplying water to the whole city.[17]

Laminated Fabric

Describing the laminated fabric produced in the state of Mu, Du Huan emphasized its quality as being "fine and soft," which echoes what the mid-tenth century Arab geographer Ibn Hawqal said: "The cotton fabric named after Mulu is well-known and it is particularly fine and soft."[18] That probably explains why Shi Huilin in the *Sound and Meaning of All Sutras* (*Yiqiejing yinyi*) has an entry entitled "Laminated Fabric of Mulu."[19] At the ruins of Erk-Kala in South Turkmenistan, archaeologists also found pieces of ancient fabric from the state of Mu, which were made of cotton, linen, wool, and silk, some of them dyed. Related literature and cultural relics show that from the time of the Sassanid Empire to the Arab Caliphate Empire, the state of Mu had been the center of fabric production in the Khurasan region. The cloth here was like "brocade fabric," soft and expensive, enjoying the same fame as the products from Samarkand and Bukhara.

Painted Jars

Describing the native products of the state of Mu, Du Huan in *Record of Travels* mentioned, in particular, the painted jars: "According to the local custom, the year begins in the fifth month, which is celebrated by offering painted jars." Then what were these jars? An explanation should be given about them here. At the aforementioned Gyaur-Kala Buddhist Temple, archeologists also found a 46-centimeter-high painted terra-cotta jar with two ears. On the surface of this jar, four scenarios of a nobleman's life were displayed: hunting, feasting, falling ill, and being buried. In the unpainted margins, red heart-shaped dots with a deep black rim on the top can be seen.[20] This kind of painted jar was entirely different from a common ceramic urn. The jars were in high demand, because they were used by local residents for the New Year's offering. In other words, if there had not been a pottery kiln nearby, it would have been very difficult to satisfy the consumers. Indeed, archaeological results proved that at Gyaur-Kala alone, there were 14 pottery kilns, which clearly shows the scale of their pottery production.[21]

The above illustration about the state of Mu, although incomplete, is significant enough to indicate that, as one of the city-states of the "Nine Surnames of Zhaowu," this nation enjoyed a noteworthy status in history.

A List of the Mu People in the Tang Dynasty

In medieval China, it was a common practice to address a Sogdian by his country name. In the historical records before the Tang period, there were descriptions of how the Mu people were favorably treated by the aristocratic society in the Northern Qi dynasty after they traveled east to China. As stated in "Accounts of the Favored" ("Enxing zhuan") in the *History of the North* (*Bei shi*), volume 80:

> During the Wuping reign (570–576), about ten crafty Sogdians, most of them from rich families such as "Hunchback" Kang and "Ancle" Mu, were selected as royal retinues. They were very close to the emperor, almost like eunuchs. Some of them were even promoted to be commanders unequaled in honor (*kaifu yitong sansi*). Of these people, there was a Sogdian named Cao Sengnu who had a son named Cao Miaoda. Both the father and the son were good at playing a Sogdian lute called *pipa*, and both of them were crowned to be kings. Besides these two, a Sogdian named He Hai and his son He Hongzhen were also crowned and were particularly favored by the emperor. But He Hongzhen abused his power. He took bribes and arbitrarily issued verdicts, and he even traded official positions for money. There were another ten people, which included "Weak" He and "Ugly" Shi, who were all promoted to be commanders simply because they were good at dancing and playing musical instruments.

Among these Sogdians, "Ancle" Mu was mentioned together with the children from the family clans of the Kang, Cao, He, and Shi. All of these people enjoyed special privileges and influenced the emperor in the same way as the eunuchs.[22] Also, in 615, of the Nine Surnames of the Sogdians [shortened as the Nine Surnames hereafter] who sent envoys and paid tribute to Emperor Yang of the Sui dynasty, the state of Mu was on the same list with other states such as An [Bukhara], Cao [Kabudhan], He [Koshania], and Bi [Baikand].[23] Thus, it is reasonable to say that during the Tang period, there were traces of the Mu people, showing the continued trend of Sogdians moving from west to east.

No systematic records can be found about the social life of the Mu people in the Tang period, and only some fragments are visible in history books, notes, poems, and excavated documents. Adopting Feng Chengjun's research method as shown in his books *Collection of the Materials on Shanshan* (*Shanshan shiji*) and *Collection of the Materials on Gaochang* (*Gaochang shiji*), I provide a list of the Mu people mentioned in historical sources, with some notes added, for the benefit of future scholars who are interested in the cultural exchange between the Hu people and the Han Chinese in the Tang period.

Mu Boxi

Among the relics excavated at the ancient tomb No. 31 of Astana in Turpan, there was a list of burial clothes from the year 620. Together with this list, there was also another list of names, but only seven lines of this list were visible, and the second one was "Mu Boxi, one person." This name was juxtaposed with the surnames of Cao, He, Kang, and An.[24] With a Sogdian name, this person was probably an immigrant from the state of Mu as his surname was Mu, and his personal name was "Boxi", which was very likely a Chinese transcription of the Sogdian loanword "Boshi."

Mu Shishi and Mu Gougou

In the Tang period, Gaochang was part of the Prefecture of Xizhou. In the land registry book of Gaochang which provides information about the size and location of the land that each Sogdian family was allocated, there were two distinctly recognizable names Mu Shishi and Mu Gougou, but the allocation information was missing.[25] Each of them had two identical characters for their personal name, the meanings of which are hard to decipher, but both undoubtedly bore the surname of Mu. After they settled down in Gaochang, they were allocated land to cultivate, like other local residents, and they also paid official rent as required. As a border prefecture in the Tang dynasty, Xizhou was inhabited by both Sogdians and Chinese, and the Mu people also enjoyed their share here. But there is no information about the details of their life.

Mu Sha'nuo

According to volume 975 of the *Prime Tortoise of the Record Bureau* (*Cefu yuangui*), in the seventh month of 725, "Mu Sha'nuo, the ruler of Persia, paid an official visit and was conferred the title of 'general who subdues' (*zhechong*), and stayed in the palace to guard the emperor." In the 11th month of 730, there is a similar entry that goes like: "Mu Sha'nuo, the ruler of Persia who paid tribute with local products, was conferred the title of 'general who subdues,' and stayed in the palace to guard the emperor." In two of his visits, Mu Sha'nuo presented himself as "the ruler of Persia," which is probably a pseudo-title. The Sassanid dynasty of Persia ended in 654, and the government-in-exile, headed by Peroz, the son of Yazdegerd II, was completely overthrown in 670. How is it possible that 50 or 60 years later there was a "ruler of Persia"? It is likely that Mu Sha'nuo did the same thing as that legendary Sogdian merchant who cut himself open to hide the precious jewels, so that nobody could take his treasure away. That is, Mu paid tribute in exchange for privileged treatment. The title of "general who subdues" conferred upon him was a favor from the Tang court. As a matter of fact, by doing so, the Xuanzong Emperor set a precedent. In "A Biography of Wang E" ("Wang E zhuan") of the *New Book of Tang* (*Xin Tang shu*), volume 170, there is a description that echoes this:

> Every year, thousands of tributary chieftains from the Western Regions, and officers from the protectorates of Anxi and Beiting, gathered in the capital. After the fall of Longyou, these people could not go back, and they needed provisions from the Protocol Office (*Libin yuan*) of the Court of State Ceremonial (*Honglusi*). Every month, forty thousand clusters of coins were distributed and this lasted for a total of forty years. These people were also given pieces of land which bore their surname, and they lived and raised their children on that land, just like registered civilians.

Mu Sha'nuo was probably one of them.

Mu Yu

Xu Hao, a calligrapher in the Tang period, wrote in his book *Records of Antiquities* (*Guji ji*):

> During the Tianbao reign (742–756), I was appointed as the imperial librarian (*tushu shi*). When I was looking for valuable books, I heard about a Sogdian merchant named Mu Yu who was dealing with rare books and antiquities. Every time he got good books, he would decorate them with precious fabrics.

Dou Gao's *Discussion about Calligraphy* (*Shushu fu*) provides Mu Yu's biographical information as follows:

> Born in Xianyang, Longyou area, young Mu Yu started his business by selling books. In 756–758, because he informed the local officials of the other businessmen's illegal search for ancient books, and because he claimed credit for having found the missing books that Empress Wu Zetian returned to Lord Shiquan, he was rewarded with the official title of 'senior officer of golden defense (*jinwu zhangshi*).' After that, he changed his name to Mu Xiang, and later, he gained profit by taking risks.[26]

Although he changed his personal name to Xiang, the previous one "Yu" had a distinct Sogdian characteristic. As a Sogdian merchant dealing in antiquities, Mu Yu gained much from nothing. The risks he took were actually the An Lushan Rebellion during which he made a huge fortune. What he did seemed to be in line with the social character of Sogdian merchants at that time.

Mu Shancai

In the "Preface" to his poem "Song of the Lute," Bai Juyi, a famous poet in the Tang period, wrote:

> In 815, I was demoted to the rank of sub-prefect (*sima*) of Jiujiang. In the autumn of the following year, I walked my friends off to Penpukou. At night, I heard someone on the boat playing a lute. Listening carefully, I recognized the tune popular in the capital. Upon inquiry, I found that the lutist was a courtesan from Chang'an who had learned from two maestros Mu Shancai and Cao Shancai, but growing old and losing her attractiveness, she had to marry a merchant.

There are four lines in this poem which read:

> At thirteen she learned to play the lute,
> enrolled in the First Section of the Court Music Academy.
> Her performances were highly lauded by maestros (*shancai*),
> her looks were gossiped by fellow players who envied her beauty.

Here, "the First Section of the Court Music Academy" was also called the Sitting Section (*zuo bu*), where most of the excellent players were found to be Sogdian. The word "Shancai" is neither a name nor a title. It is probably a way to address those musicians with superb skills. Of the two "maestros," the player with the surname Mu was listed first, indicating his musical talent. As for Li Shen's poem "Lament for the Maestro" ("Bei shancai"), it was written specifically for "Maestro Cao,"[27] a famous lutist who came from the state of Cao, which is irrelevant to the present discussion.

Palace Singer Mu

In Liu Yuxi's poem "Listen to the Former Palace Singer Mu Singing a Song" ("Ting jiu gongzhong yueren mushi changge"), there are four lines that read:

> Having accompanied the Weaver Lady to cross the River of Stars,
> you learned the best tune up in heaven.
> Sing no more the court songs in the Zhenyuan reign,
> as the court officials from the past are not legion.

This poem is generally believed to have been written on the day of the poet's first return to Chang'an in 828. He felt sad about the changed world and could not help but sigh when he heard the song. Hong Mai provided an accurate interpretation of this in his book *Notes Taken in Rong Study* (*Rongzhai suibi*):

> Liu Yuxi first served as an assistant administrator (*lang guan*) and then an imperial censor (*yu shi*) during the Zhenyuan reign. He was not recalled to the court until 24 years later. That is why he had such a poem.[28]

In 785–805, palace singer Mu stayed in one of the lateral courts. Her residence, like the place where the famous musician Kang Kunlun stayed, was the forbidden court inside the imperial palace. The "court song" she sang could be explained as a song of the inner circle among the court musicians and that is why it was lauded by Liu Yuxi as "the best tune up in heaven."

Doctor Mu

Volume seven of the *Anecdotes in the Tang Dynasty* (*Tang yu lin*) records this story:

> When Prime Minister Cui Shenyou went to the western areas of Zhejiang for an inspection, something unknown grew on his left eye, almost covering his pupil. He tried medical treatment for a long time but to no effect. Hearing that in Yangzhou there was a man surnamed Mu who was good at treating eye disease, he asked Yang Xiu, the administrative officer of Huai'nan to send for him. Shortly after that, he got a letter from Yang who told him that 'Mu is a careless person who cannot be trusted. There is another doctor named Tan Jian who is meticulous and careful, far better than Mu.'[29]

82   *The Mu Sogdians in the Tang Period*

Since Cui Shenyou worked as the prime minister in 856, the so-called careless Doctor Mu must have been a famous ophthalmologist in Yangzhou in the middle of the ninth century.

Mu Zhaosi

In volume 98 of the *Extensive Records of the Taiping Era* (*Taiping Guangji*), there is a quote from the *Trivial Tales from North of Meng* (*Beimeng suoyan*):

> A Persian man named Mu Zhaosi was keen on medicine since childhood. One day he followed his father to visit Huaijun, a famous monk of the Zigui prefecture who was good at fortune-telling. Huaijun drew a Taoist monk flying on a gourd among the clouds and captioned it as: 'Strongly recommended by Commander Gao.' Years later, because Mu Zhaosi could cure his patients, Gao Conghui, the king of Nanping rewarded him with a turban, and officially recommended him.

Nanping, located in Jingnan, was one of the states during the Five Dynasties and Ten Kingdoms period, lasting for 57 years (907–963). This story, as well as the preceding one, shows that both in Yangzhou and Jingzhou, there were Mu doctors, and these two prefectures were favored by Sogdian merchants in the Tang period. As for why Mu Zhaosi was called a "Persian man," it was probably a common way to address a Sogdian at that time, revealing nothing about his ethnic origin. The same understanding can be found in the *Miscellaneous Records by Yishan* (*Yishan zazuan*) where "a poor Persian" is listed as an example of oxymoron. Here, "Persian" was just a fixed label in the mind of Chinese people in the Tang period.

Mu Daoling

In volume six of Sun Guangxian's book *Trivial Tales from North of Meng*, there is an anecdote about what happened during 898–901:

> During the Guanghua period [Emperor Zhaozong of the Tang dynasty], Zhu Pu, an erudite man of the *Maoshi*[30], passed the imperial examination and was selected as an official. Proud to be an eloquent person, he believed that he could bring peace and prosperity to this country. Hearing about him from a king, Emperor Zhaozong summoned him to the court. In his meeting with the emperor, he analyzed and commented on current political events, and referring to each one, he would declare "I will handle this for Your Majesty." But after he was appointed, nothing happened, and gradually he lost the emperor's favor. Shortly thereafter he became a sensational joke inside and outside the court. One day when a court banquet was held, Mu Daoling, a comedian, acting as a sutra chanter, came to the emperor, and said in a pun "if it is *Zhuxiang* 朱相, then it is *feixiang* 非相," [31] meaning Zhu Pu was not a good minister. The next day Zhu was demoted and sent out of the capital.

In the same book, volume 10 also narrates a story about Mu Daoling:

> There was an assistant minister (*cheng lang*) who suddenly felt like urinating. In a hurry, he found an empty house and went inside to use the toilet, not knowing that this house belonged to the great comedian Mu Daoling. Just before he left, Mu came home and caught him in person. The assistant minister was ashamed and then apologized to him. Mu said, "Next time if Your Lordship needs to pee, please come uncovered[32]." Everyone who heard this burst into wild laughter.[33]

Among the court performers who served Emperor Zhaozong, there were singers, dancers, musicians, and actors. Mu Daoling stood out as a comedian, displaying his talent of teasing others. Not only could he respond to the emperor in a satirical manner but he also earned his own property, including an empty house. Puns in the Tang period were often used in political jokes, and the fact that Mu Daoling was skilled at this shows the degree of his localization.

Mu Simi

In volume 10 of Qian Yi's book the *New History of the South* (*Nanbu xinshu*), it is written that "when Sun Guangxian worked in Jiangling, a Sogdian guest named Mu Simi stayed at his house. This man left several bunches of daffodils in vases and the flowers did not wither through years." According to "A Biography of Sun Guangxian" ("Sun Guangxian zhuan") in *The Spring and Autumn Annals of the Ten Kingdoms* (*Shiguo chunqiu*), volume 102, Sun Guangxian stayed in Jiangling between 926 and 930. The fact that Mu Simi was only a guest at his house shows that, as an immigrant from the state of Mu, he was probably a late arriver. As for the gift "daffodils," they seemed to have been the best of their species and different from the normal type that usually blooms in winter and dies in summer. These daffodils miraculously "did not wither through years." In ancient Persia, daffodils were used as medicinal plants,[34] but Chinese people in the Tang and Song periods used them for ornamental purposes. With its name changed from Sogdian "green onions in the heaven" (*tiancong*) to Chinese "fairy in water" (*shuixian*), daffodils were elegantly transformed and poetically lauded as the flower which has "agarwood as the bone and jade as the muscle."[35]

Ranging from the early seventh century to the beginning of the tenth century, and covering the regions from Xizhou to Yangzhou, the above ten records involve the life of an envoy, a merchant, a musician, a comedian, a doctor, and a villager. Like limited clues in a sea of information, these records can only give a rough sketch of social activities of the Mu Sogdians in the Tang period. Most Mu people lived in China for generations, bearing only their Sogdian surnames. Deeply localized, they could not be ethnically listed as Sogdians though they had Sogdian lineage.[36] Nevertheless, when we review the history of the Nine Surnames in the Tang period, it is unwise to ignore them.

The State of Mu and the Nine Surnames of the Sogdians

Lying in the oasis of southern Turkmenistan, and bordering other Sogdian states along the Amu Darya River, the state of Mu used to be the capital of Khorasan province in the Sassanid Empire. In the Sui and Tang dynasties, it was regarded as one of the Nine Surnames communities. Located in the west, it was closest to Eastern Iran, so its degree of Persianization was comparatively higher. That is why it was sometimes called "Persia" in the Tang period. It connected Sogdiana and Iran and functioned as a historical and cultural bridge across the Amu Darya River.

Politically, the Arabs used this state as a base for their march into Sogdiana. In 651, the last king of the Sassanid Empire, Yazdajird III[37], met his end at the hands of the Nestorians at Merv (the state of Mu). His son Peroz fled to the Tang empire via Tokharistan. First, he was appointed as military commander (*dudu*) of a "Persian military commandery," and later, he was bestowed the title of "general of martial defense (*wuwei jiangjun*)." In 704, Qutayba Ibn Muslim[38] became the governor of Khorasan. With Merv as the capital, and gathering a troop of more than 50,000 soldiers, he led his army across the Amu Darya River for an eastward expansion. In 706–709, the state of An [Bukhara] was seized, and in 710–712, the state of Kang [Samarkand] was captured. From 713 to 715, Ibn occupied the Ferghana Valley.[39] Deep in crisis, the Nine Surnames reached out to the Tang empire for help and promised to pay tributes. In 719, Tughshada, the king of Bukhara, wrote to the Tang Emperor: "Disturbed by the Arab robbers every year, there is no peace on this land." In the same year, Gurak, the king of Samarkand, wrote: "Muslim came with his army, starting a war against my kingdom. We resisted the invasion bravely, but many of my soldiers were killed and hurt. Since the Arabs disproportionately outnumbered us, we saw no prospect of winning the war." In 741, the king of Chach [in modern Tashkent] Yina Tudun Qule addressed the Emperor Xuanzong of Tang: "If there is a threat from the west, it is the Arab empire."[40] It can be seen that the Arab Caliph used the state of Mu as a garrisoned frontier in his conquest, and this city-state played an important role in the disintegration of Sogdiana. No wonder that Du Huan, in his record about the state of Mu, particularly emphasized that "the commissioner from the Arab empire is officially positioned here."

Culturally, the state of Mu was also the converging place from which the three foreign religions, namely, Nestorianism, Zoroastrianism, and Manichaeism, spread from the west to the east. The religion mentioned in the *Record of Travels* as "they worship gods" is often interpreted as Islam, which used to be called "Tianfang" [meaning "holy land"] in China. But this interpretation is unsupported. The term "Tianfang" was not commonly used until the Ming period. Yet, the Nestorians in the Tang period talked a lot about "Tian" (godly): "A godly message of celebration should be spread to the world that, a virgin has given birth to a holy baby in the Roman Empire. Inspired by the star, Persians traveled here with gifts."[41] In Persia where numerous Zoroastrian temples could be found, there were also "many holy temples," as Xuanzang declared in the 11th volume of the *Great Tang Records on the Western Regions* (*Datang xiyu ji*). Thus, the state of Mu had a mixture of religions. First, since Mouru is mentioned as a nation in the Zoroastrian scriptures, it is reasonable to conclude that there were worshipers of Zoroastrianism in the state of Mu. Second, as early as 334, a Christian parish had been set up in this state. At the beginning of the fifth century, it was taken as the seat of a major archbishopric of the Nestorian Church to deepen the Christianization of the states along the Amu Darya River in Central Asia.[42] In 644, the metropolitan Bishop Elias (or Eliyah) converted the Tocharians to Nestorianism. On the Nestorian Monument, the inscription says that Yesbuzid "came to China from the royal city," which was Balkh in Tokharistan. Third, in the early Middle Ages, the state of Mu became one of the main centers of Manichaean preaching in the East. After the death of Mani, "the head of the Manichaean hierarchy came to Merv, where he found that all the brothers and sisters lived in piety." In the sixth century, "the Manichaean community in Merv and Balkh flourished."[43] Thus, it would not be an exaggeration to say that the state of Mu was a center of religions in the early Middle Ages.

To sum up, the state of Mu was both the political and cultural center in the Western Regions along the Amu Darya River, bearing a close connection with the fate of other Sogdian states. During the fall of the Sassanid Empire and the expansion of the Caliphate, this state became noticeable due to its important role in history. Yet, possibly due to the lack of records, its past glory seems hard to be detected among the descriptions of the Sogdians in the Tang period.

Final Thoughts

Thanks to the efforts of generations of scholars, fruitful research has been made about the relationship between the Hu and the Han in the Middle Ages. However, some fields are well-trodden, and others are neglected. This could be related to either availability of research materials or research interests, which is rather common nowadays.

With regard to the history and culture of the Nine Surnames, for years, more attention has been paid to the eastern states than the western states. For instance, there is plenty of research about eastern Sogdiana (around Samarkand) and not much about western Sogdiana (with Bukhara as the center state). Similarly, the ruins of Panjikent are frequently mentioned, but the artifacts of Varakhsha are rarely cited. As for the "Nine Surnames of Zhaowu" in the Tang period, there has been more attention to their distribution of settlements than individual studies of each state.[44] Generally speaking, the states of Kang [Samarkand], An [Bukhara], and Shi [Kesh] have attracted more attention, followed by He [Kushaniyah], Cao [Kabudhan], Mi [Maimurgh], and Shi [Chach]. Yet, the other three states such as Mu [Amol], Bi [Baikand], and Huoxun [Khwarazm] are rarely touched upon. Besides, there are a couple of puzzling cases awaiting to be demystified. For example, Lady Cao Yena, a concubine of Emperor Xuanzong of the Tang dynasty, who gave birth to the Princess of Shou'an, had a distinct Sogdian name, but there is little information about her background, nor do we know whether she was related to Sogdian dancing girls at Chang'an wine shops. We have no idea when that mystery can be disentangled.

In recent years, more and more tombs of the Hu people have been excavated. In particular, the tombs of An Jia and Shi Jun from the Northern Zhou dynasty discovered in Xi'an, whose epitaphs and stone coffin images reflected the cultural interaction between the Hu, the Han and foreigners, have aroused widespread interest.[45] Do the two paintings of "ox carts" reflect a mythological theme or real life? We might remember that in "Accounts of Khwarazm" ("Huoxun zhuan") of the *New Book of Tang*, volume 22, section 3, there is a sentence that reads: "As these Sogdian states have ox-carts, merchants can easily travel between states." Inspired by excavated cultural relics, we might consider two research directions about the study of the Nine Surnames. The first, in terms of historical periods, is to shift the timeline up from the Sui and Tang dynasties to the Northern Qi dynasty (550–577) and the Northern Zhou dynasty (557–581), looking at the Sogdian merchants in a longer time span. The second, in terms of geographical locations, is to move westward to include Sogdian states beyond the Amu Darya River and examine their relationship with other nomadic states. This kind of grid investigation is rather dialectical, responding to what previous scholars have advocated.[46] If used effectively, it will surely lead to greater innovation in the research about the relationship between the Hu and the Han in medieval times.

Notes

1. Rak, 111.
2. In Chinese history books, the Parthian Empire is called Anxi 安西. Xiao Anxi 小安西 refers to the eastern part of the empire. As a region, Parthia covered the province of Khorazan in modern Iran, and as an empire, it existed between 247 BCE and 224 CE. —Trans.
3. Cen Zhongmian, *Geographical Annotations to the "Book of the Later Han: Records of the Western Regions,"* 2004: 209. Yu Taishan, 268.
4. Oxus was the former name of the Ama Darya River. —Trans.
5. Wunahe was a former state that existed in Central Asia. —Trans.
6. Guazhou was an important town on the Silk Road in the Tang dynasty. Now it is a county in the western part of Gansu province. —Trans.
7. Gaochang 高昌 was located in Turfan, Yanqi 焉耆 in Karashahr, Qiuci 龟兹 in Kucha, Shule 疏勒 in Kashgar, Bohan 钹汗 in Ferghana, Suduishana 苏对沙那国 in modern Ura Tyube, the state of Kang 康国 in Samarkand, the state of Cao 曹国 in Ishtykan, the state of He 何国 in Koshania, the state of An 大安国 in Bukhara, the state of Lesser An 小安国 in Kharghan near Karminia, and the state of Mu 穆国 in Amol. Chongling 葱岭 was the Chinese name for Pamirs. —Trans.
8. Yang Xuanzhi, vol. 3.
9. Xiang Da, 12.
10. In "Border Defense," the name of the state is given as Zhulu, which should be Mulu. The spelling might be incorrect.
11. In the Tang dynasty, the Arab empire was called Dayi 大食. —Trans.
12. See Ding Qian, *Textual Criticism on the Geographical Positions in the "Record of Travels"* (*Jingxingji dili kaozheng* (Series of Books in Zhejiang Library, Hangzhou: Zhejiang tushuguan, 1915); See also Zhang Yichun, *Annotations to the "Record of Travels"* (*Jingxingji jianzhu*) (Beijing: Zhonghua shuju, 2004).
13. Cen Zhongmian, *Research on Geography of China and Foreign Lands,* 2004: 346–347.
14. Kosheleenko, 138–139.
15. Brykina, 26, 28, 245.

16 Huili and Yancong, vol. 2.
17 Bartold, 1965: 138. See also Wang Guowei, 620–622.
18 Bartold, 1963: 443.
19 Cen Zhongmian, *Supplement to the Tang Histories*, 2004: 261.
20 Brykina, 28; Diagram 23 on page 245. See also Stavinsky, 1992: 94.
21 Litvinsky, 413.
22 Huang Yongnian, 69–82.
23 See "A Biography of Emperor Yang" ("Yangdi benji") in volume four of the *Book of Sui*.
24 Volume three of *Documents Unearthed in Turfan* (*Tulufan chutu wenshu*), 119. Song Xiaomei, 22–25.
25 Volume six of *Documents Unearthed in Turfan,* 243–245.
26 Zhang Yanyun, volume 3, volume 6: 121, 209.
27 See *Complete Tang Poems* (*Quan Tangshi*), case 18, scroll 1, for poems by Li Shen.
28 Hong Mai, 779.
29 Wang Dang, 1987: 637.
30 The *Maoshi* is a version of the *Book of Songs* (*Shijing*) transmitted by Mao Heng and Mao Chang. —Trans.
31 Here Mu Daoling used a pun by changing the words in the sutra. The original sutra is "all the characteristic things in the world are also formless forms" (Yiqie zhuxiang, jishi feixiang) [一切诸相，即是非相]. —Trans.
32 Here Mu Daoling punned on the word "uncovered" which can either mean "in an open manner; not in a stealthy way" or "without any clothes on; naked." —Trans.
33 Sun Guangxian, 132, 210.
34 Laufer, 2001: 252–254.
35 Jia Zuzhang, 15–21.
36 Cai Hongsheng, 2004: 81–83.
37 In the Tang dynasty, the name was translated as Yisiqi 伊嗣俟.
38 His name was translated as Qudibo 屈底波 in the Tang period.
39 Hitti, 1995: 241–242.
40 Cai Hongsheng, 1998: 53–57.
41 See "The Nestorian Stele of the Tang Dynasty" ("Daqin Jingjiao liuxing Zhongguo bei").
42 Nikitin, 123. See also Lin Wushu, 2003: 48–57.
43 Litvinsky, 355.
44 Rong Xinjiang, 37–110.
45 Jiang Boqin, 2004: 95–120.
46 See Chen Yinke, *Draft for a Political History of the Tang Period* 唐代政治史述论稿, vol. 2 (Beijing: Sanlian shudian, 2001) and Chapter five of *Draft of a Brief Study of the Origins of the Sui–Tang Political System* 隋唐制度渊源略论稿 (Beijing: Sanlian shudian, 2001).

Bibliography

Bai Juyi. *Bai Juyi ji* (*Collection of Works by Bai Juyi*). Shanghai: Shanghai guji chubanshe, 1988.
Bartold, Vasily Vladimirovich. *A General History of the Cotton Industry in Central Asia.* Moscow: Nauka, 1963.
Bartold, Vasily Vladimirovich. *On the History of Irrigation in Turkestan.* Moscow: Nauka, 1965.
Brykina, Galina Anatolyevna, ed. *Central Asia in Early Medieval Period.* Moscow: Nauka, 1999.
Cai Hongsheng. *Tangdai Jiuxinghu yu Tujue wenhua* (*Nine Surnames of the Sogdians in the Tang dynasty and the Turkic Culture*). Beijing: Zhonghua shuju, 1998.

Cai Hongsheng. *Yangwang Chen Yinke* (*Homage to Chen Yinke*). Beijing: Zhonghua shuju, 2004.

Cen Zhongmian. *Hanshu xiyu zhuan dili jiaoshi* (*Geographical Annotations to the "Book of the Later Han: Records of the Western Regions"*). Beijing: Zhonghua shuju, 2004.

Cen Zhongmian. *Tangshi yushen* (*Supplement to the Tang Histories*). Beijing: Zhonghua shuju, 2004.

Cen Zhongmian. *Zhongwai shidi kaozheng* (*Research on Geography of China and Foreign Lands*, vol. 1). Beijing: Zhonghua shuju, 2004.

Chen Yinke. *Sui-Tang zhidu yuanyuan luelun gao* (*Draft of a Brief Study of the Origins of the Sui–Tang Political System*). Beijing: Sanlian shudian, 2001.

Chen Yinke. *Tangdai zhengzhishi shulun gao* (*Draft for a Political History of the Tang Period*), vol. 2. Beijing: Sanlian shudian, 2001.

Dou Gao. *Shushu fu* (*Discussions about Calligraphy*). Taipei: Taiwan shangwu yinshuguan, 1983.

Du Huan. *Jingxing ji* (*Record of Travels*). Beijing: Zhonghua shuju, 1963.

Fan Ye, ed. *Hou Hanshu* (*Book of the Later Han*). Zhengzhou: Zhongzhou guji chubanshe, 1996.

History Department of Wuhan University, ed. *Tulufan chutu wenshu* (*Documents Unearthed in Turfan*), vol. 3 and vol. 6. Beijing: Wenwu chubanshe, 1981, 1985.

Hitti, Philip K. *History of the Arabs*, vol. 1. [In Chinese.] Translated by Ma Jian. Beijing: shangwu yinshuguan, 1995: 241–242.

Hong Mai. *Rongzhai suibi* (*Notes Taken in Rong Study*), vol. 14. Shanghai: Shanghai guji chubanshe, 1978.

Huang Yongnian. *Wenshi tanwei* (*A Study of Literature and History*). Beijing: Zhonghua shuju, 2000.

Huili and Yancong, eds. *Da Tang Da Ci'en si sanzang fashi zhuan* (*A Biography of the Tripitaka Master of the Great Ci'en Monastery of the Great Tang Dynasty*). Annotated by Sun Yutang and Xie Fang. Beijing: Zhonghua shuju, 1983.

Jia Zuzhang. *Hua yu wenxue* (*Flowers and Literature*). Shanghai: Shanghai guji chubanshe, 2001.

Jiang Boqin. *Zhongguo Xianjiao yishushi yanjiu* (*A History of Chinese Zoroastrian Art*). Beijing: Sanlian shudian, 2004.

Kosheleenko, Gennady Andreevich. "A Study of Buddhist Relics at Merv," in *Ancient Cultures of Central Asia and India*. [In Russian.] Edited by Vadim Mikhailovich Masson. Leningrad: Nauka, 1984. 137–141.

Laufer, Berthold. *Sino-Iranica*. [In Chinese.] Translated by Lin Junyin. Beijing: Shangwu yinshuguan, 2001.

Li Yanshou. *Bei shi* (*History of the North*). Beijing: Zhonghua shuju, 1974.

Li Yishan. *Yishan zazuan* (*Miscellaneous Records by Yishan*). Changsha: Yuelu shushe, 2005.

Lin Wushu. *Tangdai Jingjiao zai yanjiu* (*New Reflections on Nestorianism of the Tang Dynasty*). Beijing: Zhongguo shehui kexue chubanshe, 2003.

Litvinsky, Boris Anatolyevich, ed. *History of Civilizations of Central Asia*, vol. 3. [In Chinese.] Translated by Ma Xiaohe. Beijing: Zhongguo duiwai fanyi chuban gongsi, 2003.

Nikitin, Alexander. "A Brief Survey of the History of Christianity in Central Asia from the Very Beginning till the Middle Ages," in *East Turkestan and Central Asia*. [In Russian.] Edited by Boris Anatolyevich Litvinsky. Moscow: Nauka, 1984. 121–137.

Qian Yi, ed. *Nanbu xinshu* (*New History of the South*). Annotated by Huang Shoucheng. Beijing: Zhonghua shuju, 2002.

Quan Tangshi (*Complete Tang Poems*). Collected by Peng Dingqiu et al., and edited by Cao Yin. Shanghai: Shanghai guji chubanshe, 1986.

Rak, Ivan Vadimovich. *Myths of Ancient and Early Medieval Iran Zoroastrianism.* [In Russian.] St. Peterburg: Zhurnal "Neva," 1998.

Rong Xinjiang. *Zhonggu Zhongguo yu wailai wenming* (*Medieval China and Outside Cultures*). Beijing: Sanlian shudian, 2001.

Song Xiaomei. *Gaochang guo - Gongyuan wu zhi qi shiji sichouzhilu shang de yige yimin xiao shehui* (*The Kingdom of Gaochang: An Immigrant State on the Silk Road between the Fifth and Seventh Centuries*). Beijing: Zhongguo shehui kexue chubanshe, 2003.

Stavinsky, Boris Yakovlevich. *Ancient Arts of Central Asia.* [In Chinese.] Translated by Lu Yuan. Xi'an: Shaanxi Lvyou chubanshe, 1992.

Sun Guangxian. *Beimeng suoyan* (*Trivial Tales from North of Meng*), collated by Jia Erqiang. Beijing: Zhonghua shuju, 2002.

Wang Dang. *Tang yulin jiaozheng* (*Anecdotes in the Tang Dynasty*), vol. 2, collated by Zhou Xunchu. Beijing: Zhonghua shuju, 1987.

Wang Guowei. "Xiyu jingqu kao (On the Well-canals in the Western Regions)," in *Guantang jilin* (*Collected Writings of Wang Guantang*). Beijing: Zhonghua shuju, 1984.

Wang Qinruo et al., eds. *Cefu yuangui* (*Prime Tortoise of the Record Bureau*). Beijing: Zhonghua shuju, 2003.

Wei Zheng et al. *Sui shu* (*Book of Sui*). Beijing: Zhonghua shuju, 1973.

Wu Renchen, ed. *Shiguo chunqiu* (*The Spring and Autumn Annals of the Ten Kingdoms*). Taipei: Guoguang shuju, 1962.

Xiang Da. *Tangdai Chang'an yu xiyu wenming* (*Tang Dynasty Chang'an and the Culture of the Western Regions*). Beijing: Sanlian shudian, 1979.

Xuanzang, dictated. *Da Tang xiyu ji* (*Great Tang Records on the Western Regions*). Transcribed by Bian Ji. Beijing: Wenxue guji kanxingshe, 1955.

Yang Xuanzhi. *Luoyang qielan ji* (*A Record of Buddhist Monasteries in Luoyang*). Annotated by Liu Weidong. Beijing: yanshan chubanshe, 1998.

Yu Taishan. *Lianghan Weijinnanbeichao zhengshi xiyu zhuan yanjiu* (*A Study on the Accounts of the Western Regions in the Official History of the Eastern and Western Han Dynasties, Wei, Jin, and the Southern and Northern Dynasties*). Beijing: Zhonghua shuju, 2003.

Zhang Yanyuan. *Fashu yaolu* (*Compendium of Calligraphy*), vol. 3 and vol. 6. Beijing: Renmin meishu chubanshe, 2004.

5 Worship of Fire and Sky among the Ancient Turks

For the ancient Turks (*Tujue*), the worship of fire and sky was a nationwide rite, boasting a long history. From khans to herdsmen, everybody revered the Fire Spirit and the Sky God (Tengri), the two deities that organized the bulk of Turkic religious history. In this sense, they are much more important and influential than any other gods (such as mountain spirits, water spirits, or goddesses). Now I would like to examine the relationship between the ancient Turks and their worship.

The Origin of Fire Worship

In 627, Xuanzang traveled to ancient India to look for Buddhist scriptures and was honorably treated by a Turkic khan when he passed through Suyab in Central Asia. The book *A Biography of the Tripitaka Master of the Great Ci'en Monastery* (*Da Tang Da Ci'en si sanzang fashi zhuan*) gives the following description:

> The khan lived in a large yurt which was brilliantly decorated, almost dazzling one's eyes. The officials, all dressed in embroidered garments in a magnificent manner, sat on mats in two long rows in front of the khan to attend him, while armed guards stood behind him. Although the khan was a tribal head living in a felt tent, he had an air of elegance which commanded respect. When the Master approached the camp, at a distance of about thirty paces, the khan went out to welcome and greet him, and invited him to sit inside. The Turks worshipped fire and did not use wooden couches, as wood contained the element of fire, they only covered the floor with thick carpets. But the Master was invited to sit on an iron chair with a mat on it.

Although we are not clear whether this "tribal head living in a felt tent" was Tong Yabghu Qaghan or Sy Yabghu Qaghan,[1] there is no doubt about the Turks' veneration of fire in the records. Also, we can find further evidence in the Byzantine historiographer Theophylact Simocatta's book *History*, which contains a letter that

DOI: 10.4324/9781032616353-5

Tardu Qaghan wrote to Maurice (539–602), the Eastern Roman Emperor in 598. Part of the letter reads:

> The Turks worship fire, revere air and water, and praise the earth, but they only take one as their god, the creator god who made the sky and the earth. To him they sacrifice horses, cattle, and sheep, and they have priests who are believed to prophesy the future.[2]

Worship of fire was prominent in the Turks' belief system at the turn of the seventh century, clearly shown in both exchange documents and diplomatic etiquette. With regard to the origin of fire veneration, we need to trace it back to their steppe homeland. For one thing, it is widely known that "the Western Turks and the Northern Turks had the same ancestors"[3] and that they split because of Turkic expansion from the East to the West. For another, it was unlikely for the Turks to take Persian Zoroastrianism as their religion during the period when Xuanzang traveled westward, as the Turkic Khaganate in Central Asia was in a hostile relationship with the Sassanid Empire at that time.

To begin with, let me quote a legendary tale about the ancestors of the Turks. According to "Records of the Turks" ("Tujue zhuan") in the *Book of Zhou* (*Zhou shu*), volume 50:

> The ancestors of the Turks came from the State of Suo, which was located north of the Xiongnu. The leader of this tribe was called Abangbu, who had seventeen brothers. One of them was called Yizhi Nishidu, and his birth mother was a wolf. Bangbu and his brothers were all stupid and slow-witted, so their state was destroyed. Nishidu stood out as an extraordinary brother because he had the power to summon the wind and the rain for his service. He married two women who were said to be the daughters of, respectively, the God of Summer and the God of Winter. One of them became pregnant and gave birth to four sons. One of the sons changed into a swan goose, another established a state between the Afu River and the Jian River, called Qigu [Kirghiz]. The third ruled along the Chuzhe River. The fourth one, the eldest son, lived on the Mountain Jiansi-Chuzhe-shi. On this mountain there also lived a group of people from the Abangbu tribe. It was cold and damp here. As the eldest son was able to make fire for them, warm them up and keep them all alive, they elected him to be their leader, and called him Tujue [Turk]. He was Naduliu-she [Naduliu Shad]. Naduliu had ten wives, each of whose sons took the clan name of his mother. Ashina was the son of Naduliu's concubine.

This prehistory about the Turks contains important elements of totem and nature worship. The sentence that reads "One of them became pregnant and gave birth to four sons" indicates that four clans came out of one core family, which does make some sense. On the whole, although this quote sounds more mythical than the legend of "living on the south of the Jinshan," it does provide a historical clue to the origin of the Turkic worship of fire. For one thing, if "[t]he ancestors of the Turks came from the State of Suo," then we can surely find the religious marks left by the Turks by examining the religious beliefs of this country. For another, the connection between the eldest son's ability to "make fire for them, warm them" and his being called "Tujue" presents us a possibility of analyzing their worship of fire from the word structure of "Tujue." Following these two clues, I examine and explain their worship step by step.

According to field research by ethnographers, the descendants of Suo are the Kumandins who reside in the Northern Altai region.⁴ Still known as "Suo" (co or coro), they are living among the Kachins. Similar to other ethnic groups in the Altaic region, the Kachins address all the spirits that have existed in the sky, on the earth, and in the underground realm since ancient times, as Töc⁵, among which the Fire Spirit – "Чапбак – Töc" is most worshipped. Taking a female anthropomorphic figure and painted in fiery red on a piece of white cambric approximately 30 or 40 centimeters long and 20 or 30 centimeters wide, this spirit occupies the most glorious position inside the yurt as this cloth is usually hung from the beam between the yurt owner's sleeping mat and cash cupboard. As the first spirit to whom a Kachin shaman prays in a ritual, and as the spirit to whom the yurt owner offers the first morsel of food, the Fire Spirit is regarded as the "divine housekeeper"⁶ who blesses the family, keeps them safe, and guards the hearth. Obviously, she is the spirit of yurt, a product of hearth veneration, enjoying a well-acknowledged sanctity among the Turks. As quoted above, inside the yurt of the Western Turkic khan, the Turks "did not use wooden couches, as wood contained the element of fire," and even "a tribal head living in a felt tent" would not dare to offend the Fire Spirit. What then is the relationship between the worship of the Fire Spirit and the word "Tujue"? As a Turkologist pointed out, the noun "Tujue" is composed of two parts, namely, "тÿр" and "к," where "к" can be traced back to the commonly seen suffixes "гÿн" and "кÿн," which are derived from the words "гÿні" and "кÿні" (wife). As for "тÿр"//"тöр," it is mainly understood as "a stove place" and its varied sounds are "тÿс" // "тöс" ~ "тöз," the aforementioned "Töc" that refers to "primitive spirits," with additional meanings of "idol," "icon," "place of honor," and "restricted area in the tent." Later, there appeared a derivative word тöрÿ (тöpä), meaning "custom" and "law," and even "judge" and "official." Therefore, it makes perfect sense to say that "тÿр" in the word "Tujue" means "strength" and "power."⁷

The ethnographic and linguistic sources quoted above are of great help to decode the Turkic legend from the perspective of history. First, the word "Tujue" contains information about stove veneration, which shows that what is stated in the *Book of Zhou* about the causal relationship between the eldest son's ability to "make fire for them, warm them" and his being called "Tujue," though quite implicit, is fully consistent with the logic of social life in a primitive society. Then, the Fire Spirit is presented as a female anthropomorphic figure, and the "к" in "тÿрк" comes from "кÿні," indicating that the worship of fire was rooted in a matriarchal society. The above quote, "Naduliu had ten wives, each of whose sons took the clan name of his mother," manifests the characteristic of a matriarchal society.⁸ Thus, it is clear that the Turkic custom of fire worship has its own ancient origin. Even when the Turkic Khaganate was separated into the Western Khaganate and the Eastern Khaganate, the custom remained unchanged. Therefore, it is far-fetching when some scholars took the Altaic "Töc" for "Dexi" in the state of Cao [Kabudhan] and asserted that Turkic worship of fire was "acquired" from Iran through the Nine Surnames of the Sogdians in the Central Asia.[9]

In fact, "Dexi" and "Töc" are entirely different, as detailed in "The Western Regions: Records of Kabudhan" ("Xiyu: Caoguo zhuan") in the *Sui shu* (*Book of Sui*), volume 83:

> In this state, there is the deity Dexi, worshipped by all the states east of the Western Sea. There is a golden statue of this deity, holding a golden poluo, the diameter of which is 1 *zhang* and 5 *chi*,[10] with its top and bottom in proportion. Every day, five camels, ten horses, and one hundred sheep are sacrificed to the deity. Even a thousand persons would not be able to finish the offered food.

In the Middle Ages, the land "east of the Western Sea" belonged to Sogdiana. According to an expert specializing in Sogdian, "Dexi" should be the Sogdian word Taxsič (txs' yc),[11] and it should not be mistaken for "Töc." Moreover, judging from the variety and quantity of sacrifices, we can see that this famous "divine temple,"[12] located in the city of Yueyudi, northeast of Ishitikhan, the capital of the state of Cao, boasted of a much more prosperous stream of pilgrims than any other "Töc." Even if we accept another view that traces "Dexi" back to its Persian origin Teštar,[13] Tishtrya [the deity of star and rainfall] in Zoroastrianism is quite different from the "spirit of the hearth" in shamanism.

But of course, by excluding the possibility that "Dexi" is "Töc," I am not saying that the Turkic worship of fire had no relevance at all to the Zoroastrianism prevalent at that time. Rather, what I try to argue is that the Ashina tribe's "fire" should be traced back to the area north of the Gobi Desert. In the following section, I explore the contact between the Eastern "fire" and the Western "fire" and see what miracles happened in the history of religion in Central Asia.

Zoroastrian God and Turks

The Turkic invasion of Central Asia began in the 560s. From 563 to 567, a Turkic force led by Istami Khagan defeated the Hephthalite Empire and held the area north of the Oxus River.[14] In 605–616, the king of Samarkand "Qushuzhi took the daughter of Yehu kehan [Tong Yabghu Qaghan] as his wife, thus [this state was] subjugated to the Western Turkic Khaganate."[15] By the time Xuanzang traveled westward, the Turkic Khaganate had entirely conquered the Hephthalite, extending its reign as far as Jibin [Kashmir.] This vast area was a key point of transportation between the East and the West in the Middle Ages. According to "Records of Samarkand" ("Kangguo zhuan") in the *New Book of Tang* (*Xin Tang shu*), volume 221, section 3, in Kushan:

> There is a tower on the left side of the capital city. On the northern wall of this tower are paintings of emperors from ancient China, on the east are the

king of Turkic Khanate, and the Brahman [of India], and on the west are the kings of Persia and Fulin [Byzantium]. The king of this state comes every morning to perform the ritual bow and then leaves.

Clearly, the Kushan maintained a close connection with China, Persia, India, and the Byzantine empire. Influenced by the four ancient civilizations, Sogdiana almost became an exhibition of different religions. Before the inhabitants here converted to Islam, Central Asia not only witnessed the co-existence of Zoroastrianism and Buddhism but also saw some followers of Manicheism, Sabianism, and Nestorian Christianity. Of these religions, Zoroastrianism was the most flourishing, as recorded by the Chinese literature of the Tang dynasty. At the beginning of the seventh century, when Xuanzang passed through Samarkand, he discovered that:

> The king and his subjects do not believe in Buddhism. Instead, they worship fire. There are two temples but no monks live inside. For the visiting monks, they are not allowed to stay, and would be driven away with fire.[16]

In this quote, the sentence "they worship fire" is used to show their religious belief, as the word "xian 祆" [Zoroastrianism] was only seen in non-Buddhist sources and scarcely found in the Buddhist documents in the early Tang period.[17] For example, at the beginning of the eighth century, Hyecho, a Buddhist monk from Silla, wrote that "these six states (An 安, Cao 曹, Shi 史, Shiluo 石骡, Mi 米, and Kang 康) believed in Zoroastrianism, and had no single idea about Buddhism."[18] Given such a deep-rooted belief in Zoroastrianism in this area, how would the Turks, those followers of the Fire Spirit, respond? Before citing historical texts, let us take a look at the excavated relics. According to Vasily Vladimirovich Bartold, Zoroastrianism in Russian Turkestan was different from that in the Sassanid Empire, and the difference was mainly regional, as is shown in the former's common use of ossuary in funerals. Made of pottery, and decorated with paintings or carvings on the exterior, this kind of ossuary was used to keep the bones of the deceased.[19] Different varieties and types of ossuaries appeared around the second century B.C. during the time of the Kushan Empire. It resulted from the confluence of two major burial rituals of the Eastern Iranian tribes, namely, celestial burial (corpses put out for vultures to devour) and cremation (burying ashes).[20] In the Turkic era, there was a noticeable change about its design, and a tent-style ossuary emerged. The surface of the ossuary had a decorative design similar to that of a shepherd's yurt, and the top was hollowed out to imitate the wooden frame of the tent.[21] In this way, besides its regional features from Central Asia, the ossuary betrayed the nomadic lifestyle of the Turks. Furthermore, new elements could be found in the ceramic lanterns excavated from Sukuluke. As the sacred animals that guarded the "eternal flame" of the Zoroastrians, dogs or birds (actually chickens) were painted on the surface of a lantern,[22] but in the Turkic era, sheep or goats also became fire guardians.[23]

As mentioned above, archaeological finds have revealed some new features, exemplified by the changed design of the ossuary and the use of "sheep or goat" as the "fire keeper," indicating that the Turks in Central Asia had a certain degree of

Zoroastrianization after the disintegration of the Khaganate.[24] This tendency was also evidenced in texts from the Tang period. In volume four of Duan Chengshi's *Miscellaneous Writings from Youyang* (*Youyang zazu*), there is a description about how the Turks worshipped their Zoroastrian gods:

> The Turks do not worship their Zoroastrian gods in a temple. Instead, they have sacred images painted on precious fabrics, and put the painting inside a horse-hide bag when they move. [To show respect,] they apply a moisturizing cream on the face of each god. Or they tie the painting to a pole so that they can worship at any time.

Whether the painting was kept inside a bag or tied to a pole, it was meant to serve a wandering nomadic life. That is, they worshipped their gods in a different "Zoroastrian temple." As for their preference of applying a moisturizing cream to blending musk into cream,[25] this too was a reflection of their lifestyle, a living on meat and cheese. For the Turks, their worship of Zoroastrian gods was unchangeably characterized by their identity as skillful archers.

Tengrism ant Its Social Connotations

The nomads living north of the Gobi Desert had a long history of worshipping the sky, and their way of addressing the Sky God was not much different. In the *Records of the Grand Historian: An Arrayed Account of the Xiongnu* (*Shiji: Xiongnu liezhuan*), "for the Xiongnu, sky is called 'chengli' 撑犁." In the Tang dynasty, the Turkic word for "sky" was translated into "dengli" 登里 or "tengli" 腾里. And the *Sino-Tartars Glossary* (*Dada yiyu*) translates sky into "tengjili" 腾吉里. Wen Tingshi, a scholar in the late Qing period, had long noticed this linguistic phenomenon of one homologous word with different transcriptions. He made the following assertion:

> The *Book of Han* (*Hanshu*) records that the Xiongnu call the sky "chengli," and now, Mongolians call the sky "tenggeli 腾格里," which means that "tenggeli" is chengli. They are just different transcriptions. The name for sky in the northern areas has not changed for more than two thousand years. Shiratori Kurakichi has made a precise statement: nowadays, the Turkish people of different ethnic groups still call sky "chengli." As the descendants of the Turks, the Xiongnu also call sky "dengningli 登凝梨."[26]

In the ancient Turkic language, "denningli" or "denli" was spelt as "täŋri" or "teŋiri." The root of this word "teŋ" means "ascend" or "fly" and can still be found in the names of birds. For example, a sparrow hawk is called teŋälgün in the ancient Turkic language, and this word shares the same root with "teŋiri." With the connotative meaning of "ascend," the Turkic word "teŋiri" can also be transformed to mean "offering," "worship," and "veneration." Thus, "sky" means more than the physical sky and has been endowed with an additional meaning of deity.[27]

The ancient Turks' worship of Tengri was divided into two types: seasonal worship and perennial worship. The former had specific dates and venues, with regular offerings. In a Chinese source, it is stated as "in the middle of the fifth month, [they] collect water from other people to worship Tengri," and "in the middle of the fifth month, goats and horses are killed to worship the Sky God."[28] As for the latter, it was not limited to a fixed time. Whenever necessary, a worship ceremony would be held to seek blessings from Tengri and to eliminate disasters. For instance, in 697, Qapaghan Qaghan "killed Xu Qinming, the governor of Liangzhou, in order to offer his sacrifice to Tengri."[29]

We can get a rough idea about the importance of Tengri from the local customs of the Altai people, the descendants of the ancient Turks. They call the deity of light (the sun and the moon) "Ülgen" (ульгень). Of Ülgen's sons, the eldest is the god of thunder and rain, and the second and third are the gods of war. The sacrifice offered to Ülgen is white horses, with horsehides hung on stakes and horse heads facing east; and goats are also offered.[30] This ritual echoes the aforementioned Turkic practice where "goats and horses are killed to worship the Sky God."

Tengrism originated from nature worship, and the deified "sky" has a rich social connotation. The ancient Turks had many reasons to worship the Sky God, and the three noticeable ones are as follows:

First, a khan's divine right came from Tengri. It can be seen in a khan's enthronement ceremony. When a khan

> is newly enthroned, his ministers and generals carry him in a felt rug, and they walk clockwise nine times in the direction of the sun. For every round, the ministers and generals kneel down and bow. After the bowings, they put the khan on the horse, and then strangle him with a silk scarf, almost to the point of suffocating him before they hurriedly let go of him, and then they ask him 'how many years can you be a khan?' The khan has become so dizzy that he cannot name a calculated number, so his ministers write down any number he gives, which will be used to verify his reign time.[31]

Some of the khan titles are also evidence of this belief. For example, Ishbara Qaghan was given the title "The Sage under Heaven and the Great Turkish Son of Heaven, Born from the Heaven"; Qapaghan Qaghan was given the title "The Male Divinity Nurtured by the Heaven, Heavenly Turkic Guoduolu Mochuo Khan"; and Bayanchur Qaghan was given the title "Same as the Heaven and Heavenly Granted."

Second, their military successes depended on Tengri's blessing. Accustomed to a life of fighting and wars, the Turks regarded Tengri as a god of protection. On the eastern part of the "Kul Tigin Monument," there is a line that reads: "As Tengri gave them force, the soldiers of my father, the kagan, were like wolves, and his enemies were like sheep," and "by the grace of Tengri, he took the realm of those who had had a realm, and captured the kagan of those who had had a kagan

[.]"³² They took a favorable fighting opportunity as a "godsend." As is recorded in "A Biography of Yang Su" ("Yang Su zhuan") in the *Book of Sui* (*Sui shu*), volume 48:

> In 598, Tardu Qaghan invaded the frontier border. [Emperor Gaozu] appointed Yang Su as the "army area commander-in-chief (*xingjun zongguan*)" along the Lingzhou Road to crush the Turks. Yang was bestowed 2,000 pieces of fabric and 100 *jin* [catties] of gold. At the beginning, the generals were worried that the Turkish horses might bash, bump or shove the army, so they mixed chariots, infantry and cavalry to form a phalanx. On the outside of this phalanx were chariots piled with antlers as obstacles, and on the inside was the cavalry. Yang Su said to others, "This is a way to consolidate defense, not to win a victory." So, all the original arrangements were abolished, and a cavalry phalanx was set up. When Tardu heard about this, he was exulted and exclaimed, "This is really a godsend!" Dismounting from his horse, he prayed upward to the sky, and then led special forces of more than 100,000 soldiers to attack. Yang Su and his army tried their utmost to fight back and defeated them.

Similarly, a wish for Tengri's protection of the Turkic armies was expressed when the Turks offered a sacrifice to Tengri at the Fuyun Temple before the Turkic soldiers crossed the river to invade the borders of the Tang empire.

Third, Tengri symbolized a fear of the wrath of heaven. The Turks tended to view unexpected natural disasters as the manifestation of god's wrath. For instance, in the mid-sixth century, during the reign of Muqan Qaghan, there was a time when "a fierce thunderbolt struck and destroyed their yurts and properties. The attack lasted for more than ten days. The khan was so frightened that he thought it was the wrath of heaven."³³ At the beginning of the seventh century, when Tardu Qaghan and his army were engaged in a warfare with the Sui soldiers in Lingwu, Zhangsun Sheng poisoned their water supply, thus "most of Tardu's soldiers and horses died after drinking the contaminated water. Terrified, Tardu called out: 'If the sky rains evil water, does that mean the god is going to destroy us?' Then they ran away at night."³⁴

Expressing veneration and fear, the Turks had conflicting and complementary views about the sky. They worshipped because they were afraid, and this is a typical primitive mentality. In the Turkic era, how long a khan could remain enthroned, how a military attack would continue, and whether they would be blessed or cursed, in their belief, were all decided by Tengri. In a sense, the Turks on the steppe lived in a shamanic kingdom. They were obeying the "Sky God" at all times.

"Sorcerer" as a Mediator between Heavenly Kingdom and Human World

Between the heavenly kingdom and the human world, there was a mediator – Turkic sorcerer. The *Book of Sui*: *Records of the Turks* (*Sui shu*: *Tujue zhuan*) states that the Turkic people "revered spirits and gods, and trusted witches and wizards." That is, both sorcerers and sorceresses were active in their life.

As early as the middle of the sixth century, Turkic sorcerers had performed in a way similar to later shamans, using instruments and casting spells. In 568, the Byzantine envoy Zemarchus and his entourage witnessed a rite performed by some Turkic sorcerers:

> Someone came to say that sorcerers could exorcise devils and foretell bad omens. Then they surrounded Zemarchus and his valets, put their luggage in the center. Someone stood on the luggage, shaking a bell and beating a tambourine. Some other sorcerers held flaming incense in their hands, and frenziedly walked back and forth in circles around them, pointing to the sky and drawing circles on the ground, as if the devil had really been driven out by them. After the incantation, they asked Zemarchus to pass through two piles of fire, and then his valets were asked to do the same one after another. It was said that, in this way, all the demons and devils could be expelled.[35]

On the steppes, these prophets were viewed as professionals. As stated in the *New Book of Tang*, volume 200, these "Turkic sorcerers live off divination."[36] They were also asked to predict military opportunities for a khan before he started a war. For example, in 620,[37] Chuoluo Qaghan "sought to take Bingzhou and help Yang Zhengdao[38] to settle down. However, the result of divination was inauspicious, and his men all advised him to give up this plan."[39]

The Turkic sorcery probably originated from the Ashide Cave. As noted by the *Miscellaneous Writings from Youyang*, volume four, "The ancestor of the Tujue was a sea god named Shemosheli 射摩舍利, living west of Ashide Cave." Presumably, it is a reliable story that the Ashide clan was good at producing sorcerers and sorceresses. According to Yao Runeng's *Biographical Accounts of An Lushan (An Lushan shiji)*, volume one:

> An Lushan came from a mixed Sogdian origin in Yingzhou. His childhood name was Yaluoshan. His mother came from the Ashide clan and served as a sorceress. Unable to get pregnant, she went to the Yaluoshan and prayed to the mountain spirit, and then her prayer was answered and she was pregnant. On the night of delivery, rays of red light shone all around, and the wild animals howled in all directions. Someone who watched the sky saw a freak star, the fiery light of which was falling on the yurt where the baby was born. There were also innumerable strange omens. His mother thought it was divine, so she named him Yaluoshan.

In this tale, we can get to know how a "Turkic sorcerer" viewed the world from the words used in the above quote: mountain spirit, fiery light, wild animals, and a freak star. To understand the connection between these "innumerable strange omens," we need to examine the shamanic beliefs of the Turkic descendants living in Southern Siberia. A tambourine used by a Shor depicts such a mythical world of "shamans." Between the heavenly realm and the human world, there are three layers of land. In the heavenly realm, the sky is dotted with stars, with the sun on the right and the moon on the left. The human world is centered on sorcerers, with one sorcerer sitting on a horse, led by wolves and birds, sheltered by the lord of sorcery, and then there are mountain spirits and birch tree spirits. The underworld is populated by different kinds of spirits and goblins, like those of mountains, water, birds, animals, insects, and fish.[40] From this, we can see that the grotesque and variegated childbirth scenario told by the sorceress of the Ashide clan is not a random fabrication. It has Shaman belief as its origin.

As a deified figure from conception to birth, An Lushan was more or less influenced by shamanism, although he might not be considered as a sorcerer. That explains why he generously sent gifts to a sorcerer in Fangyang who was "good at breathing techniques and who could see clearly at night without light or candle."[41] Even when he accepted the treasures sent by Sogdian merchants, there were "shamans beating tambourines, singing and dancing" there. The "tambourine" was the tool of sorcery. Named after its pronunciation, it is called "бубен" in the Turkic language.

In the history of the Turkic Khaganate, the Ashina and Ashide clans occupied the most predominant positions and were regarded as the noble families north of the Gobi Desert. These two clans stood out probably because the former was the first to hold political power, while the latter was the first to hold theocratic power. With khans on one side and sorcerers on the other side, the two pillars of the power base of the Turkic nomadic aristocracy were thus set up. In the "Tonyukuk Inscriptions" written in the Turkic language, the word "Bögü" (meaning "enlightened sage") and "Kagan" (meaning "khan") are joined together, giving a clear manifestation of theocracy.[42]

A sorcerer used to be called a "Kam." After the Turks entered Central Asia, this word was combined with the Buddhist loanword "bakši" (meaning "master of rites") to form a unique term "Kambakši" (meaning "sorcerer"). In the Timurid era, Turkic sorcerers fully displayed their capabilities. As Turkologist Emel Esin has studied this widely,[43] I will not give further details here.

Notes

1 Édouard Chavannes opines that Xuanzang "might have met Tong Yabghu Qaghan when he was still alive" (Chavannes, 1958: 139), but Cen Zhongmian is skeptical about this and holds that "it is doubtful whether the khan whom Xuanzang met was Tong Yabghu Qaghan" (Cen Zhongmian, *A Supplement to and Examination of the Historical Information of the Western Turks*, 2004: 127). Regarding the identity of this khan, Chen Yuan asserts that "the one whom Xuanzang met was the Sy Yabghu Qaghan, the son of Tong Yabghu Qaghan." See Chen Yuan, 1980: 415.
2 Simocatta, 161. As for the Turkic worship of the earth-water spirits, and Goddess Umay, see the following essays: Leonid Pavlovich Potapov, "Earth-Water Spirits in the Orkhon Inscriptions," [In Russian] *Soviet Turkology* 6 (1979): 71–77; Sergei Grigorievich Skobelev, "Iconography of Goddess Umay of Ancient Turkic Period on Ornaments," [In Russian] *Soviet Archaeology* 2 (1990): 226–233.
3 "Records of the Turks" ("Tujue zhuan") in the *Old Book of Tang* (*Jiu Tang shu*), vol. 194.
4 Potapov, 1953: 160. See also Kiselev, 494.
5 It is more commonly spelt as tös. —Trans.

6 Ivanov, 167–171.
7 Kononov, 45–47. This essay discusses the meaning of the word "Turk" and its evolution, while Paul Pelliot's "The Origin of Chinese Translation of Turkic Names" focuses on the ancient pronunciation of "Turk" and its etymology. These two papers can be read together for confirmation. For more details, see Feng Chengjun, *The Second Collection of Translated Works for the Study on History and Geography of the Western Regions and South China Sea* (Beijing: Shangwu yinshuguan, 1995). As for how the Turks were addressed in ancient Chinese sources, see Edwin G. Pulleyblank's article "The Chinese Name for the Turks," *Journal of the American Oriental Society* 85, no. 2 (1965): 121–125.
8 Ma Changshou, 1958: 17. As for the name of "Naduliu-she", Mori Masao tried to trace it back to "? – tölis Săd." See Mori Masao, 305.
9 Shiratori Kurakichi, 1936: 45. See the original Japanese version *A Historical Study of the Western Regions*, vol. 2 (Tokyo: Iwanami Shoten Publishers): 81–83.
10 There are different readings about the size of this golden poluo, which is interpreted by some scholars as a drinking vessel. This translation refers to Ching Chao-jung and Frantz Grenet's essay "The Golden Poluo in Sogdiana: An In-depth Analysis of the Suishu and Tongdian Passages," *Pis'mennye Pamiatniki Vostoka* 18, no. 3 (2021), 127–147. —Trans.
11 Henning, 1965: 253.
12 *New Book of Tang* (*Xin Tang shu*), vol. 221, section 3. Regarding the architectural form of the "divine temple," see Belenitsky, et al., 1973: 38–40. The ruins of this "divine temple" in the Eastern Cao were also discovered. For more details, see Kayama Yohei, 253–261.
13 Belenitski, 1949: 84–85. See also his essay "Sogdians' Thoughts and Beliefs," 61.
14 Chavannes, 1935: 161–162.
15 "Records of Samarkand" ("Kangguo zhuan") in the *Old Book of Tang* (*Jiu Tang shu*), vol. 198.
16 See Huili and Yancong, vol. 2; see *Taisho Tripitaka*, vol. 50: 227. See also Zhang Yichun, 8–10.
17 See Chen Yuan, 1980: 313.
18 See "Memoir of the Pilgrimage to the Five Kingdoms of India" ("Wang wu tianzhuguo zhuan") in *Taisho Tripitaka*, volume 51: 978. See also Fujita Toyohachi, 1931: 76–78; and Zhang Yi, 118–130.
19 See Bartold, *Four Studies on the History of Central Asia: A Short History of Turkestan*, 1962: 9–10.
20 Rapoport, 1962: 80–83. For a typological study of ossuaries, see Rapoport, "Some Aspects of the Evolution of Zoroastrian Funeral Rites," 1963: 127–132.
21 Bernshtam, 1950: 81.
22 Boyce, 52–68.
23 See Bernshtam, "Suyab River," 146. The goat is the most common animal image in the Turkic stone carvings. Regarding the goat-shaped mark on the top of the Kul Tigin Monument, Thomson thought that it is a changed form of "и" (as "ke" in "kehan") in the Turkic rune script. However, another scholar has compared it with 39 similar marks found in Southern Siberia, Mongolia, and Central Asia and concluded that it is a simplified way of drawing a goat. The second reading seems to be more reliable. See Grach, 413–414.
24 The disintegration happened in the middle of the seventh century, marked by the establishment of Protectorates (Mengchi and Kunling) in the Western Turkic Khaganate in 657 during the reign of the Emperor Gaozong of Tang.
25 See the *New Book of Tang*, vol. 221, section 3.
26 See Wen Tingshi, vol. 28.
27 See Tatarintsev, 79–80. See Klyashtorny, 1977: 131–132.
28 "Records of the Turks" ("Tujue zhuan") in the *Comprehensive Institutions (Tongdian)*, vol. 197, book 1. See also "Records of the Turks" ("Tujue zhuan") in the *Book of* Sui (*Sui shu*), vol. 84.

29 See Sima Guang, vol. 206.
30 Ivanov, 167–171.
31 "Records of the Turks" ("Tujue zhuan") in the *Book of Zhou (Zhou shu)*, vol. 50.
32 Cen Zhongmian, 1958: 881.
33 "A Biography of Empress Ashina" ("Ashina huanghou zhuan") in the *Book of Zhou*, vol. 9.
34 "A Biography of Zhangsun Sheng" ("Zhangsun Sheng zhuan") in the *Book of Sui*, vol. 51.
35 Zhang Xinglang, 107–108.
36 "Biographical Accounts of An Lushan" ("An Lushan zhuan") in the *New Book of Tang*, vol. 200.
37 There is a mistake about the year here. The Chinese version of this book has the year as "the seventh year of the Wude reign" (624), but it should be 620, as the *New Book of Tang* says Chuoluo Khan seized Bingzhou in the third year of Wude (620). — Trans.
38 Yang Zhengdao was the grandson of Emperor Yang of the Sui dynasty. —Trans.
39 "Records of the Turks" ("Tujue zhuan") in the *New Book of Tang*, vol. 215.
40 Alekseev, 167–169.
41 See Kang Pian, the entry entitled "Liu Ping Sees a Demonic Side of An Lushan" ("Liu Ping jian An Lushan chimei") in the *Record of True Stories (Jutan lu)*, vol. 1.
42 Wei Cuiyi, 39–41.
43 Esin, 83–94.

Bibliography

Alekseev, Nikolai Alekseevich. *Shamanism of the Turkic-Speaking Peoples of Siberia*. [In Russian.] Novosibirsk: Nauka, 1984.

Bartold, Vasily Vladimirovich. *Four Studies on the History of Central Asia: A Short History of Turkestan*. Leiden: E. J. Brill, 1962.

Belenitski, Alexandre Markovitch. "On the Superstitions in Central Asia before Islam," in *Bulletin of the Institute of the History of Material Culture*, vol. 28. [In Russian.] Edited by Alexander Dmitrievich Udaltsov. Moscow: The USSR Academy of Sciences Publishing House, 1949. 83–85.

Belenitski, Alexandre Markovitch. "Sogdians' Thoughts and Beliefs," in *Textual Research on the Ancient Murals of Penjikent*. [In Russian.] Edited by Alexander Yurievich Yakubovsky. Moscow: The USSR Academy of Sciences Publishing House, 1954. 25–82.

Belenitsky, Alexandre Markovitch, et al. *Medieval Cities of Central Asia*. [In Russian.] Leningrad: Nauka, 1973.

Bernshtam, Alexander Natanovich. *Suyab River* (Special Issues of *Archaeological Materials and Research in Soviet Union*, no. 14). [In Russian.] Moscow: The USSR Academy of Sciences Publishing House,1950.

Boyce, Mary. "On the Sacred Fires of the Zoroastrians." *Bulletin of the School of Oriental and African Studies* 31, no. 1 (1968): 52–68.

Cen Zhongmian. *Tujue Jishi* (*Compilation of Historical Records of the Turks*). Beijing: Zhonghua shuju, 1958.

Cen Zhongmian. *Xi tujue shiliao buque ji kaozheng* (*A Supplement to and Examination of the Historical Information of the Western Turks*). Beijing: Zhonghua shuju, 2004.

Chavannes, Emmanuel-èdouard. *Documents on the Western Turks*. [In Chinese.] Translated by Feng Chengjun. Beijing: Zhonghua shuju, 1958.

Chen Yuan. *Chenyuan xueshu lunwe ji* (*Collection of Chen Yuan's Academic Essays*), vol. 1. Beijing: Zhonghua shuju, 1980.

Chen Yuan. "Shu neixueyuan xin jiao Ci'enzhuan hou (After the Publication of the Newly Collated and Annotated 'Biography of Ci'en' by the China Buddhist Institute)," in *Chenyuan xueshu lunwe ji* (*Collection of Chen Yuan's Academic Essays*), vol. 1. Beijing: Zhonghua shuju, 1980. 410–421.

Duan Chengshi. *Youyang zazu* (*Miscellaneous Writings from Youyang*). Beijing: Zhonghua shuju, 1981.

Esin, Emel. "The Turkish Baksi and the Painter Muhammad Siyah Kalam." *Acta Orientalia* 32 (1970): 81–114.

Feng Chengjun. *Xiyu nanhai shidi kaozheng yicong er bian* (*The Second Collection of Translated Works for the Study on History and Geography of the Western Regions and South China Sea*). Beijing: Shangwu yinshuguan, 1995.

Fujita, Toyohachi. *Expository Notes on Huichao's "Memoir of the Pilgrimage to the Five Kingdoms of India."* [In Japanese.] Beijing: Quanshou dongwen shucang, 1931.

Grach, Alexander Danilovich. "Rock Carvings in Tuva." [In Russian.] *Collection of the Museum of Anthropology and Ethnography* 17 (1957): 385–428.

Henning, Walter Bruno. "A Sogdian God." *Bulletin of the School of Oriental and African Studies* 28, no. 2 (1965): 242–254.

Huili and Yancong, eds. *Da Tang Da Ci'en si sanzang fashi zhuan* (*A Biography of the Tripitaka Master of the Great Ci'en Monastery of the Great Tang Dynasty*). Annotated by Sun Yutang and Xie Fang. Beijing: Zhonghua shuju, 1983.

Ivanov, Sergei Vladimirovich. "On the Meaning of Symbols on Ancient Objects of Worship among the Peoples of the Sayan-Altai Highlands." [In Russian.] *Collection of the Museum of Anthropology and Ethnography* 16 (1955): 167–171.

Kang Pian. *Jutan lu* (*Record of True Stories*). Shanghai: Gudian wenxue chubanshe, 1958.

Kayama, Yohei. "Murals Discovered in Shakhristan of the Republic of Tajikistan," in *Collection of Papers Honoring Prof. Egami Namio's 70th Birthday, Archaeology and Art Edition.* [In Japanese.] Edited by Ono Katsutoshi. Tokyo: Yamakawa Shuppansha, 1976. 253–261.

Kiselev, Sergei Vladimirovich. *Ancient History of Southern Siberia*. [In Russian.] Moscow: USSR Academy of Sciences Publishing House, 1951.

Klyashtorny, Sergey Grigoryevich. "Mythological Themes of Ancient Turkic Inscriptions," in *1977 Collected Works on Turkology*. [In Russian.] Edited by Andrey Nikolaevich Kononov. Moscow: Nauka, 1981. 117–138.

Kononov, Andrei Nikolaevich. "Analysis of Turkic Terms." [In Russian.] *Soviet Ethnography* 1 (1949): 40–47.

Linghu Defen, et al., eds. *Zhou shu* (*Book of Zhou*). Beijing: Zhonghua shuju, 1971.

Liu Xu, et al., eds. *Jiu Tang shu* (*Old Book of Tang*). Beijing: Zhonghua shuju, 1975.

Ma Changshou. "Lun tujueren he tujue hanguo de shehui bian'ge (On the Social Change of the Turks and the Turkic Khanate)." *Lishi yanjiu*, no. 3 (1958): 9–22.

Mori, Masao. *Historical Studies of the Ancient Turkic Peoples*, vol. 1. [In Japanese.] Tokyo: Yamakawa Shuppansha, 1967.

Ouyang Xiu, et al., eds. *Xin Tang shu* (*New Book of Tang*). Beijing: Zhonghua shuju, 1975.

Potapov, Leonid Pavlovich. "Earth-Water Spirits in the Orkhon Inscriptions." [In Russian.] *Soviet Turkology* 6 (1979): 71–77.

Potapov, Leonid Pavlovich. *Essays on History of Altaians*. [In Russian.] Moscow: USSR Academy of Sciences Publishing House, 1953.

Pulleyblank, Edwin G. "The Chinese Name for the Turks." *Journal of the American Oriental Society* 85, no. 2 (1965): 121–125.

Rapoport, Yuri Alexandrovich. "The Astodans of Khwarazm: A Contribution to the History of Religion in Khwarazm." [In Russian.] *Soviet Ethnology*, no. 4 (1962): 67–83.

Rapoport, Yuri Alexandrovich. "Some Aspects of the Evolution of Zoroastrian Funeral Rites." [In Russian.] *Proceedings of the XXV International Congress of Orientalists*. Edited by Bobojan Gafurovich Gafurov. Moscow: Publisher of Eastern Literature, 1963. 127–132.

Shiratori, Kurakichi. *A Historical Study of the Western Regions*, vol. 2. [In Japanese.] Tokyo: Iwanami Shoten Publishers, 1981.

Shiratori, Kurakichi. *A Study on Su-t'ê or Sogdiana*. [In Chinese.] Translated by Fu qinjia. Shanghai: Shangwu yinshuguan, 1936.

Sima Guang, et al. *Zizhi tongjian (Comprehensive Mirror in Aid of Governance)*. Beijing: Zhonghua shuju, 1976.

Simocatta, Theophylact. *History*, vol. 5. [In Russian.] Moscow: The USSR Academy of Sciences Publishing House, 1957.

Skobelev, Sergei Grigorievich. "Iconography of Goddess Umay of Ancient Turkic Period on Ornaments." [In Russian] *Soviet Archaeology* 2 (1990): 226–233.

Takakusu Junjirou and Watanabe Kaikyoku, eds. *Taisho Tripitaka*. Tokyo: Taisho shinshu daizokyo kanko kai [Society for the Publication of the *Taisho Tripitaka*], 1960.

Tatarintsev, Boris Isakovich. "The Origin of the Turkic Word for Sky and its Similarity with the Word Tengri." [In Russian.] *The Soviet Turkology* 4 (1984): 73–84.

Wei Cuiyi. "Cong Weiwu'er yu bwyi de yuanliu tanqi (The Origin of the Uyghur Word bywi)," in *Collected Essays on Turkic Languages in China*. Edited by China Turkic Studies Association. Beijing: Minzu chubanshe, 1991. 38–45.

Wei Zheng, et al., eds. *Sui shu (Book of Sui)*. Beijing: Zhonghua shuju, 1973.

Wen Tingshi. *Chun Changzi zhiyu (A Lengthy and Confusing Talk of Chun Changzi)*. Nanjing: Jiangsu guangling guji keyinshe, 1990.

Yao Runeng. *An Lushan shiji (Biographical Accounts of An Lushan)*. Shanghai: Shanghai guji chubanshe, 1983.

Zhang Xinglang. *Zhongxi jiaotong shiliao huibian (A Collection of Historical Sources on Relations between China and the West)*, vol. 1. Beiping [Beijing]: Jingcheng yinshuju, 1930.

Zhang Yi. *Wang wu tianzhuguo zhuan jianzhi (Annotations of "Memoir of the Pilgrimage to the Five Kingdoms of India")*. Beijing: Zhonghua shuju, 1994.

Zhang Yichun. *Jingxingji jianzhu (Annotations to the "Record of Travels")*. Beijing: Zhonghua shuju, 1963.

6 Legal Practice in the Turkic Khaganate

Introduction

The Turkic Khaganate that emerged in the south of the Altai Mountains in the mid-sixth century was a military-administrative state headed by the Ashina family. In the reign of Muqan Qaghan (553–572):

> From its east border located on the west of the Liao River, to its west end by the wide-reaching Western Sea, from its south fringe along the north of the desert [the Gobi Desert], to its north frontier by the Northern Sea that stretches for five or six thousand *li*, all are its territory.[1]

For this huge multi-tribal country, the Ashinas ruled not only by force but also through law. Not only do Chinese sources mention the Turkic "domestic discipline,"[2] but also the Orhon inscriptions repeatedly refer to "Turkic legal system" and "ancestors' legal practice."[3] Given the importance of this topic, it is necessary to do some research on Turkic law. With no ambition to reveal its original look, I only try to examine several aspects concerning the economic structure and political system of the Turkic Khaganate from the sixth to the eighth centuries through the refraction of legal rights.

As this is a very complex issue, two points need to be clarified here.

The first concerns the scope of discussion. The "Turks" (*Tujue*) was a large political federation, a complex mixture in terms of ethnic relations. At the end of the sixth century, it was split into two major khaganates: the Eastern (Northern) Turkic Khaganate and the Western Turkic Khaganate. Since "the Western Turks and the Northern Turks had the same ancestors"[4] and their split was the result of the Turkic westward expansion, the analysis of their legal practice should be centered on the Eastern Turks. The Eastern Turks also had divisions, one being the central lineage and the other being a branch. For the Turks of central lineage, they lived around the Altai Mountains before they moved to the area "between the Wudejian shan [Otuken Mountain] and the Kunhe [Orkhon River]."[5] Therefore, my analysis of Turkic legal practice focuses on the Turkic tribes along the Orkhon River and the Yenisei River. Such a treatment is certainly not comprehensive, but it is more convenient for us to understand the essence of Turkic law.

DOI: 10.4324/9781032616353-6

The second is related to historical sources. Legal documents from the Turkic era are not complete files, but fragmentary records scattered in historical books and inscriptions. Although the discovery of the Orkhon-Yenisei inscriptions and the excavations of Turkic tombs in the Altai area and South Siberia since the end of the nineteenth century have produced an increasing number of archaeological materials on Turkic history, these cultural relics do not have sufficient information about Turkic law. Moreover, because most of the inscriptions that have been dated belong to the period after Qutlugh Qaghan (approximately 682–691), it is difficult to compare information in Chinese documents with Turkic cultural relics from the same period, and vice versa. Therefore, some legal documents of other nomadic peoples are used as circumstantial evidence. As the Turks, on the one end, were related to the Xiongnu and the Rouran, and on the other end, were related to the Uyghurs and the Mongols, one cannot examine the Turkic legal system without referring to documents from other empires, either before or after the Turkic Khaganate.

An Overview of Turkic Law

"Delimited Lands" and "Livestock Marks"

To explore the issue of property in Turkic law, we need to examine three concepts: "delimited land," "livestock mark," and "slave." Marx once pointed out, "In each historical epoch, property has developed differently and under a set of entirely different social relations. Thus to define bourgeois property is nothing else than to give an exposition of all the social relations of bourgeois production."[6] Similarly, in order to understand the above-mentioned three concepts, we need to describe "all the social relations" in the Turkic era. But due to limited sources, we can only conduct a brief description.

I first discuss property ownership that concerns the first two concepts. As for the third concept "slave," it cannot be separated from the concept of "courtier," so it is left to a later section for discussion.

"Delimited land," or "divided land," in this case, refers to a delimited pasture. According to "Records of Xiongnu" ("Xiongnu liezhuan") in the *Records of the Grand Historian* (*Shiji*), volume 110, in the second century BC, the Xiongnu "migrated for water and grass. Although they did not reside in a walled city or live a farming life, they had their own delimited lands." The same can be said of the Turks in the sixth century. As accounted in the *Book of Zhou: Records of the Turks* (*Zhoushu: Tujue zhuan*), the Turks "often migrated, but had their own delimited lands."[7] But as to who owned these "delimited lands," there is no record in the historical documents, so I try to provide an explanation below.

In 598, in a letter to Maurice – the Byzantine emperor, Tardu Qaghan mentioned the relationship between the Turkic supreme ruler and the "Golden Mountains" as follows: "The natives call it Golden Mountains because it is rich in fruits and animals. The Turks have a law that the strongest khan governs the Golden Mountains."[8] According to the textual research of Édouard Chavannes and other scholars, the "Golden Mountains" mentioned in this letter are the "White Mountains" located north of the Tarim River, near Qiuci, where the capital of the Turkic Khaganate was located.[9] As indicated in the above quote, the "Golden Mountains" were a fertile pasture, and Tardu Qaghan's jurisdiction over them was recognized by Turkic law. When Tardu Qaghan's grandson Tong Yabghu Qaghan (approximately 618–628) became the ruler, "the capital was moved to Qianquan [literally 'thousand springs'] north of the state of Shi [in present Tashkent]."[10] According to Xuanzang's *Great Tang Records on the Western Regions* (*Datang xiyu ji*), volume one, Qianquan was also a rich pasture:

> Qianquan covers a radius of over two hundred *li*, with snow-capped mountains on the south and flat plains on three other sides. The soil is fertile and the woods are luxuriant. In late spring, all kinds of flowers bloom, resembling a beautiful tapestry. There are thousands of spring pools here, so it is called Qianquan. Whenever the Turkic khan comes here for a summer vacation, he will see herds of deer, most of which wear bells and rings. These deer are very close to people, not easily scared away by anyone approaching them. Khan likes it very much, so he has issued the order that if anyone dares to kill these deer, they will be killed without mercy, and that is why the deer can live long enough to die of old age.

Clearly, Tong Yabghu Qaghan designated his summer resort as a hunting reserve[11] and used the strict law of "killing without mercy" to prevent it from being encroached upon. From the examples of "Golden Mountains" and "Qianquan," it can be seen that fertile pastures near the Turkic capital had been monopolized by the Turkic khans and turned into their crown lands.

Now let us look at the relationship between "tribal leaders" and "delimited lands." In 630, after Emperor Taizong of the Tang dynasty defeated the Turks, he summoned his ministers to discuss the border policy. Yan Shigu, an attendant gentleman of the Central Secretariat (*zhongshu shilang*), proposed to "pacify them according to their customs." As recorded in the *Institutional History of Tang* (*Tang huiyao*), volume 73, Yan said that:

> It is my humble opinion that the Turks and the Tiele should always live in the north of the river. We can assign different people to chieftainship and let them lead the tribes. As for official rankings at each level and land coverage of different sizes, they can decide by themselves and then set regulations. In this way, we can pacify those who have submitted from afar, and it will be always like this in the future.

As the Turkic "customs" had it, official rankings matched the number of tribes and the size of lands under control. In other words, "delimited land" formed the basis of power, without which a chief would not be respected as a leader. This is why in 646 when the Taizong Emperor defeated the Syr Tarduš, the envoys of 11 tribes including the Tiele and the Uyghurs remarked that "We have our own lands, so we cannot follow the Syr Tarduš."[12] Where there were delimited lands, there were tribes. What enabled Ashina She'er, the second son of Chuluo Qaghan, to declare that "Prospering tribes are sufficient enough for me"[13] is precisely due to the fact that he had obtained material security through controlling the pastures.

In the Turkic era, although pastures were controlled by chiefs, they were still collectively owned. At least, they looked so on the surface. According to "Annals of Taizong" ("Taizong benji") in the *Old Book of Tang*, volume three, in 648, "On the fourth day of the fourth month [1 May], as ethnic minorities beyond the desert had a dispute over the pasture boundary, His Majesty himself made the judgment, and everyone was convinced." After the turmoil subsided, Chu Suiliang offered high praise to the emperor: "Your Majesty's holy virtue spreads wide and far, and there is no place that cannot be reached. Minorities beyond the desert even asked Your Majesty to adjudicate their territorial disputes."[14] Since Emperor Taizong ruled over "territorial disputes," then this dispute was certainly not a personal matter. Apparently, pastoral boundaries were publicly maintained precisely because pastures were collectively owned. Given the fact that chiefs were actual controllers of pastures, then we need to answer this question: what obligations did the herders have? Some indirect sources can help to answer this question. In 599, Yami Qaghan (personal name Ashina Rangan) wrote a letter of thanks to the Wen Emperor of the Sui dynasty for giving his tribe some lands for animal husbandry, saying:

> Either south of the Great Wall or at Baidao,[15] there are sheep and horses all over the valley. [Because of Your Majesty,] Rangan is like a dead tree that grows new branches and leaves, or a dead bone that regenerates flesh and blood, therefore, we are willing to herd sheep and horses for the Sui dynasty for thousands of generations.[16]

This kind of political vassal relationship, of course, is different from economic dependency. However, it can be seen that, for the Turks, "herd[ing] sheep and horses" was the corresponding obligation of someone who grazed his herds in other people's valleys or in valleys under the protection of other people. There is a similar record in the fifth line of the "Ongin Inscription" in the late seventh and early eighth centuries: "to the north of China among the Oğuz chiefs seven were enemies. The rest called my father holy 'Mohe' [father] and grazed and worked [for him] here."[17] Obviously, the word "worked" in this line implies the price one needed to pay in exchange for the right to graze. Since the use of pastures entailed the labor of tending livestock, then controlling pastures naturally became a prerequisite for exploitation. In this sense, we can say that "delimited land" provided the basis for economic enslavement, and it was also the fundamental cause of the basic contradiction in Turkic society, "the conflict between chiefs and common people."[18]

The remnants of the Turkic "delimited lands" which were found in the Altai Yabogan horse ranch are a long row of rounded boulders dividing the valley into two sides. According to the saying that has been circulating among local residents, these huge stone columns marked the land borders for magical warriors on the ancient Yabogan Steppe. As Sergei Vladimirovich Kiselev has pointed out, this is not nonsense at all. Instead, they are the direct evidence that communal pastures (owned by communes, clan groups, and tribes) were dominated by tribal heads (chiefs, khans, and other nobles).[19]

To conclude, what is mentioned as "they had their own delimited lands" in the *Book of Zhou: Records of the Turks* can be interpreted as follows:

First, "delimited lands" appeared to be the property collectively owned by the nomadic tribes;

Second, "delimited lands" were actually controlled by tribal chiefs;

Third, the khans had their own private "delimited lands," the crown lands close to their capital;

Fourth, "delimited lands" made it possible for Turkic aristocrats to exploit herdsmen.

The livestock raised within a certain "delimited land" was the material necessity for the survival of the Turks. Its importance is best illustrated by the saying that "the rise and fall of the Turks is determined by sheep and horses."[20]

Regarding the ownership of livestock, we can examine it from the perspective of "livestock mark."

In ancient animal husbandry, livestock mark was a sign of ownership. For instance, the Gaoche, a Turkic people living in the Mongolian steppe in the fifth century, "had their own mark for their livestock, and although the animals were kept in the wild, they would not be mistakenly taken away."[21] If the livestock mark in the Gaoche era was a sign of communal ownership, then those of the Turkic tribes recorded in the *Institutional History of the Tang Dynasty*, volume 72, were the legacy of this practice. As evidenced by historical sources, private ownership of livestock was very common among the Turks.

Although the Turkic nobles did not have private livestock marks like the Mongolian aristocrats,[22] the number of livestock they owned was significantly impressive. Kul Tigin, the younger brother of Bilge Qaghan, had "four thousand stallions."[23] The "Uyuk-Turan Stele" also mentions "six thousand horses"[24] owned by the person for whom the epitaph was written. Besides natural reproduction, these noblemen also appealed to two other means to increase the number of their herds. The first was plunder by force. Ilterish Qaghan, whose personal name was Ashina Qutlugh, was the founder of the Second Turkic Khaganate in the 680s. He started his empire by "stealing livestock such as horses from the nine tribes."[25] The second was "to collect tax in the form of livestock."[26] Otherwise, it would not have been possible for the Turks to provide a large number of "tribute horses" and "market horses" in their official diplomatic contacts as well as regular trades with the Tang court.

Ordinary Turkic herdsmen also had a small number of private livestock. When someone died, his family members or relatives would pay homage to this deceased person by slaying cattle or horses as a sacrifice.[27] Also, it was the duty of the Turkic herdsmen to bring their own horses to join a war.[28] In addition, horses were used as sacrificial grave goods. There were a couple of horses found in the tombs of ancient Turkic herders in Altai.[29] All of these indicate that livestock had become private property and that explains why Turkic law made some provisions to protect the private ownership of livestock. As for why livestock were privatized earlier and more completely than other possessions, it is due to the fact that they were a "movable property" available to be "directly transferred."[30]

Based on the above discussion, we can quote Karl Marx to summarize the characteristics of pasture and livestock ownership in the Turkic era: "What is appropriated and reproduced here is only the herd and not the soil, which is always used in temporary commonality wherever the tribe breaks its wanderings."[31]

"Slave" and "Courtier"

In the Turkic era, the concept of "slave" had two meanings. First, it was synonymous with "courtier." In 584, Ishbara Qaghan once "asked his subordinates, 'What does it mean to be a courtier?' and the answer was, 'A courtier in the Sui dynasty is what we call a slave here.'"[32] Then in 725 when Bilge Qaghan mentioned two subordinate tribes, he said that "the Xi [Kumo Xi] and the Khitans used to be slaves of the Turks."[33] Clearly, from the sixth to the eighth centuries, the Turks believed the idea of "courtier as slave." This is true not only of the Eastern Turks but also of the conquered rulers in Central Asia. In the early seventh century, in order to help Xuanzang to travel to India to seek Dharma, the king of Gaochang wrote a letter to the Yabghu Qaghan of the Western Turkic Khaganate, saying that "I hope that the khan will treat the master as well as you treat me, your slave."[34] Thus, we can say that one meaning of "slave" covered a suzerain-vassal relationship. Besides, historical data also prove its usage as an indication of one's identity as a slave. Here are three examples. First, Muqan Qaghan once gifted General Shi Ning of the Northern Zhou dynasty "a hundred slaves."[35] Second, in the mid-seventh century, the Syr Tarduš suggested to Emperor Taizong of the Tang dynasty, "if Your Majesty defeats the Turks, they can be taken as slaves, and given to Your Majesty's people."[36] Third, Stele 10 at Khoshoo Tsaydam dated from the seventh to the eighth centuries has the following line, "In October of ..., I obtained slaves in Kushus."[37] It can be seen that in the sixth to eighth centuries, apart from the meaning of "courtier," "slave" had a second usage, indicating those who were given, distributed, and captured as slaves.

From the above, it can be seen that in the Turkic era, the concept of "slave" had dual meanings. When it was used in a collective sense (for instance, to refer to subordinate tribes), it denoted subordination; when it was used in an individual sense, it meant the status of being a slave. Only by clarifying the dual meanings of "slave" can we remove the misty clouds of historical data and conduct a targeted analysis of the relationship between suzerain and subordinates, slave masters and slaves in the Turkic era.

According to the Turkic text on the Kul Tigin Monument, in terms of the suzerain-vassal relationship, the subordinates were supposed to economically "send tributary delegates" and politically "lower their heads and bend their knees."[38] In brief, they were asked to pay tribute and admit their subordinate position.

Agreeing to "lower their heads and bend their knees" meant an acceptance to be governed by the Turkic tudun (*tutun*). After the Shiwei were conquered, "the Turks sent three tuduns to be governors there."[39] The same is true of the Khitan, "The Turkic ruler Ishbara Qaghan sent Pandie as a tudun to govern them."[40] In "Records of the Turks" ("tujue zhuan") of the *Old Book of Tang* (*Jiu Tang shu*), volume 194, there is also a mention of tudun: "All the kings in the Western Regions were granted the title of Xielifa. Put under the supervision of a tudun, they were responsible for tax collection."[41] Sometimes, the Turkic khans also used "marriage alliance" to strengthen their control over the subordinates. For example, Bilge Qaghan married his sister to Barsbeg,[42] and the king of Samarkand "Qushuzhi took the daughter of Tong Yabghu Qaghan as his wife, thus [this state was] subjugated to the Western Turkic Khaganate."[43] Whatever the means, it was to consolidate the suzerain-vassal relationship in order to "levy troops and horses, and collect tax in the form of livestock."[44] By "send[ing] tributary delegates," vassal tribes played a significant role in the building of the Turkic Khaganate. Take the Tiele as an example, "Since the founding of the Turkic Khaganate, wherever the Turks were fighting, they would requisition supplies [from the Tiele] so that they could defeat the northerners and control their territory."[45] Another example is Kirghiz, "Every time it rains, as the local saying goes, iron is definitely obtained. It is locally called Jiasha. Weapons made from this kind of iron are very sharp, so they are often offered to the Turks."[46] It is evident that the prosperity of the Turkic Khaganate was based on the exploitation of its subordinates. As recorded on ancient Turkic steles, if an entire vassal was "enslaved," it was probably due to the following reasons: first, this vassal had lost its khan; second, this vassal had lost its own country (or its own Yili, an independent state agency); third, it had lost the previous rules governing this country; fourth, it had lost the possibility of gaining an advantage for itself; and fifth, it had lost its "delimited lands." Thus, the antagonistic relationship between a suzerain and its subordinates became one of the fundamental contradictions of Turkic society.[47]

Regarding the sources of Turkic slaves, as Ma Changshou has conducted a detailed study,[48] here I only focus on the relationship between the owner and the slave.

"Slave" (*nu*) means the same as the word "qul" on the Orkhon inscriptions, which is derived from the verb "qulmaq" (meaning "labor"), which refers to foreign laborers. The word "qul" is part of another noun "orul" (meaning "child"), which is composed of "oq" (meaning "arrow" and referring to the clan) and "qul" (meaning "slave"), but here "r" is used to replace two "q"s.[49] The composition of these words not only indicates the external source of the Turkic slaves but also shows that slaves were treated as "children" once they were adopted by a clan. Thus, it seems reasonable to assume that there were clan-owned slaves in the Turks, equivalent to the unaganbogol in the Mongol era. There were also family-owned slaves, most of whom were prisoners of war. It is recorded in history that the Turks "distributed all the confiscated and looted property to the soldiers,"[50] which apparently followed the old Xiongnu practice of dividing the spoils of war to boost morale: "The looted property was rewarded to soldiers, and the captives were turned into slaves, so every time when there was a battle, everyone wanted to win and gain profit."[51] This is evidenced by the aforementioned inscription "I obtained slaves in Kushus." Of course, captives were of both sexes, but the Turks seemed to have had a particular need for women. In 620 when Chuluo Qaghan led his troops to Bingzhou, "most of the beautiful women in the city were taken away by him."[52] No wonder as early as 607 when Emperor Yang of the Sui dynasty defeated the Khitan, he gave half of the female captives to the Turks.[53] Probably like other nomads, the Turks turned most of the captured women into wives and concubines of their soldiers. The sons they gave birth to, as a rule, would be inferior to others. Daluobian, the son of Muqan Qaghan, was deprived of the right to inherit the khanate simply because "his mother was of humble origin, so everyone refused to obey."[54] As for what kind of work male slaves did, there is no mention in the historical sources, and archaeological results only provide vague clues. For example, archaeologists divided the Altai tombs from the sixth to the eighth centuries into three classes according to their attributes and burial objects. The second class is the tombs for slaves or those with low social status, where burial objects such as bone arrowheads were found. But in tombs for shepherds, there were iron arrowheads. As the Altai people used bone arrowheads for hunting, it is likely that male slaves may have been involved in animal husbandry and hunting. But they only looked after cattle and sheep and did not herd horses. In other words, the slaves who were responsible for production were shepherds rather than horse herders.[55]

Although slaves were regarded by the Turks as their family members, they were ultimately their masters' property. If they wanted to regain their freedom, gold and silk were the only means to buy it back. In 631, Emperor Taizong of the Tang dynasty issued an edict, "When war broke out during the Sui dynasty, many Han Chinese became captives, so it was arranged to have an envoy redeeming 80,000 men and women with gold and silk to make them free again."[56] In 653, Emperor Gaozong of the Tang dynasty also sent an envoy to redeem the "Han Chinese" captured by the Kirghiz, "more gold and silk were given so that he [the envoy] was allowed to visit where the Han people lived, and he was told that all these people need to be bought back."[57]

It is worth noting that at the end of the reign of Illig Qaghan, among the "Han Chinese" who were enslaved by the Turks, some "gathered spontaneously and occupied a favorable mountainous terrain for self-defense,"[58] and others "went to Gaochang to seek shelter after Illig Qaghan was defeated."[59] The uprising and fleeing efforts of the Han slaves in the Turkic Khaganate indicate a class struggle, showing that the antagonistic relationship between master and slave was also a fundamental conflict in Turkic society.

The social relationship embodied in the concept of "slave" shows that slavery did exist in Turkic society. Moreover, from the fact that Muqan Qaghan gave Shi Ning 100 slaves at one time, and the number of "Han Chinese" redeemed by Emperor Taizong reached as many as 80,000, it can be seen that the number of Turkic slaves was considerably large. However, if we compare it with the "400,000 soldiers"[60] who used to be free herdsmen, we can see that the proportion of slaves in the Turkic population was not that large. Also, we should remember that these slaves earned their living as clan "children" or family members. Therefore, while we acknowledge the master-slave relationship as one of the fundamental contradictions of Turkic society, we should not exaggerate the role played by slaves at that time. As we know, from the sixth to the eighth centuries, the Turks had a nomadic life of animal husbandry by "following the water and grass," which meant that these herdsmen could only enjoy a pattern of simple reproduction in good times. If they encountered "a dry climate without rain or snow so that rivers dried up, or a calamity caused by locusts," they "had to migrate to the south of the desert because they could not live on the bare land." Even worse, they had to "live by digging holes to catch wild rats, feeding themselves on grass roots, or eating human flesh."[61] The lack of material reserves greatly limited the use of slave labor, not to mention the difficulty of supervising slave laborers in a nomadic life of animal husbandry. In addition, the excessive number of slaves could hinder the mobility of nomadic herdsmen to follow the needs of their livestock that were chasing water and grass. All of these factors forced the Turks to limit the number of slaves and to stabilize them by means of dependency (through taking them as a wife or concubine or adopting them as a "child"), thus forming a patriarchal slavery system.

Family and Marriage

The smallest economic unit of the Turkic nomadic society in the sixth and eighth centuries was the patriarchal family, which is called the "account" (*zhang*) or "household" (*hu*) in Chinese sources, corresponding to the ancient Turkic words "inijügün" and "arqarun," respectively. The word "inijügün" means "house of young kids," with "ini" (meaning "young brother") as its root, while the word "arqarun" means "family," the root of which is arqa (meaning "back, people standing behind"). These two words illustrate a shared fact from the perspective of either family members or parents, i.e., families are made up of young offspring. In this sense, "inijügün" and "arqarun" are a pair of synonyms, the word structure of which echoed the historical reality: with the collapse of the Turkic clan system, what took its place was the patriarchal family that was based on younger offspring with inheritance rights.

Regarding the historical conditions for the emergence of the patriarchal family among the nomads, Friedrich Engels made the following assertion:

> The herds were the new means of producing these necessities; the taming of the animals in the first instance and their later tending were the man's work. To him, therefore, belonged the cattle, and to him the commodities and the slaves received in exchange for cattle. All the surplus which the acquisition of the necessities of life now yielded fell to the man; the woman shared in its enjoyment, but had no part in its ownership.[62]

In the Turkic era, women in Turkic families had long been relegated to the secondary place, burdened with domestic work. For example, in the *Extensive Records of the Taiping Era* (*Taiping guangji*), volume 297, there is a quote from *The Extended Ancient and Modern Records of Five Elements* (*Guang gujin wuxing ji*), which provides this account: "A man asked the tent owner for food. The husband led him in and ordered his wife to prepare a meal." A stone hand-powered mill has been found in an eighth-ninth-century tomb of a woman in the Kurai Tombs of Sayan Altai,[63] which serves as strong evidence of the fact that a "meal-preparing" "wife" did the housework. However, since "vestiges of mother-right were found as late as the Middle Ages,"[64] it would certainly have been preserved among the Turks of the sixth and eighth centuries. As the Turks followed water and grass to graze and they were frequently involved in military conflicts, male Turks were often not at home, leaving the financial right to women who were taking care of the family. This division of labor, governed by nomadic life, was the basis for the high status of Turkic women and the material conditions for the preservation of the vestiges of matriarchy. The following two concepts of kinship, which were branded with the importance of female lineage, are examples of the remnants of matriarchy. First, the son-in-law was treated the same as the son. Ishbara Qaghan once wrote to Emperor Gaozu of the Sui dynasty, "Your Majesty is my wife's father, and naturally my father. I am the husband of Your Majesty's daughter, and naturally I am Your Majesty's son."[65] In a letter thanking Emperor Xuanzong for promising to marry the princess to him, Bilge Qaghan wrote: "A humble person like me is Your Majesty's son."[66] Second, a nephew on the maternal side (*waisheng*) was treated the same as a nephew on the paternal side (*zhizi*). Both the Turkic Kul Tigin Monument and Bilge Khan Inscription were signed "Nephew Yeli Tigin." According to the Turkic official system, "Tigin" was the title bestowed to the royal family of the khan. The two nephews on the maternal side were also given the title of "Tigin," which proves that the Turks treated the sons of sisters and brothers equally.[67]

The remnants of matriarchy in Turkic society made it possible for Turkic women to gain a certain foothold in social life. The following are a few examples recorded in historical sources, proving that "among the northern minorities, wives mostly participated in politics":[68]

1 A khatun knew about military arrangements. For example, in "A Biography of Xiao Yu" ("Xiao Yu zhuan") of the *Old Book of Tang*, volume 63, it is written that:

> There was a practice among the northern ethnic minorities that a khatun knew about military arrangements […] Princess Yicheng sent a messenger to Shibi Qaghan to inform him of an emerging crisis in the north, and because of this message, the Turks were saved.

2 A khatun was involved in deciding who would be the next khan. In "Records of the Turks" ("Tujue zhuan") of the *Old Book of Tang*, volume 194, section one, there is an account that:

> After the death of Chuluo Qaghan, Princess Yicheng deprived his son Aoshe Shad of the right to inherit the khanate on account of his ugly looks and weak personality. Instead, she made Chuluo Qaghan's younger brother Duobi as the khan, who was later known as Illig Qaghan.

3   A khatun met foreign envoys together with the khan and courtiers. In "Records of the Turks" ("Tujue zhuan") of the *New Book of Tang* (*Xin Tang shu*), volume 215, section three, we read this:

> Yuan Zhen, the minister of Court of State Ceremonial (*Honglusi*), conveyed the emperor's order to the Turks. Mojilian [Bilge Qaghan] arranged a banquet in a yurt where he was seated with his khatun, [and his subordinates] Kul Tigin, and Tonyukuk.

4   A khatun had a good knowledge of lawsuit. In "Records of the Uyghurs" ("Huihe zhuan") in the *Old Book of Tang*, vol. 195, we read this sentence: "His [Yaoluoge Pusa] mother Uluohun was familiar with lawsuit. She redressed the injustice in a fair and strict manner, so the tribe was highly disciplined."
5   A khatun prevented a khan from killing people. In "A Biography of Qibi Heli" ("Qibi Heli zhuan") in the *Old Book of Tang*, volume 109, there is a statement like this: "The khan was furious and tried to kill him, but was stopped by his wife."

In the extant literature, there are merely documents related to noble women, and no direct records have been found about the social status of ordinary women. Yet, from the records about other nomads in ancient times, we can see that ordinary Turkic women might have enjoyed a limited voice in social life.[69] At that time, the tenacious remnants of the matriarchy made it possible for certain customs from the clan era to pass into the patriarchal system. The following are two examples:

The first is the practice of adoption. An Lushan was adopted by the family of An Zhenjie.[70] Some other evidence about this practice can be found on the Turkic inscriptions. For instance, on Stele No. 2 in Barlyk, we read "(1) I, Künitirig, lost my father at the age of three. (2) My brother, the well-known governor, brought me up."[71] According to Alexander Natanovich Bernshtam, the name "Künitirig" is composed of two words küni (meaning "concubine") and tirig (meaning "living"), indicating "one born of a concubine." What is meant here is, after Künitirig's father died, he was adopted by a dignitary.[72] The life experiences of both An Lushan and Künitirig prove that adopted children lived as family members in the Turkic nomadic society in the eighth century. From the fact that An Lushan "raised many adoptive sons at home"[73] to prepare for his rebellion, it can also be inferred that adoptees at that time were treated as servant boys.

The second is the practice of foster care. According to "Records of the Turks" in the *New Book of Tang*, volume 215:

> In 634, Illig Qaghan died. [...] He had an old courtier with the title of Külüg Tarkhan, who was a Tuyuhun man surnamed Xie, a servant that Illig's mother Poshi brought with her when she married his father. After his birth, Illig was sent to the Xie family to be raised. [After Illig Qaghan died,] Külüg Tarkhan was so heartbroken that he committed suicide.

Illig was fostered by the Tuyuhun Xie family since his childhood. It is possible that, after he ascended the throne, Illig Qaghan rewarded the Tuyuhun man with an official title of Tarkhan to repay the Xie family for their upbringing. As the two leftovers of the clan system, both adoption and foster care were preserved in the Turkic Khaganate, and they opened up a wide source of labor for patriarchal families. In a sense, the ancient tradition of mutual assistance from the clan era became a cover for exploitation among the Turks.

Based on the above analysis, we can summarize the characteristics of the Turkic family during the sixth and eighth centuries as follows: it was predominantly patriarchal, but with some matriarchal remnants.

Now let us turn to the topic of marriage, as it is closely related to the family. In "Records of the Turks" ("Tujue zhuan") of the *History of the North* (*Bei shi*), volume 99, there is a section especially devoted to the account of the Turkic marriage:

> Men and women put on their best dress and gather at the place where the dead are buried. When a man sees a woman he likes, he will send someone to inquire about the dowry, and usually the woman's parents do not interfere. If a man's father, brother, or uncle dies, this man or his cousin can marry his stepmother, aunt, or sister-in-law, but the elder should not marry the spouse of the younger generations.

The last sentence in this quote – "the elder should not marry the spouse of the younger generations" – indicates that it was compulsory in nature. Thus, this must have been a customary marriage law among the Turks rather than a mere marriage custom. What follows is a detailed discussion from three perspectives.

The first is about how to get into a marriage.

From the above quotation, we can see that a Turkic young man sought his future wife at funeral meetings. The reason why Turkic youth had to pursue their love at funerals where they "cut their faces and cry, with blood and tears flowing downward" was not due to superstition, but to the fact that dispersion and mobility of nomadic life prevented them from having regular social activities, even if only in a limited sense, so they had to make use of funeral meetings to choose their future spouse. This special custom may have seemed ludicrous to people living to the south of the Great Wall, but for the Turkic youth, it was a "mixed occasion of joy and sorrow." From the sentence "he will send someone to inquire about the dowry, and usually the woman's parents do not interfere," it is clear that parents tended to approve of their child's love affair. As for the dowry, although it is not recorded in the historical source cited above, there is no doubt that a dowry was required if a man wanted to get a wife, and this is evidenced in the Turkic criminal law that mentions a compensation method of using "wife's property." Probably because of the unequal wealth distribution, it was hard for ordinary Turkic herdsmen to accumulate sufficient wealth to marry a woman, and thus, they had a particular favor for female captives.

The second concerns the topic of levirate.

In the history of the Turkic Khaganate, Princess Yicheng was a famous case of levirate. She was successively married to Yami Qaghan, Yami Qaghan's son Shibi Qaghan, Shibi Qaghan's younger brother Chuluo Qaghan, and Chuluo Qaghan's younger brother Illig Qaghan. This case proves that Turkic law allowed levirate between a woman of the elder generation and a man of the younger generation as well as levirate between peers. According to the *History of the North*, levirate is prohibited in the following circumstances:

a the woman's husband is still alive;
b the woman is the birth mother of the inheritor;
c the inheritor is the woman's elder.

If the condition for levirate was not met, the widow could remarry. For example, the *Biographical Accounts of An Lushan* (*An Lushan shiji*) describes that An Lushan "lost his father when he was a child and lived with his mother among the Turks. His mother later married An Yanyan, brother of the Sogdian general An Bozhu." As An Lushan was his mother's biological son, he was not allowed to be her "inheritor." As for whether her deceased husband had adopted sons, younger brothers, or nephews, there is no clear account in the historical sources, so it remains unknown. It is likely that An Lushan's mother remarried because she did not meet the condition for levirate marriage. From this case, it can be assumed that when there was no legal "inheritor" in the husband's family, the widow had the right to remarry, and she was allowed to bring her biological child to her new marriage. The practice of levirate was continued after the Turks invaded Central Asia. For example, in the early seventh century, after the death of Tardush Shad, Tong Yabgu Qaghan's eldest son, "Tigin, the son of Tardush's former wife, usurped his position as a shad and married his wife."[74]

The third concerns the so-called Turkic law, which was believed to be prevalent in the Imperial Music Office (*jiaofang*) in Chang'an during the Tang period.

In Cui Lingqin's *Records of the Imperial Music* (*Jiaofang ji*), there is an entry entitled "Girls in the Imperial Music Offices":

> Similar in temperament, girls in the Imperial Music Office tend to form a sisterhood, which is called sworn brothers. There are as many as 14 or 15 of them in a big group, and no fewer than eight or nine for a smaller one. After one of them is picked up by a young man and offered a betrothal gift, she will be addressed in a feminine way. Those who are older than her call her 'bride,' and those younger call her 'sister-in-law.' [...] After a dowry is put down on her, her sworn brothers will go to her place, saying that they are 'following the Turkic law,' and that 'this man is in love with my brother, and I want to know how it feels to be his wife.' The woman who is about to marry the man is not jealous. This practice is not applicable to other groups of sworn alliance.

The meaning of the word "law" in this quote refers to a marriage custom. The term "sworn brothers" looks similar to but essentially different from the alliance prevalent in the Eastern Turkic Khaganate. Presumably, among the Turks, in addition to the levirate marriage and the practice of polygyny,[75] there was also a form of fraternal polyandry, the variant of which was teased as "Turkic law" by the performers in the Imperial Music Office. This practice resembled what Engels called the "marriage-club." That is, the group of "sworn brothers" functioned in the same way as a "marriage-club" did.[76] However, except the above-mentioned *Records of the Imperial Music*, nowhere else can this "Turkic law" be spotted.[77] Neither was this marriage custom found in the Mongolian steppe after the Xiongnu took control.[78] As most performers in the Music Office came from Sogdiana or had Sogdian ancestors,[79] their habits were likely to have originated from Central Asia.[80] Therefore, whether the so-called Turkic law was actually the "law" of Turks is really doubtful.

Existing historical sources reveal that fraternal polyandry was a unique marriage custom among the Hephthalites. As narrated in "Records of the Hephthalites" ("Yanda zhuan") of the *Book of Zhou*, volume 50:

> The criminal law and the customs here are roughly the same as those of the Turks. It is a local custom for a man and his brothers to marry one wife. If this man has no brothers, his wife wears a hat with one horn. If this man has brothers, then the number of his brothers decides the number of horns on her hat.

Similarly, in "Records of Tokharistan" ("Tuhuoluo zhuan") of the *Comprehensive Institutions* (*Tongdian*), volume 193, there is an account that reads:

> [They] mix with the Hephthalites. [...] As men outnumber women, brothers share a wife. If a woman has five husbands, she wears a head ornament with five horns; if she has ten husbands, she wears one with 10 horns. If a man does not have a brother, he can choose to become a sworn brother of somebody else so that he can obtain a wife. Otherwise, he would remain single for his whole life. The children born belong to the eldest brother.

In the *Memoir of the Pilgrimage to the Five Kingdoms of India* (*Wang wu tianzhuguo zhuan*), Huichao also wrote:

> In countries such as Tokharistan, the Kingdom of Kapisa, Bamian, and Zabulistan, fifteen, five, three, or two brothers marry a wife. A man is not allowed to take a woman as his own wife, as that might financially ruin his family.

From the above quotes, we can see that the region where fraternal polyandry was prevalent was the home of the Hephthalites. What is mentioned in the *Book of Zhou* as "It is a local custom for a man and his brothers to marry one wife" is meant to emphasize the point that the Hephthalites had slightly different customs although they had roughly the "same laws as the Turks," while what is recorded in the *Comprehensive Institutions* as "he can choose to become a sworn brother of somebody else" speaks to the practice among performers of the Imperial Music Office who formed a group called "sworn brothers." Based on the research results of numismatic study, we can know that the horned hat, which was the external symbol of this marriage custom, appeared as early as the Kushan period. It originated in Kafiristan (present Nuristan of Afghanistan), which was the main settlement of the Hephthalites.[81] After 556, the Turks entered the land of the Hephthalites, so some Hephthalites moved away to settle in the oasis between the Syr Darya River and Amu Darya River. By the eighth century, they had been assimilated by the local residents. No wonder Syrian historical records refer to the Hephthalites as "Turks."[82] These facts tell us two points. First, due to political changes, the fraternal polyandry of the Hephthalites later became a marriage custom in the Western Turkic Khaganate. Second, due to ethnic migration, the Hephthalites had partially merged with the "Nine Surnames of Zhaowu," and their marriage custom may have been introduced to the Bukhara Oasis and the Zeravshan Valley. By the mid-Kaiyuan period [Kaiyuan reign: 713–741], the time for the narration of the *Records of the Imperial Music*, the country of the Hephthalites had perished, and the Western Turkic Khaganate had just fallen apart. Therefore, when performers of the Imperial Music Office called the variant form of fraternal polyandry that they had imitated from the Hephthalites "Turkic law," they probably attributed this practice to a wrong source, showing their lack of knowledge about their own history. If this hypothesis is valid, then we can say that the so-called Turkic law, which was popular in the Imperial Music Office of Chang'an during the Tang period, was in fact a "Hephthalite law." If one insists on the term "Turkic law," then it can only be counted as a law of the Western Turks rather than of the Eastern Turks.

Principles Governing the Throne Succession

No direct references to the Turkic law of property inheritance have been found in the extant literature. As a result, the present discussion is limited to the succession to the khanate and centered on the change of succession principles in history.

Succession to the throne is an important part of a country's superstructure. With the establishment of class relations in the Turkic society and the expansion of political power of the khaganate, the throne succession went through some changes from son inheriting from father, to younger brother inheriting from elder brother, then to nephew inheriting from uncle. The following is a detailed examination about this process.

According to "Records of the Turks" of the *Book of Zhou*, volume 50:

> Neduliu had ten wives, and all of his sons adopted their mothers' surnames. Ashina was the son of his youngest wife. After Neduliu's death, a successor should be chosen from the sons born to his ten wives, so they gathered under a tree and made an agreement: 'Everyone jumps towards the tree, and whoever jumps the highest will be elected as the successor.' Although Ashina was the youngest, he jumped the highest, so all the other sons elected him as the leader and called him Axian Shad.

The statement that "all his sons adopted their mothers' surnames" indicates a society of matrilineality, but the practice that the right of succession was limited to "sons" reveals the traces of patrilineality. Therefore, the era of Neduliu was likely a transitional time from a matriarchal to a patriarchal society as it had both characteristics. Also, the Turks called their "leader" "shad," which was obviously a military chief, and that explains why they "call a military leader of other countries shad."[83] The legend of several sons jumping under a tree implies that, at that time, ultimogeniture was not a fixed system. Otherwise, there was no need for Ashina to "jump."[84] This is not contradictory to the aforementioned statement that Turkic families adopted ultimogeniture. After all, the succession to the position of "shad" was different from the inheritance of property, and the choice of a military chief should be decided by the candidates' ability rather than the order of seniority. But Axian Shad's victory was, after all, a turning point, which meant "the first rudiments of segregated families of aristocrats"[85] had already sprung up within the clan, and thus opened up the era of monopoly by the Ashina clan.

After Axian Shad's succession to the throne, between 435 and 460,[86] as narrated in "Records of the Turks" ("Tujue zhuan") of the *Book of Sui* (*Sui shu*), "the Ashina tribe of five hundred households moved to Ruru [Rouran Khaganate]. They lived in the Jinshan 金山 area for generations, good at producing iron tools." In "Records of the Turks" of the *Book of Zhou*, we read: "Axian Shad's descendants were called Tumen. As the tribe gradually thrived, they began to trade silk and cotton at the border, showing an interest in interacting with the Han Chinese." The title "Tumen" is a transcription of the Turkic word "Tümän," which means "a military unit of 10,000 soldiers" or "a leader of 10,000 households." The literal meaning of this title reflects the situation at that time – "the tribe gradually thrived." It indicates that after their migration to Jinshan (the Altai Range), the Turks had the following socioeconomic characteristics:

First, they were "good at producing iron tools." That is, they had a remarkable skill of making and using iron tools. According to the *Book of Zhou: Records of Turks*, the Rouran called the Turks "blacksmith slaves," because the latter was a dependent tribe that took iron products as tribute.

Second, the sentence that "they began to trade silk and cotton at the border" indicates an exchange of goods, showing that the Turkic nobility already had surplus products that exceeded their consumption.

Third, the fact that the Ashina clan changed from a "Shad" that controlled 500 families to a "leader of 10,000 households" not only indicates the growing Turkic population but also implies the expanding power of military chiefs who held their titles by hereditary right. The characteristics of a "heroic age" including the use of iron tools, emergence of commerce, and aristocratic control marked that the Turks had already stepped into a period of civilization.

In 546, "when Tiele was about to invade Ruru, Tumen led his troops to attack the enemies on the way, and defeated them. More than 50,000 Ruru families surrendered."[87] This victory provided the Turks with a strong material backup for their "numerous conquests." In 552, Tumen defeated Rouran in northern Huaihuang, gaining full independence for the Turks and bringing about their change from "blacksmith slaves" to suzerainty. What followed was a remarkable change. As Engels pointed out:

> But the immediate representative of the conquering people was their military leader. To secure the conquered territory against attack from within and

without, it was necessary to strengthen his power. The moment had come to transform the military leadership into kingship: the transformation was made.[88]

Not surprisingly, Tumen, the former leader of 10,000 households, started to "call himself Illig Qaghan."[89]

After the death of Tumen, his son Keluo inherited the throne, with the title of Issik Qaghan. In 553, "Keluo died. His younger brother Yandou became the new khan with the title of Muqan Qaghan." From this year on, the old practice of "son inheriting the throne from father" was replaced by "younger brother inheriting from elder brother." Why did the throne succession of the Turkic Khaganate undergo such a significant change in the era of Muqan Qaghan? For an easier explanation, let me quote the *Book of Sui: Records of the Turks* as follows:

> When Keluo was very ill and was about to die, he did not pass the khanate to his son Shetu. Instead, his brother Yandou ascended to the throne with the title of Muqan Qaghan.
>
> After ruling for twenty years (553–572), Muqan Qaghan died. He did not let his son Daluobian inherit the khanate either. Instead, he passed the throne to his younger brother, who was known as Taspar Qaghan.
>
> After reigning for 10 years (572–581), Taspar Qaghan fell ill and was about to die. Before his death, he told his son Anluo, 'I have heard that among the kinship, the father-son relationship is the closest. My elder brother was not close to his son, so he passed the khanate to me. After my death, you should avoid Daluobian.' After Taspar Qaghan's death, Daluobian was about to ascend the throne. However, because his mother was of humble origin, everyone refused to obey. But Anluo had a noble birth, and the Turks had a high regard for him. Later, Shetu came and he said: 'If Anluo is elected as khan, I will command my people to serve him; if Daluobian takes the throne, I will guard the border, and fight against him with sharp broadswords and spears!' Shetu was a towering and brave figure. People in this country were so afraid of him that no one dared to resist, so finally Anluo took the throne. Having failed to succeed the khanate, Daluobian refused to obey Anluo, and he often sent people to insult the new khan. Knowing that he was unable to control Daluobian, Anluo intended to cede the throne to Shetu. Seeing this, the Turks said to each other: 'Of the sons of the four khans, Shetu was the wisest.' So they made Shetu their khan, who was known as 'Il Kul Shad Bagha Ishbara Qaghan' or simply Ishbara.
>
> At first, believing that his son Yongyulv was weak and cowardly, Shetu left an order before his death to appoint his younger brother Yabgh Chuluohou as khan. Yongyulv sent an emissary to take him back and prepared to make him the khan. But Chuluohou said, 'Since the time of Muqan Qaghan, Turkic khanate was passed from the elder brother to the younger brother, that is, having the concubine's son to take the place of the wife's son, which is

contrary to the practice of our ancestors, and that made us have no respect and fear for each other. You should inherit the khanate, and I am not afraid to bow down to you.' Yongyulv sent a messenger to Chuluohou again with a reply: 'Uncle and my father share the same root, while I am just a branch. I am only a humble and young man, so how can I be the lord of the Turks and place such a noble man as Uncle under me? It is unreasonable to let the root subordinate to the branch. Besides, this is an order issued by my father before he passed away, how can I disobey it? I hope Uncle can put down your doubts.' After five or six rounds, Chuluohou finally succeeded to the throne. He was Tong Yabgh Qaghan (581–587).

From this quote, it is clear that the Turks had two types of succession: one is "the practice of ancestors," which is legal inheritance, and the other is "a dying father's order," which is testamentary inheritance. The latter took the form of an oral will. When the succession principle of "replacing the elder brother with the younger one" replaced "the practice of ancestors," there must have been a stronger force in real life that prompted the Turks to defy the traditional force on account of "a dying father's order." It is interesting to note that once the new succession principle was established, it was so powerful that a strong leader like Shetu who helped Anluo become the new khan by force had to make an oral will to "appoint his younger brother Yabgh Chuluohou as khan" when he was dying. Historical sources explain this phenomenon by the account that "Yongyulv was weak and cowardly," but that does not touch upon the essence of the problem. It is no coincidence that the new succession practice of "replacing the elder brother with the younger one" emerged in the middle of the sixth century. By the time Keluo died, the Turks had already gained independence and embarked on the outward expansion. Under Muqan Qaghan's rule, the Turks completely destroyed the forces of Rouran and the Hephthalites, laying the foundation for the Turkic Khaganate. The expansion of the territory brought new political problems to the Ashina clan. On the one hand, "the tribes were not purely Turkic. Among the various ethnic groups, there were resentments and hostilities"[90]; on the other hand, "brothers were fighting for the khanate, and father and uncle were suspicious of each other. They looked united to the outside world, but each had his own secret plan inside his mind."[91] Under such circumstances, if the "practice of the ancestors" was still followed and the khanate was passed on to the son, there might have appeared a "child khan" who was unable to take charge of the government. In the meantime, even if the crown prince had come of age, the khan's brothers, each of whom was dominant in a region, would never settle down in peace. That explains why the khan was forced to be "not close to his own son" and had to look for a strong successor from among his brothers. For example, Keluo's brother Muqan "was good at conquering and crushing enemies."[92] Muqan's younger brother Taspar was also an ambitious ruler.[93] Taspar's nephew Shetu, as quoted above, was "a towering and brave figure." Shetu's younger brother Chuluohou was equally qualified to be a successor, as he was "brave and wise."[94] The character traits of the above-mentioned leaders spoke for their political strength. As a result, when old khans died, young crown princes were deprived of the right of succession. For instance, when Shibi Qaghan died:

> His son Shibobi was too young to succeed the khan, so he was appointed as Nibu Shad and was asked to live in a small town on the eastern border to manage the northern part of Youzhou. Shibi Qaghan's younger brother Ilteber Shad was enthroned with the title of Chuluo Qaghan.

A similar situation occurred after the death of Chuluo. As narrated in the *Old Book of Tang: Records of the Turks*, "because of his ugly looks and weak personality, Aoshe Shad was deprived of the succession to the throne. Then Chuluo's younger brother Duobi was appointed as the khan, who was known as Illig Qaghan." From Muqan Qaghan to Illig Qaghan, there were many cases of "younger brother replacing the elder one, and nephew succeeding uncle," indicating that these could be a general rule of throne succession. Even by the end of the seventh century when Qutlugh had led the Turks to rebuild the Khaganate, the throne still fell into the hands of his younger brother Mochuo, with the reason that "his [Qutlugh] son was too young." But in Mochuo Qaghan's reign, he "appointed his son Fuju as a sub-khan (*xiao kehan*), a rank higher than shad," paving the way for his son to succeed. But what became of that? As described in "Records of the Turks" in the *Old Book of Tang*, "Qutlugh's son Kul Tigin gathered his subordinates, and killed Fuju, Fuju's brothers and his trusted aides. Then, Kul Tigin sent his brother Mojilian who then was a Left Wise Prince (*zuoxianwang*) to the throne, known as Bilge Qaghan." This shows that the succession principle of the former Turkic Khaganate still had a strong vitality in the later period. As for why it remained active for such a long time, it is probably due to the fact that this principle was more flexible than "the practice of ancestors" and was thus more adaptable to the complex political situation of the Turkic Khaganate.

In short, in terms of the throne succession in the Turkic era, there was a change from the son succeeding the father, to the younger brother taking the place of the older brother, and also the nephew inheriting the uncle. On the surface, it was manifested as obeying "a dying father's order" which went against "the practice of ancestors." In essence, it was determined by the complicated political struggle of the khaganate and the deepening conflicts within the khanate nobility.[95]

Regarding the throne succession, two other issues also deserve a mention.

The first is related to the succession ritual. According to "Records of the Turks" in the *Book of Zhou*:

> When a khan is newly enthroned, his ministers and generals carry him in a felt rug, and they walk clockwise nine times in the direction of the sun. For every round, the ministers and generals kneel down and bow. After the bowings, they put the khan on the horse, and then strangle him with a silk scarf, almost to the point of suffocating him before they hurriedly let go of him, and then ask him 'how many years can you be a khan?' The khan has become so dizzy that he cannot name a calculated number, so his ministers write down any number he gives, which will be used to verify his reign time.

Legal Practice in the Turkic Khaganate 123

Obviously, the succession ceremony is a reflection of the religious custom of the Turks who worshipped the sun and the sky. Through this ritual, the khan was deified and the divine right of the khan gained a religious basis.[96] However, it can be seen from here that the secular power at that time was only covered with a layer of "divine will." That is, among the Turks, there was the concept of divine power, but not the supremacy of the khanate.

The second concerns the succession procedure. According to the aforementioned *Book of Sui: Records of the Turks*, the dispute about who could be the next khan after Taspar's death revealed that succession to the throne "also required the consent of the Turks in the form of an assembly."[97] But, as recorded in historical sources, when faced with the threat of "sharp broadswords and spears," "[p]eople in this country were so afraid of him that no one dared to resist, so finally Anluo took the throne." Thus, it is reasonable to assume that "the choice of a khan at the assembly" was mostly a procedure of formality. But this long-standing principle was not a useless fossil in history. When Anluo "was unable to control Daluobian," and "the Turks said to each other: 'Of the sons of the four khans, Shetu was the wisest.' So they made Shetu their khan," we can see that even for Shetu, a powerful and eminent figure, he had to use the cover of "election" to ascend to the throne.

To summarize, in the Turkic era, the acquisition of the khanate was determined by three factors: heredity right, divine will, and election. Heredity right was the basis for determining the khanate, which was approved by election, and divine will was to cover the khan with a layer of divine halo and turn him into a "messenger from the sky." In this sense, the three factors are not contradictory, but complementary.

Criminal Law

The most complete account of the Turkic criminal law can be found in "Records of the Turks" of the *History of the North*, volume 99, where we read:

> Their criminal law goes like this: whoever rebels, murders, rapes another man's wife, or steals horse lassos, shall be punished with a death penalty; whoever is lecherous in behavior shall have his genital cut and then chopped into halves at the waist; whoever rapes another person's daughter shall be punished by a heavy fine of his property and then marry his own daughter to this person; whoever hurts another person shall pay compensation according to the severity of the victim's wound. If the victim is hurt in the eyes, the perpetrator shall pay compensation by offering his daughter to the victim. In case this perpetrator does not have a daughter, he pays with his wife's property. If the perpetrator breaks the victim's arms or legs, he pays with his horse. Whoever steals horse lassos and other personal belongings shall compensate the victim with a monetary value ten times of the stolen property.[98]

124 *Legal Practice in the Turkic Khaganate*

Based on the quoted text, I divide the criminal acts into the following four categories:

1 Crimes against the state, such as rebellion, including "betrayal of the Turks"[99] and murder of the khan.[100] Delaying military arrangements[101] and leading the army astray[102] also fell into this category.
2 Crimes against property, such as stealing horse lassos, horses, and other personal belongings.
3 Crimes against the family, such as raping another person's wife or daughter, or behaving in a lecherous manner.
4 Crimes against the person, such as killing, or injuring someone in a fight (injuring eyes, breaking arms or legs).

Penalties can also be divided into four categories:

1 *Death penalty.* The death penalty was imposed on whoever committed crimes against the state, behaved in a lecherous manner, or stole horse lassos. In addition to the special punishment of "hav[ing] his genital cut and then chopped into halves at the waist," there were also other methods of execution, such as "being chopped into halves at the waist,"[103] beheading,[104] and burying alive.[105]
2 *Corporal punishment.* In "Records of the Turks" of the *Old Book of Tang*, volume 194, there is an account that Tuli was "imprisoned and whipped" by Illig Qaghan. There was also the punishment of "hanging [the victim] upside down."[106]
3 *Fines and compensation.* The amount of the fine depended on the severity of the crime, and compensation included property, horses, or women.
4 *Punishment in the form of hard labor, exile, or "confined service in the army."* This punishment was imposed on foreign envoys. For example, in the fifth year of Wude [622/623], Wen Yanbo was "exiled to the harsh and cold area of the Yin Mountains"[107] by Illig Qaghan, and Pei Huaigu was forced to have a "confined service in the army"[108] at the order of Mochuo Qaghan.

The following features of Turkic criminal law can be seen from the provisions concerning crimes and penalties:

1 *Protection of property rights.* The inviolability of private property, such as horses and horse lassos, was legally guaranteed by severe penalties. It is also worth noting that those who stole horses were punished with fines, while those who stole horse lassos were punished with a death penalty. This indicates that the Turks considered horse lassos more important than horses, probably because lassos were not only a herding tool but also a weapon.
2 *Defense of aristocratic privileges.* The crime of "rebellion" included both "betrayal of the Turks" and "murder of the khan," which indicates that the concept of "monarch as the personality of the state" had already existed in the legal thoughts of the Turks. That is why Turkic inscriptions often referred to "Yili" [meaning "an independent state agency"] and "khan" in the same breath.

As for khan's relatives who should have been sentenced to capital punishment but were only "deposed and sent back to their own tribes,"[109] they were also enjoying a privilege. This is quite similar to "Mercy on Relatives" of the Eight Deliberations system (*ba yi*)[110] in feudal Chinese law.

3 *Priority of the husband's interests.* Turkic law stipulated that whoever raped another man's wife should be sentenced to death, while raping the daughter of another person should be punished with a heavy financial penalty. Both crimes involved females (whether it was adultery or rape is not clearly stated in historical sources), but the criminal liability of the offender differed in accordance with the victim's social role. The law offered greater protection to the "wife" than the "daughter" precisely because the former was more closely associated with the husband's interests.

4 *Emphasis on the father's rights.* The fact that daughters were used as a means of compensation to indemnify others suggests that it was legitimate for a father to use his daughter to offset his own crime. Clearly, Turkic law reduced the daughter to a status similar to the object possessed by the head of the family.

As for the judicial proceedings closely related to the criminal law, we are unable to conduct a detailed discussion because of the scarcity of related materials. All we know is that in the Turkic official system, there was a "Rehan 热汉 who supervised the officials to prevent them from violating the law, and took responsibility for the rectification of the officialdom."[111] This could be the official in charge of justice. Moreover, in "A Biography of Lai Junchen" ("Lai Junchen Zhuan") of the *Old Book of Tang*, volume 186, section one, there is an account that:

> Ashina Huselo, one of the Sogdian chieftains had a servant girl who was good at singing and dancing. Junchen wanted this girl, so he instigated his followers to fabricate a false accusation, suing Huselo for conspiracy against the government. Many chieftains went to the capital, complaining of injustice on his behalf by ripping their ears and cutting their faces. In the end, the Ashina were exempted from the clan execution.

It is clear that in the minds of Turkic chieftains, the act of ripping ears and cutting faces was regarded as important judicial evidence. This practice of using mourning rituals as a means of litigation indicates that the Turkic law at that time was still in an immature stage.

Conclusion

The word "torü" on the Orkhon Turkic inscriptions means "custom," "law," "power," etc.[112] The multiple meanings contained in this word indicate that the formation of Turkic law was, without exception, subject to the following rule:

> At a certain, very primitive stage of the development of society, the need arises to co-ordinate under a common regulation the daily recurring acts

of production, distribution and exchange of products, to see to it that the individual subordinates himself to the common conditions of production and exchange. This regulation, which was at first a custom, soon became a law. With law, organs necessarily arise which are entrusted with its maintenance - public authority.[113]

The Turkic Khaganate from the sixth to the eighth centuries was a military administration headed by khans and characterized by a hierarchical and hereditary system, with "officials such as yabghu (*yehu*), followed by shad (*she*) and tigin (*tele*, also called *teqin*), then elteber (*yilifa*), and then tudun (*tutun*), and many other minor officials. There were 28 ranks in total, all hereditary."[114] As members of the bureaucratic system, they were "[r]epresentative of a power which estranges them from society, and they have to be given prestige by means of special decrees, which invest them with a peculiar sanctity and inviolability."[115] What the Turkic Khaganate upheld was the customary law, which changed from the common regulation that represented the will of the whole society in the tribal era into a tool that enabled the ruling class to realize its own will. This was evidenced by the distinct feature of Turkic criminal law that emphasized the difference between social classes.

However, this does not mean that a khan, as the head of state, had unlimited power over the law. In fact, it was only within the political circle of the Turkic Khaganate that the khan was able to go against "the practice of ancestors," passing the throne not to his son but to his younger brother. In the general social domain, the khan was always the enforcer of the law, someone who "organized and rectified public life in accordance with the legal system of his ancestors"[116] since "the customs had been around for such a long time that they could not be changed."[117] For example, the governing philosophy relished by Bilge Qaghan (716–734) – "Let the naked be clothed, the poor be enriched, and the underpopulated be multiplied"[118] was extracted from the ancient practice of mutual assistance within clans. Since the khan's power was still constrained by tradition, the Turks did not believe in the supremacy of the khanate, though they did take their "monarch as the personality of the state."

How is it that the ancient customs of the Turks still managed to retain a certain authority in the process of their own metamorphosis? It is probably because the social basis on which they emerged had not been completely destroyed. As mentioned earlier, there were still substantial remnants of the clan system in the Turkic era. Not only do we see the coexistence of private ownership of livestock and collectively owned pastures (although only on the surface) but also we find the glory of the matriarchal era casting its shadow on patriarchal families through the kinship concepts that valued female lineage and the custom that "wives mostly participated in politics." Even the exploitation of labor was cloaked with a cover of mutual assistance, revealing itself in the form of practices such as foster care and adoption. Since social life was still inextricably linked to the "military-democratic period," it is natural that the concept of law could not be isolated from ancient customs. That is why the original face of Turkic law that was derived from customs was still vaguely discernible, although it had a distinct feature of class hierarchy.

All of the above reminds us of the similar legal practice in the early Middle Ages in the Germanic kingdoms of Western Europe: the law was derived from customs, and the monarchy was under the law. Since the evolution of legal practice in the Germanic tribes showed a direct transition from clanship to feudal system, the materials related to Turkic law, which was a contradictory combination of customary law and prerogative practice, may help with the exploration of the nature of Turkic society from the sixth to the eighth centuries.

Notes

1. "Records of the Turks" ("Tujue zhuan") in the *Book of Zhou* (*Zhou shu*), vol. 50.
2. "Records of the Turks" ("Tujue zhuan") in the *Book of Sui* (*Sui shu*), vol. 84.
3. The east side on the Kul Tigin Monument, line 13. See Cen Zhongmian, 1958, vol. 2: 881.
4. "Records of the Turks" ("Tujue zhuan") in the *Old book of Tang* (*Jiu Tang shu*), vol. 194.
5. "Records of the Uyghurs" ("Huihu zhuan") in the *New Book of Tang* (*Xin Tang shu*), vol. 217.
6. Marx, *The Poverty of Philosophy*, 1979: 180.
7. Regarding Altai before the rise of the Turks, see Jettmar, 135–223.
8. Simocatta, 161.
9. Simocatta, 212. Chavannes, 1958: 212.
10. "Records of the Turks" in the *Old book of Tang*, vol. 194.
11. The Mongol Khanate also had a hunting reserve, see *The Travels of Marco Polo*, translated by Feng Chengjun, 1954: 373–374.
12. Su Mian, et al., vol. 96.
13. "A Biography of Ashina She'er" ("Ashina She'er zhuan") in the *New Book of Tang*, vol. 110.
14. Wang Qinruo, et al., vol. 37.
15. Baidao was located in the present Baidaoxi in the north of Hohhot. —Trans.
16. "Records of the Turks" in the *Book of Sui*.
17. Malov, 1959: 10. "Mohe" in this quote means "father." Pelliot believed that this way of addressing one's father as "Mohe" was borrowed from the Rouran. See Pelliot, 1957: 33. Clauson had a different translation for line 5 of the Ongin Inscription, which reads: "Then to the north of China among Atiğ (?) and Oğuz seven men started hostilities (against us). My father . . . thereupon marched behind His Majesty and gave him his services." See Clauson, "The Ongin Inscription," 1957: 188.
18. Cen Zhongmian, 1958, vol. 2: 880.
19. Kiselev, 514–515. See also Klyashtorny, 1979: 98–99.
20. "A Biography of Zheng Yuanshu" ("Zheng Yuanshu") in the *Old Book of Tang*, vol. 62.
21. "Records of Gaoche" ("Gaoche zhuan") in the *Book of Wei* (*Wei shu*), vol. 103.
22. In *The Travels of Marco Polo*, it is written: "It is usual for every chief of a tribe or other person possessing large cattle, such as horses, mares, camels, oxen, or cows, to distinguish them by his mark, and then to suffer them to graze at large, in any part of the plains or mountains, without employing herdsmen to look after them; and if any of them should happen to mix with the cattle of other proprietors, they are restored to the person whose mark they bear." See Marco Polo, 284.
23. Cen Zhongmian, 1958, vol. 2: 887. See also his note on page 907.
24. Malov, 1952: 19.
25. "Records of the Turks" ("Tujue zhuan") in the *New Book of Tang*, vol. 215.
26. "Records of the Turks" in the *Book of Zhou*.
27. "Records of the Turks" in the *Book of Zhou*.
28. Cai Hongsheng, 1963: 45.
29. Kiselev, 531.
30. Marx, *Capital*, 1953: 75.

31 Marx, *Pre-Capitalist Economic Formations*, 1953: 75.
32 "Records of the Turks" in the *Book of Sui*.
33 "Records of the Turks" in the *Old Book of Tang*, vol. 194.
34 Huili and Yancong, vol. 1.
35 "Biography of Shining" ("Shining zhuan") in the *Book of Zhou*, vol. 28.
36 "Records of the Turks" in the *Old Book of Tang*, vol. 194.
37 Malov, 1959: 53. Malov believed that Kushus probably means "winter."
38 This can be seen from the inscriptions on the Kul Tigin Monument, in particular the eighth line of the small stele and the second line of the large stele. see Malov, 1951: 35–36. There is actually physical evidence of this subordinative posture of "lower[ing] their heads and bend[ing] their knees." On the right bank of the Chulyshman River in the Gorno-Altai Autonomous Oblast, the Soviet Union, a tomb from the end of the seventh century was unearthed. In this tomb, a circular stone carving was found, the picture of which has the following three parts: on the left is the face of a noble minister, which resembles the appearance of the existing ancient Turkic stone statues. In the middle, there are three animal-faced knights, who dismount and kneel to noblewoman sitting on the right, accompanied by her son. This stone inscription also confirms the record of "among the northern ethnic minorities, a khatun knew about military arrangements."
39 "Records of Shiwei" ("Shiwei zhuan") in the *Book of Sui*, vol. 84.
40 "Records of the Kitans" ("Qidan zhuan") in the *Book of Sui*.
41 "Records of the Turks" in the *Old Book of Tang*, vol. 194.
42 Cen Zhongmian, 1958, vol. 2: 882.
43 "Records of Samarkand" ("Kangguo zhuan") in the *Old Book of Tang*, vol. 198.
44 "Records of the Turks" in the *Book of Zhou*.
45 "Records of the Tiele" ("Tiele zhuan") in the *Book of Sui*, vol. 84.
46 "Records of the Kirghiz" ("Xiajiasi zhuan") in the *New Book of Tang*, vol. 217.
47 Klyashtorny, 1986: 335.
48 Ma Changshou, "On the Social Change of the Turks and the Turkic Khaganate," no. 4 (1958), 52. Regarding the sources of Turkic slaves, the first and second sources are quite convincing, but the third source that is based on the following translation seems problematic: "These seven hundred people had lost their country and their khan. According to the law of our ancestors, those who have lost their country and khan can be taken as slaves as they are thought to have disobeyed the Turkic law." Sergey Efimovich Malov in his book *Ancient Turkic Documents* gave a different translation to the 13th line of the large stele of the Kul Tigin Monument, which reads "When [he] obtained seven hundred people, he started to organize and teach these people who have lost their 'Yili' (that is, their own independent state agency) and their khan, these people who were made into slaves, who abandoned [their] Turkic legal system. In accordance with the law of our ancestors, he consolidated and educated [these people]." See Malov, 1951: 37–38. The German-Chinese translation by Han Rulin and English-Chinese translation by Cen Zhongmian mean roughly the same as Malov's interpretation. See Han Rulin, "Annotations to the Translation of Kul Tigin Monument" ("Tujuewen queteqinbei yizhu"), *Guoli beiping yanjiuyuan yuanwu huibao* 6, no. 6 (1935): 20; and Cen Zhongmian, *Compilation of Historical Records of the Turks*, vol. 2 (1958): 881.
49 Bernshtam, 1946: 116, 125.
50 "A Biography of Zheng Yuanshu" in the *Old Book of Tang*, vol. 62.
51 "Records of the Xiongnu" ("Xiongnu liezhuan") in the *Records of the Grand Historian* (*Shiji*).
52 "Records of the Turks" in the *Old Book of Tang*, section 1.
53 See "A Biography of Wei Yunqi" ("Wei Yunqi zhuan") in the *Old Book of Tang*, vol. 75.
54 "Records of the Turks" in the *Book of Sui*.

55 Kiselev, 534. See also Sergey Grigoryevich Klyashtorny, "Slaves of the Ancient Turkic Community," in *Ancient Mongolian Culture* [In Russian], edited by Ruslan Sergeyevich Vasilevsky (Novosibirsk: Nauka, 1985) 166.
56 "Records of the Turks" in the *New Book of Tang*, vol. 1.
57 "Records of the Kirghiz" in the *Universal Geography of the Taiping Era* (*Taiping huanyu ji*), vol. 199.
58 "A Biography of Zhang Gongjin" ("Zhang Gongjin zhuan") in the *Old Book of Tang*, vol. 68.
59 "Records of Gaochang" ("Gaochang zhuan") in the *Old Book of Tang*, vol. 198.
60 "Records of the Turks" in the *History of the North* (*Bei shi*), vol. 99.
61 Cen Zhongmian, 1958, vol. 1: 314.
62 Engels, 1954: 155.
63 Kiselev, 543, 551.
64 Engels, 1954: 134.
65 "Records of the Turks" in the *Book of Sui*.
66 Wang Qinruo, et al., vol. 979.
67 Cen Zhongmian, 1958, vol. 2: 891–892.
68 Wu Jing, vol. 9.
69 For instance, in "Records of Wuhuan" ("Wuhuan zhuan") of the *Book of the Later Han* (*Hou Hanshu*), vol. 89, there is a statement that "they adopt women's stratagem." In Tacitus's *Germania*, there is also an interesting account: "They [Germanic men] never despise women. They discuss matters with women and respect women's opinions." See Tacitus, 58.
70 "A Biography of An Lushan" ("An Lushan zhuan") in the *Old Book of Tang*, vol. 200.
71 Malov, 1952: 21.
72 Bernshtam, 1946: 115.
73 "A Biography of An Lushan" in the *New Book of Tang*, vol. 225.
74 Huili and Yancong, vol. 2
75 It was a common practice for a Turkic nobleman to have several wives. See the scripts on the northern side of the Kul Tigin Monument, line nine. See also Cen Zhongmian, 1958, vol. 2: 886.
76 Engels, 1954: 59.
77 In the *Great Tang Records on the Western Regions* (*Datang xiyu ji*), vol. 20, it is recorded that in Himatala, a married woman wore a wooden horn over her heads, because "their territory [Himatala] is adjacent to that of the Turks, so they take their custom." But this cannot be taken as the evidence to argue that the fraternal polyandry came from the Turks. After all, the "wooden horn" that symbolized the presence of her husband's parents are dramatically different from the "horned hat" that symbolized the number of her husbands.
78 In his book *Compilation of Historical Records of the Turks*, vol. 2, page 1117, Cen Zhongmian asserted that the marriage custom of the Xiongnu that "a son married his stepmother after the death of his father and a man took all the wives of his brother after the latter's death" is "roughly similar" to the "Turkic law" mentioned in the *Records of the Imperial Music* (*Jiaofang ji*). This actually has confused levirate with fraternal polyandry. Ren Bantang followed Cen's argument in his monograph *Annotations to "Records of the Imperial Music"* (*Jiaofang ji jian ding*, Beijing: Zhonghua shuju, 1962) 51.
79 Chen Yinke, 1955: 149.
80 Xiang Da opined that performers in the Imperial Music Office followed the "Turkic Law" because "the Turkic Khaganate at that time was powerful and prosperous, and there were so many Turks in Chang'an that the local customs were also influenced in an invisible way." See Xiang Da, 44. In fact, the "Sogdianization" of Chang'an during the Kaiyuan period was much more obvious than the "Turkicization."
81 Regarding the marriage customs of the Hephthalites, See Enoki Kazuo, 51–55.
82 Frye and Sayili, 205.

83 "Records of the Turks" in *Comprehensive Institutions* (*Tongdian*), vol. 1.
84 I gained this understanding after Dai Yixuan's insightful explanation.
85 Engels, 1954: 102.
86 Ma Changshou, "On the Social Change of the Turks and the Turkic Khaganate," no.3 (1958), 13.
87 "Records of the Turks" in the *Book of Zhou*.
88 Engels, 1954: 147.
89 "Records of the Turks" in the *Book of Zhou*.
90 "Records of the Turks" in the *Book of Sui*.
91 "Records of the Turks" in the *Book of Zhou*.
92 "Records of the Turks" in the Book of Zhou.
93 Taspar Qaghan once said, "As long as my two sons (the Northern Qi dynasty and Northern Zhou dynasty) in the south show filial respect to me, there is nothing I need to worry about!"
94 "Records of the Turks" in the *Book of Sui*.
95 The issue of khanate in the Turkic era involved not only the succession system but also the power structure, i.e., the relationship among the "Middle Khaganate," the "Eastern Khaganate," and the "Western Khaganate." Regarding the second point, Mori Masao concluded that "starting from the reign of Shibi Qaghan, the 'Turkic' countries turned from a decentralized 'feudal' state to a centralized 'feudal' state." See Mori Masao, *Historical Studies of the Ancient Turkic Peoples* (Tokyo: Yamakawa Shuppansha, 1967) 277.
96 Ishbara Qaghan had a title that claimed himself to be "Born from the Heaven," see "Records of the Turks" in the *Book of Sui*. Similarly, Beilge Qaghan's title also had words such as "Same as the Heaven and Heavenly Granted." See Cen Zhongmian, 1958, vol. 2: 908.
97 Ma Changshou, 1957: 22.
98 In the collated version of the *Universal Geography of the Taiping Era* which was completed in the eighth year of Jiajing [1529/1530], there is a different expression that reads: "If the perpetrator breaks the victim's arms or legs, he compensates by becoming the victim's slave 折肢体者输为奴隶." Since both the Hualongchi edition of this book during the reign of Qianlong [1736–1795] and the *Comprehensive Institutions* have the wording that "he pays with his horse 输马," Cen Zhongmian then concluded in his annotation that "what is written here as 'he compensates by becoming the victim's slave' is a mistake." See Cen Zhongmian, *Compilation of Historical Records of the Turks*, vol. 2 (Beijing: Zhonghua shuju, 1958) 605. But I believe it is not that simple. The two Chinese characters "马 [mǎ] (horse)" and "奴隶[nú lì](slave)" are noticeably different both in sound and form, so they could not be easily mistaken in the block print. Besides, although it was based on the *Comprehensive Institutions*, the *Universal Geography of the Taiping Era* made some supplements. For example, in the second part of "The Turks," there is a section entitled "Local Products and Customs" where more than thirty additions are made at the end, covering names of mountains, water, and cities. Thus seen, the wording that "he compensates by becoming the victim's slave" in the same section might not be a wrong addition. After all, we can have doubts about the wording here, but there is no need to deny it.
99 As recorded in "A Biography of Liu Wuzhou" ("Liu Wuzhou zhuan") of the *Old Book of Tang*, vol. 55, in 620, Song Jingang betrayed the Turkic Khaganate and fled. When he was about to return to his hometown Shanggu county, he was captured by the pursuing cavalries and was chopped into two halves at the waist.
100 According to the second part of the "Records of the Turks" in the *New Book of Tang*, vol. 215, in 734, Bilge Qaghan "was poisoned by Buyruk Chor. Enduring his pain before death, Bilge Qaghan had Buyruk Chor and his entire clan executed."

101 In his book *Compilation of Historical Records of the Turks*, vol. 1, Cen Zhongmian quoted from the *Comprehensive Mirror in Aid of Governance* (*Zizhi tongjian*), volume 206, to give this account: in 697, Sun Wanrong sent five people to Heisha Ridge to pass on military messages, and "Two of them arrived late. Mochuo Qaghan was irritated by their delay, and killed them." See Cen Zhongmian, 1958, vol. 1: 338.
102 On line 26 of the first stele of the "Tonyukuk Inscriptions," there is a sentence that reads "The guide led us astray, so we killed him." See Cen Zhongmian, 1958, vol. 2: 860.
103 "A Biography of Liu Wuzhou" of the *Old Book of Tang*, vol. 55.
104 Cen Zhongmian, 1958, vol. 1: 132.
105 According to "Records of the Uyghurs" in the *New Book of Tang*, vol. 217, Chuluo Qaghan once "summoned hundreds of powerful chieftains and buried them all alive."
106 Cen Zhongmian, 1958, vol. 1: 335.
107 Cen Zhongmian, 1958, vol. 1: 162.
108 Cen Zhongmian, 1958, vol. 1: 340.
109 In the second part of the "Records of the Turks" of the *New Book of Tang*, volume 215, it is recorded that "After the death of Mochuo Qaghan, Kul Tigin killed all of Mochuo's trusted subordinates. Only Tonyukuk was absolved from death penalty because his daughter Pofu was Mojilian's khatun. He was deposed and sent back to his own tribe." On the Kang Ayiqu Tarkhan Inscription, there is also an account about the nobleman's privilege: "Mochuo Qaghan's younger brother Baximi Tigin tried to poison him, but Kang Ayiqu found the poison, hid it away, and secretly informed Mochuo of this plan. Mochuo was infuriated, and intended to kill his brother. Kang Ayiqu interceded for him. So finally his brother was sent back to his own tribe." See Cen Zhongmian, 1958, vol. 2: 851. Baximi's attempt to kill the khan was an unpardonable crime and he should have been sentenced to capital punishment. He escaped from death probably not because of Kang Ayiqu's help, but due to the fact that the murder did not succeed.
110 The "Eight Deliberations" was a set of principles used by traditional Chinese law to lessen legal punishment on the royals, nobles, and members of upper classes. —Trans.
111 "Records of the Turks" in the *Comprehensive Institutions*, vol. 197.
112 Radlov, 1905: 1254, photocopied in 1963. See also Tekin, 385.
113 Engels, 1962: 559–560.
114 "Records of the Turks" in the *Book of Sui*.
115 Engels, 1954: 164–165.
116 Cen Zhongmian, 1958, vol. 2: 881.
117 "Records of the Turks" in the *Book of Sui*.
118 Cen Zhongmian, 1958, vol. 2: 883.

Bibliography

Bernshtam, Alexander Natanovich. *The Socio-Economic System of the Orkhon Yenisei Turks from the Sixth to Eighth Centuries.* [In Russian.] Moscow: The USSR Academy of Sciences Publishing House, 1946.

Cai Hongsheng. "Tujuehanguo de junshi zuzhi he junshi jishu (Military Organization and Military Technology of the Turkic Khaganate)." *Academic Research*, no. 5 (1963): 42–51.

Cen Zhongmian. *Tujue jishi* (*Compilation of Historical Records of the Turks*), vol. 2. Beijing: Zhonghua shuju, 1958.

Chavannes, Emmanuel-èdouard. *Documents on the Western Turks*. [In Chinese.] Translated by Feng Chengjun. Beijing: Zhonghua shuju, 1958.

Chen Yinke. *Yuanbai shijian zhenggao* (*Annotations to and Evidence in Yuan and Bai's Poems*). Beijing: Wenxue guji kanxingshe, 1955.

Clauson, Gerard. "The Ongin Inscription." *Journal of the Royal Asiatic Society of Great Britain and Ireland*, no. 3/4 (1957): 177–192.

Cui Lingqin, ed. *Jiaofang ji (Records of the Imperial Music)*. Shenyang: Liaoning jiaoyu chubanshe, 1998.

Du You, ed. *Tongdian (Comprehensive Institutions)*. Beijing: Zhonghua shuju, 1988.

Engels, Friedrich. *Origin of the Family, Private Property and the State*. Translated by Compilation and Translation Bureau of the CPC Central Committee. Beijing: Renmin chubanshe, 1954.

Engels, Friedrich. "The Housing Question." *Selected Works of Marx and Engels*. Beijing: Renmin chubanshe, 1962.

Fan Ye, ed. *Hou Hanshu (Book of the Later Han)*. Zhengzhou: Zhongzhou guji chubanshe, 1996.

Frye, Richard N. and Aydin Sayili. "Turks in the Middle East before the Seljuqs." *Journal of the American Oriental Society* 63, no. 3 (1943): 194–207.

Huichao. *Wang wu tianzhuguo zhuan (Memoir of the Pilgrimage to the Five Kingdoms of India)*. Lanzhou: Lanzhou guji shudian, 1990.

Huili and Yancong, eds. *Da Tang Da Ci'en si sanzang fashi zhuan (A Biography of the Tripitaka Master of the Great Ci'en Monastery of the Great Tang Dynasty)*. Annotated by Sun Yutang and Xie Fang. Beijing: Zhonghua shuju, 1983.

Jettmar, Karl. "The Altai before the Turks." *Bulletin of the Museum of Far Eastern Antiquity* 23 (1951): 135–223.

Kazuo, Enoki. "On the Nationality of the Ephthalites." *Memoirs of the Research Department of the Toyo Bunko* 58, no.18 (1959): 1–58.

Kiselev, Sergei Vladimirovich. *Ancient History of Southern Siberia*. [In Russian.] Moscow: USSR Academy of Sciences Publishing House, 1951.

Klyashtorny, Sergey Grigoryevich. "Forms of Social Attachment in Nomadic Countries of Inland Asia," in *Slavery in Medieval Eastern Countries*. [In Russian.] Edited by Oleg Georgievich Bolshakov and Evgeny Ivanovich Kychanov. Moscow: Oriental Literature Publishing House, 1986. 305–412.

Klyashtorny, Sergey Grigoryevich. "On Land Ownership in the Turkic Khaganates," in *Forms of Feudal Land Ownership in the Near and Middle East* (Proceedings of the 1975 Conference on Bartold). [In Russian.] Edited by Bobojan Gafurovich Gafurov. Moscow: Nauka, 1979. 97–101.

Li Fang et al., eds. *Taiping guangji (Extensive Records of the Taiping Era)*. Beijing: Zhonghua shuju, 1961.

Li Yanshou. *Bei shi (History of the North)*. Beijing: Zhonghua shuju, 1974.

Linghu Defen, eds. *Zhou shu (Book of Zhou)*. Beijing: Zhonghua shuju, 1971.

Liu Xu, et al., eds. *Jiu Tang shu (Old Book of Tang)*. Beijing: Zhonghua shuju, 1975.

Ma Changshou. "Lun tujueren he tujuehanguo de shehui bianqe (On the Social Change of the Turks and the Turkic Khaganate.")" *Lishi yanjiu*, no. 3 (1958): 9–22.

Ma Changshou. "Lun tujueren he tujuehanguo de shehui bianqe (On the Social Change of the Turks and the Turkic Khaganate.")" *Lishi yanjiu*, no. 4 (1958): 47–69.

Ma Changshou. *Tujueren he tujue hanguo (The Turks and the Turkic Khaganate)*. Shanghai: Shanghai renmin chubanshe, 1957.

Malov, Sergey Efimovich. *Ancient Turkic Documents*. [In Russian.] Moscow: The USSR Academy of Sciences Publishing House, 1951.

Malov, Sergey Efimovich. *Monuments of Ancient Turkic Writing in Mongolia and Kirghizia*. [In Russian.] Moscow: The USSR Academy of Sciences Publishing House, 1959.

Malov, Sergey Efimovich. *Orkhon-Yenisey Script.* [In Russian.] Moscow: The USSR Academy of Sciences Publishing House, 1952.
Marx, Karl. *Capital.* Translated by Guo Dali and Wang Ya'nan. Beijing: Renmin chubanshe, 1953.
Marx, Karl. *Pre-Capitalist Economic Formations.* Translated by Ri Zhi. Beijing: Renmin chubanshe, 1953.
Marx, Karl. *The Poverty of Philosophy* (*Completed Works of Marx and Engels*, vol. 4.). Beijing: Renmin chubanshe, 1979.
Mori, Masao. *Historical Studies of the Ancient Turkic Peoples*, vol. 1. [In Japanese.] Tokyo: Yamakawa Shuppansha, 1967.
Ouyang Xiu, et al., eds. *Xin Tang shu* (*New Book of Tang*). Beijing: Zhonghua shuju, 1975.
Pelliot, Paul. "Tuyuhun as a Mongolic Language." [In Chinese.] Translated by Feng Chengyun and collected in *Xiyu nanhai shidi kaozheng yicong sanbian* (*The Seventh Collection of Translated Works for the Study on History and Geography of the Western Regions and South China Sea*). Beijing: Zhonghua shuju, 1957.
Polo, Marco. *The Travels of Marco Polo*, vol. 1. [In Chinese.] Translated by Feng Chengjun. Beijing: Zhonghua shuju, 1954.
Radlov, Vasily Vasilievich (Friedrich Wilhelm Radloff). *Experimental Dictionary of Turkic Dialects*, vol. 3, 1st fascicule. [In Russian.] Saint Petersburg: Imperial Academy of Sciences, 1905. Photocopy version in 1963.
Ren Bantang. *Jiaofangji jianding* (*The Annotation of "About the Instruction Quarters"*). Beijing: Zhonghua shuju, 1962.
Sima Qian. *Shiji* (*Records of the Grand Historian*). Beijing: Zhonghua shuju, 1982.
Simocatta, Theophylact. *History*, vol. 5. [In Russian.] Translated by Sergey Petrovich Kondratiev. Moscow: The USSR Academy of Sciences Publishing House, 1957.
Su Mian, et al., eds. *Tang huiyao* (*Institutional History of Tang*). Shanghai: Shangwu yinshuguan, 1936.
Tacitus, Publius Cornelius. *Germania.* Translated by Ma Yong and Fu Zhengyuan. Beijing: Sanlian shudian, 1958.
Tekin, Talat. *A Grammar of Orkhon Turkic.* The Hague: Mouton and Co., 1968.
Wang Qinruo, et al., eds. *Cefu yuangui* (*Prime Tortoise of the Record Bureau*). Beijing: Zhonghua shuju, 2003.
Wei Shou. *Wei shu* (*Book of Wei*). Changchun: Jilin renmin chubanshe, 1995.
Wei Zheng, et al. *Sui shu* (*Book of Sui*). Beijing: Zhonghua shuju, 1973.
Wu Jing, ed. *Zhenguan zhengyao* (*Essentials of the Government of the Zhenguan Era*). Shanghai: Shanghai guji chubanshe, 1978.
Xiang Da. *Tangdai Chang'an yu xiyu wenming* (*Tang Dynasty Chang'an and the Culture of the Western Regions*). Shanghai: Sanlian shudian, 1957.
Xuanzang, dictated. *Da Tang xiyu ji* (*Great Tang Records on the Western Regions*). Transcribed by Bian Ji. Beijing: Wenxue guji kanxingshe, 1955.
Yao Runeng. *An Lushan shiji* (*Biographical Accounts of An Lushan*). Shanghai: Shanghai guji chubanshe, 1983.
Yue Shi. *Taiping huanyuji* (*Universal Geography of the Taiping Era*). Taipei: Wenhai chubanshe, 1963.

7 Local Products of the Turks

Historical documents about the Turks (*tujue*) in the Tang period describe the Turkish customs in detail, but contain little about local products. Except for "Marks for Horses from Foreign States" (*zhufan ma yin*) which provided a special record for horses, there are few references to local products. The same is true for the excavation of tombs in southern Siberia and Mongolia – the land where Turks used to live, where the unearthed relics were mostly horse harnesses and weapons, and there were few other artifacts. This makes it difficult for historians to assemble a comprehensive understanding of the nomadic life in the Turkic era.

But life inside the Turkish yurts can still be traced if we sift through historical sources, and knowledge about their unique local products can be gained. The following is a categorized description of Turkish products that I gleaned from history books and notes, and I hope it will be useful for future research.

Iron

Before the Turkic history was recorded, it had been believed that the Turks mastered the technique of making wrought iron. As recorded in the *Book of Sui – Records of the Turks* (*Suishu: Tujue zhuan*):

> The Turkic ancestors were mixed Hu people from Pingliang, under the surname of Ashina. After the Juqu tribe was subjugated by the Grand Emperor Wei [*Cao Cao*], the Ashina tribe of five hundred households moved to Ruru [Rouran Khaganate]. They lived in the Jinshan area for generations, good at producing iron tools.

After joining the Rouran Khaganate for protection, the Ashina tribe began to pay tribute with iron products. The ruler of the Rouran Khaganate, therefore, referred to them as "blacksmith slaves."[1] Even after the founding of their own country, this nomadic tribe was still renowned for "producing iron products." In early 568, a Byzantine delegation visited the Western Turkic Khaganate. When they "arrived at Kangju [Sogdiana], many Turks sold iron products to them. The famous historian Menander interpreted this as a message from the Turks to the envoys that their country was rich in iron mines."[2]

Within the Turkic Khaganate, Kirghiz 黠戛斯 had the richest deposits. After a heavy rainfall, some iron ore veins would be exposed, thus the saying that "iron rain falls from the sky." Volume 199 of the *Universal Geography of the Taiping Era* (*Taiping huanyu ji*) offers a reasonable explanation as follows:

> This place is rich in iron ores, some of which are exposed to the air after the torrential rain. As they become corrosion-resistant, they make the excellent material for sharp iron products. It does not make sense to say that iron falls from the sky, as that would definitely hurt both inhabitants and livestock. According to Jia Dan: "What is called meteoric iron comes from the Turkic Khaganate."

The Turks were good at producing iron products, particularly harnesses and weapons. In addition to iron stirrups and bridles, they were famous for making exquisite iron arrows of different types, which were widely used in hunting and fighting. As archaeologists have shown, in terms of shape, the iron arrows used by the ancient Turks can be divided into eight categories and 30 different types. In the first category called three-bladed whistling arrows, there were as many as ten types. Among the 220 iron arrows unearthed, 180 were whistling ones, accounting for 81% of the total.[3] They were popular in the ancient Turkic era and were highlighted in the historical records of the Tang period as standard military equipment. In the article "An Appeal to Yao Chong and Others to Start the Northern Expedition" ("Ming Yao Chong deng beifa zhi") written during the Xuanzong reign in the Tang dynasty, there is a line that reads "Mo Chuo [Qapaghan Qaghan] is tough and uncompromising, aided by whistling arrows produced in Langju."[4] Apparently, whistling arrows were seen as a clear indication that the Turks had invaded the Tang empire.

In terms of iron craftsmanship, although the Turks were good at producing iron arrows, they were not as good at making farming tools. During the Xianheng reign (670–673), when the captured Turks coming from "Liu Hu Zhou" were repatriated, Qapaghan Qaghan demanded "three thousand pieces of farming tools and about ten thousand *jin* [catties] of raw iron"[5] from Empress Wu Zetian to meet the need of farming settlement.

Apparently, the Turks who started their life by producing iron products were actually blacksmiths on the steppe. But their skill was one-sided, unable to make them stand out both in herding and husbandry, or farming and warfare.

Horses

Horses were also the regional specialty of the Turks. According to volume 73 of the *Institutional History of Tang* (*Tang huiyao*): "The Turkish horses are extremely well-trained, with excellent muscles and bones. They can reach very far, and are superb at hunting. They are called Taoyu in historical records." The quality and quantity of horses are an indication of the national power of the Turkic Khaganate. This is also stated in the *Old Book of Tang: Biography of Zheng Yuanshu* (*Jiu Tang shu: Zheng Yuanshu*): "The rise and fall of the Turks depended entirely on sheep and horses." Unsurprisingly, the wealth of the Turkic nobles was also measured by the number of horses they owned. For example, Kul Tigin, the brother of Bilge Qaghan had "four thousand male horses."

On the "exchange market" between the Turkic Khaganate and China, silk and horses were the most important trading goods. In 588:

> The heads of the Turkic tribes arranged to have about ten thousand horses, twenty thousand sheep, five hundred camels and five hundred cows on the national border. They sent envoys to China with the proposal that a trading center should be established along the border, which was approved by the emperor.[6]

Emperor Taizong of Tang, whose personal name was Li Shimin, was very familiar with Turkish war horses as he had fought his way to the throne on horseback. In the eighth month of 647, he made a "Bole-style"[7] comment on the famous horse that was gifted to him by the Kurykans:

> With the mere sight at this horse, you notice its large bones, and thick mane. Its eyes look like hanging mirrors, and its head is as square as a brick when viewed sidewise. The legs are like that of a deer but less round, and the neck is similar to that of a phoenix yet thinner. Underneath the hip, the bones rise to form peaks, and beneath the saddle, the veins are thick, strewn like petals on a flower. Judging by the ears which are sharp and strong as a beveled bamboo, you might say it is a Turkish horse, but its brawny tail which can almost dig out the bricks in the ground, shows a Korean origin. With a flat belly, and a small barrel, it is strong enough to run afar; and with a big nose, it does not pant when running.[8]

In times of peace, horses were traded on the exchange market for Chinese silk which benefited both countries. Emperor Xuanzong of Tang remarked in 721:

> When we were on good terms with the Turks, both countries enjoyed a happy time, with soldiers at rest, and traders busy. We bought the Turkish horses and sheep, and the Turks purchased our silk. We satisfied each other's need at a fair price.[9]

However, this situation did not last forever. When a trade deficit occurred, the Tang court felt pressure from the Turkic Khaganate. In 736, Emperor Xuanzong expressed his dissatisfaction with Yollig Khagan's dumping policy:

> During the reign of your father [Bilge Qaghan,] the number of horses traded each year was no more than three or four thousand. It was comparatively easier for us to handle such a manageable quantity. But now, on and off, you brought us 14,000 horses. As you have just been enthroned, and I have adopted you as my son, it is unwise to turn you down, so I have kept them

all. These horses are worth 500,000 bolts of silk. At present, we are in a time of national amnesty and the whole country is exempt from taxes, but our expenditure remains unchanged. As this trade does not serve the special purpose of a marriage alliance (*heqin*), and the quantity of silk fabric needed for the exchange of horses is huge, the delivery time is slightly delayed. Chuluo Dagan still stays with us. When you understand that he is not deliberately detained, you will be relieved. Now the transaction is back on, and shortly the silk fabric will be ready, and then Chuluo will return, which you can count on. Our place is like home to him, so what is the difference between going back and living here? In the future, when you plan to trade horses for silk, you should remember not to bring so many. It is better to follow your father's footsteps and make trading pacts with us. Anyway, a long-term trading relationship is not a one-day business.[10]

In the large-scale horse-for-silk trade, the total cost of horses reached the startling figure "500,000 bolts of silk." It is no wonder that Emperor Xuanzong, who was in the prime of his rule, had to ask his "Khagan son" to curb his appetite. Later, this trading situation deteriorated. By the time Bai Juyi wrote his poem "Yinshan Road" ("Yinshan dao"), it had become an unbearable financial burden for the Tang court: "Silk away and horses back, the business goes on and on, never ending."

Turkish Sparrow

Information about Turkish birds is rare, and thus, the related study is also limited. Fortunately, linguists have listed a number of bird names, offering us a glimpse into the bird world. In 1975, Dolores Habibovna Bazarova published an article entitled "Interpreting Names of Various Birds in the Ancient Turks,"[11] listing the following birds: crake, swan, Pallas's sandgrouse, magpie, ruddy shelduck, quail, lark, crow, swallow, sparrowhawk, chicken, crane, merlin, and owl. Of these birds, Pallas's sandgrouse was the only one mentioned in the Tang records related to the Turks. Living before the founding of the Turkic Khaganate, and still alive after the fall of the empire, sandgrouse is known by its nickname "Turkish sparrow" (Chinese name: Tujue que), enjoying fame as the "national bird."

Also known as chukar, partridge, or invading sparrow, Pallas's sandgrouse lives around the Gobi Desert. In his book *Sound and Meaning of All Sutras* (*Yiqiejing yinyi*), volume 73,[12] Shi Huilin provided a clear description:

As big as a dove, or a partridge, an invading sparrow (*duo*) looks like a hen pheasant. The feet look like that of a rat, but without a hind toe. It has a forked tail. When stirred, invading sparrows fly in flocks and they are active around the northern desert. Their meat tastes good. Commonly known as Turkish sparrows, they breed on grasslands.

In the ancient Turkic language, "Turkish sparrow" is spelt as kekälik or keklik. According to Bazarova, its pronunciation is derived from the bird's sound "kek,

138 *Local Products of the Turks*

kek", and it is still called кек илик in modern Kyrgyz. Beginning in the later years of Emperor Gaozong, Turkish sparrows became well known in the Tang period:

> After the reign of Tiaolu [679], a bird called invading sparrow or Turkish sparrow was found. It is as big as a dove, and has a color similar to a crow. When flying, it produces a sound like the wind. They like to fly in thousands. If they fly here, the Turks would come. This always proved to be true.[13]

Regarding how the border people thought of them, "Treatise on the Five Agents" ("Wuxing zhi") in the *Old Book of Tang*, volume 37, gives a clear clue:

> In 679, we were still in alliance with the Turks and no rebellion happened. Then suddenly, flocks of invading sparrows flew across the frontier fortress. There were so many of them that they almost covered the entire land. The border people were frightened and said: "When the Turkish sparrows fly south, the Turkic invaders are certain to come."

From then on, until the end of the Ming dynasty, for nearly a thousand years, "Turkish sparrows flying south" had become a warning sign, frightening the border people living along the Gobi Desert. Yang Shicong,[14] an examining editor (*jiantao*) of the Hanlin Academy (*Hanlin yuan*) in Chongzhen's reign (1627–1644) in the Ming period, wrote in the *Record of the Jade Hall* (*Yutang huiji*):

> There is a kind of bird outside the frontier fortress called sandgrouse which does not have a hind toe. From 1632 onwards, they were caught and sold on the market. Every time this kind of bird was spotted, there was a crisis along the border, so this sandgrouse is probably what people called Turkish sparrow in the past. In 1636, it was announced that there was an emergency along the border, yet no one in the court knew about it until an imperial edict was passed to the minister of war. As no guard was stationed there, there has been no information from that place. What a waste of value of these messenger birds!

The interaction between mankind and Turkish sparrows, although fairly superstitious, reveals the rise and fall of a dynasty. Clearly, misfortune or blessing is not decided by birds. As a matter of fact, after the Manchu rose to power from Manchuria, the sign of Turkish sparrows flying south was no longer an emergency warning, but a "sign of Mongolia's surrender":

> In the seventh year of Tiancong [1633], Pallas's sandgrouse flocked in Liaodong. Local people said: There is no such bird in Liaodong, and now these Mongolian birds have come, it must be a sign of the surrender of Mongolia. The following year, Chahar surrendered. In 1753 and 1754, for two consecutive winters, tens of thousands of such birds flew to the northwest part of the capital, and the next year Dzungar surrendered. He Tai'an

had a poem about this, the title of which is "A Poem about Turkish Sparrows" ("Tujue ji shi"): "These poor invading sparrows inhabit sandy areas, and yet they have full brownish features to fly in elegance. /Flocking twice to the capital to offer signs of good fortune, they are natural messengers ahead of a gifted person." Note: "A Turkish sparrow is actually a Pallas's sandgrouse, and it tastes like a hen pheasant."[15]

For ancient Chinese, Turkish sparrows were either interpreted as a warning shot or a sign of good fortune, corresponding to the change of dynasties. Underneath the dusty pages of history, there is an anthropological trace left by birds. What an amazing surprise that is!

Turkish Wine

The Turks were horse herders, and the beverage they drank is called kumiss. In "Records of the Turks" ("Tujue zhuan") of the *Universal Geography of the Taiping Era*, volume 196, it is stated that the Turks "drink beverage made from fermented cheese to get drunk." Before horse milk became drinkable, it had to be turned sour. Here is the Mongolian method recorded in *A Brief History of the Black Tatars* (*Heida shilue*):

> The colostrum is consumed by foals in the daytime, but at night, it is collected, filtered and then stored in a horse-hide bag. Kept for several nights, and constantly shaken until it tastes slightly sour, it will be good enough to drink. It is also called airag.

In the ancient Turkish language, "wine is called funi," and "daluobian is the wine vessel, which looks like a horn but is rather stubby."[16] "Funi" and "daluobian" were also two Turkic official titles. The Turks had a long history of drinking kumiss and followed a very interesting drinking etiquette. According to the *Book of Sui: Records of the Turks* (*Sui shu: Tujue zhuan*), when they drank, they would "call each other loudly." If we refer to the *Book of Sui: Records of the Ryukyu* (*Sui shu: Liuqiu zhuan*), we can get a rough idea about how nomadic people held their banquet:

> On the banquet, the person who holds the beverage bag must wait for his name to be called before he drinks, and the person who proposes a toast to the king also calls the king's name. People drink together, as the Turks do.

This quote explains what it means to "call each other loudly."

At the beginning of the 20th century, Paul Pelliot published two essays about the names of Turkish wines: "The Names of Wines in Odoric's Books" and "The Turkish Word for Wine – Funi."[17] According to Han Rulin's interpretation in *A Study of Turkic Official Titles* (*Tujue guanhao kaoshi*), in the ancient Turkish language, Funi was pronounced as bak-ni, the transcription of which is bagni, but this pronunciation is no longer heard in any Turkish dialect. However, this word can still be found in many ancient Turkish documents, for example, the Uyghur stone inscription of Shineusu in Mongolia, the Turkish documents discovered by Sir Marc Aurel Stein in Dunhuang, the *Complete Turkish Dictionary* edited by Mahmud Kashkarii in 1073, and the *Arabic-Turkic Lexicon* compiled by Ibn Muhanna. As for sources in other languages, besides the above-mentioned article "The Names of Wines in Odoric's Books," there is also Rashid al-Din's multi-volume book *Compendium of Chronicles*.[18]

Turkish Medicine

As ancient Turks were frequently involved in wars, medicines for stab wounds were quite necessary for them. Here is a valuable record by Li Shizhen, the author of the *Compendium of Materia Medica* (*Bencao gangmu*):

> Tujuebai, bitter in taste, is mainly used to treat injuries by metal objects. It helps to stop bleeding and grow new muscles, and it can also tonify the kidney and boost the reconnection of torn tendons. Originating from the Turks, it looks off-white and about grey, and it is said to be synthesized from lime and other medicines.[19]

As to how this medicine was applied in treatment, no description can be found in historical sources. However, after An Lushan castrated Li Zhu'er, he applied a kind of grey dressing on Li to stop his bleeding. That dressing was very close to Tujuebai. The following is taken from "Biographical Accounts of An Lushan" ("An Lushan zhuan") in the *Old Book of Tang*, volume 200:

> Li Zhu'er came from a Khitan tribe. When he was about ten years old, he started to serve An Lushan. He was a pretty sly page. After Lushan castrated him with a sharp knife, he lost a lot of blood and was about to die. Then Lushan applied ash on his wound. A day later, he recovered. As a eunuch, Li Zhu'er was favored by Lushan and was most trusted.

Li Zhu'er was An Lushan's most favored servant. He was castrated because Lushan wanted to turn him into a henchman. If there was no medicine available to stop his bleeding, Lushan would not have carried out the castration. As for the "ash" that was applied to the boy's wound, it seemed to be "synthesized from lime and other medicines." It seemed really effective, as it enabled a person who had lost several liters of blood to recover after a day. Although this example might not reveal what Tujuebai is, it provides some information about this medicine.

Turkish Yurt

Turkish yurt, a felt tent, was the dwelling place for nomads. This crown-like structure was a unique cultural feature for the inhabitants along the Gobi Desert in the Turkic era, marking its huge difference from agricultural civilization: "Relying on animal husbandry, the Turks follow water and grass, living a nomadic life in felt tents."²⁰ The following dialogue reflects the difference between the Turks and the Han Chinese:

> Lu Kai from Fanyang, the minister of rites (*libu shangshu* 礼部尚书) and minister of personnel (*libu shangshu* 吏部尚书), appointed Da Ye, his guest counselor to be the governor of Lanzhou. Ye declined by asking, "What wrong did I do so you would send me off to be neighboring the Turks by a single wall?" Kai was surprised, "How could the Turks have a wall?" Ye replied, "Meat is their staple food, ice is their main source of drink, and yurt is their house which is walled by felts."²¹

One of the ancient rock paintings about a Turkish yurt found in the Yin Mountains vividly illustrates what is meant by the saying "yurt is their house which is walled by felts." Chiseled on a rock at the top of the Bulhada Mountain in the Urad Rear Banner, the painting shows a Turkish tent much higher than today's Mongolian ger. With skylights on the top, this yurt has a latticework of wood for walls, on one of which a door is made. With thick ropes to horizontally bind two different sections, the latticed space is divided into three parts, making the yurt spacious enough for easy access.²²

For a better understanding of the Turkish yurt, we may refer to the tent structure of later nomads:

> There are two types of yurts. The one popular in Yanjing, is made of willow wood so that it is easy to be rolled up, just like the screen used in the southern areas. On the front, the yurt has a door; on the top, it is shaped like an umbrella, but with a skylight. On the surface, it is covered by felts which can be taken down and put on a horseback. The second type, the one commonly used on the grasslands, has a fixed ring of willow wood and is covered with felt fabric which cannot be rolled up. This type of yurt needs to be loaded onto a cart and carried away when water dries up and grass withers. [As to when people need to move away,] there is no fixed time schedule.²³

The cart on which a felt tent is loaded is probably a "Turkish tent cart."²⁴ From the above quote, it can be inferred that the second type was long in use among the Turks. This mobile equipment was also one of the "loads" that the Turkish soldiers carried along to serve their camping purpose in the Tang period.

With animal husbandry and hunting as the main modes of production, handicraft industries such as iron forging, winemaking, and tent-cart assembling as the auxiliary forms of production, the Turkic herdsmen displayed a good mastery of "grassland craftsmanship," proving that they did not live a dull and monotonous life, as was commonly assumed. The famous verse recited by generations of Chinese readers, "when the wind blows and grass lowers, cows and sheep can be seen," indeed epitomizes the main characteristics of nomadic animal husbandry. If we take into consideration records of local products, we can see its rich economic meaning that goes beyond its surface simplicity.

Notes

1. See the *Book of Zhou: Records of the Turks* (*Zhou shu: Tujue zhuan*).
2. Chavannes, 1935: 168.
3. Khudyakov, *Arms of Medieval Nomads of Southern Siberia and Central Asia*, 1985: 149. See also his essay "Iron Arrowheads from Mongolia," 1985: 96–114.
4. Li Fang, et al., vol. 459.
5. "Records of the Turks" ("Tujue zhuan") in the *New Book of Tang* (*Xin Tang shu*), vol. 215.
6. "Records of the Turks" ("Tujue zhuan") in the *History of the North* (*Bei shi*), vol. 99.
7. Bole was a famous connoisseur of horses in the Spring and Autumn period. Now Bole is used in Chinese to refer to someone who is good at spotting a talented person and functioning as a mediator. —Trans.
8. Wang Pu, vol. 27.
9. Wang Qinruo, et al., vol. 980.
10. See "To the Turkic Khans" ("Chi Tujue kehan shu") in the *Collected Works of Zhang Qujiang* (*Zhang Qujiang ji*), vol. 6.
11. Bazarova, 11–22.
12. See also an entry entitled "Shuangduo" in volume 99.
13. Here is a quote from the *Record of the Imperial Court and Beyond* (*Chaoye qian zai*). See Yue Shi, vol. 139.
14. Yang Shicong (1597–1648), born in Jining, was a scholar who passed the imperial examination in the fourth year of Chongzhen [1631]. The *Record of the Jade Hall* (*Yutang huiji*) was finished in the 12th month of the 16th year of Chongzhen [1643], just about a hundred days before the fall of the Ming dynasty. It is a book of concern about the nation's fate.
15. Yang Zhongxi, vol. 5.
16. Du You, vol. 197.
17. See Pelliot, *Le Nom du vin dans Odoric de Pordenone*, TP. 1914. Also Pelliot, *Le mot bigni (ou begni) "vin" en turc*, TP, 1926.
18. Han Rulin, 1982: 310–311.
19. Li Shizhen, vol. 18: 1307.
20. "Records of the Turks" ("Tujue zhuan") in the *Book of Sui* (*Sui shu*), vol. 84.
21. See Li Fang, et al., vol. 173.
22. See figure 700 in Gai Shanlin's book *Petroglyphs in the Yinshan Mountains*, 382.
23. See Peng Daya, *A Brief History of the Black Tatars* (*Heida shilue*), particularly the entry about "Yurts," annotated by Xu Ting.
24. "Records of the Shiwei" ("Shiwei zhuan") in the *Book of Sui*, vol. 84.

Bibliography

Bazarova, Dolores Habibovna. "Interpreting Names of Various Birds in the Ancient Turks." [In Russian.] *The Soviet Turkology* 4 (1975): 11–22.

Chavannes, Édouard. *Documents on the Western Turks*. Translated by Feng Chengjun. [In Chinese.] Beijing: Shangwu yinshuguan, 1935.

Du You, ed. *Tongdian* (*Comprehensive Institutions*). Beijing: Zhonghua shuju, 1988.

Gai Shanlin. *Yinshan yanhua* (*Petroglyphs in the Yinshan Mountains*). Beijing: Wenwu chubanshe, 1986.

Han Rulin. *Qionglu ji* (*Ethnic Minorities Living in Yurts*). Shanghai: Shanghai renmin chubanshe, 1982.

Khudyakov, Yuliy Sergeyevich. *Arms of Medieval Nomads of Southern Siberia and Central Asia*. [In Russian.] Novosibirsk: Nauka, 1985.

Khudyakov, Yuliy Sergeyevich. "Iron Arrowheads from Mongolia," in *Early Cultures of Mongolia*. [In Russian.] Edited by Ruslan Sergeyevich Vasilyevsky. Novosibirsk: Nauka, 1985. 96–114.

Li Fang, et al., eds. *Taiping guangji* (*Extensive Records of the Taiping Era*). Beijing: Zhonghua shuju, 1961.

Li Fang, et al., eds. *Wenyuan Yinghua* (*Finest Blossoms in the Garden of Literature*). Beijing: Zhonghua shuju, 1966.

Li Shizhen. *Bencao gangmu* (*Compendium of Materia Medica*). Beijing: Renmin weisheng chubanshe, 1985.

Li Yanshou. *Beishi* (*History of the North*). Beijing: Zhonghua shuju, 1974.

Linghu Defen, et al., eds. *Zhou shu* (*Book of Zhou*). Beijing: Zhonghua shuju, 1971.

Liu Xu, et al., eds. *Jiu Tang shu* (*Old Book of Tang*). Beijing: Zhonghua shuju, 1975.

Ouyang Xiu, et al., eds. *Xin Tang shu* (*New Book of Tang*). Beijing: Zhonghua shuju, 1975.

Peng Daya and Xu Ting. *Heida shilue* (*A Brief History of the Black Tatars*). Shanghai: Shangwu yinshuguan, 1937.

Shi Xuanying and Shi Huilin, eds. *Yiqiejing yinyi* (*Sound and Meaning of All Sutras*). Shanghai: Shanghai guji chubanshe, 1986.

Su Mian, et al., eds. *Tang huiyao* (*Institutional History of Tang*). Shanghai: Shangwu yinshuguan, 1936.

Wang Qinruo, et al., eds. *Cefu yuangui* (*Prime Tortoise of the Record Bureau*). Beijing: Zhonghua shuju, 2003.

Wei Zheng, et al., eds. *Sui shu* (*Book of Sui*). Beijing: Zhonghua shuju, 1973.

Yang Shicong. *Yutang huiji* (*Record of the Jade Hall*). Beijing: Zhonghua shuju, 1985.

Yang Zhongxi. *Xueqiao shihua yuji* (*Poetry Criticism of Xueqiao*). Beijing: Beijing guji chubanshe, 1992.

Yue Shi. *Taiping huanyuji* (*Universal Geography of the Taiping Era*). Taipei: Wenhai chubanshe, 1963.

Zhang Jiuling. *Zhang Qujiang ji: Chi Tujue kehan shu* (*Collected Works of Zhang Qujiang: To the Turkic Khans*). Shanghai: Shangwu yinshuguan, 1946.

8 Tracing the History of Pugs

In the Tang period, a new breed of dog called "wozi," which is later known as the pug, was introduced from the Western Regions. From a royal tribute to a folk pet, wozi has left traces in historical documents, cultural relics, and poems.

In *Chen Yinke's Poems* (*Chen Yinke shiji*), there is an untitled seven-syllable poem (*qilv*) written in 1954. This poem is impressive and has a profound meaning. Right below it, Chen added an intriguing long note of more than 70 words on wozi:

> *The Unofficial Biography of Yang Taizhen* (*Taizhen waizhuan*) has a description about pugs from Samarkand. They are known as "Pekingese" to foreigners, and "pugs" to us Chinese. They are also mentioned in Yuan Zhen's two poems "Dream of Wandering in Spring" ("Meng you chun") and "Spring Dawn" ("Chun xiao") where we read these two lines - "the cute puppy still looks angry in his sleep 娇娃睡犹怒" and "when the puppy snorts, the bell rings too 猧儿撼起钟声动." The pets mentioned here are wozi, and "娃 [wá] (human baby)" in "Dream of Wandering in Spring" should be "猧 [wō](pug)." Some ignorant person gave the wrong spelling in his so-called revision.

This serious-sounding note, aside from explanations and corrections, has a dual structure of classical and contemporary interpretations, given Chen's research style as evident in two of his articles entitled "Reading 'Lament for the South'" ("Du 'ai jiangnan fu'") and "On 'Reincarnation'" ("Lun 'zaisheng yuan'"). For the contemporary one, it is related to the "Redology" turmoil[1] that swept the Chinese academia in 1954. As there have been some vague allusions about it, it won't be the focus of my discussion here. As for the classical one, by means of cultural research, we can trace the history of pugs back to more than a thousand years ago, from the time when they were tributary animals offered by the states in the Western Regions in the seventh century, and then were localized and commercialized during the Tang, Song, Yuan, Ming, and Qing periods, to their present status as an ordinary house pet. Like the Chinese lion, the pug is listed as one of the "Chinese cultural icons," witnessing the cultural exchange between China and its western neighbors. Yet, as few scholars have paid attention to this cultural mirror, what really happened during this long period remains hidden underneath the dust of history.

Wozi originated from the Eastern Roman Empire, namely, the Byzantine empire, which was called "Daqin" or "Fulin" in the Tang period. According to "Records of Gaochang" ("Gaochang zhuan") in the *Old Book of Tang* (*Jiu Tang shu*), volume 198:

> In the seventh year of the Wude Emperor [624], Qu Wentai offered a pair of dogs as tributes, one male and one female, both about six *cun* high and one *chi*[2] long. Assumed to come from Fulin, these dogs were remarkably intelligent, capable of chasing horses and holding candles. This marked the beginning of the "Fulin dog" in China.

Located in the Turpan Basin in Xinjiang, the state of Gaochang was a protectorate of the Tang empire, offering yearly tributes to the latter, including dogs. The silk painting named "Two Kids"[3] unearthed in Astana, Turpan county in 1972, which vividly shows a child on the left side holding a black wozi, could be regarded as the evidence of the Fulin dog's early arrival in China. As for the wozi that Imperial Consort Yang cuddled and petted in the harem, although it was also a kind of Fulin dog, it was actually a tribute from Samarkand, a city-state in Central Asia. As stated in a historical source, in 724, Samarkand offered "two horses and two dogs" and continued offering tributes until the Tianbao reign (742–756).

Before Yue Shi (930–1007) in the Song period wrote his book *The Unofficial Biography of Yang Taizhen* (*Yang Taizhen wai zhuan*), Wang Renyu's book *Anecdotes of the Kaiyuan and Tianbao Periods* (*Kaiyuan tianbao yishi*) completed in the period of the Five Dynasties and Ten Kingdoms had given a detailed description about how "a wozi disrupted the chess game":

> One day, Emperor Ming of Tang [685–762] played chess with one of his kings, accompanied by a famous musician He Huaizhi playing Chinese lute in solo. Imperial Consort Yang stood aside and watched the game. When the emperor was about to lose, Yang set loose the wozi and allowed it to run on the chessboard so that the game was messed up, which made the emperor very happy.

This kind of naughty puppy was a common "buffoon" in the harem. "Palace Verse" (*Gong ci*) written by Wang Ya, an "imperial scholar" (*jinshi*) during the Zhenyuan reign, is quite evocative in describing its loveliness, "A snow-white pug drags on the ground as it walks / Used to sleeping on the red carpet with no fears." This lively image of a pet dog can also be found in Zhou Fang's famous painting "Ladies Wearing Flowers in Their Hair." Following the imperial fashion, the nobles in the outer court also kept wozi as their pet. In the *Extensive Records of the Taiping Era* (*Taiping guangji*), volume 386, there is a quote taken from the *Mysterious Strange Record* (*Xuan guai lu*) which goes like this: "Lu Xu, the governor of Mingzhou (now in Yongping, Hebei province) had an aunt on his mother's side. This aunt had an adorable wozi named Flowery, and she cared a lot for it." In the famous quatrain "A Dog Separated from its Master" ("*Quan li zhu*") written by Xue Tao, a socialite lady during the Shu Han Kingdom [221–263], a wozi becomes the tool to vent the sadness of an abandoned woman:

> Behind crimson gates for four or five years, it has been trained to be obedient,
> its sweet-smelling coat and clean feet won the master's heart.
> For no reason at all, it bit a dearly beloved friend and acted deviant,
> no more is it allowed to sleep upon the red silk rug, looking jubilant.

For this gifted social butterfly, bemoaning her own situation in terms of a dog's experience cannot be viewed as self-degradation, because at her time no other animal but this extraordinary dog was capable of gaining the owner's affection after being disfavored.

The above anecdotes in the Tang period indicate that, after they were introduced to Chang'an by Gaochang officials, the Fulin dogs, either through breeding or importation, had been raised in different areas of China, and around the eighth and ninth centuries, they reached as far as Chengdu in Sichuan province and Yongping in Hebei province. But, how to keep a wozi "white, clean, and fragrant"? Was it done by spraying the dog with "rose water" from the Western Regions, or was it done through other means? Due to the lack of records, there is no way to figure it out.

In the middle of the 10th century, when Zhao Kuangyin set up the Northern Song dynasty in Bianjing (now Kaifeng, Henan province), there were also traces of wozi in the imperial palace. Song Bai, an "imperial scholar" in the reign of Emperor Taizu of Song, had a palace poem that reads:

> Spring night sees a palace girl in a thin dress of gauze,
> the bell rings when no wind is found to be the cause.
> Underneath the bead curtain lies a wozi in his day sleep,
> shaded by a scarlet banana is the lady who gazes at green leaves in the haws.

By drawing the picture of a wozi and a palace girl on one spring night, this poem conveys a sense of peace and tranquility. Emperor Taizong of the Song dynasty, who ruled for 20 peaceful years (976–997), was a big fan of wozi dogs. When alive, he enjoyed their companionship; after his death, they were arranged to guard his mausoleum. In the *Events on Poetry of the Song Period* (*Songshi jishi*), volume two, one of Li Zhi's poems "Song of the Dog Named Peach-blossom" ("Cheng xiushi qian shilang taohua quan ge") goes as follows:

> Inside the imperial palace, there is a dog named Peach-blossom,
> with a golden bell hung from the deep red silk around her neck to add charm.
> Well trained and sensitive,
> she echoed the late emperor in a manner quite intuitive.
> Before the bead curtain rolled sideways, or the paper fan was thumbed open,
> wagging her tail, Peach-blossom had already arrived in one swift motion.
> Sleeping by the flower patch on quiet nights,
> she sat close to the imperial bed in the morning for a couple of bites.

On beautiful days of gorgeous clouds, she can easily find her way,
with breeze blowing through the scented grass, she barks occasionally [as if she has something to say].

This understanding dog, as a rare breed, was given special treatment in the Harem of the Northern Song dynasty. Not only did she stay "close to the imperial bed" but also she had "a golden bell hung from the deep red silk around her neck to add charm." Obviously, she was more brilliant than her "fragrant and clean" ancestors. Although Taizong was not a mediocre and ruthless monarch, his excessive adoration for dogs did not bode well for the dynasty's future.

After the Mongols entered China, they took Beijing as the capital. With the change of life from domes to palaces, they were going through an accelerated process of urbanization. Of the ethnic groups in the Yuan dynasty, "Semu" from the Western Regions rose to be the elites and some of them were immersed in all kinds of sensuous pleasures including horses, dogs, lust, and banquets, leading a luxurious and corrupted life. In the *Records of Discontinuing Farming in Nan Village* (*Nancun chuogeng lu*), volume 24, Tao Zongyi described the "grand gathering" in the Yuan period as follows:

Every time when an imperial banquet was hosted to treat the kings and ministers, there was a "a grand gathering." On this day, some fierce beasts would be shown as a spectacle at the Wansuishan [Longevity Hill]. After tigers, leopards, bears, and elephants were led out one by one, there were the lions which were so small in size that they resembled exactly those golden-haired lapdogs that ordinary people kept at home.

Here, the "grand gathering" was also an exposition of beasts. From the way Tao Zongyi described the rare lions – comparing "the beast of the imperial court" to a folk pet – the "golden-haired lapdogs," we can see that these lapdogs had already entered the life of common people in the Yuan period.

These "golden-haired lapdogs" were actually pugs, often seen in the variety play (*zaju*) of the Yuan period. In their co-authored book *A Thorough Explanation of Qu and Ci of the Song, Jin, Yuan, Ming and Qing Dynasties* (*Song Jin Yuan Ming Qing quci tongshi*), Wang Xueqi and Wang Jingzhu listed the following occasions when a pug is mentioned.

In Meng Hanqing's play *The Moheluo Doll* (*Moheluo*), Act 2, there is a line that goes like this: "A red door, a green window, a curtain made of mottled bamboo hanging on the door, and a pug lying under the curtain."

In Zheng Guangzu's play *The Battle of Hulao Pass* (*Hulao Sanzhan Lvbu*), Act 1, we read: "There are two leading flags in front of the tent, each bearing the image of a pug."

In an anonymous play entitled *Tactics in a Series* (*Lianhuan ji*), Act 2 has this sentence: "If I lie, I'll be turned into a pug."

In *A Tale of the Fisherman and the Woodcutter* (*Yuqiao ji*), another anonymous play, Act 2 mentions, "Oops, *Lian'er*, *Pan'er*, chicken-head, pug, thorny plum, and bird's beak[4], listen to me, our lord is coming back. Let us greet him."

According to Fang Linggui, the word "哈叭 [hābā](pug)" is the transcription of a Mongolian word "*qaba*" (*-n, -ng*), which means "doggie."[5] As a loanword in the Chinese language, it has been widely used for more than 700 years. But during the Ming period, everything concerned with the Hu people became a taboo; therefore, "haba" was changed into "xièbā." But in his book *Tea Room Notes* (*Chaxiang shi congchao*), volume 23, Yu Yue claimed that among the folks, xieba rather than "haba" was used. As transcription involves different choices of words, this is still debatable.

The replacement of "haba" with "xieba" happened at the beginning of the Ming period when an order was issued to eradicate the old Hu-related customs from the Yuan period. In 1368, Emperor Zhu Yuanzhang issued an imperial order to forbid the Hu style of dress, language, and revoke the Hu surnames.[6] Firm and resolute, the edict shocked the whole country. Amid the anti-Hu hustle and bustle, what became of pugs? From the literature of that period, we know that they were not totally rooted out. But whether they were treated well and lived an easy life is difficult to verify. Yet, there is evidence that they were still favored by eunuchs in the late Ming period. This can be affirmed by Liu Ruoyu's book *A Palace History of the Ming* (*Ming gongshi*). In the entry entitled "Directorate for Imperial Temples" ("Shen'gongjian"), there is a sentence that reads: "During the reign of the Wanli Emperor (1573–1620), a eunuch named Du Yong kept a xieba which was really adorable."

According to job specification in the Directorate for Imperial Temples, Du Yong was responsible for sweeping the floor and lighting the lamps at the Imperial Ancestral Temple, and this made it possible for his beloved dog to play around the solemn palace. As for pugs outside of the imperial city, Tian Yiheng detailed the features, quantity, and origins of Hangzhou wozi in the late Ming period in the *Miscellaneous Records of the Social Customs of the Ming Dynasty* (*Liuqing rizha*), volume 30:

> Today's short-legged dogs are the variant of ancient pugs. After crossbreeding with Chinese dogs, they have grown taller. In Hangzhou, there are plenty of stirrup dogs, about four or five *cun* long, so small that they can be hidden in the stirrups. […] The smallest pair, purple-haired and lovely, are kept by a provincial graduate (*juren*) named Shen Renwen. He got them as a gift from Grand Secretary Xu (*Xu gelao*).

"Grand Secretary Xu" – Xu Guangqi (1562–1633) held himself really high, yet he kept pugs at home and gifted Shen with a pair, indicating that in the late Ming period, scholars both in Beijing and Hangzhou picked up this hobby. This social fashion is also depicted in artistic works. For instance, Xu Lin's play *The Story of Embroidered Ru* (*Xiuru ji*), volume 31, describes a presented panache of "riding a piebald horse, followed by a xieba"; and in the 50th volume of *Journey to the West* (*Xiyou ji*), there is also a fictional scene: "A haba [pug] ran out from behind him and barked furiously at the Monkey King."

During the Qing period, the fashion of keeping pugs was more prevalent than ever before, and its golden age appeared during the 17th and the 18th centuries. From the north to the south, there co-existed three breeding centers: Beijing,

Yangzhou, and Canton, where pet dogs were sold to the Han people, the Manchu people, and foreigners. On the market, pugs were tradable for a fair price, and pug-owning was completely commercialized.

Beijing

In the second volume of *Casual Remarks North of the Pond* (*Chibei outan*), Wang Shizhen (1634–1711), a famous poet in the Qing period, wrote down his experience at a temple fair in Beijing during the Kangxi period:

> I once saw a Persian dog on the market at the Ciren si [Benevolence Temple]. It was less than one *chi* high, with fur as smooth as that of a brown sable. Its ears pricked up, mouth pointy and legs very short, with a thick woolen cloth covering its back. The seller said it knew hundreds of tricks and bid 50 silver ingots for it.

Referring to its history, Wang added that it was "the offspring of those peach-blossom dogs during the Taizong Emperor's reign."

Li Zhensheng, in *Bamboo Ballads for Acrobatics* (*Baixi zhuzhi ci*), a book about social customs during the Kangxi reign, introduced the acrobatic skills of dogs in the preface entitled "Pugs": "These small dogs are taught to arch the paws as if to greet people, or produce a certain sound as if they were singing, or are trained to run through metal loops which is called 'dog looping.'"

This kind of pug that "knew hundreds of tricks" and could do acrobatics on the street was well known to people. It is no wonder that in the 37th chapter of *Dream of the Red Chamber* (*Honglou meng*), when Skybright and Ripple make fun of Flower Aroma, they ridicule her as "a flowery pug from the Western world."

The late Qianlong and early Jiaqing eras saw more pugs than the Kangxi period, but the price of dogs did not drop. In *New Poems for Today* (*Rixia xin'ou*), below the line "On the colorful bamboo sheet lies an adorable Fulin flowery dog," Huang Zhutang added this note: "The tiny Fulin dog has become a local speciality of the capital city, with the good breed selling for more than ten silver ingots each. Some owners care more about them than their kids." The note not only points out the fact that Fulin dogs were localized but also discloses the bizarre mentality of "valuing dogs more than humans," thereby admonishing people not to pay excessive attention to amusement.

Localized pugs were the pet of noble families in the late Qing period. In Chen Shizeng's famous picture book "Beijing Custom" ("Beijing fengsu"), a poem is attached to the 16th painting entitled "A Young Woman in Manchu Dress" ("Qizhuang shaofu") revealing the fashion of that time:

> Much goes to the design and sewing of a new set of dress,
> a light red shirt matching skillful make-up is no less.
> Followed by a bell-hanging pug,
> she enjoys her after-meal time by smoking a cigarette and strolling through the market at an easy pace.

Affection for wozi is also found in the second volume of *Fishermen's Song of the East China Sea* (*Donghai yuge*) authored by Gu Taiqing, a famous Manchu noblewoman and writer of the Song lyric (*ci*). In one piece entitled "The Tune of Silk Washing – Ode to Shuanghuan" ("Huanxisha – Yong shuanghuan wo'er"), the depiction of a wozi is vivid and full of emotion:

> Held in arms or hidden in a sleeve with care,
> the puppy has two fluffy ears hanging with a pair of golden bells.
> "Annular buns [Shuanghuan]" is a fitting nickname matching her hair.
> When bamboo leaves cast shadows on the curtain, disrupting the image
> of the moon,
> she barks at the flare, which silhouettes the flowers against the screen
> wall so well.
> Not until late at night does she fall into a sleep next to my pillow, light and fair.
>
> Gentle and simple,
> she is charming and clever.
> To be a delight is its nature forever.
> In slumber, she seems to be posturing for a painting,
> at play, the tiny body to be lifted high is a thing.
> Not yet mature, she fails to make a full sound when learning to bark, which is
> really entertaining.

After Shuanghuan died, the bereaved owner commemorated her pet dog by writing another piece entitled "The Tune of Courtyard Full of Fragrance – Epigraph for the Burial of Shuanghuan" ("Mantingfang – Yi Huan ming"):

> The moon is not full,
> the cloud is scattered,
> they knew what a grieved situation I am in.
> Why would this happen to me?
> Is it because you were a too lovely thing?
> Still remember your simple and innocent look,
> with the golden bells hanging and jingling.
> At the dressing table,
> putting on make-up,
> I cannot rid the memory of you, this little being.
>
> A strong wind brought the pain,
> As if your life was snatched away by an invisible chain.
> For such a fleeting time that we were together,
> then you left me and drifted on another plain.
> The owner's eyes are drying up and the tears wouldn't stop like rain.
> Too sad to approach the poplar tree underneath which you were buried,
> as the green grass becomes a sad scene.

At the corner of the railing,
I gathered a cup of yellow earth, and with a tablet of inscription,
for your death, I built a shrine.

As mentioned above, the tiny pug that could be hidden in the sleeve was commonly known as a "shoe dog" and was regarded as a "mini treasure" on Beijing's pet markets. In the late Qing period, to satisfy the curiosity of those "palace people," dog dealers in Beijing did not hesitate to manipulate the breeding of dogs so that an extremely small-sized "shoe dog" could be bred:

> In 1900–1901, a foreigner traveled from Beijing to Shanghai, carrying three "shoe dogs" for sale. Declaring that he got them from inside the imperial palace, he bid a hundred silver ingots for them. They were actually the products of manipulated breeding. First, an ordinary pug is fed with meals that contain cinnabar so that it might give birth to a baby dog that is smaller in size when it grows up. Then, this baby dog is raised the way its mother was fed so that next generation is even smaller. After three and four generations, they are as small as shoes. Sold to those "palace people," these dogs can fetch a very high price.[7]

In her book *Imperial Incense* (*Yuxiang piaomiao lu*), Princess Der Ling offered a detailed description about the royal dog stables (*Yuquan jiu*) attended by four eunuchs and about Empress Dowager Cixi's obsessive affection for pugs, so no further explanation is needed here.

Yangzhou

Located at the confluence of the Yangtze River and the Huai River, Yangzhou has been known as the "Famed City East of the Huai River" since the Song period and functioned as the base for the "Lianghuai Salt Administration" in the Qing period, enjoying wealth and fame in southeastern China. For the inhabitants of Yangzhou during the 18th century, one of the leisure activities was "raising little tiger-headed dogs." As Lin Lanchi stated in the eighth volume of *Three Hundred Songs of the Hanjiang River* (*Hanjiang sanbai yin*):

> There are different types of dogs, among which the tiger-headed is the most vigorous. People in Yangzhou mostly buy pugs from Beijing. They pick up the ones that are agile, in particular those resembling a tiger. Then they raise them in a secret place. In terms of the size, the smaller ones are more valued.

As shown here, people in Yangzhou preferred a "vigorous, agile, and small" pug when they shopped for dogs in Beijing.

Jin Nong (1687–1763), one of the "Eight Eccentrics of Yangzhou," was also a dog lover. He was a hermit, a man of peculiar style, and disdainful of officialdom. In the *Yangzhou Art Gallery Records* (*Yangzhou huayuan lu*), volume three,

Wang Jun detailed the close bond between this outstanding painter and his pet dog "Magpie" as follows: "He had a dog of foreign breed named Magpie and he fed it with meat every time. When Magpie died, he cried and wrote a poem for it." His grief was so genuine that this story spread among his peers. For example, Yuan Mei, a famous poet, mentioned Jin Nong's mourning for his dog in his poem "The Portrait of Mr. Dongxin" ("Ti Dongxin xiansheng xiang"): "sometimes talking with a chicken, sometimes writing a poem for his dog." [8]

Canton

In the Qing period, the most famous pug owner in Canton was Shang Zhixin, the son of Shang Kexi who was the king of Pingnan. Shang Zhixin had a "doghouse" where he kept "Guandong hounds and tiny pugs." He also had an "insect house," a "house for canaries and sparrows," and a "house for eagles and hawks," all on the sandy land at the foot of the Yuexiu Mountain. These pets were well taken care of and meticulously attended to by servants. "Some dogs were called 'Xianggong [lord],' and others 'Xiaoge [cute big brother].' Every day, eunuchs dressed them with embroidered clothes and took them to the downtown area to show them off." [9] It was not hard to imagine, under the bloody rule of the king of Pingnan, how ordinary people in Canton would shun these dogs when they saw "cute big brothers" taken for an outing.

In 1680, there was a "withdrawal of power from kings" and Shang Zhixin was given an imperial order to commit suicide. After that, his doghouse was also closed. Then in 1685, when the Maritime Customs office was established in Guangdong, more foreigners came. With their arrival, dogs of foreign breeds also came, thus making the Thirteen Hongs a new center of pet animals. Xu Chenglie, whose art name was Qingliang Daoren, gave the following description in his book *Chronicle of Hall of Raindrops* (*Tingyu xuan biji*):

> I saw several pairs of foreign breed dogs at the Thirteen Hongs. They look like giant eggplants, not much different from ordinary newborn baby dogs. Their colors are black, white, or pale brown. Wagging tails and shaking heads, they are well tamed. It is worth 20 to 30 yuan per pair in foreign cash.

In 1782, Zeng Qiru, a provincial graduate (*juren*) from Jiaxiang, Shandong province, also saw a foreign "short-legged dog" at the Dutch factory in Canton.[10] It is possible that dogs traded in foreign currency at that time were imported directly from Macau, and they were of the same species as pugs. The only difference is that one came from the Western Regions, and the other came from the South China Sea. This is also what Qu Dajun (1630–1696) claimed long ago in his book *A New Encyclopedia of Guangdong* (*Guangdong xinyu*), volume 21, "Macau has many dogs of foreign breed. They are short and small, with hair resembling that of a lion, worth about 10 silver ingots." As for the traits of various types of foreign dogs, the second volume of the *Local Chronicle of Macau* (*Aomen jilue*) has a detailed record for reference.

Finally, a few words about pugs in artistic works. A famous poet named Wang Yan from the Southern Song period once wrote a poem entitled "For Consultant Xu's Painting 'A Tang Person Bathing her Child'" ("Ti Xu canyi suo cang tangren yu'er tu")[11] which has a line of praise about the dog: "A gorgeous dog enjoys being cuddled and petted, so familiar is it with people that no fear or misgivings can be found." Although pugs were painted long ago, it was the Guangdong painters in the Qing period that first discussed their aesthetic value in paintings. Zheng Ji, a well-known southern scholar from Xinhui during the Jiaqing and Daoguang periods, proposed a new idea in his book *A Comprehensive Guide to Painting* (*Menghuanju huaxue jianming*). The following is what he wrote in a chapter entitled "On Animals" ("Lun qinshou"):

> As domestic animals, dogs are of different shapes. There is one kind of tall foreign breed dog which is three *chi* high like a pony, either black, white or livid, and there is also a kind of small dog, with hair as long as that of a lion, which is even more adorable in paintings. This small dog has a head like a gourd, and its ears are like a clamshell. Its belly is big on the front and small on the rear, and its tail wags up and down. For the small dog, although there are varieties, mostly they are of two types: solid-haired and fluffy-haired. They can be painted in the same way as one draws a lion or a horse.

Here, Zheng clearly states that foreign-breed dogs can be subjects for Chinese paintings, and he gives detailed suggestions about techniques and shapes. In a certain sense, it is not an overstatement to say that this was the first time that a "painterly style" was created for pugs.

Since the Tang period, wozi became a favored pet of the Chinese people. As to why this was the case, the word Zheng Ji used above might provide a clue, "adorable." Unlike guard dogs, hunt dogs, or load-bearing snow dogs, pugs might be categorized as one of the "useless" breeds, if utility is taken as the standard of judgment. However, in the past or in the present, they have been adored. Like the goldfish or the parrot, the pug as an ornamental animal has a symbolic value that is scarcely seen in other ordinary dogs. They stirred up human emotions, and attracted harem beauties or literati who enjoyed their shape, sensed something of their wisdom, and were enchanted by their "neither close nor distant" attachment to their owners. As objects of empathy, they played a unique role that cannot be replaced by any other breeds. The Fulin dogs from the Western Regions, although not much help with the national livelihood, brought pleasure to the Chinese people. It is in this sense that the pug has become a cultural wonder in China and has been endorsed by both scholars and ordinary people for thousands of years. But of course, from the perspective of economics, as Thorstein Veblen pointed out in *The Theory of the Leisure Class*, raising this breed of dog is actually a manifestation of conspicuous consumption by the privileged class.

Tracking the history of pugs was a "long time" effort that involved five dynasties including the Tang, Song, Yuan, Ming, and Qing. The related information is scattered or even lost, like copper coins dropping to the ground and rolling away

Table 8.1 Names of Pugs in Different Dynasties

Dynasty	Name	Region/City
Tang	Fulin gou [Fulin Dog]	Gaochang
	Kangguo wozi [Pug from Samarkand]	Chang'an
	Baixue woer [Snow-white pug]	Chang'an
	Huazi [Flowery]	Mingzhou
Song	Wozi [Pug]	Bianjing
	Taohua quan [Peach-blossom dog]	Bianjing
Yuan	Jinmao naogou [Golden-haired lapdog]	Dadu
	Haba gou'er [Pug]	Haozhou
Ming	Xieba xiaogou [Xieba dog]	Beijing
	Ai pa gou [Short-legged dog]	Hangzhou
	Madeng gou [Stirrup dog]	Hangzhou
Qing	Bosi quan [Persian dog]	Beijing
	Haba gou [Pug]	Beijing
	Xiyang hua'dian'zi haba gou [Flowery pug from the West]	Beijing
	Fulin hua [Fulin flowery dog]	Beijing
	Xie gou [Shoe dog]	Beijing
	Hutou gou [Tiger-headed dog]	Yangzhou
	Yang gou [Foreign dog]	Yangzhou
	Haba xi gou [Tiny pug]	Canton
	Duan gou [Short dog]	Canton
	Fan gou [Foreign dog]	Canton

into different directions, it is really hard to thread it together, so this research can only function as a brief survey. If it succeeds in proving the function of pugs in the cultural exchange between China and the West, then the energy spent in tracing their history in numerous ancient texts is not a waste.

Attached is a list of 21 names for pugs in different dynasties.

Notes

1 "Redology" turmoil arose from different interpretations of *Dream of the Red Chamber* (*Honglou meng*), a masterpiece by Cao Xueqin in the Qing period. It started in September, 1954, when two Chinese young scholars sharply criticized a famous scholar Yu Pingbo (1900–1990) for his failure to read this book from the perspective of literary realism. Their attacks on Yu Pingbo started a more theory-based and ideological rereading of the classics. —Trans.
2 The *chi* 尺 and *cun* 寸 are both Chinese units of length. One *chi* is equal to 10 *cun*. In the Tang period, one *chi* was about 30.7 centimeters. In the Qing period, when used for measuring distances, one *chi* was about 30.9 centimeters. —Trans.
3 *Relics Unearthed in Xinjiang* (*Xinjiang chutu wenwu*), 74.
4 These are the names the speaker has invented to show her sarcasm and contempt for her husband. The first two *Lian'er, Pan'er* are names for kids. — Trans.
5 Fang Linggui, 401–402.
6 Tan Xisi, vol. 1.
7 *A Collection of Strange Things throughout the History* (*Gujin guaiyi jicheng*), vol. 3.
8 Dongxin was the art name of Jin Nong. See Yuan Mei, *Collected Poems from the Studio of Mt. Xiaocang* (*Xiaocangshan fang shiji*), vol. 28.

9 Huang Foyi, vol. 1.
10 Zeng Yandong, "Travel Notes from South China" ("Nan zhong xing lvji") in *The Little Bean Arbor* (*Xiao doupeng*), vol. 16.
11 Li E., vol. 56.

Bibliography

Chen Yinke. *Chen Yinke shij* (*A Collection of Chen Yinke's Poems*). Beijing: Qinghua daxue chubanshe, 1993.

Fang Linggui. *Gudian xiqu wailaiyu kaoshi cidian* (*A Dictionary of Loanwords in Classical Dramas of China*). Shanghai: Hanyu da cidian chubanshe, 2001.

Gu Taiqing. *Donghai yuge* (*Fishermen's Song of the East China Sea*), in *Gu Taiqing Yihui shici heji* (*A Combined Collection of Gu Taiqing and Yihui's Poems and Lyrics*). Edited by Zhang Zhang. Shanghai: Shanghai guji chubanshe, 1998.

Huang Foyi. *Guangzhou chengfang zhi* (*A Historical Survey of Guangzhou City and its Surrounding Areas*). Guangzhou: Guangdong renmin chubanshe, 1994.

Li E., ed. *Songshi jishi* (*Events on Poetry of the Song Dynasty*). Shanghai: Shanghai guji chubanshe, 1983.

Li Fang, et al., eds. *Taiping guangji* (*Extensive Records of the Taiping Era*). Beijing: Zhonghua shuju, 1961.

Lin Sumen (also known as Lin Lanchi). *Hanjiang sanbai yin* (*Three Hundred Songs of the Hanjiang River*). Nanjing: Jiangsu guangling shushe, 2005.

Liu Xu, et al., eds. *Jiu Tang shu* (*Old Book of Tang*). Beijing: Zhonghua shuju, 1975.

Minguo zhonghua shuju, ed. *Gujin guaiyi jicheng* (*A Collection of Strange Things throughout the History*). Beijing: Zhongguo shudian, 1991.

Qu Dajun. *Guangdong xinyu* (*A New Encyclopedia of Guangdong*). Beijing: Zhonghua shuju, 1985.

Tan Xisi, ed. *Ming dazheng zuanyao* (*The Greatest Political Events of the Ming Period*). Taipei: Wenhai chubanshe, 1987.

Tao Zongyi, ed. *Nancun chuogeng lu* (*Records of Discontinuing Farming in Nan Village*). Beijing: Zhonghua shuju, 1997.

Tian Yiheng. *Liuqing rizha* (*The Miscellaneous Records of the Social Customs of the Ming Dynasty*). Shanghai: Shanghai guji chubanshe, 1992.

Wang Renyu, ed. *Kaiyuan Tianbao Yishi* (*Anecdotes of the Kaiyuan and Tianbao Periods*). Taipei: Taiwan shangwu yinshuguan, 1983.

Wang Xueqi and Wang Jingzhu. *Song Jin Yuan Ming Qing quci tongshi* (*A Thorough Explanation of Qu and Ci of the Song, Jin, Yuan, Ming and Qing Dynasties*). Beijing: Yuwen chubanshe, 2002.

Xinjiang, weiwu'er zizhiqu bowuguan, ed. *Xinjiang chutu wenwu* (*Relics Unearthed in Xinjiang*). Beijing: Wenwu chubanshe, 1975.

Xu Chenglie. *Tingyu xuan biji* (*Chronicle of Hall of Raindrops*). Shanghai: Shangwu yinshuguan, 1931.

Yu Yue. *Chaxiang shi congchao* (*Tea Room Notes*). Beijing: Zhonghua shuju, 1995.

Yuan Mei. *Xiaocangshan fang shiji* (*Collected Poems from the Studio of Mt. Xiaocang*). Shanghai: Shanghai guji chubanshe, 1988.

Zeng Yandong. *Xiao doupeng* (*The Little Bean Arbor*). Wuhan: Jingchu shushe, 1989.

Zheng Ji. *Menghuanju huaxue jianming* (*A Comprehensive Guide to Painting*). Beijing: Zhongguo shudian chubanshe, 1984.

9   Lions in China

Placed at the intersection of Western culture and Chinese culture, lions in Chinese history went through polarized treatments. On the one hand, as tributes from the Western Regions, they were not favorably bred and trained like Akhal-teke or Ferghana horses because they were believed to be more ornamental than practical. From the Tang dynasty to the Ming dynasty, occasionally they were even listed as "declined tributes" and were officially denied entry into China. On the other hand, as an auspicious beast, the lion enjoyed a prominent position like other Chinese "spirit animals." Widely accepted by both prospering cities and remote villages, and embraced as a mascot by the folk, the image of lion has become part of Chinese culture. Thus, a study of lions in China is of special significance, as it not only reflects the transformation of the lion from a physical entity to a spiritual sign in the process of cultural dissemination but also reveals the fusion of foreign and Chinese cultures.

Lions from the Western Regions

In the book *Origin of Chinese Characters* (*Shuowen*), there is no such word as "lion." A famous linguist Luo Changpei conducted textual research on this loanword in the Chinese language as follows:

> Inferring from its transcription, Thomas Watters proposed that the word ši 狮 [lion] is derived from the Persian word sēr. But Berthold Laufer was not so sure about this statement, "because there was no such language as 'Persian' when the first lion was brought to China as a tribute by the Yuezhi in the year 88 AD. Coming from some East Iranian language, this word was introduced to China via the Yuezhi around the end of the first century. In its root language, the morphological form of this word is šē or ši (Tocharian A, śisāk) and it has no final consonant, just like the Chinese word ši 师 (š'i)." French sinologists such as Édouard Chavannes, Paul Pelliot and Henri Cordier also examined the transcription of this word. Pelliot stated that "about the Persian word šēr, some Iranian linguists used to take xša-θrya as its etymological form. This idea should be dropped, as Cordier has pointed out that this word is derived from the Sogdian expression šryw, or šaryə ('lion')." In short,

DOI: 10.4324/9781032616353-9

although some scholars do not take this word as 'Persian," there is hardly a denial that it is Iranian. Bernhard Karlgren also quoted Georg Morgenstierne, asserting that "'si' (lion) is the transcription of the Iranian word šary."[1]

Ancient Western Regions were a land of lion worship. From India to Persia, lions were mythologically renowned in both religious and secular worlds, and taken as a symbol of divine power and kingship.

Lions in India

Buddhist scriptures confer a supreme position to lions. As stated in volume 10 of the *Great Collection of Sutras* (*Daji jing*), "In the past, there was a lion king who often chanted in the deep mountain cave: I am the king of beasts, and I can guard them all." As "the king of beasts," the mighty lion was the protector animal of the Buddha from the very beginning. In the Buddhist scripture *Sutra of the Original Endeavour of the Prince in Accordance with All Good Omens* (*Foshuo taizi ruiying benqi jing*), it is written: "When the Buddha was born, five hundred lions came from the snow-capped mountains and guarded at the door." From then on, the Buddha preached sutras on the lion seat and expounded the Law as loudly as a lion's roar, becoming "a lion among men." In the third century BC, a column was erected by the Mauryan Emperor Ashoka in Sarnath to promote Buddhism, and the lion capital was featured by four life-sized lions set back to back on an abacus.[2]

Lion Worship in Persia

Lion worship in Persia has a long history. According to "Records of Persia" ("Bosi zhuan") in the *Book of Sui* (*Sui shu*), volume 83, "The king wears a golden crown and sits on a golden lion seat." In the epic *The Book of Kings* written by the ancient Persian poet Ferdowsi in 994, most of the heroes take nicknames related to "lion," such as "lion Dastan" and "lion Suhrab".

Lions in the Arab Empire

The legend about the founding of the Arab empire is allegedly related to the oracle of a lion. In "Records of the Arab Empire" ("Dayi zhuan") of the *Old Book of Tang* (*Jiu Tang shu*), volume 198, it is stated that:

> In 605–617, a Persian man herded camels in Mount Jufenmodina. Suddenly, a lion-man appeared, telling him, 'On the west side of this mountain, there are three caves where a great number of weapons are stored. You can go and take them. There is also a black stone where white texts are carved. You will be enthroned if you can read them!

Tribute lions from the ancient Western Regions came from the states where lion worship was part of their religious and cultural background.

In extant documents, there is no record about China as being home to lions, and scholars from the past and present have unanimously agreed that lions came from the Western Regions. Shi Huilin, an eminent monk in the Tang period, asserted that "Suanni[3] is lion, and it came from the Western Regions."[4] Li Shizhen, a herbalist and naturalist of the Ming period, also believed that "Lions came from the Western Regions."[5] Wen Tingshi, a scholar in the late Qing period, gave more details:

> Suanni is a species of lion. It is not native to China. If there were lions before the Three Dynasties [the Xia, Shang and Zhou], it does not make sense that poems or documents record rhinos and elephants but omit lions.[6]

Historically, lions were introduced into China as a tribute from the Western Regions. The earlier record can be found in volume three of the *Book of the Later Han* (*Hou Hanshu*): In the year 87, the Yuezhi offered lions; in the second year (88), the Parthian Empire offered lions. There had been tribute lions in the following dynasties until 1678 when the Portuguese envoy Rento offered an African lion as a gift. For as long as 16 centuries, these tribute lions from the Western Regions came to China mostly by land. Because of scarce sources, it is hard to find out where all these tribute lions ended up. The only complete record was the one "offered by the king of Persia" in 525. It is documented that after staying in China for six years:

> In 531, when King Guangling ascended the throne, he issued an edict, declaring that 'it is against the nature of animals to imprison them, so they should be released back to mountains and forests.' Then this lion was arranged to be returned to its home country. However, those who were sending the lion back thought that it was too far to go to Persia, so they killed the lion on their way and then returned.[7]

As for the fate of other tribute lions, Niu Shangshi, a poet in the middle Tang period wrote ruefully in "Preface to the Rhapsody on Lion" ("Shizi fu bing xu") about this:

> Locked by golden locks for a long time, I grow to be lethargic,
> trapped in an iron prison, I am bound in everlasting control.
> Engrieved by this constraining life,
> I recall my motherland in a sad and nostalgic emotional flow.[8]

If an order to return tribute lions from the Western Regions is a comparatively mild outcome, being listed as a "declined tribute" is a much more embarrassing response. In April/May of 696, in his memorial entitled "Please decline the tribute lions offered by the state of Shi [Chach]," Yao Shu explained why lions were not a suitable tribute: "Lions are ferocious carnivores. It is too costly to move them from Suiye [Suyab] to our capital and feed them here."[9] In the Ming period, besides the cost, new reasons were added for the rejection. In 1481, when the sultan of Samarkand offered two lions as tribute, Lu Rong, the director of the Bureau of Operations (*zhifang langzhong*) submitted a memorial to Emperor Chenghua: "Although lions are a rare beast, they can neither be taken as the sacrificial offering in the royal temple nor be used as horses to pull a carriage. They should be declined." In 1489, Samarkand offered a lion again. Ni Yue, the minister of rites (*libu shangshu*), in a more confident and forceful way, suggested rejecting the tribute:

> I think the tribute lion from Samarkand is a wild beast from an uncivilized state. It is not suitable to be kept in our country. Having it in the inner court does not add beauty to the palace, and placing it with the troops does not help with military force. If we accept it, it is like exchanging our valued asset for their useless gift.

Emperor Xiaozong of the Ming dynasty praised him and took his suggestion. Later, Li Dongyang, a grand secretary, wrote a poem entitled "Poem of Declining the Tribute Lion" ("Que gongshi shi") to extol the emperor:

> As Suanni from thousands of miles away was declined,
> officials in central government agencies all rejoiced in cheer.
> It is known that the study of Confucianism must start from the heart,
> but about the difficulty of taking unfavorable advice, who in the world is not clear!
> In the Han dynasty a dragon was bragged as a horse,
> in the Sui dynasty the bird was believed to be a phoenix.
> For this bright court, an untalented person like me dares to write an ode of praise,
> with a single voice, I express my loyalty and sincerity in a new poem here.[10]

With a label of "declined tribute," the lion in China was declared to be an unwelcome animal. This reaction is in sharp contrast with the lion worship in the Western Regions. To find out why this was the case, we should turn to the views of ancient Chinese for a cultural explanation.

Lions in the Eyes of Ancient Chinese

Although not a place of origin, China had a history of accepting tribute lions which enabled a direct observation. Generally speaking, descriptions of lions in the ancient Chinese documents are highly documentary. Huang Xingzeng, a scholar of the Ming period, wrote a featured article about lions in *The Beasts Classic* (*Shoujing*),[11] but it is too sketchy, unable to show us what lions looked like for ancient Chinese people. Now, based on the materials that I have collected, I provide a textual description about lions as follows.

Shape

In the *History of the Han Compiled at Dongguan* (*Dongguan Han ji*), a lion is described as "having a tiger's shape, with whiskers, and a hairy tail as big as a round-bottomed bucket. The body is pure yellow." This description is the same as that recorded in "Tiaozhi"[12] of the *Comprehensive Institutions* (*Tongdian*), volume 192.

In "Rhapsody on the Lion" ("Shizi fu") written by Yu Shinan, there is an account that goes:

> A lion is rather different from other beasts in shape, with a wide chest and a long tail. Its tendons and bones are tightly bound. Its hair looks soft, yet strong. The claws look like hooks and the teeth as sharp as a saw. With its drooping ears and kneeling posture, it nevertheless hides its vigor and strength for a big push whenever an opportunity arises.

In the *Records of the Expedition to the West* (*Xishi ji*) authored by Liu Yu, we read this: "A male lion has a mane. Its tail looks like a tassel, one flick of which might hurt people. When it roars, the sound comes out of its abdomen."

In volume 24 of the *Records of Discontinuing Farming in Nan Village* (*Nancun chuogeng lu*), Tao Zongyi wrote:

> Though it is not that tall, it is nothing like the golden-haired lapdog that people keep as a pet. When other beasts see it, they fall prostrate in fear and dare not look up. It overwhelms them in an imposing manner.

In *The Overall Survey of the Ocean's Shores* (*Yingya shenglan*) written by Ma Huan, there is one chapter about Adan [a country in Southeast Asia] which mentions lions:

> A lion here looks like a tiger. The whole body is blackish yellow, without speckles. It has a big head and a wide mouth. The tail, hairy and pointed, is black and long as a tassel. When it roars, it sounds like thunder. When other beasts see it, they all lie on the ground and dare not rise. It is the king of beasts.

Characteristics

In volume one of *The Legend of Emperor Mu* (*Mu tianzi zhuan*), a sentence reads: "Suanni[…][13] a wild horse travelling 500 *li* a day."

In volume three of *A Record of Buddhist Monasteries in Luoyang* (*Luoyang qielan ji*), Yang Xuanzhi included a story like this:

> Emperor Zhuang said to Li Yu, a palace attendant (*shizhong*): 'I heard that a tiger lies prostrate when it meets a lion. Get one for me, and let us have a look.' Then an edict was issued to catch the tigers in the mountain regions. Two counties - Gongxian and Shanyang brought in two tigers and one leopard. In the Hualin yuan [Hualin Garden], the emperor had his observation. When the two tigers and one leopard met the lion, they all closed their eyes and did not dare to look up. Knowing that there was also a blind tame bear in the garden, the emperor issued the order to bring it here. When the official in charge of forestry (*yu ren*) led it in, the blind bear smelled the lion. Immediately it jumped away in horror and ran afar with chains still on its body.

In Tao Zongyi's *Records of Discontinuing Farming in Nan Village*, volume 24, it is stated:

> When fed with wide animals or chickens and ducks, other beasts usually pressed them with claws, and removed feathers with teeth and tongue. But a lion lifted a fowl up with its paw and blew on it, then feathers dropped off like snowflakes. It looked as if the fowl had been plucked in hot water. This is how a lion is different from other beasts.

Diet

According to Zhang Tingyu's book *History of Ming: Records of the Western Regions* (*Ming shi: Xiyu zhuan*): "For one day alone, a lion eats two live sheep. It also drinks two bottles of each of these: vinegar, bitter wine, honeyed cheese."

In *The Pearl Boat* (*Zhenzhu chuan*), Hu Shi wrote that:

> Each day, lion No. 2 from the lion enclosure gobbles up one and a half live sheep, eats four *liang* [taels] of white sugar, drinks two bottles of goat milk, two bottles of vinegar, and consumes one *liang* and three *qian* [mace] Sichuan peppers.[14]

Taming

In "A Record of the Foreign Countries in the Western Regions" ("Xiyu fanguo zhi"), Chen Cheng offered this account:

> After birth, it does not open its eyes until seven days later. For those who want to capture and domesticate it, it is best to get it when its eyes are still closed. When a lion grows up, it will be hard to tame, as it becomes ferocious and brutal.

In volume six of *A Wanderer's Talk* (*Langji congtan*) authored by Liang Zhangju, there is a description of the lion enclosure in the Ming period:

> In the enclosure where a lion dwells, unwrought iron is used to make pillars from which two iron chains spread out, each wrapping around the lion's neck, one to the left and the other to the right. Before the lion is led out, a large iron stake which is about six or seven *chi*[15] in length and one *chi* in diameter with two large iron rings on one end is nailed into the ground, leaving only the rings above the surface. When a lion is let out, two tamers fasten the chains to the rings, and then pull the chains in opposite directions to prevent the lion from moving. Then the eunuch gives the order to play the ball game. Taking out two colorful yarn balls that are as big as a round-bottomed bucket, one tamer starts to play with the ball first. The lion lies on the ground, watching his moves. When the tamer sees that the lion is getting up to grab the ball, he

immediately throws one to the lion. Holding the ball between two paws, the lion then plays for a long time without putting it down.

This is similar to what Tian Yiheng recorded in the *Miscellaneous Records of the Social Customs of the Ming Dynasty* (*Liuqing rizha*), volume 29.

Wang Youguan, in volume one of *Couplets and Adages from the Suzhou Area* (*Wuxia yanlian*), also noted the ball game:

> Lions are fond of rolling balls, but balls are not available in the wilderness. When a small lion comes in as a tribute, a tamer takes a ball which is a trimmed cluster of bright silk pieces and plays with this lion. By making it happy, a tamer can mold its character, making it a rare beast in the royal garden.

Check and Balance

In Ma Huan's book *The Overall Survey of the Ocean's Shores*, there is a country called Hulumosi [now Hormuz in Iran] where:

> There is a rare beast nicknamed Caoshangfei [flying on grass]. Its native name is siyāhgōs.[16] It is as large as a big cat, and the whole body looks like a tortoiseshell or a spotted cat, and its pointed ears are black. It is guileless in nature and does not harm others. But ferocious beasts like lions or leopards lie prostrate on the ground when they see it coming. It is really the king of beasts.

In *Guest News* (*Kezuo xinwen*), Shen Zhou recorded something about the tribute lion from the Western Regions in the Ming period:

> There are two small beasts called Hou[17]. They look like a rabbit, with long pointed ears about one *chi* long. When a lion gets tyrannical, it will be brought to face a Hou. When the Hou stares at the lion, it is too scared to move. If a Hou's urine splashes on a lion's body, that place rots immediately.

As seen above, for ancient Chinese people, a lion from the Western Regions was merely an "exotic beast" or a "rare beast" rather than an "auspicious beast." In volume four of *The Six Statutes of the Tang Dynasty* (*Tang liu dian*), when a list of "auspicious objects" is given, the lion is nowhere to be found. It is not taken as a grand auspice (*darui*), or upper auspice (*shangrui*), nor viewed as a medium auspice (*zhongrui*) or lower auspice (*xiarui*). That is, the lion was completely excluded from the list of "auspicious objects" in the feudal ritual system. With the lion regarded as a "ferocious and sinister beast," to quote Han Ding in the Ming period, it is not surprising that cases of "declined tribute" ensued, revealing a deep-rooted selective pattern in the process of cultural exchange.

In 1678, an Italian Jesuit P. Ludovicus Buglio (1606–1682) published his book *Talks on the Lion* (*Shizi shuo*) in Beijing. In the preface, he wrote: "We talk about a lion's appearance, shape, temperament, and ability, but it is not just for amusement or enjoyment. It must be known that the Creator in this world has created and nurtured, dominated and arranged, and put everything in its place. We should always praise that."[18] Mixing Catholic theology and modern zoology together, Ludovicus' book did not succeed in changing the view of lions in China. Probably, that was an impossible task for him.

After a brief survey of real lions in Chinese history, I now examine the lion as a cultural image and explore how it became a shining star in Chinese culture.

Sinicized Lion Image

The dissemination of lion culture in China is related to the far-reaching impact of Buddhist arts. Through Buddhist paintings and statues, the image of the "lion king" in the Buddhist scriptures is concretized. According to *The Nirvana Sutra* (*Niepan jin*), volume 25, an Indian-style lion looks like this:

> With square cheeks and huge bones, a lion is plump in figure and fatty in flesh. It has a large head, long eyes, high and wide eyebrows, and an embedded nose above a square mouth which has neat and sharp teeth and a light red tongue sticking out. The ears are high up. It has a straight spine and a thin waist, and its abdomen is invisible. Its tail is soft yet strong. With lustrous mane, sharp teeth and claws, the lion seems to know its own strength and power. Walking on four feet, it settles in a cave with ease. When it shakes the tail, a loud sound can be heard. When anyone sees such a beast, this person knows that here is the true lion king.

In a Buddhist art, Manjusri Bodhisattva riding a lion is a common theme. At two historical sites in the Tang period, there were vivid expressions of this scene. One is the Bodhisattva Hall on Mount Wutai. As recorded in the *Ennin's Diary: The Record of a Pilgrimage to China in Search of the Law* (*Ru Tang qiufa xunli xingji*), volume three:

> In each of the five halls, there is a lion-riding statue. These lions look spirited. They look so real that it is as if they are about to move. Their mouths seem moist and there is breath out of an open mouth. If you look at them for a longer time, you feel that they are moving.

The other is the fresco in Cave No. 25 at Yulin Cave in Gansu province. This painting shows Manjusri Bodhisattva riding a mighty and majestic blue lion, with a Kunlun slave guarding him. A lion in a Buddhist painting is not a real animal, so it differs greatly in shape from a living lion, which confused the ancient Chinese. Some people complained that lion paintings were inaccurate. For example, Song

Yun, an envoy of the Northern Wei dynasty, saw two live lions in Balkh in the early sixth century and sighed: "I found these two lions majestic and brave. Painters in China have not touched upon the essence of a real lion."[19] There were also people who suspected the authenticity of tribute lions. In the Yuan period, "when a blueish black tribute lion was found to have a tiger's head, and a dog's body, people in the imperial palace thought it doesn't look like the lion in paintings, and suspected that it isn't a real one."[20] How can we explain about this true or false images of the lion?

Coming from the ancient Western Regions, lions could not escape the shaping power of traditional Chinese culture, whether they previously bore an Indian style or had a Persian look. Thus, a threatening Persian lion with sharp teeth and lacerating claws becomes amiable, and an Indian lion with "a light red tongue sticking out" retracts its tongue. After a long period of localization and transformation, a Sinicized lion image presented itself to the world in a unique way.

Positioned Beneath the Dragon

The ancient Chinese people worshipped "four spirit animals": Kylin, phoenix, turtle, and dragon. For instance, the primogenitors of Chinese civilization, Fuxi and Nüwa were said to have a human head and a dragon body, and emperors were revered as the descendants of dragons. It is not exaggerating to say that ancient China was the land of dragon dominance. To make a living in such a land, lions from abroad could not enjoy a predominant position as they did in the Western Regions and they had to be placed "beneath the dragon." This explains why the ancient legend has this saying: "Of the nine sons of the dragon, lion is the fifth one."[21] This positioning is also reflected in Chinese social life. Here is some evidence in Chinese history. First, after Wu Zetian of the Tang dynasty ascended the throne, she had the Axis of the Sky Exalting the Merits of the Great Zhou built and erected. At the top of a huge octagonal Buddhist bronze pillar are dragons guarded by lions. Second, inside the Yongling Mausoleum built for Wang Jian, the founding emperor of the Former Shu before the Five Dynasties, there is a stone bed resembling a real royal bed in the rear chamber. On the front of this bed is a relief sculpture where a coiled dragon is placed in the middle, surrounded by lions.[22] Third, the embroidered Tang official attires indicated the difference between the dragon and the lion: "A king's robe is decorated with coiled dragons and deer" while "a robe of left guard or right guard (*zuoyoujian menwei*) is patterned with a pair of lions."[23] This system of dragon and lion attires corresponding to distinct hierarchical officialdom did not change until the Qing dynasty when princes and kings had coiled dragons on their robes, and lion robes were restricted to the first rank (*yipin*) and second rank (*erpin*)[24] military officers. Obviously, in the secular and feudal rituals of ancient China, the lion could neither go above the dragon nor enjoy an equal status. Having completely lost their prominent position as a symbol of divine power and kingship in the Western Regions, they could only condescend to join ceremonial guards, positioned on the road leading to imperial mausoleums of the past dynasties, in the posture of either a walking lion or a crouching lion, to guard "mausoleums of the Han dynasty amid the Autumn wind and the sinking sun."[25]

Awe-inspiring Appearance

In the Southern Dynasties period when Buddhism was prevalent, an Indian-style lion with its tongue sticking out was fairly fashionable in the plastic arts. Xiao Dan, a royal member in the Liang dynasty whose posthumous title was King Zhongwu, died in 522. The stone lions on the east side of his mausoleum, large or small, all had their long tongues sticking out. Xiao Jing, another royal member entitled Duke of Pingzhong, died in 523. Of the stone lions in front of his tomb, "the east lion is the only one left. It is a male beast with a plump figure, with a protruding chest, a hunched back, a lifting head and a tongue sticking out."[26] In traditional Chinese culture, a tongue is viewed as one's "spiritual root" and should be hidden instead of sticking out. That is why in the Tang period, the statue of a lion with "a light red tongue sticking out" became rare, and the commonly seen lion statue was the one with its mouth open and teeth exposed. The change of tongue design is an important step in the Sinicization of the lion image. Yan Suihou, a scholar in the Kaiyuan reign (713–741), in his prose "Rhapsody on the Seat-holding Stone Lion" ("Zhenzuo shishizi fu") described for us what a lion in the prosperous Tang period looked like:

> For hundreds of cities, a lion's formidable power can be felt, intimidating those lower-ranking officials who come to visit. For thousands of miles, a lion's commanding force is unchallenged, unlike the meaningless show of force by a tiger. With huge claws that do not grab, people know that it is domesticated; with sharp teeth that do not bite, people know that it is kind and gentle.[27]

As shown by historical facts, this kind of awe-inspiring stone lion not only became a symbol of the prosperous Tang period, but also set a standard for the lion image as it evolved in the future.

Harmony between Humans and Lions

In ancient Persian art, the theme of a human-lion fight is common. It was called "Sassanian style" as it prevailed in the Sassanid era (226–642). This style is evident in fabric designs and silverware ornaments of West and Central Asia, manifested by the familiar hunting scene at that time: a knight in full armor, turning around and shooting the lion that pounced on him. On the two artifacts typical of the "Sassanian style," "Brocade with Lion Hunting" at the Horyuji Temple in Japan and "Silver Bowl with a Hunting Scene," excavated along the bank of the Amu Darya River,[28] we can see the two sides, one displaying a ferocious intent to kill, the other making threatening gestures by baring fangs and brandishing claws. This "spectacular" fighting scene between a man and a lion was popular in the Western Regions, but it could not be accepted in China, because in traditional Chinese culture, the relationship between humanity (the realm of the human) and heaven (the realm of nature) is harmonious, not antagonistic. The artistic expression of this belief is depicted in the well-known painting "a lion playing with an embroidered ball" (modeled on the Chinese way of lion-taming) found in almost every household from the Tang and Song dynasties to the late Qing period. This image has been used not only as a decoration on bronze mirrors and porcelain but also functioned as an important subject for Spring Festival pictures and papercutting designs.

Lion Family

The personification of lions is common in Buddhist stories and Aesop's Fables, but treating lions as a family is unique to Chinese culture. As in ancient Greek group sculpture, an adult lion, a lioness and their cub form a lion family. In ancient China, the gates of temples, official offices, and shrines were usually guarded by a pair of squatting stone lions, with the female on the left and the male on the right. The male lion holds an embroidered ball with its left paw, and the female one caresses her cub with its right paw. Resembling human life, this familial group has become the model for all gate lions later. For example, in Biyun Temple of Fragrant Hill in Beijing in the Qing period, there was a pair of such stone lions:

> The mountain gate faces east, and in front of it there are two stone lions. The male is so thin that its bones are visible. Its skin looks smooth and black as if washed by rain. The female is so fat that its flesh bulges. Its skin looks green as if covered by moss. Their bellies are both pure white. The carving of the stone lions is exquisite.

The design of the stone lions here, according to Wanyan Linqing who provided explanations for illustrations, is nothing more than a combination of two patterns, a ball-playing lion and a lioness with her cub.[29] In the *Dream of the Red Chamber* (*Honglou meng*), the famous stone lions sitting at the gate of Jia's mansion are also paired. This lion family image reflects the family-centered Chinese culture and its ability to assimilate foreign elements. It also indicates the unique artistic skill of ancient stonemasons.

By the Qing period, the lion image had been completely fixed in Chinese paintings and sculptures, and corresponding artistic instructions also emerged. Regarding how to paint a lion, Zheng Ji wrote in his 1866 treatise *A Comprehensive Guide to Painting* (*Menghuanju huaxue jianming*):

> Lion is the king of beasts, and that's why it is called shi 狮.[30] A lion has either a yellow or blue coat, with a large head and a long tail. Its claws are like hooks, teeth like saws. The ears droop submissively but the nose is held very high. Its gaze is like a lightning bolt, and there are whiskers around its huge mouth. The mane hair is fluffy enough to cover its face, and the tuft on the tail is as huge as a big ball. Its skin is as loose as that of a dog. As Yu Shinan said that a lion is so fierce and sturdy that it can pull down a tiger and swallow up a Pixiu,[31] tear apart a rhinoceros and dismember an elephant, so those who only focus on its smile and neglect its ferocity are not good painters of the lion.[32]

Regarding how to carve a lion, Li Dou in his 1795 book *Records of the Yangzhou Barges* (*Yangzhou huafang lu*), volume 17, gave the following instruction, "Carving a lion covers all of the following: head, face, body, legs, teeth, crotch, embroidered belt, bell, neck hair, embroidered ball, and a lion cub."[33] The "neck hair" refers to the lion's mane in the style of ushnisha. It is still in use among folk stonemasons today.

Lions in Folklore

As shown in Chinese history, the image of a Sinicized lion was widely known, and generally accepted in urban and rural areas, greatly enriching Chinese custom. Passed down from the Tang or Song periods, lion-related culture such as lion dance, lion candy, and snow lion is still embraced today.

Lion Dance

The lion dance has been popular among the Chinese people since the Tang period and it has spread over the northern and southern provinces. According to the *New Book of Tang: Account of Rites and Music* (*Xin Tang shu: Liyue zhi*), with regard to the "Lion Dance of the Five Directions," there are specified requirements about both performers and props:

> Five lions of different colors are set in five directions, each about one *zhang* high, operated by 12 performers. The person who wears a costume and holds a red whisker is called a "lion lad." The lion lad has a red band over his forehead.

By referring to other related sources, I want to highlight two points here, regarding the above-mentioned lion dance. The first is the physical description of lions. Bai Juyi described in "New Yuefu: Dancer of Xiliang" ("Xin yuefu: Xiliang ji") this way:

> Having a wooden head and a silk tail,
> the lion has its eyes gilded with gold and teeth plated with silver.
> Quickly shaking its coat and swiftly moving its ears,
> it resembles miles of quicksand gliding over from afar to be here.

What is portrayed in this poem also becomes the prototype of a modern lion dance - "Awakened Lion" (*xing shi*). The second pertains to the color of lions. Among the five colors, "yellow" is the color for emperors, which means that no one other than an emperor can dance in a yellow lion. Wang Wei, a famous Chinese poet, was once severely punished because he broke this taboo:

> When he served as the deputy master of the Music Department (*dayue cheng*), Wang Wei was instigated to perform a lion dance inside a yellow lion and was thus demoted. A yellow lion can only be performed by an emperor. This should be born in mind by younger generations.[34]

After generations of localization and transformation, the lion dance has become a popular Chinese folk dance, recalling only a faint association with the Western Regions. It has become part of the celebratory activities during the Spring Festival or appeared on other festive occasions such as welcoming gods or holding a competition. As the customs in the North and the South China are different, their performing styles also vary. In the eastern part of Guangdong in the Qing period, the combination of "lion dance" and "kung fu" became a wonderful work of art. The Chaozhou lion dance in the Tongzhi reign (1862–1874) described by Zhang Xintai is quite an eye-opener:

> In Chaozhou and Jiaying, a lion dance is performed around the New Year. The lion's body is made of five-colored silk, and its head is also painted and decorated. The lion dance is like a play. One person holds the head while the other forms the rear end of the lion. The third man acts as Sha Wujing from *Journey to the West*. This man wears a huge red mask over his head, dressed in short jacket, revealing the clothes underneath his jacket. He also holds a bamboo whisker in the right hand, and a cattail-leaf fan in the left hand. The fourth man is short but plucky, with an imp mask over his face. Accompanying them upstage in a loud gong-beating sound are ten teenagers who hold spears, shields, tridents, or sticks. Each of these kids has his hair tied with a red band. On the first day of the first lunar month, the performers visit the family ancestral shrines of villagers. This is called a "lion visit." On this day, no performance of Chinese boxing and cudgel play is arranged. It is only an occasion to pay homage to the deceased. On the second day, Sha Wujing fights against the lion. After the fighting, a bamboo frame is set up for the imp to jump over it. This is called "imp jumping over frame." Then the teenagers gather at a square, showing off their martial arts. It starts with Chinese boxing, followed by a performance with spears, shields, tridents, and sticks, and finally concludes with a knife stunt. On a large table, machetes with sharp points are placed upright in front of the table. When an agile teenager leaps over the table, the machete tips almost rub against his abdomen and cut him open. It is so dangerous that audiences watch with trepidation and fear. In ancient times, this was probably meant to exorcise demons. However, according to the custom passed down, it is believed that "狮 [shī] (lion)" is "师 [shī](master). Around the end of a year, villagers have more leisure time so they start to learn martial arts. To learn from a martial master, they need to follow his instructions and thus a lion dance becomes an occasion for practice.[35]

A lion dance such as this one is a mixture of dance, acrobatics, and martial arts. It is no wonder that in the modern Chaozhou dialect, a martial arts master is known as a "Lion Master of Fist."[36]

Lion Candy

Chinese food culture not only values color, smell, and taste but also attaches great importance to shape. As early as the Northern Song dynasty, "lion candies" had been sold at food stores of Bianjing (now Kaifeng).[37] In the Qing period, lion candies were popular in areas south of the Yangtze River. Kong Shangren, a dramatist and poet in the Qing period, had a poem about this:

> Prosperity in the southeast China starts with Yangzhou,
> a city filled with valued products like silk dresses transported through land or by tides high or low.
> Red tangerines, yellow oranges, and fragrant citrons are abundant,
> sugar-made spirits and lion-shaped candies are put row upon row.[38]

Lion candies are a form of "animal candies," the production of which includes boiling sugar, molding, and stripping etc. Song Yingxing, a scientist in the late Ming period, detailed "the method of making white sugar" in his book *The Exploitation of the Works of Nature* (*Tiangong kaiwu*).

Snow Lion

As the name suggests, the fun associated with building "snow lion" belongs to the northern part of China. The noble families of the Northern Song dynasty held feasts in midwinter, where building a snow lion was a show of extravagance. Volume 10 of *The Eastern Capital: A Dream of Splendor* (*Dongjing menghua lu*) by Meng Yuanlao has this record:

> In this month [12th month in the lunar calendar], although there are no festivals, the noble family would have a feast once it started to snow, building snow lions, installing snow lamps, and using snow [...][39] to greet relatives and friends.

Fresh snow was used to build snow lions for good luck, but that did not last long. When the temperature rose, they melted immediately. Poets in the Song period made fun of this in their poems, as is evidenced in the *Records of the Miscellaneous Delicacies* (*Houqing lu*), a book written by a Song scholar Zhao Delin. In volume eight, Zhao quoted one of Zhang Wenqian's poems "A Play on Snow Lions: A Quatrain" ("Xi zuo xueshi jueju") which has the following two lines: "Liuchu [snow] is used to build a fake king of beasts, /when the sun comes out it becomes small bits!" The word "liuchu" here is short for "six petals of a snowflake." It is also a term for lion dance in the Tang and Song periods. We can find this term in a Zen talk between Master Yaoshan (also known as Weiyan) and Master Yunyan (also known as Tansheng), two eminent monks of the middle Tang period:

> Yaoshan asked again: "I've heard that you performed lion dances, did you?"
> Yunyan answered, "Yes."
> Then, "how many did you perform?"
> Reply: "Liuchu (six sets)."
> Yaoshan: "I can perform too."
> Yunyan: "How many?"
> Reply: "Only one."
> Yunyan: "One is six, and six is one."[40]

"Liuchu" here is six sets, forming a series of lion dances. The monks were also good at performing a lion dance, so it is clear that it was popular among both monks and laymen.

In addition to festivals and banquets, lions also played a unique role in funeral services. Among the folks of Jinan in the Qing period, there was a funeral ceremony called "sending over a lion and a leopard":

> During the funeral, close relatives or best friends sent over a couple of fabricated lion and leopard here. They have a patterned tapestry for the body, wood for the head and tail, with a person hidden underneath each of them. When the condolence begins, the lion and the leopard are placed at the left and right sides of the gate. When the coffin is about to be taken away, they dance in front of it. The family of the deceased prepares one or two thousand copper coins, and puts them on the table where the casket is placed. After the dance, the lion and the leopard lie beside the coffin, and then a lion cub is taken out of the lion's belly to ask for money. After they grab the coins on the table, they leave. Occasionally, after the lion and leopard dance, several people put on costumes borrowed from a theatrical troupe and perform one act of a play before the coffin is taken away. In rural areas, these performers are all relatives or friends; in the cities, poor people are hired to perform. Recently, a "lion and leopard service center" has been set up near Bianzi xiang ["Whip Lane"], but those who need the service "invite" rather than hire the performers. The lion and leopard dancers at the funeral are not supposed to go to the graveyard.[41]

Lions were not only related to the social life of mankind, but also regarded as a protector of farm animals. In "Rhapsody on Lion King" ("Shiwang shenshu") widely spread in Chengdu in the Qing period, we read the following:

> Regarded as the king of beasts, the lion enjoys the highest respect. That is more so when the lion has become a deity! In our land, the lion god shows its power when the livestock are sick, offering magic water (*fushui*) to cure disease. This god benefits animals and humans, protecting them from disaster and harm. Now we have a sick cow that neither eats nor drinks. With incense and paper money ready, we pray to the lion god for magic water so that this cow can recover quickly to be as strong as a tiger, remain free from plague, become as mighty as a dragon, and always live by lush grass. All the living beings in this world will thank you for your nurturing love and feel grateful for your benevolence. We write down this statement in sincerity to let you know about this.[42]

As shown above, in the folk tradition, a lion was involved in human joy and sorrow and was regarded as a mysterious power benefitting both humans and animals. This is how Chinese lion culture differentiates itself from that of the Western Regions in its historical and ethnic dimensions.

From transplantation, naturalization, to innovative transformation, the lion image in China has gone through a long process of change, embodying the efforts of generations of skilled craftsmen. After years of subtle influence, the Chinese lion has shown itself independently among the world arts, and become "a rare treasure of China." Its uniqueness cannot be simply explained by "spiritual resemblance," a term often used in traditional painting theory. As shown above, the lion became a shining star in Chinese culture precisely because of cultural assimilation, which on the one hand preserved its mighty manner and on the other hand bestowed an amiable look to it.

"Lion's Roar": From the Buddha's Dharma Sound to A Rallying Cry

In Buddhist scriptures, the Buddha is called "a lion among men" and the phrase "lion's roar" is used to describe the solemn sound of the Dharma. It is said that this roar can shake heaven and earth, and sweep away evil, revealing its great power.

With the localization of Buddhism and Sinicization of the lion in China, the "lion's roar" also stepped down from the sacred altar and landed in folk life, becoming a rallying cry for earthly struggles.

In China, nobody forgets that when China was oppressed and bullied by the Western powers, it was described as a "sleeping lion," a term that indicates unawakened national consciousness. In Wang Kangnian's famous book *Notes of Wang Rangqing* (*Wang Rangqing biji*), it is stated that:

> Westerners called China a sleeping lion. If it were only a sleeping lion, it would eventually wake up. I asked Westerners about this, but they all laughed and did not answer, so I had no idea about what they meant. Later I saw a lion tamer and asked him for an explanation. The tamer said: "This term has a deep meaning. In the past, when we were learning to tame a lion, we caught a cub and fed it with a dog's milk. We thought that when the cub grew up, it would have the shape of a lion and the nature of a dog, so it would be easy to tame it for play. One day, someone played with this lion and counted its teeth when its mouth was open. The lion was hungry at that time, so it took advantage of this opportunity to bite off the man's head. People who saw this were horrified, blaming me for my poor lion-taming skill. So I thought it over and got an idea. I rubbed some raw opium on beef as a bait and fed it to the lion. At first, only a little was used, then a bit more was added until the increasing dosage kept the lion drowsy all day long. Kept in a state of deep sleep, it allowed people to do whatever they wanted with it. Although it could move its claws, and opened its mouth to howl or roar, it was like shouting in the dream, unable to hurt anyone. Now, with a lion's shape, it did not act like a lion at all, and the previously acquired dog behavior was also gone. If this state of slumber went on, it would never wake up. China is a big country, just like a huge lion. But it has been far more poisoned, yet not just by opium! This close analogy might help with your understanding of this term." How horrifying! I hope all the Chinese people will wake up and know how serious this is.

In modern China, in the form of the "lion's roar," Chinese people joined national and democratic revolutions to challenge the harsh reality of "streets full of wolves." Chen Tianhua, an activist during the 1911 Revolution, titled his revolutionary novel *The Lion's Roar* (*Shizi hou*),[43] and urged people to "raise the lion flag and sweep the wolf's den," and to fight for the republic.

In 1934, facing the national peril, Xu Beihong, a famous Chinese painter, full of grief and indignation, drew a picture of a lion with the caption: "New life comes alive!"

Both Chen Tianhua's novel and Xu Beihong's painting encouraged Chinese people to fight and save the nation in a time of misery and plight, expressing deep and sincere feelings for the land where the descendants of the Fiery Emperor and Yellow Emperor have lived for generations. Today China has taken on an entirely new look, and there is no need to add figurative meanings to lions when we review Chinese history. But two points can be summarized about lions which help to reveal the relationship between Chinese and foreign cultures. On the one hand, lions as "exotic animals from the Western Regions" were believed to have no practical value, and therefore were declined, repatriated, or died of old age in an enclosure before they finally disappeared into obscurity, producing no impact on the course of Chinese history. On the other hand, due to the impact of Chinese culture, the lion became one of the "four spirit animals," and acquired the Chinese style both in appearance and spirit, adored by folks and adopted into artworks. All these demonstrate that the lion's spirit rather than appearance won the heart of Chinese people.

Notes

1. Luo Changpei, 19–20. See also Schafer, 86–87.
2. Stavisky, 1985: 193–194.
3. In Chinese mythology, Suanni is said to be a creature which is a hybrid of the lion and the dragon. It is one of the nine sons of the dragon. —Trans.
4. Shi Xuanying and Shi Huilin, vol. 71.
5. Li Shizhen, vol. 51.
6. Wen Tingshi, vol. 23.
7. Yang Xuanzhi, vol. 3.
8. Dong Gao, et al., vol. 398.
9. Dong Gao, et al., vol. 169.
10. Yan Congjian, vol. 15.
11. Zhou Lvjing, vol. 21.
12. Tiaozhi was a state near the head of the Persian Gulf. When the Chinese envoy Gan Ying reached this land in 97 CE, it was a dependency of the Parthians. —Trans.
13. This quote comes from an ancient Chinese text, and one word is missing in this sentence. —Trans.
14. *Liang* [tael] and *Qian* [mace] are the Chinese units of weight. 1 *Liang* equals 50 g, and 1 *Qian* equals 5 g. —Trans.
15. In the Ming period, 1 *chi* was about 0.30 to 0.32 meters. —Trans.
16. According to Feng Chengjun, siyāhgōs is a type of wild cat called Felis Caracal.
17. Commonly referred to as Wangtianhou, Chaotianhou, or Denglong, the hou was a legendary beast in Chinese mythology. —Trans.
18. Xu zongze, 307. See also Wu Zhenyu, vol. 26, where it mentions that "In 1678–1679, the kingdom of Guli [now Calicut in India] offered a lion as tribute, and ministers were invited to have a look. Mao Qiling once wrote a poem about this."

19 Yang Xuanzhi, vol. 5.
20 Zhou Mi, *Sequel to* "Miscellaneous Knowledge from the Guixin Street" (*Guixin zashi xuji*).
21 See Chen Yuanlong, vol. 90.
22 Feng Hanji, 37–38, diagram 39.
23 Wang Pu, vol. 32.
24 The Qing dynasty used an "official rank" system (*pin*). This system had a total of 19 ranks. —Trans.
25 Cheng Zheng and Li Hui, 97–107. The earliest record of tomb-guarding stone lions is from the middle of the second century AD, in the tomb of Yin Jian, the head commissioner of Anyi county in the Eastern Han dynasty. As is stated in Yang Kuan's book, "in the south of the tomb, there are two lions facing each other." See Yang Kuan, 73.
26 Yao Qian and Gu Bing, photos 73, 74, 76, 77.
27 Dong Gao, et al., vol. 400. The gilded bronze lions in the palace of the Tang dynasty triggered a well-known story of promoting Buddhism: When Master Fazang expounded the Buddhist doctrine for Empress Wu Zetian, he used the "golden lion" in the palace as a metaphor, and wrote the famous paper "Essay on the Golden Lion" ("Huayan jinshizi zhang") in *Avatamsaka Sutra*.
28 Kuwayama Shoshin, 143–150. Regarding the lion hunting pattern of the Sassanian style and its influence on the goldware and silverware of the Tang period, see Gyllensvard, 117–119, photo 65.
29 Wanyan Linqing, *Geese Tracks on the Snow* (*Hongxue yinyuan tuji*), illustrated by Wang Chunquan, etc., book 3, in particular the chapter entitled "Clouds in the Clear Blue Sky Touching the Lions."
30 In ancient Chinese language, "狮 [shī] (lion)" is also written as "师 [shī](master)," that might explain why Zheng Ji wrote so. —Trans.
31 Pixiu 貔貅 is a legendary animal in Chinese mythology. It is described as having a head of a dragon and a lion's body, often with hoofs, wings and tail. —Trans.
32 Yu Jianhua, 1200.
33 Li Dou, 387.
34 Wang Dang, vol. 5.
35 Zhang Xintai, *Short Records of Travels in Guangdong* (*Yueyou xiaozhi*), in volume nine of *Collection of Documents on World Geography* (*Xiaofanghu zhai yudi congchao*) edited by Wang Xiqi.
36 In Chinese language, "lion" 狮 has the same pronunciation as "master" 师. That is why a martial art master can be called a "Lion Master of Fist." —Trans.
37 See the entry entitled "Food and Snacks" ("Yinshi guozi") in Meng Yuanlao, *The Eastern Capital: A Dream of Splendor* (*Dongjing menghua lu*), vol. 2.
38 Kong Shangren, vol. 2.
39 Here one word is missing in the original quote. —Trans.
40 Shi Puji, vol. 5.
41 Sun Dian, *Travels in Lixia* (*Lixia zhiyou*), in volume six of *Collection of Documents on World Geography*.
42 Fu Chongju, 531.
43 See People's Journal (*Minbao*), issue 2, 1906.

Bibliography

Chen Yuanlong, ed. *Gezhi jingyuan* (*Mirrored Contexts for Thorough Investigations*). Shanghai: Shanghai guji chubanshe, 1992.

Cheng Zheng and Li Hui, eds. *Tang shiba ling shike* (*Stone Carvings of the Eighteen Tombs of the Tang Dynasty*). Xi'an: Shaanxi renmin meishu chubanshe, 1988.

Dong Gao, et al., eds. *Quan Tangwen* (*Complete Tang Prose*). Beijing: Zhonghua shuju, 1983.

Du You, ed. *Tongdian* (*Comprehensive Institutions*). Beijing: Zhonghua shuju, 1988.

Ennin. *Ru Tang qiufa xunli xingji* (*Ennin's Diary: The Record of a Pilgrimage to China in Search of the Law*). Shanghai: Shanghai guji chubanshe, 1986.

Fan Ye, ed. *Hou Hanshu* (*Book of the Later Han*). Zhengzhou: Zhongzhou guji chubanshe, 1996.

Feng Hanji. *Qianshu Wangjian mu fajue baogao* (*Report on the Excavation of the Tomb of Wang Jian in Former Shu*). Beijing: Wenwu chubanshe, 1964.

Fu Chongju. *Chengdu tonglan* (*An Overview of Chengdu*). Chengdu: Bashu shushe, 1987.

Guo Pu, ed. *Mu tianzi zhuan* (*The Legend of Emperor Mu*). Shanghai: Shanghai guji chubanshe, 1990.

Gyllensvard, Bo. *Tang Gold and Silver* (Contained in The Museum of Far Eastern Antiquities Bulletin No. 29, 1957). Stockholm: The Museum of Far Eastern Antiquities, 1957.

Hu Shi. *Zhenzhu chuan* (*The Pearl Boat*). Shanghai: Shangwu yinshuguan, 1936.

Kong Shangren. *Kong Shangren shi* (*Poems of Kong Shangren*). Edited by Wang Weilin. Beijing: Kexue chubanshe, 1958.

Kuwayama, Shoshin. "Dating of the Brocade with Lion Hunting at the Horyuji Temple." *Collection of Papers Honoring Prof. Egami Namio's 70th Birthday, Archaeology and Art Edition*. [In Japanese.] Edited by Ono Katsutoshi. Tokyo: Yamakawa Shuppansha, 1976. 137–161.

Li Dou. *Yangzhou huafang lu* (*Records of Yangzhou Barges*). vol. 17. Nanjing: Jiangsu guangling guji keyinshe, 1984.

Li Shizhen. *Bencao gangmu* (*Compendium of Materia Medica*). Beijing: Renmin weisheng chubanshe, 1985.

Liang Zhangju. *Langji congtan* (*A Wanderer's Talk*). Fuzhou: Renmin chubanshe, 1981.

Liu Xu, et al., eds. *Jiu Tang shu* (*Old Book of Tang*). Beijing: Zhonghua shuju, 1975.

Liu Yu. *Xishi ji* (*Records of the Expedition to the West*). Shanghai: Shangwu yinshuguan, 1936.

Luo Changpei. *Yuwen yu wenhua* (*Language and Culture*). Beijing: Yuwen chubanshe, 1989.

Ma Huan. *Yingya shenglan* (*The Overall Survey of the Ocean's Shores*). Beijing: Zhonghua shuju, 1985.

Meng Yuanlao. *Dongjing menghua lu* (*The Eastern Capital: A Dream of Splendor*). Beijing: Zhongguo shangye chubanshe, 1993.

Minbao (People's Journal), Issue 2, 1906.

Ouyang Xiu, et al., eds. *Xin Tang shu* (*New Book of Tang*). Beijing: Zhonghua shuju, 1975.

Schafer, Edward. *The Golden Peaches of Samarkand: A Study of T'ang Exotics*. Berkeley: University of California Press, 1963.

Shen Zhou. *Kezuo xinwen* (*Guest News*), in *Xuxiu siku quanshu* (*Supplement to the Complete Library in Four Sections*), vol. 1167. Shanghai: Shanghai guji chubanshe, 1995.

Shi Puji. *Wudeng huiyuan* (*Compendium of Five Lamps*). Beijing: Zhonghua shuju, 1984.

Stavisky, Boris Yakovlevich. "Stone Lions on a Column Unearthed in Old Termez," in *The Cultural Heritage of the East*. [In Russian.] Edited by Julian Vladimirovich Bromley. Leningrad: Nauka, 1985. 190–197.

Su Mian, et al., eds. *Tang huiyao* (*Institutional History of Tang*). Shanghai: Shangwu yinshuguan, 1936.

Sun Dian. "Lixia zhiyou (Travels in Lixia)," in *Xiaofanghu zhai yudi congchao, bubian and zaibubian* (*Collection of Documents on World Geography*, with the first and second supplements), vol. 6. Edited by Wang Xiqi. Hangzhou: Hangzhou guji shudian, 1985.

Tao Zongyi, ed. *Nancun chuogeng lu* (*Records of Discontinuing Farming in Nan Village*). Beijing: Zhonghua shuju, 1997.

Tian Yiheng. *Liuqing rizha* (*The Miscellaneous Records of the Social Customs of the Ming Dynasty*). Shanghai: Shanghai guji chubanshe, 1992

Wang Dang. *Tang yulin* (*Anecdotes in the Tang Dynasty*). Shanghai: Shijie shuju, 1959.

Wang Kangnian. *Wang Rangqing biji* (*Notes of Wang Rangqing*). Shanghai: Shanghai shudian, 1997.

Wang Xiqi, ed. *Xiaofanghu zhai yudi congchao, bubian and zaibubian* (*Collection of Documents on World Geography*, with the first and second supplements). Hangzhou: Hangzhou guji shudian, 1985.

Wang Youguan. *Wuxia yanlian* (*Couplets and Adages from the Suzhou Area*). Beijing: Zhonghua shuju, 1982.

Wanyan Linqing. *Hongxue yinyuan tuji* (*Geese Tracks on the Snow*). Illustrated by Wang Chunquan, etc. Beijing: Beijing guji chubanshe, 1984.

Wei Zheng, et al. *Sui shu* (*Book of Sui*). Beijing: Zhonghua shuju, 1973.

Wen Tingshi. *Chun Changzi zhiyu* (*A lengthy and Confusing Talk of Chun Changzi*). Nanjing: Jiangsu guangling guji keyinshe, 1990.

Wu Zhenyu. *Yangji zhai conglu* (*Collected Notes from Yangji Studio*). Hangzhou: Zhejiang guji chubanshe, 1985.

Xu zongze. *Ming Qing jian yesu huishi yizhu tiyao* (*A Summary of the Publications by Jesuits during the Ming and the Qing Dynasties*). Beijing: Zhonghua shuju, 1989.

Yan Congjian. *Shuyu zhou zi lu* (*Records of the Surrounding Foreign Countries*). Beijing: Gugong bowuyuan tushuguan, 1930.

Yang Kuan. *Zhongguo gudai lingqin zhidu shi yanjiu* (*Research on the History of the Ancient Chinese Mausoleum Systems*). Shanghai: Shanghai guji chubanshe, 1985.

Yang Xuanzhi. *Luoyang qielan ji* (*A Record of Buddhist Monasteries in Luoyang*). Annotated by Liu Weidong. Beijing: Beijing yanshan chubanshe, 1998.

Yao Qian, et al., eds. *Nantang lingmu shike* (*Stone Carvings of the Mausoleums in the Southern Dynasty*). Beijing: Wenwu chubanshe, 1981.

Yu Jianhua, ed. *Zhongguo hualun leibian* (*Chinese Painting Theory by Category*). Beijing: Renmin meishu chubanshe, 1986.

Zhang Tingyu, et al., eds. *Ming shi* (*History of Ming*). Beijing: Zhonghua shuju, 1974.

Zhang Xintai. *Yueyou xiaozhi* (*Short Records of Travels in Guangdong*). Shanghai: Shanghai guji chubanshe, 2002.

Zhao Delin. *Houqing lu* (*Records of the Miscellaneous Delicacies*). Beijing: Zhonghua shuju, 1985.

Zheng Ji. *Menghuanju huaxue jianming* (*A Comprehensive Guide to Painting*). Beijing: Zhongguo shudian chubanshe, 1984.

Zhou Lvjing, ed. *Yimen guangdu* (*Numerous Books from the Peaceful Gate*). Beijing: Shumu wenxian chubanshe, 1990.

Zhou Mi. *Guixin zashi* (*Miscellaneous Knowledge from the Guixin Street*). Beijing: Zhonghua shuju, 1988.

10 Variation of Manichaeism in the Coastal Areas during the Tang and Song Periods

The interaction between Manichaeism and ancient China varied across time and place, highly visible in the coastal areas of China during the Tang and Song periods, particularly in the Jinjiang River Basin in Fujian, forming a unique religious and cultural landscape. The extant documents and cultural relics in Quanzhou have proved, to varying degrees, that when the place was called Qingyuan prefecture, it was the "land of the Buddha" where Manichaeism gained popularity among local inhabitants and took very distinctive regional characteristics, becoming almost entirely localized. As early as 90 years ago, two world-renowned Sinologists, Édouard Chavannes and Paul Pelliot, had noticed that in China, the practice of Manichaeism in western regions was substantially different from that in the coastal areas. The former is viewed as "true Manichaeism," while the latter is called "Sinicized Manichaeism."[1] Thanks to the persistent efforts of Chinese and foreign scholars, particularly the careful investigation by local personages, the Religion of Light (*Mingjiao*) in Quanzhou as one historical exemplar of the Sinicized Manichaeism turned out to be a fact for all to see. But to further this research in a more empirical and systematic way, more collaboration and cooperation are still needed. Let me quote a great thinker to clarify this point:

> It is, in reality, much easier to discover by analysis the earthly core of the misty creations of religion, than, conversely, it is, to develop from the actual relations of life the corresponding celestialized forms of those relations. The latter method is the only materialistic, and therefore the only scientific one.[2]

Revived in Exile

The *Book of Fujian: Records of Local Histories* (*Min shu: Fangyuzhi*), offers a clear description of how Manichaeism flourished in Fujian, giving information about when it originated, where it started and who was the pioneering figure:

> In 841–846, Buddhist monks were repelled, and followers of the Religion of Light were also suppressed. A Manichaean missionary called Master Hulu [Ulug] fled to Futang. Then he started to teach disciples in Sanshan.

Wandering around, he came to Quanjun. After his death, he was buried at the foot of a mountain in northern Quanjun. During the reign of Zhidao [995–997], Li Tingyu, a scholar from Huai'an, found an image of the [Mani] Buddha in a divination shop at the capital city. He bought it with 50,000 coins. After that, the auspicious image began to be circulated in Fujian. In 998–1022, Lin Shichang, a scholar in Fujian who was well-versed in the Manichean scriptures, passed the imperial civil examination and was conferred the honor of "Master of Literatures of Fuzhou" (*Fuzhou wenxue*).

The repelling of monks was actually a large-scale persecution of missionaries by Emperor Wuzong [840 to 846] of the Tang dynasty. Manichaeism bore the brunt and was publicly banned in 843. As a result, temples were closed, properties were confiscated, and Manichaean missionaries, regardless of gender, were all scared away like frightened birds with approaching death threats. According to the *Topical Compendium of the Buddhist Clergy* (*Seng shilue*) written by Zanning,[3] volume three, section three:

> In 843, Emperor Wuzong banned Manichaeism and all the Manichean temples were revoked by the government. Seventy-two Manichean nuns in the capital were killed. Many Uighurs and Manichaeans who had been trapped at the capital were exiled to other prefectures, and most of them died. In 845, Wuzong issued another edict, forcing more than 2,000 Daqin [Nestorians], Muhu [Zoroastrian priests], and Huoxian [Zoroastrians], to return to secular world. But these religious groups were not uprooted and they later spread to other places.

Because of Master Ulug, a branch of Manichaeism spread to the coastal area. There is no information about where he used to preach, but it is obvious that he escaped to Futang. Hence, the question arises: in an abyss of misery, why did he choose to go east instead of seeking refuge in the west, the south, or the north? In my opinion, Master Ulug's choice of Fujian which was east of the two capitals, Chang'an and Luoyang, was not a rash or random decision. Rather, it was the result of double constraints, one being the realistic situation, and the other religious doctrine. That is, he had no other choices available.

Manichaeans during the Huichang era [841–847] found themselves in a dire situation. In 840–843, the Uighur Khanate north of the desert was defeated by Kirghiz, and thus, it could no longer shelter the Manicheans. The Karluks on the west could be a choice, because they had previously accepted Uighur refugees, but it was too far and too dangerous. As for other prefectures like Jingzhou, Yangzhou, Hongzhou, and Yuezhou, each of which had a Manichean temple called Dayun Guangming Monastery, governors there followed the order of the emperor and were ready to catch Manichaeans; hence, there was no chance for these missionaries to survive. Also the repelling order was forcefully and frighteningly carried out in the north. The Japanese monk Ennin who had experienced and witnessed all kinds of cruelties put everything down in his book *Ennin's Diary: The Record of a Pilgrimage to China in Search of the Law* (*Ru Tang qiufa xunli xingji*):

> Dengzhou is the northeastern extremity of China. Built along the North Sea, this city is about a couple of *li* away from the sea. Although it is a remote place, it is no different from the capital in terms of regulating monks and nuns, destroying monasteries, banning scriptures, breaking statues, and confiscating monastery properties. They peeled off gold from the Buddhas, smashed bronze and iron statues, and measured their weight. What a pain!

Since the west and north were a dead end, the only exile choice left for Master Ulug was the south or east. As to why he finally gave up the south and went east, the doctrine of Manichaeism might help to explain, in the situation that there is no other available evidence. According to the Manichaean doctrine of light and darkness, which has been repeatedly mentioned by classical Christian writers, the world of space is divided into primary and secondary levels, with the realm of light three times larger than that of the darkness, and that each is located in a distinct position. If we use a tree analogy, as Evgeniya Borisovna Smagina explained in her 1998 book *Translation and Interpretation of Kephalaia*, the precious tree of light flourishes in the east, the west, and the north, but the deadly tree of darkness grows in the south. Since the south meant a dead end, it is no wonder that, contrary to the habitual choice of fleeing to the south for survival whenever there was a crisis on the Central Plains, Master Ulug headed east to the comparatively safer coastal area and sought refuge there.

Master Ulug's exile led to the rebirth of Manichaeism. As he wandered and taught in Fujian, a deified "Religion of Light" finally emerged and became popular among local residents.

Secularization among the Folk

As Blaise Pascal remarked, miracles served as the foundation of religion, and the same can be said of Manichaeism. As for how Manichaeans used supernatural means to win the support of local inhabitants of Quanzhou, the third volume of Xu Xuan's *Record on the Investigation of the Divine* (*Ji shen lu*) in the mid-tenth century provides the following exorcism record:

> Someone surnamed Yang was a native of Qingyuan county. He was a vice general (*fujiang*) of the county's Containment Battalion (*fang'e'ying*), living in a mansion in the western suburb. One morning, before he came back from the office, and when his family members were having breakfast, a big goose suddenly walked in from the front gate, carrying false paper money on its back and went straight to the west room. Yang's family were puzzled, "Did this goose come from the divine temple?" Then they told a servant to chase it away. But when the servant rushed to the west room, he only saw a white-bearded old man there. The family were scared and fled out of the

house. When Yang came home and heard about this, he was really enraged. Getting hold of a stick, he chased the ghost, and tried to hit him. But the ghost was running around, constantly changing his shape, and Yang could not get him. Yang was infuriated, shouting, "I'll kill you when I finish my meal!" The ghost bent over to salute him, saying, "As you please." Yang had two daughters. The elder daughter went into the kitchen to cut meat for her father, but the meat disappeared when it touched the cutting board. Still holding the kitchen knife in hand, she hastened to her father, "A big dark, hairy hand emerged from under the chopping board, and it said, 'Please chop!'" Running away in scare, she soon got sick. When the younger daughter scooped salt from the big urn, a monkey suddenly jumped out of it and got on her back. Rushing to the sitting room, she found the monkey gone. After that, she fell sick, too. Yang then hired a shaman to set up an altar to exorcise the ghost, but the ghost did the same thing, and it even beat the shaman. Unable to conquer the ghost, the shaman was also scared away. Shortly, Yang's wife and two daughters died. Later, he learned about a person called Mingjiao who was good at exorcism, whom he invited to chant scriptures in his house for one night. Cursing him angrily, the ghost left. Later in the same year, Yang too died.

This absurd narrative is noteworthy for two points. One is that the Religion of Light gained an upper hand over witchcraft, and the other is that chanting scriptures was a necessary step for exorcism. This miraculous story made a sensation among the folk, but it could only last for a short time. To have a lasting effect, Manichaeans needed to blend practical social interests into their doctrine. The reason why the "Manichean worship" in the Song period was popular in Fujian and Zhejiang provinces can be explained by the secular function of "mutual care" which served as the basis of their religious beliefs. Wang Juzheng, an imperial diarist (*qiju sheren*) in the Southern Song dynasty, understood this clearly:

> I heard that, for every village, Manichean worshipers gather around a headman, who is fierce and sly, and who would register the other villagers and gang up with them. Anyone who joins has to be a vegetarian, and when one family is in trouble, the other members need to offer their assistance to get this family through. Being vegetarian means a reduction in living costs, which also suggests an easier way to satisfy the demand for food, while ganging up means a closer relationship and mutual care, which indicates an easier access to relief.[4]

The mutual care of "Manichean worshipers" reinforced the ancient principle of life in rural society, in other words, it attested to both the moralization of religion and the religionization of morals.[5] What is advocated in the *Fragments of the Manichaean Manuscripts* (*Monijiao canjing*), "collaboration leads to unification, and mutual help brings about collective achievements," has been turned from preaching into practice. Compared with western Manichaeism, the Religion of Light practiced in China shows more concern for social life.

Idolized and Deified

Through a secularization among local residents, Manichaeism fulfilled its transformation in exile. But their scriptures, articles, treatises, and songs were nothing but a manifestation of heterodoxy in the eyes of traditional Buddhists. Indeed, an examination of this religious sect reveals a regional variation in terms of idol, fasting meals, funeral rites, and congregation. Still following the Manichaean doctrine of "the supreme and perfect truth, the Buddha of Light," the Religion of Light in Quanzhou nevertheless showed clear features of idolization and deification.

Idol

As mentioned earlier, Li Tingyu in the early Northern Song dynasty bought a Mani Buddha image in Bianjing. But what kind of image that was still remains unclear today. Nevertheless, the wall carving of Mani in Cao'an of Jinjiang, passed down since the Yuan period, is kept intact. Judging from his appearance, dress, posture, and waves of light behind him, we can see that this image is dramatically different from those on the frescoes of Gaochang. Indeed, we might say that it is a statue of a Sinicized idol with a Buddhist figure but a Taoist appearance. The eighteen rays of light behind him are also inconsistent with the "twelve rays of light" in Manichaeism. It is very likely that the eighteen rays of light symbolize "the eighteen perfections of purity in a Buddha's enjoyment body," among which, the first perfection – "Perfect purity of visible color" which means "Light illuminates the unenlightened world," aligns with the dualistic belief of light and darkness in Manichaeism, and echoes the Manichean verse of "purity and light."

Fasting Meals

In her note to the Turkish version of *Repentance*, Lyudmila Vasilyevna Dmitrieva remarked that followers of Manichaeism are not allowed to harm animals, birds, fish, and insects. That explains why during the fasting days Manichaeans in Gaochang mainly lived on melons which are believed to have the seeds of light. In Fujian, however, melons were replaced by fungi. Lu You, in the 10th volume of the *Jottings from the Life-Long Learning Hut* (*Laoxue an biji*), wrote that in Fujian, followers of the Religion of Light at that time "burned nothing but frankincense, and ate nothing but red fungi, leading to high prices of both." Except the poisonous ones, generally speaking, fungi are delicious and good for health, accepted as one of the famous varieties of dietary herbs. These people probably acquired the habit of eating fungi from monks, if we recall what is described in the *Miscellaneous Writings from Youyang* (*Youyang zazu*), authored by Duan Chengshi from the late Tang period:

> In the second year of the Wuzong Emperor, in Mount Pogang, Putian county, Song prefecture, fungi as big as a basket were found growing on the rocks. The stem and cap of this type of fungus were yellowish-white, the other parts light red. The monks passing by ate them all, and commented that they were more tasteful than any other fungi.

Funeral Rites

In the Song period, Manichaean funeral rites were not only performed in Quanzhou but also spread to Wenzhou, and then to Zhexi and Zhedong. Zhuang Chuo offered this description in his book *Chicken Rib Chronicles (Jilei bian)*:

> About the funeral, there is no drinking, no feasting on meat, no worshipping of gods, Buddha or ancestors of the deceased, and no visits from guests. Naked burial is preferred. Before being entombed, the deceased will be fully dressed. Then two people sit beside the corpse, and start a dialogue. One of them asks: 'Did he wear a hat when he was born?' The other answers: 'No.' Then they take off the dead person's hat. In this manner, they get rid of his apparel one by one until there is nothing left. Then one asks: 'What was he born with?' 'With the afterbirth.' Then they put the body into a sack.[6]

Although naked burial was an act of Manichaean doctrine, putting the corpse into a sack was actually a legacy from Taoism in the Han period. According to the *Book of Han: Biography of Yang Wangsun (Han shu: Yang Wangsun zhuan)*:

> In the period of Emperor Xiaowu [510–535], Yang Wangsun devoted himself to the study of the thoughts of Huang-Lao [Huangdi and Laozi]. He owned properties, enjoying a very affluent lifestyle, and taking care of his health by all possible means. When he was about to die of illness, he left his last will to his son, saying: 'after death, I want to be buried naked so I can return to nature, and you should not disobey me! After I die, you should put my body into a sack, and bury me seven *chi* under the ground. After my body is lowered down, just pull down the sack from my feet, that way, my body can be close to the soil.'

This quote indicates that the concept of "afterbirth" in the Religion of Light matched the "return to nature" idea of the Huang-Lao. With regard to funeral rituals, there was a hidden but traceable connection between this Manichean sect and Taoism. Thus, the deification of Chinese Manicheanism was further proved, aside from the evidence in Cao'an where we see a Buddhist figure with a Taoist appearance.

Congregation

In a manner similar to the "Buddhist Assembly in White Robes" (*Baiyi fohui*) in Wenzhou, the "Community of the Religion of Light" in Quanzhou (as evidenced by the unearthed porcelain bowls) gathered its followers as a congregation which served as the social foundation of monastic Manichaeism. More than two centuries after Master Ulug taught his disciples in Sanshan and Quanjun, worshipers of Manicheism in coastal areas in the early years of Emperor Xuanhe [1119–1126] in the Northern Song dynasty were no longer loose followers, but rather an organized congregation. As narrated in the *Draft to an Institutional History of the Song Dynasty: Penal Law No. 2, Prohibitions* (*Song huiyao jigao: Xingfa 2, jinyue*):

> Around Wenzhou, there are recalcitrant people who claim to be disciples of the Religion of Light. In each village where they live, they build a "vegetarian hall." In Wenzhou, there are about forty such establishments which are actually privately built and unlicensed Buddhist temples. In the first month of each year, on one of the *Mi* days [Sundays][7] in the calendar, they gather followers such as attendants, hearers, paternal aunts, sisters who donate vegetarian food, et al., and set up a Buddhist rite where they instigate naïve local residents. They assemble at night and will not leave until dawn.

"Fasting on Sundays" used to be a monastic rule in Manicheanism, but in the quote above, it became a folk custom. The excavated "Community" bowl shows that special cutlery used to be popular in Quanzhou. The information disclosed by this unearthed cultural relic is not insignificant for understanding the popularity of Chinese Manichaeism and its folk base.

Historical Trend of Manichaeism's Variation in the Coastal Areas

The Religion of Light in Quanzhou, though idolized and deified, did not ease the tension between political rule and religious forces, or reconcile conflicts between heterodox factions. Therefore, it was hard for this religious sect to gain a strong position among the folk in the coastal areas. By the time of the Southern Song dynasty, there had been further variations of Manichaeism as it became more diversified and heretical. This can be attested by what Lu You wrote below:

> Since ancient times, the imperial court has not been bothered by rebels who, due to flood, drought or famine, suffered from hunger and then ganged up to attack and rob, as they could be pacified so long as their case was properly handled. However, those who practice heterodoxy are a real worry, as they bewitch naive people, form gangs, and bide their time, and it is hard to predict when this harm might surface. Such cults can be found everywhere. In Huai'nan, it is called "Er gui zi [People of the Double Collar-Crossings]," in Liangzhe [Zhexi and Zhedong], it is called "Mouni jiao [Teachings of Mouni]," in Jiangdong, "Si guo [Four Fruits]," in Jiangxi, "Jin-gang chan [Vajra Chen]," and in Fujian, "Mingjiao [the Religion of Light]" or "Jie di zhai [Teaching of Gate and Abstinence]," and so on. They are addressed by different names, and among them, the Religion of Light is the most influential.[8]

Comparatively speaking, the Religion of Light was probably the "most authentic heterodoxy," as it originated from Master Ulug. That might explain why this sect fared comparatively well in the early years of the Ming period. According to the *Book of Fujian: Records of Local Histories:*

> After Emperor Hongwu [1328–1398] of the Ming period united the country, three religions [Confucianism, Taoism and Buddhism] were employed to educate the people. As Mingjiao [the Religion of Light] was believed to have offended the official dynastic name, the followers of this sect were disbanded and their temples destroyed. Yu Xin, the minister of revenue, and Yang Long, the minister of rites, presented a memorial to the emperor pleading that this sect should be retained, thus it was left unattended. At present, there are people who follow its practice through incantations and call their doctrine the "Shi fa [Teaching of the Masters]," but they are not very visible. Behind the Thatched Hut [Cao'an in Mount Huabiao, Jinjiang], there is the Wanshifeng [Ten-Thousand-Rock Peak], the Yuquan [Jade Spring], one-hundred-step stone ladder and some stone inscriptions.

What is inscribed on the cliff next to the Thatched Hut are not scriptures, but a sixteen-character incantation-like verse:

> The Immaculacy and Brightness
> The Great Power and Wisdom
> The Highest Perfection
> Mani the Buddha of Light.⁹

As a condensed tenet, this verse indicates to future followers that for the Religion of Light, its essence remains unchanged although the appearances may vary. That is to say, the variation of Chinese Manichaeism does not mean a digression from its origins. This distinction is a matter of principle. Otherwise, religion might be undistinguishable from superstition.

Notes

1 See Paul Pelliot and Edouard Chavannes, "A Manichaean Treatise Found in China." The Chinese version was translated by Feng Chengjun and it is included in the second volume of Feng's multi-volume works *Translated Works for the Study on the History and Geography of the Western Regions and South China Sea* (*Xiyu nanhai shidi kaozheng yicong*) (Beijing: Shangwu yinshuguan, 1995).
2 Karl Marx, *The Capital*, 1975: 410.
3 Shi Zanning [Master Tonghui, 919–1001] was a Buddhist scholar-official renowned for his knowledge of Buddhist history and institutions in China. The following quote comes from the edition of the Jinling kejingchu.
4 Li Xinchuan, vol. 76. See also *A Collection of Enlightened Judgments by Famous Officials* (*Minggong shupan qingming ji*), 535–537.
5 Chen Yuan opines that "Manichaeism can yet be regarded as a kind of moral religion." See Chen Yuan, 1980: 370.
6 Zhuang Chuo.

7 The Chinese term is 密日, which, according to some researchers, is the transcription of the Sogdian word "Mir" which means Sunday. —Trans.
8 Lu You, "Item-by-Item Reply" in the *Collected Works of Weinan* (*Weinan wen ji*), vol. 5. See also Lin Wushu, 1997: 141–155. [This translation refers to Lin Wushu's essay "A Study of Equivalent Names of Manichaeism in Chinese," in *Popular Religion and Shamanism*, edited by Ma Xisha and Meng Huiying. Leiden and Boston: Brill, 2011. 55–121. —Trans.]
9 This translation comes from Lin Wushu's essay "A Study of Equivalent Names of Manichaeism in Chinese," 55–121. —Trans.

Bibliography

Chen Yuan. *Chenyuan xueshu lunwenji* (*Collection of Chen Yuan's Academic Writings*). Beijing: Zhonghua shuju, 1980.

Dmitrieva, Lyudmila Vasilyevna. "Translation and Interpretation of Repentance," in *The Turkological Studies*. [In Russian.] Moscow & Leningrad: The USSR Academy of Sciences Publishing House, 1963. 214–232.

Ennin. *Ru Tang qiufa xunli xingji* (*Ennin's Diary: The Record of a Pilgrimage to China in Search of the Law*). Shanghai: Shanghai guji chubanshe, 1986.

Feng Chengjun. *Xiyu nanhai shidi kaozheng yicong* (*Translated Works for the Study on the History and Geography of the Western Regions and South China Sea*). Beijing: Shangwu yinshuguan, 1995.

He Qiaoyuan, ed. *Min shu* (*Book of Fujian*). Fuzhou: Fujian Renmin chubanshe, 1994.

Li Xinchuan, ed. *Jianyan yilai xinian yaolu* (*Annual Records of the Most Important Events since the Jianyan Reign*). Beijing: Zhonghua shuju, 1988.

Lin Wushu. *Monijiao jiqi dongjian* (*Manichaeism and its Dissemination in the East*). Taipei: Shuxin chubanshe, 1997.

Lu You. *Laoxue an biji* (*Jottings from the Life-Long Learning Hut*). Beijing: Zhonghua shuju, 1979.

Lu You. *Weinan wen ji* (*Collected Works of Weinan*). Beijing: Zhonghua shuju, 1976.

Marx, Karl. *The Capital*. [In Chinese.] Translated by Compilation and Translation Bureau of Works of Marx, Engels, Lenin and Stalin of the CPC Central Committee. Beijing: Renmin chubanshe, 1975.

Shi Zanning. *Dasong seng shilue* (*Topical Compendium of the Buddhist Clergy*). Edition of Jinling kejingchu at Nanjing.

Xu Song, ed. *Song huiyao jigao* (*Draft to an Institutional History of the Song Dynasty*). Beijing: Zhonghua shuju, 1957.

Xu Xuan. *Ji shen lu* (*Record on the Investigation of the Divine*). Taipei: Taiwan shangwu yinshuguan, 1983.

Zhongguo shehui kexueyuan lishi yanjiusuo Song Liao Jin Yuan shi yanjiushi, ed. *Minggong shupan qingming ji* (*A Collection of Enlightened Judgments by Famous Officials*). Beijing: Zhonghua shuju, 2002.

Zhuang Chuo, ed. *Jilei bian* (*Chicken Rib Chronicles*). Beijing: Zhonghua shuju, 1997.

11 The Kunlun Slaves in Buddhist Books of the Tang and Song Periods

In the early twentieth century, when Chen Yinke was reading the collection of Dunhuang Buddhist songs edited by Luo Zhenyu, he made detailed notes on "A Romance Derived from 'Manjushri's Inquiry about Illness' in *Vimalakirti Sutra*" ("Weimojiejing wenshushili wenjipin yanyi"). In particular, he cited ten pieces of literature to explain what is meant by the saying "led and followed by Gulun lions." In 1932, his essay "A Romance Derived from 'Manjushri's Inquiry about Illness' in *Vimalakirti Sutra Illustration in Dunhuang* – An Afterword" ("Dunhuangben weimojiejing wenjipin yanyi shuhou") was published. He declared that "骨仑 (gulun)" is "昆仑 (Kunlun)."[1] This research shows that Buddhist texts of the Tang and Song periods cannot be ignored for the study of the "Kunlun slaves."

The Kunlun slaves in the Tang and Song periods were believed to be a group of "dark-skinned and curly-haired" South China Sea islanders who were good at swimming and taming elephants. After their arrival in China, owing to their distinctive physical features and skills, they enjoyed higher fame than "Sogdian dancing girls" or "Korean handmaids," and they were frequently mentioned in poems, personal notes, or romances. As an exotic group participating in the cultural exchange between China and foreign countries, they have caught the attention of international sinologists. In 1915, Japanese scholar Kuwabara Jistuzo published *Studies on Pu Shougeng*.[2] In 1919, the French sinologist Gabriel Ferrand published *Kunlun and Navigation across the Ancient South China Sea*.[3] Delving deeply into the Kunlun civilization in the ancient South China Sea, these books are the earliest research accounts of the Kunlun slaves.

If we take Wen Tingshi's posthumous book *A Lengthy and Confusing Talk of Chun Changzi (Chun Changzi zhiyu)*,[4] published in the late Qing period, as the starting point in China, then the study about the Kunlun slaves has been ongoing for about a hundred years. Setting aside its merits and demerits, I now pick up what was left by Wen and carry on with this research. Wen's work is an encyclopedic book of essays, revealing a prominent feature of Sino-Western cultural interaction. Volume 13 provides the account about the Kunlun slaves as follows:

> As Shi Daoxuan in the Tang period mentioned in his book *Continued Biographies of Eminent Monks (Xu gaoseng zhuan)*: "On the newly conquered land Linyi 林邑 [now central Vietnam], the Buddhist scriptures that

we have got total 564 cases, more than 1,350 books, all written in the Kunlun language on pattra [palmyra] leaves." In his book *A Record of Buddhist Practices Sent Home from the South China Sea* (*Nanhai jigui neifa zhuan*), Shi Yijing also stated that "there are more than ten countries in the South China Sea, but they have been put under one name – the Country of Kunlun since some Kulun people first arrived at Cochin and Guangdong. But the Kunlun people on this land are curly-haired and dark-skinned.[5] This country goes as far south as Zhanbo [Champa] which is also known as Linyi. Here, most people are followers of the Saṃmatīya, and a small number are believers of the Sarvāstivādins." In my understanding, the Kunlun language should be today's Wulaiyou [Melayu]. I have read some Wulaiyou [Melayu] which is similar to Arabic. Kunlun is also mentioned in *A Brief Account of Island Foreigners* (*Daoyi zhilue*): "In ancient times, the Kunlun Mountain, also known as the Juntun Mountain, was high and square, extending for several hundred of *li* into the middle of the sea, facing Zhancheng [Champa] and Xizhu [India]. It is named for the Kunlun Ocean below it."[6]

From the perspective of academic study, Wen Tingshi's textual research of Kunlun geography and racial identity might not be as detailed as those of later scholars. However, his focus on Buddhist texts from the Tang period and the extensive use of historical materials set a new direction worthy of our attention. He noticed the cultural phenomenon of "explaining Buddhism with Confucian books, and approaching Confucianism with Zen Buddhism." This trend of exploring different sources developed into a unique research style, which is applicable to the study of Kunlun slaves. Many contemporary scholars have noticed the necessity of matching documents with their corresponding cultural relics, such as the Dunhuang frescoes and the unearthed pottery figurines.[7] However, there is still a lack of academic efforts and awareness in using comparative studies between historical documents and Buddhist texts. This is the reason why I have chosen to examine historical materials about the Kunlun slaves in Buddhist texts from the Tang and Song periods. I focus more specifically on the Kunlun slaves in Zen texts, which has been overlooked by previous scholars. My hope is that a critical analysis will help to disclose social and cultural significance of these accounts.

"Kunlun" in Shi Huilin's *Sound and Meaning of All Sutras*

Born in a Pei family in the state of Shule during the Tang period, Shi Huilin later became a monk in the Ximing Temple of Chang'an. He was an educated monk "well versed in Indian Buddhism or Chinese exegesis." [8] From 788 to 810, he spent 23 years on his book *Sound and Meaning of All Sutras* (*Yiqiejing yinyi*), totaling hundreds of volumes. In volume 61, he classified the knowledge about the "Kunlun" and people living there as follows:

> According to the *Extended Elegance* (*Guangya*), "*bo*" is a kind of vessel on the sea. *Kunlun bo* has a draft of sixty *chi*, capable of carrying more than a

thousand people and goods. Many Kunlun sailors work on the vessel to get it going. They connect coconut exocarps to form a chain and fill gelan syrup in between the strands so that they are waterproof. The vessel is made of layers of plank as thin deck might break, but no nails are used, as iron at a certain high temperature might start a fire. Divided into front, middle and rear, the vessel has a length about several *li* (?). When on full sail, it goes faster than what manpower can make it sail.

In volume 81, he explained the "Kunlun language" this way:

> Although the first character is read as "kun 昆" and the second as "lun 论," for the sake of convenience, it is also pronounced as "gulun 骨论." The gulun people are foreigners from the South China Sea islands. They are dark-skinned and naked, and they can tame wild beasts like rhinos and elephants. There are different ethnic groups, such as Sengzhi [Zanj], Tumi, Gutang, or Gemie [Khmer], all inferior people. This is an uncivilized land where people plunder for a living, and behave like cannibals, similar to demons or evil spirits. They are different from people of other vassal states, and speak a strange language. But they are really good swimmers and can stay in the water all day without drowning.[9]

These two paragraphs in the *Sound and Meaning of All Sutras* are often quoted, enjoying a fame as classical interpretation. What is mentioned about the place, identity, language and skills reveals Shi Huilin's view of the Kunlun people. Although there are some biased words such as "inferior," the descriptions are rather documentary. Concerning the "South China Sea islands" and "different ethnic groups," Feng Chengjun explained:

> The Country of Kunlun was a general name for all the countries in the South China Sea, ranging from Champa in the north, Java in the south, the Malayan peninsula in the west, to Borneo in the east. It even went beyond to the east coast of Africa. All these places were brought under one name - Kunlun.[10]

Apart from these explanations, there are two more points that can be gleaned from the records of the Tang and Song periods. First, animal taming and swimming are described as the two major skills of the Kunlun people and tend to be attributed to all of them. But it should be pointed out that mahouts and sailors actually came from different regions. According to Zhu Yu's *Notes on Pingzhou* (*Pingzhou ketan*), volume two, published in the Northern Song dynasty, although the Kunlun people were all islanders, they were divided into two groups: "savages in the mountains" and "savages on the sea."[11] The former were "cannibals" who might be called "Beastmaster Kunlun", and the latter were known as "Swimmer Kunlun" who "did not wink their eyes a bit when diving underwater." After their move to China, they had different identities. One group became official slaves and the other group, private slaves.

Second, the gelan syrup used to build a Kunlun vessel was actually olive gum. Although it was difficult to know how it developed, there was no doubt that Lingnan people in the Tang period had used this technology. In his *Record of Strange Things of the Far South (Lingbiao luyi)*, Liu Xun provided an explanation for "olive":

> For the wild lush trees that bear a lot of fruits, it is hard to get to the top even with a ladder, but if you carve a few inches into the lower trunk, you may find salty pulp inside. Overnight, the fruits fall. The resin on the branches is like peach gum. After being collected, it is cooked together with bark and leaves until something like dark brown syrup is formed. That is called olive gum. It can be used to fix holes in a boat and it sticks better than glue. When dipped in water, it becomes even more sticky.[12]

Clearly, the adhesive material used on the Kunlun vessel was a mixture of resin and bark. It was named that way just because it looked like syrup, but it had no sweet flavor whatsoever.

The Kunlun Civilization in Yijing's Works

Yijing was a famous dharma-seeking monk in the Tang period. His secular surname was Zhang, and he was born in Qizhou of Shandong. In 671, he sailed across the sea from Guangzhou to India, worshipped sacred sites, and stayed in Srivijaya (now Sumatra) for ten years. By 691, he had completed two famous Buddhist books: *A Record of Buddhist Practices Sent Home from the South China Sea* (*Nanhai jigui neifa zhuan*); and *The Great Tang Biographies of Eminent Monks who Sought the Dharma in the Western Regions* (*Da Tang xiyu qiufa gaoseng zhuan*). Both books are records of his personal experience and have important historical value. Readers can refer to Wang Bangwei's annotated version of these two books for a better understanding.

Although the Kunlun civilization in the ancient South China Sea is not fully covered in Yijing's works, it includes some chronicles that can be cross-referenced with other books. The first point worthy of mention is local products. As stated in the third volume of *A Record of Buddhist Practices Sent Home from the South China Sea*:

> In Gulun, a country in the South China Sea, a large water-filled copper cauldron with a hole at the bottom is used to measure time. The moment when water is completely gone, a drum is beaten once. With four strokes, it is midday. Then with another four beats, it is dusk. The same goes for the night. With eight beats for the day, and another eight for the night, there is all together 16. This is the practice ordained by the king. Owing to the clepsydra, even on a cloudy day, there is no mistake about whether it is afternoon or night, and even if it rains all night long, there is no fear of missing the beats that mark time.[13]

In addition to the time-measuring copper pot, this country is described as rich in lilacs. In the same volume, there is a mention of the lilacs used in medicine: "For lilacs of two different colors, both grow in Gulun 堀沦."[14] There were large female lilacs and small male ones, the former useful for its fruit and the latter good for its flower buds.[15] Based on this, Cen Zhongmian assumed that "Since Gulun 堀沦 was in the east and it specialized in lilacs, it is probably somewhere near the Moluccas."[16]

The second point that deserves our attention is the relationship between "Juelun 掘伦" and "Kunlun 昆仑." The foreword of the first volume of *A Record of Buddhist Practices Sent Home from the South China Sea* gives the reason why "more than ten countries in the South China Sea" were called by one general name "Kunlun":

> These countries are wide apart in the sea, some about a hundred *li* from others, some hundreds of *li*, or even hundreds of sea stations away. Though it is difficult to calculate the distance, those merchants who ship around know the places. It is probable that some Juelun people first arrived at Cochin and Guangdong. As they are curly-haired and dark-skinned, then the whole area in the South China Sea was called Kunlun.[17] Inhabitants in other Kunlun countries look similar to us Chinese.

In this quotation, "Juelun people first arrived at Cochin and Guangdong" is really important, as it touches upon the questions of "who" and "when." From the extant documents, the arrival can be traced back to the Liang dynasty during the "Southern Dynasties" period. When the Emperor Wu of the Liang dynasty held a court meeting with his ministers on the lunar New Year's Day, "In the east stood Kunlun envoys from Ru [It should be Ruru], and in the west were guests from Gaogouli [Goguryeo] and Baiji [Paekche]."[18] While there were "Kunlun envoys" as court guests, there were also "Kunlun mahouts." In his book *Commented Rhapsodies on Categorized Matters* (*Shilei fuzhu*), volume 20, Wu Shu from the Song period quoted from the book *Summary Documents of the Three Kingdoms* (*Sanguo dianlue*) to define the word "elephant":

> The army of the Northern Zhou approached Jiangling, and the Liang army fought back. The Liang soldiers sent out two elephants, each of which wore an armor on back and had a dagger fastened to the end of its trunk, and two Kunlun slaves led them to the fight. As Yang Zhong shot at the elephants, the animals turned backwards and ran into the Liang troops.[19]

This is the first time Kunlun slaves' participation in the war was mentioned.

Third, in his book *The Great Tang Biographies of Eminent Monks Who Sought the Dharma in the Western Regions*, Yijing spoke of the "Kunlun language" and the "Kunlun accent" several times. Wen Tingshi in *A Lengthy and Confusing Talk of Chun Changzi* assumed that "Kunlun language should be today's Melayu." Due to the scarcity of sources, it is hard to know. But an anecdote from the Northern Song period told a story about a man from Srivijaya who joined others in Guangzhou to recite sutras, and that might provide some information. In the second volume of *Notes on Pingzhou*, Zhu Yu recorded this intriguing episode:

> When I was in Guangzhou, I held a banquet and many foreigners gathered in my mansion. Their leader invited a man from Srivijaya to come here, saying that he was good at chanting the "Peacock King Sutra." I reckon that this is a brilliant chance, as what is meant by the Mantra in a Buddhist text is hardly comprehensible and possibly misunderstood, so I asked him to do it. This man put his hands behind his back, leaned against the hall column and shouted. His voice sounded like pouring boiling water into a bottle, not in the least bit similar to the legendary way of chanting the "Peacock Sutra." I said to the others that this scripture has been re-translated, so it is understandably different, but if we pay homage to the deceased this way, I have no idea how Chinese ghosts might get it.

As this man from Srivijaya spoke like "pouring boiling water into a bottle," it was impossible for Chinese listeners to understand him. No wonder literati in the Song period spoke of this in a teasing way and treated it as a "drunkard's dream talk." For instance, Wang Junyu of the Song period, in his book *Collected Aphorisms – Continued* (*Zazuan xu*), cited the anecdote of "a Persian chanting the Peacock Sutra"[20] as an example for an entry entitled "Incomprehensible." In the Song period, "Persia" in the South China Sea was part of Srivijaya, as explained in detail by Gabriel Ferrand's "Persia in the South China Sea,"[21] so there is no need to dwell on this topic here. It seems that the "Peacock King Sutra" translated by Amoghavajra, when chanted by speakers of strong Kunlun accents, really shocked people in the Song period.

Swimmer Kunlun in *A Forest of Pearls from the Dharma Garden* (Fayuan zhulin)

Shi Daoshi [secular name Xuanyun] was a Buddhist monk at the Ximing Temple in Chang'an during the Tang period. His book *A Forest of Pearls from the Dharma Garden* (*Fayuan zhulin*), which was finished in 668, is a compilation of Buddhist stories and historical documents. In volume 38, the section about "Guta" ["Ancient Pagoda"] in the sixth entry records the miracle about the base of Chaohua Temple in Zhengzhou in the Sui dynasty:

> I climbed up to the second floor of the pagoda and saw in the south a pool of spring water. The water is splashing and surging, but no single sound can be heard. Isn't that produced by divine force? There is a 105- year-old splendid-looking monk from Youzhou called Daoyan who wanted to find out why. This monk's secular surname is Li, and he used to serve his religion in four famous temples during the reign of Emperor Yang in the Sui dynasty, but later he changed into his secular clothes and started a reclusive life in

the mountain. For seven days every year, he would come and stay in this pagoda, trying his best to make offerings to gods here. Surprised to see water gushing and gurgling yet soundlessly, he sent a Kunlun slave who is good at swimming to find out why. Underneath the water, the swimmer saw the neatly arranged stone pillars whose edges are unmeasurable. In the middle is a pagoda, about three feet high, suspended in the air, and surrounded by water. The diver was brave enough to explore the base of the pagoda but could not reach it. As to its origin, there is no way to find out. The folklore has it that it was authorized by Aśoka. Nevertheless, this pagoda has been in existence since the reign of the Emperor Wen in the Sui dynasty.[22]

In the Tang period, it was a common practice for dignitaries or noble people to send Kunlun slaves into the water to pick up things. The book *Extensive Records of the Taiping Era* (*Taiping guangji*) has many records about this. As for Buddhist temples' use of Kunlun slaves for this purpose, the above account about what happened in the Chaohua Temple provides an example. Presumably, the Kunlun slaves served both monks and laymen. Thus, among the people who employed the Kunlun slaves, after Li Deyu, Tao Xian, and Zhou Han, Monk Daoyan should be added. Given this background, it is not surprising to see "Kunlun slaves" mentioned in Zen texts.

"Kunlun Slaves" in the Zen Talks

From the mid-Tang to the Song periods, the marine trade in the South China Sea prospered, and Zen Buddhism also rose to its zenith. In their practice of "talking Zen indirectly," the monks touched extensively upon secular life, including the topic of "Kunlun slaves." Although "the first tenet of Zen is unsayable," for the sake of research, we need not worry about the implied profound theories, and just read these talks literally. In what follows, I divide the quotations from the Song period documents – Shi Puji's *Compendium of Five Lamps* (*Wudeng huiyuan*) and Zezangzhu's *Recorded Sayings of the Ancient Worthies* (*Gu zunsu yulu*) into six talks and briefly comment on each for future reference.

First, in *Compendium of Five Lamps,* volume 12, there is a sermon given by Zen master Shi Jicheng from Jingyin Temple in Bianzhou, which contains an impressive description about how some Kunlun slaves were publicly punished:

> Convocation sermon: "Wearing iron leggings, Kunlun slaves could hardly walk. Whipped once, they took a step forward. It was really like catching a soft-shelled turtle out of the fire, hiding ice in the sun, finding sprites in the shadow, and binding hemp rope with nothing."[23]

The four situations listed above are included to allegorically show reliability of the first two sentences. However, even the situation revealed in these two sentences is illusionary, as Kunlun people in the South China Sea did not wear leggings, let alone "iron leggings." For a man, he would wrap his waist with a piece of cloth, which was called "heman" [uttariya]. This is clearly shown in the 81st volume of Huilin's *Sound and Meaning of All Sutras:* "It is a Sanskrit word, meaning a piece of cloth around the waist, covering the lower part of the body. It is a whole piece, not cut or sewn, just wrapped around the waist. It is called heman."

Second, in the *Compendium of Five Lamps*, volume 19, there is another reference to the Kunlun slaves:

> Zen master Shi Haiping at the Dawei Temple, Tanzhou, stepped into a dharma hall and gave a public sermon: "Dancing on lanterns, hiding behind pillars. Spirit of the Deep Sands loses temper (*e fa*), and a Kunlun slave goes furious." After a shout, he went on: "A single phrase and you've come up with words in the head; for ten thousand 'kalpa,' you will be like in a maze."

Literally speaking, "a Kunlun slave goes furious" and "Spirit of the Deep Sands loses temper" are phrases used to describe the moments when a person or a god loses control. Yet in both of these two cases, it is hardly believable. Here it is helpful to explain the related Buddhist tale and idioms in the Song period. As legend has it, Sha Wujing used to be a demon in the Sha River. After he meets Master Xuanzang who is traveling west to seek dharma, he is subdued. Roaring like thunder, this demon performs magic, and creates and holds the golden bridge with his hands for Xuanzang and his disciples to cross the river. After being transformed into a good spirit, he reads out a four-line epiphany:

> For five hundred years I have sunk in the deep sands, and all my family members have been punished and tortured. Holding the golden bridge with my hands for the Master to cross the river, I begged him to get permission from the demon lord to offer me a second birth.[24]

As for "*e fa*" ("losing temper,") it was an idiom used in the Song period. Lu You in the eighth volume of the *Jottings from the Life-Long Learning Hut* (*Laoxue an biji*) explained that "*e fa* is another way to say one loses temper." Since Sha Wujing has already become a good spirit, he won't be benevolent if he "loses [his] temper." For a Kunlun slave, it is also unbelievable that he would "go furious," as Kunlun slaves had always been known as "simple and honest servants who never run away."[25] Apparently, what Zen master Haiping mentioned in the public sermon were quite uncharacteristic.

Third, in the *Recorded Sayings of the Ancient Worthies*, volume 23, there is a dialogue between Zen Master Guixing and his disciples in Guangjiao Temple, Ye county, Ruzhou:

> Someone asked: "What does it mean by saying Bodhidharma is coming from the West?"
> Master responded: "A Kunlun lad carries ivory."[26]

The literal meaning of this sentence is very clear – a Kunlun slave carries goods from Kunlun, but it does not answer the question. As in the famous reply – "The cypress in the courtyard" which answers the same question, Master Guixing's response follows a similar pattern.

Fourth, in the 24th volume of the same book, the second chant of "Improvised Eighth Chants" ("Oushu baji") records the remarks of Zen master Hongyin in Shending Mountain, Tanzhou:

> There is an apparatus in the Shending Mountain,
> which you should agree without any suspicion.
> It strikes midnight at noon,
> Just like a Kunlun lad with a fair complexion.

In the last four lines of a seven-syllable poem "A Kunlun Lad" ("Kunlun er") by Zhang Ji, a poet of the Tang period, this portrayal is provided:

> He has dangling gold earrings, and his pierced nose is like that of livestock,
> bare-headed, a ushnisha keeps his long curly hair in lock.
> Proud of his pitch-black skin,
> he is half dressed with kapok [cotton] garments in his walk.[27]

It is clear that there is no "Kunlun lad with a fair complexion," and the claim that an apparatus "strikes midnight at noon" is also spurious. In other words, both are deliberately made up. The Shending sentence might be a paradoxical saying that is meant to help the disciples to unravel a "puzzle."

Fifth, also in this book, the 34th volume records the dialogue between Monk Foyan and his disciples in Longmen, Shuzhou:

> When Panshan Baoji was about to die, he said to monks, "Is there anyone among you who can draw a portrait for me?" Many of the monks made drawings, but none was accepted. Then Puhua stepped forward and said, "I can draw it." Panshan said, "Why don't you show it to me?" Puhua then turned a somersault and went out, saying:
>> Master is too ugly to be portrayed,
>> that everybody tried all means to get a good one for him laughs
>>   my head off indeed.
>> Not a bit of essence is obtained from his congregational address,
>> just like a white-nosed Kunlun lad celebrating the lunar new year
>>   for his need.

As mentioned above, a Kunlun lad had "pitch-black skin," then how is it possible that he had a "white nose"? Similarly, the "true portrait" of Panshan can never be "depicted." If a portrait is persistently demanded, the "ugliness" would be shown, and he would become a "white-nosed Kunlun."

Sixth, the 38th volume of this book mentions the talk between Monk Shouchu and his disciples in the Dong Mountain, Xiangzhou:

> Someone asked: "The golden crow rises from the sea to illuminate the world, how does it relate to time?"
> Master responded: "The Kunlun people cross the sea to sell their treasures, and the Persians have heavy beards."

It is well known that Kunlun people crossed the sea by ship and brought their treasures to sell to Chinese people, just as Persian men liked to grow beards. Nothing is uncommon.

From the six quotes above, it can be seen that references to "Kunlun slaves" by Zen monks in the Tang and Song periods were not documentary, but rather allegorical. They should deserve our attention not because of their historical value, but on account of their function to reflect social reality, revealing the role that Kunlun slaves played in the life of ordinary people and Zen monks. Moreover, since these Zen talks spread across regions such as Bianzhou, Tanzhou, Ruzhou, Shuzhou, and Xiangzhou, it can be seen that, besides local residents of Lingnan, people around the Yangtze River also knew about the Kunlun slaves. In previous research about them, Zen texts have been neglected and assumed to be empirically unhelpful. That is really a pity.

Conclusion

Kunlun slaves, Kunlun vessels, and Kunlun goods were all part of the Kunlun civilization in the ancient South China Sea, disclosing noticeable historical facts about the international trade in the Tang and Song periods.

As skilled laborers (good at swimming and taming elephants), the Kunlun slaves not only played a unique role in Chinese social life but were also important for their cultural influences. They can be seen in romances and tales like *Kunlun Slaves* (*Kunlun nu*) written by Pei Xing in the Tang period, and some derivative poetic dramas created in the Yuan and Ming periods, as well as in visual arts, such as terra-cotta figures and murals. In the Song period, in order to exhibit royal grandeur and majesty, Kunlun slaves riding on elephants were arranged to lead the guard troop. The word "Kunlun" is even rhetorically used to describe the color "black," not to mention its use in Zen talks, as I discussed above. All these demonstrate that there is still much room for exploration on the topic.

From the perspective of research sources, scholars have found materials from official histories, notes, and poems.[28] More efforts can be made in the analysis of correspondences between literature and cultural relics, literature and romances, literature and Buddhist texts. For instance, with Buddhist texts, there are different categories such as monks' biographies, travel notes, phonetic exegesis, quotes, and bianwen [religious storytelling that combines singing and narration.] Information gleaned from Buddhist scriptures not only makes up for what is not included in the external sources, but also enables us to propose the following hypothesis: In China, the enslavement of Kunlun people might not necessarily start in secular life, yet it probably matched the eastward spread of Buddhism. In fact, in the Buddhist songs, there are descriptions about Manjusri Bodhisattva riding a lion to a dharma hall, attended by two Kunlun slaves. In a word, previous studies about Kunlun slaves merely focus on the transportation history, which is somewhat partial and incomplete. In fact, the relationship between the history of Buddhism and Kunlun slaves was particularly close, especially in the initial stage. The word "奴 [nú](slave)" in "Kunlun nu" 昆仑奴 (Kunlun slaves) originally referred to "mahouts," but later took the meaning of a "domestic servant." The study about the origin of Kunlun slaves in China is twofold and may be further clarified by future research.

Notes

1. See *Two Episodes of Reading Notes* 读书札记二集 (Beijing: Sanlian shudian, 2001); and *The Second Collection of Manuscripts from the Jinming Studio* 金明馆丛稿二编 (Shanghai: Shanghai guji chubanshe, 1980).
2. Kuwabara Jistuzo, 84–87.
3. Ferrand, 27–32.
4. Wen Tingshi, courtesy name Daoxi, art name Yunge, was a regular metropolitan graduate (*jinshi chushen*), who was posted to be academic reader-in-waiting (*shidu xueshi*) in the Hanlin Academy (*hanlin yuan*), helping the emperor reading documents, and was entrusted with the duty to plan imperial daytime activities. After the failure of "The 1898 reform" (*wuxu bianfa*), he went to Japan for a living and studied Western politics. He died in 1904 in his hometown, Pingxiang, Jiangxi province.
5. Literary sketches in the Tang period described the Kunlun people as slaves, and that is how they got this nickname.
6. Wen Tingshi, 198. See also Wang Shuzi, ed., *Collected Works of Wen Tingshi* 文廷式集, vol. 2 (Beijing: Zhonghua shuju, 1993): 982–1020.
7. See Bu Liansheng, "Images of the Kunlun in Ancient Chinese Sculpture and Other Related Issues" ("Shilun woguo gudai diaosu de kunlunren jiqi youguan wenti" in *Collected Papers in Memory of Xiang Da* 向达先生纪念论文集 (Urumqi: Xinjiang renmin chubanshe, 1986): 635–648; Qin Hao, "An Archaeological Interpretation of Kunlun Slaves in Tang Tombs" ("Tang mu kunlun nuyong kaoshi"), *Nanjing daxue xuebao*, no. 2 (1983): 106–113; Cui Dayong, "A Preliminary Study of the Images of Black People in the Tang Dynasty" ("Tangdai heiren xingxiang chutan"), *Zhongguo wenwu shijie*, no. 108 (1994): 110–121, published in Hongkong; Ge Chengyong, "Tracing the Origin of Black People in Chang'an during the Tang Period" ("Tang Chang'an heiren laiyuan xunzong"), *Zhonghua wenshi luncong*, no. 1 (2001): 1–27.
8. Chen Yuan, 81–89. See also Xu Shiyi, *Studies on Sound and Meaning by Huilin* 慧琳音义研究 (Shanghai: Shanghai shehui kexueyuan chubanshe, 1997): 113–133.
9. This description is racially coded, indicating that Shi Huilin considers himself racially superior to the Kunlun people. Similar views can be found in other quotes from the Tang and Song documents. —Trans.
10. Feng Chengjun, 1984: 51.
11. Zhu Yu, 28. These terms are racially coded.
12. Liu Xun, 19.
13. Shi Yijing, 170.
14. Shi Yijing, 153.
15. Zhao Rushi, 181.
16. Cen Zhongmian, 1962: 305.

17 In the Tang period, besides its association with the famous Kunlun Mountains, the word Kunlun was also used to describe something dark or black. — Trans.
18 Zhou Yiliang, 239–240.
19 Wu Shu, 412.
20 Wang Junyu, 63. See also Kong Zhiyuan, *Indonesia-China Cross Culture Relation* 中国印度尼西亚文化交流 (Beijing: Beijing daxue chubanshe, 1999): 112–117.
21 Feng Chengjun, 1995: 79–95.
22 Shi Daoshi, vol. 1: 590.
23 Shi Puji, vol. 2: 767.
24 *The Story of How Tripitaka of the Great Tang Procures the Scriptures* (*Datang Sanzang qujing*): 23.
25 See Zhu Yu, vol. 2.
26 Zezangzhu, vol. 1: 438.
27 *Complete Tang Poems* (*Quan Tangshi*) vol. 1: 961.
28 Li Jiping, 292–298.

Bibliography

Cen Zhongmian. *Zhongwai shidi kaozheng* (*Inquiries in the Historical Geographies of China and Foreign Countries*), vol. 1. Beijing: Zhonghua Book Company, 1962.

Chen Yuan. *Zhongguo fojiao shiji gailun* (*An Introduction to the History of Chinese Buddhism*). Beijing: Zhonghua Book Company, 1962.

Feng Chengjun. *Xiyu nanhai shidi kaozheng yicong* (*Translated Works for the Study on the History and Geography of the Western Regions and South China Sea*), vol. 1, book 2. Beijing: Shangwu yinshuguan, 1995.

Feng Chengjun. *Zhongguo nanyang jiaotong shi* (*The History of China's Communication with Nanyang*). Shanghai: Shanghai shudian chubanshe, 1984.

Ferrand, Gabriel. *Kunlun and Navigation across the Ancient South Seas*. [In Chinese]. Translated by Feng Chengjun. Beijing: Zhonghua shuju, 1957.

Kuwabara, Jistuzo. *Studies on Pu Shougeng*. [In Chinese]. Translated by Chen Yuqing. Beijing: Zhonghua shuju, 1954.

Li Jiping. "*Tangdai Kunlunnu kao* (Studies on Kunlun Slaves in the Dang Dynasty)." *Literature and History* 16 (1982): 292–298.

Li Shiren and Cai Jinghao, collated. *Datang Sanzang qujing* (*The Story of How Tripitaka of the Great Tang Procures the Scriptures*). Beijing: Zhonghua shuju, 1997.

Liu Xun. *Lingbiao luyi* (*Record of Strange Things of the Far South*). Collated by Lu Xun. Guangzhou: Guangdong renmin chubanshe, 1983.

Lu You. *Laoxue an biji* (*Jottings from the Life-Long Learning Hut*). Beijing: Zhonghua shuju, 1979.

Quan Tangshi (*Complete Tang Poems*). Collected by Peng Dingqiu et al, and edited by Cao Yin. Shanghai: Shanghai guji chubanshe, 1986.

Qu Yanbin, ed. *Za zuan qizhong* (*Seven Types of Collected Aphorisms*). Shanghai: Shanghai guji chubanshe, 1988.

Shi Daoshi, ed. *Fayuan zhulin* (*A Forest of Pearls from the Dharma Garden*). Beijing: Zhonghua shuju, 1991.

Shi Puji. *Wudeng huiyuan* (*Compendium of Five Lamps*). Beijing: Zhonghua shuju, 1984.

Shi Xuanying and Shi Huilin, eds. *Yiqiejing yinyi* (*Sound and Meaning of All Sutras*). Shanghai: Shanghai guji chubanshe, 1986.

Shi Yijing. *Nanhai jigui neifa zhuan* (*A Record of Buddhist Practices Sent Home from the South China Sea*). Collated and Annotated by Wang Bangwei. Beijing: Zhonghua shuju, 1995.

Wang Junyu. "Zazuan xu (*Collected Aphorisms - Continued*)," in *Zazuan qizhong* (*Seven Types of Collected Aphorisms*). Edited by Qu Yanbin. Shanghai: Shanghai guji chubanshe, 1988. 47–80.

Wen Tingshi. *Chun Changzi zhiyu* (*A lengthy and Confusing Talk of Chun Changzi*). Nanjing: Jiangsu guangling guji keyinshe, 1990.

Wu Shu. *Shilei fuzhu* (*Commented Rhapsodies on Categorized Matters*).Beijing: Zhonghua shuju, 1989.

Zezangzhu, ed. *Gu zunsu yulu* (*Recorded Sayings of the Ancient Worthies*). Beijing: Zhonghua shuju, 1994.

Zhao Rushi. *Collation and Annotation of "Records of Foreign People"* (*Zhufanzhi jiaoshi*). Collated and annotated by Yang Bowen. Beijing: Zhonghua shuju, 1996.

Zhou Yiliang. *Wei Jin nanbeichao shi zhaji* (*Notes on the History of the Wei, Jin and Southern and Northern Dynasties*). Beijing: Zhonghua shuju, 1985.

Zhu Yu. *Pingzhou ketan* (*Notes on Pingzhou*). Shanghai: Shanghai guji chubanshe, 1989.

12 "Caravan Tea"

The tea trade with Europe in the Qing period took two routes. In the south, tea was exported to Western Europe from Canton by sea, and in the north, it was transported to Russia by land through Kiachta. Due to the difference between Southern Fujian dialect and Northern Mandarin, Europeans developed different loanwords for "tea":

> The British called it "替 [tì](tea)," the French "代 [dài](thé)," and the Russian "柴 [chái](чай)." Probably on account of the northern route, Russian pronunciation is similar to that in Mandarin.[1]

Tea transportation in the north primarily relied on caravans, thus the name "caravan tea." In the modern European tea market, Russian "caravan tea" was more competitive than the tea that other countries imported by sea. As Gerard Fridrikh Miller highlighted in his book *Conquest of Siberia and The History of the Transactions, Wars, Commerce, Etc. Carried on between Russia and China from the Earliest Period*:

> The teas which are brought into Russia are much superior in flavor and quality to those which are sent to Europe from Canton. The original goodness of the teas is probably the same in both cases; but it is conjectured, that the transport by sea considerably impairs the aromatic flavor of the plant.

Wei Yuan, in the *Illustrated Gazetteer of the Sea Kingdoms* (*Haiguo tuzhi*), volume 83, explained this situation as follows: "For the tea transported by land, exposure to wind and frost adds its flavor, whereas for the tea shipped across the South China Sea, the taste is weakened owing to summer heat."

The uniqueness of "caravan tea" and its significance in European commercial competition had long ago attracted Karl Marx's attention. According to Marx, of the tea sold to the Russians at Kiachta, "the larger part was of superior quality well known to continental consumers as caravan tea, which formed a contradistinction with the inferior article imported by sea," and in the Russia-China relationship, "as an indemnification for this exclusion from the maritime trade, the Russians enjoy an inland and overland trade peculiar to themselves."[2] It is no wonder that as early as 1840, someone in Russia hailed that "one Kiachta is worth three provinces."³ The monopoly over land trade gave Russia the commercial advantage during the two Opium Wars and also directly affected Western countries' spheres of influence in China. Furthermore, it provided economic incentive for some major political events in Sino-Russian relations during the Qing period. For example, the reason why the Tsarist government carried out armed intervention against the Taiping Heavenly Kingdom (*Taiping tianguo*) was clearly expressed during its address to the Court of Colonial Affairs (*lifan yuan*): "Civil unrest in your country [China] has made our business at Kiachta stagnate for years, and our country [Russia] would like to quell the rebellion for you as soon as possible."⁴ The "caravan tea" trade also echoed the change in the international situation. The Napoleonic Wars of 1812, for instance, caused turmoil in Russian social life and resulted in a sharp decline in the quantity of Chinese tea transported to Russia. In 1811, there were 46,405 poods of Pekoe tea transported via Kiachta,⁵ while in 1812, the tea shipment was reduced by half to a mere 24,729 poods.⁶ Apparently, the importance of the "caravan tea" trade via Kiachta should not be underestimated.

In modern times, the Kiachta trade was synonymous with the tea trade. From 1839 to 1845, tea accounted for 91% of all Kiachta exports.⁷ However, for a long time, no sufficient attention has been paid to the "tea routes" that linked China and Russia in the 18th and 19th centuries. In a sense, if seaborne tea was notable because it was related to the opening of treaty ports, then "caravan tea" was neglected precisely because of inland transshipment. Due to the lack of systematic records about "caravan tea" in historical sources passed down from the Qing period, whether they are official documents or private writings, researchers find it hard to carry out comprehensive research in this field. By examining some important historical materials as a starting point, I explore the reasons for the rise of "caravan tea." Then I discuss the ups and downs of Chinese merchant tea consortiums and analyze the phenomenon of the "inversed flow of Russian tea." Finally, I turn to the relationship between the Russian Hotel and "caravan tea." Although these factors only form a small part of the bigger picture, they are indispensable in establishing a comprehensive understanding of the relationship between Sino-Russian business and diplomacy.

Introduction of Chinese Tea into Russia

The Russians were not pioneers of the tea trade. Long before the rise of "caravan tea," maritime countries in Western Europe had already shipped tea in from southern China. According to Xue Fucheng's *Diary of an Embassy to Four Nations* (*Chushi Ying De Yi Bi riji*), dated "the 22nd day of the third month in the 16th year of Guangxu" [10 May 1890]:

> Chinese tea appeared in Europe in 1612 when the Dutch East India Company imported some tea out of curiosity. In 1651, Dutch merchants began to ship tea to Europe for sale. Over the next ten years, the tea trade thrived, and the law concerning tea tax was then made by the British government. Still very

precious at that time, only one or two pounds of tea was offered to aristocrats as a gift. After another 30 years, the tea trade was becoming more prosperous, and the British government began to increase taxes on tea.[8]

Similarly, "caravan tea" also experienced a transformation from gift to commodity, but it was slightly later than maritime tea. It was only in 1616, four years after the Dutch first brought tea to Europe, that Petrov, the Head of Ten Men from Cossack, tasted tea for the first time in Kalmyk Khanate. He was amazed by this "indescribable leaf." In 1640, Vassily Stalkov, a Russian envoy, returned from Kalmyk Khanate with 200 bags of tea (each bag weighed 3 Russian pounds, 1 Russian pound was 409.51 grams) and offered them as presents to his Tsar. That marked the beginning of Chinese tea into Russia.[9]

In the early Qing period, Russian envoys to China continued to bring tea back to Russia as gifts. In 1675, the Russian envoy Nikolai received four boxes of tea as an "imperial gift" after a formal audience. He was also asked to take another eight boxes to his Tsar.[10] Apart from being used as a gift for official contacts, tea was also sold in Russia. By the late 17th century, there had been a small amount of tea available on the Tobolsk Market.[11] In 1674, there were shops in Moscow selling tea at a retail price of 30 kopecks per pound, but the consumers were mostly wealthy people, and the quantity of tea imported was still small.[12] After the Treaty of Nerchinsk was signed in 1689, border trade began to increase and the quantity of Chinese tea entering Russia via Nerchinsk rose slightly, as one of the regulations stipulated that "from now on, if travelers have road stamps [licenses], they shall be permitted to trade." For example, in 1698, Russian merchant Gavrila Romanovich Nikitin purchased Chinese goods worth 32,000 rubles, including tea that weighed 5 poods and 7 pounds, with each pood of tea selling for 20 to 25 rubles on the Moscow market.[13] In 1699, Russia's national caravan headed by Spiridon Yakovlevich Lyangusov arrived in Beijing.[14] Every three years thereafter, they came regularly. They traded in gold, silver, cotton, silk, and porcelain, but there were no large quantities of tea involved in these transactions. From 1729 to 1755, Russia stopped sending caravans to Beijing for trade and officially opened Kiachta as the exchange market. Then, tea gradually became the biggest business in this "trading town." According to Russian records, in 1750, there were 7,000 poods of tea bricks and 6,000 poods of Pekoe tea exported to Russia via Kiachta. In 1810, the quantity of these two types of tea reached 75,000 poods, almost six times more.[15]

The prosperity of the Kiachta exchange market attracted more Russian merchants. By the time the Kiachta Trade Agreement was signed in 1792, there were six major commercial consortiums in Russia. First, there was the Moscow group, dealing in woolen cloth, walrus hides, sea otter pelts, and other Russian goods. Second, the Tura group, dealing in lamb fur, cat fur, and small hardware. Third, the Arzamask and Vologda groups, dealing in Finnish fox fur and Arctic fox fur. Fourth and fifth, the Tobolsk and Irkutsk groups, both dealing in leather, marten, fox fur, and furry coats. The last was the Kazan group, specializing in leather products.[16]

These Russian consortiums bartered for tea with animal furs, thus setting the trade convention of "arriving with furs and returning with tea"[17] and making "caravan tea" completely different from maritime tea not only in the form of transportation but also in the items exchanged.

Trading Activities of the "Shanxi Tea Merchants"

On the exchange market of Kiachta, the rivals of the Russian commercial groups were Shanxi merchants, known as "Shanxi consortium." As stated in the *Peregrinations in the North* (*Shuofang beicheng*), volume 37:

> More than half of the inland merchants at Kiachta are from Shanxi province. They buy tobacco, tea, satins, and groceries from Zhangjiakou, and bring them here to barter for leather sheets and felts sheets, etc.

It had long been known in Chinese history that Shanxi people were "good at doing business." According to "A Biography of the King of Changshan, a Royal Member of the Northern Wei" ("Wei zongshi changshan wang zun zhuan") in the *History of the North* (*Bei shi*), volume 15, "villagers living east of the river prefer business to farmwork. Some of them do not know how to plow when they are about 30 years old." The long-lasting custom in this area persisted until the Qing dynasty. In the *Jottings from the Thatch Hut of Subtle Views* (*Yuewei caotang biji*), volume 23, it is also stated that:

> Most people from Shanxi leave hometowns for trade. When children are about 10, they follow adults to learn how to conduct business. After accumulating enough capital, they return home to get married. After that, they go out again for business profits.

In the early Qing period, the "eight merchant families" that brought in animal skins for the Imperial Household Department (*neiwufu*) were all from Shanxi. The *Annals of Wanquan County – Appendix* (*Wanquan Xianzhi: Zhiyu*) in the reign of the Qianlong Emperor gives a detailed account of this:

> The eight merchant families are all from Shanxi and they came to Zhangjiakou for business around the end of the Ming dynasty. Headed by Wang Dengku, Jin Liangwang, Fan Yongdou[18], Wang Dayu, Liang Jiabin, Tian Shenglan, Zhai Tang and Huang Yunfa, these families have been sending traders to conduct business in Zhangjiakou since the founding of this dynasty along the east of the Liao River. After His Majesty ascended to the throne, they were summoned to the capital city, treated to an imperial dinner at the banquet hall and bestowed with high-quality clothing. Since then, every year, they have brought in animal furs and left them with the Storage Office (*guangchusi*) of the Imperial Household Department (*neiwufu*).

Shanxi merchants had a long business tradition and gained a high political status in the early Qing period; therefore, the commercial contacts within and beyond the Shanhai Pass had long been in their control. The trade of "caravan tea," for example, attracted a large number of Shanxi merchants to venture into the Wuyi tea area. In his book *Miscellaneous Chants of the Tea Market* (*Chashi zayong*),[19] Zhonggan described their financial strength and business manner this way:

> In the early Qing period, the tea trade fell entirely into the hands of Shanxi merchants who transported tea first to Jiangxi, then to Henan before they were transferred beyond the Pass to be sold. These "western traders" are actually Shanxi merchants, each of them rich in capital, ranging from two or three hundred thousand taels to one million. The goods were transported back and forth like running water in an endless stream. Every spring they came. After receiving a warm welcome at the estuary port by the tea shop owners, they would hand over both money and an order form to shop owners, who made all the arrangements. When the tea business was finished, they settled the accounts and left.

Zhangjiakou was the transit station for Shanxi tea merchants. Tea purchased from Fujian was picked up here and then sent to Kiachta via the "trading route." According to what Qingyun, the commander-in-chief (*dutong*) of Chahar reported to the emperor in the ninth month of 1860:

> Except for the military stations, there are three routes that connect Zhangjiakou and Kiachta - the east, the west, and the middle. The east route starts from Ulanba, goes to Plain Blue Banner[20] of Chahar, then passes through the nomadic areas of King Abag Banner, Prince Abahanar Banner, etc. in Xilin Gol League, Inner Zasak, before it enters the nomadic areas of Ahaigong Banner of Sechen Khan Aimag in Outer Zasak. Then it passes through east Dariganga and enters the nomadic areas including Prince Banner of Sechen Khan, and arrives in Kulun. From Kulun it reaches its destination Kiachta. The west route starts from Wenggunba and Heluoba of Tumd Banner, passes through Shalamuleng of Sizi Aimag and Tushiyetu Khan Banner, and arrives at Sanyinnuoyan Banner where it is divided into two separate routes, one of which goes west to Uliassutai's Khovd, another goes east to Kulun, and then from Kulun to Kiachta. The middle route starts from Sengjituba of Xigou which is outside Dajingmen, passes through Dahonggou, Heichengzi and Baichengzi, and nomadic areas such as Niuqun of Bordered Yellow Banner, Damaqun, and Yangqun of Bordered Yellow Banner, and enters King Sonid Right Banner. Then it passes through Sechen Khan, and Prince Banner, Ahaigong Banner, etc. in Tushiyetu Khan Aimag before crossing the Kherlen River to Kulun and finally to Kiachta.

From Zhangjiakou to Kiachta, the distance was about 4,300 *li*.[21] The land was so sparsely populated that merchants had to brave wind and dew, grazing cattle on their way. Since all the three routes were extremely difficult, Shanxi tea merchants had to go in groups, and their organization was roughly as follows:

> Transporting goods across the Pass, Shanxi merchants worried about potential robberies, so they formed cart groups, similar to "caravans" in the Western countries. Each group might have as many as over one hundred carts, which looked more or less like a big Gulu cart [a kind of cart in Dahuli[22]], with a small wheel gap. Pulled by an ox, each cart could load up to 500 *jin*[23][catties] of goods. One rider could take care of more than ten carts. They set off at sunset and rested at dusk, camping near a river where they could graze the oxen. They usually traveled 30 or 40 miles a day, without a fixed schedule. For each group, dogs were brought along. They were chained among the carts when moving, and tied around as guards when the carts were arranged in two oval-shaped rows for defense. While the riders gathered inside tents, several armed escorts took turns patrolling. When it was the time to rest, they would be replaced by dogs, thus the name of guard dogs.[24]

Shanxi tea merchants treated the ox cart as their home, which was known as "One Room." Wu Jiabin, a poet who was sent to guard the military station during the Daoguang era [1821–1850], compiled a collection of poems entitled *Eight Poems of the New Yuefu on the Front* (*Saishang xinyuefu bashou*). For his poem "One Room," he added a note which reads: "Riding on ox carts from Zhangjiakou to Kiachta, merchants traveled back and forth for many years. As the cart was taken as their home, hence the name 'One Room.'"

Nevertheless, the ox carts were not the only means of transportation. In winter, when grass withered outside the Great Wall, camels seemed more suitable for long-distance travel. The third volume of *Miscellaneous Notes of the Bamboo Leaves Pavilion* (*Zhuyeting zaji*) written by Yao Yuanzhi describes how the camel caravan arrived at Kiachta from Kulun:

> Camels were used to carry both traders and goods. Each time when the Russians spotted caravans through their telescopes, from counting the number of camels, they could get a rough idea about the amount of goods that were about to arrive. They could know this about four or five days in advance, because the telescope enabled them to see as far as three or four hundred *li* away.

Russian commercial commissioners at Kiachta also used camel and cart as two units of measurement to calculate Chinese goods. For example, in 1817, there were 2,500 camels and 1,420 carts of Chinese goods arriving at this trading town. In 1818, there were 3,450 camels and 1,420 carts. During the Daoguang reign, the trade continued to grow. In 1829, it reached 9,670 camels and 2,705 carts.[25]

Clearly, before the Opium War, the quantity of tea transported by Shanxi merchants was considerably large. As is stated in the *Illustrated Gazetteer of the Sea Kingdoms*, volume 81:

> The Russians bought tea in northern Mongolia. In 1830, they purchased 563,440 pounds of tea, and in 1832, it was 6,461,000 pounds. All of it was black tea. It was transported from Kiachta to Danse [Tomsk] by road, and then to Nuo'a'e'luo [Nizhny Novgorod] by water and land.

Although the Kiachta tea market was expanding day by day, it was still a barter trade controlled by commercial operators. So even in the first half of the 19th century when business was booming, the "caravan tea" trade was still following a medieval pattern. Just as Friedrich Engels pointed out: "Russians have almost unparalleled skills in conducting low-level trade, by taking advantage of favorable circumstances and some deceptive practices relating to this."[26] The Kiachta exchange market was a place where Russian merchants could display these skills. According to Russian records, in the mid-1850s, the number of Chinese shops in the trading town approached 100: "90 of them had their own stores. Only 37 were engaged in wholesale business with Russian merchants. The rest were all small dealers."[27] After years of wholesale business, Chinese shops were burdened with uncashed "foreign checks" and fell into an extremely disadvantageous position. According to a report submitted by Amban (*banshi dacheng*) of Kulun on 29 November 1852:

> Currently, the shop owners' foreign checks amount to more than 80,000 *liang* [taels], if valued in silver. If those checks were suddenly banned and foreign merchants refused to cash them with silver, these owners would be heavily burdened and unrest would ensue.[28]

With the deepening of the semi-colonization of China, Shanxi tea merchants found themselves in increasing trouble. During the Second Opium War, they were forced to sell goods without the ability to buy. This is also what Karl Marx pointed out in "A Contribution to the Critique of Political Economy":

> According to the Treaty [Treaty of Kiachta], the border trade at Kiachta is, in fact, one of barter. Silver only plays the part of being a measure of value. The war of 1857–1858 compelled the Chinese to sell without the ability to buy. Silver now suddenly appeared to be the only means of purchase. To literally act on the treaty, the Russians casted the French five-franc silver coins into crude silverware and used them as a means of exchange.[29]

After the Opium War, Russia hastened its commercial expansion into China, and the long-established position of Shanxi tea merchants at Kiachta faced a new challenge. Meanwhile, the Russian government tried all means to gain tea transportation right so that "Russian merchants could travel in and out of China by land to southern provinces, purchase goods and then send them back to Russia."[30]

Just as the opening of treaty ports caused the "thirteen hongs" (*shisan hang*) of Guangdong to lose control of maritime tea, the decline of Shanxi tea merchants was also inseparable from Tsarist Russia's privileges over land trade. According to the memorial submitted by Prince Gong and other ministers in the eighth month of 1868:

> Trading activities at Kiachta used to be prosperous mostly because of the fact that Russians were not allowed to enter inland provinces. After the land trade was permitted, Russian merchants were able to buy tea on their own. They were not required to exchange goods with Chinese merchants at the ports. That is how they took away profits. [For Chinese merchants,] blocked roads led to decreasing goods, and repeated attacks by the armed forces around Hankou and other places of Hubei forced them to relinquish all their capital. All these made their business worse and worse.

The Convention of Peking for the Land Trade between Russia and China was signed in 1862. In 1869, the Revised Land Trade Regulations was signed in order to loosen the original restrictions and reduce taxes. The blow to Shanxi tea merchants was extremely serious in the early years of Guangxu. On 28 November 1880, Wang Xianqian pointed out that:

> Zhangjiakou used to have more than a hundred shops owned by Shanxi tea merchants, who bartered with Russian merchants at Kiachta. When Russians transported goods on their own, most Chinese shops closed down, leaving only about 20 open.[31]

Within a mere 30 years, Shanxi tea merchants went out of business one after another, with only one-fifth of the shops remaining active. Although this drastic decline was mainly caused by "Russians' buying tea on their own," it was inseparable from the ruthless feudal exploitation of commercial capital, evident in the managing way of the Qing government.

The "Bureau Stamp" (*bupiao*) System

As a rule, the Qing government imposed a strict control over the exchange market on the national border, like it had done with the port trade. The "bureau stamp" (*bupiao*) system, which was closely related to Shanxi tea merchants, was formally established in the fourth year of the Jiaqing reign [1799]. As is explained in *Peregrinations in the North*, volume 37:

> In the fourth year, the proposed regulation stipulated that merchants needed to obtain a stamp to trade. After the commander-in-chief of Chahar, the general of Guihua city, or vice-prefect's office (*tongzhi yamen*) of Dolon Nor issued the stamps, the ministers, officials, or yamen of the destination city should not allow merchants to trade without license. If a merchant used the excuse

that he was not able to get a stamp in time so he used a pass (*luyin*) issued by another yamen, and if he was found doing that, this person would be penalized for committing the crime of "trading without the stamp." Checked and filed by officials in charge, stamps would be revoked a year later to prevent merchants from staying out, getting out of control, and causing trouble. For the merchant who had arrived at the destination, and wanted to send goods to another place for sale, he should apply to the local yamen for a credit stamp (*xinpiao*). The yamen at the next destination would then be informed. For those merchants who were engaged in illicit trade without stamps, they would be imprisoned for two months, and punished with 40 lashes on the day of release. They would then be sent back to their home provinces. As for their goods, half would be confiscated by the government.

In 1862, this regulation was approved by Emperor Tongzhi, so that:

> Merchants who traded at Kiachta used to apply for tea stamps from the Court of Colonial Affairs. Now they still need to follow this regulation. For every three hundred boxes of tea, one stamp is issued, and fifty *liang* of silver is charged. The stamp issued is still to be withdrawn a year later.[32]

It is quite clear that a bureau stamp was the business license, different from "*luyin*" which was used as a pass. Referring to other records related to the above-mentioned regulations and ensuing implementation, I briefly explain the system of "bureau stamp" as follows:

First, "bureau stamp" was also known as "court stamp" (*yuanpiao*). It was issued by the Court of Colonial Affairs, and its application and inspection went to the "Zhangliting" – Zhangjiakou vice prefect's yamen for managing affairs (*Zhangjiakou lishi tongzhi yamen*). Qingyun, the commander-in-chief of Chahar clearly knew his power:

> For wealthy merchants who trade around Kiachta, to get the tea stamps, they should first register with Zhangliting. Then they pick up stamps at the Court of Colonial Affairs and bring them back to Zhangjiakou. Before their commercial goods are shipped off, a notice must be sent in advance. Then their stamps will be sealed on the stub for inspection and release.[33]

Second, after a "bureau stamp" was picked up, a merchant also needed to change this stamp for a credit stamp at Kulun before journeying to the border. Upon arriving at the trading town, he was supposed to present his stamp for inspection, thereby concluding all the procedures for a legal trade. In the *Miscellaneous Notes of the Bamboo Leaves Pavilion,* volume three, there is a clear record of this: "Our outgoing merchants got stamps at Zhangjiakou, changed for new ones at Kulun, and handed them in upon arrival." Those who had no stamps or used a pass as a stamp were considered to be equally guilty. What is meant by the penalty that "half would be confiscated by the government" does not mean that the other half was returned to the original owner. As was shown by the cases handled by Baketang'a, an official at Kiachta in the eighth month of 1855, "half is confiscated as usual, and the other half is rewarded to the bounty hunter," that is, the smuggler catcher. This actually means, once arrested, all the goods were confiscated.

Third, a "bureau stamp" was valid for one year. There were two methods to decide the legal freight for each stamp. The first was to measure by the number of tea boxes, and "300 boxes of tea would earn one stamp." According to the Agreed Terms of Settlement about the Burning of Tacheng Trade Circle between China and Russia signed in 1858, the packing specification of Wuyi tea was that "the net weight of one box of tea is 55 catties in accordance with the Chinese Kuping[34], and the tare weight is 80 catties." The second was to calculate according to the number of camels, "200 camels would be given one stamp." The convention for transportation beyond the Great Wall was that "each camel carries less than 250 catties of tea."[35] For owners of small shops who were not qualified to acquire a stamp, they had to attach themselves to a large shop and share a stamp. This was called "friend stamp" (*pengpiao*). But each of the two parties would have to prepare their checklist separately for inspection.

Clearly, controlled by the stamp system, Shanxi tea merchants did not have freedom either in time or space. The regulation which stipulated that "stamps would be revoked a year later to prevent merchants from staying out, getting out of control, and causing trouble" clearly shows the nature of feudal compulsion. As for the number of stamps issued each year at Zhangjiakou, there was no systematic record in the Qing documents. But the Russian diplomatic archives give the following numbers: 268 stamps were issued in 1850, and they were distributed to five or six shops. Large shops got more than six, and medium or small shops got four, two, and one accordingly. From 1851 to 1855, a total of 400 to 500 stamps were issued each year to 60 big shops at Zhangjiakou so that they could conduct business at Kiachta.[36] Regarding the situation in the Tongzhi period, only fragments of data can be quoted here to explain. In Zhangjiakou, from the ninth month of 1862 to the third month of 1863, "254 court stamps were issued to merchants who transported their goods to Kiachta for sale."[37] Burdened by heavy taxes, these merchants found themselves in a very disadvantageous position compared to their Russian counterparts. As revealed by Prince Gong's memorial in the first month of 1868:

> When Russian tea merchants transport tea back to Russia, they only pay the regular tax. For our tea merchants who export tea abroad, besides the regular tax, they must pay another fifty *liang* of silver for each stamp upon arrival at Kiachta. In 1860, owing to the shortage of the military budget for soldiers, it was decided that merchants should donate sixty *liang* as a likin (*lijin*)[38] tax for each commercial stamp. This went to the General Headquarters (*dutong yamen*) of Chahar, which became the perennial wages for the soldiers stationed in Chahar. With a heavy likin tax, and with few profits to make, our merchants' livelihoods became more difficult, and their businesses gradually declined and withered.[39]

For one stamp of transported tea, the total value was "6,000 *liang* of silver" (that is, 20 taels per box). The profits were squeezed three times. First, there was the regular tax where each box of tea would be taxed four taels, and one stamp of tax money would amount to 1,200 taels. Second, there was the stamp tax (*piaogui*), which was 50 taels. It eventually became 76 taels in total during the early years of Guangxu, because it then included 13 taels levied in the name of guardians (*mending*) and 13 taels for corporals (*lingcui*). Finally, there was the 1% likin tax (60 *liang*). Thus, it was natural that there were "few profits to make." Obviously, the situation that Shanxi tea business "has gradually declined and withered" since the late 1860s was related to the fact that the Qing government increasingly turned the system of "bureau stamp" into a means of extorting money.

Cornered by "a harder livelihood," Shanxi merchants made an attempt to change from land transportation to maritime shipping. But they still could not regain profits from the hands of Russian merchants. As Liu Kunyi analyzed in his submitted memorial "Discussion of and reply to merchants' transporting tea to Russia by shipping cargoes abroad" dated "the 15th day of the first month in the seventh year of Guangxu" [13 February 1881]:

> After Jianghan Customs was set up for foreign trade, Russian merchants set up their firms in Hankou, from which they loaded both black tea[40] and tea bricks onto ships, transporting them from Hankou to Tianjin and then to Russia. Due to the low cost of freight and the increasing quantity of cargo, Russians took away two-thirds of Shanxi merchants' business. For Shanxi merchants who transported tea out through the West Gate, they would still take the land route; for those who took the East Gate, there was a change. In 1873, there was an official petition asking for the exemption of re-import half duty in Tianjin. The petitioners required to follow the pattern set for Russian merchants so that they could have the tea which was formerly transported to Russia by land shipped from Hankou to Tianjin via the arrangements made by the Bureau of Merchants. The petition was approved by Li Hongzhang and put into practice. But unlike Russian merchants, the stipulation stated that Shanxi merchants still needed to pay the inland likin tax. After they paid the regular tax and half duty, there would be no more taxes levied on them. Even in this case, it was still difficult to make profits. As a result, only 20% of the merchants chose the new route from Hankou to Tianjin. The rest of them continued the land transportation. Compared with Russian merchants, Shanxi merchants had a higher cost of freight and fewer profits. There was a worry that Russian merchants in the future might ship more tea out and Shanxi merchants would then undoubtedly be forced out of business.[41]

With the competition against Russian merchants on the one side and the extortion from the Qing government on the other side, Chinese tea merchants found their "caravan tea" trade in dire straits. During the reigns of the Tongzhi and Guangxi, the "trading route" already became a daunting road in the eyes of Shanxi tea merchants.

The Change of Route by "West Merchants" and the Rise of "Southern Counter"

In terms of land trade between China and Russia, besides Kiachta, Yili and Tacheng were also opened after the China-Russia Yili/Tal Bahatai Trade Regulations was signed in 1851. This increased the number of trade ports to three. Then, the transportation of "caravan tea" was divided into two routes, "west route" and "north route."

The tea merchants on the west route were called "west merchants." Like those "north route merchants" trading on the exchange market at Kiachta, they also came from Shanxi. Their trading activities, however, were quite different from their fellow countrymen. On the whole, there were three different aspects:

1. *Tea Types*: "West merchants" purchased Zhulan tea (also known as Qianliang tea) in Jiande of Anhui province, while "north merchants" shopped for Wuyi tea or Pekoe tea.
2. *Transportation route*: "West merchants" did not choose the Zhangjiakou-Kiachta line:

    This Qianliang/Zhulan tea was transported by tea merchants from Jiande to Shizidian in Henan. Then it went from Shizidian to Xinzhou which is located in Qi county of Shanxi province. Then it went from Xinzhou to Guihua where it was sold to those who did business in Xinjiang. Merchants would transport them to Urumqi, Tal Bahatai and other places for sale.

3. *Targeted customers*: "West merchants" did not trade with Russians – "While this Qianliang/Zhulan tea met the daily necessity of Europeans, Russians did not consume it, nor would they buy it."[42]

It can be seen that merchants on the west and north routes had their own zones of activity, independent of each other. However, this state of equal profitability was disrupted by the political crisis in the Qing period in the mid-1860s.

In 1864, under the influence of the Taiping Rebellion, peasant uprisings broke out in Kuqa and Yili. The revolt against the Qing government spread to the north and south of the Tianshan Mountains. The "caravan tea" transportation on the west route was blocked and they had to seek diversion. In 1867, "west merchants" like Cheng Huapeng, Yu Pengyun, and Kong Guangren et al. petitioned the general stationed in Suiyuan for permission to "travel through Kiachta for business," and

> the route to be taken will start from Guihua to the Khalkha tribe, then to Kulun, and then from Kulun to Kiachta, from Kiachta to the Russian border where the tea will be sold to Western countries by Russian merchants.

This petition seriously states: "The Wuyi tea that Zhangjiakou merchants have been transporting and selling is a native product of Fujian while the goods sold by Cheng Huapeng and others come from Anhui, and they do not interfere with each other."⁴³ In the following year, the Foreign Office (*zongli yamen*), the Ministry of Revenue (*hubu*), and the Court of Colonial Affairs sent people to investigate. It was confirmed that "West merchants transported and sold tea to Kiachta, and there is no hindrance to the livelihoods of north merchants."⁴⁴ Therefore, after a formal discussion, the Foreign Office replied: "It is tentatively agreed that tea merchants on the west route can take the north route to Kiachta and the original practice will be restored when the western frontier is recovered."⁴⁵

In 1871, Tsarist Russia invaded and occupied the Yili area and imposed colonial rule for ten years. During the entire Yili crisis, the west route business could not be revived, and "being restored to the original practice" was not possible. In 1872, Rong Quanzu, the general of Yili, petitioned:

> Please give an order to purchase tea, as we plan to recruit merchants from cities. We hope that the old practice can be restored so we won't be burdened by the use of Russian stamps. Please buy for us tin-lined packing boxes in Suiyuan, each weighing about sixty or seventy catties, two hundred boxes of red plum tea, two hundred boxes of fine Zhulan tea, all of which are sent to Khovd and stored for later use.⁴⁶

Nevertheless, it was difficult to recruit "west merchants" due to the change of route to Kiachta. Accordingly, there were also major changes in the Jiande tea area. According to a report in the 267th issue of the newspaper Yiwen Lu (Record of Good News):

> Jiande is a tea-producing area, with green leaves, buds, and fragrance everywhere. As a convention, the tea here has been transported by Shanxi merchants to the northern Guihua city for sale. In the early years of Tongzhi, Guangdong merchants changed to black tea, and packed and shipped it to Hankou. This had created lucrative profits for the superrich merchants. After 1878, the price of tea was temporarily reduced, and the tea business was declining day by day. This year (1883), the price is even lower, and the losses are even worse. Compared with previous years, only half of the tea merchants came to Jiande, and the market is so desolate that few customers visit.

After "west merchants" changed the transportation route, a replacement emerged. That was the Hunan tea consortium, which was brought out and supported by Zuo Zongtang, the governor-general (*zongdu*) of Shaanxi and Gansu provinces. "Guangzhuang black tea" in Hunan, also known as "Yangzhuang black tea," appeared during the Taiping Rebellion. According to the *Annals of Anhua County* (*Anhua xianzhi*), volume 33, in the Tongzhi reign:

> In the Xianfeng reign, as the rebellion was rampant, the merchants stopped coming and the tea sale has been stagnant for several years. Tongshan in Hunan, as a tea-producing area with some history, had attracted merchants. As the rebels fled out of Changsha and haunted the areas between the Yangtze

River and Han River for several years, tea transportation in Tongshan was hindered. For this reason, the tea merchants took the route to Xiangtan, and finally arrived at Anhua where they encouraged the locals to make black tea which would then be sold to Western countries. The tea thus made was called Guangzhuang black tea.

"Guangzhuang" was named after the Guangdong merchants who initiated the making of black tea. For the tea industry in the Qing period, almost all the change regarding black tea was related to Guangdong merchants. Jiande was one case, and Anhua was no exception. With the tea industry becoming more and more prosperous, since 1856, the Hunan government began levying a duty on tea. For example, merchants of "Yangzhuang black tea," in addition to the likin tax, had to pay an extra 6 *qian* [mace] of silver for each trunk of tea.[47] There was no shortage of entrepreneurs who started up with tea. For example, Zhu Zigui, a well-known Hunan tea merchant, rose up during the period of Xianfeng and Tongzhi reigns. The *Classified Anecdotes of the Qing Dynasty* (*Qingbai leichao*), volume 17, shows how he became rich:

> Zhu Zigui, born in the countryside of Hunan, was impoverished in his early life. He went to a private school at the village, but quitted after three months, and then he made a living by chopping wood. In his teenage years, he helped with cooking in a rice shop, working diligently. A very rich merchant with the surname of Liu let him manage the shop, and he did an outstanding job. Over the years, with the salary dividends, he set up his own shop, and with more than a thousand silver ingots that he had saved, he went into the black tea business. By the year of 1867, he had earned an annual profit far exceeding ten thousand [taels]. After he became rich, Zigui felt a strong sense of regret for having dropped out of school in his childhood, so he tried to make up by reading more books. At the same time, he continued doing tea business every year and accumulated nearly one million [taels] of wealth. There was almost no one around the Xiang River or the Han River who had not heard about him.

As mentioned above, it can be seen that the time when Cheng Huapeng changed his business route was the time when Zhu Zigui earned wealth from his tea business. It is noteworthy that the two things happened in the same year, indicating that from then on, Hunan tea merchants would gradually dominate the tea market in Xinjiang.

In the Qing period, there had long existed an economic pattern that the goods produced in Hunan and Hubei provinces were transported from Hubei to Gansu before they were sold in the northwestern cities. Therefore, during Zuo Zongtang's tenure as the governor-general of Shaanxi and Gansu from the 10th month of 1869, to the 11th month of 1880, the "Southern counter" was added to introduce the Hunan black tea into Xinjiang, which can be viewed as an innovation upon the old practice. According to the memorial entitled "Gansu tea business long abandoned, please adapt to manage," dated 2 April 1874:

> The tea business in Gansu province used to be divided into two counters: eastern and western. Merchants of the eastern counter were all natives of Shanxi and Shaanxi; for the western ones, they were mostly the Muslim merchants who were born in Shaanxi. Because of the war, many Muslim merchants were either threatened, or died later, with very few survivors. Shanxi merchants also went into hiding. After the looting, their business capital was entirely gone. Where does the tax come from if there is no one to pay it?
>
> The tea transported from Gansu province to be sold abroad is mainly produced in Hunan, though some from Hubei, and the rest from Sichuan and Jiangxi.
>
> Since merchants from eastern and western counters are not willing to get involved in tea business, it is suggested that "Southern counter" should immediately be added to attract the southern tea vendors and thus business capital can be expanded during this difficult time.[48]

After Zuo Zongtang's cultivating support, "Southern tea vendors" completely replaced "Shanxi merchants," and finally, "in the 1870s, the Chinese government implemented a monopoly on the tea trade in the western border area, only allowing Hunan merchants to do tea business."[49] Thus, the three Hunan "giant merchants" in the late Qing period emerged. Liu Shengmu, in the *Sequel to Chang Chu Zhai* (*Changchu zai xubi*), volume nine, detailed this:

> During the reign of the Guangxu Emperor, Hunan merchants became wealthy after transporting Anhua black tea to Russia for sale. Among them, the most wealthy were Ye Huanbin (courtesy name Dehui) from the Ministry of Civil Appointments (*libu*), Yu Jieqing (courtesy name Jinsheng) who worked as a surveillance and supervisory commissioner (*guanchashi*), and Zhu Yutian, a grand academician (*neige xueshi*). Of the three, Zhu Yutian was the richest.

Zhu Yutian was the courtesy name of Zhu Changlin who was the chief merchant of the "Southern counter." He established a private bank called "Qianyi" in Changsha, set up a tea house called "Qianyisheng" in Xinjiang, and obtained stamps for exclusive transportation of tea to the northwest for sale to Russia. In 1895, Chen Baozhen, the governor (*xunfu*) of Hunan, "established an official money office, a money-making factory, and a mint for producing foreign silver coins, all with Zhu Changlin as the head."[50] Employing the wealthiest person to run a money office, Chen was really somebody who knew how to place a person in the most suitable position.

When the "Southern counter" was at its peak, Hunan scale and Korla scale co-existed in the Xinjiang tea market, enjoying an extraordinary momentum. However, when Hunan black tea enjoyed its popularity, a shadow was already approaching. This was the threat posed by the dumping of Indian black tea in Europe. As Huang Zunxian lamented in his poem "In Memory of Friends at the End of the Year"

("Suimo huairen shi"): "In the competition against Indian new tea and Japanese silk, merchants in the Central Plain of China had small profits to yield." In 1887, Miao Yousun, head of the Ministry of Revenue, was sent to Russia to investigate business matters. He had a conversation with Lev Rabinovich, a tea merchant from Odessa. He was told that "British merchants used Indian tea to take over two or three tenths of the profits from Chinese merchants, and similarly, there were also some vendors in Russia who participated in this business."[51] This "participation" method against Chinese traders was what Russian merchants learned from their British counterparts:

> Although tea from Southeast Asia, India, and Japan was not as rich in flavor as Chinese tea, British merchants cheated in a cunning way. When only 30 or 40 percent were adulterated, it was hard to be distinguished. Even more cunningly, they mixed Indian tea with Chinese tea, saying that this was Indian tea. Everybody rushed to buy it because of the lower price, and thought that it is not much different from Chinese tea. At the beginning, there was more Chinese tea than Indian tea in the mixture, so it cannot be easily discovered. Over time, Chinese tea and Indian tea were evenly mixed, and later there was more Indian tea than Chinese tea, thus the "hidden transfer" was completed covertly.

The above-mentioned secret was revealed by Wang Zhichun in the sixth volume of the *Manuscript of My Mission to Russia* (*Shi E cao*), dated "the 10th day of the third month in the 21st year of Guangxu" [4 April 1895]. Due to the "hidden transfer" of Chinese tea by Indian tea, Hunan's "Yangzhuang black tea" became a victim of foreign merchants' "cunning cheat." As the sales grew stagnant day by day, tea merchants had to find another way out.

Wu Dacheng's Purchase and Shipping of Black Tea for a Trial Sale in Russia

The decline of Hunan tea industry in the late Qing period raised the concerns of the local governor-general (*zongdu*) and provincial governor (*xunfu*). Wu Dacheng's purchase and sale of black tea to Russia was an effort to turn the tide. Dacheng, whose courtesy name was Qingqing, as well as Zhanzhai, was a native of Wu county, Jiangsu province. Good at seal script (*zhuanshu*), talented in bronze and stone inscription (*jinshi*), and rich in book collections, he was an official, as well as a scholar, enjoying a good fame at that time. In his tenure as the governor of Hunan, on 26 September 1894, Wu Dacheng, together with Zhang Zhidong, who was the governor-general of Hunan and Hubei provinces, petitioned the emperor as follows:

> In recent years, tea merchants in Hubei and Hunan provinces have lost quite a lot of money. For one thing, due to rainy days and wet weather, or adulteration with rough and assorted mixtures, the unsatisfactory tea quality has

214 *"Caravan Tea"*

made it hard to sell at a good price. For another thing, foreign merchants deliberately reduced the weight, canceled orders, or reduced prices, making trouble in various ways. However, as black tea can only be sold to foreign merchants, they have to endure the extortions and oppression.

In fact, tea traders and planters were unwilling to be extorted by Russian merchants. Zhang Zhidong disclosed an example of this in his "Notice to Tea Planters," on 10 June 1894:

> In the third month of this year, a merchant named Danilov from the Russian Baichang Tea Company [also known as K.S. Popoff Bros], went to Yangloudong [now in Xianning, Hubei province] to purchase tea. When he reached a place called Xindian, he was surrounded by idlers there, and later he was injured because an urchin threw a stone at him. Meanwhile, there was an anonymous poster in the Yangloudong area [...], saying that the tea business in China had always been prosperous, but recently it suffered losses, mostly because of the foreigners who came here.[52]

In response to the loss and burden of tea merchants and the increasing public discontent, the governor-general of Hubei and Hunan provinces decided that the government would take over the business and purchase black tea as a trial sale in Russia:

> Yun Zuyi, supervisor of Jianghan Customs, was ordered to select two hundred boxes of high-quality black tea, half coming from Hubei province, and the other half from Hunan province. After negotiating with Russian merchants, he tried to gain the permission to ship the chosen tea via their tea ship to Odessa, Russia for a trial sale. Then I sent a telegram to Xu Jingcheng, our ambassador to Russia and entrusted him to take care of it. The price of tea, packing fee, miscellaneous expenses, export duties, etc., totaled 5,472 in Hankow taels (*Yang liyin*).
>
> Later, I sent a telegram to the Russian merchant Yuweiluofu 余威罗福 [It should be Sheweiluofu 佘威罗福] that I planned to purchase more boxes of black tea and transport them to Russia by land and water for a trial sale. I entrusted this merchant to take care of them. Soon he telegraphed back his consent, so I asked Yun Zuyi to do it. Shortly thereafter, I received the reply, saying that the first shipment of tea had already been sold out. Later, we managed to buy 120 boxes of top-quality black tea, respectively from Hubei and Hunan provinces, and entrusted them to Shunfeng yanghang [S. W. Litvinoff & Co.] for distribution to Russia, by sea to Kiachta and overland to Moscow for separate trial sales. The price of tea, packing fee, miscellaneous expenses, export duties, etc., totaled 1,816.05 in Hankow taels.[53]

The Russian merchant Mikhail Grigoryevich Shevelev (Михахл Григоръевич Щевелев), in the Qing documents, was translated as "Sheweiluofu 佘威罗伏"

or "Sheweiliefu 佘威列甫." In 1863, Shevelev graduated from Kiachta Chinese Language School.⁵⁴ Miao Yousun, in the *Compilation of Travel Diaries in Russia*, volume eight, wrote about him as follows:

> Shevelev was in Vladivostok. Years ago, he served as an interpreter when the two countries were demarcating the border in Hunchun. He could do this because he is good at Chinese, which is probably due to his learning experience in China during his youthhood. He was also an expert in handling interpersonal relationships, both in China and abroad.

The border demarcation was carried out in 1886. At that time, Wu Dacheng participated in the negotiations as the chief representative of the Qing government with the title of "imperial commissioner for handling Beiyang affairs (*Qinchai huiban beiyang shiyi dachen*), and left vice censor-in-chief of the Censorate (*Duchayuan zuo fu duyushi*)." He had three out-of-conference contacts with the Russian "translator" Shevelev:

> On the 21st day of the fourth month [24 May], he met with some Russians, and one of them was "Shevelev from Steamboat Foreign Trade Company";
> On the 16th day of the sixth month [17 July], "Baranov [governor of the east coast provinces and general of Military Affairs, chief representative of Russia] and Ma Qiuning [Nikolai Gavrilovich Matyunin, a border officer of South Ussuri], Domozhilov, and Shevelev all came along and chatted for an entire day."
> On the 29th day of the sixth month [30 July], Wu Dacheng "rode in the same carriage with Baranovo to Shevelev's house for the night."⁵⁵

Wu's record that Shevelev worked for the "Steamboat Foreign Trade Company" is consistent with Miao Yousun's account stating that "Shevelev was in Vladivostok." According to Russian documents, Shevelev established a shipping company in Vladivostok as early as 1880 and owned the steamer "Baikal." He was funded by the Tsarist government for 6,000 rubles each year, and he traveled back and forth between Hankou, Shanghai, and Nagasaki. He was specifically engaged in the business of transporting passengers, delivering cargo and mail.⁵⁶ Since 1876, he and Tokmakov set up a joint venture tea shop in Hankou. Around the beginning of 1883, Shevelev started to conduct business independently and changed the name to "Tokmakoff, Molotkoff, & Co." Now that Wu Dachen had acquainted himself with this entrepreneur who engaged both in tea and shipping, it is not difficult to understand why the black tea shipped to Russia for a trial sale would be "taken care of by this merchant" in the future. As for the S. W. Litvinoff & Co. (*Shunfeng yanghang*) which Wu entrusted to have the black tea delivered, it was a tea brick factory founded by Russian merchant Litvinov in Hankou in 1863. In the 1890s, the plant had an annual output of 150,000 boxes of tea, establishing its position as the controller of black tea processing and transportation around Hubei and Hunan provinces.

As the governor of Hunan province, Wu Dacheng would condescendingly seek help from Shevelev whom he met by chance to clear the channels for the export of Hunan black tea. He was really giving a lot of thought to this. In 1899, Zhang Zhidong was satisfied with the trial sale and proposed an expansion of the business. This is shown in the memorial entitled "Proposal to increase business when chances come as the trail sale of tea purchased and shipped to Russia works well":

> The total price of tea commissioned for sale by Shevelev was just about 1,900 taels, but the profit was more than 800 taels, showing an outstanding commercial interest. Silk and tea constitute the bulky portion of Chinese and foreign trade, critical to our tax money which is huge. Recently, the tea market has declined year by year, far worse than before. If no great efforts are made to improve the situation, and if we let it go down the slope, there will be few profits from tea business, and that might pose a risk to national economy and people's livelihoods. Since the black tea shipped to Russia last year proved to be truly profitable, it should be continued and expanded. The rule is, when the government advocates, the merchants will surely follow. So, if an order is given to the Bureau of Merchants to allow them to build their own tea ships, establish their own companies, set up their own warehouses for sales in Russia, thereby taking back economic rights, it will be beneficial for both business and tax revenues. As is known, last time when the tea was shipped to Russia through a Russian merchant ship, we confronted a refusal. After we repeatedly pleaded, they reluctantly agreed but said that they could not do this again in the future. Although Russians specialize in building tea ships which can travel the fastest to make more profits, their cost of human labor is also the highest, so they do not want Chinese tea to be attached to share their benefits. As to whether Shevelev would agree to sell tea for us in the future, it is still unclear. I will take chances to discuss tactfully with Russian merchants and shipowners. If they are willing to help us transport and sell tea, I will meet with the two governors from Hubei and Hunan provinces, and ask them to raise some funds and continue to purchase, transport and sell, and see how business goes.

But relying on Russian merchants and Russian ships is tantamount to throwing oneself into the trap where the weak is swallowed by the strong. Even though you get part of the profit, you cannot prevent the business from going down the slope, just as a cup of soup cannot keep a person away from hunger. As Russian merchants had stated that there would be no next time, because "Chinese tea attached might share the benefits," reliance on Russians was doomed to fail. Unsurprisingly, with only one trial, the Russian-dependent "water and land trial sale" plan failed and vanished into thin air.

"Inversed Flow of Russian Tea": The End of "Caravan Tea"

The end of "caravan tea" was inseparable from the Siberian Railway which replaced traditional tea routes. On 26 July 1900, Yang Ru, left vice minister of the Ministry of Industry (*gongbu zuo shilang*), stated in a legal reform proposal, "I heard that the Siberian Railway would be completed on schedule. While land transportation is beneficial for business, powerful neighboring countries would also come, causing changes in Manchuria and Mongolia." [57] This foresight was accurately proved by the coming facts:

> The railway connected Europe and Asia like an iron chain. It has revolutionized immigration patterns and economic development in the east area, which indicates that the entire balance of power in the Far East will be broken, creating a favorable situation for Russia.[58]

The unusual phenomenon of "inversed flow of Russian tea" is a manifestation of "creating a favorable situation for Russia."

As early as the 1880s, a small quantity of "inversed flow of Russian tea" had appeared in northwestern China. In 1880, there were 41 Russian caravans that traded in Tacheng, Gucheng, and Khovd, importing a total of 175,381 rubles of cotton textiles, 12,140 rubles of Central Asian fabrics, and only 11,760 rubles of tea.[59] If this happened because of Russia's forceful occupation of Yili and the following exclusion of Chinese merchants, then, after the completion of the Siberian Railway, the transportation of "caravan tea" had undergone a fundamental change.

As to what happened to the north route, we can get a hint from the memorial delivered by the Court of Colonial Affairs on 27 May 1911:

> As for business with Mongolians, tea is the mainstay. The Court of Colonial Affairs has, as a rule, practiced the regulation of issuing tea stamps, which brings a large amount of income. In recent years, there has appeared a sudden reduction of sales, totaling less than three or four tenths of the previous quantity. This, in fact, is attributed to the opening of the Siberian Railway which has made transportation more convenient. [Confronted with] an inversed flow of Russian tea, [Chinese merchants find it] hard to compete [against their Russian counterparts] when their tea is not that good in quality but high in price.[60]

On the west route, it was the same case. As early as 18 October 1880, Zhang Zhidong claimed ardently in a memorial:

> It is reported that, along Zhangjiakou and Kiachta, there used to be 28 tea houses making great profits. Towards the end of the Xianfeng reign, Russian business has prevailed, and now there are only three left open. If Russian business is introduced to Xi'an and Hanzhong, it is not hard to imagine how our people's livelihood would be impacted![61]

As for those Chinese merchants who set up shops to sell tea in Siberia, it was even more difficult for them to make ends meet. In the ninth month of 1888, Miao

Yousun, the head of Ministry of Revenue, returned to China. When he passed Tomsk,

> He went to a Chinese tea house called Wanhexing for a short visit, and heard that recently there had been a slump in tea business, because Russian merchants themselves shipped in more tea and sold it at a much cheaper price. There are about a thousand residents in this city, with few rich families or wealthy merchants, and the people here are tough. It is said that someone owed another person more than a thousand rubles. He was sued and the case was brought to the county magistrate, but in the end, there was still no payment returned.[62]

When he arrived at Irkutsk, he didn't see much improvement in Chinese business: "There are more than 10 Chinese tea shops, most of the owners are from Fenzhou [in Shanxi province]. They do not have a big profit, either. The Russians east of the Urals mostly despise the Chinese."[63] Since 1906, after the signing of the Charter Concerning Russian Merchants' Use of Yili and Tacheng to Export Tea, Russian merchants had dumped tea that they purchased inland along their way back, heavily hurting the tea business of the Hunan merchants in Xinjiang and deteriorating the situation. According to Guangfu, the general of Yili, who handed in a memorial in the 12th month of 1910:

> In the past, "Hunan/Hubei merchants" in Gansu sold tea all the way to the tribes of Mongolia and Kazakhs, as well as to residents along Russian borders, enjoying a fairly booming market. In 1906, the new charter about Russian merchants' use of Yili and Tacheng to export tea was signed. Now it is not just that we are prohibited from selling Chinese tea in Russia, but Russian vendors transport Chinese tea to Yili and Tacheng for dumping, not to mention the overwhelming number of tea smugglers. With private tea everywhere, markets are really sluggish."[64]

Obviously, by the eve of the "1911 Revolution," the distribution and sales of "caravan tea" had entirely changed. Heavily hit by the "inversed flow of Russian tea," the highly feudal tea business – "Shanxi consortium" and "Southern counter" failed one by one, finally dying from "fatigue and stagnation" in the death knell of the Qing dynasty.

The Russian Hotel and Transportation of "Caravan Tea"

The change of "caravan tea" trade from an exchange market to one-way transportation, and the rise and fall of China's northern and southern tea consortiums have been briefly discussed above. As for the relationship between the Russian Hotel and the transportation of "caravan tea," some historical materials can be used for a further exploration.

The Russian Hotel in Beijing during the Qing period seemed to have nothing in common with "foreign factories" in Canton. The "lamas in Beijing"

(Russian missionaries) gave people a more "noble and upright" impression than the "supercargoes in Guangdong." But in fact, in terms of seeking commercial rights, the role that the former played was by no means inferior to the latter. As some Russians admitted:

> Although the Russian missions sent to Beijing are not directly related to trade, they are still of great benefit to us. Stationed at the center of China, they can know the national characteristics and the needs of its residents, and gather a good knowledge about the favorable selling conditions for those goods suitable for use in China.[65]

The special position of the Russian Hotel had long aroused the envy of Western countries that shipped their goods in by sea. That is also mentioned in the second volume of *Illustrated Gazetteer of the Sea Kingdoms* which quotes from the *Macao Monthly*, "with a learning center in Beijing, Russia can know whatever happens in China." Indeed, the Russian Hotel's collection of "whatever happens in China" is all-encompassing, including a large volume of commercial information. As early as 1731, the Russian Privy Council had instructed students at the Russian Hotel to "use study as a coverup to stay in Beijing and familiarize themselves with Chinese business."[66] With the increasing proportion of tea trade, the focus of their attention was then turned to "caravan tea."

For the "caravan tea" trade, both lamas and students from the Russian Hotel provided comprehensive information. Da Lama Bichurin of the ninth mission, in his book *Statistical Description of the Chinese Empire* published in 1842, devoted one chapter to the Chinese tea industry; Nechaev, a student from the 13th mission, edited and translated the *Regulations about Chinese Tea,* which was submitted to the Asian Department of the Russian Ministry of Foreign Affairs in 1851[67]. In addition, they were also committed to the collection of Chinese tea plant seeds and tea samples. After returning to Russia in 1840, the medical doctor on the 11th mission, Kirilov, conducted an experiment successfully at home by planting tea plant seeds in clumps. In 1853, he published his results in the Russian newspaper Northern Bee.[68] When the supervisor of the 13th mission, Kovalevsky, returned to Russia in 1850, he took away a large number of tea samples and sent them to the Russian Ministry of Trade, boasting that his collection was "Number one in Europe."[69]

The intelligence work of the Russian Hotel during the two Opium Wars was particularly eye-catching. For several times, Russian lamas stationed in Beijing sent timely commercial reports to the Asian Department to reflect the trend in the Chinese tea market.

On 8 March 1844, Policarp (Chinese name: Tong Zhenghu), Da Lama of the 12th mission of the Russian Hotel, submitted a written report to the Asian Department on the current situation of China's tea industry:

> The number of tea gardens has increased year by year. In the past ten years, Chinese tea merchants have benefited greatly. Although the demand for tea has increased, the price of tea in the producing area, compared with previous

years, has almost fallen by half. Planters in the tea district attributed the price drop to the growing number of tea gardens and the shortage of silver caused by the large purchase of opium.[70]

On 25 February 1853, Da Lama Pallady of the 13th mission wrote a secret message to the Asian Department in invisible ink, detailing the serious consequence of the Taiping Army's control of the lower reaches of the Yangtze River on the trade of "caravan tea":

> According to hearsay from Zhangjiakou, the current turmoil in China has more and more negative effects on trade volume. Chinese merchants engaged in the Kiachta trade have lost 2 million taels (4.31 million rubles) because the armed insurgents have destroyed the business town of Hankou and looted the local stores where these merchants kept their promissory notes. As for the 200,000 boxes of tea ordered for Kiachta, only half have arrived in Zhangjiakou and there is no confirmation about when the remaining will arrive. It is even believed that, due to the turbulence in southern China, there will be very few merchants traveling to Fujian to order tea this year, thus, probably next year (?) we will not have new tea coming. The terror caused by the rebels throughout the lower reaches of the Yangtze River has cut off the traffic route via Fancheng. In such a chaotic period, Shanxi merchants may not dare to take risks with their money.[71]

In the sixth month of 1857, Pallady again did not hesitate to report the situation in the Wuyi tea area to the Tsarist government:

> The mob marched towards Fujian and surrounded the western border of this province. In February of this year, the major force entered Fujian, and soon occupied several cities of this industrial and commercial province. They not only controlled the waterway traffic between the Wuyi mountains and Fuzhou prefecture, but also occupied Chong'an county, which is adjacent to the Wuyi tea district.[72]

These messages about Chinese tea areas, tea roads, and tea merchants not only played a significant role in helping the Tsarist government to formulate their invasion strategy but also directly enhanced Russian merchants' ability to predict the market and gain an upper hand over their Chinese counterparts, making it easier for them to suppress the latter and make huge profits from the "caravan tea" trade. As for how Lama Polikarp (Tong Zhenghu) of the Russian Hotel repeatedly asked the Court of Colonial Affairs to establish trade ports in Yili and Tacheng, and how two Russian consuls Dmitry Alekseevich Peshchurov (Chinese name: Mengdi) and Konstantin Adrianovich Skachkov (Chinese name: Kongqi), who started up as "officially sponsored students," sought and expanded Russia's land trade privileges during their tenure in Tianjin, those are known facts and there is nothing secret about them. It is clear that in the history of Sino-Russian relations in the Qing period, the economic part of the Russian Hotel coexisted with its diplomatic role.[73]

Based on the above discussion, we can see that, generally speaking, the history of "caravan tea" can be divided into two phases, with the signing of the Land Trade between Russia and China in 1862 as the dividing line. The early stage saw a cross-border exchange where Russian merchants "arrive[d] with furs, and return[ed] with tea." The leading role of transportation was entirely in the hands of Chinese merchants. Although in 1851, the newly-set two trade ports with Russia – Yili and Tacheng demonstrated certain characteristics different from that of the Kiachta exchange market but did not cause a fundamental change. As for the later land trade period, Russian merchants bought and transported tea by themselves and did not have to exchange with Chinese merchants at the port. With the emergence of Russian tea shops and tea factories in Tianjin, Hankou, Fuzhou, and Jiujiang, the business of "Shanxi tea merchants" deteriorated, and gradually, shops closed one after another. During this period, the "Southern counter" rose, but it could not prevent the tea industry from declining although it did reflect the ups and downs of the tea consortiums in the Qing period. Affected by the "inverted flow of Russian tea," it also fell into the desperate situation of having a "sluggish sales market."

The decline of the "caravan tea" trade during the Tongzhi and Guangxu reigns, as an economic manifestation of the border and ruling crisis of the Qing dynasty, was so serious that even high-ranking officials like a governor-general or a provincial governor could not stop it. The "water and land trial sale" plan jointly formulated by Zhang Zhidong and Wu Dacheng was nothing more than a painstaking "utopian" project in the history of the "caravan tea" trade. Its failure undoubtedly declared to future generations that, without the revival of Chinese society, there would be no revival of the Chinese tea industry.

Supplement: Kiachta Tea market and its Business Language

The Kiachta tea market was a seasonal bazaar. As reported by the Yili General Yishan, "Kiachta is dozens of stops away from Zhangjiakou, and it is at this remote location that Chinese merchants and Russian merchants trade regularly. They return home after transactions are completed."[74]

Every year, the period from the end of winter until the beginning of next spring was the peak season for the Kiachta trade. "Big business usually started in early February, lasting for one or two months. Sometimes it would just take two weeks to complete a successful transaction."[75] Take the tea market in 1838 as an example. For businesses shops among the "Shanxi tea merchants," such as Wangshouqiao, Daxingfa, Longqingyuan, Guofacheng, Qiaofacheng, Dexingxi, Xidecha, Meiyoukang, and Xingyou[76], they all had a turnover of more than 2,000 boxes. The consignors of various brands returned to Zhangjiakou immediately after the transaction, leaving only the assistants to guard shops, waiting for the market to reopen in the coming year. Therefore, it is not the shop owners who maintained constant contact with Russian merchants in Kiachta, but those assistants, who, because of this division of labor, were prompted to learn Russian, thus forming a unique business language.

The tea market itself was a school to train assistants. As stated in a document from the Qing period, an assistant grew up like this:

> Choose a lad about 20, who knows a bit about how to read and calculate, to work as an assistant in the store. If, after a few years, he has proved to be potentially talented and can be promoted, he will be asked to join with his labor share, without any salary and with just a little money to buy clothes each year. Three years later, he will be rewarded with his share of dividends.
>
> Living at the Russian border, one is supposed to master the Russian language. Every day at dusk or at sunset, each assistant holds a book in hand, learning to read and write. They are far more diligent than students in village schools.[77]

According to Russian documents, as early as the 1820s, it had become a common practice for assistants in Kiachta to learn Russian. In the absence of formal training, with "each assistant hold[ing] a book in hand," it is inevitable that the language they were learning was diversified – "Almost every shop had a hand-written dictionary, which was compiled by merchants in so-called Sinicized Russian."[78] Therefore, although "Chinese merchants used the Russian language to do business, only the residents of Kiachta could understand them. To people who were not used to this language, their talk was just like speaking Chinese."[79] Obviously, the Russian language that they claimed to have mastered was nothing more than the Sinicized Russian known as the "trading town dialect," which was nonstandard in terms of word order, declension, or tense. As this unique "Shanxi consortium" business language had a close relationship with Sino-Russian trade, it also attracted the attention of some Russian researchers. In 1831, "Moscow Telecom" published a letter from Kiachta, introducing 15 sentence examples. In 1854, the St. Petersburg News published a feature article, commenting on this business language. But no such record can be found in the extant Qing documents.

From the above, it can be seen that, before the Opium War, there was a mixture of Chinese and foreign languages used for foreign trade both over land and by sea, and each had developed into a strange business language. If the pidgin English popular at the Canton port emerged with seaborne tea,[80] then the "trading town Russian" commonly used in Kiachta was a derivative of "caravan tea." However, those "assistants" did not turn into "western houseboys," because after the 1870s, the business of "Shanxi tea merchants" was declining, and they had to abandon the tea houses in the north and go inland to engage in private banking business.[81]

Notes

1 Zhang Deyi, vol. 14. See the entry dated as "The sixth day of the eighth month in the fifth year of Guangxu [21 September1879]."
2 Karl Marx, 1995: 9–10.
3 Parshin, 136.
4 Wen Qing, et al., vol. 16.

"Caravan Tea" 223

5 Pood is a Russian unit of weight equal to about 16.4 kilograms (36.1 pounds). One pood is equal to 40 Russian pounds. —Trans.
6 Korsak, 110.
7 Khokhlov, 93.
8 Xue Fucheng, *Completed Works of Yong'an* (*Yong'an quanji*). See also Schlegel, 468–472.
9 Baddeley, 118.
10 Baddeley, 398.
11 Vilkov, 110.
12 Korsak, 51.
13 Bakhrushin, 242.
14 Wang Zhixiang and Liu Zerong, 274–275.
15 Skarikovsky, 141.
16 Korshak, 94–95.
17 He Qiutao, vol. 37.
18 The ninth volume of the *Annals of Jiexiu County* (*Jiexiu xianzhi*) has the name "Fan Yongnian" 范永年 instead of "Fan Yongdou" 范永斗.
19 Quoted in Peng Zeyi, 1957: 304.
20 The Eight Banners were the military and social structure in the Qing dynasty. They were Bordered Yellow Banner, Plain Yellow Banner, Plain White Banner, Plain Red Banner, Bordered White Banner, Bordered Red Banner, Plain Blue Banner, and Bordered Blue Banner. —Trans.
21 The *li* 里 is a Chinese unit of distance. In the Qing dynasty, one *li* was approximately 537–645 meters. —Trans.
22 Dahuli was the region inhabit by the Daur people. Now it is located in Russia's amur region and northeast part of Chita. —Trans.
23 The *jin* 斤 [catty] is a Chinese unit of weight. In the Qing dynasty, one *jin* (about 0.6 kilograms) was equal to 16 *liang*/tael (one *liang* was about 0.04 kilograms). —Trans.
24 Xu Ke, vol. 17: 73. See also Terada Takanobu, 303–313.
25 Khokhlov, 96–97. See also Pang Yicai and Qu Shaomiao, 12–21.
26 Engels, 1995: 325.
27 Korsak, 328.
28 Wen Qing, et al., vol. 6.
29 Marx, 1998: 140.
30 Barsukov, 204–205.
31 Wang Yanwei, et al., vol. 24.
32 Kun Gang, et al., vol. 983.
33 Wen Qing, et al., vol. 15.
34 Kuping was a standard weight for monetary silver ingots adopted by the Qing government. It was used for tax collection and measuring government expenditure. —Trans.
35 Wen Qing, et al., vol. 51.
36 Khokhlov, pp. 94–95.
37 Wen Qing, et al., vol. 15.
38 The likin tax was an internal tariff on the transport of goods introduced in the mid-19th century in the Qing dynasty. —Trans.
39 Wen Qing, et al., vol. 58.
40 In this quote, it is written as hong cha (red tea). As red tea is the Chinese name for what is called "black tea" in the West, the term "black tea" is used hereafter. —Trans.
41 Liu Kunyi, 607–608.
42 Wen Qing, et al., vol. 56.
43 Wen Qing, et al., vol. 51 and vol. 56.
44 Wen Qing, et al., vol. 61.
45 Wen Qing, et al., vol. 54.

46 Wen Qing, et al., vol. 88.
47 Wen Qing, et al., vol. 5.
48 See volume 45 of Zuo Zongtang, *Memorial Drafts by Zuo wenxianggong* (*Zuo wenxianggong zougao*).
49 Bogoyavlensky, 170.
50 Chen Sanyuan, vol. 5.
51 Miao Yousun, vol. 8, dated "the 18th day of the fifth month in the 14th year of Guangxu [27 June 1888]."
52 Zhang Zhidong, vol. 28.
53 Wang Yanwei, et al., vol. 96.
54 Skachkov, 1977: 113.
55 Gu Tinglong, 135–145.
56 Skachkov, 463.
57 Jin Yufu, et al., vol. 47.
58 Korsak, 151.
59 Cahen, 261.
60 Skachkov, 156.
61 Skachkov, 1958: 143–144.
62 Quoted from Miao Yousun, *Travel Diary in Russia* (*E you riji*).
63 Quoted from Miao Yousun, *Exchange of Letters between Friends of Yifengtang* (*Yifengtang youpeng shuzha*), letter 66 from Miao Yousun to Miao Quansun.
64 Wang Yanwei, et al., vol. 149.
65 Lensen, 1978: 136.
66 Skachkov, 156.
67 Jin Yufu, et al., vol. 53.
68 Wang Yanwei, et al., vol. 23.
69 Valskaya, 147.
70 Khokhlov, 107.
71 G.L., 154.
72 Popov, 195.
73 Cai Hongsheng, 1979: 119–128. See also Widmer, 148–167.
74 Wen Qing, et al., vol. 5. See also Xu Shuming, 11–16.
75 Korsak, 329.
76 Parshin, 48–49.
77 Xu Ke, vol. 17: 70–71.
78 Skachkov, 1977: 109.
79 Parshin, 50.
80 Hall, 95.
81 As to how Shanxi tea merchants turned to private banking business, further research is needed. Some useful information is given in *Historical Materials of Shanxi Private Banks* (*Shanxi piaohao shiliao*), edited by Zhongguo Renmin Yinhang Shanxi Fenhang and Shanxi Caijing Xueyuan (Taiyuan: Shanxi jingji chubanshe, 1990): 776–793.

Bibliography

Baddeley, John F. *Russia, Mongolia, China*, vol. 2. London: MacMillan, 1919.

Bakhrushin, Sergey Vladimirovich. *Academic Works of Bakhrushin*, vol. 3. [In Russian.] Moscow: The USSR Academy of Sciences Publishing House, 1955.

Barsukov, Ivan Platonovich. *Count Muravyov-Amursky*, vol. 2. [In Chinese.] Translated by Department of Foreign Languages of Heilongjiang University. Shanghai: Shangwu yinshuguan, 1974.

Bogoyavlensky, Nikolai Vasilyevich. *Western China beyond the Great Wall*. [In Chinese.] Translated by Russian Teaching Group in Department of Foreign Languages of Xinjiang University. Beijing: Shangwu yinshuguan, 1980.

Cahen, Gaston. *Russian Relations with China during the Reign of Peter the Great*. [In Chinese.] Translated by Jiang Zaihua and Zheng Yongqin. Beijing: Shangwu yinshuguan, 1980.

Cai Hongsheng. "Shuofang beicheng Eluosi guan jishi buzheng (Supplements and Corrections to the Chronicle of the Russian Mission in *Peregrinations in the North*)." *Wenshi* 7 (1979): 119–128.

Chen Sanyuan. *Sanyuan jingshe shiwenji (Collected Works of Sanyuan Jingshe)*. Shanghai: Shanghai guji chubanshe, 2003.

Engels, Friedrich. "Social Problems in Russia," in *Selected Works of Marx and Engels*, vol. 3. [In Chinese.] Translated by Compilation and Translation Bureau of the CPC Central Committee. Beijing: Renmin chubanshe, 1995. 323–336.

G. L. "Peking Missions and Russia-China Trade from the 1930s to the 1950s." [In Russian.] *Red Files*, no. 4 (1932): 162–164.

Gu Tinglong. *Wu Kezhai xiansheng nianpu (Biographical Chronology of Wu Kezhai)*. Peking: Hafo yanjing xueshe, 1935.

Hall, Robert A. "Chinese Pidgin English: Grammar and Text." *Journal of the American Oriental Society* 64, no. 3 (1944): 95–113.

He Qiutao. *Shuofang beicheng (Peregrinations in the North)*. Taipei: Wenhai chubanshe, 1964.

Ji Xiaolan. *Yuewei caotang biji (Jottings from the Thatch Hut of Subtle Views)*. Changsha: Yuelu shushe, 1993.

Jin Yufu, et al., eds. *Qing shilu - Xuantong zhengji (Veritable Records of the Qing Dynasty - Records of the Politics of the Xuantong Reign)*. Beijing: Zhonghua shuju, 1987.

Khokhlov, Alexander Nikolayevich. "China's Foreign Trade from the 1890s to the 1940s," in *State and Society in China*. [In Russian.] Edited by Lev Petrovich Delyusin. Moscow: Nauka, 1978. 86–120.

Korsak, Alexander Kazimirovich. *Historical and Statistical Review of Trade Relations between Russia and China*. [In Russian.] Kazan: The Publication of Bookseller Ivan Dubrovin, 1857.

Kun Gang, et al., eds. *Daqing huidian shili (Collected Statutes of the Qing Dynasty with Precedents and Regulations)*. Beijing: Zhonghua shuju, 1991.

Lensen, George Alexander. *Russia's Eastward Expansion*. [In Chinese.] Translated by Yang Shigao, Proofread by Yan Siguang. Beijing: Shangwu yinshuguan, 1978.

Li Yanshou. *Bei shi (History of the North)*. Beijing: Zhonghua shuju, 1974.

Liu Kunyi. *Liu Kunyi yiji (Posthumously Collected Writings of Liu Kunyi)*, vol. 2. Beijing: Zhonghua shuju, 1959.

Liu Shengmu. *Changchu zhai xubi (Sequel to Changchu Zhai)*. Beijing: Zhonghua shuju, 1998.

Marx, Karl. "A Contribution to the Critique of Political Economy," in *Completed Works of Marx and Engels*, vol. 13. [In Chinese.] Translated by Compilation and Translation Bureau of Works of Marx, Engels, Lenin and Stalin of the CPC Central Committee. Beijing: Renmin chubanshe, 1998.

Marx, Karl. "Russian Trade with China," in *Selected Works of Marx and Engels*, vol. 2. [In Chinese.] Translated by Compilation and Translation Bureau of the CPC Central Committee. Beijing: Renmin chubanshe, 1995.

Miao Yousun. *E you huibian* (*Compilation of Travel Diaries in Russia*). Shanghai: Shanghai xiuwen shuju, 1889.
Miao Yousun. *E you riji* (*Travel Diary in Russia*). Shanghai: Zhuyitang, 1891.
Miao Yousun. *Yifengtang youpeng shuzha* (*Exchange of Letters Between Friends of Yifengtang*). Shanghai: Shanghai guji chubanshe, 1981.
Pang Yicai and Qu Shaomiao. "Lun Qingdai Shanxi tuobang de duie maoyi (Shanxi Camel Gang's Trade with Russia in the Qing Dynasty)." *Jinyang Academic Journal* 4 (1983): 12–21.
Parshin, Vasily. *A Journey to the Transbaikal Region*. [In Chinese.] Translated by Russian Translation Group of Beijing International Studies University. Beijing: Shangwu yinshuguan, 1976.
Peng Zeyi, ed. *Zhongguo jindai shougongye shi ziliao* (*Records of China's Modern Handicraft Industry*), vol. 1. Beijing: Sanlian shudian, 1957.
Popov, Alexander Ivovich. "Tsar Diplomacy in the Age of the Taiping Rebellion." *Red Files* 2 (1927): 182–199.
Qiu Yuquan and He Caihuan. Anhua Xianzhi (*Annals of Anhua County*). Anhua: Yiyang Anhua, 1862.
Schlegel, Gustav. "First Introduction of Tea into Holland." *T'oung Pao* 2. ser., no. 1 (1900): 468–472.
Skachkov, Peter Emelyanovich. "Doctors of the Russian Mission in Beijing." [In Russian.] *China Studies in the Soviet Union* 4 (1958): 136–148.
Skachkov, Peter Emelyanovich. *A History of Russian Sinology*. [In Russian.] Moscow: Nauka, 1977.
Skalkovsky, Konstantin Apollonovich. *Russian Trade in the Pacific*. [In Russian.] St. Petersburg: The Publication of Aleksei Sergeyevich Suvorin, 1883.
Terada, Takanobu. *A Study on Shanxi Merchants*. [In Chinese.] Translated by Zhang Zhengming etc. Taiyuan: Shanxi renmin chubanshe, 1986.
Valskaya, Bluma Abramovna. *The Journey of Egor Petrovich Kovalevsky* (In Russian). Moscow: State Publishing House for Geographic Literature, 1956.
Vilkov, Oleg Nikandrovich. "On the Chinese Goods in the Tobolsk Market in the 17th Century." *History of the USSR* 1 (1958): 105–124.
Wang Yanwei, et al., eds. *Qingji waijiao shiliao* (*Sources to the History of Foreign Relations during the Qing Period*). Beijing: Shumu wenxian chubanshe, 1987.
Wang Zhichun. *Shi E cao* (*Manuscript of My Mission to Russia*). Taipei: Wenhai chubanshe, 1967.
Wang Zhixiang and Liu Zerong, eds. *Gugong ewen shiliao* (*Documents in Russian Preserved in National Palace Museum*). Peking [Beijing]: Gugong bowuyuan, 1936.
Wei Yuan. *Haiguo tuzhi* (*Illustrated Gazetteer of the Sea Kingdoms*). Zhengzhou: Zhongzhou guji chubanshe, 1999.
Wen Qing, et al., eds. *Chouban yiwu shimo* (*A Complete Record of the Management of Foreign Affairs*). Shanghai: Shanghai guji chubanshe, 1979.
Widmer, Eric. *The Russian Ecclesiastical Mission in Peking During the Eighteenth Century*. Cambridge: Harvard University, 1976.
Xu Ke, ed. *Qingbai leichao* (*Classified Anecdotes of the Qing Dynasty*). Shanghai: Shangwu yinshuguan, 1917
Xu Shuming. "Yong Qian shiqi beifang bianjing maoyi xincheng: Maimai cheng (Trading Towns on the Northern Border during the Yongzheng and Qianlong Reigns)." *Qingshi yanjiu tongxun* 1 (1984) 11–16.

Xue Fucheng. *Chushi Ying De Yi Bi riji* (*Diary of an Embassy to Four Nations*). Changsha: Yuelu shushe, 1985.

Yao Yuanzhi. *Zhuyeting zaji* (*Miscellaneous Notes of the Bamboo Leaves Pavilion*). Beijing: Zhonghua shuju, 1982.

Zhang Deyi. *Si shu qi* (*Fourth-told Strange Tales*). Shanghai: Zhuyitang, 1883.

Zhang Zhidong. *Zhang wenxianggong gongdu gao* (*Official Documents Drafted by Zhang Wenxianggong*). Photocopy archived in Zhongguo renmin daxue tushuguan, 1920.

Zuo Chengye, ed. *Wanquan Xianzhi* (*Annals of Wanquan County*). Beijing: Xinhua chubanshe, 1992.

Zuo Zongtang. *Zuo wenxianggong zougao* (*Memorial Drafts by Zuo wenxianggong*). Shanghai: Guxiangge, 1902.

13 Russian-American Company and the Canton Port

As a trading port of the feudal empire, Guangzhou [Canton] in the Qing dynasty had long been subject to the impact of colonialism, and it was a place where numerous disputes over "foreign affairs" occurred. The year 1805 witnessed the "Russian vessels sailed to Canton for business" incident, indicating that Tsarist Russia was to follow the footsteps of other Western countries and entered the Guangdong Maritime Customs.

In accordance with the Qing government's foreign policy, Tsarist Russia was one of those "Northern countries for land trade" and was legally allowed to conduct business at Kiachta, but no other coastal ports. Since Guangdong Maritime Customs was established in 1685, no Russian vessels had ever come here for business. That is why the unexpected arrival of the vessels from the Russian-American Company (RAC) in 1805 was seen as a serious violation of the old rule, immediately upsetting the Qing court. Emperor Jiaqing himself took an earnest concern in this matter. Within the span of one month in 1806 (between 28 January and 26 February), the Council of State (*junji chu*) sent three letters to the governor-general of Guangdong and Guangxi provinces (*liangguang zongdu*), and the Court of Colonial Affairs (*lifan yuan*) sent out two official inquiry letters to the Privy Council of Russia. When the case was finally closed, following the "imperial edict," the Grand Secretariat (*neige*) imposed the following penalties on those who were involved in this incident: Yanfeng, the former customs superintendent, was dismissed from his post; Yanfeng's replacement Akedang'a, together with Wu Xiongguang, the governor-general of Guangdong and Guangxi, and Sun Yuting, the governor of Guangdong (*xunfu*), were all sent to the Ministry of Punishment (*xingbu*) to await coming decisions about them.

With regard to this incident, "foreign merchants" (*yi shang*) and Hong merchants (*hang shang*) in Canton were also involved in varying degrees. James Drummond, the chief supercargo of the British East India Company in Canton, and Thomas Beale, the president of the British Select Committee in Canton, and his successor John Roberts, all offered "guidance" to the Russian captains about how to be put "under security" (*cheng bao*) and gain "customs clearance" (*fang guan*). As for the head merchant of the "thirteen hongs" – Pan Youdu [also known as Pan Qiguan, Poankeequa] from Tongwen Hang, and other merchants like Lu Guanheng from Guangli Hang and Li Yanyu from Xicheng Hang, they were caught in the fight

DOI: 10.4324/9781032616353-13

between the Qing government and "foreigners." Used by both sides as pawns, they once again found themselves in fear and trepidation, as was typical with the Hong merchants in the past.

In terms of the impact of this incident, this case was invoked again and again by the Qing officials when they were making preparations for the coming "foreign affairs." For example, in the eighth month of 1824, when Ruan Yuan, the governor-general of Guangdong and Guangxi provinces, and Chen Zhongfu, the governor of Guangdong province, together with the superintendent of Guangdong Maritime Customs, were handling the case concerning "foreign vessels from Xiaoxiyang [Goa],"[1] they carefully went over the whole incident so as to learn from this lesson and avoid any possible mistakes. Even He Qiutao, the secretary (*zhushi*) of the Ministry of Punishment, did not forget to take account of the Jiaqing Emperor's "imperial edict" regarding this as one of the "sacred instructions" when he wrote the book *Peregrinations in the North* (*Shuofang beicheng*) in the Xianfeng reign [1850–1861].

However, in the Qing documents about "foreign affairs," this notable trading dispute in the Jiaqing era [1796–1820] is only briefly mentioned. Even treatises like the *Gazetteer of Guangdong Maritime Customs* (*Yuehaiguan zhi*) do not clearly outline the whole story, leaving details of this incident obscure. Based on the available information, I try to make some interpretations from several aspects, with the hope that they can provide some reference for scholars who are interested in the study of the RAC and the Canton port.

The Rise of the Fur Market in Canton

As a result of the trade deficit between Western maritime countries and China, the fur market in Canton emerged in the 1780s.

In his 1853 article "Revolution in China and in Europe," Karl Marx declared, "Up to 1830, the balance of trade being continually in favor of the Chinese, there existed an uninterrupted importation of silver from India, Britain and the United States into China." That is also shown in the report of Wu Dunyuan, a Hong merchant when he addressed Jiang Youxian, the governor-general of Guangdong and Guangxi in 1814:

> When foreign merchants come to Guangdong, as a rule, they barter for goods. They bring woolen fabrics, serge, cotton, hides, clocks and watches, and exchange them for satin, cloth, Huzhou silk, tea, and porcelain from the mainland of China. There is a trading agreement between them and us. All price differences that occur are settled in foreign currency, and no perfunctory excuses should be made. One silver dollar is counted as seven *qian* [mace] and two *fen* [candareen][2], with no additional compensation. As we have more exportation than importation, foreign money is often used to make up the difference. There is no such thing as smuggling sycee silver (*wenyin*) abroad.[3]

"Bartering" does not guarantee a trade balance. In fact, with "more exportation than importation," Mexican eagle silver coins (called *"huabian"*[4] in Chinese) and Spanish silver dollars (called *"fanmian"*[5] in Chinese) and other foreign currencies flowed into Canton in large quantities. This not only brought out a situation that "money from the trade deficit was piled up in the thirteen hongs" but also caused the circulation of silver dollars in the prefectures and provinces from the north to the east of Guangdong where "people in Nanxiong, Shaozhou, Lianzhou, and Zhaoqing mostly used Spanish silver dollars, while people in Chaozhou, Leizhou, Jiayingzhou and Qiongzhou took Mexican silver coins."[6] For example, in 1788 alone, the silver imported that year amounted to 2.72 million *liang*. In order to reduce payment in silver coins, "foreign merchants" in Guangdong tried all means to find other substitutes so that a trade balance could be achieved. After some search, they finally landed on the tradable objects from the northwest coast of America – precious furs taken from sea otters (nicknamed "sea dragons" in China) and seals (nicknamed "sea tigers" in China).

In 1776, commanding two vessels – the *Resolution* and the *Discovery*, British captain James Cook (1728–1779) sailed to the northwestern coast of America and bought some sea otter pelts from aborigines at a low price at Nootka Sound. In 1779, Cook and his men arrived at Huangpu [Whampoa Anchorage]. They sold these pelts at a high price of 120 yuan each, showing a promising future for other "foreign merchants" to follow.

In 1787, two other British vessels – the *King George* (320 tons) and the *Queen Charlotte* (200 tons) – commanded by Captain Nathaniel Portlock and Captain George Dixon, respectively, came to Canton with 2,500 furs and sold them for 50,000 yuan. In the same year, the *Imperial Eagle*, a 400-ton British vessel under the command of Captain Charles William Barkley, sailed to Macau where 700 North American furs were sold, gaining a profit of 30,000 yuan. Given the scale of supply and distribution, it can be said that in 1787, the fur market in Canton was officially established.

Although the United States was a latecomer, it was no slouch in this business. In 1784, the *Empress of China* made her maiden voyage to Canton, ushering in an era of direct commerce between America and China. In 1787, Boston merchants sent the *Columbia* (212 tons), captained by John Kendrick, and the *Lady Washington* (90 tons), captained by Robert Gray, to the northwest coast in exchange for furs. By 1789, the entire cargo was shipped by the *Columbia* to Canton and dumped on the market. In 1790, the *Columbia* returned to the United States via the Cape of Good Hope with a full cargo of Chinese goods, becoming the first American vessel to sail around the world. In 1792, the *Margaret*, a merchant vessel from Boston, sailed to Canton via Hawaii with about 1,200 sea otter pelts, all of which were sold successfully.

American merchants were vigorous in promoting the fur trade in Canton, as one voyage meant "three opportunities to make money": shipping out cheap goods such as knives and felts from the United States to the northwest coast in exchange for valuable Indian furs, then sailing to Canton to sell them and buy tea, and then selling tea at a high price in the United States or European markets on the return voyage.[7] Layers of profits were the secret of the so-called fur fever.

During the late eighteenth and early nineteenth centuries, Europe was witnessing the French Revolution and the Napoleonic Wars, while the United States was enjoying relative peace. The favorable international situation made it possible for the shipping industry on the northwest coast of the United States to develop by leaps and bounds. As a result, between the British and American vessels that sailed to the northwest coast for furs, there appeared an obvious contrast of reduction and growth: 35 British vessels and 15 American vessels in the years 1785–1794; 9 British vessels and 50 American vessels in 1795–1804; and 3 British vessels and 40 American vessels in 1805–1814.[8] In addition, after Americans discovered new fur resources off the coast of California and in the Spanish territories of South America at the end of the eighteenth century, they organized major seal hunting expeditions. Between 1793 and 1807, about 3.5 million seal skins were shipped from Más Afuera Island alone to Canton for sale.[5] The above two factors finally led to the monopoly of American traders in the Canton fur market. According to Tyler Dennett, from the early nineteenth century to the 1930s, the total value of furs imported from the United States to Canton amounted to 15–20 million dollars.[9]

The rise of the fur market in Canton would certainly stir up Tsarist Russia's craving for profits. As we all know, in the sixteenth century, Russia conquered Siberia that was rich in furs; then expanded to Kamchatka Peninsula, the Bering Sea, and the Aleutian Islands; and finally brought the "Fur Kingdom" Alaska into its sphere of influence, becoming the largest fur exporter in modern times and the pioneer of the fur trade with China. At the end of the Kangxi reign [1661–1722], Russian furs were flooding the Beijing market, so the Court of Colonial Affairs issued an official note to Russia in 1719, informing Russians that the caravan trade would be temporarily suspended:

We have abundant furs of different varieties. Moreover, in Guangdong, Fujian and other coastal areas, there are also merchant vessels from Western countries coming to trade every year. With sufficient supply of various commodities, no one would buy your goods.[10]

After the opening of the mutual market in Kiachta, the number of furs entering China increased dramatically, accounting for about 70%–80% of the total value of Russian exports. In 1784, for example, among the 1.8 million rubles of Russian goods, furs accounted for 1.17 million rubles. It is evident that fur sales had become the lifeline of Russia's trade with China. No wonder Tsarist Russia kept a close watch over fur resources in North America and actively planned to squeeze into the Canton market and seize the fur business from the United States. In 1794, a wealthy Russian merchant Grigory Ivanovich Shelikhov, who specialized in American furs, asked the Russian government to allow him to send vessels "to transport products obtained in the Americas as well as some Russian products to Canton and Macau."[11] In 1799, Tsar Paul I approved the establishment of the RAC. This colonial company was described in the document of the Qing government as "a Russian company set up in a place to the extreme east of its country, specializing in furs in the northwest of America,"[12] which is quite accurate. One of the urgent tasks that

232 *Russian-American Company and the Canton Port*

this company had faced was to take advantage of its "specialization in fur trade" to eliminate the impact of the Canton fur market on Kiachta and to preserve years of commercial interests from the fur trade with China. However, it was a very tough job, as shown in the report written by Alexander Andreyevich Baranov, RAC's General Manager in 1800:

> A large quantity of furs have been imported into Canton after numerous changes of hands, and then shipped from here to everywhere else in China, causing so heavy a blow to our cheap trade in Kiachta that in the end our profit is probably unable to cover tariff. According to an American merchant, the closing of Kiachta market has benefited them by raising the price of furs and hides by 20 percent, so the conclusion to be drawn from this, as he has said, is that the Canton trade has had a great impact on the trade in Kiachta. [13]

The frequent "closing of Kiachta market" during the Qianlong reign was actually an economic sanction imposed by the Qing government on Russia for their disturbance of border peace. From 1744 to 1792, the market was "closed" ten times, and the last one, also the longest one, went on for seven years (1785–1792).

While the sale of Russian furs in the north was blocked, Boston merchants fully displayed their commercial capabilities in Canton. The RAC, in their jealousy, sought to unblock the channels for the transportation of furs from the north to the south and took the risk of violating the "old rule" of Sino-Russian land trade. In the winter of 1805, two RAC vessels, the *Hope* and the *Neva*, were sent south to "open up business in Canton with a vision for future trades with Japan and other Asian regions." Bringing various furs to Canton for a trial sale, their arrival shocked and greatly upset the Qing court.

The Mystery of "Patrol Vessel" or "Cargo Vessel"

The first report about the Russian vessels that came to Canton for trade was delivered by Yanfeng, the superintendent of the Guangdong Maritime Customs. In his memorial dated 19 December 1805, he wrote:

> On the eighth day of the tenth month this year [28 November 1805], the Macau commissioner (*weiyuan*) reported that a patrol vessel came to Macau. It was captained by a foreign merchant called Luchendun 嚕呧吨 from a country called Luchen 咯呧. As to which country this Luchen is, a further investigation should be made jointly by the sub-prefect of Macau (*Aomen tongzhi*), the Macau commissioner and Hong merchants. On the 17th day [7 December 1805], the commissioner reported that another vessel from this Luchen country came, carrying fur and silver to Canton for trade. This one is captained by a merchant named Erzanshi 呃赞吋. Later, Hong merchants asserted that Luchen is actually Russia, because the crew spoke a foreign language similar to Russian. Then they submitted the translated version of the foreign statement to me. After reading and reviewing their request,

I, Your Majesty's servant, found that the second foreign vessel, like the first one, had sailed from Russia all the way east [to North America]. For a long time, the trade between Russia and our Celestial Empire (*tianchao*) has been conducted outside our capital beyond the border. Probably because it is difficult to travel back and forth by land between two countries, so they have decided to send vessels to Canton as a trial. Although sailing to Canton is much farther, it can save a lot of travel expenses. The earlier vessel captained by Luchendun is not a patrol vessel, because it has furs and hides on board and it is for trade. The two vessels now are begging Your Majesty to allow them to unload their cargo.[14]

There are two points worth noting here. First, the two Russian vessels not only arrived at different times but also asked for inspection in a different way. The *Hope* initially reported itself as a "patrol vessel" and then changed to a "cargo vessel" upon the arrival of the *Neva*, asking the Guangdong Maritime Customs to allow them to unload their cargo. Thus, it is not historically accurate to say in a general way that the two Russian vessels "forced their way into Whampoa." [15] Second, the altered statement that it "is not a patrol vessel" was directly quoted by Yanfeng from the "foreign statement" in his memorial; therefore, it is not a "false claim" [16] at all. The *Hope* gave a contradictory statement to the maritime customs. Obviously, there must be something hidden, awaiting further disclosure.

Foreign vessels coming to Guangdong in the Qing period can be roughly divided into three types, namely, tribute vessels, cargo vessels, and patrol vessels (also known as "escort vessels," that is, naval ships). Except for "tribute vessels" that were treated with special courtesy, the other two types of vessels must follow the rule of "cargo vessel inside and patrol vessel outside" when they were looking for a mooring place. As is recorded in the *Gazetteer of Guangdong Maritime Customs*: "It is a long-time practice that after a cargo vessel to Guangdong enters the port, the escorting naval vessel should sail to Lingding and Tanzai [Taipa] for berthing."[17]

All cargo vessels entering the port must be guided by a pilot boatman who had a licensed waist plate with a given number. There were 14 vessel guiders hired by the sub-prefect of Macau. After being inspected by the Whampoa general inspectorate (*zong xunguan*), these vessels would be measured by customs officials and then taxed. The method of levy is as follows:

When the Guangdong Maritime Customs handled the taxation, they divided foreign vessels into three types - first, second or third class, and taxed them in the same way as they did with the vessels from Southeast Asia, namely, each vessel would be levied 20% off. The vessel's length and width decided the amount it was supposed to pay, in an increasing or decreasing pattern. For large vessels of the first class, the charge ranged from about 1,100 taels to 2,100 or 2, 200 taels, and for medium and small vessels of the second and third classes, the charge ranged from about 800 taels to 400 taels. This was the old practice adopted by the Guangdong Maritime Customs to collect taxes on foreign vessels. When collecting cargo taxes, they would levy according to type and grade of the goods, as well as the vessel's weight and size. In addition to vessel tax and cargo duty, they would also collect regulatory fees of importation (*jinkou guiyin*), which were required of all vessels, regardless of class or size.[18]

As clearly shown here, in accordance with the old practice of the Guangdong Maritime Customs, a ship entering Whampoa as a "cargo vessel" would have to pay vessel tax, cargo duty, and regulatory fees. But if it declared itself as a "patrol vessel," it would be exempt from the above charges, although this vessel was not allowed to enter the Humen [Boca Tigris] waterway. These were the two choices that the *Hope* faced when it had to report itself to the office of the sub-prefect of Macau. Why did it finally choose the latter?

Let us have a closer look at these Russian vessels. Both the *Hope* and the *Neva* were three-masted vessels, purchased by the RAC in London in 1802 for a circumnavigation at a total cost of 25,000 pounds.[19] The former had 16 gun positions, a displacement of 450 tons, and a crew of 76, while the latter had 14 gun positions, a displacement of 370 tons (another source says 350 tons), and a crew of 53.[20] The captain of the *Hope*, "Luchendun" (Adam Johann von Krusenstern, 1770–1846), and the captain of the *Neva*, "Erzanshi" (Yuri Fedorovich Lisianski, 1773–1839), both graduated from the Naval Academy and were naval officers of the new generation trained under the guidance of the famous Russian Empress Catherine II. They had personal experience in naval battles (having fought in the war against Sweden), and they knew about long-distance voyages (having sailed to North America and India). Before coming to China, both of them had attained the rank of first lieutenant. Krusenstern was also known for a unique experience. As early as 1798, he had sneaked into Canton by boat from Malacca and stayed there for a whole year, which enabled him to gain first-hand knowledge about the navigation conditions of the South China Sea and the trading activities of the fur market in Canton.[21] He was familiar with various rules and regulations of the Guangdong Maritime Customs in those days. That is why, by analyzing the local situation at the time, he was able to make a favorable choice for Tsarist Russia when his vessel anchored in Macau.

According to Krusenstern's voyage log, the *Hope* sailed into Taipa at 2:00 p.m. on 21 November 1805. Early the next morning, he went to the office of the sub-prefect of Macau to apply for inspection in the name of a "patrol vessel."[22] Why would he do this? The reason was clearly explained in the report of Fedor I. Shemelin, RAC's commissioner on the *Hope*. Writing to RAC's general manager from Canton on 21 December 1805, Shemelin stated:

> The *Hope* has a small cargo of only 412 sea otter pelts and 10,000 fur seal skins, which is not a good deal if it sailed into Whampoa. We were told that all we have to pay, including vessel tax, miscellaneous donations and charges, and regulatory fees for the Qing officials, would greatly exceed the total value of our goods. Even if the *Hope* has managed to declare itself as a cargo vessel, according to the Chinese regulation, it is not allowed to anchor

in Macau for more than one day and one night. After that, it would have to move to Whampoa or find another place to anchor.

Whatever awaits us, to make minor repairs to the vessel, or wait for the missing *Neva*, we have to gain some time. In order to find a decent excuse, Captain Krusenstern had to report to the Chinese authorities in Macau that his vessel is a patrol vessel.[23]

Obviously, it was expedient for Krusenstern to apply for inspection in the name of a "patrol vessel" so that he could "gain some time" to carry out the scheduled trade plan for the two vessels after their rendezvous in Canton. As soon as the *Neva* arrived in Macau on 3 December 1805 and its cargo was sufficient to pay fees for both vessels (there were as many as 4,007 pieces of sea otter pelts, not to mention other commodities), the "patrol vessel" that had been moored for two weeks, immediately confessed that it was "not a patrol vessel." For Akedang'a, the new customs superintendent who took office in the 11th month of 1805,[24] "Since this was two cases in one, there was no need to handle them separately, so permission was granted to Luchendun [Krusenstern] to unload the cargo."[25] The Guangdong Maritime Customs did not conduct a serious investigation into the Russian vessel's contradictory and fraudulent statement. This is really a sign of administrative corruption. If officials at the Canton port had not been so lax in law and so incompetent with their work, it would not have been that easy for the two Russian expedition vessels to pass as "cargo vessels" and get by without revealing their flaws!

A Pretense of "Trading in Canton in Partnership"

After the Qing government learned about the "record-breaking incident" of the Russian vessels coming to Canton to trade, which was not in line with the old rule, the Council of State sent a letter to Wu Xiongguang, the governor-general of Guangdong and Guangxi provinces on 28 January 1806, pressing him with a list of questions. One of the questions concerned the nature of the incident: "Did these two foreign vessels bring cargo here for their own profits, or did they come to trade on the order of their king?"[26] The answer Wu Xiongguang received was that "They came to Canton for trade in partnership on their own rather than on the order of their king."[27] Yet, this reply came from "an English merchant who was informed by one of the Russian merchants." This is an entirely false statement, with an ulterior motive of disguising their official background and the true nature of the incident.

As "a product of the Russian aristocratic government," [28] the RAC was officially established in 1799 with the approval of Tsar Paul I (1796–1801) and was granted a charter by the Privy Council for a full monopoly of trade and mineral deposits "on the northeast coast of Americas from 55 degrees north latitude to the Bering Strait and beyond, as well as in the Aleutian Islands, the Kuril Islands and other islands located in the northeast ocean."[29] In order to strengthen the cooperation with the government, the general manager's office was moved from Irkutsk, the seat of the governor's office of East Siberia[30] to Saint Petersburg. Due to the strong support of the Tsarist government, the RAC grew to have a fleet of vessels, warehouses, and fortresses in the "fur kingdom" of Alaska. By the beginning of the nineteenth century, it had risen to prominence in the Pacific region like an upstart of the Romanov dynasty, becoming a powerhouse similar to the British East India Company, with its own commercial authority, military force, and land control. From the time of its establishment to 1818, the company exported a total of 870,000 sea otter pelts from the Bering Sea in 20 years.[31] Before 1805, the year when the Russian vessels came to Guangdong, there were as many as 470 Russian colonialists who had forced their way into North America.[32] Without giving further details about the history of the RAC and how it ended, I can simply cite two important facts to reveal the absurdity of the aforementioned pretense.

First, the Tsar and his prominent ministers were shareholders of the RAC. When the company was founded, its total capital was 724,000 rubles or 724 shares of 1,000 rubles each. The "Register of Shareholders" in 1802 reveals that Tsar Alexander I and the Dowager Empress Maria Feodorovna invested in the name of "special contribution from His Majesty." The high-ranking officials who held shares of this company were also easy to spot, such as Count Nikolay Petrovich Rumyantsev, the minister of commerce, and Admiral Mikhail Ivanovich Mordvinov, the minister of the navy.[33] How similar was this to the exemplary precedent set by Queen Elizabeth in the colonial history when she had a share in Francis Drake's privateering expedition 200 years ago! Seen in this light, it is no coincidence that the RAC was able to get a loan of 250,000 rubles from the Tsarist government to equip the *Hope* and the *Neva* for an ocean voyage.[34] Their status as government-sponsored vessels was so obvious that the claim of "com[ing] in partnership on their own to Canton for trade" could only be interpreted as a deliberate lie that Russian captains such as Krusenstern spread in Canton back then.

Second, the Russian vessels coming to Guangdong carried with them a major political mission. The intercontinental expedition of the *Hope* and the *Neva* marked the beginning of 38 Russian circumnavigations, 16 of which were organized by the RAC, in the first half of the nineteenth century (from 1803 to 1848). As a pioneering team of maritime expansion, these two Russian vessels were entrusted with important tasks by the Tsarist government. In a message sent to Alexander I, dated 8 April 1803, the minister of commerce Rumyantsev claimed that the trip "will help the government to carefully examine the results in North America, open up business in Canton with a vision for future trades with Japan and other Asian regions."[35] Following this intended goal, a group of astronomers, hydrographers, cartographers, and botanists were ordered to participate in the global voyage. On 7 August 1803, the two Russian vessels departed from the port of Kronstadt. After arriving in Honolulu, they sailed separately to carry out their respective missions: the *Hope* was responsible for transporting RAC's general manager, Nikolai Petrovich Rezanov, to Japan and for breaking into the estuary of the Heilongjiang to conduct an illegal survey, so that it could provide information for Tsarist Russia's invasion of Sakhalin and the northeastern coastal areas of China. Immediately after that, it sailed south from Kamchatka and then arrived in Macau. The *Neva* sailed straight to Kodiak on the west coast of North America and acted as an accomplice of the Tsarist colonial leader Baranov in suppressing the Indians. After reestablishing a colonial stronghold in Sitka in 1804, it came to join the *Hope* with a cargo of hides and skins in an attempt to "open up the Canton market" in one fell swoop and realize Tsarist Russia's long-cherished wish of commercial expansion on the southeast coast of China.

Since the RAC was "private in form, but official in nature,"[36] it is not surprising that these two Russian vessels were very secretive about the official intentions of their voyage. Now, let us look back and see what attitude the Privy Council of Russia took at that time.

From the diplomatic archives released by the Russian side, it can be seen that the Court of Colonial Affairs of the Qing dynasty and the Privy Council of Russia exchanged messages about the Russian vessels coming to Guangdong. In the official note dated 28 January 1806, the Court of Colonial Affairs demanded an answer as to whether the two Russian vessels were dispatched by the government or whether the merchants came to Canton of their own accord, and they also pointed out that this was not in line with the existent practice of mutual market in Kiachta. The Privy Council received this letter on 14 March, but did not reply. It was not until the arrival of the second letter from the Court of Colonial Affairs, dated 9 March 1806, with the original copies of two captains' statements requesting to enter Whampoa to unload cargo, that the Privy Council made a reply on 27 May. The response time does not seem like a random choice, because at that time the Russian vessels had already left Canton and were sailing in European waters north of Saint Helena, about to return to Russia, but had not yet arrived. About the incident, this letter betrays a deliberate shirking of responsibility and sounds rather weird in its tone. What is particularly striking is that the Privy Council claimed to have authorized Count Yuri Alexandrovich Golovkin to explain personally to the Qing government during his mission to China about RAC's merchant vessels in Canton, yet unexpectedly, the two Russian vessels had already arrived in Canton at the time when Golovkin reached Kiachta.[37] In this way, a long-planned expansion was coated with contingency by the Privy Council. In fact, this is only one of the commonly used diplomatic techniques of the Tsarist government, namely, the Russian vessels created a fait accompli for trade in Canton, and then Golovkin negotiated to officially obtain the privilege of sea trade. This is similar to its territorial expansion tactic of "occupying land before demarcating national borders."[38] In the end, their plans were foiled because the Qing government insisted on the old rule and did not give in.

How Li Yanyu from Xicheng Hang Agreed to Secure the Russian Vessels

The initial contact between the RAC and the "thirteen hongs" in Guangdong was shown in "Li Yanyu from Xicheng Hang acting as a security merchant (*bao shang*)" for the Russian vessels.[39] It constitutes an important part of the entire incident and therefore deserves discussion.

The Qing government's feudalistic management of the Canton port, including the practice related to "security merchants," first came out in 1745 and continued until the Jiaqing period. Also called a "guarantor" (*baojia*), a security merchant had a clearly defined duty. As recorded in the *Gazetteer of Guangdong Maritime Customs*, volume 25:

> Every foreign vessel coming to Canton to export goods need to pay taxes at the Guangdong Maritime Customs, through an entrusted Chinese consignee before its return voyage. For a foreign vessel importing goods, it should also pay taxes through its security merchant. The import duty will be charged when the goods are purchased, and no further payment is required later.

It is clear that a security merchant was responsible for accepting foreign goods, paying taxes, and purchasing goods for foreign merchants. As for who would act as a security merchant, it was not officially designated. Rather, the foreigners themselves chose among the Hong merchants. In 1801, Jiqing, the governor-general of Guangdong and Guangxi, sent a memorial to the emperor, claiming that:

> We found out that when foreigners import or export goods, they always choose their own trading partners, which is similar to the inland shopkeepers trading with merchants. When dealing with rich and trustworthy dealers of foreign goods, foreigners will certainly take out more goods for sale; for those poor merchants who are not doing well, they are naturally unwilling to do so.[40]

There is no doubt that when the Russian vessels came to Guangdong, they would also look for "rich and trustworthy dealers of foreign goods." So, did "Xicheng Hang" meet their requirements?

Founded by Li Yanyu, a native of Shunde, in 1804[41], Xicheng Hang had been open for only one year when the Russian vessels came to Guangdong, and thus, it was a new dealer without much experience among the "thirteen hongs." Compared with the famous Tongwen Hang and Guangli Hang, Xicheng Hang was neither "rich" nor "trustworthy." Why would such a "poor merchant who is not doing well" act as a security merchant for the Russian vessels? This is a story full of twists and turns.

As revealed in the Russian literature, the *Neva* arrived at Whampoa on 8 December 1805.[42] On the next day, Krusenstern went into the city of Canton on a small boat and stayed at a "foreign house" (*yiguan*) of his old acquaintance, the British merchant Thomas Beale. That night they agreed that he would pay a 5% commission to Beale who would find for him a security merchant to unload the cargo.[43] According to Krusenstern's own account, the result of Beale's search was as follows:

> The most qualified old merchants were afraid to deal with us, because they were aware of the fact that Russia is adjacent to China and the two countries have some kinds of commercial transactions. They clearly knew the temperament of their own government, and could not help but fear the trouble that the Russians would cause by sailing to Guangdong to trade. Beale tried to find reliable agents for us among the established merchants, but to no avail. None of them wanted to deal with newcomers. Finally, he had to give up

his original plan and use his own personal credit to persuade the new Hong merchant Official Li [Li Yanyu] to guarantee our two vessels.[44]

The usual practice of the "thirteen hongs" is that, for a Hong merchant, besides his personal name, the name of his firm, he also had an official name, so what is given in the preceding quote as "Official Li" was actually Li Yanyu from the Xicheng Hang. Then how could Beale succeed in securing his agreement? That is because Beale was the owner of a prosperous firm called "Beale & Magniac" (the predecessor of Jardines) and had succeeded his brother Daniel Beale as Prussian consul in Canton since 1797. He had a strong capital and was well known among the British "private merchants" (i.e., those private merchants not serving the British East India Company). For this reason, Li Yanyu dared to take a risk on his recommendation.

The Russian representative in the trade talk with Xicheng Hang was Shemelin, who later reported the process of negotiation to his general manager, detailing the terms of unloading, bargaining, and purchasing, which can make up for what is not covered in the Qing documents such as the *Gazetteer of Guangdong Maritime Customs*.

First, about the date of unloading. On 14 December 1805, Xicheng Hang sent a barge to Whampoa to unload furs and hides in the capacity of a "security merchant." In the Qianlong period, the unloading capacity of Whampoa was roughly like this: "four boats per day, each with more than 400 *dan*[45], and the entire cargo could be unloaded in a few days."[46] In the Jiaqing period, it must have been roughly the same. After three days, Shemelin and his men were able to send the goods to the warehouse of Xicheng Hang. After the unloading, the Russians joined the lads of Xicheng Hang for another three consecutive days, removing the outer packaging, sorting, and inspecting the goods.

Second, about the price of furs and hides. According to Shemelin, the fur market in Canton at that time was suffering from a drop in price due to the massive import of sea otter pelts year by year. In 1804, about 8,200 pieces were imported, and the price was 23–24 piasters per piece (Spanish currency, with a weight of 27 grams). In 1805, three more American vessels brought 14,002 pieces. Together with 4,007 pieces from the *Neva* and 414 pieces from the *Hope*, the total number of sea otter pelts exported to Canton that year reached 18,423 pieces. The oversupply led to the decrease of price to 18–16 piasters per piece. With Beale's socializing influence, Shemelin agreed to accept the following prices set by his Hong merchant and sell them at a moderate price:

One sea otter pelt	Whole piece	17 piasters
Sea otter tails	Ten tails as one bunch	17 piasters
One river otter pelt	One piece	2.5 piasters
One otter pelt	One piece	4 piasters
Red fox furs	100 pieces	120 piasters
Gray fox furs	100 pieces	60 piasters
One brown fox fur	One piece	2 thalers
One white fox fur	One piece	1 thaler
One blue fox skin	One piece	1.5 thalers
American bear furs	100 pieces	120 thalers
Fur seal skins	100 pieces	75 piasters

The sale of furs and hides on the two vessels was 176,605.25 piasters for the *Neva* and 12,000 piasters for the *Hope*, totaling nearly 190,000 piasters.[47]

Third, purchased goods. Shemelin intended to buy less tea and more cotton, so he handed over a purchase order to Beale like this:

Premium flower tea	30,000 piasters
Nanjing cloth [Nankeen]	30,000 piasters
Fine porcelain	5,000 piasters
Coarse porcelain	15,000 piasters
Shellfish beads	3,000 piasters

Because there was an oversupply of tea in Canton that year, the Hong merchant Li Yanyu insisted that half of the payment must be used to buy tea; otherwise, he would not make this deal. As the Russian vessels were eager to return, they reluctantly agreed. As a result, in their application for customs duty, it was recorded as "of the goods purchased, they are tea and porcelain."[48]

In getting Xicheng Hang to act as a security merchant for the two Russian vessels, the British merchant Beale, as a broker, played a very important role as a "guider." In the following part, I clarify how the supercargo of the British East India Company in Guangdong did the RAC a great favor at a crucial moment to help the Russian vessels get "customs clearance."

The British Supercargo in Canton

In the official documents of the Jiaqing reign concerning the Russian vessels, "the British supercargo in Canton" was mentioned twice, but he was only associated with one role, that is, he had agreed to act as an assignee. To be specific, after the departure of the Russian vessels, if the emperor's edict came, he would "send it back to Russia."[49] This is far from complete, leaving out too much information. In fact, the role of this man went far beyond what has been mentioned.

Among the idioms prevalent in the Canton port in the Qing period, "supercargo" (*daban*) and "supercargo in Canton" (*liuyue daban*) were two different titles, which should not be confused with each other. The former is rather clear: "The captain of a vessel is called a supercargo (*daban*)." As for the latter, we can get a clue from the memorial submitted by Jiqing, the governor-general of Guangdong and Guangxi: "The shipping company from the United Kingdom has the largest business, and this country has a supercargo to handle trade affairs in Guangdong."[50] From this, we can know that the "supercargo in Canton" was not an ordinary captain, but a "company supercargo" (*gongsi daban*) who "came to Guangdong to manage trade," that is, he was the resident agent of the British East India Company in Canton. Wu Xiongguang did not reveal the name of this supercargo in Guangdong in his memorial, but Russian records tell us that he was actually James Drummond [Друммонд] and his English name was translated into Cantonese as Duolinwen.

Among the Hong merchants, Duolinwen [Drummond] was well known, and what he did was often mentioned in the Qing documents. For example:

1. In the sixth month of the sixth year of Jiaqing [July/August 1801], Pan Changyao, a merchant from Liquan Hang, was in trouble on account of smuggling a thin textile called Yusha.[51] He wrote urgent letters to "red-haired company supercargoes" to ask for immediate help and one of the people he turned to was Duolinwen [Drummond].[52]
2. In the 12th month of the ninth year of Jiaqing [January 1805], Duolinwen [Drummond] handed over "a letter and some local specialties" from the King of England and was honored with a chance to meet Woshenbu, the governor-general of Guangdong and Guangxi, in person.[53]
3. In the tenth year of Jiaqing [1805/1806], Duolinwen [Drummond] arrived at the east of Canton with a "method of cowpox vaccine inoculation." This refers to the *Revised Guide to the Cowpox Vaccination* published in 1804. The signature at the end of the book reads "Edited by Duolinwen [Drummond], the chief supercargo of the United Kingdom who handles trade affairs in Canton."[54]

The above shows that Drummond had been an active figure in the business world of Canton before the Russian vessels came. He was also an old friend of Krusenstern whom he acquainted during his stay in Canton in 1798.[55] Therefore, when Krusenstern found themselves in trouble and were "not allowed to leave," it is quite natural that he relied on Drummond's help to seek ways out of this predicament. We will see how, guided and planned by Drummond, a tense contest between the government, the Hong merchants, and the foreigners unfolded at the Canton port.

In mid-January 1806, when the Russian vessels were loading their cargoes and preparing to return, there suddenly emerged hearsay among the Hong merchants and foreigners, saying that Nayancheng, the former governor-general of Guangdong and Guangxi, decided to "release the vessels only when the emperor's approval arrives." On 22 January, Li Yanyu officially informed the Russian side of this confirmed decision.[56] All at once, a tense atmosphere was formed around Whampoa: "The military officers and soldiers were stationed near the vessels with loaded guns, and no Chinese were allowed to come near them, and even the compradors (*maiban*), who came here every day, were nowhere to be seen."[57] Krusenstern had planned to leave Canton on the 25th and set sail from Whampoa on the 27th or 28th, now the entire schedule was about to fail. Seeing that the disaster was imminent and average British merchants could not help him, he had to pin all his hopes on the "supercargo in Canton" and went to visit Drummond to seek a possible solution. At the latter's suggestion, Krusenstern immediately asked his "security merchant" Li Yanyu to file a complaint with the customs superintendent.[58] On the following day, stationed soldiers were evacuated, and the security line around the Russian vessels was lifted. However, when they would get "customs clearance" remained unknown.

From the Hong merchants, Krusenstern learned that there would be a change of the governorship and that the new governor-general would take office in a few days. He seized the opportunity to write a letter of protest in English and planned to have it delivered to the new head, Wu Xiongguang. To achieve this purpose, he asked Lisyansky to join him for another visit to Drummond. Together, they analyzed the situation and concluded that the new leader would probably decline to meet foreign merchants directly and that the only viable way was to do it indirectly, i.e., they should ask a Hong merchant to submit the letter to the customs superintendent who would then forward it to Wu Xiongguang. This was a more challenging choice, which required Drummond to use his socializing skills. With his prestige as the "supercargo in Canton," Drummond invited the heads of "thirteen hongs" to meet up for a discussion, and they decided that it was left to Roberts (who later succeeded Drummond), to organize a special committee for a more effective negotiation. They also reached a consensus that it was imperative to get the head merchant Pan Qiguan from the Tongwen Hang to participate, "because he had a capital of six million piasters and was the mainstay of other merchants, particularly favored by the customs superintendent."[59] Drummond visited Poankeequa and invited him to take part in the 3:00 p.m. meeting held at a "foreign office." Pan agreed but he did not keep his promise. At this meeting, Drummond retold the contents of Krusenstern's letter and entrusted the second most important person among the Hong merchants, Lu Guanheng from Guangli Hang, to deliver the letter to the customs superintendent Akedang'a. Noticing the absence of the head merchant Pan, Lu was quite apprehensive about the possible trouble, but he accepted the letter reluctantly because he did not want to make the "supercargo in Canton" unhappy. Yet the next morning, he told them that he could not do it because the tone of the letter was not respectful enough. Then, he took out his own version and asked Krusenstern and Lisyansky to sign on that, but the Russians refused. Finally, at the suggestion of Drummond, a new, concise letter was drafted on the spot. This "foreign statement," which was revised several times, is shown in a Qing document as follows:

> Our country is located in an extremely northern place. [If we don't leave now], as the wind becomes weaker, we might be delayed here for a whole year, so we beg for an earlier issue of a "red card" and a chance to be released from the customs. If His Majesty's edict arrives after our departure, please leave it with the British supercargo in Guangdong so that he can forward it to us. Once we receive the letter, we will definitely do as required.[60]

Six days after Lu submitted the letter on behalf of the Russians, no news came. Really worried, Krusenstern went to see Drummond again and asked him to organize another meeting with the Hong merchants, hoping to give it a little push and get an earlier permission to leave. This time, the head merchant Poankeequa could not decline but come to join their discussion. It was agreed that the next day, with Pan as the head, Hong merchants would visit the customs superintendent and beg him for a permission. As recorded in the *Historical Materials on Qing Diplomacy: The Reign of Jiaqing*, a few days later:

> Akedang'a himself came to Whampoa, summoned the foreign merchant and tried to talk him round. The foreign merchant did nothing but to plead with

Akedang'a, begging to have his vessel released so he could return to his country. He looked really worried and anxious.[61]

In Krusenstern's account, the customs superintendent was indeed accompanied by Lisyansky to board the Russian vessels for an inspection, and then two days later, a "red card" was issued, i.e., a license to leave the port was officially granted. It is said that this decision to "act before reporting" was the result of an "interactive consultation" between Wu Xiongguang, the governor-general of Guangdong and Guangxi; Sun Yuting, the governor of Guangdong; and Aketang'a, the customs superintendent. They thought that they had handled this matter properly and sounded very confident about it:

> Considering that we need to comfort foreign merchants, it is natural that we should show to them that we are trustworthy people. As we have given them permission to unload their goods, it would not be good to detain them for a long time and prevent them from returning to their country, because to do so would make foreigners from afar think that we do not have enough goodwill.[62]

These feudal bureaucrats were important ministers responsible for the security of the sea frontier, but they were so muddle-headed and derelict in their duty that they were entirely unaware of the secret activities between the Hong merchants and foreigners. It is not surprising that they could not see through the real intention of the Russian vessels coming to Guangdong.

The Russian Hotel in Beijing and the Incident of Russian Vessels Coming to Canton

During the Russian-Chinese negotiations at that time, the role of the Russian Hotel in Beijing cannot be overlooked. In the memorial submitted by Wu Xiongguang and other officials on 15 February 1806, it is stated:

> We are submitting in deference, a list of all the unloaded goods, the original statement of this foreign merchant and its translated copy, to Your Majesty for review. We ask Your Majesty's permission to send the foreign documents to the Russian Hotel for a Chinese translation. That way, we can know whether there is a discrepancy between the alleged statement and the reality.

From this, we can see that the Russian Hotel rather than the Center of Russian Language in Beijing was the one that took the translation task. Here there are two questions that merit a discussion. First, why did the Center of Russian Language not undertake the task of translation? Second, who was the "translator" in the Russian Hotel? By referring to some historical evidence, I give the following explanation.

The Center of Russian Language, also known as the "Russian Studies in the Grand Secretariat" (*neige Eluosi xue*), was founded in 1757 in the west of Beichi

Street outside the Donghua Gate. In the *Peregrinations in the North*, volume 13, there is a brief mention about the source of students and the purpose of its establishment: "Also called the Russian Studies, it was a special program set up by the Grand Secretariat for the Eight Banners students to learn the Russian language so that they could be prepared for a future task of translation."

This center was scheduled to have 24 students who would study for five years. By the year 1803, there also formulated a set of assessment and promotion methods:

> Every five years, there will be an examination to evaluate the performance of students at the Center for Russian Studies. The first rank students will become eighth rank (*ba pin*) officials, students in the second rank ninth rank (*jiu pin*) officials, and students in the third rank should be sent back to the center and get more lessons. After a student enjoys the treatment of the eighth rank officials, if he still gets a good grade and lands again in the first rank in an examination, he then can be treated as a seventh rank official. If a student takes an examination as a seventh rank official and still scores high, then he can be promoted to be a secretary (*zhushi*) and can get an internship at a Branch Office (*fenbu*), and if there is a vacant position of officialdom, he can fill it immediately.

How did such painstaking efforts go? The memorial from Grand Secretary (*da xueshi*) Tuojin in 1824 gives a clue:

> Before the 29th year of the Qianlong reign [1764/1765], official school students (*guan xuesheng*) at the Center for Russian Studies could learn Russian from those native speakers who were studying Manchu in Beijing, but later only Chinese teachers were employed there. Although the center has been established for a long time, students can only produce fragmented translation of Russian documents. As for taking a translating task about a major event, there has been no record until now. To improve this situation, we suggest that one Russian teacher should be picked out of those who are studying Manchu in Beijing to collaborate with Chinese teachers at the center.[63]

It is clear that the "Russian Studies in the Grand Secretariat" was a school in name only, without any real training results. More than half a century after its foundation, students in this center were still incapable of independent translation, and the head here had to go to the Russian Hotel to ask Russian missionaries in Beijing to "collaborate with Chinese teachers" and "improve this situation." If this was the case in the early years of the Daoguang period [1821–1850], how could it be better in the Jiaqing period [1796–1821] to take a "translating task about a major event"?

Now let us move on to discuss the second question. The Russian Hotel was located at the site of the former Rites-Bureau offices (*huitong guan*). Since 1729, this place had been officially allocated to the Russian Orthodox missionaries in Beijing, called the "South Hotel" (*nan guan*). The students there were not clergymen. They were sent to "study the Manchu in Beijing" and often served as "student translators," translating official documents from the Court of Colonial Affairs. In the first month of the tenth year of the Jiaqing period [January/February 1805], the Council of State intercepted a map privately given away by the Catholic priest Adeodato Santo Agostino and asked "Sitieban and Yiwan, the two Russian students in Beijing to translate the Western words on the top of the map."[64] Both of them were students of the eighth Russian Mission (1794–1807). "Sitieban" was Stepan Vasilevich Lipovtsov (1770–1841), and "Yiwan" was Ivan Malyshev (1770–1806). As mentioned above, since the translation of documents related to the Russian vessels (a "foreign statement" and a manifest in Russian and English) was beyond the capability of the Eight Banners students, and they had to be sent to the "Russian Hotel" for Chinese translation, as a rule, this task would fall on the Russian students there. After cross-checking with the Russian archives, I found that Ivan, who died in 1806 in Beijing, was not involved, and the translation task was entirely left to Stepan. In 1819, Stepan was elected as a Corresponding Member of the Russian Academy of Sciences (Department of Oriental Literature and History). In 1828, he published in Petersburg two volumes of the Russian translation of the *Rules and Cases of the Court of Colonial Affairs* (*lifan yuan zeli*). In his posthumous manuscripts, there is a copy of the letter from the Court of Colonial Affairs to the Privy Council, which proves his connection with the Russian vessel incident when he was a "student translator."[65]

When the Qing court was in full swing to handle the Russian vessel incident, the Center of Russian Language had no ability to translate "Russian language" into Chinese, so they had to find Russians in the Russian Hotel to do that, what a weird situation! This ominous sign of having "foreigners" running "foreign affairs," similar to the Guangdong Maritime Customs officials' brazen "pacification of the foreigners," heralded the tragic end of the feudal diplomacy of the Qing dynasty about a third of a century before the Opium Wars.

Negotiation Records

The incident of the Russian vessels coming to Canton for trade lasted for 3 months and 20 days, from 20 November 1805, when the *Hope* was berthed in Macau, to 9 March 1806, when the last "imperial edict" was issued. The whole process can be divided into three stages: inspection and unloading (from 20 November 1805 to 14 January 1806), release from customs (from 14 January 1806 to 9 February 1806), and closure (from 9 February 1806 to 9 March 1806). The second stage could be regarded as the climax of the incident.

As for the sources of the negotiation records, except for the "imperial edict" of the Jiaqing Emperor and the memorials of Yanfeng and Wu Xiongguang, the rest were mainly taken from the sailing records of two captains, Krusenstern and Lisyansky, as well as from Shemelin's business reports to the RAC's general manager. The following list gives the dates in the Chinese lunar calendar, the Gregorian calendar (first date in parentheses), and the Russian calendar (second date in parentheses).

The tenth year of Jiaqing (1805)

The 30th day of the ninth month (20 November; 8 November): At 7:00 p.m. that night, the *Hope* arrived in Macau.

The first day of the tenth month (21 November; 9 November): At 2:00 p.m., the *Hope* entered Taipa and anchored there.

The second day of the tenth month (22 November; 10 November): In the morning, Krusenstern went to the office of the sub-prefect of Macau to apply for inspection in the name of a "patrol vessel."

The eighth day of the tenth month (28 November; 16 November): Guangdong Maritime Customs superintendent Yanfeng received a report from the Macau tax commissioner (*shuikou weiyuan*) about the arrival of a patrol vessel captained by Krusenstern.

The 13th day of the tenth month (3 December; 21 November): The *Neva* captained by Lisyansky was berthed in Macau.

The 15th day of the tenth month (5 December; 23 November): The *Neva* left Macau for Whampoa, taking Krusenstern and others on board. The *Hope* was at anchor in Taipa.

The 17th day of the tenth month (7 December; 25 November): The Guangdong Maritime Customs superintendent received a report from the Macau tax commissioner about the arrival of a vessel carrying fur products and silver coins to Canton for trade.

The 18th day of the tenth month (8 December; 26 November): At 2:00 a.m., the *Neva* arrived at Whampoa.

The 19th day of the tenth month (9 December; 27 November): Krusenstern took a boat to Canton and stayed at the British merchant Beale's "foreign house" in order to discuss how to find a "security merchant" to unload goods.

The 21st day of the tenth month (11 December; 29 November): Shemelin, RAC's commissioner on the *Hope*, received a message in Whampoa from Krusenstern and rushed to Canton that night with the manifest.

The 24th day of the tenth month (14 December; 2 December): Xicheng Hang sent barges to Whampoa to unload furs and hides in the capacity of a "security merchant."

The 27th day of the tenth month (17 December; 5 December): RAC's commissioner on the *Neva*, Nikolai Ivanovich Korobitsyn, went to Canton and, in cooperation with Shemelin, delivered the cargo to the depot of Xicheng Hang, where everything was unloaded at 11 p.m. that evening.

The 28th day of the tenth month (18 December; 6 December): At 10:00 a.m., Yanfeng, the Guangdong Maritime Customs superintendent, went to Whampoa to inspect the *Neva*.

The 29th day of the tenth month (19 December; 7 December): Yanfeng submitted a memorial about the Russian vessels coming to Canton for trade and asked for the emperor's order so that he could handle it.

The second day of the 11th month (22 December; 10 December): The two Russian captains jointly submitted a "foreign statement" to the Guangdong

Maritime Customs superintendent, declaring that the *Hope* was a cargo vessel rather than a patrol vessel, and requesting that it be moved to Whampoa.

The fifth day of the 11th month (December 25; December 13): The newly appointed Guangdong Maritime Customs superintendent Akedang'a approved that the *Hope* was levied as a cargo vessel and unloaded in Whampoa.

On the same day, the British merchant Beale conveyed to Shemelin the terms of the deal proposed by Xicheng Hang, that is, half of the payment must be used to purchase tea.

The seventh day of the 11th month (27 December; 15 December): RAC's two shiploads of hides and skins were sold on the terms agreed by the Hong merchants.

The 23rd day of the 11th month (11 January; 30 December): The Russian vessels seized the time to load the return cargo.

The 25th day of the 11th month (14 January; 2 January): A Danish merchant vessel was about to return to Europe from Canton. Shemelin entrusted someone aboard this ship to bring a business report to the RAC's general manager.

The third day of the 12th month (22 January; 10 January): The security merchant Li Yanyu informed the Russians of the delayed release of the Russian vessels.

The sixth day of the 12th month (25 January; 13 January): British, Russian, and Hong merchants held the first meeting.

The seventh day of the 12th month (26 January; 14 January): The Russian merchants prepared another "statement" and asked the Hong merchant Lu Guanheng to forward it to the Guangdong Maritime Customs superintendent.

The ninth day of the 12th month (28 January; 16 January): The Council of State sent the emperor's edict to Wu Xiongguang, the governor-general of Guangdong and Guangxi, inquiring about the Russian vessels in Canton.

On the same day, the Court of Colonial Affairs sent a message to the Russian Privy Council regarding the Russian vessels in Canton, accusing them of violating the existing regulation.

The 13th day of the 12th month (1 February; 20 January): British, Russian, and Hong merchants held the second meeting.

The 14th day of the 12th month (2 February; 21 January): The head merchant Pan Youdu (who became the head merchant in 1796 and died in 1820) led the Hong merchants to visit the Guangdong Maritime Customs superintendent and begged him to issue a "red card" to the Russian vessels.

The 15th day of the 12th month (3 February; 22 January): The Council of State sent Wu Xiongguang the emperor's edict that Russian vessels should not be allowed to stay in Guangdong.

On the same day, the Grand Secretariat passed on the "imperial edict" to Yan Feng, the former Guangdong Maritime Customs superintendent, and Sun Yuting, the governor of Guangdong, informing both that they would be sent to the Ministry of Punishment to await coming punishments.

The 17th day of the 12th month (5 February; 24 January): Akedang'a, the Guangdong Maritime Customs superintendent, went to Whampoa to inspect the Russian vessels.

The 18th day of the 12th month (6 February; 25 January): Wu Xiongguang asked the emperor for instructions and obtained approval to allow the Russian vessels to return to their country.

The 19th day of the 12th month (7 February; 26 January): Wu Xiongguang issued the release order for the Russian vessels to sail back.

The 21st day of the 12th month (9 February; 28 January): The *Hope* and the *Neva* set off from Whampoa and returned to Europe from the South China Sea via the Indian Ocean.

The 27th day of the 12th month (15 February; 3 February): Wu Xiongguang and other officials reported to the emperor about the Russian vessels coming to Canton for trade and requested penalties on them from the Ministry of Punishment.

On the same day, they also proposed that if Russian vessels come to Canton in the future, they should be prohibited from trading there so that the old rule can be respected.

The 11th year of Jiaqing (1806)

The fourth day of the first month (21 February; 9 February): The Council of State reported to the emperor about their interrogation of the former Guangdong Maritime Customs superintendent Yanfeng who allowed Russian vessels to unload cargo without getting permissions from the Qing court.

The ninth day of the first month (26 February; 14 February): The Council of State sent the emperor's edict to Wu Xiongguang and other officials, ordering that Russian vessels sailing to Canton should be strictly prohibited to trade.

The 20th day of the first month (9 March; 25 February): The Grand Secretariat received the imperial edict that Yanfeng was dismissed from his post; Wu Xiongguang, Sun Yuting, and Akedang'a were all sent to the Ministry of Punishment to await coming decisions about them.

On the same day, the Court of Colonial Affairs sent a second message to the Russian Privy Council about the two Russian vessels, reiterating that the old rule should be observed and stating that if Russian vessels came to trade in Canton again, the market of Kiachta would be closed as a sign of sanction.

Conclusion

The arrival of the RAC vessels *Hope* and *Neva* to Guangdong for "a trial trade" was an organized exploratory activity of the Tsarist government to "open up the Canton market." This long-planned expansion can be traced back to at least 1725 when Savva Lukich Raguzinsky-Vladislavich, the Russian plenipotentiary in China, received the following instruction: "Efforts to investigate Canton should be made, because of all the cities in China, it is the most convenient one for Russia to have trade with China."[66] It is obvious that the attempt to extend power to the southeast coast of China with Canton as a target city was not an improvised whim of Peter I (1682–1725) in his later years, but was connected with the transformation of Tsarist

Russia from a landlocked state to a seafaring empire in the eighteenth century. It showed a shift in policy from territorial encroachment to worldwide aggression.[67]

The year when the Russian vessels came to Guangdong saw the heavily fought Napoleonic Wars, and it was less than two years apart from the coming Franco-Russian alliance (marked by the Treaty of Tilsit of 7 July 1807). Struggling between choices of "war or peace," the Tsarist government still sent vessels for a round-the-world voyage via Canton, showing that although its plan for world domination was focused on Europe, it never neglected the expansion to the East.

The Russian-British relationship in 1805–1806 created a favorable situation for the Russian vessels to come to Guangdong. At that time, the Tsarist government had not yet joined the Continental System, and both Russia and Britain were allies of the Third Coalition against Napoleon's France in Europe. The captain of one Russian vessel was also a friend of the British "supercargo in Canton." Both of these factors made it possible for the RAC to use the commercial credit of the British East India Company in Canton to exert an influence upon the Hong merchants again and again. Directly guided by a British merchant, the Russian vessels were finally able to troubleshoot the problem and move from "inspection and unloading" to "release from customs."

Faced with the joint operation of two colonial companies from Russia and Britain, the "thirteen hongs" were placed at the mercy of others. Rooted in feudalism, the Hong merchants in Canton could not be strong, and this weakness made their decline inevitable. Apparently,

> What the decline of the Hong system really indicates is the disparity between the level of the Chinese economy, where 'domestic' industry and capital accumulation were at a low level, and the rapidly developing British economy in the era of what is generally called the 'industrial revolution.'[68]

After the Opium War, the Hong system in Canton completed its painful course from decline to death and was finally abolished in Article 5 of the Treaty of Nanjing.

The Qing government's strong insistence on the "old rule" openly curbed the attempt of Tsarist Russia at the Canton port. This, of course, did not eliminate its desire to expand, but it did force Russia to change its mode of activity from directly sending Russian vessels to "entrusting foreign vessels to bring commodities to Canton for trade." On 2 May 1812, the RAC and the American Fur Company (founded by the wealthy New York merchant John Jacob Astor in 1808) signed a trade agreement in Petersburg, the fifth article of which obliged the latter to carry Russian furs on each vessel that came to Guangdong and to have its agents sell furs and purchase Chinese goods in Canton for Russians.[69] With the emergence of this "shadow trade," Russian goods continued to flood the southern Chinese market though no Russian vessels sailed to Canton. From then on, the business of Tsarist Russia in Canton entered a new and delicate period, becoming "seemingly forbidden yet practically operational."

Notes

1 *Historical Materials on Qing Diplomacy: The Reign of Daoguang (Qingdai waijiao shiliao: Daoguang chao)*, vol. 2: 3–4. *In the Local Chronicle of Macau (Aomen jilue)*, "Xiaoxiyang" is written as "Woya 我呀," which is Goa.
2 The *qian* 钱 [mace] and *fen* 分 [candareen] are units of traditional Chinese measurement of weight. They were also used as a currency denomination. One *qian*, which is 1/10 of a tael or approximately 3.78 grams, *is equal to 10 fen*. —Trans.
3 *Historical Materials on Qing Diplomacy: The Reign of Jiaqing (Qingdai waijiao shiliao: Jiaqing chao)*, vol. 4.
4 It was called "huabian" (meaning "edge of flowers") probably because its obverse has oak tree branches and leaves around an eagle, just like leaves of a flower. —Trans.
5 It was called "fanmian" (meaning "face of a foreigner") probably because its obverse has the image of the King of Spain. —Trans.
6 Liang Shaoren, vol. 3.
7 Latourette, 31. See also John Frazier Henry, 63–90, 173–194.
8 Howay, 7.
9 Dennett, 35.
10 *A Selection of Archival Materials on Sino-Russian Relations during the Qing Period (Qingdai Zhong E guanxi dangan shiliao xuanbian)*, 400.
11 Okun, 1982: 29.
12 Wenqing et al., *A Complete Record of the Management of Foreign Affairs (Chouban yiwu shimo)*, vol. 79.
13 Korsak, 261–262.
14 *Historical Materials on Qing Diplomacy: The Reign of Jiaqing*, vol. 1: 37.
15 Liu Xuanming, 196.
16 In Ding Zeliang's article "The First Russian Voyage around the World and China" "Eguoren diyici huanqiu hangxing yu Zhongguo" which was published in *Lishi yanjiu*, vol. 5, 1954, no reason is given to explain why the Russians changed their statement. To declare that "Yanfeng falsely reported to the Qing emperor that neither vessel was a patrol vessel" (p. 127) is clearly inconsistent with the fact.
17 Liang Tingnan, vol. 29: 13, 17.
18 *Historical Materials on Qing Diplomacy: The Reign of Daoguang*, vol. 3: 22.
19 Lensen, 1959: 130.
20 Nevsky, 54.
21 Nevsky, 26.
22 Krusenstern, 250–251. Here I would like to thank Dai Yixuan who pointed out to me that the Russian name Типа or Тайпа is a transliteration of the Portuguese word Taipa, which refers to Tanzai 潭仔 in the vicinity of Macau. This place was called by local people as Dangzai 氹仔.
23 Gromyko, vol. 3: 17.
24 According to the *Gazetteer of Guangdong Maritime Customs*, Akedang'a "served [as the customs superintendent] in the 11th month of the tenth year, and stayed in this position in the eleventh year." (38) He was nicknamed "God of Wealth A" (*A caishen*) among the officials. As described in the *Spring Songs at the Water Window (Shuichuang chunyi)*, "During the Jiaqing and Daoguang periods, Akedang'a was an extremely wealthy person. Serving as the director of the Lianghuai Salt Administration for more than ten years, he was called God of Wealth A. When he socialized with others, the expenses involved were no less than five hundred taels of gold. He made friends all over the country." (63)
25 *Historical Materials on Qing Diplomacy: The Reign of Jiaqing*, vol. 1: 45–48.
26 *Historical Materials on Qing Diplomacy: The Reign of Jiaqing*, vol. 1: 45–48.
27 *Historical Materials on Qing Diplomacy: The Reign of Jiaqing*, vol. 1: 45–48.
28 Makarova, 347.

29 Vernadsky, 478.
30 It is called E'erkucheng in the *Memoirs Regarding the Foreign Lands* (*Yiyu lu*), authored by Tulisen (1667–1740). This book was published in 1723.
31 Skalkovsky, 444.
32 Bolkhovitinov, 318. See also Wheeler, 485–494.
33 Bolkhovitinov, 306–307. See also Alexander Alexandrovich Preobrazhensky's article "On the Shares of Russian-American Companies in the Early 19th Century," *Historical Notes* 67 (1960): 286–298.
34 Nevsky, 54.
35 Gromyko, vol. 1: 405.
36 Okun, 1939: 258.
37 Gromyko, vol. 3: 175–177.
38 Wenqing et al., *A Complete Record of the Management of Foreign Affairs*, dated 15 June 1863.
39 *Historical Materials on Qing Diplomacy: The Reign of Jiaqing*, vol. 1: 47.
40 *Historical Materials on Qing Diplomacy: The Reign of Jiaqing*, vol. 1: 6.
41 Liang Jiabin, *Study of the Thirteen Hongs of Canton* (Nanjing: Guoli bianyiguan, 1937): 321–325.
42 Lisianski, 234.
43 Gromyko, vol. 3: 18. After the incident of the Russian vessels, Thomas Bill lived a luxurious life in Macau for a long time. After going bankrupt in debt, he committed suicide on the Black Sand Beach in Macau in December 1841 and was buried in a cemetery near Pak Kap Chao.
44 Krusenstern, 254. See also Peng Zeyi, 1957: 21. Based on Krusenstern's record on pages 274–275, we can add two more items: 8 firms in 1798 and 11 firms in 1805.
45 One *dan* 担 in the Qing period was about 60 kg.
46 See "A Report on the Abuses of the Customs Service Submitted to the Customs Superintendent of Guangdong by Foreign Merchants from France" ("Fulanxi guo yishang Weideli deng wei jingchen haiguan bihai shi cheng yuedu bing"). Xiang Da had a copy of this report in his collection. This report was also cited in *Renwen kexue xuebao*, no. 1, published in Kunming, 1942. Regarding the corruption of the Guangdong Customs during the Jiaqing period, we can get an idea about the situation from the novels completed during that time. For instance, Yuling Laoren's *The Mirage of Love* (*Shenlou zhi*), Chapter 18, is a good source.
47 The transaction of the *Hope* is quoted from Krusenstern, on page 254. For more information, see Gromyko, vol. 3: 21.
48 *Historical Materials on Qing Diplomacy: The Reign of Jiaqing*, vol. 1: 6.
49 *Historical Materials on Qing Diplomacy: The Reign of Jiaqing*, vol. 1: 47, 49.
50 *Historical Materials on Qing Diplomacy: The Reign of Jiaqing*, vol. 1: 6.
51 *Yusha* is a thin textile woven from a mixture of cotton, wool, silk, etc. —Trans.
52 Xu Dishan, 203.
53 *Historical Materials on Qing Diplomacy: The Reign of Jiaqing*, vol. 1: 18. See also Liang Tingnan, *The Foreign Tributes via Guangdong Province* (*Yuedao gongguo shuo*), vol. 6.
54 Xiang Da, 1957: 647.
55 Krusenstern, 237.
56 Lisianski, 237.
57 Krusenstern, 254.
58 In Russian language, Guangdong Customs Superintendent is called a гоппо, which is a transliteration of the English word "hoppo." According to Huang Pusheng, "there are three possible explanations regarding "hoppo." First, it refers to the Ministry of Revenue (hoo-poo); second, it is the variant form of "ho-poh," which means maritime police; third, it comes from the Cantonese word hoi-pu, which means mutual guarantee. Judging from its sound and meaning, I believe the first statement is more plausible." (175)

59 Krusenstern, 255.
60 *Historical Materials on Qing Diplomacy: The Reign of Jiaqing*, vol. 1: 47–48.
61 *Historical Materials on Qing Diplomacy: The Reign of Jiaqing*, vol. 1: 47–48.
62 *Historical Materials on Qing Diplomacy: The Reign of Jiaqing*, vol. 1: 47–48.
63 *Veritable Records of the Daoguan Reign (Qing Xuanzong shilu)*, vol. 74: 20.
64 *Historical Materials on Qing Diplomacy: The Reign of Jiaqing*, vol. 1: 20.
65 Skachkov, 1977: 406–407.
66 Cahen, 335.
67 Marx, 1979: 80.
68 Greenberg, 65.
69 See Nina N. Bashkina et al., eds. 519.

Bibliography

Bashkina, Nina N. et al., eds. *The United States and Russia: The Beginning of Relations 1765-1815*. [In Russian.] Moscow: Nauka, 1980.
Bolkhovitinov, Nikolai Nikolaevich. *The Formation of Russian-American Relations 1775–1815*. [In Russian.] Moscow: Nauka, 1966.
Cahen, Gaston. *Russian Relations with China during the Reign of Peter the Great*. [In Chinese.] Translated by Jiang Zaihua and Zheng Yongqin. Beijing: Shangwu yinshuguan, 1980.
Dennett, Tyler. *Americans in Eastern Asia: A Critical Study of the Policy of the United States with Reference to China, Japan and Korea in the 19th Century*. Translated by Yao Zengyi. Beijing: Shangwu yinshuguan, 1959.
Korsak, Alexander Kazimirovich. *Historical and Statistical Review of Trade Relations between Russia and China*. [In Russian.] Kazan: The Publication of Bookseller Ivan Dubrovin, 1857.
Lensen, George Alexander. *The Russian Push Toward Japan*. Princeton: Princeton University Press, 1959.
Liang Tingnan. *Yuehaiguan zhi (Gazetteer of Guangdong Maritime Customs)*. Guangzhou: Guangdong renmin chubanshe, 2002.
Liu Xuanmin. "*Zhong E zaoqi maoyi kao* (An Examination of Early Sino-Russian Trade)." *Yanjing xuebao* 25 (1939): 151–212.
Greenberg, Michael. *British Trade and the Opening of China 1800–42*. [In Chinese.] Translated by Kang Cheng. Beijing: Shangwu yinshuguan, 1961.
Gromyko, Andrei Andreevich, edited. *Russian Foreign Policy in the 19th and Early 20th Centuries*. [In Russian.] Moscow: Politizdat, 1963.
Gugong bowuguan, ed. *Qingdai waijiao shiliao (Historical Materials on Qing Diplomacy)*. Beijing: Gugong bowuyuan, 1933.
Henry, John Frazier. *Early Maritime Artists of the Pacific Northwest Coast, 1741–1841*. Seattle: University of Washington Press, 1984.
Howay, Frederic William. "An Outline Sketch of the Maritime Fur Trade: Presidential Address." *Report of the Annual Meeting* 11, no. 1 (1932): 5–14.
Huang Pusheng. "Qingdai Guangdong maoyi jiqi zai Zhongguo jingjishi shang zhi yiyi (Guangdong Trade in the Qing Dynasty and its Significance in Chinese Economic History)." *Lingnan xuebao*, no. 4 (1934): 157–196.
Krusenstern, Adam Johann von. *Journey around the World in the Years 1803, 1804, 1805, and 1806 at the Command of His Imperial Majesty Alexander I in the Ships Nadezhda and Neva*. [In Russian.] Moscow: State Publishing House of Geographical Literature, 1950.

Latourette, Kenneth Scott. *The History of Early Relations between the United States and China, 1784–1844*. Translated by Chen Yu. Beijing: Shangwu yinshuguan, 1963.

Liang Jiabin. *Guangdong shisan hang kao* (*Study of the Thirteen Hongs of Guangdong*). Nanjing: Guoli bianyiguan, 1937.

Liang Shaoren. *Liangban qiuyuan suibi* (*The Essay of Two Kinds of Autumn Rain Temple*). Shanghai: Shanghai guji chubanshe, 1982.

Lisianski, Yuri Fedorovich. *Voyage of the Neva around the World*. [In Russian.] Moscow: State Publishing House of Geographical Literature, 1947.

Makarova, P. B. "A Brief History of Russia's Far East Policy in the Late 18th Century." [In Russian.] *Collection of Papers Published by Moscow State Institute for History and Archives* 14 (1960): 322–348.

Marx, Karl. *Secret Diplomatic History of the Eighteenth Century*. [In Chinese.] Translated by Compilation and Translation Bureau of Works of Marx, Engels, Lenin and Stalin of the CPC Central Committee. Beijing: People's Publishing House, 1979.

Nevsky, Vladimir Vasilievich. *Nevsky. The First Russian Voyage Around the World*. [In Russian.] Moscow: State Publishing House of Geographical Literature, 1951.

Ogden, Adele. *The California Sea Otter Trade 1784–1848*. Berkeley: University of California Press, 1941.

Okun, Semen Bentsianovich. *The Russian-American Company*. [In Chinese.] Translated by Yu Qixiang, et al. Beijing: Shangwu yinshuguan, 1982.

Okun, Semen Bentsianovich. *The Russian-American Company*. [In Russian.] Moscow-Leningrad: The State Social and Economic Editorship, 1939.

Ouyang Zhaoxiong, and Jin Anqing. *Shuichuang chunyi* (*Spring Songs at the Water Window*). Beijing: Zhonghua shuju, 1984.

Peng Zeyi. "Qingdai Guangdong yanghang zhidu de qiyuan" (The Origin of Foreign Companies in Guangdong during the Qing Dynasty)." *Lishi Yanjiu* 1 (1957): 1–21.

Qingdai Zhong E guanxi dangan shiliao xuanbian (*A Selection of Archival Materials on Sino-Russian Relations during the Qing Period*). Edited by First Historical Archives of China. Beijing: Zhonghua shuju, 1981. 1–1.

Skachkov, Peter Emelyanovich. *A History of Russian Sinology*. [In Russian.] Moscow: Nauka, 1977.

Skalkovsky, Konstantin Apollonovich. *Russian Trade in the Pacific*. [In Russian.] St. Petersburg: The Publication of Aleksei Sergeyevich Suvorin, 1883.

Vernadsky, George. *A Source Book for Russian History from Early Times to 1917*, vol. 2. New Haven: Yale University Press, 1972.

Wenqing, et al., eds. *Chouban yiwu shimo* (*A Complete Record of the Management of Foreign Affairs*). Shanghai: Shanghai guji chubanshe, 1979.

Wen Qing, et al., eds. *Qing Xuanzong shilu* (*Veritable Records of the Daoguan Reign*). Taipei: Huawen shuju, 1985.

Wheeler, Mary E. "The Origins of the Russian-American Company." *The Yearbooks for the History of Eastern Europe* 14, no. 4 (1966): 485–494.

Xiang Da. *Tangdai Chang'an yu xiyu wenming* (*Tang Dynasty Chang'an and the Culture of the Western Regions*). Beijing: Sanlian shudian, 1957.

Xu Dishan, ed. *Dazhong ji: Yapianzhanzheng qian Zhong Ying jiaoshe shiliao* (*Arriving at the Inner Truth: Historical Materials of Sino-British Negotiations before the Opium War*). Shanghai: Shangwu yinshuguan, 1931.

Yin Guangren, and Zhang Rulin. *Aomen jilue* (*Local Chronicle of Macau*). Guangzhou: Guangdong gaodeng jiaoyu chubanshe, 1988.

14 "Qin Huan" from the Russian Hotel

The Jesuits who practiced medicine in the inner court of the Qing dynasty, such as Pierre Frapperie and Giovanni Giuseppe da Costa, were widely known as they left their names in the book *In Praise of the Orthodox Church* (*Zhengjiao fengbao*).[1] But there is insufficient literature about the contact between doctors of the Russian Hotel in Beijing and imperial clans at that time. To fill this gap, I examine some historical materials on Sino-Russian cultural relations and present my findings for future reference.

In He Qiutao's book *Peregrinations in the North* (*Shuofang beicheng*), volume 40, a chapter entitled "Russian Chronicles" ("Eluosi congji") gives a noteworthy entry as follows:

> Wang Shoutong[2] from Gaoyou said: I used to know an officially sponsored student (*guan xueshe*) from Russia through Zizhang - Prince Yihui.[3] I do not know his Russian name, but Zizhang calls him "Qin Huan" owing to his excellent medical skills. He can speak Chinese, and every year when he comes to the court to receive audience, he holds a name tablet that reads "Qin Huan."

The above information is described in more detail in the *Guo Songtao's Diary* (*Guo songtao riji*), in an entry dated "The seventh day of the 11th month in the eighth year of Xianfeng [11 December 1858]." According to this record, in 1829, Wang Shoutong passed the examination and became an instructor in an official school (*guan xue*) for the Eight Banners students, and then, he came to know "Qin Huan" through Yihui. Wang once visited the Russian Hotel, namely, the "South Hotel" located on the West Street of the Yuhe Bridge and witnessed something He Qiutao did not mention in his book:

> As Qin Huan said, Russian platinum is just like Chinese silver. When asked why, he said that a piece of silver weighs 5 *liang* [taels], gold 16 *liang*, and platinum 21 *liang*. He also said that Russians pay much attention to the production site and the property of those precious metals, as they might be used to either make utensils or serve the purpose of medical treatment.
>
> Once in the Russian Hotel, in Qin Huan's room, I saw two statues resting on the niches, each protected with a glass case. He told me that one is

God, and the other is the Russian Tsar. These two figures look just like those Westerners.

There are two points worth noting here. The first one is about who deserved more respect. As Eastern Orthodoxy was the state religion in Russia, and a Tsar was honored as the "Supreme Patriarch,"[4] it was no wonder that in the Russian Hotel, the statues of God and Tsar were put alongside each other. The second is about who was the bearer of this titular name "Qin Huan." In Chinese history, Qin Huan was a famous doctor in the Qin state during the Spring and Autumn Period, and out of his medical records emerged the four-character idiom "病入膏肓 [the disease having attacked the vitals so it is beyond cure]." As details about this can be found in the entry entitled "The Tenth Year of Duke Cheng" in the *Zuo's Commentary on Spring and Autumn Annals* (*Chunqiu zuozhuan zhengyi*), volume 26, there is no need for me to quote more here. Considering that officially sponsored students living in the Russian Hotel referred to all the secular members except lamas,[5] and the student that Yihui introduced to Wang Shoutong as "Qin Huan" had "excellent medical skills," we can be sure that this person must have been a doctor who served on a Russian mission in Beijing. With this specific role clarified, it is fairly easy to unravel the puzzle surrounding this Russian doctor.

Yihui was the grandson of Yongqi, Prince Rong of the First Rank. He inherited his imperial title as a Prince of the Third Rank in the reign of Emperor Jiaqing and served as the commander-in-chief (*dutong*) of the Han army in the Plain White Banner. His mansion was located on the Taiping Street close to the Taiping Lake, which was actually a gathering place for nobility and celebrities. It was an aristocratic "literary salon" that was very famous in Beijing before the Opium War. Yihui's princely lady (*ce fujin*)[6] Gu Taiqing was a famous Ci poetess and the couple collaborated on many works. From the note given in the *Poems Written at Tianyou Pavilion* (*Tianyouge ji*) by Gu Taiqing, "my late husband passed away on the seventh day of the seventh month, the year of Wuxu [26 August 1838]," it can be seen that the contact between Yihui and "Qin Huan" could only happen before this day, that is, before 26 August 1838. For information about the Russian Hotel, historical records show that it started to have a doctor on duty in 1821. Up to the year of Yihui' death, there were two missions in total, each with one doctor. They were Joe Pa Voyzekhovsky (1793–1850) on the tenth mission (1821–1830) and Porphyrii Yevdokimovich Kirilov (1801–1864) on the eleventh mission. Both of them had "excellent medical skills," so who was this "Qin Huan"? Voyzekhovsky enjoyed a good name within the imperial clans as "changsang" [meaning "a good doctor"]. In 1829–1830, he cured a patient who suffered from scrofula. That person was the brother of Prince Li of the First Rank.[7] Voyzekhovsky was therefore rewarded with a complementary plaque that read "Excellent Medical Skills of a Wonderful Doctor." Therefore, he could not possibly be "Qin Huan." Thus, it seems more likely that Kirilov was the person honored with the name "Qin Huan." Kirilov's previous experiences provide more proof for this conjecture. He had graduated from a surgical medical school in

Saint Petersburg and had practiced medicine before he came to China with the 11th Orthodox mission at the age of 29. Over the years, this young doctor in the Russian Hotel had cured many patients from royal families. In the one-year period from 1835 to 1836, for example, he had already been honored with two plaques. One of them was from Xi'en, defender general of the state (*zhenguo jiangjun*), and it reads: "Spreading Benefits Far and Wide." The other one was from Mianxiu, a "Prince of the Fourth Rank," and it reads: "Practicing Virtue at Home and Abroad." Both plagues addressed him simply as a "doctor," with no specific family name given. This is probably why Wang Shoutong confessed that "I do not know his Russian name." Kirilov had also cured the disease of Yiji's mother when Yiji served as the vice director (*Yuanwai lang*) of the Supervisorate of Medical Relief (*guangji tiju si*).[8] This experience would have definitely left a deep impression on Yihui, as they belonged to the same extended family and bore the same generational name of "Yi." These factors are probably why "Zizhang calls him 'Qin Huan' owing to his excellent skills in medicine." There is further evidence in the "Flowing Water" ["Liushui bian," meaning "daily records"] from the eighth volume of the *Mingshantang Collection* (*Mingshantang wenji*). It is a collection of books written by Yihui. In the 12th month of 1835, Yihui's youngest son Zaitong died of smallpox, and the bereaved father wrote eight poems to lament his son. The second poem reads:

> Vaccine inoculation in the ninth month made my baby fall ill,
> misdiagnosis led to a father holding a dead bluish body in the 12th month in tear.
> Too late an acquaintance with Doctor Qin failed to save my elderly friend Mr. Pan,
> leaving me to reflect on my fatherhood and the mistrust of a quack, a lesson too dear.

Below this poem, he added a note as follows:

> Mr. Pan passed away this spring, which brought back my memory of my fourth son. In the ninth month, unwillingly, my child was inoculated with a smallpox vaccine but there was no blister or scab on his arm. The doctor was invited to examine him, but he talked nonsense that my child did not have smallpox. When my child fell ill in the early 12th month, this doctor took extremely drastic measures and prescribed an antidote that was supposed to quickly "put out the fire inside the body." He made this decision probably because he worried that "the fire inside the body" might develop into a "flame." This did not work at all. About the middle of this month, my child was about to die, and then we turned to a Qin-Huan-like Russian doctor called Po'erfeili for help. This doctor applied balm on my child's body and had him bathed with fragrant herbs, thereby delaying the death for seven days.

There is no doubt that "Po'erfeili" in the above quote is the Chinese transcription of a Russian name Порфирий, and "Qin Huan" is the synonym of a "famous doctor." This is why Wang Shoutong did not know his Russian name. Yihui, however, actually knew the name. In the early Qing dynasty, when people were scared by a mere mention of chickenpox, Kirilov had succeeded in "delaying the death for seven days," which explains why he enjoyed such widespread fame.

Although he was a Western doctor, Kirilov attached great importance to the curative effect of Chinese herbal medicine. After living in Beijing for ten years, he collected more than 100 specimens of medicinal plants, six of which were unknown to European scientific academia, thus enriching the plant classification in Europe. He also managed to introduce tea seeds into Russia.

According to Russian records, Kirilov not only spoke Chinese but also studied *Laozi* intensively. On 1 May 1837, he wrote a letter from Beijing to his close friend Basnin, a wealthy businessman in Siberia, and said that: "The five thousand words handed down by Laozi are more precious in my mind than five thousand gold coins."[9] It is no wonder that the famous Orthodox priest Avvakum, who was on the same mission in Beijing with Kirilov, commented that "Kirilov adores Laozi, the philosopher, so much that he seems to think that Laozi not only surpasses Pythagoras and Plato, but also transcends Kant and Schelling."[10] Such admiration for Laozi's Taoism naturally resonated with Yihui's taste, the latter giving himself a courtesy name "simple and pure Taoist" (*Taisu daoren*).

Kirilov was quite familiar with Chinese etiquette. The statement that "every year when he comes to the court to receive audience, he holds a name tablet that says 'Qin Huan'" reveals the dominant social manner of the capital city during the reign of Daoguang. This fashion is also shown in one of Yang Jingting's poems in the collection entitled *Miscellaneous Poems about the Capital*" (*Dumen zayong*), which reads:

Delivering a visiting card in the new year is a customary pattern,
but presenting it in regular and small characters seems too poverty-stricken.
Envious of the Hanlin academicians' enlarged spelling,
we all wrote our names large on a red sheet in fashion.

Besides his familiarity with the custom, Kirilov also imitated the Beijing nobility by growing orchids and collecting snuff boxes in the Russian Hotel.

The contact between Yihui and Kirilov shows that doctors in the Russian Hotel in the Qing dynasty had ready access to nobility and imperial society. This can be attributed to their outstanding medical skills, their ability to speak Chinese, their knowledge of the Chinese classics, and their familiarity with social norms. After Kirilov, there were several other "China Hands," such as "Ming Chang" (Doctor Tatarinov of the 12th mission) and "Sai Shan" (Doctor Bazilevsky of the 13th mission), who, aside from being professional doctors, played an important role in Russia's contact with China in the mid-nineteenth century. Apparently, these "Qin Huan" doctors in the Russian Hotel fulfilled their unique role in history.

Notes

1. This book is mostly known as *Zhengjiao fengbao*, though occasionally, it is called *Shengjiao fengbao*. —Trans.
2. Wang Shoutong (1804–1852), courtesy name Jiru, and art name Zilan, was the son of Wang Yinzhi, a famous exegetist in the Qing dynasty. His life experience was detailed in "A Biographical Note for Zilan," collected in the sixth volume of the *Copies of Six Lineages of Historical Records Engraved on Tomb Tablets of the Wang Family from Gaoyou* (*Gaoyou wangshi liuye zhuanzhuang beizhi ji*). See Luo Zhenyu, ed. *Gaoyou Wangshi yishu* (*Documents Left by the Wangs of Gaoyou*). Nanjing: Jiangsu guji chubanshe, 2000.
3. Prince Yihui was a "Beile," Prince of the Third Rank. His courtesy name was Zizang. —Trans.
4. Cai hongsheng, 1978: 59–65.
5. Cai hongsheng, 1979: 119–128.
6. In the Qing dynasty, a princely lady (*ce fujin*) was the designation of secondary wives of an imperial prince whose principal wife was called princess-consort (*fujin*). —Trans.
7. Prince Li of the First Rank was the title of a princely peerage of the Manchu-led Qing dynasty of China. Starting in 1636, this title was passed down for many generations without being downgraded until it was ended in 1914. —Trans.
8. Skachkov, 1958: 140, 143.
9. Myasnikov, 153.
10. Skachkov, 1977: 146.

Bibliography

Aixinjueluo Yihui. *Mingshantang wenji jiaojian* (*Collation and Annotation of "Mingshantang Collection"*). Collated and annotated by Jin Qicong.Tianjin: Tianjin guji chubanshe, 1995.

Cai Hongsheng. "Sha'e guojia jiaohui xingcheng de lishi guocheng (The Historical Formation of the Russian State Church)." *Zhongshan daxue xuebao* 6 (1978): 59–65.

Cai Hongsheng. "*Shuofang beicheng Eluosi guan jishi buzheng* (Supplements and Corrections to the Chronicle of the Russian Mission in *Peregrinations in the North*)." *Wenshi* 7 (1979): 119–128.

He Qiutao. *Shuofang beicheng* (*Peregrinations in the North*). Taipei: Wenhai chubanshe, 1964.

Myasnikov, Vladimir Stepanovich. "Dr. Kirilov's Letters from Beijing." [In Russian.] *Far Eastern Affairs*, no. 4 (1988):146–155.

Skachkov, Peter Emelyanovich. *A History of Russian Sinology* (Russian version). Moscow: Nauka, 1977.

Skachkov, Petr Emelyanovich. "Russian Doctors at the Russian Mission in Beijing." [In Russian.] *China Studies in the Soviet Union*, no. 4 (1958): 136–148.

15 The *Three Character Classic* in Russia

The translation and dissemination of the *Three Character Classic* played a remarkable role in the history of cultural communication between China and Russia. According to Miao Yousun, head of the Ministry of Revenue (*hubu*), who was commissioned to visit Russia in 1887, "Of the Chinese books translated into Russian, there are *Book of Documents, Classic of Filial Piety, Three Character Classic* and some miscellaneous songs."[1] Speaking of the spread of the *Three Character Classic* in Europe, scholars often refer to its English translation published by Elijah Coleman Bridgman in 1835, an American missionary who then served as the editor-in-chief of *The Chinese Repository* in Canton. Yet about a hundred years earlier, Russians had already started their efforts to know China through the *Three Character Classic*.

Early Translations

After the signing of the Treaty of Kiachta in 1727, the Tsarist government sent some "Russian child learners" (adults actually) to Beijing. In the Russian Hotel, these students started their basic training in Sinology by studying the *Three Character Classic*. Written in triplets of rhyming characters, with 378 sentences, 1,134 words in total, this small book for Chinese children gained its lasting popularity from the Southern Song to the Qing periods. It worked equally well for foreigners who wanted to learn Chinese history, culture, and morality, as it touched upon "the humbleness of human life, the wonders of geography and landscape, the changing regimes of past emperors, and the core credos of the Hundred Schools of Thought." That is why Russian students in the earlier missions made repeated attempts at the translation of the book. Larion Rossokhin (1717–1761) from the second mission was the first translator, and his version is now kept in the Manuscript Department of the Library of the Soviet Academy of Sciences in Leningrad. From 1741 to 1751, in Petersburg, he ran a Chinese language school where he used the *Three Character Classic* as his textbook. Through teaching this book, he officially introduced it to Russians.[2]

In 1779, the Imperial St. Petersburg Academy of Sciences published *The Three Character Classic and Collections of Other Writings by Chinese Sages*, translated by Aleksei Leontiev (1716–1786). Leontiev used to be a student in the third mission. After leaving the Russian Hotel and returning to Russia, he served as a lower-ranking civil servant in the Asian Department of the Foreign Ministry. When the Russian translation came out, Catherine II, the Empress of Russia, put into practice what Karl Marx mentioned in his book *The History of the Polish Question* "a hypocritical act of enlightenment and humor." Because the *Three Character Classic* is characterized by Chinese feudal ethics and moral preaching, it suited the Russian political atmosphere and the so-called enlightened autocracy. That is why the St. Petersburg Bulletin, the Russian state mouthpiece, published a book review in the following year, recommending this "poetic aphorism" to the Russian public.[3]

Bichurin's Translation and Its Influences

The second Russian version of the *Three Character Classic* was translated by archimandrite Nikita Yakovlevich Bichurin (1777–1853), who was "the founding father of Russian Sinology" in the 1820s. As the head of the ninth mission who lived in Beijing for 13 years, Bichurin was clear about this book's rich contents and significance and spoke of it as "the encyclopedia of the 12th century." Published by Genz Publishing in Petersburg in 1829 under the title *Chinese-Russian Version of The Three Character Classic*, this annotated translation provides a preface and lists the original Chinese characters. Only a few months after the publication, four book reviews came out, causing a great sensation.

The first book review was published in the Russian newspaper Northern Bee on 21 December 1829. It paid particular attention to the following lines of the *Three Character Classic*: "Silkworms silk educe, / Bees honey produce. / Such you learn, / Or receive spurn." and "Learn when young, / Act while strong. / Benefit each one, / Under the sun."

The second book review, published in the 24th issue of *Moscow Telecom* in 1829, gave this comment: "Although the Eastern philosophy may seem quaint to Europeans, its grandeur, depth and simplicity are amazing." This review also explained sentence by sentence what is meant by "Senior to young, / The ethical rung. / Lord loves subjects, / And enjoys respects."

The third one, published in the first issue of *Athena* in 1830, claimed that the *Three Character Classic* reveals "Chinese virtues and wisdoms" by referring to some Confucian moral norms illustrated in Bichurin's annotation.

The most striking review was the fourth one published in the New Year's Day special issue of *Literaturnaya Gazeta* in 1830. This review gave a detailed introduction to Chinese stories like "Three Moves by Menciu's Mother" and "Menciu's Mother Cuts the Cloth." As to why lines like "Then Mencius' mother, / Chose her neighbor. / At Mencius cloth, / She cut th' cloth" received particular attention from the commentator, we can find an answer by referring to the situation in Russia in the late 1820s. At that time, there was a heated debate about the relationship between environment and education among Russian educators, and the core issue was whether the environment was the sole factor influencing a child's education.[4] Undoubtedly, this review used the story of Mencius' mother as historical evidence for the debate.

The fact that Bichurin's translation was received with undiluted enthusiasm has much to do with the time of its publication when feudal autocracy in Russia strengthened its control after the failure of Decemberists and when Pushkin was calling on "Russia to wake up from its slumber." Each of the above-mentioned four reviews responded with a covert or manifest intention, some emphasizing the order between monarch and minister, senior and junior, while others explored the relationship between mankind and the environment. It is somewhat thought-provoking if we examine how the *Three Character Classic* was culturally appropriated.

Due to Bichurin's translation, the influence of the *Three Character Classic* was further expanded in Russia. From the 1830s to the 1850s, in both Kazan University and St. Petersburg University, the *Three Character Classic* was listed as a primary reading material for the Chinese majors in the Oriental Department. Similarly, in the Chinese language schools run by Russian businessmen in Kiachta in 1832, and in the training program organized in Kazan for the 12th Russian mission to Beijing in 1839, this book was used as a textbook. All these indicate that the *Three Character Classic*, which was originally written for Chinese children, left a much deeper trace in Russia than in other Western European countries.

Notes

1 Miao Yousun, vol. 8.
2 Skachkov, 1977: 45–46.
3 Skachkov, 1932: 473.
4 Belkin, 129–132.

Bibliography

Belkin D. I. "A. S. Pushkin and Sinologist Father Iakinth Bichurin." [In Russian.] *Asians and Africans*, no. 6 (1947): 129–132.
Miao Yousun. *E you huibian (Compilation of Travel Diaries in Russia)*. Shanghai: Shanghai xiuwen shuju, 1889.
Skachkov, Peter Emelyanovich. *A Bibliography of China*. [In Russian.] Moscow-Leningrad: The State Social and Economic Editorship, 1932.
Skachkov, Peter Emelyanovich. *A History of Russian Sinology*. [In Russian.] Moscow: Nauka, 1977.

16 The "Russian Case" in the Tianjin Missionary Incident

After the Opium War, Western missionary activities in China extended from coast to inland and were drastically different from the time when the Jesuits entered China during the late Ming and early Qing periods. As Huang Zunxian revealed in his poem:

> Recently there has been an increasing number of Christians,
> busy spreading the Old and New Testaments.
> Their stacks of Bibles help with their marine trade,
> and when necessary, assist with artillery barrages.[1]

Given this situation, boycotting foreign goods and resisting Western missionary activities became the consensus of both the officials and the populace.

After the Second Opium War, the Qing government was forced to sign the Treaties of Tianjin with Britain, France, the United States, and Russia, respectively, and had to rescind the prohibition against Western missionaries. Article 13 of The Sino-French Treaty of Tianjin (1858) states, "all previously written and inscribed official documents that were directed against Catholic Christianity - regardless of where they had been issued - should now be abrogated." Moreover, the Xianfeng Emperor also issued "The Imperial Decree on Missionary Activities" across the entire country. With the "green light" on, Western missionaries became more presumptuous and arrogant, and the "affray between local people and Christians" finally erupted in the Tianjin Missionary Incident of 1870.

The culprit in this incident was the French Consul Henri Victor Fontanier (Chinese name: Feng Daye). As Zeng Guofan explained in his memorial to the emperor, the whole thing "changed drastically owing to the rash behavior of Consul Feng [Fontanier]." On the same day, when the newly built Wanghailou Church [Notre-Dame-des-Victoires] next to the French Consulate was burned, three Russians were killed by an angry crowd near a place called Yaowangmiao [literally "King of Medicine Temple"]. This incident came to be called the "Russian Case."

The "Russian Case" was unique for several reasons. First, three traders instead of three priests were killed. Second, the death resulted from mistaken assumptions rather than a desire for vengeance. Third, the case was settled in a rather liberal manner, which was not because China had lax law enforcement but rather because Russia "pleaded for a reprieve." The decisive force behind the entire negotiations is not reparation and reprisal, but rather concerns about Russia's practical trade interests with China.

The Origin of the "Russian Case"

Regarding the origin of the "Russian Case," the official document of the Qing dynasty describes it as follows:

> In the afternoon of 21 June 1870, having heard that some Frenchmen were making trouble and hitting local magistrates, Tian Er and his fellow villagers were furious. Tian Er and Duan Da each held a watermelon knife in hand, and Zhang Guoshun and Xiang Wu grabbed the weapons from the local militia - a dagger-like knife called "shundao" and a spear, all rushing in to rescue the officials. They saw two male and one female Russians resting on their sedan chairs near the Yaowangmiao in the Hedong area, surrounded by some folks. Mistaking them to be the French who hit the local officials, Tian Er grabbed the woman out of the sedan chair and Zhang Guoshun hacked her back with the watermelon knife. Upon seeing this, a male foreigner immediately ran behind the woman to hold her. But then Tian Er slashed her left rib. The man had to loosen his hold on her because he himself was hacked on the right waist by Duan Da. Both of them fell to the ground. As for the other male foreigner, his sedan chair was torn so he had to exit it. Then Zhang Guoshun lunged in and stabbed him in the center of his head with the shundao. As the man was trying to protect himself with his hands, the back of his right hand was injured. At the same time, Xiang Wu threw his spear into this man's left leg, forcing him down to the ground. With the understanding that the three foreigners had died from fatal injuries, Tian Er and Xiang Wu left and returned home. After dumping the corpses and weapons into the river, Duan Da, Zhang Guoshun and several others also returned. After an official investigation, they were all arrested one after the other.[2]

Of the four criminals, Xiang Wu was unemployed, Zhang Guoshun was a hired laborer, Duan Da earned his living by selling watermelons, and Tian Er was a fishmonger. None of them knew or heard about these Russians. As for the Russians killed – "merchant Protopopov and his wife" and "merchant Basov,"[3] they were not Orthodox priests. Instead, they were tea merchants working at "Sabaoshi Yanghang,"[4] namely, "Shunfeng Yanghang" [S. W. Litvinoff & Co.] in Tianjin. Because the deaths resulted from a case of mistaken identity, this case was entirely different from the anti-Christian incident of "Burning the Wanghailou Church."

Consul Skachkov's "Reprieve" Strategy

After the killing happened, and after the autopsy and burial, the Russian consul in Tianjin, Konstantin Adrianovich Skachkov (Chinese name: Kongqi), began the process of negotiation. On 25 June, the Russian embassy's interim head, Evgeny

Karlovich Bytsov, submitted an official protest to the Foreign Office (*zongli yamen*) of the Qing dynasty. He demanded "punishment against the perpetrators who beat the Russians to death." On 8 July, Zeng Guofan, the governor-general (*zongdu*) of Zhili, was ordered to leave Baoding for Tianjin to handle the case. Zeng made the following decisions: First, a negotiation should be made between Chinese representatives and the Russian Consul Skachkov about the amount of reparation. The plan was that each family of the deceased should be paid 5,000 *liang* [taels]. In the ninth month of 1870, the amount was changed to 10,000 *liang*. Second, it was temporarily decided that Tian Er and the other three people involved should be executed to pay for their crime of killing the Russians.[5] On 29 August, Li Hongzhang succeeded Zeng Guofan as the governor-general. In order to settle the "Russian Case" as soon as possible, he followed the previous decision: to make reparation and execute the killers. And then he let the magistrate of Tianjin inform Skachkov. However, the Russian consul responded in an unexpected way. He "pleaded for a reprieve for Tian Er and the other three offenders who killed the Russians." Li Hongzhang reported the situation to the emperor as follows:

> As far as I know, the Russians only demanded restitution for the deceased, and they did not want to take away more lives. The reason behind it was that, more killings would drag them into the French Missionary Incident, and ignite the hatred and vengeance against Russian merchants in Tianjin. With these concerns and worries in mind, the Russians delayed the execution with the excuse that the criminals' confessions were not true. Then Russia's new envoy to Beijing, Alexander Georgievich Vlangali, arrived in Tianjin. He notified the Three-port Commerce Minister (*sankou tongshang dacheng*) Cheng Lin to forward the message that, in this case, what mattered was to get the real offenders punished in accordance with the law, regardless of how many criminals there might be. I immediately wrote to the prefect of Tianjin and ordered him to take the four criminals' detailed confessions again and send them to the Russian consul so that he would know whether these men were the real criminals and culprits. I also ordered Ma Shenwu, the magistrate of Tianjin, to inform the consul that we Chinese handle murder cases according to our own regulations. Being the local magistrate, he would follow the imperial edict to enforce the law and this should not be intervened by the Russian government. Then, the Russian consul came to my place to see me, saying that as the confessions did not clarify where the Russians were killed, who killed them, which parts of the body were injured, who the ringleader was, or who the accessory criminals were, it was hard to report the case to his superior. As for the rule that Chinese criminals should be convicted by the Chinese official according to Chinese laws and regulations, he only hoped that this case could be carefully studied, and that the interrogation would reveal the facts, so that the truth would be clear and credible. And he also said that although three Russians were killed, he did not want to haggle over the amount of reparation, nor did he worry about the speed of the verdict.[6]

On 19 December, the Russian consul went to see Li Hongzhang in person. Concerning the Russian consul's seemingly accommodating gesture, it was merely done for the sake of his "business considerations." Li Hongzhang was very clear about this:

> A close observation shows that although the consul spoke the official language, he is being very flexible. He has pleaded for an alleviation of the crime, and also shown his intention of delaying the conviction. This being the case, a message forwarded by Ma Shou [also known as Ma Shengwu] about the consul's request for a lighter sentence is not unreliable. What is holding Russian merchants in Tianjin [from vengeance] is probably related to their fear that taking away more lives might breed enmity among the Chinese.[7]

Russia's commercial interests in Tianjin were indeed more important than three lives. If there were no such concerns, then how is it possible that Consul Skachkov was being so "flexible"? Obviously, the strategy of "reprieve" had more far-reaching intentions. At its foundation was the need to maintain Russian merchants' position in the Tianjin tea port.

Russian Merchants and Tianjin Tea Port

In the late 19th century, Tianjin was a famous tea port for the transshipment of "caravan tea." In the second month of 1870, before the "Missionary Incident" took place, the Russian consul in Tianjin had already been promoted to consul general:

> On 14 March 1870, there was a diplomatic note from Russia which states that the previous consul in Tianjin has become the consul general who supervises all of the other Russian consuls, and Skachkov, the former consul of Tianjin, is now assigned to take this position.[8]

When Tianjin became the leading port above the other trade cities, whatever happened in Tianjin was important in the shaping of Russia's overall trading pattern in China. Having just stepped into this important position, Skachkov was cautious and careful with regard to the "Russian Case," because he was aware of their top priorities. A brief explanation is given below about the role of Tianjin in the Russia-China trade and the position of S. W. Litvinoff & Co. in that trade.

First, ever since the signing of the Sino-Russian Land Trade Regulations in 1862, Russian merchants had been entering the inland provinces of China to buy tea. With Tianjin being the transshipment base for "caravan tea," the difficulties with overseas shipping had been successfully overcome. As Wang Xianqian noted:

> After the Russians bought tea in China, they used to ship it through Shanghai to France, then to Britain before reaching Russia. As the distance of transportation was too long and the transshipment taxes in these two countries were extremely heavy, they changed the route and shipped tea to Tianjin, and then through Tongzhou to Zhangjiakou before arriving at Kiachta for storage and wholesale business.[9]

According to the previous trade regulations, when Russian merchants transported tea from Hankou to Tianjin, and then to Kiachta, in addition to paying an export tax in Hankou, they needed to pay half duty in Tianjin. Thus, they were expected to pay both "regular tax" and "sub-tax." In 1869, the land trade regulations were revised, and Article 10 stipulates that:

> For the Russian merchants who buy local goods in other ports, when they return via Tianjin, if they do not trade here, and if they have already paid the regular tax at the other port and have got a receipt, no taxes will be levied in Tianjin so that re-collection can be avoided.

With frequent favors granted to Russian merchants at the cost of Chinese commercial interests, the amount of tea transported through Tianjin to Zhangjiakou increased steadily. Between 1870 and 1875, an average of 14,995,276 pounds of tea were shipped from Tianjin to Russia each year.[10] Considering the interests of the tea industry, the Russians tried to avoid being implicated in the French Missionary Incident, as that might have worsened their situation in Tianjin. In a sense, this was a rather calculating choice.

Second, S. W. Litvinoff & Co. was the main party in the "Russian Case," as the three Russians who were killed by mistake all worked in this company. For the "caravan tea" trade during the Tongzhi and Guangxu reigns, S. W. Litvinoff & Co. was a well-known trade name. Located on the west bank of the Sancha River in Tianjin, the firm was founded by Litvinov, the owner of Hankou Shunfeng Tea Brick Factory. Also known by the name "Sabaoshi", it was the accountant office and warehouse for the distribution of Hankou brick tea. It had abundant financial resources and was the head of several branches in Zhangjiakou, Yili, Jiujiang, and Fuzhou. If the firm was implicated in the "Russian Case" and became a target of attacks, the entire inland trading network was bound to suffer from a serious drawback, which would bring huge economic losses to Russian tea merchants. After weighing the gains and losses, it was no wonder that the Russians were unwilling to "ignite the hatred and vengeance against Russian merchants in Tianjin."

Not surprisingly, as Consul Skachkov "did not want to haggle over the amount of reparation, he did not worry about the speed of the verdict." His attitude not only won the affirmative comment from Li Hongzhang as being "fairly decent," but also produced an immediate social impact that favored the Russians. In the 12th month of 1870, "when the gentry and folks in Tianjin heard that the execution of four offenders was postponed, everyone cheered. Some of them made a public petition," jointly requesting that "the offenders be forgiven and that their offense be compensated." The petitioners included 145 gentry and 115 shopkeepers. In the *Memorial Drafts by Li Wenzhonggong* (*Li Wenzhonggong zougao*), volume 18, there is a sincere statement on this petition:

> For us, the gentry and merchants, we believe that Tian Er and the other three offenders bore no grudges against the Russians, nor did they know the latter. When they heard that foreigners had made trouble and hit magistrates, they were so infuriated that they mistook the three Russians for the French and beat

them to death. As for why they were infuriated and lost control, it was probably out of their eagerness to protect and rescue the local officials. Concerning the death of the three foreigners, it was entirely the result of a reckless mistake. This case is totally different from the one where an offender harbors personal hatred and premeditates murder by gathering accomplices. After the murder, the four people deeply regret what they have done. Although they deserve the punishment, their motivations are excusable. As their fellow villagers, we feel that we cannot prioritize our own safety and keep silent about this matter, so we made a public petition, begging the Grand Secretary (*zhongtang*), who is also the Grand Tutor of the Crown Prince (*taibao*), to diminish the charge against our silly folks and consider making an exception in this case. If His Excellency shows his benevolence by consulting with the Foreign Office, and sending a diplomatic note to the Russian Imperial Commissioner to ask for extrajudicial grace so that "the offenders [can] be forgiven and their offense [can] be compensated," then, not only will Tian Er and other culprits be grateful for a chance of rebirth, but we gentry and the folk will appreciate His Excellency's benevolence.[11]

It is worth noting that the victim side in the "Russian Case" secretly contacted the petitioners, and "a merchant named Starr from the Sabaoshi Yanghang made the mistake" of sending the above petition to the Russian envoy.[12] As a result, the Russians left a completely different impression from that of the French on the gentry, merchants, and other commoners in Tianjin. They not only succeeded in freeing themselves "from being implicated in the French Missionary Case," but also earned a good reputation for offering "extrajudicial grace."

From the "Russian Case" to the Tsar Diplomacy

The "Russian Case" lasted one year and four months, starting in June 1870 and ending in October 1871. It was also a critical time when Russia's armed forces invaded the Yili region of China. As the official document in the Qing dynasty states, "This country has not only succeeded in carrying out its plan of occupying Yili, but also schemed to encroach everywhere, showing a fairly treacherous intention."[13] Comparing Russia's threatening posture of military readiness in Xinjiang with its response to the Tianjin Incident, we can see that Russia's policy towards China in the 1870s was aimed at devouring China as a piece of "fat meat," through both "simmering" and "frying." Prince Gong, who was in charge of the Foreign Office at that time, had long ago realized the cunning and deceitful nature of the Tsar diplomacy after comparing it with that of Britain and France:

Among the countries, Britain has the most competitive financial power, thus commerce is prioritized. France has the strongest temperament, thus missionary activity becomes its choice. As for Russia, it is deceitfully kind and soft, yet malevolent and insidious, always coveting China's borderland. With the tripartite pattern set, the remaining countries go along with them, with nothing but their own interests in mind.[14]

In handling the "Russian Case," the Russian consul general of Tianjin Skachkov showed himself to be an expert in carrying out this "deceitfully kind and soft, yet malevolent and insidious" diplomatic strategy. As a matter of fact, with his background in the 13th Russian mission, this "China Hand" had established his image as an experienced and knowledgeable diplomat during his tenure as a consul in Tacheng (1859–1862). Ivan Fyodorovich Babkov, the chief of staff of the Russian West Siberia Military Region, had this comment about him: "His actions are cautious and well-thought-out. For every step, he would weigh, measure and ponder."[15] When the Tianjin Missionary Incident happened, Consul Skachkov had been in office for three years (he took over in 1867 and left in 1879), so he was familiar with the local life and custom in Tianjin, and that is why he adopted "reprieve" as the best strategy, choosing foresight (economic benefits) over immediate worries (reparation and reprisal). The strategy of dissolving "hatred and vengeance" consolidated the position of Russian merchants in the Tianjin tea port, and promoted the development of the "caravan tea" trade. The following table shows the growth of exported Pekoe tea transported by Russian merchants from Hankou to Tianjin and then to Kiachta during the last five years of Consul Skachkov's tenure (1875–1879):[16]

Year	Boxes	Loads	Pounds	Tael (Liang)
1875	43,717	28,896	4,276,638	954,079
1876	61,898	39,652	4,868,516	1,239,809
1877	66,268	44,012	6,513,768	986,092
1878	66,814	43,725	6,471,130	982,256
1879	121,435	81,542	12,068,216	1,840,108

Within five years, the value of tea shipped from Tianjin to Russia had doubled. From the perspective of business transaction, Skachkov's diplomatic strategy clearly paid off.

Although the "Russian Case" in the Tianjin Missionary Incident was only an episode, it provided an occasion to compare the diplomatic policies of Russia and France. Judging from the actual effect, the "soft position" of the Russian Consul Skachkov was superior to the "strong posture" of the French Consul Fontanier. The event itself and its impact once again confirmed Engels' assertion that "Wherever Russian diplomacy meets English and French, it is always successful."[17]

Notes

1 Huang Zunxian, vol. 6.
2 Li Hongzhang, vol. 18.
3 See "Russian Interim Envoy Bytsov's Diplomatic Note about Punishing the Culprits who Killed the Russians" in *Historical Materials on Missionary Cases in the Qing Dynasty (Qingji jiao'an shiliao)*, vol. 1, edited by Guoli gugong Beiping bowuyuan wenxianguan.

4 In different sources, "Sabaoshi" in Chinse is written as "萨宝实", "萨宝石," or "萨宝时." —Trans.
5 See "A Second Report about What Happened in Tianjin" in Zeng Guofan, vol. 29.
6 Wen Qing, et al., eds., vol. 83.
7 *Archives Concerning Incidents Involving Foreign Missionaries* (*Jiaowu jiao'an dang*), collection 2, vol. 1: 348.
8 Tianjin shi dang'an'guan, 227–228.
9 Wang Yanwei, vol. 24.
10 Skalkovsky, 305. About the position of Tianjin in the Sino-Russian tea trade, see Chen Ciyu, *The Development of Modern China's Tea Industry and the World Market* 近代中国茶业的发展与世界市场 (Taipei: Taiwan zhongyang yanjiuyuan jingji yanjiusuo, 1982): 142–145.
11 *Archives Concerning Incidents Involving Foreign Missionaries*, collection 2, vol. 1: 377.
12 *Archives Concerning Incidents Involving Foreign Missionaries*, collection 2, vol. 1: 381.
13 Wen Qing, et al., vol. 808.
14 Wen Qing, et al., vol. 50.
15 Babkov, 193.
16 See Skalkovsky, 258–259.
17 See Engels, "Russia's Successes in the Far East."

Bibliography

Babkov, Ivan Fyodorovich. *Memories of My Service in West Siberia*, vol. 1. [Chinese version.] Translated by Wang Zhixiang, Proofread by Chen Hanzhang. Beijing: Shangwu yinshuguan, 1973.

Engels, Friedrich. "Russia's Successes in the Far East," in *Completed Works of Marx and Engels*, vol. 12. [In Chinese]. Translated by Compilation and Translation Bureau of Works of Marx, Engels, Lenin and Stalin of the CPC Central Committee. Beijing: Renmin chubanshe, 1998.

Guoli gugong Beiping bowuguan wenxianguan, ed. *Qingji jiao'an shiliao* (*Historical Materials on Missionary Cases in the Qing Dynasty*). Beijing: Guoli gugong Beiping bowuyuan wenxianguan, 1937.

Huang Zunxian. *Renjinglu shicao* (*Draft of Poems from the Hut within the Human Realm*). Beijing: Zhongguo qingnian chubanshe, 2000.

Li Hongzhang. *Li Wenzhonggong zougao* (*Memorial Drafts by Li Wenzhonggong*). Shanghai: Shanghai guji chubanshe, 1995.

Skalkovsky, Konstantin Apollonovich. *Russian Trade in the Pacific*. [In Russian.] St. Petersburg: The Publication of Aleksei Sergeyevich Suvorin, 1883.

Taiwan zhongyang yanjiuyuan jindaishi yanjiusuo, ed. *Jiaowu jiao'an dang* (*Archives Concerning Incidents Involving Foreign Missionaries*), vol. 1. Taipei: Taiwan zhongyang yanjiuyuan jiudaishi yanjiusuo, 1974.

Tianjin shi dang'an'guan, ed. *Sankou tongshang dachen zhi Jin haiguan suiwusi zhawen xuanbian* (*Selected Texts from the Three-Port Commerce Minister to the Commissioner of Customs of Tianjin*). Tianjin: Tianjin renmin chubanshe, 1992.

Wen Qing, et al., eds. *Chouban yiwu shimo* (*A Complete Record of the Management of Foreign Affairs*). Shanghai: Shanghai guji chubanshe, 1979.

Zeng Guofan. *Zeng Wenzhenggong zougao* (*Memorial Drafts by Zeng Wenzhenggong*). Huhehaote: Neimenggu renmin chubanshe, 2000.

17 The Dutch Factory in Canton during the Qing Period

The beginning of the seventeenth century marked the start of Sino-Dutch relations. In the winter of 1601, the Dutch fleet led by Jacob Corneliszoon van Neck came to Guangdong, asking for an opportunity to trade. Although this effort failed, it left the nickname "red-haired foreigners" (*Hongmao yi*) with the local residents.[1] In 1602, the Dutch East India Company (VOC) was officially established and obtained from the Parliament the exclusive right to trade in the area from the east of the Cape of Good Hope to the Strait of Magellan. After that, the "red-haired foreigners' vessels" (*Hongmao chuan*) appeared more and more frequently in the South China Sea. That is why ships and merchants from the Netherlands were no strangers to Cantonese in the early Qing dynasty. Qu Dajun (1630–1696), a famous poet, had a five-syllable poem entitled "Sea-conquering Tower" ("Zhenhai lou"):

> From Haikou to Humen,
> foreigners' vessels spread over the waters.
> The red-haired are the Dutch,
> the black-toothed are the Vietnamese.[2]

He also boarded a Dutch ship and witnessed different customs, leaving the following visual description for readers:

> A Dutch vessel came to Canton, and I was able to board it for a tour. There are several decks, so I went down by ropes. This ship has water tanks and patches of vegetables. For the turbid water inside the tanks, alum is used to make it clean again. Water is poured into a pot and boiled before drinking. They sleep on what they call a soft bed, which is spread with white felt fabric. Everybody wears soft gloves and takes them off when eating. For food, steamed bread and beef are fried and baked in sweet gum oil, ready to be served when the color turns golden. They eat with a knife which can be flexed and stretched like a snake. Twisting and turning powerfully from left to right, it also looks like an ancient fish-intestine sword. From time to time, they play a musical instrument that has brass strings. Clapping their hands, shaking their shoulders, they dance face-to-face to entertain the guests. It seems they are very polite people.[3]

In this passage, Qu sketches a picture of how the Dutch merchants in the early Qing era cooked, lived, and treated guests.

In the "foreign affairs" management system of the Qing dynasty, the Netherlands was one of the "tributary countries via Guangdong," which naturally bore a close connection with Canton. In 1655, the first mission sent by the governor-general of the Netherlands to Beijing via Canton failed to achieve the expected purpose of establishing trade relations, and made only modest progress, as revealed by the following edict:

> They can come to China every eight years, with no more than a hundred staff members, and only twenty of whom are allowed to come to our capital. The goods they have brought are to be traded at the Dutch factory rather than sold privately at sea in Guangdong.

In 1685, the Guangdong Maritime Customs was set up. With the approval from the Qing government, there was a change about the Sino-Dutch trade: "The Netherlands was originally scheduled to pay tribute every eight years. Now the Dutch king, feeling the benevolence of the emperor, requested a change of the schedule to every five years."[4] This only shortened the "tribute period," yet no regular trading relationship was established. It is "not until 1727 that the Dutch were allowed to set up a trading post in Canton."[5] From then on, the VOC's trade with China entered a new phase:

> From the 17th century to the early eighteenth century, the VOC conducted their Chinese tea trade between Europe and Asia mainly from their base in Batavia. On 5 December 1728, the company directly sent a vessel from the Netherlands to Canton to buy tea and other goods. Loaded with 300,000 guilders of silver, it returned to the Netherlands on 13 July 1730 after the transaction was completed, bringing back tea, silk and porcelain, etc. The net profit was more than double of the investment. From 1731 to 1735, eleven more Dutch vessels were sent to Canton to trade. Since 1739, Chinese tea had become the most valuable commodity shipped from the East to Europe by Dutch ships.[6]

Different from the Russian Hotel in Beijing which was a missionary base and a learning center, the Dutch factory in Canton specialized in purchasing and exporting tea, silk, porcelain, and other goods.[7] In the foreign market of Canton, the Dutch factory was also known as the Hong of Justice, revealing a clear mercantile purpose.[8] However, as the only Dutch organization in China in the early Qing period, it was inevitably involved in foreign affairs and cultural exchanges, playing a unique role. With this as the focus, I go through the accounts in historical books, particularly those shown in the Qing poems, to gain a more comprehensive understanding of the importance of the Dutch factory in Sino-Dutch relations.

The Dutch Factory in the Poems of the Qing Dynasty

In the Ming and Qing eras, there were various transliterations of the word "荷兰 [Hélán] (Holland)": Hèlán 贺兰, Hélán 和兰, Ālántuó 阿兰陀, Nítèlán 尼特兰, and so on.[9] It was only in 1794 that the translation was standardized in accordance with the emperor's decree that "Hèlán 贺兰 should be rewritten as Hélán 荷兰."[10]

Le Jun, a poet during the Qianlong and Jiaqing reigns, was a provincial graduate (*juren*) in Linchuan, Jiangxi province. He wrote a set of poems entitled "Lingnan Yuefu" during his tour to Guangdong. There is a poem specifically entitled "Thirteen Hongs" which mentions Dutch merchants as follows:

> There are thirteen foreign firms in Canton,
> measured in a round-bottomed bucket, their wealth you can know.
> With the outer railings painted pink or white, and company flags flying high
>   in front of the building,
> You see the ocean far away with a telescope hanging by the window.
> The Dutch, the Spanish, or the British,
> all have deep eyes and noses that are not low.
> Dressed in foreign clothes made of woven tweed, showing unmatched
>   exoticism and peculiarity,
> they come here every year when the sea tides towards a certain direction flow.[11]

The thirteen foreign firms, also known as the "thirteen foreign factories," were located in the west of Canton. Their office buildings stood side by side along the Pearl River. What is mentioned in the poem as "company flags flying high in front of the building" means that each firm had a flag in front of the building to indicate its nationality. The Dutch factory, which was adjacent to the British factory, had a tricolor flag in "red, white and blue." This building belonged to Cai Zhaofu from Yifeng Hang, the annual rent of which was about 600 taels of silver. In 1783, as Merchant Cai Zhaofu, widely known as Tjobqua, sold this house to cover his debts,[12] there was a change of owners, but the Dutch factory kept the tenancy right until 1822 when the entire area for foreign firms was destroyed by fire.

As a firm with a long-established reputation in Canton's "maritime market" (*bo shi*), the Dutch factory was well known. As early as the Qianlong period, it had become the target of praise for the literati. Zhang Jiuyue, a native of Xiangtan, Hunan province, who once served as the magistrate of Shixing county and Haiyang county in Guangdong province, wrote a poem called "Foreign Firms" ("Fanhang pian") in 1770. It is a rarely known seven-syllable poem with 78 lines, detailing the foreigners and their life in Canton in those days, with a focus on the Dutch factory.[13] The last stanza is sentimental, and rather banal, therefore, instead of analyzing it in full, I only quote some lines that are descriptive and add some explanations to the best of my understanding:

> There are the thirteen hongs in the maritime market of Canton by the sea,
> positioned like the wings of a wild goose and clustered like honeycombs
>   surrounded by many a bee.

In front of the Pearl River there is a vast expanse of water,
where each day ships of brocade sails and fancy cables soar free.
Clams move towards a fairy island with branch-like corals,
sharks spout out watery silk as if painting on the vast white ocean in glee.
Tall buildings here have become the prototype for Macau to follow suit,
wonderful houses are inhabited by foreign merchants you never see.
Lofty residences and eye-catching houses come in many forms,
exotic roses are never monochromatic, beautiful as a flower tree.
Red agates are threaded, and gold leaves are paired,
green glazed tiles slant down, about to touch the windows to some degree.
Colorful banners of leno cloth are fluttering in the air,
jasper-paved balustrades are straight against the sky for miles to see.

In the landscape of the "maritime market," the color of green is the dominant feature, revealed by the words like "green glazed tiles" and "jasper-paved balustrades" which are realistic depictions. There are three other texts that can be used for reference. In Yuan Mei's set of six poems entitled "Farewell to Xiangting" ("Liubie Xiangting"), the third one reads:

If you go to the distant city of Wuyang[14],
you will see temples and flower fields lining the seashore.
Music and songs echo throughout the night on the island of Shamian,
shining in bluish green are the resplendent foreign buildings that are tall.

In Shen Muqin's poem "Climbing the Building where Westerners Reside" ("Deng xiyang guizi lou"), we read these four lines:

The building is so tall that it is about to touch the clouds,
over the pinkish white walls are roof ridges of design and decoration.
The railings are painted bright green,
guarding the gate is a brass lock that works better than any weapon.

Lidou, in his book *Records of Yangzhou Barges* (*Yangzhou huafang lu*), volume 12, offered an explanation about this:

Probably because Westerners like green, there is a Bitang [Green Hall] in the area of thirteen hongs of Canton. It was built with a design concept that a wide building with rooms can block direct sunlight out and allow moonlight in.

In Zhang Jiuyue's poetic work "Foreign Firms," more information about the Netherlands can be found in the following lines:

We welcomed an unknown ship owner,
and learned through the interpreter that he is from Heguo [Holland].
Wearing whiskers and having deep-set eyes like those of a large eagle,
he was dressed flamboyantly as if displaying his wealth to other people.

When talking about prices, he understands the Wu-Yue dialect,
when dealing with guests, in Han and Tang manners he will surely act.
The silver coin that he presents has a foreign king's head,
the glass mirror in his house shows a beautiful woman in a fancy dress.
Locked in the fence are calves and *luquan*,[15]
spread on the staircase steps are *suofu* and *tuoni*.[16]
If products made of *tuoni* and *suofu* need to be counted in total,
Du'nou and *qinan*[17] can be limitlessly taken as they are extremely ample.
A lotus-shaped clock strikes out the time of sunrise and sunset,
a jewelry-adorned watch marks midnight and noon by its hands' motion.
Randomly piled among the beautiful jade ornaments is suhe ointment,
what is poured out of the bottle is a yellow or purple grape-juice-like lotion.
Water music can imitate the chirping of a small phoenix,
an accordion produces the sound of a red parrot.
There are also men jumping together arm in arm,
showing their tight cotton shirts and restraining narrow pants.
The men with short swords in their chests come from Italy,
those with hidden guns in sleeves are from France.
The black slave watching the door holds a musket in his hand,
the *hongmao guizi* [red-haired foreigner] polishes a curve dagger of a good brand.

In this account about the "ship owner," both "*Heguo*" and "*hongmao*" refer to the Netherlands. The quote above also touches upon both the ancient allusions and the modern usage. For example, *suhe* and *du'nou* were the spices for medicine from the South China Sea in the Tang and Song dynasties, not the Western goods imported in the early Qing dynasty. As for "*suofu* and *tuoni*" on "staircase steps," they were Dutch woolen cloth imported in large quantities in those years. This can be confirmed by referring to Zhang Yu'nan's collection of poems entitled "Bamboo Branch Lyrics of the Maritime Nations" ("Haiguo zhuzhi ci"). The sixteenth poem "Holland" and its original note read as follows:

The woolen cloth is unchangingly exquisite,
whose dyed color emits a precious light indeed.
Loaded onto merchant ships and sailed to Linghai,[18]
at the thirteen hongs they were sold neat.
(Note: The woolen cloth woven in this country is very well sold, especially in Canton).

In addition, a lotus-shaped clock (*lianhua zhong*), a jewelry-adorned watch (*baibao biao*), a glass mirror, an accordion, and so on are the novelty furnishings unique to the foreign houses. No wonder Zhang Jiuyue takes a serious tone about them as if he is counting his own treasure.

The following is the last part of Zhang's poem:

Hearing that the red-haired foreigners have arrived at Whampoa,

consignees and carriers run around with the message with hope.
Wooden oars fly on the centipede-shaped speedboat,
several *Polan*[19] of bundled cargo cover the boat like a hill of some scope.
Calling each other's name, they could scarcely hear the reply,
Some are happy and some are angry, who can predict who is going to fly high!
The maritime merchants and Hong merchants are cheerful,
with banquets and music, they compete over bigger bowls and bottles on the table.
Which ship has more *Huoqi*[20] and *Mu'nan*[21],
which place has more strange ostriches and what Buddha deer is more fun?
Scattered among the common households and known to traveling businessmen,
the Co-hong among the firms is the largest broker then.
Superficial obedience covers their secret embezzlement,
they win over both domestic and foreign merchants, far from being benevolent.
Huzhou silk and Guangdong brocade of different colors and patterns,
Wenzhou tea and Raozhou ceramics,[22] all of the latest fashions.
From time to time, they put on their fancy dress to visit a high-ranking official,
planning a large deal that negotiates the impossible.

In this poem, whatever happened after the Dutch vessels had arrived at Whampoa, such as finding a consignee, unloading the cargo, making a deal, and purchasing goods for the return trip with the support of the Co-hong merchants, is provided a full description.

Compared with the official documents about the Dutch factory around the same time, "Foreign Firms" offers more invaluable information about the maritime market, ship owners (*bo zhu*), and vessel merchants. However, limited by sentence patterns and rhythms unique to classical poetry, its accuracy of description is still slightly inferior to that of the prose. The following quote is taken from "The Journey to Nanzhong" ("Nanzhong xing lvji") authored by Zeng Qiru,[23] a provincial graduate of Jiaxiang county, Shandong province. Directly based on a personal visit Zeng made on 23 June 1782, this piece is believed to be an authentic report on the Dutch factory in Canton in the Qing period:

Going out of Guide Gate, I visited the thirteen hongs, accompanied by an interpreter surnamed Xu. The houses here are built near the water, with pink walls and green fences, in octagonal or hexagonal shapes. Some are square, some are round, and some are spiral, which is really incredible. In front of the houses are slopes. The doors open on the side, resembling the gate of an ancient walled city. With white carvings, and much drapery, their houses look resplendent. Patrolling in front of the houses with Folangji [muskets] are the guards. These foreign servants have deep-set eye sockets, green pupils, twinkling eyes, and curly hair. They look like a yellow horse with a protruding nose. Most of the foreigners are dressed in tweeds, and on their waists hang sharp daggers that seem to be emitting a cold light which can illuminate tiny hair on one's body. If one had not already asked for permission to go inside, he would not dare to enter. Embroidered curtains hang on the windows, the lattices of which are all made of crucible steel, which look spectacular yet strong enough to stop outsiders from entering. For each window, large glazed tiles are used.[24] When many people walk indoors, there is a resonant sound like that of an echo in the valley. The floor is covered with a foreign carpet, scarlet in color, and as clean as a boulder hit by waves in the river. One is reluctant to step on it, fearing that their shoes might bring dust in. The small table takes the shape of a moon, or half-moon, with many fruits and flowers placed on it. The person with white skin and green eyes is a well-known businessman, wearing a black velvet tricorn hat which looks like a monk's hat. He was dressed with a tight-fitting blue tweed with large golden buttons which look like strings of gold beads. His neckwear was of a mixed color, tightly wrapped around the neck in a neat way. He wore leather shoes. In his hand was a walking stick made of Sargentodoxa cuneata. It is said that there is a sharp dagger hidden within this stick. The interpreter told me that this kind of stick is the most expensive. The house owner indicated with a gesture that he would dispense with the etiquette and we should treat each other only as the guest and the host, to which I bowed with my hands folded in front of the chest. The host handed me a golden box of tobacco, the smell of which was pungent and unbearable for me, yet in both hands, he held it in front of his nose and sniffed hard without giving a single sneeze. Soon after, the meal was served. The tableware was also made of Yuzhan porcelain, but with resplendent patterns and colors, greatly different from those used by common households. Each utensil can hold ten liters of food, the capacity of which goes beyond the ones we use. The meat on the table was served whole without being cut into small pieces, but the head and claws were removed. No chopsticks were used, only forks made of iron. The main dish was wheat products, interspersed with small pieces of barbecued meat which was sprinkled with fennel, ground pepper, and chili powder. The wine was served in white glasses, each of which is crystal clear, with a small opening and a straight middle part. The taste was aromatic and refreshing. I drank three glasses at once. The host was very happy, making a gesture by pointing at a wine glass and touching his lips for three times, and the interpreter told me that it meant "I envy you for being able to drink so much." After the meal, we walked together in the corridor and saw all kinds of novel things. There is a clock that can play music, and when it is the time, different kinds of sound will come out without any mistake in rhythm. It does this without missing a single hour. There is also a thousand-mile-seeing glass (*qianli jing*, i.e., a telescope), with which you can look far away when standing at a high place. Holding this glass in front of your eyes, you can see clearly the face of people two or three *li* away. There are treasures like a microscope, a multi-treasure glass (*duobao jing*)[25], and a watch. Put this kind of watch next to your ear, you can hear a tick-tock sound like a bug pecking wood. There are also: a map of world oceans, plumeria, lilac vines, leiothrix, rainbow lorikeet, animals that hang upside-down, meerkats, and short-legged dogs. From the eaves are suspended crystal chandeliers, the bottoms of which have strings of pearls or beads. When the wind blows, these decorative hangings sway in the air and collide with each other, making clanking sounds. Fifty lamps can be placed on one chandelier. Every time I go to the Pearl River, I can see these lights from a distance in the middle of the night. In 1781, I also saw this kind of chandelier in the capital city. When a house hangs a flag of red saltire, you know that the residents are Dutch merchants.

The furnishings inside the house were exotic. Various gadgets and pets were eye-opening. As some of the items mentioned above will be discussed in the third section, I skip this part for the time being. What I want to point out is that the "well-known businessman" in the above quote was a supercargo of the Dutch factory. According to the Dutch archives, in 1782, Cornelis Heijligendorp held this post.[26] Therefore, the "person with white skin and green eyes" who invited Zeng Qiru to a banquet in his factory and praised him for his drinking capacity must have been Heijligendorp, the merchant holding "the most expensive" walking stick.

The successive supercargoes of the Dutch factory in Canton were far less famous than the British supercargoes in Guangdong. However, there was one person who enjoyed a lasting fame in history for his participation in foreign affairs with China. His experience was so unique that it deserves a special mention.

Van Braam and the Sino-Dutch Relations

Flipping through documentary files of the Qing dynasty, we find very few Dutch supercargoes in Canton who left a record in history. The only exception is van Braam who served continuously from 1791 to 1794 in this position. Because of his work and his writings, van Braam occupied a prominent place in the Sino-Dutch relations.

Andreas Everardus van Braam Houckgeest (1739–1801) was born on 1 November 1739 in Utrecht, the Netherlands. In 1759, he joined the Dutch Navy as a midshipman. After eight years of trading in Macau and Canton for the VOC, he returned to his country, running a farm and living there as a squire until 1773. After he acquired American citizenship in 1774, he became a dual-citizen maritime merchant. Later, he returned to the East and stayed in Malacca and Batavia. On 8 July 1790, he arrived at Canton and took office in the Dutch factory.[27]

In terms of personal characteristics, van Braam was a man of pioneering spirit: "He is very interesting, lively, cautious, wise, good at adapting, quite pompous and self-proclaimed, but he has a broad mind and a thirst for new knowledge."[28]

Van Braam's most significant achievement during his tenure as a supercargo was the planning of and participation in the Dutch mission to the Qing court. This mission, which followed the British Macartney Embassy to the imperial palace in 1793, received the same friendly reception from the Qianlong Emperor and became another major event in Sino-Western relations at the end of the eighteenth century.

Van Braam was a smart Dutchman who was good at seizing opportunities. When he learned from the Macartney mission that Beijing would celebrate the 60th anniversary of the Qianlong Emperor's accession to the throne, he requested that the Dutch general in Batavia send an embassy to take part in the celebration. After this suggestion was accepted, a Dutch mission was formed with Isaac Titsingh (1745–1812)[29] as the chief envoy and van Braam as his deputy. The mission's itinerary was as follows:

15 August 1794: They set sail from Batavia on the *Siam* and came to Canton via Macao.

13 October 1794: Changlin, governor-general of Guangdong and Guangxi provinces, met with the diplomatic mission at the Haizhuang Temple and inspected the credentials.

22 November 1794: The embassy of 27 people went from Canton to Beijing by ship.

9 January 1795: The embassy arrived in Beijing.

12 January 1795: At an audience with the Qianlong Emperor, the members of the embassy performed the formal etiquette of kneeling three times and kowtowing nine times, and then attended the imperial banquet at the Hall of Purple Light.

31 January 1795: The embassy visited the Longevity Hill.

8 February 1795: The embassy bid farewell to the Qianlong Emperor in the Summer Palace and accepted the "special imperial edict."

9 May 1795: The Dutch embassy returned to Canton.

As for the meeting between Changlin and the Dutch embassy at the Haizhuang Temple, we can find a detailed description in Wang Wengao's poems,[30] which can fill the gap in the Qing literature.

The diplomatic activities arranged for the Dutch mission were carried out under the tributary system of the Qing government. The congratulatory gifts they brought were mainly Western novelties, but some famous products from the South China Sea were also included. The list is as follows:

The gifts from the tribute envoys to Beijing are: a pair of eight-tone clocks with engraved patterns symbolizing longevity and fortune, four pairs of very lovely gold watches, a pair of gold lockets inlaid with jewels, four pairs of belts inlaid with jewels, 108 coral beads, 108 amber beads, two sets of thousand-mile-seeing glass [telescopes], a pair of fine guns, 30 *jin* [catties] of gold and silver thread, 40 catties of amber, 10 embroidered tapestries, 10 pieces of satin-smooth fabric, 10 pieces of tweed, 10 pieces of Western cloth, two carpets, a pair of large looking-glasses, a pair of wall mirrors made of stained glass, four pairs of glass lamps, 100 catties of bird's nests[31], 500 catties of sandalwood, and 100 catties of cardamoms, 250 catties of cloves, 30 bottles of sandalwood oil, and 30 bottles of clove oil.[32]

The return gifts from the Qing court were divided into "regular rewards" (in accordance with Kangxi's practice of giving rewards) and "additional rewards." More details can be found in the reports submitted by the Council of State (*junji chu*) on the first day and the 27th day of the 12th month in the 59th year of Qianlong [22 December 1794 and 17 January 1795, respectively].[33] As a "deputy envoy" and a supercargo, van Braam received "additional rewards" at the Longevity Hill and the Summer Palace.

The Dutch mission to Beijing failed to make the expected progress in trade. The Qing court treated the congratulatory visit as a sign of "submission" and, in a condescending manner, gave the Dutch king the following imperial edict in the first month of the 60th year of Qianlong:

> For the 60th anniversary of the Celestial Empire (*tianchao*), the *Gongban ya* (Dutch East India Company) failed to report to thee, the king, in time because of the long journey, so they vicariously performed the task and came to the court. As the edification they got from me would be the same as when thou, the king, came here, so I have given them preferential treatment, to show my care and concern. All the tributary envoys to the capital were careful and courteous. After they were led by the ministers to an audience with me, I rewarded them with a feast, and arranged for them to visit the forbidden gardens and various scenic spots so that they could feel the favor and enjoy the peaceful life. The multiple rewards given to the envoys, the regular rewards and additional rewards given to officials, interpreters, soldiers, etc., are all listed separately to inform thee of these items. In addition, because thy envoys are returning to thy country, I have issued a special edict to give thee not only gorgeous fabrics and precious jewels as listed before, but also various treasures such as silk and satin, antiques and valuable utensils, which are on a separate list. Surely thou, the king, will accept my gifts with respect. I hope thou will be more and more faithful, try thy best to protect thy country, and never fail to meet my expectations. Respect this special edict!"[34]

The praise of their being "careful and courteous" is not an overstatement for van Braam who had stayed in China on and off for 13 years. Moreover, in this comment, there is an implicit comparison with the arrogant Macartney mission.

After the end of the Dutch mission, van Braam resigned from his position as the Dutch supercargo in Canton. On 3 December 1795, he boarded the *Lady Louisa* and went to the United States. After settling in Philadelphia, he worked on horticultural business and wrote a book in French about his mission. This book, entitled *An Authentic Account of the Embassy of the Dutch East-India Company, to the Court of the Emperor of China, in the Years 1794 and 1795*, was published in Philadelphia in 1797. Van Braam dedicated this masterpiece describing his trip to Beijing to George Washington, in order to express a Dutch-American's respect for the president of the United States. In 1798, he left the United States for England, and in 1800, after a year in Germany, he returned to his home country to live out his days. He died in Amsterdam on 8 July 1801.[35]

For the Sino-Western relations in the eighteenth century, van Braam's book and Sir George Leonard Staunton's official report *An Authentic Account of an Embassy from the King of Great Britain to the Emperor of China* can be regarded as the two exemplary records of Western envoys to China.[36] From a Western perspective and with their own observations as the starting point, both of them have revealed the weakness of the Qing empire during the Qianlong era, and in a similar vein, fired a warning shot over the "Celestial Empire" at its heyday.

French scholar Alain Peyrefitte (1925–1999) compared the British and Dutch missions and gave an account of van Braam's changed perception of China as follows:

> Both embassies, the British and the Dutch, ended in failure, the former with dignity, the latter in humiliation. Van Braam's experience made him a sadder but wiser man. "This people," he wrote, "is so secluded that it can forgo all those artificial needs from whose lack we would suffer were they to go unsatisfied. The sight of the masterworks of European technique, though delivered annually to the Chinese, will not open their eyes, for they regard these marvels as mere superfluities."[37]

Van Braam was the last deputy envoy of the Dutch mission to China and the last supercargo of the Dutch factory in Canton. He was active at a time when the VOC was in decline. In 1795, a coup d'état occurred in the Netherlands, and Stadtholder William V fled to England. In 1796, the VOC was reorganized, and two years later, the entire company was disbanded. Given this trend, it can be said that the day when van Braam left Canton was also the end of the Dutch factory.

The Dutch Factory and the Cultural Exchange between China and the West

The "maritime market" of Canton in the Qing dynasty was an economic exchange. It was also a unique cross-cultural communication between different nations and heterogeneous cultures. As a well-known trading post run by "red-haired" foreigners, although the Dutch factory did not play a pivotal role, it definitely left something on the promotion of cultural exchange between China and the West.

In the eighteenth century's Europe, there was a noticeable "Chinese Vogue" that lasted for some time. Although this fashion was formed through multiple channels and on different levels, it is an undeniable fact that the Dutch factory in Canton offered its contribution. Besides the spread of tea consumption in Europe, garden design also betrayed the intermediary role that it played in this "vogue." This is not hard for us to see. The following is what Leonard Blussé, a Dutch historian has described in his book:

> In 1760, the first garden was built in the Netherlands. Claimed to be an "Anglo-Chinese garden" which integrated the traditions of both cultures, it presented a stunning layout with twists and turns: a bridge, a cave, a Chinese pagoda, a pavilion, a suspension bridge, and even the ruins of a Gothic building. The most striking garden of this type in the Netherlands is undoubtedly Baarn's "Chinese Garden," which was built in 1790 by R. Scherenberg,

a commercial officer of the VOC. In this now defunct garden, there were two Chinese-style pavilions painted in red, purple, and white, among rockery and ponds, named Beijing Pavilion and Canton Pavilion respectively. These two pavilions were customized in Canton, and then transported to the Netherlands by a VOC merchant vessel.[38]

As for how the Dutch factory in Canton introduced Western species into China, a general discussion of the wide variety of "tributes" and commodities seems unnecessary, yet it would be helpful to look at several Dutch novelties that were historically recorded and use them as examples for future research.

Clocks and Watches

For the Chinese people in the Qianlong era, a pocket chronograph was an extremely rare treasure from the West. No wonder it is called a "jewelry-adorned watch" in Zhang Jiuyue's poem. Zeng Qiru, as mentioned above, describes the tick-tock sound produced by this kind of watch with a simile "like a bug pecking wood," making readers feel as if they could hear it. The "four pairs of very lovely gold watches" that van Braam's mission presented to the Qianlong Emperor were probably of the same kind. Zhang Wen'an, a provincial graduate (*juren*) from Sichuan in the late Qianlong reign, wrote a set of poems entitled "Six Miscellaneous Poems Playfully Written in Summer about Foreign Ships in Canton" ("Xiari zai Guangzhou xi zuo yangbo zashi liushou") and the fourth one reads:

> The mechanical gears rotate continuously, dividing the day in a neat way,
> colorful ornaments can match a maiden's embroidered belts, it is needless to say.
> What is comparable to high-quality watches manufactured by the red-haired
>   foreigners?
> It is the French brand featuring shadowed flowers under the half-moon ray.

Below this poem, he also added a note: "Foreign watches come in two types: one made in Holland and the other in France. Dutch watches mostly have gold cases, while French ones use silver cases. For silver watches, those that are bigger and flatter are more expensive."[39] At that time, only noble families could afford such kind of foreign watch. In Chapter 45 of *Dream of the Red Chamber (Honglou meng)*, Jia Baoyu, a noble son growing up in the Grand View Garden, is one of the few who are able to "take out a gold watch the size of a walnut out of his chest pocket." Based on Zhang Wen'an's observation that "Dutch watches mostly have gold cases," we can make the inference that, in *Dream of the Red Chamber*, there is a Dutch watch, a top-end product inside the Happy Red Court of the Jia Residence.

Telescope

The telescope was an important decorative device in the Dutch factory. It was introduced into China in the late Ming period. The literati in the early Qing dynasty gave detailed descriptions of its structure and performance. In *Twelve Towers*

(*Shi'er lou*), a collection of tales completed by Li Yu in the 15th year of the Shunzhi Emperor (1658), there is a story entitled "Xiayi Tower" ("Xiayi lou") in which the marriage between scholar Qu Ji and a maiden surnamed Zhan is related to a telescope:

> This kind of sight glass [telescope] is composed of multiple tubes of different sizes, with the thinner inside the thicker, making it free for the user to pull it out or push it back. What is called "a thousand-mile-seeing glass" is to have a piece of glass embedded in either end of the device, so when you pull it out, you can see far away, with a clear vision. Although the modifiers "a thousand-mile" sound a bit exaggerated, and this kind of sight glass cannot guarantee that you can see the state of Yue from the state of Wu, or you can view Chu from Qin[40], you will not feel deceived if your search is limited within a thousand *li* or less. As for using it within tens of *li* or thousands of steps, you will feel that the vision you get is clearer than looking from the opposite side. It is truly a treasure.

Those who once visited the Dutch factory would certainly notice this treasure. That is why Le Jun provided this line: "You see the ocean far away with a telescope hanging by the window," and Zeng Qiru emphasized that:

> There is also a thousand-mile-seeing glass, with which you can look far away when standing at a high place. Holding this glass in front of your eyes, you can see clearly the face of people two or three *li* away.

During the Qianlong and Jiaqing periods, wealthy merchants or prominent officials were probably the only group of people in Canton who could afford a telescope and write about it. Pan Youdu, the head merchant of the thirteen hongs had a set of poems entitled "Miscellaneous Verses about the West" ("Xiyang zayong") and the 12th one describes his use of a telescope in a vivid way:

> On ten thousand hectares of land stand palaces of glazed tiles and spacious houses of sumptuous decoration,
> which I see clearly from thousands of miles away though it is an illusion.
> As smoke rises from the moon on the hazy night, I cannot help but wonder,
> are there people living in the Moon Palace[41] for certain?

Below this poem, Pan also added a note:

> The largest telescope is about one *chi* wide and one *zhang* long. There is a side lens which enables one to see the moon. Observing the moon through this lens, you will see a magnified planet several times larger than the one you actually see. It is spherical and clear, radiating lights like those of fish scales. Inside the moon, there are dark shadows as if the mountains and rivers are viewed upside down. You cannot see them all at a glance. You can

only look from the middle to the east, west, south, and north respectively. If you look at them for a long time, the heat might make your eyes uncomfortable. At midnight, when someone observed the moon through a telescope, he seemed to see smoke rising from its surface. It looked like cooking smoke.[42]

The other person who wrote about the telescope is Ruan Yuan, the governor-general of Guangdong and Guangxi provinces. His poem "Moon through a Telescope" ("*Wangyuanjing zhong wangyue ge*") completed in Canton in 1820 is descriptive, emotional, and imaginative:

Within the concentric sphere of the universe is the earth,
rotating fast and tight as a whirlpool of force.
Yin and Yang wax and wane, like ice and water,
all change depends on the sun that is so close to us.
There is also the celestial body- the moon,
relying on the sunlight to appear concave or convex.
As the Moon Palace, or the Jade Rabbit is merely a legend,
what is there? baffled and beguiled, we guess.
I think it is similar to the earth,
with the dark mountains and bright water on the surface.
Ships sail over the sea,
people live in the mountainous recess.
A moon day is fifteen days on the earth,
a lunar eclipse in my eyes is their solar eclipse.
If they look at the earth from the moon,
they will see similar moonlight emitting from the earth.
Not a loquacious talker on astronomy like Zou Yan[43],
I can use a large telescope to explore its secrets.
The shades of the moonlight I can discern,
the bright red sun I can study in boldness.
Not as small as the one we usually see,
flat moon lands resemble ocean waves, and protruded places look like islands.
Where the bright and dark divide, flow bubbles of light and shadow,
shaped like big and small pearls.
Moon residents should be intelligent as well,
observing the sun and the five planets.
Among them is an outstanding figure well learned in astronomy,
holding a telescope to peer at our planet- a star with the moon's face.
We observe each other secretly but cannot meet in person,
both submerged in beautiful moonlights.
If their telescope is more sophisticated,
Wu Gang should be able to see clearly my face.
Separated by two continents,
who of us can sail to the end of the waves?
Xi He[44] drove the sun chariot through the sky, silhouetting the two "moons,"

differentiating the large from the small, both made of glass.
Seen from 400,000 *li* away,
The bright moon takes more of the autumn color under my device.[45]

By writing about "a large telescope," Ruan Yuan addressed his "heavenly questions" (*tianwen*). In his poems, a product of the Western industrial civilization brings out a new understanding of the Chinese mythology about the moon. As a result, the "Tao" (*dao*) is also enriched, which is really thought-provoking. In this sense, the telescope not only broadened the physical horizon of the Chinese people in the Qing dynasty but also brought them into a new spiritual realm. This kind of infiltrating influence, epitomized by the term "eastward dissemination of Western learning" (*xixue dongjian*), requires a more detailed analysis in the future.

Short-legged Dogs

The short-legged dogs that Zeng Qiru saw in the Dutch factory were pugs. They were a pet animal for foreigners at that time. Xu Chenglie, who was known as Qingliang Daoren, recorded the pugs that he saw at the Thirteen Hongs in his book *Chronicle of Hall of Raindrops* (*Tingyu xuan biji*):

> I saw several pairs of foreign breed dogs at the Thirteen Hongs. They look like giant eggplants, not much different from ordinary newborn baby dogs. Their colors are black, white, or pale brown. Wagging tails and shaking heads, they are well-tamed. It is worth 20 to 30 yuan per pair in foreign cash.[46]

In early 1834, along the streets of Canton, a foreigner posted a surprising search notice for two lost foreign dogs as follows:

> On the 10th day of the first month of the present year, two foreign dogs strayed, one from the Sui Hong and one from the Dutch Hong, and have not been seen to return. Long ears and a long tail adorned the one, which had also a brown star on its breast, the body being of the color of "fragrant ink." The other was a small dog, with cropped ears and a tail of no length. His body was spotted in variegated colors of brown and white. The larger dog was named "Lo-Wā," and the smaller "Pŏ-Pā." This is to give notice that should any "superior man" know where they are, or if they have been "misled," and will inform, he shall be rewarded with flowered red money - two great rounds for the big one, and one great round for the little one. Even should they have been stolen (an inconceivable thing!), if the person who took them will bring them to Sui-Hong No. 2, he Shall still be rewarded, and clemency used towards him. This placard is real; its words will not be eaten.[47]

The above quote seems like a long-winded statement about dogs, yet as it concerns the difference between the Chinese and Western cultures and values, it may not be meaningless, even if it is trivial. If we make a comparison between this poster and Fu Xuan's "Rhapsody on Dogs" (*Zougou fu*) in the *Complete Jin Prose* (*Quan Jinwen*), volume 46, we will have some rough ideas.

The Snow Pea

Concerning the relationship between the Dutch factory and the snow pea (called *helan dou* in Chinese), there is also a great story to look back on.

During the Jiaqing period, Liu Shixin from Yangchun, Guangdong province, completed his book *Odds and Ends about Guangdong* (*Yue xie*). In volume one, he wrote:

> Snow peas came from abroad. No such plants had been found in Guangdong before. In the 50th year of the Qianlong Emperor, some seeds were brought to the Thirteen Hongs via a foreign ship and given to the local residents. They were sown around the Double Ninth Festival (*chongyang jie*) in the ninth month of that year. The seedlings reached two or three *chi* tall, with green leaves and white flowers. In the first month of the next year, beans grew inside the pods. They were sweet and crisp. At the very beginning, nobody else but an experienced vegetable farmer in Xiguan knew how to plant snow peas by season. Every year, at the end of the eighth month, he put seeds in a small basket and sold them on the street, and everyone rushed to buy. They were very expensive at first, but now you can find them everywhere in Guangdong and Guangxi provinces. Some time ago, I quit my job and went back to my hometown to take care of my parents. I dug out a vegetable plot and planted some peas to meet my needs. I also wrote a poem about this: "In the garden I planted some snow peas, which came all the way from overseas. /Around the Double Ninth Festival, from the Thirteen Hongs I bought the seeds. /Picking the ripe beans home, I filled the burner with foreign incense for my needs. / Inhaling the unmatchable fragrance from the morning flowers, I started my first taste of the savory food as a Cantonese." Because the seeds came from the Netherlands (*helan*), thus the name snow peas (*helan dou*).

As the introduction and spread of snow peas in Fujian, Guangdong and Taiwan, have been well researched by Yang Baolin,[48] here I would only clarify a couple of points about the above quotation by referring to some Dutch sources. First, there were four Dutch vessels that arrived in Guangdong in 1785, and two of them sailed directly from Amsterdam to China: the *Voorschoten* and the *Pollux*. Therefore, the "foreign ship" that brought the seeds of snow peas should be one of them.[49] Second, Pieter Kintsius served as the supercargo of the Dutch factory in Canton in 1785. As he was an experienced "red-haired" foreigner who worked at the Dutch factory since 1759, he knew the city and the people pretty well. Thus, it was highly likely that he was the person who gave the seeds to the local residents. As a result, "Xiguan" became the first place for planting snow peas.

Conclusion

The thirteen "foreign factories" (*yiguan*) and the thirteen hongs were trading partners in Canton during the Qing period. Both are worthy of in-depth study in the history of Sino-Western relations, and only in combination can this study be furthered. Yet there has not been much attention to the first research field so far.[50] As for the second one, no significant progress has been made either. As a result, the interaction between the "foreign factories" and the Co-hong (*gong hang*) has been regrettably unclear.

It can be said that cultural exchanges between China and the West during the Qing period were a two-track process, one through the Church and the other through the "foreign factories," that is, one religious and the other secular. It is self-evident that merchant chambers were not cultural halls, and there is no need to discuss their cultural functions in detail. However, the trade between China and foreign countries was, after all, a "cross-cultural" trade. Therefore, although researchers should "emphasize commerce," they should not "belittle culture." In other words, any parochialism in understanding is not conducive to a comprehensive view. In human civilization, economy and culture have always been intertwined, and there is no insurmountable divide between the two fields, so how can we "imprison our thoughts and confine ourselves to a restricted area"?

With regard to the history of the Dutch factory in Canton, I have relied on some poetry written in the Qing dynasty to make up for the missing details in the related literature. As Guangdong was the first province to open its trading port, it is natural that Guangdong poets revealed more of the foreign style and fashion. The literati who came to Guangdong from other provinces were also affected by the atmosphere here. To quote Wei Yuan, the author of the *Illustrated Gazetteer of the Sea Kingdoms*, "Their poetic styles have changed since they passed through Lingnan, and they doubt that these islanders speak a different language from their mother tongue." Very often, these literati could not help but write about foreigners and foreign affairs. Therefore, their poems and writings about their travels to Guangdong are also a source of historical materials to be used. If we make an effort to sort them out and read between the lines, we will be able to benefit from this legacy and gain a better understanding of the "foreign factories."

Notes

1 Zhang Weihua, 90–91.
2 Ou Chu and Wang Guichen, 38.
3 Qu Dajun, 482.
4 Liang Tingnan, vol. 3.
5 Blussé, 10.
6 Quan Hansheng, 12.
7 Cai Hongsheng, 1994: 18–19.
8 Jorg, 54.
9 Du Zongyu, vol. 3.
10 Quoted from *The Foreign Tributes via Guangdong Province*.
11 Zhang Yingchang, 923.

12 Liang Jiabin, 365.
13 Zhang Jiuyue, vol. 11. Of the paintings and porcelain designs that describe foreign people or foreign buildings in Canton, some were exported during the Qing period. A number of them can illustrate Zhang's poem "Foreign Firms." For more information about the paintings, see *Views of the Pearl River Delta* (compiled and published by the Urban Council of Hong Kong, 1996): 149–183.
14 The city of Wuyang is another name for the city of Guangzhou. —Trans.
15 The *luquan* is a legendary beast in the Chinese mythology. —Trans.
16 Both *suofu* and *tuoni* are woolen fabrics, with the first woven from bird feathers and the second from camel hair. —Trans.
17 Both *du'nou* and *qinan* are spices made from trees. —Trans.
18 Linghai refers to the Guangdong and Guangxi area. —Trans.
19 The *Polan* was an ancient unit of weight assumed to be used by foreigners. One *Polan* was about three hundred catties. —Trans.
20 According to ancient Chinese literature, *Huoqi* was a decoction for treating gastrointestinal diseases. —Trans.
21 *Mu'nan* 木难, also written as 莫难, was a kind of jewel in ancient Chinese literature. —Trans.
22 Huzhou and Wenzhou were in Zhejiang province. Raozhou was in Jiangxi province.
23 Zeng Yandong, *The Little Bean Arbor* (*Xiao doupeng*), vol. 16. The description about the Dutch attire in this book can be cross-referenced with the entry entitled "Foreigners from the Netherlands" ("Helan guo yiren") in the *Imperial Tributary Illustrations* (*Huang qing zhigong tu*), vol. 1.
24 Here "the large glazed tiles" are probably window glass, which Zeng saw for the first time.
25 A multiple-treasure glass was believed to be able to produce millions of the images of a person standing afar. —Trans.
26 Jorg, 204.
27 Duyvendak, 1–2; 5–7.
28 Boxer, 1984: 265.
29 In Chinese documents, the name of Titsingh was translated as Desheng 德胜, Desheng 得胜, or Yusongdisheng 余悚第生.
30 The group of poems is entitled "Poems Written Respectfully about Governor-general Changin Who Led the Tribute Envoy from the Netherlands to Receive the Imperial Edict at the Haizhuang Temple." See the anthology authored by Wang Wen'gao, *Collected Poems from Yunshan Hall* (*Yunshantang shiji*), vol. 1.
31 Bird's nests usually refer to the saliva nests built by the cave swifts. They are used to cook a special soup in Chinese cuisine. —Trans.
32 See *The Foreign Tributes via Guangdong Province*.
33 See "Rewards to Envoys from the Netherlands" ("Helan guo jiaopin an") in Gugong bowuyuan, eds., *Collection of Documents* (*Wenxian congbian*), vol. 5.
34 Gugong bowuyuan, *Collection of Documents*, vol. 5.
35 Duyvendak, 97–107.
36 George Leonard Staunton's book *An Authentic Account of an Embassy from the King of Great Britain to the Emperor of China* was translated into Chinese by Ye Duyi, and was published by the Joint Publishing HK in 1994. For more information, see also *Proceedings of the Symposium on the Bicentenary of Sino-British Diplomatic Relations* (*Zhong ying tongshi erbai zhounian xueshu taolunhui lunwenji*) published by Zhongguo shehui kexue chubanshe in 1996.
37 Peyrefitte, 564.
38 Blussé, 102.
39 Zhang Wen'an, vol. 3.
40 These were four states during the Spring and Autumn period (approximately 770 to 476 BC). Wu bordered Yue; Qin and Chu were adjacent to each other. —Trans.

41 In the Chinese legend, the Moon Palace (*Guanghan gong*) is a palace on the moon, where Chang E lives, together with a three-legged toad, a rabbit, and the woodcutter Wu Gang. —Trans.
42 Pan Yizeng, *Poems by the Pan Family of Panyu* (*Panyu panshi shilue*), block-printed edition in the 20th year of Guangxu.
43 Zou Yan was a pioneering figure of the School of Yin-Yang, a Chinese Warring States-era philosophy that synthesized the concepts of yin-yang and the Five Elements. —Trans.
44 Xi He is a legendary figure in the ancient Chinese mythology, the god who drives the sun chariot.
45 Ruan Yuan, 971–972.
46 Huang Foyi, vol. 5. See also Cai Hongsheng, "Tracing the History of Pugs" in this book.
47 Hunter, 91–92.
48 Yang Baolin, 313–316.
49 Jorg, 200, 203–204.
50 For research about this topic, see Cai Hongsheng, "Historical Accounts of Sweden in the Qing Dynasty and the Sui Hong's Trading Activities in Guangzhou" ("Lun Qingdai Ruidian jishi ji Guangzhou ruihang shangwu"), *Zhongshan daxue xuebao*, no. 2, 1991: 72–79. The English version of this essay is included in Bengt Johansson, ed., *The Golden Age of China Trade: Essays on the East India Companies' Trade with China in the 18th Century and the Swedish East Indiaman Götheborg* (Hong Kong: Viking Hong Kong Publications, 1992): 90–104. See also Zha Shijie, "Robert Morrison and the Thirteen Hongs in Guangdong" ("Malixun yu shisan yiguan"), in *Proceedings of the Symposium "Modern China and Asia,"* vol. 2 (Hong Kong: Xianggang Zhuhai shuyuan yazhou yanjiu zhongxin, 1995): 629–661.

Bibliography

Blussé, Leonard. *A History of Sino-Dutch Relations*. [In Chinese.] Translated by Zhuang Guotu and Cheng Shaogang. Amsterdam: Otto Cramwinckel, 1989.

Boxer, Charles Ralph. "The Dutch Embassy to China in the 18th Century," in *Zhongwai guanxishi yicong* (*Collected Essays of Translation about the History of Sino-Foreign Relations*). [In Chinese.] Translated and compiled by Zhu Jieqin. Beijing: Haiyang chubanshe, 1984. 248–268.

Cai Hongsheng. *Eluosi guan jishi* (*Accounts of the Russian Hotel*). Guangzhou: Guangdong renmin chubanshe, 1994.

Du Zongyu. *Yinghuan yiyin yiming ji* (*Different Translations of Names around the World*). Block-printed edition in Echeng, 1904.

Duyvendak, Jan Julius Lodewijk. "The Last Dutch Embassy to the Chinese Court (1794–1795)." *T'oung Pao* 34, no. 1 (1938): 1–137.

Gugong bowuyuan, ed. *Wenxian congbian* (*Collection of Documents*), vol. 5. Beijing: Gugong bowuyuan, 1930.

Huang Foyi. *Guangzhou chengfang zhi* (*A Historical Survey of Guangzhou City and its Surrounding Areas*). Guangzhou: Guangdong renmin chubanshe, 1994.

Hunter, William C. *The "Fan Kwae" at Canton Before Treaty Days, 1825–1844*. [In Chinese.] Translated by Feng Shutie. Guangdong: Guangdong renmin chubanshe, 1993.

Jorg, C. J. A. *Porcelain and the Dutch China Trade*. The Hague: Martinus Nijhoff, 1982.

Li Yu. *Shi'er lou* (*Twelve Towers*). Nanjing: Jiangsu guji chubanshe, 1991.

Liang Jiabin. *Guangdong shisanhang kao* (*A Study of the Thirteen Hongs in Canton*). Shanghai: Guoli bianyiguan, 1937.

Liang Tingnan. *Yuedao gongguo shuo* (*The Foreign Tributes via Guangdong Province*). Beijing: Zhonghua shuju, 1993.

Liu Shixin. *Yue xie* (*Odds and Ends about Guangdong*). Shanghai: Shen baoguan, 1877.

Ou Chu and Wang Guichen, eds. *Qu Dajun quanji* (*Complete Works of Qu Dajun*). Beijing: Renmin wenxue chubanshe, 1996.

Pan Yizeng, ed. *Panyu panshi shilue* (*Poems by the Pan Family of Panyu*). Block-printed edition of 1894.

Peyrefitte, Alain. *The Immobile Empire: The Collision of Two Civilizations*. [In Chinese.] Translated by Wang Guoqing and Mao Fengzhi. Beijing: Sanlian shudian, 1993.

Qu Dajun. *Guangdong xinyu* (*A New Encyclopedia of Guangdong*), vol. 18. Beijing: Zhonghua shuju, 1985.

Quan Hansheng. "Luelun xinhanglu faxian hou de zhongguo haiwai maoyi" ("A Brief Discussion of China's Overseas Trade after the Discovery of the New Route," in *Zhongguo haiyang fazhanshi lunwenji* (*Collected Essays on the Maritime China*), vol. 5. Edited by Zhang Bincun and Liu Shiji. Taipei: Zhongyang yanjiuyuan zhongshan renwen shehui kexue yanjiusuo, 1993. 1–16.

Ruan Yuan. *Yanjing shi ji* (*Collected Writings from the Yanjing Studio*). Beijing: Zhonghua shuju, 1993.

Zeng Yandong. *Xiao doupeng* (*The Little Bean Arbor*). Wuhan: Jingchu shushe, 1989.

Zhang Jiuyue. *Zixianshanren shiji* (*Collection of Poems by Zhang Jiuyue*). Shanghai: Shanghai guji chubanshe, 1995.

Zhang Weihua. *Mingshi Ouzhou siguo zhuan zhushi* (*Annotations to the Sections on the Four European Countries in the "History of the Ming"*). Shanghai: Shanghai guji chubanshe, 1982.

Zhang Wenan. *Haibai shicao* (*Drafted Poems of Zhang Wen'an*). Block-printed edition of 1816, archived in Hunan tushuguan.

Zhang Yingchang, ed. *Qingshi duo* (*Poems as a Warning Bell to the Qing Dynasty*). Beijing: Zhonghua shuju, 1983.

18 Wang Wengao's Historical Poems about the Dutch Tribute

The visit of the Dutch mission to China in 1794–1795 was another important event in the relations between China and the West, following the British Macartney embassy. In recent years, the British embassy to China has attracted widespread attention,[1] but the Dutch mission has been almost forgotten, which is quite regrettable.

In the "foreign affairs" management system of the Qing dynasty, the Netherlands, like the United Kingdom, was one of the "tributary countries via Guangdong." Before going to Beijing, the Dutch mission had to undergo some formalities related to foreign affairs at the governor's office in Canton, such as having their credential documents inspected, listening to someone reading the imperial edict to them, being rewarded with a banquet, and so on. Clearly, a study of the "Dutch tribute" should take Canton as a starting point. Yet, these ritualistic formalities are scarcely mentioned in the official documents of the Qing dynasty. Leaving aside the *Donghua Record* (*Donghua lu*) and the *Veritable Records of the Qing Dynasty* (*Qing shilu*) where details about this "tribute" are omitted, we cannot find records in Liang Tingnan's *Guangdong Maritime Customs* (*Yuehaiguan zhi*) or *The Foreign Tributes via Guangdong Province* (*Yuedao gongguo shuo*). Fortunately, the Lingnan poetry[2] of the same period left behind some descriptions, which makes it possible for us to fill in the blanks in historical sources. From these poems, we get to know how Changlin, the governor-general of Guangdong and Guangxi provinces, in the last years of Qianlong's reign, received the Dutch mission at the Haizhuang Temple in Canton, and gain a deeper understanding of the role played by the merchants from the Thirteen Hongs.

Wang Wengao and *Collected Poems from Yunshan Hall*

Wang Wengao, whose courtesy name was Chunsheng, art name Jianda, was born in Renhe, Zhejiang province. In 1792, he traveled around in Guangdong and wrote quite a few poems about the local customs of Lingnan and foreigners living there. His poems boast of elegance and grandeur. Completed in 1798, his Lingnan poems were grouped together under the title of *Collected Poems from Yunshan Hall* (*Yunshantang shiji*). In 1830, the engraved edition was published by the Zhejiang

Publishing House. There were seven volumes, 605 poems in total.³ In the preface that he wrote in 1798, Wang offered a brief explanation as follows:

> I am not a smart person. Thanks to my late father, I have gained a bit of learning. In the 57th year of Qianlong [1792], I traveled around in Lingnan, and wrote down my feelings in plain and direct language. As I had no study of poetry, [I was not sure if they could be called poems]. In the winter of the third year of Jiaqing [1798], before going to another place, I sorted out those manuscripts kept in the box at my residence, and after a quick scan, I found that 70% of them are sentimental poems, so they can be included in this collection. As I lost one volume of manuscript in Longtan in the 58th year of Qianlong [1793], so in the 59th year of Qianlong [1794], I rewrote some poems and put them in a safe place. All these manuscripts were put together under the title of *Collected Poems from Yunshan Hall*.

In volume one of this collection, there are two groups of poems about the Dutch mission in Canton, both recording what Wang witnessed there. Of the two groups, "Poems Written Respectfully about Governor-general Changlin Who Led the Tribute Envoy from the Netherlands to Receive the Imperial Edict at the Haizhuang Temple," and "Sending off Circuit Intendant Wang Xiangyu and Department Magistrate Zhao Zaoting Who Escort the Dutch Tribute Envoy to the Capital," the first one has eight seven-syllable quatrains. As it is the focus of my textual interpretation, I cite all the eight poems as follows:

> (1) His Majesty's imperial prestige spreads far and wide,
> sensed at close range in Lingnan from the imperial commissioner in sight.
> No waves are spotted over the purplish sea,
> amid the colorful clouds is the red haze around the sun that looks arty.
> (2) Over the mountains and across the sea, thou travelled thousands of miles,
> to southern China where early spring is heralded by blooming plum blossoms.
> Year after year, we study the clouds until an auspicious sign is spotted,
> guests from an exotic land have come to the imperial court to send congratulations.
> (3) At Humen anchorage, the Dutch tribute ship was allowed to dock and stay,
> after sailing through Macau like uproarious buildings on the bright mirror-like bay.
> A gold leaf memorial has to be submitted before they offer tribute,
> and they straighten their green leather jackets for the grand ceremony under way.
> (4) Eminent monks and solemn-looking halls make the Haizhuang Temple distinctive,
> Spinulose wood ferns and tala trees shade the clear river, making the scene alive.
> Kind and amiable faces look up to the direction of the imperial majesty,
> one day's glory is to be shared by all the sea states that are attentive.

(5) Ten thousand glass-made oil lamps hang at the colorful gates,
woolen carpets have been spread on the ground, matching crimson flags.
The morning saw the governor acting on the emperor's edict,
Amid the euphonious fairy music, we heard him speaking soft words.
(6) A coral finial, a peacock feather,[4] and fluttering red silk tassels on an official hat,
as well as an embroidered crane over a four-clawed-dragon court robe,[5]
overwhelmingly set thee apart from other officials among whom thou sat.
The chiming of the dawn bell ushered in a royal guard of honor,
as if bringing in ministers who wait outside the palace gate for the morning audience, an important occasion to expect.
(7) Like a good horse used to running in the sand for years, thou, a provincial official of outstanding talent,
will go up to the capital in a fast stagecoach to receive a special commendation from the emperor for thy achievement.
From now on, sea countries lean on the imperial court in the north just like a sunflower following the sun,
and the map of the Chinese empire will become clearer and more easily recognizable because of thy commitment.
(8) Music from jade *xiao* and gold *guan*[6] can be heard across blooms,
a feast is held amid the flowers that stand around like ravishing screens.
Officials of varying ranks all kneel down and kowtow to the emperor's tablet,
censer smoke rises and floats in the pavilion carved with nine dragons.[7]

The above eight poems "that were respectfully written" reflect how a scholar of the late Qianlong period viewed the "foreign affair." Dedicated to the topic of the "Dutch tribute," these poems are filled with words such as "imperial prestige," "come to the imperial court," and "offer tribute," misinterpreting the equal relationship between China and foreign countries as a suzerain-vassal connection. Nevertheless, there are some descriptions of historical value, and therefore, these poems can help to fill the gap of the Qing dynasty documents. Based on the above poems that contain issues such as the tribute envoys, the tribute ship, the tribute memorial, the process of receiving the imperial edict, holding the feast, and leaving for the capital, I try to provide an interpretation by referring to both Chinese and Dutch sources, in the hope that they might be helpful for scholars who study the history of Sino-Dutch relations and the history of Canton Port.

The Dutch Tribute Envoy Titsingh

The Dutch embassy was headed by a chief envoy, with van Braam (1739–1801) serving as the deputy envoy. As the previous chapter has a detailed account of van Braam, the supercargo at the Dutch factory in Canton, who is addressed as "the deputy envoy and supercargo" in the official documents of the Qing dynasty, I will turn to the other envoy here.

The chief envoy was Isaac Titsingh (1745–1812). In Chinese sources, he is called Desheng 德胜/得胜 or Yusongdisheng 余悚第生. He was born in a prominent family in Amsterdam and belonged to the upper middle class which almost had a monopoly of important administrative posts in the Netherlands in the eighteenth century. From 1766 on, he worked for the Dutch East India Company (VOC) and mostly lived in Batavia. Later, he was appointed to be VOC's Chief factor on the island of Dejima in Japan. In 1779 and 1784, Titsingh paid a visit of homage to the shogun in Edo. Highly regarded by the VOC, he was then transferred to Bengal and served as director of the Dutch factory at Chinsurah for seven years (1785–1792). After leaving that post, he joined the Government Council in Batavia and thus became a leading figure in the colonial administration of the VOC.[8]

As a well-educated Dutch business official, Titsingh had a strong interest in burgeoning oriental studies. He was one of the founding members of the Asiatic Society in Calcutta. He collected cultural relics and documents from the early Edo period, including *The History of Japan* compiled by the feudal lord Tokugawa Mitsukuni, and he also searched for a Chinese-Latin dictionary compiled by the Jesuits. Moreover, he once employed two Chinese clerks of Fujian origin. Titsingh's cultural background indicated that he was an expert in the "Oriental research" and that the Batavia VOC's decision to make him the chief envoy of the Dutch embassy to China was the result of careful selection rather than random choice.

The Dutch colonial empire at the end of the eighteenth century was decimated by the French Revolution. Before Titsingh's visit to China, Batavia had shown signs of decay everywhere. The Macartney mission, which passed through this place in April 1793, gave the following observation:

> In the districts round Batavia, immediately subject to the Dutch, it is calculated that near 50,000 Javanese families are settled, containing six persons, upon an average, to a family, or 300,000 persons in the whole. The city of Batavia, including the suburbs, contains near 8,000 houses. Those of the Chinese are low, and crammed with people. The Dutch houses are well built, clean, and spacious, and their construction, for the most part, well suited to the climate. The doors and windows are wide and lofty. The ground floors are covered with flags of marble, which being sprinkled frequently with water, give a pleasant coolness to the apartment; but a considerable proportion of those was untenanted; which denoted a declining settlement. Among other circumstances which announced the same, were those of the Company's vessels lying useless in the road, for want of cargoes to fill, or men to navigate them.[9]

When Titsingh visited Beijing, the VOC was just on the verge of disintegration. Therefore, what is mentioned in one of the poems – "guests from an exotic land have come to the imperial court to send congratulations" which literally means that they came to celebrate "the great emperor of the Celestial Empire for his sixtieth year on the throne" – was just a fitting excuse. The real motive was to seek new interests for the VOC's trade with China. After Titsingh's efforts failed, he left Batavia and arrived in London in December 1796 for a life of leisure. He then moved to Paris, where he joined a group of Orientalists for in-depth discussions about China and Japan. For example, he was a close friend of the French scholar Joseph de Guignes, who was the first to propose that "Fusang 扶桑 is Mexico." Unfortunately, Titsingh's manuscripts were not published. On 9 February 1812, Titsingh died of illness in Paris at the age of 66.

"The Dutch Tribute Ship" and Captain Gas

The two lines "At Humen anchorage, the Dutch tribute ship was allowed to dock and stay, / after sailing through Macau like uproarious buildings on the bright mirror-like bay" are inverted for the sake of rhyming. As a matter of fact, this Dutch ship sailed through Macau before it entered Humen [Boca Tigris]. During the eras of the Kangxi Emperor and the Qianlong Emperor, Dutch ships were known for their many trips to Huangpu [Whampoa] in Canton. The famous poet and scholar Qu Dajun and Zhao Yi both boarded Dutch ships and wrote down what they had seen. In Qu Dajun's *A New Encyclopedia of Guangdong* (*Guangdong xinyu*), volume 18, we read this account:

> There are several decks, so I went down by ropes. This ship has water tanks and patches of vegetables. For the turbid water inside the tanks, alum is used to make it clean again. Water is poured into a pot and boiled before drinking. They sleep on what they call a soft bed, which is spread with white felt fabric.

Zhao Yi, who served as the prefect (*zhifu*) of Canton in the mid-Qianlong period, was very enthusiastic about "their peculiar sails": "Each of the vessels owned by red-haired foreigners has dozens of sails that can convert crosswind and headwind into tailwind."[10] He once "stepped on the hanging ladder to visit the ship" at Humen and wrote a long poem entitled "A Foreign Ship" to note down his impressions in detail. First, regarding its length and capacity, there is a stanza that reads:

> A majestic ship of a hundred *zhang*,
> across the tide, it looks like a mountain-shaped screen that is impressively long.
> Fully loaded, it carries the cargo weighing a thousand *Polan*,[11]
> the huge capacity of which is hard to be measured in ton.

Second, with regard to its decks and equipment, the description is given in this stanza:

> The ship has several floors, separated by horizontal boards.
> Poking out of the decks are cannons, placed on the shelves are cargo in boxes.
> Numerous water tanks are filled with clear water, and rice containers boast of abundant grain ready to be cooked and served on platter.
> A rope is needed for stepping down, also for going up to exit later.

Finally, regarding its navigation, sails and masts, we can refer to the following stanza:

> The helmsman's eyes are fixed on the compass, while carefully identifying the various sounds.
> The sails are hoisted on three masts, each folding and unfurling serves a clear purpose.
> When sails hang down, they look like clouds falling from the sky, when they are fully stretched, they seem to block the red sun.
> In a flash, the ship has traveled a thousand miles, fast and unrestrained, it rises high upward on the waves.
> It needs no labor to steer the ship, as the sails have turned blustery winds into able-bodied workers.[12]

Descriptions of Dutch ships coming to Guangdong in the poems of the Qing dynasty are consistent with the Japanese historical sources of similar age. Shihei Hayashi (1738–1793), also known as Rin Shihei, was a painter in the late Tokugawa shogunate period. In his "Orandasen zusetsu" ["Illustration of a Dutch Ship"], there is an illustration that goes as follows:

> Length of the ship is more than 14 *zhang*, beam three *zhang* and eight *chi*, draught three *zhang* and five *chi*. Height of the mast is more than 14 *zhang*, and flagpole is more than three *zhang*. There are 18 sails, 36 guns. Its height of chimney is more than three *zhang*. The crew number is about 100.[13]

The Dutch tribute ship that Titsingh was riding in back then was also this kind of "red-haired foreigners' ship," and its shape was likewise similar to the latter. In Wang Wengao's *Collected Poems from Yunshan Hall*, volume three, there is a poem entitled "Foreign Ship" ("Yang bo") where we read the following lines:

> *Duqiang*, *Niutou*, or *Liaohe*,[14] of all these ships,
> the largest one can carry cargo of a thousand *Polan*.
> Pitch, naphtha, and steel, with these materials, [builders] made the hull as fitting and firm as they can.
> With nails tempered in *Shegao*,[15] and alkaline water in clever use,[16] the ship can venture into any dangerous rapids.

Apart from these, there are two more lines that read: "To see Geluoba, one needs to travel through Linghai,[17] / With four hundred sails kept full, the ship crosses the huge waves up and down." As Geluoba is a transcription of the Malay word "coconut" which stands for Batavia, so from this sentence, we can know that the ship mentioned in Wang Wengao's poem is the said Dutch ship. According to a Dutch source, the ship was named *Siam*, which set sail from Batavia on 15 August 1794, and arrived at Humen one month later. The ship was originally owned by the Chamber of Commerce in Delft, a city in the western part of the Netherlands, but it diverted to Norway on the homeward voyage.[18]

In the official documents of the Qing dynasty, the captain of the Dutch tribute ship *Siam* is called "Ship Merchant Jishi,"[19] which is a Cantonese transcription of Captain Gas. Before the ship started its homeward voyage, the Qing government decided to exempt the Dutch merchants from paying taxes, including duties on the ship as well as on the purchased goods, and then on 3 March 1795, the superintendent of the Guangdong Maritime Customs conveyed the emperor's order to "Hong merchants Cai Shiwen and Pan Zhixiang." According to Titsingh's letter to the VOC head in Batavia, dated 20 March 1796, the *Siam* was exempted from paying taxes for a total of 8,670 taels of silver.[20]

The "Dutch tribute ship" had a different mission from that of the *Lion* serving the British Macartney embassy. The *Siam* was a commercial ship, so it carried neither the chief nor deputy envoys on their return journey, but the *Lion* was the assigned ship for the British envoy and his entourage. Actually, the two Dutch envoys went their separate ways. On 3 December 1795, van Braam boarded the *Lady Louisa* in Canton and headed to the United States, and on 25 March 1796, Titsingh left Canton for England in the East-Indiaman *Cirencester*.[21] After the tribute ship left, and the tribute envoys bid farewell to each other, the Dutch embassy quickly disintegrated, and that might really have surprised Wang Wengao, who had predicted that "from now on, sea countries lean on the imperial court in the north just like a sunflower following the sun."

People and Places Mentioned in the "Gold Leaf Memorial"

What is mentioned as the "gold leaf memorial" in Wang Wengao's poem is actually a letter of credence drafted by the VOC in Batavia. To put it another way, the VOC "prepared memorial and credential documents on behalf of the king." This letter was translated into Chinese by an overseas Chinese[22] who signed in this way: "Written by Zhu Geqiao[23] in the Tuku [the Castle] of Galaba [Batavia]." The full text of the letter is as follows:

> Entrusted by the King of Holland Bolian [William], the Dukes of the Country of Ba [Commissioners-general of Batavia], who also administer the local affairs of the Island of Niu [Cape of Good Hope] and Gongbanya [Compnay] and other places, Nilvmaolu [Nederburgh], Woliding [Alting], Bolijinian [Frijkenius], Shimeili [Siberg] and others, present this letter in kowtow: May Your Majesty the Emperor, reigning by virtue, walk in the happiness of the Four Seas [the world]; cherishing the multitudes with benevolence, may Your Majesty reach a boundless age. We recall how our fiefdom from the days of Emperor Shengzu [Kangxi] till now has traded in Guangdong and always has received the wide-reaching sacred blessings, so that everyone far and near has submitted to the civilizing influence. Next year we shall respectfully witness Your Majesty's anniversary, an occasion on which the entire world jubilates, and a period in which all the people rejoice over the imperial virtue. From the beginning of the world, there has never been such a glorious reign as that of our emperor. Although I, William, have territories in a remote

area, I often receive Your Majesty's favor. So, upon hearing this news, how dare I not come to pay my respects and congratulate! I now respectfully send Yusongdisheng [Titsingh] as my envoy to proceed reverently to the palace and present tribute, and at the same time to congratulate the Heir-apparent for His Royal Highness's enthronement in the coming year. We wish His Royal Highness the universal peace of all the countries and the grand good fortune of a thousand years. In case my envoy is negligent in etiquette, I earnestly pray that Your Majesty will graciously pardon him and will permit him a speedy return in his ship. How excited I am and how much I admire you, Your Majesty! Prostrating myself, I hope that Your Sacred Kindness will deign to glance down at this and respectfully I present this memorial for Your Majesty's information. The 30th day of the sixth month of the 59th year of Qianglong; the 26th day of the seventh month of Holland.[24]

Besides the Dutch "gold leaf memorial," there was also "A Letter to the Governor-general of Guangdong and Guangxi provinces," with the same dating and the writer's signature as the above-mentioned letter. This copy is quoted as follows:

Entrusted by the King of Holland Bolian [William], the Dukes of the Country of Ba [Commissioners-general of Batavia], who also administer the local affairs of the Island of Niu [Cape of Good Hope] and Gongbanya [Compnay] and other places, Nilvmaolu [Nederburgh], Woliding [Alting], Bolijinian [Frijkenius], Shimeili [Siberg] and others, present this letter in kowtow: Your Excellency the Governor-general, we recall that for more than a hundred years, our fiefdom has maritime trade with the provinces that are currently under Your Excellency's dominion and we have abundantly received Your Excellency's condescending kindness. We have indeed witnessed that the sacred blessings have been granted far and wide so that all the outlying territories have submitted to the civilizing influence. Next year we shall respectfully witness the 60th anniversary of His Sacred Majesty on the throne, and the entire world will respectfully celebrate the longevity of the sovereign. This is really a period of peace for the whole world and felicity for all the countries. Examining former history and inspecting the present, [we find that] there has never been a more prospering time than this one. I, William, although far away in a distant region, upon hearing this news, must show my sincerity. I have therefore respectfully sent Yusongdisheng [Titsingh], who holds the office of Xilili [Edeleer] and co-administers the Gongbanya [Company], as my chief envoy, and Banwunan Houyi [van Braam Houckgeest], the Guangban Helan [Head of the Dutch factory in Canton] in Your Excellency's dominion, as the deputy envoy, to jointly proceed to the palace to respectfully celebrate the longevity of the sovereign, and to congratulate the Heir-apparent for His Royal Highness's enthronement in the coming year. We wish His Royal Highness the universal peace of all the countries and the grand good fortune of a thousand years. In case my envoys are negligent in etiquette, I shall be grateful if Your Excellency bears with them and instructs them how to behave properly so that they will not commit any errors. In case anything untoward should happen to my chief envoy, the deputy shall replace him. When my ship arrives, I plead for Your Excellency's condescending care, for which I shall be extremely grateful. When it is time to put down my thoughts on paper, they just fly away, so I will not go into details, but just pray that Your Excellency will cast a luminous glance on this letter.[25]

The above-quoted two letters have some wording differences, but the tone remains the same. As for names of people, their titles, and places, they are obscure and difficult to understand. Thanks to the textual research of the famous Dutch sinologist Duyvendak (1889–1954), we can gain a better understanding.[26] The following is a brief explanation taken from Duyvendak's article:

1 The King of Holland "Bolian" should be the Prince of Orange. The name "William" is pronounced as "Bolian" in Hokkien.
2 The Dukes of the Country of Ba refer to the Commissioners-general of Batavia.
3 "Niuyu," which refers to the Cape of Good Hope, is a translated name combining sound and meaning. The pronunciation of the word "niu" in Hokkien is similar to the English word "good." As for the other four names mentioned in the letters, Nilvmaolu is Sebastiaan Cornelis Nederburgh, Woliding is Willem Arnold Alting, Bolijinian is Simon Hendrik Frijkenius, and Shimeili is Johannes Siberg.
4 With regard to "Xilili," it is an interesting transcription of the word "edeleer." Titsingh was a member of the Council of India, and those who held this position in Java were respectfully designated as "Edeleer" [the Right Honorable], and that explains why he was addressed this way.
5 Regarding "Guangban Helan" and "Banwunan Houyi," it is just another transcription for van Braam Houckgeest [the other one is Fan Balan]. Here, "Ban" stands for "Van," "wunan" for "Braam," and "Houyi" for "Houckgeest." As for "Guangban Helan," it refers to his official position at that time, the supercargo of the VOC in Canton.
6 The word "my ship" in the second letter refers to the *Siam* that brought the embassy to China.

In both the "memorial" to the emperor and the "statement" to the governor-general, the two Dutch letters mentioned the issue of "etiquette," the ceremony of "three kneelings and nine kowtows" which has been much discussed in the relation between China and the West during the Qianlong and Jiaqing period. As to how the governor-general of Guangdong and Guangxi provinces "instructed them [the Dutch envoys] to behave properly," thus paving the way for their visit to Beijing, it will be explained in the following section.

Changlin and "Receiving the Imperial Edict at the Haizhuang Temple"

Changlin, the governor-general of Guangdong and Guangxi provinces who received the Dutch mission, was a fairly accomplished official who showed his talent in governing the coastal areas in the late Qianlong era. Zhaolian, his contemporary, said that he "gained his fame as a competent official governing both Guangdong and Guangxi provinces." Zhaolian offered the following description about Changlin's life experience, achievements, and personality:

> Minister Changlin,[27] courtesy name Mu'an, was a descendant of Emperor Jingzuyi. He became an imperial scholar (*jinshi*) at the end of the 40th year of Qianlong [1775/1776]. Previously working in the central government, he was later promoted to be a governor. Smart in nature, he served as a high-ranking provincial official in different provinces, and was well-known for being honest and wise. When he served as the governor of Jiangsu province, he ordered to have robbers and thugs captured, and forbade extravagance. He often went around streets and alleys to investigate the living situation of the locals in his personal capacity, and then ate at a noodle shop. This has become an anecdote popular among the local residents.
>
> I was on duty with him in the imperial palace, and I asked him about visiting people in his personal capacity. I said something like this: you are a high-ranking official and common people all know you, so I am afraid this action of yours might not change the reality. But he said: "Jiangsu has a cunning and treacherous local custom, so I want people here to know that I often make private visits among them, which can serve as a warning to everyone." His reply sounded really convincing to me.
>
> Changlin was fair-skinned, long-bearded, handsome in appearance, and elegant in his speech. One might have forgotten his fatigue even if he talked to him all day long. People were also happy to befriend him. However, he had a taste for luxury and had bought thousands of private houses, which joined streets and alleys together. Tieyeting, the minister of personnel (*zhongzai*), once tried to persuade him, but he responded that "I have been an official in places away from the capital for a long time, and I know that I have bought too many houses, but if in the future I can make people on this street know that Governor-general Chang once lived here, that will be enough." Well, he was undoubtedly good at rejecting advice.[28]

This smart, elegant, and luxury-loving governor-general of Guangdong and Guangxi provinces, not long after he took office, had to handle the matter concerning the Dutch "tribute." The official reception he arranged for the Dutch mission took place on 13 October 1794. The ceremony must have taken place in the morning, as evidenced by Wang Wengao's poetic lines: "The morning saw the governor acting on the emperor's edict," and "The chiming of the dawn bell ushered in a royal guard of honor." As for the venue, following the arrangement of receiving the Macartney mission, it was arranged at a Buddhist temple instead of an official office. Regarding the reason for this arrangement, Changlin told Titsingh that it was not customary to receive foreign guests at the official office and that he had likewise received Lord Macartney in the same temple when the latter returned from

Beijing in December of the previous year.²⁹ Then why was the Haizhuang Temple chosen as a meeting place?

The Haizhuang Temple is located on the south bank of the Pearl River in Canton, across the river from the Thirteen Hongs, a business area where Chinese merchants and foreigners traded. It was one of the famous temples in Lingnan in the Qing dynasty. As described by Ruan Yuan in the *General Chorography of Guangdong* (*Guangdong tongzhi*):

> The Haizhuang Temple, situated in the south of the river [the Pearl River], is a blessed area in Wansongling. It was the location for the Qianqiu Temple in the Southern Han dynasty. After being abandoned for some time, it became a residential house. Later, Monk Guangmu solicited donations from Guo Longyue [the land owner] who offered this place. After some restoration and renovation, it was named "Haizhuang." When Monks Chiyue and Jinwu were abbots here, Buddhist halls, sutra chambers and an abbot's chamber were built one after another. In the 11th year of Emperor Kangxi [1672/1673], the king of Pingnan helped to build the Hall of the Heavenly Kings, and later, the temple gate was built by Governor Liu Bingquan. The eagle-claw orchids in the temple, which were planted by the previous owner, grow luxuriantly although the land has been turned into a temple. And because of the orchids, a pavilion was built here. Sutra chambers are magnificent and bodhisattva statues are more majestic than those in other temples.³⁰

On 15 October 1794, that is, the third day after the reception, Changlin wrote a memorial to ask for further instruction from Emperor Qianlong:

> We will immediately arrange for the tribute envoy Titsingh to have the audience. It is reported that the tribute envoy looked towards the direction of the imperial palace in the north, knelt three times and kowtowed nine times, and said in prostration, "The King of Holland, Weilin Hualanzhi Nasou [William of Orange-Nassau] has admired the great emperor's benevolence and virtue for a long time. But the long distance between Holland and the Celestial Empire makes it hard for him to get the news early whenever there is a celebration. And because he lives in a remote place overseas, he has no idea about the rituals and customs of the Celestial Empire and does not dare to act in a rash and presumptuous way. But the king has arranged for four officials, including Nedebo [Nederburgh], who is in charge of national affairs, to inquire around Batavia, so that when there is any news about a celebration in the Celestial Empire, they would inform the king on the one hand and prepare the tribute on the other, and then send officials to Guangdong without delay. Recently, Nederburgh and the other officials in Batavia have heard that a great celebration will take place next year in honor of the great emperor's sixtieth year on the throne. If they had returned to their country to prepare documents and tribute, they would certainly have been late and

missed the celebration, as Batavia is more than 100,000 *li* away from the Celestial Empire. So they chose to inform their king while at the same time, obeying their monarch's order, prepared memorial and credential documents on behalf of the king, and respectfully got the tribute ready. Then they immediately dispatched the Grand Chief (*da toumu*) Titsingh as tribute envoy from Batavia to Guangdong province, requesting me and other officials to submit a memorial for them, begging Your Majesty for the favor of allowing them to go to the capital to kowtow and offer congratulations." We noticed that he spoke in an obedient and respectful manner, so following usual practice, we first respectfully read the imperial decree to them, rewarded them with a banquet, and properly accommodated the tribute envoy, then we respectfully presented this memorial to request Your Majesty's imperial edict. If by Your Majesty's grace, they are permitted to have an audience at the imperial court, we can order them to depart from Guangdong, probably in the 10th month of this year, so that they can arrive at the capital in the 12th month of this year to join the officials of other foreign countries in kowtowing with sincerity to Your Majesty for the celebration. Or we can let him stay and wait respectfully in Guangdong until Your Majesty's birthday comes next year. Then we will arrange for him to go to the capital. Or we can submit the tribute memorial on his behalf. If there is no need for the tribute envoy to enter the capital, we will respectfully follow Your Majesty's imperial edict.[31]

The meeting at the Haizhuang Temple was a key factor in determining whether the Dutch mission could go up to the capital from Guangdong. From the above-quoted memorial, it can be said that both sides achieved the expected goal. Titsingh justified why they "prepared memorial and credential documents on behalf of the king" and therefore won the understanding from the local governor, and eliminated the doubts arising from the signature on the "gold leaf memorial." Changlin, on the other hand, succeeded in "instruct[ing] them how to behave properly" as the Dutch envoys tamely "looked towards the direction of the imperial palace in the north, knelt three times and kowtowed nine times"[32] which was believed to uphold the prestige of the "Celestial Empire." After Changlin "respectfully presented this memorial to request [the] imperial edict," he finally won the emperor's approval, which enabled Titsingh and his entourage to visit the imperial court in time.

"A Feast Held amid the Flowers" and the Wu Family of Hong Merchants

After the Dutch mission's "receiving the imperial edict at the Haizhuang Temple," Changlin immediately "rewarded them with a banquet," although he himself did not attend. Wang Wengao's poem describes the feast as "Music from jade *xiao* and gold *guan* can be heard across blooms, / a feast is held amid the flowers that stand around like ravishing screens." This is really a lively scene, in sharp contrast with the pure world of Sanskrit sounds. Regarding the place where the banquet was held, the Dutch source provides a clear record: "After the interview the ambassadors were entertained at an Imperial banquet in the adjoining garden of the Hong merchant Lopqua [Wu], where Macartney had lodged during his stay in Canton."[33] For this garden-like building, George Leonard Staunton described it as follows:

> Its quarters consisted of separate buildings sufficiently spacious and convenient. Some of them were fitted up in the English manner, with glass windows and fire-grates. The use of the latter was then found, in the winter solstice, to be very comfortable, though in a situation bordering upon the tropic. A large garden with ponds and parterres surrounded the buildings. On one side of them was a temple,[34] and on the other, a high edifice, the top of which commanded a view of the river and shipping, as well as of the city and the country to a considerable distance.[35]

The garden-like building south of the Pearl River, where the Dutch and English embassies lodged, was the estate of the Wu family which had generations of Hong merchants. The names and owners of this estate are roughly as follows: (1) Nanxi Bieshu, located in Wansongyuan of Anhai, near the present-day Xixia Street. Within this residence, there was the famous Baolun Hall. The owner was Wu Bingyong, who had used the courtesy names of Xuzhi and Dongping. Born in Nanhai [now Canton], he became a tribute student (*gongsheng*) and then worked as an official in Yuecanglidao of Hunan province. He was the author of *Poems Written at the Mountain Hut Striving for Excellence as that of Ziyuan and Ziyun* (*Yuan yun mo miao shanfang shichao*). (2) Qinghuichi guan, located in Wansongyuan of Anhai. This estate had been owned by Wu Pinghu, a native of Nanhai, who was also a member of the Wu family, before it was transferred to Wu Chongyao. (3) Tingtaolou, owned by Wu Yuanhua, whose courtesy name was Liangyi, art name Chunfan, a member of the Wu family. He was good at painting and known for his rich collection of calligraphy, paintings, and stone inscriptions. He was the author of *Manuscripts from Yanhui Hall* (*Yanhui lou yin gao*). (4) Yueyatang, located in Anhai, leaning against Wulonggang, and facing the Pearl River, with Shuzhuyong stream flowing around the residence. Inside this estate, there were ponds, hills, and stone bridges of considerable size. The owner was called Wu Chongyao, whose original name was Wu Yuanwei, with a courtesy name Liangfu, and art name Ziyuan. He was the owner of Yihe Hang, one of the Thirteen Hongs. He was confirmed as a provincial graduate (*juren*) by the emperor himself and later appointed provincial administration commissioner (*buzheng shi*).[36] The owner had a rich collection of books and he really loved block printing. Because of the books he printed such as *The Surviving Works from Lingnan* (*Lingnan yishu*) and *Collection of Works from Yueyatang* (*Yueyatang congshu*), this residence became well known throughout the country.

Wu's Residence had a beautiful scenery of pavilions, water, and rocks, and it was rich in culture. No wonder it was chosen as the venue for a royal banquet. During the reigns of Emperor Jiaqing and Emperor Daoguang, the area around Wansongyuan and the Haizhuang Temple became an officially designated place for foreigners to visit. This makes good sense, given the historical background of this place.

The Dutch Mission's Journey to the Capital

Shortly after the imperial edict was read and the bestowed banquet was held, there came the emperor's order from Beijing:

> Changlin and other officials reported that the Netherlands sent an envoy to present a document and pay tribute, begging to come to the capital to kowtow and present his congratulations, which is really good. Reading the translated version of the original document, as submitted by Changlin and others, [I learned that] the king of the said country, considering that the following year is the 60th anniversary of my ascension to the throne, which is an occasion for universal celebration, has specially arranged for a tribute envoy to come to the capital with a document and to congratulate in prostration. The feelings and expressions are extremely submissive. Because their document was issued under the names of gongban dachen [company officials] Nedebo [Nederburgh] and others who acted for their king, which somewhat deviates from our statutory practice, Changlin and other officials have questioned them again and again. What need is there to go deep into this matter? We should allow him to come to the capital for an audience so that his passionate admiration can be satisfied. Now I order Changlin and others to convey my decree to that envoy to let him know about this, and then appoint some reliable officials to escort him on the journey. It is preferable that he can arrive at Beijing one or two days before the government offices are closed on the 20th day of the 12th month, so that he can join princes and dukes from Mongolia and ambassadors from various foreign countries for banquets and presents. Orders should also be sent to the provinces he will pass along the way, and have governors-general and local governors to coordinate with each other and dispatch officials to take care of him in accordance with regulations so that he can arrive in Beijing in due time. Also, as the document submitted by the Netherlands cannot be read by any foreigner residing at Beijing, I order Changlin and others to look for people who know Dutch and Chinese among the Westerners living in the interior and send one or two of them to Beijing in the suite of the embassy, so that they may act as interpreters. Respect this.[37]

On 20 November 1794, Changlin, the governor-general of Guangdong and Guangxi provinces, and other officials saw off the Dutch mission at the Haizhuang Temple. On 22 November 1794, they set off from Canton by waterway, and the first part of their journey was done in 30 boats. The mission was made up of 27 persons, including the envoy and the deputy envoy, as well as de Guignes the younger who acted as an interpreter, J. H. Bletterman who was a doctor, C. H. Petitpierre-Boy who was a Swiss watchmaker, two Malay servants, and a body-guard of 11 soldiers.[38]

The Chinese escort officials included Circuit Intendant (*daoyuan*) Wang Shiji, Assistant Regional Commander (*canjiang*) Mingshan, Department Magistrate (*zhizhou*) Zhao Hongwen, Assistant Brigade Commander (*shoubei*) Zhang Yongcheng, and five other officials including registrars (*jingli*) and squad leaders (*bazong*).[39]

Wang Shiji and Zhao Hongwen were friends of the poet Wang Wengao who was proud of them for taking on this important task. In order to see them off, Wang Wengao wrote a poem entitled "Sending off Circuit Intendant Wang Xiangyu and Department Magistrate Zhao Zaoting[40] Who Escort the Dutch Tribute Envoy to the Capital," which is included in the *Collected Poems from Yunshan Hall*, volume one. The poem reads:

> Together you are escorting the tribute envoy for an audience in the palace,
> two types of flags are intermingled and cast their reflections on the waters of the Qujiang.[41]
> Against the Shao Rock,[42] we happily enjoy grand music piece by piece,
> soon you will leave me to wait for the envoys, and I can only ask postmen to send plum blossoms to indicate that you are the very friends that I miss.
> With tribute envoy paying homage to the emperor, and receiving imperial care,
> we know that ten thousand countries admire our emperor, the source of our happiness.
> After following others to congratulate longevity in an auspicious atmosphere,
> you should wait a little longer to be the first visitors to the royal garden in spring, which is a bliss.

Conclusion

The Canton port in the Qing dynasty was a frontier of trade and cultural exchange between China and the West. That is why both local poets in Lingnan and poets from other provinces who came to Guangdong to serve as officials expressed varying degrees of interests in foreigners, foreign business, or exotic products from the West. By the eighteenth century, there even had emerged a theme of "foreign aura" in Lingnan poetry. Although we cannot sense an open mind from these poems, they did show a broader vision and to some extent a fresh atmosphere of that time.

In *Collected Poems from Yunshan Hall*, Wang Wengao claimed that "70% of them are sentimental poems." Indeed, his historical poems centering around the Dutch tribute do reveal a scholar-official's feelings about "foreign aura." Although the lines such as "guests from an exotic land have come to the imperial court to send congratulations" and "we know that ten thousand countries admire our emperor, the source of our happiness" are heavily branded with laudatory marks of "tribute" ode, his account of receiving the imperial edict, holding the banquet and the following departure can well support the historical facts and visualize the experience of the Dutch mission in Canton.

Because of the arrangement by Changlin, the governor-general of Guangdong and Guangxi provinces, the non-governmental estates of the Haizhuang Temple and Wu's Residence developed a connection with "the Dutch tribute" in the history of Sino-Dutch diplomacy, which is really surprising. But it is quite intriguing to see official affairs carried out in civil residences. In the prosperous Qianlong era of feudalism, this was not an indication of the government's favor for the religious and the rich, but a burden of inescapable servitude.

Notes

1 In May 1996, China Social Sciences Press published *Proceedings of the Symposium on the Bicentenary of the Sino-British Diplomatic Relations* which include 22 papers by Chinese, British, American, French and German scholars. In August 1996, China International Culture Press Limited published *Archives and Historical Materials of British Envoy Macartney's Visit to China*, compiled by the First Historical Archives of China, with a total of 605 pages.
2 Lingnan is a geographic area referring to the lands in the south of the Wuling [Literally "Five Mountains"]. The region covers the modern Chinese subdivisions of Guangdong, Guangxi, Hainan, Hong Kong, and Macau. The "Lingnan school of poetry" was formed by poets who mostly came from this area. In the Ming dynasty, it was listed as one of the great schools of poetry in China. —Trans.
3 Yuan Xingyun, 1765.
4 With regard to the Qing official headwear, it should be noted that an official's rank decided the color and shape of the hat finial as well as the number of "eyes" (with one to three "eyes") attached to his peacock feather. The "coral finial" in this line indicates that the wearer was a second-rank official. —Trans.
5 The embroidered crane on the court robe was a rank badge that identified a first-rank civil official in the Qing dynasty. A four-clawed-dragon court robe could only be worn by the royal family and high-ranking officials in the Qing dynasty. —Trans.
6 Both the *xiao* and the *guan* are Chinese musical instruments. The former is a vertical end-blown flute, which is often made of bamboo, while the latter is an ancient wind instrument made of jade. Like a flute, the guan has six holes. —Trans.
7 Wang Wengao, vol. 1.
8 Boxer, 1988: 3–4.
9 Staunton, 123.
10 Zhao Yi, vol. 4.
11 One *Polan* 婆兰 was about 300 catties.
12 Zhao Yi, 1997: 334.
13 Boxer, 1988: 69.
14 *Duqiang* [literally "single high mast"], *Niutou* [literally "bullhead"], and *Liaohe* [literally "a boat of a considerable size that travels over water"], all refer to ships, of which *Duqiang* has the largest loading capacity, carrying cargo of 1,000 *Polan*. What comes next is *Niutou*, and then *Liaohe*. — Trans.
15 *Shegao*, often called *Shexiangao* or simply *Shexian*, is a kind of Chinese herbal medicine for treatment of fever, cough, ulcer, and erysipelas. It is said that it can make broken fingers grow back. — Trans.
16 Probably, in Wang Wengao's time, people believed that the use of alkaline water could prevent ship hulls from rotting. — Trans.
17 Linghai refers to the area of Guangdong and Guangxi provinces, as this place is adjacent to Wuling in the north and the South China Sea in the south. — Trans.
18 Jörg, 201.

19 Liang Tingnan, vol. 3.
20 Duyvendak, 93–94.
21 Boxer, 1988: 29.
22 Judging from the transliteration of the characters, it is inferred that the translator might have come from Fujian.
23 For the name "Zhu Geqiao," Duyvendak believes that it is not a person's name. Rather, it should be interpreted as a phonetic rendering of the word "secretary," as the Hokkien word for "secretary" has a similar pronunciation to that of Chu Ko-chiao. See Duyvendak, 31, note 1. —Trans.
24 This translation, with some changes, is based on Duyvendak's rendering in his essay "The Last Dutch Embassy to the Chinese Court (1794–1795)." See Duyvendak, 30–31. —Trans.
25 This translation refers to the same essay by Duyvendak. See Duyvendak, 36–37. —Trans.
26 Duyvendak, 1938: 29–30.
27 In the Ming and Qing dynasties, an academician of the Grand Secretariat was honored as a Xiangguo [minister]. Changlin was Assistant Grand Secretary, so he could be honorably addressed as a minister. —Trans.
28 See the entry entitled "Mu'an Xiangguo" ("Minister Mu'an") in Aixinjueluo Zhaolian, *Miscellaneous Records of Whistling Pavilion (Xiaoting zalu)*, vol. 3.
29 Boxer, 1988: 14–15.
30 Quoted in Huang Foyi, *A Historical Survey of Guangzhou City and its Surrounding Areas (Guangzhou chengfang zhi)*, vol. 6.
31 Liang Tingnan, vol. 3.
32 In van Braam's book *An Authentic Account of the Embassy of the Dutch East-India Company, to the Court of the Emperor of China, in the Years 1794 and 1795*, there is a figure captioned "Haizhuang Temple Ceremony, 1794" as well as a description about the ritual.
33 Boxer, 1988: 15.
34 This refers to the Haizhuang Temple which was called "Temple in the South of the River" by foreigners.
35 Staunton, 431.
36 Huang Guosheng, 43.
37 Liang Tingnan, vol. 3.
38 Boxer, 1988: 15–16.
39 "List of rewards prepared by the Council of State for those officials who have escorted the Dutch envoys," in Gugong bowuyuan, eds., *Collection of Documents (Wenxian congbian)*, vol. 5.
40 Wang Xiangyu and Zhao Zaoting were the courtesy names of Wang Shiji and Zhao Hongwen. —Trans.
41 Qujiang was a county in Guangdong province. —Trans.
42 The Shao Rock was located in Qujiang county. —Trans.

Bibliography

Aixinjueluo Zhaolian. *Xiaoting zalu (Miscellaneous Records of Whistling Pavilion)*, with a supplement in 3 volumes. Beijing: Zhonghua shuju, 1997.

Boxer, Charles Ralph. *Dutch Merchants and Mariners in Asia, 1602–1795*. London: Variorum Reprints, 1988.

Duyvendak, Jan Julius Lodewijk. "The Last Dutch Embassy to the Chinese Court (1794–1795)." *T'oung Pao* 34, no.1 (1938): 1–137.

Gugong bowuyuan, ed. *Wenxian congbian* (*Collection of Documents*), vol. 5. Beijing: National Palace Museum, 1930.

Huang Foyi. *Guangzhou chengfang zhi* (*A Historical Survey of Guangzhou City and its Surrounding Areas*). Guangzhou: Guangdong renmin chubanshe, 1994.

Huang Guosheng. "Qingdai Guangzhou de yuanlin dizhai (Gardens and Residents in Guangzhou during the Qing Dynasty)." *Lingnan wenshi*, no. 4 (1997): 41–45.

Jörg, Christiaan J. A. *Porcelain and the Dutch China Trade*. The Hague: Martinus Nijhoff, 1982.

Liang Tingnan. *Yuedao gongguo shuo* (*The Foreign Tributes via Guangdong Province*). Beijing: Zhonghua shuju, 1993.

Qu Dajun. *Guangdong Xinyu* (*A New Encyclopedia of Guangdong*). Beijing: Zhonghua shuju, 1985.

Ruan Yuan, ed. *Guangdong tongzhi* (*General Chorography of Guangdong*). Shanghai: Shanghai guji chubanshe, 1990.

Staunton, George Leonard. *The Authentic Account of an Embassy from the King of Great Britain to the Emperor of China.* Translated by Ye Duyi. Hong kong: Xianggang sanlian shudian, 1994.

Wang Wengao. *Yunshantang shiji* (*Collected Poems from Yunshan Hall*). Hangzhou: Zhejiang shuju, 1888.

Yuan Xingyun. *Qingren shiji xulu* (*Anthology of Qing Dynasty Poems*). Beijing: Wenhua yishu chubanshe, 1994.

Zhao Yi. *Oubei ji* (*Collected Writings of Oubei*). Shanghai: Shanghai guji chubanshe, 1997.

Zhao Yi. *Yanpu zaji* (*Miscellaneous Notes from Under the Exposed Eave*). Beijing: Zhonghua shuju, 1982.

19 Chinese Workers in Southeast Asia Before 1912

In the late nineteenth century when capitalism progressed from free competition to imperialist monopoly, Western colonialists turned to Southeast Asia for the economic resources, thereby deepening and expanding their economic exploitation in this region.

In 1870, under the impetus of the industrial bourgeoisie, the Dutch government changed its management of the Indonesian colony, and replaced the forced cultivation system that had been in effect for 40 years bringing 900 million guilders in profits, with decrees such as the Sugar Law and the Agrarian Laws. This facilitated the influx of huge amounts of capital into Indonesia. As a result, in metropolitan regions such as Java and Madura, large plantations sprang up in succession. On peripheral islands, this was even more prominent.

As for Malaya, it had long attracted the attention of Britain on account of its rich economic resources. As competition among capitalist countries intensified, Malaya's position in the British economic system became increasingly important. Thus, in 1863, the British government changed the Straits Settlements (including Singapore, Penang and Malacca), which were formerly controlled by the governor-general of Bengal, into a Crown colony; and in 1895, it forced Perak, Selangor, Negeri Sembilan, and Pahang to form the Federated Malay States. Political control paved the way for economic plunder. These measures both reflected the need and foreshadowed the arrival of large-scale extortion.

But both in Indonesia and Malaya, plantation owners and mine proprietors faced a labor shortage. This happened for the following reasons. First, in Indonesia, the process of encroachment on cultivated land in peripheral islands had not been as rapid as in Java and Madura, and therefore, local farmers were not so bankrupt that they had to sell their labor. They "would rather live a half-starving life as farmers and hunters than accept the servile terms to toil in the mines and plantations of the Europeans."[1] As for Java and Madura:

> Although there was a large surplus of labor force in Java, Javanese workers were not welcome to work on other islands, because Dutch plantation owners feared the consequent increase in local wages. That is why plantation owners in Sumatra adopted the method of recruiting Chinese workers.[2]

Second, in Malaya:

> For a long time, British colonists had hardly employed Malay farmers in tin mines or plantations. Until the Second World War, such work had been left to Chinese and Indian laborers imported by the British colonists. This shows that the Malayan farmers were still strongly attached to the land during this period. Also relevant is the fact that the Malayan population was small and they lived in areas far away from tin mines and plantations.[3]

It is no coincidence that both Dutch and British colonialists chose China as a source of labor supply. After the Opium War, in the rural areas of China, as the combination of agriculture and cottage industry became increasingly loose, the combination of agricultural labor and means of production gradually entered a significant state of forced separation. As a result, a group of bankrupt farmers emerged, which constituted the main labor source for other production fields.[4] As Engels said:

> The war in China has given the death blow to the old China. Isolation has become impossible; the introduction of railways, steam-engines, electricity and modern large-scale industry has become a necessity, if only for reasons of military defense. But with it the old economic system of small peasant agriculture, where the family also made its own industrial products itself, falls to pieces too, and with it the whole old social system which made a relatively dense population possible. Millions will be turned out and forced to emigrate; and these millions will find their way even to Europe, and en masse.[5]

This explains why ordinary Chinese went abroad to make a living. The explanation is generally applicable to the "pigs" (*zhuzai*) but does not touch upon their miserable fate of being plundered, cheated, and sold abroad. Here, what should be pointed out in particular is that, oppressed by Western capitalist states, the feudal government of the Qing dynasty was so weak that it failed to maintain the labor force, which was essential to the feudal system. Prohibitions were issued, but to no avail. Even if there were protests, they were nothing but a change of tune to beg for mercy. In practice, the "subjects" of the Qing government still had to be "whipped, branded, tortured by laws grotesquely terrible, into the discipline necessary for the wage system."[6]

The above explains why the Dutch and British colonialists turned to China to plunder the labor force. As for how this was carried out, we need to trace it back to these colonialists' predecessors from whom they directly inherited this vile tradition. As Marx pointed out:

> Holland was the head capitalistic nation of the 17th century. [...] Nothing is more characteristic than their system of stealing men, to get slaves for Java. The men stealers were trained for this purpose. The thief, the interpreter, and the seller, were the chief agents in this trade, native princes the chief sellers.

The young people stolen, were thrown into the secret dungeons of Celebes, until they were ready for sending to the slave ships.[7]

The British colonists did the same. It is recorded that "in 1662, an African company was established for the sole purpose of capturing blacks to be sold as slaves. To rob and enslave blacks in an ordered way, the British established fixed outposts in Gambia and the Gold Coast."[8] In the nineteenth century, the blacks were replaced by "pigs" in the southeast coast of China, "human traffickers" became "pig brokers" (*zhuzai tou*), and "fixed outposts" were similar to "pig houses" (*zhuzai guan*). Despite the change in characters and settings, the directors were the same as before – the Dutch and British colonists, the two veterans of human trafficking. Like what happened 200 years ago, this "traditional play" revived in China was also "written in the annals of mankind in letters of blood and fire."[9]

After a brief analysis of the historical background of the "pig" trade, it is necessary to look at the meaning and alias of the word "pig." There are quite a few Chinese documents on this subject, some of which are listed below. According to the supplementary note in the revised *Annals of Xiangshan county* (*Xiangshan xianzhi*), volume 22, which was completed in 1879:

> Since the peace agreement, the anti-drugs movement has slackened off. Unable to make profits from franchised business, foreign businessmen in Macau gradually fell into poverty. At this time, the Peruvian and Cuban merchants bought Chinese to work as enslaved laborers, calling them 'pigs.'

In *A Description of Singapore* (*Xinjiapo fengtu ji*) finished in 1887, Li Zhongjue wrote:

> Over the past two decades, Westerners have been recruiting laborers for farming work, causing a rapid rise in the labor cost. Thus some people started the business of selling people abroad, calling it 'selling pigs.' They set up offices in Macau and openly engaged in human trafficking. People in coastal areas were either cheated or forced into foreign vessels and loaded aboard as if they were big or small pigs.

Guo Songtao, in his memorial entitled "Request for modification of the regulation about human trafficking in Guangdong" ("Guangdong daofan kenqing biantong tiaoli banli shu") stated:

> As the British and French adventurers reclaimed islands of Southeast Asia (*Nanyang*), a large number of workers were needed and recruited. Some treacherous people sought profit by selling laborers. After repeated cases without severe punishment, human trafficking became increasingly rampant. Being coerced or enticed, dozens or even hundreds of ignorant people were shipped abroad and sold to foreigners for a high price. Those who were bought did not speak the foreign language, and they thought they were workers employed by

foreigners. Once they were shipped abroad, they could never be found again. These traffickers colluded and conspired with the shipowners, so there was no distinction between first offenders and accomplices. Laborers were locked up in the bottom of a vessel in dozens. It was called "selling pigs."[10]

As indicated above, the meaning of 'pig' is revealed in these two quotes: when "cheated or forced into foreign vessels," they were "loaded aboard as if they were big or small pigs," and "Laborers were locked up in the bottom of a vessel in dozens." Besides "pig," there are also four similar terms:

1. "New guest (*xin ke*)": The distinction between the "old guest" and the "new guest" was originally used to mark the order in which overseas Chinese went abroad, but in the late nineteenth century, the term "new guest" took on a specific content and became synonymous with "pig." This is evidenced by a Hakka folk song: "getting up early and taking a cold shower every morning, and in less than three years [the house] is full of new guests."
2. "Blue ticket guest (*Qingdan ke*)": It is said that,

> After pigs signed the contract prepared by recruiters, they were paid a certain sum of wages in advance. Then they were gathered in an inn and each was given a blue ticket, and that is how a 'blue ticket guest' came into being.[11]

3. "Indentured laborer."
4. "Coolie (*ku li*)": In the documents about Chaozhou, coolies are called "guli,"[12] and in Jinjiang folk songs, they are called "guili."[13] Both are translations of the Hindi word "hired worker" (kuli or coolie). The word "coolie" comes from the "Malabar coolie" as people from Malabar of India were the first to work in Malaya.[14] After this loanword was widely used, it became a fixed term to address indentured laborers in India, Indonesia, Malaya, Australia, Africa, and the Americas.[15]

Among these five appellations, I use "pigs" to refer to Chinese laborers, because this term is not only more primitive, expressive and familiar to the Chinese people, but more importantly, it reveals the anti-humanitarian nature of the "pig" trade in a profound way.

Recruiting Centers of the "Pig" Trade and Their Activities

In the early nineteenth century, the "pig" trade was still in its initial stage, and a complete trading net had not yet been established. Later, as the colonialists hastened their economic plundering, it became a regular need to supplement and expand the labor force in plantations and mines. This necessitated the establishment of regular offices to take on the task of recruiting large numbers of workers. In this context emerged "pig houses" that spread from abroad to China.

The following is a description of "pig" markets in chronological order. I will focus on foreign markets first.

As the largest center of the "pig" trade in Southeast Asia, Singapore was the place where most Chinese "pigs" were shipped and then transferred elsewhere.[16] Naturally, it became the base of "pig houses." Here, inns such as Luanxing, Wanyuanlong, Chengli, and Sidexing were engaged in selling "pigs." Most of those "pig houses" were controlled by heads of secret societies:

> [They] sought huge profits by force, without any mercy. New guests [pigs] were oppressed to the utmost. As they often sought escapement from the inns, the control here became more stringent. The rooms in an inn had high and tight windows, and people from the Three Dots Society (*Sandianhui* or *Sanxingdang*) were sent to guard the doors.[17]

The most famous "pig brokers" in Singapore were Liang Yabao and Mai Jun, both from secret societies.[18] Mai was the head of the Ghee Hin Kongsi (*Yixing hui*), an offshoot of the Three Dots Society. It is recorded that:

> He would send sampans to pick up 'pigs' when they arrived at Singapore. As he had guaranteed that these laborers could not escape, buyers paid him three to four dollars per head as a protection fee. Without his 'protection,' no one would dare to buy these 'pigs,' or there might be an escape.[19]

Another stronghold of "pig trade" in Southeast Asia was Penang. Every April or May, when the southwest monsoon on the Indian Ocean started, Chinese merchants hired vessels to sail from Penang to Macau or Xiamen and sent their agents to abduct ignorant residents. For each "new guest," an agent got a reward of one dollar. New guests were driven aboard a sailing vessel, and during the storm, they were nailed and chained at the bottom of the ship.[20] Chen De was the most powerful "pig broker" in Penang. He "was also the head of the Tua Pek Kong Society (*Dabogong hui*). 'New guests' who landed ashore were left in his 'care' until the handover was completed."[21]

When some heads of secret societies acted as managers of the "pig trade," the British colonialists were actually manipulators behind the scene. Since there was a division of labor, they did not run those "pig houses" in a direct way,[22] as this was more conducive to concealing their hypocrisy. In reality, they interfered in China's internal affairs through diplomatic means. The British consul in Guangzhou, for example, intervened with the governor-general's administration and forced him to withdraw the prohibition on selling "pigs" in the Circuit of Chao, Hui and Jia.[23] The British consul in Shantou, in his diplomatic note to Zhang Zhidong, embellished the practice of "credit-ticket system" (*shedan zhi*) in an attempt to trick Zhang into granting more convenient terms for the "pig trade." His note is as follows:

> As the British consul, I hereby explain about the credit-tickets, as I am afraid that the esteemed governor-general is not clear about the details. If someone has decided to go abroad but did not have money, we would give him

a ferry ticket on credit to facilitate his journey. When he lands in Singapore or Penang, we would let him first stay at a licensed inn. If this person has friends or relatives, they will pay for his travel expenses, ransom him, and then he can stay wherever he wants to; if this person has no friends or relatives, he can be ransomed by anyone, but only after the consent of this worker. Regarding the ransom fee, there is a fixed standard, therefore not a penny more can be charged. After ransoming this person, a broker will take the worker to the Chinese Protectorate, where his name, place of origin, age, and other information will be registered. As to where the worker plans to work, it is up to him, and nobody can force him. After the terms of agreement are made, the Protector explains the employment regulations paragraph by paragraph so that listeners understand everything. Then the contract is signed by the two parties in person. Brokers and recruiters are not allowed to have fraudulent behavior such as coaxing and luring, and if there is a need for investigation in the future, the registration book can provide the clues.[24]

There are two points that deserve a careful examination here. The first is about the fate of "pigs" after their arrival in Singapore. Based on his personal observation, Li Zhongjue described the situation in his book *A Description of Singapore* as follows:

For those Chinese who sought employment in Southeast Asia (*Nanyang*), after their arrival in Singapore, they would first be arranged to stay in an inn, which is actually a "pig house" run by an unscrupulous profiteer. For those who could afford their own travel expenses, nobody dared to mistreat them. But for those who had no money and rushed abroad for a living, the moment they stepped into an inn, they lost control of everything. Although this person was not necessarily abducted, he would fall into a trap in the end. The Chinese officials in Singapore wanted to clean it up from the source of the problem several times, but because of British officials behind this matter, they couldn't do it.

To have a better understanding of what is meant by "[a]lthough this person was not necessarily abducted, he would fall into a trap in the end," let me quote Xie Yudi, a native of Haiyang (now Chao'an) county. In a statement he submitted to the Chinese Protectorate in Singapore, he wrote:

This statement was written to beg the government to investigate the abduction of my own brother. My name is Xie Yudi, and I have a younger brother, formerly known as Xie Yurou. In the 11th month of 1889, he left Shantou and came to Singapore by ship. Since he did not find a fixed place to settle down, he stayed temporarily with relatives in Chwee Long Tow. During the second leap month of this year (1890), he went out, and unexpectedly he disappeared, without leaving any trace. After our friends and relatives helped to ask around, we are now fortunate enough to know his whereabouts. It is confirmed that on the 20th day of the second leap month of this year

[9 April 1890], he was deceived and taken away by two fellow countrymen, a man named Xie Tongqin and his brother Xie Tongzhu, into an inn under the control of Chengli. They changed his name to Xie Dengke and sold him to Sandakan as a servant.[25]

The second concerns the function of the Chinese Protectorate. From the report submitted by Zhang Zhidong's subordinates who visited the overseas Chinese in Southeast Asia, it is not difficult to see its real nature:

[It is] not registered with the Chinese Consular Office, neither does it liaise with the Office. Witnessing recruiting agents' fraudulent and deceptive practices, it does nothing to intervene or stop, thus losing its stated purpose of protection for Chinese laborers.[26]

In order to better observe how a Chinese laborer who just arrived in Singapore lost his personal freedom under the "protection" of the British colonial authorities and to reveal the malicious means of "pig" traffickers, I would like to quote Zhuang Dukan's statement so that we can hear the denouncement from a "pig":

My name is Zhuang Dukan. I was born in Jinjiang county, Quanzhou prefecture, Fujian province. Around the end of the ninth month of this year, I took a ship in Xiamen and went abroad to make a living. Arriving at Singapore in the early 10th month, I went ashore with the crowd. Then suddenly a couple of abducting bandits appeared. They came up to me, pretending to greet friends and relatives. As I was unfamiliar with this place, and did not know the way, so one of them took the chance to show concerns for me, asking me questions courteously, and offering to be my guide. Then he led me to the Luanxing Inn in the Kampong Malacca district and locked me in a secret room. Of course, I was terrified, and wanted to escape but I could not get out. The next day the trafficker brought me to the office of the British government. Before that, he coaxed me with sweet words, and taught me what to say, to which I agreed perfunctorily. When the British officer asked me if I was willing to work as an indentured laborer, I replied that I would not. The British officer immediately ordered the innkeeper to bring me back. What then happened was that the bandit locked me in another secret room, and beat me cruelly, telling me that if I said yes, I could live, and if no, I must die. Then he sprinkled the Western sulphuric acid onto my body and let it soak into my skin, putting me in a misery and pain that was indescribable and unbearable. I was just an ordinary person. After being subjected to all sorts of torture, I had no choice but to proclaim my willingness. Then I was taken into the ship and brought to a remote place in Deli and sold as a coolie.[27]

From what happened to Zhuang Dukan, we can see that, in the process of declaring a person to be a "pig," the British colonial government only asked him whether he was "willing" or not, regardless of any hidden reluctance. Therefore, in the Singapore "pig" market, there was a "theatrical double act" on show: a "pig" trafficker acted as an abductor, and the Chinese Protectorate was the one to approve. Obviously, what Zhang Zhidong's subordinates declared about its "losing its stated purpose of protection for laborers" was not quite right. The fact is, as long as the Chinese Protectorate legalized the "pig" trade by symbolically "touching the head" of a victim, it was considered to have completed its task. It must be noted that until the mid-twentieth century, the ghost of colonialism was still alive, and there were still people repeating the cliché of the British consul in Shantou:

> All Chinese workers must report to the Chinese Protectorate when they disembark in any commercial port in Malaya. The debt they owed from the vessel fare must be borne by themselves and registered in the record. The purpose of this procedure and other formalities is to prevent them from being cheated by traffickers who were appointed by secret societies and from being exploited by employers.[28]

But lies written in ink cannot hide facts written in blood. From their experience, "pigs" knew that the "Chinese Protectorate" was not a savior, and the British colonialists also proved themselves to be nothing but white-gloved murderers.

From 1864 to 1888, the "pigs" sent to Sumatra were transshipped at Malaya.[29] According to the *Donghua Chronicles of the Reign of Guangxu* (*Guangxu chao donghua lu*), Zhang Zhidong submitted a memorial in the 10th month of Guangxu [1887], which says:

> There are more than 10,000 Chinese emigrant workers[30] from Shantou and other places. They were first gathered in Shantou and then brought to Singapore and Penang. After British officials confirmed that they were willing to work as indentured laborers, they signed the contract in Chinese and then were sent to work in Deli.

The above quote shows that, with the British side involved, the "pig" trade in Sumatra at that time was not independent. As for "those who volunteered to become indentured laborers" after the confirmation by British officials, it was just another version of the "Zhuang Dukan" story. For example, at the beginning of 1877 in Singapore, "a large number of coolies were herded onto sailboats by armed men, transported to Sumatra and other areas, and brutally oppressed."[31] The Chinese contract mentioned here is the one recorded in the Straits Settlements' Labor Committee Report for the Sumatra Tobacco District in 1890, which states that "pigs" being transferred to Sumatra were "paid 30 dollars in advance at the time of signing the contract in the Straits Settlements, of which 19.50 was deducted for reimbursement of travel fare and other expenses, and the balance of 10.50 was paid in cash."[32] Since "pigs" recruited to the Strait Settlements and other states did not get cash in advance, this provision served as a bait, enabling the colonialists to use "lure" as a supplement to "coercion."

This indirect trade ensured a source of labor for Sumatra, but it forced local employers to pay a higher price. At that time:

> When a pig broker recruited one laborer from Chaozhou or Shantou to the Straits Settlements, the cost was just about 14 to 16 dollars. But when this laborer was transferred to east of Sumatra, Deli, or Borneo, someone who hired him had to pay 80 to 90 dollars. The majority of the benefit was earned by brokers.[33]

In order to relieve the burden of employers and protect them from the exploitation of brokers, the Dutch government sent an officer to Shantou in 1888 to sign a regulation about indentured laborers with Liao Weijie, the foreign affairs commissioner of the Qing dynasty. From then on, "pigs" were directly transported to Deli without detours to Singapore.[34]

As soon as the door of direct trade was opened, Dutch recruiting agencies immediately started to work in an unchecked and unrestrained way:

> Holland's Hotz S'Jacob and Company [a member of the Association of Deli Planters] acted as the head agency for the Dutch East Indies to buy pigs. Mines and tobacco plantations all entrusted this company with the transaction. It had branches in Hong Kong, Xiamen and Shantou.[35]
>
> Every year, Hotz S'Jacob and Company sent staff to Shantou, Beihai, Guangzhou, Zhaoqin and other places to recruit workers. After the completion of recruitment, these people would be sent abroad on a Dutch company's vessel and carried to Punjab to disembark.[36]

When "pig vessels" arrived, the Dutch colonial government gave special privileges to recruiters:

> When pigs were imported, they did not have to pay in full the landing tax of 150 guilders. Instead, they were given a special privilege to enjoy a 50% discount. As for passports and other routine formalities, they could be exempted.[37]

After landing, "pigs" were kept as prisoners. The *Donghua Chronicles of the Reign of Guangxu* records a memorial submitted by Yang Shiqi on 18 March 1908, which reads: "After their entry into a foreign country, Chinese workers were immediately imprisoned by foreigners. They were fed with coarse food, and they lived in thatched huts." The "thatched hut" here is known as the "lodge for new guests." The following description of a "lodge for new guests" in Tanjong Panlan [Tanjung Pandan] of Billiton [Belitung] enables one to take a look at the miserable life of "pigs." As soon as they set foot on the pier, the heavily armed Javanese soldiers stopped "pigs" with hemp ropes and took them in groups to a row of long bridge-style wooden houses surrounded by barbed wire: this "lodge for new guests" was modeled after a Dutch prison. Here "pigs" had to go through the following formalities: registration, fingerprinting, physical examination, and vaccination. As for the "coarse food," they were "brown rice mixed with lots of chaff and grain, rotten bean sprouts that stank of oil, and smelly salted fish that was scorched black by fire." "Pigs" had to live in such a "concentration camp" for five to seven days before they were sent to a work site:[38]

> If a Chinese worker was physically weak and was thus unqualified, or if this person was qualified but he was unwilling to work as an indentured laborer, in principle, Hotz S'Jacob and Company ought to have sent him back by ship and there should not have been any compulsion involved. However, if Hotz did send him back, it would lose a lot of money. So, whenever an unqualified worker was spotted, he would mostly be resold to somebody else as a gardener to grow pepper. It is definitely very rare to send someone back immediately.[39]

About this deceitful trick played by Hotz S'Jacob and Company, the officials of the Qing dynasty once tactfully reprimanded: "Recently, the Dutch government has continuously revised the regulations in order to show empathy for workers. But there are no practical benefits involved, so the overseas Chinese workers keep appealing [for a change]."[40]

From diplomatic efforts for direct recruitment to the centralized control after the import of "pigs," it is easy to see how the Dutch colonial government served the interests of mine proprietors and plantation owners, working as a political servant in the "piracy business" so that they could win the applause of the Dutch bourgeoisie.

After a brief description of the "pig" market abroad, now, let us look at how the domestic market was formed in China and how human traffickers cooperated with their overseas counterparts.

Before the Opium War, there had been "pigs" who were taken abroad from the coastal areas of Guangdong and Fujian.[41] But colonialists at that time mainly relied on raids and capture to get laborers to meet their urgent demands. The following historical data can prove this. On 16 August 1860, Qiling submitted a memorial that states:

> In Guangdong, foreigners enticed Chinese bandits into abducting people. They called this "buying pigs." It had been going on for a long time. Since their permitted entry into cities after 1857, this had become more rampant. But at that time, no trading house was set up, and they mostly lured and forced people aboard a barge. Once there were sufficient victims, they would sail away. More than 10,000 people have been abducted successively.[42]

Similar evidence can be found in the entry entitled "Shell Digging Song" ("Daxu ge") in Lin Dachuan's *Accounts along Han River* (*Hanjiang ji*), volume eight:

> During the first and second months of the eighth year of Xianfeng [1858], dozens of foreign ships came, buying people to work abroad. It is called

"going as a coolie" (*guo guli*). At the beginning, it was a fair transaction, then it became a luring trap, finally it became a captive robbery. The situation in the coastal area was even worse than that in the inland provinces. Coastal residents, whether they were sedan chair bearers, beggars or people digging shells along the beach, were all taken away. At that time, there was also a shell-digging song with the lyrics going like this: Come back, man! Come back, man! Stop making money from digging shells, as the "coolie catchers" (*guli zei*) are already in sight. Calling on each other to return, [you come home to hear] your wife's complaint that there is no rice for cooking, and you see your children crying because of hunger. If these robbers do not leave in a month, there will certainly be no more shell diggers along the beach.[43]

As can be seen from the passage above, "pig houses" had not yet appeared in China until around 1857. By 1876, however, there were around 20 to 30 "pig houses" in Shantou alone[44]. Therefore, it is possible that domestic "pig" markets were formed and developed in these two decades. There is no doubt that colonialist expansion was the catalyst. In the late 1840s, a huge tin mine was discovered in Larut which was developed in the 1850s; in the 1860s, the Billiton Maatschappij[45] with a capital of 5 million guilders started to mine in Larut; in the 1870s, companies like the Deli Tobacco Company (1870), the Deli-Batavia Company (1875), and the Tobacco Company Arendsburg (1877) were established, growing tobacco extensively. All of these put an immediate strain on the Malayan "pig" market, and correspondingly, domestic "pig houses" came into being, ensuring a continuous supply of labor. At that time, Shantou, Xiamen, and Haikou were the main domestic "pig" markets,[46] while Hong Kong and Macau were the transit cities for the exportation of "pigs."

The following is an overview of the "pig" trade in Shantou:

According to the evidence provided by eyewitnesses in the second year of Guangxu [1876], there were already around 20 to 30 trading houses in Shantou. The owners were informed by their customers in Singapore and Penang on a regular basis, thus they knew the updates about the coolie market in each port of the Strait Settlements. Following the guidance in the received report, they paid a considerable amount of money to the recruiters, entrusting them to recruit coolies from various villages in Guangdong to travel southward. They were also responsible for hiring vessels to send these laborers to the Straits Settlements. As for the travel expenses, they would charge the employers for reimbursement upon their arrival.[47]

About how a recruiter "recruit[ed] coolies from various villages [...] to travel southward," we can get a rough idea from the statement submitted to the county magistrate by Huang Wulong and Wu Tian, the natives of Yushi town, Song Xiu district, Haiyang (now called Chao'an) county. This document was later forwarded to the governor-general of Guangdong and Guangxi provinces, who mentioned this in his diplomatic protest to the Singapore government:

> Huang Shunxiao, a native of Gezhou town, spread the information that a foreigner in Penang was recruiting workers to plant sugarcane, and that each worker would be paid seven dollars per month, among which four dollars would go to this worker's family members in Shantou while the rest would be paid to the worker himself in Penang. Over 100 workers went there. Several months after their departure, there had not been any news about their safety. Recently, a fellow villager suddenly returned from work, and when asked for details, he said that workers had been brutally abused after arriving at Penang, and that they were hungry and desperate, living an unbearable life. Fortunately, he was able to escape back to his hometown and avoided a horrible death abroad. He also said that workers had been cheated by Huang Shunxiao, and they were already resold to other foreigners, with no hope of returning home.[48]

The "pig" trade left an indelible impression on the local residents. The related descriptions even went into a folk song of Chaozhou, called "Panic in My Heart" (*Xin huanghuang*), which vividly records the experience of Chaozhou workers going abroad, their life on the work site, and how they missed their family members. The song is as follows:

> With a panicking heart, I rushed to a trading house in Shantou. When the recruiter saw me, he asked me to come in and sit down, and then asked me if I wanted to go abroad. Sailing all the way to Shile Po [Singapore], I found no job at all. [Having no other way,] I signed to work in a mountain, praying to Elder Lord (Bogong)[49] to have pity on me and keep me safe. When it rains, I am soaked to the bone, when the sun comes out, I feel burnt inside and out. From morning to night, I carry thick fir trees on my shoulders. When the rooster crows, I go to take a shower, and after the shower, I start working again. Separated by the sea, I have no way to talk to my wife in Tangshan [China]! With two dollars, I send a letter to my wife, asking her not to worry, telling my son to help my wife, and ordering him not to gamble, to help with the farm work, to feed pigs, and wait until I earn enough money to return to Tangshan [China] so that we can be reunited.[50]

The statement cited above and this folk song, each from a different perspective, reveal two ways in which a person became a "pig" around Chaozhou and Shantou. The former describes how a recruiter went deep into the countryside, luring workers into a trap, and the latter depicts how a person threw himself into a trap and became a "pig." As for sending a letter "with two dollars," it reveals a life of blood and tears experienced by early overseas Chinese laborers.

Apart from Chaozhou and Shantou, human trafficking was also rampant in other prefectures and counties of Guangdong. According to the *Donghua Chronicles of the Reign of Guangxu*, Zhang Zhidong submitted a memorial on 20 February 1887, which states:

> I have been recently informed by prefectures and counties that cases of abduction happen almost every month. This is probably because Guangdong is a coastal province with many harbors and ports. Hong Kong and Macau are foreign settlements that are not subject to our laws or regulations. When fugitives on the run arrive here, they can board any ship and go wherever they want to go. Compared with the inland provinces, this place is easier for them to hide and avoid chase. Moreover, the price of selling a worker abroad is much higher than doing it inland. For those who are sold abroad, less than one or two out of a hundred are lucky enough to survive. People dying of this horrible and cruel death outnumber those in other provinces. When one person is abducted, the whole family is thrown into panic and misery. His parents may commit suicide because of this, and his family may disintegrate. People who go abroad suffer from hard labor, get trapped in a foreign land and lose their lives there. There is really no agency to appeal to and no place to rest their dead bodies.

The above-mentioned "price of selling a worker abroad," according to the "Price Board of New Guests" (*xinke pai*) in Singapore, fell into four types:

> Those who go to Deli to plant tobacco are sold for 120–130 dollars per head; those who go to Penang to grow sugarcane and plantains are sold for 60–70 dollars per head; those who go to Johor to reclaim wasteland are 50–60 dollars per head; and those who go to Singapore or Johor to grow gambir are 30–40 dollars per head.[51]

Abduction was certainly an important means used by recruiters to trap a large number of "pigs," but it was not the only way. Although some scholars wrote about the diversified sources of "pigs,"[52] none of them have mentioned convicted prisoners, although the latter only constituted a minor part of the entire "pig" population. The following is an excerpt from an official document written by Zhang Zhidong to the administrative authority (*niesi*) of Guangdong province on 13 June 1889,[53] discussing about sending convicted prisoners to work as indentured laborers in foreign countries:

> Excerpted report from Zuo Dao, magistrate (*zhixian*) of Shunde county: There are 102 convicted prisoners in our county [...] After I, your humble servant, had a discussion with our county's protector of sandy land (*husha*) and some of the local gentry, we had the following proposal. Employers in places near Singapore are now recruiting people to work at plantations, to dig rivers, and build roads. If we allow these convicted prisoners to go abroad to work as indentured laborers, they would undoubtedly find a way to make a

living [...] After the approval of Your Excellency, I will make arrangements to distribute clothes to these prisoners, and have them sent to Hong Kong under the supervision of county officers and guards arranged by protector of sandy land and the local gentry. In Hong Kong, they can be handed over to a trading house and then arranged to board a vessel to places like Singapore to work as laborers. When they are allowed to return ten years later, they can be exonerated.

Excerpted response from Zhang Zhidong: Approved [...] Extra care is needed so that foreigners cannot learn that these are Chinese criminals. Leaving a tiny trace is likely to start trouble [...] Shunde county handles this matter as proposed. For other prefectures or counties, they can imitate in an appropriate way, taking their own situations into consideration.

To sum up, the "pig" market in Southeast Asia first appeared in Malaya and later gradually expanded to Sumatra. In this vile and sordid trade, the Dutch colonial government acted in a blatant manner, while the British colonial government behaved more cunningly. This reflects different characteristics of the Dutch and British colonial empires: the former was known for its "villainy"[54] and the latter for being "flexible."[55] As for why secret societies in Southeast Asia acted as accomplices in the "pig" trade, it is not difficult to understand. For one reason, a secret society was a folk organization linked by religious superstition and organized by the patriarchal system. Although it had pursued mutual assistance in social life and waged struggles against oppression, it could be destructive as it was often blind in its fights and therefore easily manipulated and exploited by reactionary forces.[56] For another reason, secret societies in Southeast Asia were immersed in the colonial system that enhanced their awareness of exploitation, causing their human nature to be gradually eroded and their inherent weakness deepened. As a result, some heads of secret societies stood out and acted as leading figures of the "pig" trade. Manipulated and deployed by the Dutch and British colonialists, they became an endangering force in their society.

The domestic "pig" market was affiliated with the foreign market. Its emergence in the 1850s and 1870s not only resulted from the intensification of colonialists' economic plundering of Southeast Asia but also related to the crisis of domestic political rule at the time. This period coincided with the rise of the first revolutionary movement in modern Chinese history, and the conflict between the landowning and peasant classes unfolded into a huge outbreak: the Taiping Rebellion.[57] From the severe shock it suffered, the feudal government of the Qing dynasty realized that letting bankrupt peasants go abroad to work as indentured laborers could "quell civil strife and broaden their livelihoods."[58] Taking this as a motive, the Qing government adopted "protective measures" for overseas Chinese[59] and used the "pig" trade as a means to ease the social crisis. Such a cowardly and shameless act betrayed a unique ruling philosophy of the "Celestial Empire," a decadent feudal regime.

Living Conditions of Chinese Coolies

The place where Chinese coolies were gathered was commonly known as a "Coolie hub" (*guli bu*). In Southeast Asia, famous hubs could be found in Sumatra's Deli, Banka (Bangka), and Billiton, as well as Malaya's Penang and Perak.

Here I start with the situation in Sumatra, given that "the Netherlands was the first European country to open ports in the island countries of Southeast Asia. As the number of Chinese people who came here to make a living was multiplied over the years, they were subjected to uncontrolled exploitations by foreign officials, and torrents of abuses by local landlords. The worst situation was found in the Dutch companies."[60]

Deli

Deli in Medan was a tobacco-growing region in northeast Sumatra. Since the Dutch set up a capitalist tobacco plantation here in 1863, a large number of Chinese coolies were recruited to engage in enslaved labor. In the *Sources to the History of Foreign Relations during the Qing Period* (*Qingji waijiao shiliao*), volume 166, there is "A Petition from Chinese Merchants in Southeast Asia to the Minister of Trade Treaties Stating the Abuses over Chinese Laborers and Requesting the Establishment of a Consulate" ("Nanyang huashang cheng shangyue dacheng lichen beinue qingxing qing sheli lingshi bing") dated the 26th day of the ninth month of Guangxu 29 [27 October 1902]. The petition states:

> The contract clearly stipulates that the service lasts three years during which they can buy their freedom with the money earned from planting tobacco. After they are deceived into working at tobacco plantations in Deli, they go to work on time, regardless of weather. Anyone who lags behind is whipped. Every month, each worker is given only four dollars for food, and his earning from tobacco is calculated on the minimum basis. As the Dutch plantations have the rule that no outsiders are allowed in, Chinese laborers are not allowed to go out, so all the grocery shopping is managed by the foremen. Thus, for every ten dollars they give to a foreman, they can only get goods worth five or six dollars. When tobacco plants are ripe, casinos are set up so that gambling might drain up all their savings, or prostitutes are sent in to lead them astray. Anyway, there is always a way to put workers in a bind. After that, next year's wage is used as a bait to keep them here. If their arrears are not paid off, even if there is only a difference of one dollar or half a dollar, they will be ordered to labor for another year. This has actually doubled their debts. But nobody can be exempt from that. [...] Since the second year of Guangxu [1876/1877], a rule has been set by this country. Comparatively speaking, the rule is quite fair. For all the Chinese laborers, regardless of the price at which each was sold, everyone's debt is taken to be 36 dollars. After the calculation, if a worker's debt is equal to his earning from planting tobacco, the debt will be deducted in one year. After three

years of work, regardless of arrears, a worker is free of any debt. However, Western owners only pay lip services to the rule and do not comply with it in reality. As for foremen and Chinese chiefs (called captains by workers), they just act submissively and collaborate with the cheating, and deduct cruelly with a harsh heart. Dejected and desperate, laborers can only swallow their suffering in tears. Physically unable to exit the plantation, a place similar to a tiger or leopard den, to whom can they complain of injustice over them? Verbally unable to communicate with foreign leaders as they do not speak their language, to whom can they narrate that they are dying of exhaustion?

This historical text covers a wide range of issues. Leaving aside the topic of revolt which will be analyzed in the next section, I here cite more supplementary materials to discuss about the following four points:

The first is about working conditions and job specifications of "pigs." These coolies worked under strict controls. Regarding the organization of a tobacco plantation, there were a chief inspector (general manager) and a headman (deputy manager), who were Dutchmen. Beneath them, there were chief foremen and acting foremen, who were Chinese. The foremen were free to beat and mistreat "pigs" and were entitled to sending a rebellious worker to the manager's office (*guandu*) or even to the government office for punishment.[61] In a tobacco plantation, going to work was called "going to a dyke" (*shangba*). After a foreman measured the cultivation area, lots were drawn to divide the dykes which were then numbered. Skilled workers could grow 20,000 tobacco plants, semi-skilled about 17,000, and new workers 15,000–16,000. After dykes were divided, it was the time to plow the land. And then workers were allotted ridges, each about 100 square feet and each worker would work on 30 to 40 ridges. After that, they would start to trellis, sow seeds, transplant seedlings, remove tobacco pests, and top upper leaves, until the harvest time came.[62]

The second concerns the living environment of "pigs." "After entering a plantation, laborers are prohibited from moving freely. Even between father and son, or between brothers, no meeting is allowed."[63] This even went into a proverb that has been passed down to the present Chaozhou and Shantou, "Deli den, a place you can get in, but never can you get out."[64] "Pigs" live in a dwelling covered with palm leaves which is called "Yadaliao." It was about 100 meters long and 20 meters wide. With many people living inside, and little space between them, the air was stagnant and foul. And they lived on brown rice and cheapest meal.[65]

The third is related to the exploitation by foremen:

These foremen flatter their superiors for their own benefit, and there is literally nothing they cannot do. They deducted workers' wages, forced them to do extra work, tempted them into gambling and money borrowing, which left workers in debt. These foremen also falsely fabricated charges and brought legal accusations against workers, putting them under severe punishment. What they have done is really abhorrent.[66]

Apart from that, foremen also opened grocery stores[67] inside a plantation for "pigs" to buy daily necessities, food, and opium on credit. All debts were paid off during the harvest period.[68] However, in the grocery stores, everything was sold at a higher price.[69] This is why "for every ten dollars they give to a foreman, they can only get goods worth five or six dollars."

The last pertains to the recruitment policy. As recorded in the *Donghua Chronicles of the Reign of Guangxu*, Zhang Zhidong submitted a memorial in the 10th month of the 13th year of Guangxu [1887], which points out that:

> A careful reading of the official Dutch policy written in the foreign language reveals that, a plantation owner is allowed to send those workers who have misbehaved to the government office for investigation, but no private whipping is allowed; and that after three years of maximum working time, regardless of whether a worker still owes a debt, a plantation owner should pay him for his return journey and cannot force him to stay. But plantation owners only pay lip service to the policy and they do not include this article in the contract written in Chinese. They mistreat Chinese workers at their will.

A similar description can be found in the *Sources to the History of Foreign Relations during the Qing Period*, volume 204, where Qian Xun stated in his memorial that:

> After a work contract expires, although it is expressly stipulated that plantation owners should release their workers, they often make excuses or simply follow the practice of other plantations to detain workers. Some of them do not apply for departure documents on behalf of workers and thus keep the Chinese coolies in a trap for life until their death.

From these historical texts, it can be seen that Dutch plantation owners dared to "pay lip service to the policy" precisely because the government officials "collaborate[d] with the cheating." Again, the cover-up nature of the recruitment policy is revealed here.

Banka

Banka is an island in the southeast sea of Sumatra, famous for its tin production. At the end of the eighteenth century, "many people from Fujian and Guangdong came here to work as tin miners."[70] Later, the Netherlands took possession of the tin ore on the entire island, and in 1853, they sent experts to explore and expand the mining areas and innovate the mining methods. Since then, production had rapidly increased, reaching 100,000 quintals in 1890.[71]

Regarding the working condition of "pigs" on this island, we can get a hint from the *Donghua Chronicles of the Reign of Guangxu*, which includes a memorial submitted by Lv Haihuan in the 12th month of 1901:

> Most of the mines are located in valleys. When mountain rivers flow downward, and yet mine owners have not set up pumps to drain water, Chinese

workers are soaked in water every day. Suffering from humidity and hunger, they are most susceptible to diseases. Coupled with the extremely hot weather, and frequent attack of various seasonal diseases, a large number of workers have died. Grocery stores are owned by mine owners, so Chinese workers have no way but to buy goods here, which are of incredibly low quality and excessively high price. As their meager income can hardly cover their daily expenses, so when there is an urgent need for money, they have to apply for an earlier pay, but that amount of money needs to be paid with interest on a monthly basis: for one tael, an interest of five maces is demanded. As a result, although these people are diligent, they can only afford rough food.

More supplementary explanations can be added to the above quote. First, Banka was rich in alluvial tin ore which was partly deposited in the sea, locally known as the "tin sea." Tin mining in this place required labor-intensive dredging.[72] Every day, workers had to carry on their shoulders three cubic meters of tin mud from the bottom of the "tin sea" 30 to 40 meters deep and moved to the shore along a wooden flat ladder called "springboard." They were not allowed to rest until the required amount of work was completed. This is the so-called three bucketloads of mud,[73] a deceptive job description in the mouth of a "pig broker." Second, about their "merger income," it is said that:

> Their working contract is limited to three years. How much they could earn was calculated from the day they started to work. If their service was still within 180 days, the daily wage was two *kupang*方[74] and four *sen* 仙 [cents]. Beyond 180 days, it was increased to be three *kupang* and six *sen* per day. The contract expired after 36 months of work. If someone chose to continue working, the daily wage would be four *kupang* and two *sen*. If they continued to work for more than two years, they would be paid four *kupang* and six *sen* per day. This was the highest wage one could get.[75]

The third is about persecution and exploitation of "pigs" by foremen and mine owners (called "kepala parit"). Without an "exit permit," "pigs" were not allowed to go out. Otherwise, they would be punished as escapees. If they dared to resist, they would be brutally mistreated. For example, they might be bound and bitten by "ginger ants," or even executed after being arrested. It is not exaggerating to say that mine owners' exploitation of "pigs" went into every corner of the latter's life. In the early years, women were bought from Java at the price of 15 or 16 guilders per head. They were sold to "pigs" as wives at 25–30 guilders per head. In addition, casinos and opium dens were also opened in the plantations so that fees could be charged from the services provided.[76]

Billiton

Billiton, located east of Banka, had its tin production second only to Banka. In 1852, the Billiton Maatschappij signed a contract with the Netherlands Indies government, gaining the right of tin mining on the entire island. The monthly wage for a "pig" was like this: For a newcomer, it was seven guiders and five *kupang*, for a second-year worker, nine guiders, and for a third-year worker, 18 guiders. Wages were paid once a year. If one needed money for daily use, he had to borrow money from a foreman, at 30% interest.[77] A system of reward and punishment was also set up. First, there was a three-day break. If a "pig" worked continuously for 27 days in a month, he could enjoy a full attendance even if he did not work for the remaining three days. Second, one could be rewarded for extra work. Prior to mining, a "pig" could claim a certain number of mining areas and he could earn more by working extra time if the quota was met early. Third, if a "pig" failed to meet the requirement, part of his wage would be deducted as a punishment.[78] As for other details, since they were similar to those in Deli and Banka, there is no need to repeat them here.

Below is the situation of "pigs" in Malaya.

Penang

Penang is an island off the northwestern coast of Malaya. On 17 July 1786, Captain Light from the British East India Company obtained the island from the Sultan of Kedah. In 1800, a treaty gave the British permanent sovereignty over Province Wellesley. The following discussion concerning Penang includes both parts.

In the 1830s and 1840s, there were about 2,000 to 3,000 "new guests" in Penang every year.[79] In Wellesley's sugarcane plantations, "they were mistreated, and often beaten. They had terrible food. They were chained up at night so that they could not escape. On the whole, no medical equipment was provided, and disease was prevalent."[80] In pepper plantations in Penang, a "pig" was paid two dollars per month for the first year and given a set of clothes; in the second year, he was paid three dollars per month; and in the third year, plantation owners leased half of the land to workers for five years.[81]

In the late nineteenth century, the situation of "pigs" did not improve. In a sugarcane plantation in Penang, although workers fulfilled the contract, they were still in debt. Most of them were ill, and "the only hospital was a small hut inside the stable yard of an employer's private residence, where coolies were said to die of starvation. Yet this place was less than 50 yards from the police station." According to these coolies:

> Even if they escaped from here, they could not leave this island. The rule here was that no ferry guard would let go of any unknown coolie unless a pass was presented, and most of the boatmen were unwilling to take coolies as passengers.

Established under the third act of 1877 at the request of plantation owners in Wellesley, the rule "provides that any person who, by deceitful or unlawful methods, entices any person to leave the colony to work in other areas, shall be punished."[82]

However, "pigs" were not so submissive. They often rebelled under the leadership of secret societies:

> When coolies in a plantation heard someone blowing horns, they would get together to fight robbers, or stop policemen from carrying out their duties. When a person was arrested, they always tried to rescue him. This practice lasted until secret societies were dissolved in 1890.[83]

Perak and Malacca

Perak, located in the west of the Malay Peninsula, is rich in tin ore. The first several mining settlements were concentrated around Larut. "Obviously, Chinese miners in Larut came from Penang. They also brought two opposing forces 'Ghee Hin Kongsi' and 'Hai San Secret Society' to this place."[84] From 1873:

> About 2,000 to 3,000 Chinese coolies were directly sent from China to Larut every year. When they were ordered to work in new forests, about 10 to 20 percent of them died of fever, and when the mining started, 50 percent had already died.[85]

Malacca is in the southwest of the Malay Peninsula. Most "pigs" there worked in the local cassava plantation. A survey of nine overseas Chinese farms in 1902 showed that two farms had more than 30 "new guests," one farm had more than 20 new guests, three farms had more than 10, and three farms had less than 10 new guests. Of the 154 "new guests," eight escaped and eight died.[86]

After a survey of the situation of Chinese workers in different districts, we can see different confrontations between labor and capital in Sumatra and Malaya. In Sumatra, Chinese workers labored in plantations and mines that were owned by Europeans. It was a combination of class oppression and racial oppression. In Malaya, in addition to European companies, Chinese-run farms and mines also accounted for a certain proportion. Therefore, industrial relations here bore a more complex feature. That is to say, apart from the aforementioned double oppression in European plantations and mines, there was also class oppression shown in Chinese farms and mines. And it is the latter that was beneficial for the British colonial government, as they could produce misunderstandings among Chinese laborers and make these people feel that the British were the "liberators" who could free them from the bondage of their employers. When an assistant officer of the Chinese Protectorate in Penang inspected a Chinese sugarcane farm, thirty "pigs" ran two miles behind his car, pleading him to take them away, and when another assistant officer in Malacca inspected a Chinese cassava farm, and announced that they should be paid 12 dollars a month, "the crowd immediately cheered."[87] All these facts illustrate the true nature of the British colonial government. It is meant to distort some workers' understanding to make the situation favorable to itself.

Second, the life prospects of Chinese workers in "coolie hubs" are also worth discussing. Based on available data, we can see four patterns. The first was to become a "lifelong pig" on account of increasing debt from gambling and usury that could not be paid off. The second was to end up being an "old guest" after the change of his identity from a newcomer to the second-year coolie and then the third-year coolie. The third was to manage to escape. The fourth was to become a farmer on lease:

> There were about 100,000 Chinese indentured laborers working on farms in the vicinity of Tanjung Morawa, Lubuk Pakam, South Pagai, Binjai, Tegal, and Labuhan. They rented land from the local people to build farms and raise pigs, chickens, and ducks. [...] For daily use, they bought on credit food, fertilizer, livestock fodder and other necessities from the stores owned by local overseas Chinese. After a year of hard work, when the pigs grew to be 100 kilograms, they sold them to pay off their debts.[88]

These are the four types of life paths for "pigs" in Southeast Asia. Huang Zunxian in "Account of the Overseas Chinese" ("Fanke pian") described a different situation:

> On the left is the suntanned son,
> whose father has been engaged in mineral mining for long.
> Returning empty-handed from a treasure mountain,
> he suffered a great loss, hard to shun.
> Suddenly he found tin ore,
> which was truly a great treasure to be won.
> Just like a poverty-stricken scholar,
> who finally scored high in an imperial examination, promising a future not to be outdone.
> Covered with layers of green vegetation,
> tremendous treasure is hidden underneath known to none.
> With the marked tin ore worth millions,
> nobody knows how many treasure bowls will be filled in the long run.[89]

Huang's description in this poem is an exceptional case, about "one or two astute people who accumulated their wealth in the past,"[90] which did not apply to the majority of coolies.

Regarding opium addiction and gambling among "pigs," which are evidence of how the colonial system turned a person into a ghost-like existence, much has been revealed by other scholars, so there is no need to repeat it. By setting up casinos and opium dens, the Dutch and British colonialists and their accomplices had achieved two purposes: gambling caused "pigs" to lose their freedom that might be obtained when a contract ended and replacing weapons of resistance with opium pipes turned the labor struggle into a chronic suicide of "pigs." That explains all!

The Revolt of Chinese Workers against Exploiters

After being inhumanly mistreated, "pigs" stood up against exploiters, which is an inevitable result. Due to the limited information available, it is not possible to give a complete account of struggles and revolts in Southeast Asia in the late nineteenth century. By listing a couple of cases, with a particular focus on "Liu Yi Rebellion," I make some preliminary explorations about the protests of Chinese workers.

In 1876, Chinese workers in a Deli tobacco plantation rioted, "killing and wounding more than 10 westerners. Over a thousand Chinese were killed." [91]

On 17 February 1877, a group of Chinese workers who had been recruited to work in Singapore, after landing, were resold to employers in Sumatra by a "pig house." They refused to board the ship and started a riot. [92]

Around 1900, there was an uprising by "pigs" in Banka, which was called the "Liu Yi Rebellion." The two central figures were "pigs" Zheng Shiwu and Zheng Shiliu, who were sworn brothers of the Three Dots Society. Both were masters in boxing. In the name of "Liu Yi", an alias of Liu Yongfu[93], they gathered Chinese workers to rebel in Koba. They all wore red turbans and red belts and used choppers, guns, and sticks as weapons. After they destroyed Tung Shing Company and killed the mine owner and company employees, they moved to Pangkal Pinang, burning mines along the way, and attracting more "pigs" to join them. In response, the Dutch colonial government mobilized a large group of police from Sungailiat to suppress the uprising. The two sides were involved in a fierce battle. As they were poorly armed, the rebels were finally defeated. After this battle, the "Liu Yi" force was greatly weakened and they had to retreat to a mountainous area near a village called Faxing in Sungaliat. In 1900, after being denounced, the head of "Liu Yi Rebellion" was caught by the Dutch colonial government.[94] Later, the rebel leader was hanged in Jakarta. At the time of execution, numerous followers expressed their admiration of and regret for the heroic miners, eulogizing them with the saying "Liu Yi, you were born as a man and you died as a god!"[95]

According to Chinese documents, at the same time when the "Liu Yi Rebellion" happened, there was also an uprising by the "pigs" in Banka. In the *Donghua Chronicles of the Reign of Guangxu,* there is a memorial submitted by Lv Haihuan in the 12th month of the 27th year of Guangxu [1901], which mentions that:

> More than 300 workers gathered in the name of the Three Points Society (*sanzhi hui*) and instigated a sudden uprising. Informed in advance, the mine owner and his men fired first, resulting in countless deaths and injuries. The local officials caught many rebels and after repeated questioning, they found out that the rebellion arose from the unbearable harsh treatment by the owner and his foremen.

This "sudden uprising" coincided with the "Liu Yi Rebellion" in time and place, but whether it is the same incident awaits further research.

From the above, we can see the characteristics of Chinese workers' fight against their exploiters. First, most of these revolts were connected with Chinese secret societies either directly or indirectly. Second, they were purely economic struggles,[96] or in some cases spontaneous protests against the violation of human rights. Therefore, such rebellions had a clear feature: killing Westerners and destroying mines. Third, from the way "Liu Yi Rebellion" gathered followers, like using the name of Liu Yongfu and dressing themselves as the Red Turbans (*Hongjin jun*), we can see that these rebels "anxiously conjure up the spirits of the past to their service, borrowing from them names, battle slogans, and costumes in order to present this new scene in world history in time-honored disguise and borrowed language."[97] Thus seen, we might say, Chinese coolies' fight was more of a replica of Chinese peasant revolts in the feudal era than workers' movement in its preliminary stage. This was shaped by the demographic structure of "pigs" – they were a labor force composed mainly of insolvent peasants.

Facts have proved that revolts with the aforementioned features cannot lead Chinese workers to a complete liberation. However, because of these protests, the colonialists were forced to make some adjustments about those extremely barbaric rules and regulations,[98] and thus "pigs" were able to have their living conditions slightly improved.

Conclusion

"Indentured labor" of "pigs" is a variation of slavery under colonial conditions. From its labor structure, we can see two points. First, this practice deprived workers of their freedom to sell their labor on their own will. Second, when there was a shortage of labor force, a continuous input of "pigs" would help to solve the problem. In any enterprise that adopted this system, the basis of capitalist production would be gone, because the free wage labor was replaced by indentured slave labor. As the purpose of capitalist production was fulfilled through an exploitative slavery system, the practice of "indentured labor" can be said to have facilitated the development of capitalism, although it was not the hotbed of capitalism. That explains why the Dutch and British colonialists spared no effort to preserve it.

After the "1911 Revolution," in order to "respect human rights and protect national dignity," Sun Yat-sen approved the "Requirement for the Ministry of Foreign Affairs Concerning the Prohibition of Selling 'Pigs' Abroad and the Protection of Overseas Chinese" ("Chi waijiaobu tuo chou jinjue fanmai zhuzai ji baohu huaqiao banfa ling") on 19 March 1912, which reads:

> In the coastal provinces, some villainous profiteers abducted and trafficked "pigs" abroad, trapping them in a miserable situation, but the Qing government turned a blind eye to this, leaving the suffering compatriots in poverty and desperation. Now that the Republic of China has been established, it is imperative to immediately rescue them so that human rights can be respected and national dignity can be protected. Chinese expatriates are scattered across the islands, and some run their own businesses, but they are repeatedly

mistreated by foreigners. Although they have endured all sorts of hardships, they have never ceased to love their motherland. Now that everybody in China enjoys freedom and happiness, how can we bear to see our expatriates around the world being bullied and not lend a helping hand? In addition to urging the governor of Guangdong to strictly prohibit the trade of selling "pigs" abroad, we ask the Ministry of Foreign Affairs to immediately take effective measures to stop human trafficking and to protect the overseas Chinese, making sure that fraternity and equality are put into vigorous promotion. This command needs to be executed with urgency.

Thus, by the beginning of the twentieth century, "indentured labor" in Southeast Asia had come to an end. What it left to future generations are two facts: the achievements of "pigs" in developing Southeast Asia and the criminal evidence of colonialists' plunder of Southeast Asia.

Notes

1 Reisner and Rubtsov, 251.
2 Zabozlaeva, 101.
3 Rudnev, 353–354.
4 For more details, see Li Wenzhi, 175–193, 233–250, 939–942, 502–508.
5 Engels, 1957: 143. This letter, dated 10 November 1894, was addressed to Friedrich Adolph Sorge. Engels' accurate analysis echoed what Xue Fucheng stated in his memorial in the seventh month of 1893: "Nowadays, trains and ships travel everywhere without hindrance, and people from all over the world have almost arrived at our doorstep. We can no longer rule in isolation. Moreover, because of more than 200 years of benevolent and nurturing rule, China is becoming overcrowded and we have to guide people out to work as laborers in order to expand their livelihoods." This memorial is included in Zhu Shoupeng, ed., the *Donghua Chronicles of the Reign of Guangxu* (*Guangxu chao donghua lu*).
6 Marx, *Capital*, 1953: 932.
7 Marx, *Capital*, 1953: 949–950. In 1623, Jan Pieterszoon Coen, governor-general of the Dutch East Indies, instructed his successor to send vessels to the coastal areas of China to capture Chinese men and women. See Li Changfu, 1929: 33, note 3.
8 *Selected Translations of the Encyclopedia of the Soviet Union: The British Empire* (*Sulian dabaike quanshu xuanyi: Buliedian diguo*), 275.
9 Marx, *Capital*, 1953: 904.
10 See Guo Songtao, vol. 4, block printed edition in 1893. The word 崽 (*zai*) is a phonetic loan character of 仔 (*zai*). In *The Essay of Two Kinds of Autumn Rain Temple* (*Liangban qiuyuan suibi*), volume three, Liang Shaoren gave the explanation like this: 仔 is the same as 崽, both pronounced as "*zai*." In *The Commentary on the Water Classic* (*Shuijing zhu*) edited by Li Daoyuan, there is a sentence that reads "a catamite, an underage girl, a young kid (崽), this is what they are supposed to look like."
11 Phua Chay Long, 31.
12 See Lin Dachuan, vol. 8, in particular the song "Shell Digging Song" ("Daxu ge").
13 Zhuang Weiji, et al., 106.
14 Middlebrook and Pinnick, 159, 169. See also Taketomi Santoka, 50.
15 See the entry about "Kùli" on page 13 in the "*Great Soviet Encyclopedia*, vol. 24.
16 Li Changfu, 1929: 50.
17 Yun Yumin, 28.
18 Liu Jixuan and Shu Shicheng, 143.

19 Phua Chay Long, 31.
20 Purcell, 1950: 41.
21 Campbell, 149.
22 This is about what happened in Malaya, not in China. For example, James Tait, a British merchant who acted as the consul of Spain, Portugal, and the Netherlands in Xiamen, was the owner of Tait & Company, the largest company that operated human trafficking in Xiamen. See Ding Mingnan, et al, 63.
23 Li Zhongjue, 1937: 195. In the Qing dynasty, there were divisions of administration. There were provinces 省, circuits 道, prefectures 府 (including independent departments 直隶州 and independent sub-prefectures 直隶厅), and counties 县. The Circuit of Chao, Hui and Jia was one of the circuits in Guangdong back then. Under its control were Chaozhou prefecture, Huizhou prefecture and the independent department of Jiaying. —Trans.
24 See the document entitled "A Diplomatic Note to the British Consulate in Shantou about the Prohibition of Using Credit-tickets to Get Chinese Emigrant Workers Abroad" ("Zhaohui Shantou Ying lingshi huamin chuyang rengying jinzhi shedan"), dated the 19th day of the third month of Guangxu [18 April 1889], in Zhang Zhidong, *The Complete Works of Zhang Wenxianggong (Zhangwenxianggong quanji)*, vol. 95, Official Document 10.
25 Phua Chay Long, 31.
26 See the memorial entitled "Governor-general of Guangdong province Zhang Zhidong's memorial - About the life of overseas Chinese in Southeast Asia and a proposal to set up a consulate general in the Philippines for their protection" ("Yue du Zhang Zhidong zou chafang nanyang huamin qingxing nishe xiao lvsong zonglingshi yizi baohu"), dated the 12th month of the 13th year of Guangxu [January/February 1888], in Wang Yanwei, et al. eds., *Sources to the History of Foreign Relations during the Qing Period (Qingji waijiao shiliao)*, vol. 74.
27 Quoted from Li Changfu, 1937: 276–277.
28 Middlebrook and Pinnick, 163.
29 Purcell, 1958: 134.
30 In the "Treatises on Diplomatic Relations - Holland" ("Bangjiao zhi qi: Helan zhuan") of the *Draft History of the Qing Dynasty (Qingshi gao)*, it is "more than 10,000 people"; in the *Sources to the History of Foreign Relations during the Qing Period*, volume 74, it is written as "more than 60,000 people."
31 Blythe, 7.
32 Blythe, 9.
33 Yao Guansong, 84.
34 Xu Tongshen, 61–62. See also "To Liao Weijie, the foreign affairs commissioner in Shantou and the Circuit of Chao, Hui and Jia ("Zhi Chaozhou Huichaojia dao dedao Shantou yangwu weiyuan Liao Weijie") in *The Complete Works of Zhang Wenxianggong,* vol. 131. Regarding the year when "pigs" were directly transported to Sumatra, Japanese scholar Fukuda Shozo asserted in his article "Immigrants from China" that it should have started in 1888 (*Nanyang yanjiu* 5, no. 5, 1935) 64. But Cambell concluded that it was 1880 (*Nanyang yanjiu* 2, no. 5, 1929) 153. Li Changfu adopted the latter statement in his book *A History of Chinese Colonization*, but he gave no explanation about the inconsistency between Cambell's assertion and Chinese sources.
35 Qiu Shouyu, 88.
36 Tiannanlangzi, 80.
37 Shen Leiyu, 124–125. According to Tan Mengyan, "Ordinary people entering the territories governed by the Dutch government were subject to a dock tax (150 guilders, about 170 yuan in our currency), but pigs were secured by the company so they were not taxed. Those who could redeem their freedom in the future and wished to stay in the Dutch territories were required to pay half the dock tax (75 guilders)." See Tan Mengyan, 411.

38 Tian Yu, 33–34.
39 *Tiannanlangzi*, 80.
40 See Qian Xun's memorial "A report and analysis of the situation of overseas Chinese in the Dutch-controlled territories from Qian Xun, an envoy to the Netherlands" ("Shi he Qian Xun zou he shu huaqiao qingxing jin ju wenjian suoji lv chen") dated the 22nd day of the seventh month of Guangxu [30 August 1907], in the *Sources to the History of Foreign Relations during the Qing Period*, vol. 204.
41 Li Changfu, 48. See also Ding Mingnan, et al., 61. The article "Coolie" in the *Encyclopædia Britannica* states that the arrival of "indentured immigrants from China began around 1845" (14th ed., vol. 6), 387, and the Chinese version of Hosea Ballou Morse's book *The International Relations of the Chinese Empire*, vol. 1, states that "the first shipment of Chinese coolies on foreign ships was made on 7 March 1847" (Beijing: Sanlian shudian, 1957), 409. I think both sources have given a much later time.
42 Jiang Tingfu, 559.
43 Judging from the two phrases "going as a coolie" (*guo guli*) and "coolie catchers" (*guli zei*), we can see that local people at that time did not know the exact meaning of "coolie" (*guli*), thus this song could be the first account of foreigners' capture of "pigs" around the coastal areas of Chaozhou and Shantou. Regarding the meaning of *Daxu* 搭蚋, there is a brief mention in the entry entitled "Customs - Fishing and Shell Digging" in the *Annals of Chenghai County* (*Chenghai xianzhi*) in 1814, volume 6, "Xu 蚋 can be found in the seashore mud. There are people who go digging but get nothing. [...] People living in the coastal areas row boats to go digging, then they sell them to a kiln workshop where the shells are processed into ashes, which are used in house building or used as fertilizer for soil."
44 The details about these "pig houses" are given in the following section.
45 This company was called "Moshijiapi" by Chinese workers.
46 In the *Overview of Overseas Chinese from Qiongzhou in Singapore*, Yun Yumin gave this information: "After the opening of Qiongzhou [Hainan]as a commercial port (1858), colonies in the Strait Settlements, in their active development, were in an increasing need of coolies. That made the pig trade better than before. After Shantou and Xiamen, profiteers in Haikou also operated this business." (p. 28)
47 Campbell, 146.
48 Phua Chay Long, 31.
49 Also called God of the Soil and the Ground (*Tudishen*).
50 Jin Tianmin, 78. The in-text notes are original. Judging from some words used here, we can see that this song has been embellished by the literati.
51 Phua Chay Long, 31. Regarding the selling price of "pigs," there are many records, but most of them are either vague in time, unspecified about regions, or confusing in terms of measurement units. Therefore, readers can only garnish a general impression without accurate information. The following is a list of sources for reference: (1) Lv Haihuan's memorial in the 12th month of the 27th year of Guangxu [1901] included in Zhu Shoupeng, ed., the *Donghua Chronicles of the Reign of Guangxu*; (2) "A Petition from Chinese Merchants in Southeast Asia to the Minister of Trade Treaties Stating the Abuse over Chinese Laborers and Requesting the Establishment of a Consulate" ("Nanyang huashang cheng shangyue dacheng lichen beinue qingxing qing sheli lingshi bing") dated the 26th day of the ninth month of Guangxu 29 [27 October 1902] in the *Sources to the History of Foreign Relations during the Qing Period*, volume 166; (3) Huang Jingchu, *Overseas Chinese in Southeast Asia*, 74–75; (4) Tian Yu, "The Situation of Chinese Workers in Billiton," 32; (5) Yao Guansong, "The Past and Present of Chinese Laborers in North Sumatra," 84; (6) Tiannanlangzi, "The Current Situation of Chinese Workers in Banka," 80; (7) Fukuda Shozo, "Immigrants from China," in *Nanyang yanjiu* 5, no. 5 (1935): 64; (8) Situ Meitang, "I Hate American Imperialists," in the Guangming Daily (1951): 91; (9) Campbell, "The 'Pig' Trade in British Malaysia," 147; (10) Victor Purcell, *The Chinese in Malaya*, 41–44; (11) Blythe, *Historical Sketch*

of Chinese Labour in Malaya, 6–7, 9, 19; (12) Wen Xiongfei, *A General History of Overseas Chinese in Southeast Asia* (Shanghai: Dongfang yinshuguan, 1929), 181–182.
52 For more details, see Zheng Jianlu, 182–183; Shen Leiyu, 127; Morse, 194.
53 Zhang Zhidong, vol. 95, Official Document 10.
54 Marx, 1953: 949.
55 Stalin, 22.
56 Mao Zedong, "Analysis of the Classes in Chinese Society" in the *Selected Works of Mao Zedong*, vol. 1: 11.
57 Hu Sheng, 10.
58 See "A Telegram from Li Hongzhang, the Governor-general of Zhili, Asking the Foreign Office to Suspend the Signing of a New Treaty with the U.S. as It Prohibits Chinese Workers from Going There." ("Zhi du Li Hongzhang zhi zongshu Mei xinyue jin huagong wang Mei qing huan ding dian"), dated the 15th day of the sixth month of Guangxu [23 July 1888], in the *Sources to the History of Foreign Relations during the Qing Period*), vol. 76. Although this document is not that early as other materials, it is still illustrative, because the quotation part looks back to the past.
59 The original sentence is "The protective measures are meant to eliminate immediate concerns rather than plan a long-term strategy." See "Zhang Zhidong's Memorial" dated the tenth month of the 13th year of Guangxu [1887] in the *Donghua Chronicles of the Reign of Guangxu*.
60 "Memorial from the Ministry of Foreign Affairs" dated the 26th day of the second month of the 28th year of Guangxu [4 April 1902], in the *Donghua Chronicles of the Reign of Guangxu*.
61 Yao Guansong, 85.
62 Qiu Shouyu, 89.
63 See "Lv Haihuan's Memorial" dated the 12th month of the 27th year of Guangxu [1901], in the *Donghua Chronicles of the Reign of Guangxu*.
64 For a long time, "Deli den 日里窟" in this proverb has been mistaken as 入鯉窟, literally meaning "getting into a carp pond," which is rather confusing.
65 Yao Guansong, 85.
66 See Qian Xun's memorial "A report and analysis of the situation of overseas Chinese in the Dutch-controlled territories from Qian Xun, an envoy to the Netherlands" dated the 22nd day of the seventh month in the 33rd year of Guangxu [30 August 1907], in the *Sources to the History of Foreign Relations during the Qing Period*, vol. 204.
67 This kind of store was also called "Dianzai," literally "a small store," or "Yuanqiu dian," literally "a store inside a plantation."
68 The harvest time was commonly known as "Luo tu ku," literally [tobacco leaves] pulled and kept in a storage room.
69 Yao Guansong, 85. See also Tan Mengyan, 412; Li Changfu, 1937: 279.
70 Xie Qinggao, *Maritime Journals: An Annotated Edition* (*Hai lu zhu*), 42.
71 Qiu Shouyu, 168.
72 Dobby, 193.
73 Li Xu, 92.
74 In the northern states of Peninsular Malaysia, denominations of 10 *sen* are called *kupang*.
75 Tiannanlangzi, 80–81. Regarding the daily pay after the full service stipulated in the contract, Li Xu gave the information as follows: in the first year after that, one was paid three *kupang* and five *sen*, in the second year, four *kupang* and two *sen*, and in the third year, five *kupang* and two *sen*. See Li Xu, 92.
76 Li Xu, 93, 95.
77 Huang Jingchu, 74–75.
78 Tian Yu, 41.
79 Purcell, 1958: 41.

80 Blythe, 5.
81 Purcell, 1950: 32.
82 Blythe, 8–10.
83 Purcell, 1950: 43–44.
84 Purcell, 1950: 71.
85 Blythe, 23. According to "Yang Shiqi's Memorial" ("Yang Shiqi zou") dated the 16th day of the second month in the 34th year of Guangxu [18 March 1908], in the *Donghua Chronicles of the Reign of Guangxu*, "there were 200,000 Chinese workers in Perak."
86 Blythe, 10–12.
87 Blythe, 10–12.
88 Yao Guansong, 86.
89 Huang Zunxian, 223.
90 See "Qian Xun's Memorial" ("Qian Xun zou") dated the 22nd day of the seventh month of the 33rd year of Guangxu [30 August 1907], in the *History of Foreign Relations during the Qing Period*, vol. 204.
91 "A Petition from Chinese Merchants in Southeast Asia to the Minister of Trade Treaties Stating the Abuse over Chinese Laborers and Requesting the Establishment of a Consulate" ("Nanyang huashang cheng shangyue dacheng lichen beinue qingxing qing sheli lingshi bing") dated the 26th day of the ninth month of Guangxu 29 [27 October 1902] in the *Sources to the History of Foreign Relations during the Qing Period*, vol. 166.
92 Yun Yumin, 28.
93 Liu Yongfu was a Chinese warlord and commander of the celebrated Black Flag Army. Liu won fame as a Chinese patriot fighting against the French empire in northern Vietnam in the 1870s and early 1880s. —Trans.
94 But no historical information can be found about the details here, like who was arrested, Zheng Shiwu or Zheng Shiliu, or both.
95 Li Xu, 93–95. See also Wang Chengzhi, 184, 187–188.
96 This assertion does not conflict with the uprising of Chinese miners in Kuching, British Borneo and the establishment of an interim government in 1857, because Chinese workers were imported into Borneo from Malaya in 1887.
97 Marx, 1954: 223.
98 For example, after the "pig" riot in a Deli tobacco plantation in 1876, the Dutch colonial government made a new regulation, and after the revolt in Singapore in 1877, the British colonial government revised the immigration regulation.

Bibliography

Blythe, Wilfred Lawson. *Historical Sketch of Chinese Labor in Malaya.* [In Chinese.] Translated by Wang Lu. *Nanyang wenti ziliao yicong*, no. 2 (1957): 2–24.
Campbell, Persia Crawford. *Chinese Coolie Emigration to Countries within the British Empire*. Excerpt translated into Chinese with the title of "The 'Pig' Trade in British Malaysia." Translated by Wang Danhua. *Nanyang yanjiu* 2, no. 5 (1929): 145–161.
Ding Mingnan, et al. *Diguozhuyi qinhuashi* (*History of Imperialist Invasion of China*), vol. 1. Beijing: Kexue chubanshe, 1958.
Dobby, Ernest Henry George. *Southeast Asia.* [In Chinese.] Translated by Zhao Songqiao, et al. Beijing: Sanlian shudian, 1958.
Engels, Friedrich. "Engels to Friedrich Adolph Sorge," in *Marx and Engels on China*, 2nd edition. [In Chinese.] Translated by Compilation and Translation Bureau of Works of Marx, Engels, Lenin and Stalin of the CPC Central Committee. Beijing: Renmin chubanshe, 1957.

Guo Songtao. *Guoshilang zoushu* (*Memorials from Vice Minister Guo*). Taipei: Wenhai chubanshe, 1968.

Hu Sheng. "Zhongguo jindai lishi de fenqi wenti (Periodization of Modern Chinese History)." *Lishi yanjiu* 1, no. 1 (1954): 5–15.

Huang Jingchu. *Nanyang Huaqiao* (*Overseas Chinese in Southeast Asia*). Shanghai: Shangwu yinshuguan, 1930.

Huang Zunxian. *Renjinglu shicao jianzhu* (*Draft of Poems from the Hut within the Human Realm with Commentaries and Annotations*). Annotated by Qian Zhonglian. Shanghai: Gudian wenxue chubanshe, 1957.

Jiang Tingfu, ed. *Chouban yiwu shimo buyi* (*Supplement to "A Complete Record of the Management of Foreign Affairs"*), vol. 3, the Xianfeng reign. Beijing: Beijing daxue chubanshe, 1988.

Jin Tianmin, ed. *Chaozhou Nursery Songs*. Singapore: Nanyang Technological University (NTU) Books, 1929.

Li Changfu. *Nanyang huaqiao shi* (*A History of the Overseas Chinese in Southeast Asia*). Guangzhou: Jinan daxue nanyang wenhua shiyebu, 1929.

Li Changfu. *Zhongguo zhimin shi* (*A History of Chinese Colonization*). Beijing: Shangwu yinshuguan, 1937.

Li Daoyuan, ed. *Shuijing zhu* (*The Commentary on the Water Classic*). Beijing: Shangwu yinshuguan, 1939.

Li Shuji, et al., eds. *Chenghai xianzhi* (*Annals of Chenghai County*). Taipei: Chengwen chubanshe, 1974.

Li Wenzhi, ed. *Zhongguo jindai nongye shi ziliao* (*Materials on Modern Chinese Agricultural History*), vol. 1. Beijing: Sanlian shudian, 1957.

Li Xu. "Xidao he xidao de huagong (Banka and Chinese Workers in Banka)." *The 10th Anniversary Issue of Shenghuo Bao*. Jakarta: Indonesia Shenghuo Bao, 1955.

Li Zhongjue. "Jin zhuzai yi" ("A Talk about Prohibiting the 'Pig' Trade"), in *Late Qing Writings*. Edited by Zheng Zhenduo. Shanghai: Life Bookstore, 1937. 194–195.

Li Zhongjue. *Xinjiapo fengtu ji* (*A Description of Singapore*). Singapore: Nanyang Bookstore, 1947.

Liang Shaoren. *Liangban qiuyuan suibi* (*The Essay of Two Kinds of Autumn Rain Temple*). Shanghai: Shanghai guji Chubanshe, 1982.

Lin Dachuan. *Hanjiang ji* (*Accounts along Han River*). Collated by Peng Miaoyan. Zhongzhou guji chubanshe, 2000.

Liu Jixuan, and Shuang Shibai. *Zhonghuaminzu kaituo nanyang shi* (*A History of the Chinese People's Exploration of Southeast Asia*). Shanghai: Shangwu yinshuguan, 1935.

Mao Zedong. *Mao Zedong xuanji* (*Selected Works of Mao Zedong*), vol. 1. Beijing: Renmin chubanshe, 1952.

Marx, Karl. "The Eighteenth Brumaire of Louis Bonaparte," in *Selected Works of Marx and Engels*, vol. 1. Translated by Compilation and Translation Bureau of the CPC Central Committee. Beijing: Renmin chubanshe, 1954. 219–321.

Marx, Karl. *Capital*, vol. 1. Translated by Guo Dali and Wang Ya'nan. Beijing: Renmin chubanshe, 1953.

Middlebrook, Stanley Musgrave, and Alfred William Pinnick. *How Malaya Is Governed*. [In Chinese.] Singapore: Translated and printed by Malayan Ministry of Education, 1951.

Morse, Hosea Ballou. *The International Relations of the Chinese Empire*. [In Chinese.] Translated by Zhang Huiwen, et al. Beijing: Sanlian shudian, 1957.

Phua Chay Long, ed. *Malaiya chaoqiao tongjian* (*A General Chronicle of Overseas Chaozhou People in Malaya*), vol. 3. Singapore: Nantao Publishing House, 1950.

Purcell, Victor. *The Chinese in Malaya*. Translated by Liu Qiandu. Penang: Kwong Wah Yit Poh Press Berhad, 1950.

Purcell, Victor. *The Chinese in Southeast Asia*. [In Chinese.] Translated by Xu Ping and Wang Lu. *Southeast Asian Studies: A Quarterly Journal of Translations*, no. 2 and 3 combined, 1958.

Qiu Shouyu, ed. *Dong Yindu yu huaqiao jingji fazhan shi* (*East India and the History of Economic Development by Overseas Chinese*). Taipei: Zhengzhong shuju, 1947.

Reisner, Igor Mikhailovich and Boris Konstantinovich Rubtsov, eds. *Modern History of Eastern Countries*, vol. 2. Translated by Ding Zeliang, et al. Beijing: Sanlian shudian, 1958.

Rudnev, Vladimir Sergeyevich. "Land Relations in Malaya," in *Land Relations in Eastern Countries*. [In Russian.] Edited by N. Vaganov and V. Maslennikov. Moscow: The USSR Academy of Sciences Publishing House, 1958. 66–73.

Shen Leiyu, edited. *Sumendala yipie* (*Sumatra at a Glance*). Taipei: Zhengzhong shuju, 1936.

Stalin, Joseph. *An Interview with H.G. Wells*. [In Chinese.] Translated by Liu Guang. Beijing: Renmin chubanshe, 1953.

Taketomi, Santoka. *A Malay Dictionary*. [In Japanese.] Tokyo: Obunsha Co., Ltd., 1942.

Tan Mengyan. "Nanyang zhuzai de shenghuo jiqi weilai mingyun (Life of the 'Pigs' in the Southeast Asia and their Future Fate)." *Monthly Report of Current Events* 4 (1931): 411–413.

Tian Yu. "Wulidong huagong zhuangkuang (The Situation of Chinese Workers in Billiton)." *Nanyang yanjiu* 2, no. 4 (1928): 31–44.

Tiannanlangzi. "Pengjia huagong zhi jinkuang (The Current Situation of Chinese Workers in Banka)." *Oriental Magazine* 16, no. 7 (1919): 80–82.

Vvedensky, Boris, et al., eds. *Great Soviet Encyclopedia*, vol. 24. [In Russian.] Moscow: Sovetskaya Entsiklopediya, 1953.

Wang Chengzhi. *Nanyang fengtu jianwen lu* (*Travels to Southeast Asia*). Shanghai: Shangwu yinshuguan, 1931.

Wang Yanwei, et al., eds. *Qingji waijiao shiliao* (*Sources to the History of Foreign Relations during the Qing Period*). Beijing: Shumu wenxian chubanshe, 1987.

Wen Qing, et al., eds. *Chouban yiwu shimo* (*A Complete Record of the Management of Foreign Affairs*). Shanghai: Shanghai guji chubanshe, 1979.

Xie Qinggao, dictated. *Hai lu zhu* (*Maritime Journals: An Annotated Edition*). Transcribed by Yang Bingnan and annotated by Feng Chengjun. Beijing: Zhonghua shuju, 1955.

Xu Tongshen, ed. *Zhangwenxianggong nianpu* (*Chronicles of Zhang Zhidong*). Shanghai: Shangwu yinshuguan, 1946.

Yao Guansong. "Beisu huaqiao laodongjie de guoqu yu xianzai (The Past and Present of Chinese Laborers in North Sumatra)." *The 10th Anniversary Issue of Shenghuo Bao*. Jakarta: Indonesia Shenghuo Bao, 1955.

Sulian dabaike quanshu xuanyi: Buliedian diguo (*Selected Translations of the Encyclopedia of the Soviet Union: The British Empire*.) [In Chinese.] Beijing: Sanlian shudian, 1957

Yun Yumin. *Xinjiapo qiongqiao gaikuang* (*Overview of Overseas Chinese from Qiongzhou in Singapore*). Haikou: Hainan shuju, 1931.

Zabozlaeva, Olga Ivanovna. "The Formation of the Indonesian Working Class." [In Chinese.] Translated by Gu Xuejia. *Translated Essays in Historical Study*, no. 6 (1957): 95–113.

Zhang Zhidong. *Zhang wenxianggong quanji* (*The Complete Works of Zhang Wenxianggong*). Taipei: Wenhai chubanshe, 1963.

Zheng Jianlu. *Nanyang sanyue ji* (*Three Months in Southeast Asia*). Shanghai: Zhonghua shuju, 1935.

Zheng Zhenduo. *Wanqing wenxuan* (*Selected Writings of the Late Qing Dynasty*). Shanghai: Shenghuo shudian, 1937.

Zhu Shijia. *Meiguo pohai huagong shiliao* (*Historical Materials of American Persecution of Chinese Workers*). Beijing: Zhonghua shuju, 1958.

Zhu Shoupeng, ed. *Guangxu chao donghua lu* (*Donghua Chronicles of the Reign of Guangxu*). Beijing: Zhonghua shuju, 1984.

Zhuang Weigi, et al. "Fujian Jinjiang zhuanqu huaqiao shi diaocha baogao (An Investigation Report on the History of Overseas Chinese in Jinjiang of Fujian Province)." *Xiamen daxue xuebao*, no. 1. (1958): 95–129.

Index

Note: **Bold** page numbers refer to tables and page numbers followed by "n" denote endnotes.

Abridged Collection of Rhymes of the Ancient and Modern 20
Accounts along Han River (Lin Dachuan) 317
agate 19, 22
Agostino, Adeodato Santo 245
Agrarian Laws 308
Agreed Terms of Settlement about the Burning of Tacheng Trade Circle between China and Russia 207
Ahura Mazda 68, 69, 71
Akedang'a 228, 235, 242, 243, 247, 248
Amoghavajra 48, 190
Amu Darya River 12, 25, 66, 74, 84–86, 118, 165
An Dahan 56
An Hushufen 55
An Jia 86
An Jiasha 56
An Liaoyan 55
An Lushan 53, 54, 98, 99, 114, 116, 140; *Biographical Account of An Lushan* 33, 52
An Moyan 55
An Pantuo 54
An Pu 36, 37
An Shi 36, 37
An Sishun 39
An Zhenjie 114
ancient Turkic belief 63
Anecdotes in the Tang Dynasty (Wang Dang) 81
Anecdotes of the Kaiyuan and Tianbao Periods (Wang Renyu) 145
animals, tributes from the Nine Surnames 12–15

Annals of Anhua County 210
Annals of Wanquan County – Appendix 201
Annals of Xiangshan county 310
Annotations of Li Changji's Poems (Wang Qi) 19
Arab empire 9, 10, 36, 75, 84; lions in 157–159
Arabic-Turkic Lexicon (Ibn Muhanna) 140
Article 13 of The Sino-French Treaty of Tianjin 262
Asha Vahishta 69
Ashina Duzhi 2
Ashina Huselo 125
Ashina Qutlugh 108
Ashina She'er 107
Ashina tribe 93, 119, 134
Asian Department of the Russian Ministry of Foreign Affairs 219
An Authentic Account of the Embassy of the Dutch East-India Company, to the Court of the Emperor of China, in the Years 1794 and 1795 (van Braam) 279
Authentic Records Transmitted from the Kaiyuan and Tianbao Eras (Zheng Qi) 7
Avvakum (Orthodox priest) 257

Babkov, Ivan Fyodorovich 268
Bai Juyi (poet): "New Yuefu: Dancer of Xiliang" 167; "Song of the Lute" 80; "Twenty Rhymes for Green Felt Tents" 21
Bamboo Ballads for Acrobatics (Li Zhensheng) 149
Banner, Abag (King) 202

Banner, Abahanar (Prince) 202
Banner, Tumd 202
Bao Fang (scholar) 13, 46; Random Thoughts 1
Baranov, Alexander Andreyevich 232
Barkley, Charles William 230
Bartold, Vasily Vladimirovich 41, 77, 94
The Battle of Hulao Pass (Zheng Guangzu) 147
Baximi Tigin 131n109
Bazarova, Dolores Habibovna 137
Bāba(Bāmi)-Khwāra 50
Beale, Daniel 239
Beale, Thomas 228, 238
The Beasts Classic (Huang Xingzeng) 159
Behistun inscription of the Persian empire 25, 67
Beijing 149–151, 166, 200, 255, 257, 259–261, 271, 278, 279, 300, 303; Russian Hotel in 218–221, 243–245
Bernshtam, Alexander Natanovich 114
Bichurin, Nikita Yakovlevich 219, 260–261
Bilge Khan Inscription 113
Bilge Qaghan 38, 108–110, 113, 122, 126, 130n100, 136
Biographical Accounts of An Lushan (Yao Runeng) 33, 52, 98, 116
Al Biruni 50, 67
Bletterman, J. H. 304
Blue ticket guest (*Qingdan ke*) 311
Blussé, Leonard 280
Bodhisattva, Manjusri 163, 195
Book of Documents 259
Book of Fujian: Records of Local Histories (He Qiaoyuan) 176, 183
Book of Han: Biography of Yang Wangsun (Ban Gu) 95, 181
The Book of Kings (Ferdowsi) 157
Book of Sui: Records of Persia (Wei Zheng) 45
Book of Sui: Records of the Ryukyu (Wei Zheng) 139
Book of Sui: Records of the Turks (Wei Zheng) 17, 18, 20, 33, 36, 71, 74, 97, 119, 157
Book of the Later Han: Records of the Western Regions (Fan Ye) 24, 74, 158
Book of Wei: Records of the Western Regions (Wei Shou) 3, 12, 17, 18, 44, 66
Book of Zhou: Records of the Turks (Linghu Defen) 54, 91, 92, 105, 108, 117–119, 122
Boyce, Mary 68

A Brief History of the Black Tatars (Peng Daya and Xu Ting) 139
A Brief History of Xi'an (Wu Bolun) 37
British economic system 308
British supercargo in Canton 240–243, 277
Buddhist Dharma 40
Buglio, P. Ludovicus 163
Bureau of the Imperial Saddlery 13–14
bureau stamp (*bupiao*) system 205–208
business, Sogdian society and culture in Middle Ages 50–53
Bytsov, Evgeny Karlovich 264

Cai Zhaofu 272
calendar, Sogdian society and culture in Middle Ages 47–48
Cang Ci 38
Canton 152–154, 198, 218, 222, 234, 248–249; British supercargo in 240–243; Dutch factory (*see* Dutch factory in Canton, during Qing period); fur market in 229–232; Russian Vessels in 243–245; trading in 235–237
Canton Maritime Customs 233, 238
Cao Alanpen 56
Cao Alanyan 55, 56
Cao Fudiyan 55
Cao Miaoda 78
Cao Mopen 55
Cao Pantuo 54
Cao Poyan 55
Cao Sengnu 78
Cao Shancai 80
Cao Yanyan 55
caravan tea 198–199; bureau stamp (*bupiao*) System 205–208; Chinese into Russia 199–201; end of 216–218; Kiachta tea market 221–222; trading activities of Shanxi Tea Merchants 201–205; transportation of 218–221; Western Merchants and Southern Counter 209–213; Wu Dacheng's purchase and shipping of Black Tea 213–216
Casual Remarks North of the Pond (Wang Shizhen) 148
Catalog of Paintings of the Xuanhe Era 52
Catherine II (Empress) 260
Celestial Empire 300–301, 321
Cen Shen 46; "Song of General Gai at Yumen Pass" 20
Cen Zhongmian 42, 76, 129n78, 130n98, 131n101, 131n109, 189; *Compilation of Historical Records of the Turks* 129n78, 131n101

Center of Russian Language 243, 245
Chach lads 43–45
chalcopyrite (*tou*) 17–18
Changlin 298–301, 303, 305
Charvi 15
Chavannes, Édouard 105, 156, 176;
  Documents on the Western Turks 11
Chen Baozhen 212
Chen Cheng 12, 161; "A Record of the Foreign Countries in the Western Regions" 66
Chen De 312
Chen Shizeng 149
Chen Tianhua 172
Chen Yinke 53, 144, 185
Chen Yuan 195n8
Chen Zhongfu 229
Cheng Huapeng 209–211
Cheng Lin 264
Cheng Zheng 173n25
Chicken Rib Chronicles (Zhuang Chuo) 181
China-Russia Yili/Tal Bahatai Trade Regulations 209
Chinese coolies, living conditions of 322; Banka 324–325; Billiton 325–326; Deli 322–324; Penang 326–327; Perak and Malacca 327–328
Chinese Protectorate in Singapore 313
Chinese workers in Southeast Asia 308–311; against exploiters 329–330; living conditions of Chinese coolies 322–328; pig trade 311–321
Chronicle of Hall of Raindrops (Xu Chenglie, known as Qingliang Daoren) 152, 284
Chuluo Qaghan 98, 107, 110, 113, 115, 122
Chu Suiliang 107
civil marriage, Sogdian society and culture in Middle Ages 36–37
Classic of Filial Piety 259
Classified Anecdotes of the Qing Dynasty (Xu Ke) 211
Clauson, Gerard 127n17
Collected Aphorisms – Continued (Wang Junyu) 190
Collected Poems from Yunshan Hall (Wang Wengao) 290–292, 295, 304
Collected Verdicts of Tang Cases 35
Collection of the Materials on Gaochang (Feng Chengjun) 78
Collection of Translated Buddhist Terms (Fa Yun) 16, 19
Collection of Works from Yueyatang (Wu Chongyao) 302

Commented Rhapsodies on Categorized Matters (Wu Shu) 189
Compendium of Chronicles (Rashid al-Din) 140
Compendium of Five Lamps (Shi Puji) 191, 192
Compendium of Materia Medica (Li Shizhen) 16, 19, 140
Compilation of Historical Records of the Turks (Cen Zhongmian) 129n78, 131n101
Compilation of Travel Diaries in Russia (Miao Yousun) 215
Complete Essentials for the Military Classics 10
Complete Turkish Dictionary (Mahmud Kashkarii) 140
Comprehensive Examination of Literature: Ceremonial Music (Ma Duanlin) 49
A Comprehensive Guide to Painting (Zheng Ji) 153, 166
Comprehensive Mirror in Aid of Governance (Sima Guang) 3
Comprehensive Records on the Mongol Tartars 38
Conquest of Siberia and The History of the Transactions, Wars, Commerce, Etc. Carried on between Russia and China from the Earliest Period (Gerard F. Miller) 198
Continued Biographies of Eminent Monks: A Biography of Xuanzang (Shi Daoxuan) 51, 185
Convention of Peking for the Land Trade 205
Cook, James: the *Resolution* and the *Discovery* 230
Cordier, Henri 156
corporal punishment 124
cosmological structure of Zoroastrianism: seven holy immortals 69; seven stages of creation 68–69; seven years of meditation 68
Couplets and Adages from the Suzhou Area (Wang Youguan) 162
Court of Colonial Affairs 199, 206, 210, 217, 220, 228, 231, 237, 245, 248
Creator's Day 48
credit-ticket system (*shedan zhi*) 312
Cui Lingqin 116
Cui Rong 50
Cui Shenyou 81, 82

dancing rugs (*wuyan*) 21
Daoguang (Emperor) 153, 203, 244, 257, 302

Darius (King) 25, 68
Da Ye 141
Dayun Guangming Monastery 177
death penalty 123, 124, 131n109
defense of aristocratic privileges 124–125
Dennett, Tyler 231
Der Ling (Princess) 151
A Description of Singapore (Li Zhongjue) 310, 313
Dharma (King) 109
Diary of an Embassy to Four Nations (Xue Fucheng) 199
diet, Sogdian society and culture in Middle Ages 46–47
Differentiation of Ancient and Modern Family Names 53
Ding Qian 76
Ding Zeliang 250n16
Discussion about Calligraphy (Dou Gao) 80
Dixon, George 230
Dmitrieva, Lyudmila Vasilyevna 180
Dmitry Alekseevich Peshchurov 220
Documents on the Western Turks (Édouard Chavannes) 11
Documents Unearthed in Turpan 54, 55
Dong Gao 173n27
Donghua Chronicles of the Reign of Guangxu (Zhu Shoupeng) 315, 316, 319–320, 324, 329
Dowager Cixi (Empress) 151
Draft to an Institutional History of the Song Dynasty (Xu Song) 182
Drake, Francis 236
Dream of the Red Chamber (Cao Xueqin) 154n1, 166, 281
dress, Sogdian society and culture in Middle Ages 43–46
Drummond, James 228, 240
Du Fu 45; Appreciating General Cao's Horse Painting at the Residence of Secretary Wei Feng 19; Ballad of a Piebald Horse 14
Du Huan 76, 77, 84; *On the History of Irrigation in Turkestan* 77; *Record of Travels* (*Jingxing ji*) 21, 23, 37, 42, 45, 47, 75, 77, 84
Du Yong 148
Du You: *Comprehensive Institutions* 7, 34, 40, 49, 64, 117, 130n98, 159
Duan Chengshi: *Miscellaneous Writings from Youyang* 18, 45, 95, 98, 180; Presenting a Playful Interpretation of an Ancient Text to Feiqing 16–17

Duan Da 263
Dutch East India Company 199, 270, 279, 293
Dutch factory in Canton, during Qing period 270–271; clocks and watches 281; cultural exchange 280–281; poems of 272–277; short-legged dogs 284–285; snow pea 285; telescope 281–284; van Braam and Sino-Dutch relations 277–280
Dutch mission 290, 298, 299, 301
Dutch tribute ship 294–296
Duyvendak, Jan Julius Lodewijk 298

The Eastern Capital: A Dream of Splendor (Meng Yuanlao) 169, 306n23
Eastern Iranian tribes 94
Eight Poems of the New Yuefu on the Front (Wu Jiabin) 203
Emel Esin 99
Emir Qutaiba 9
Encyclopedia of Arts and Letters 23
Engels, Friedrich 69, 112, 117, 119, 204, 309, 331n5
enlightened autocracy 260
Ennin's Diary: The Record of a Pilgrimage to China in Search of the Law (Ennin) 163, 178
Essential Criteria of Antiques (Cao Zhao) 17, 19
exorcising evil spirits 65–66
Explaining Unit Characters and Analyzing Compound Characters 16
Explanations of Silks (Ren Dachun) 45
The Exploitation of the Works of Nature (Song Yingxing) 169
exploitative slavery system 330
Extensive Records of the Taiping Era (Li Fang) 82, 112, 145, 191

family, Sogdian society and culture in Middle Ages 33–36
Fan Yongdou 201
Fang Linggui 148
Feng Chengjun 27n11, 78, 172n16, 187
Ferdowsi (Poet): *The Book of Kings* 157
Ferghana 13, 14, 17, 33, 42, 84, 86n7, 156
Ferrand, Gabriel 185; *Kunlun and Navigation across the Ancient South China Sea* 185; Persia in the South China Sea 190
festivals, Sogdian society and culture in Middle Ages 48–50
feudal ritual system 162

fire worship, origin of 90–93
Fishermen's Song of the East China Sea (Gu Taiqing) 150
folk calendar 66–67
Fontanier, Henri Victor 262
food, tributes from the Nine Surnames 22–24
A Forest of Pearls from the Dharma Garden (Shi Daoshi) 190
Fragments of the Manichaean Manuscripts 179
Franco-Russian alliance 249
Frazer, James: *The Golden Bough* 48
French Revolution 231, 293
friend stamp (*pengpiao*) 207
Fudifen (pwtypnn) 56
Fudiyan (pwty'n) 56
Fujita Toyohachi 20

Gao Chuo (King) 41
Gao Conghui (King) 82
Gao Xianzhi 39
Gaozong (Emperor) 22, 100n24, 111, 138
Gayōmard 68
Gazetteer of Guangdong Maritime Customs (Liang Tingnan) 229, 233, 238, 250n24
Geluopulu (King) 10–12, 47
General Chorography of Guangdong (Ruan Yuan) 300
Geographic Writings of Shazhou and Yizhou 50, 52, 54, 65
Giovanni Giuseppe da Costa 254
The Golden Bough (Frazer) 48
gold leaf memorial 291, 296–298, 301
Gong (Prince of) 205, 207, 267
Gray, Robert 230
Great Collection of Sutras 157
The Great Tang Biographies of Eminent Monks who Sought the Dharma in the Western Regions 188, 189
Great Tang Records on the Western Regions (Xuanzang) 7, 15, 17, 32, 42, 84, 129n77
Gu Taiqing: *Fishermen's Song of the East China Sea* 150; *Poems Written at Tianyou Pavilion* 255
Guangdong Maritime Customs 228–247, 271, 296
Guangzhuang black tea 210, 211
Guest News (Shen Zhou) 162
A Guide to Shazhou Commandery 51, 55
Guignes, Joseph de 294
Guo Longyue 300

Guo Songtao 254, 310
Guo Yuanzhen 39
Gurak (King) 47, 84

Haizhuang Temple 278, 290, 291, 298–301, 303, 305
halite 18–19
Han dynasty 12, 13, 24, 33, 147, 159, 164, 260
Haneda Toru 55
Hankou 205, 208, 210, 215, 220, 221, 266, 268
Haurvatat 69
He Fudifen 55
He Hai 78
He Hongzhen 78
He Junzheng 36–37
He Moheduo 56
He Poyan 55
He Qiutao 229, 254
He Tai'an 138–139
He Tutun 56
He Wenzhe 36
Heijligendorp, Cornelis 277
Hephthalites law 118
Herodotus 40
Hijri calendar 10
Historical Materials on Qing Diplomacy: The Reign of Jiaqing 242
History (Simocatta) 90
The History of Japan 293
History of Ming: Records of the Western Regions (Zhang Tingyu) 161
History of the Han Compiled at Dongguan 159
History of the North (Li Yanshou) 116, 123, 201
The History of the Polish Question (Marx) 260
Hong Mai: *Notes Taken in Rong Study* 81; *Records of Yijian* 70
Hong merchants (*hang shang*) 228, 232, 238, 241–243, 247, 249, 275, 296, 301
Hong system in Canton 249
Hope 232–234, 236, 237, 239, 240, 245–248
horses 1, 2, 11–14, 25, 38, 46, 48, 51, 96–99, 107, 108, 111, 123, 124, 134; local products of Turks 135–137
Hou 162
Hu Shi 161
Huang Pusheng 251n58
Huang Shunxiao 319

Huang Wulong 318
Huang Xingzeng 159
Huang Yunfa 201
Huang Zunxian 262; "In Memory of Friends at the End of the Year" 212–213
huchuang 22
huizhe 18
Hulumosi 162
Huzhou silk 229, 275

Ibn Muhanna: *Arabic-Turkic Lexicon* (*Dashi Tujue zihui*) 140
'Il Kul Shad Bagha Ishbara Qaghan' 120
Illig Qaghan 111, 113–115, 120, 122, 124
Illustrated Gazetteer of the Sea Kingdoms (Wei Yuan) 198, 204, 219, 286
Ilterish Qaghan 108
Imperial Consort Yang 15, 24, 33, 145
Imperial Incense (Der Ling) 151
indentured labor of pigs 330
India 1, 15, 21, 25, 26; indentured laborers in 311; lions in 157, 164; wild burial or forest burial (*shilin*) in 40, 42
Institutional History of Tang (Su Mian) 13, 47, 106, 108, 135
international academic community 53
inversed flow of Russian tea 216–218
iron 56, 90, 119, 161, 187, 276; local products of Turks 134–135
Ishbara Qaghan 109, 110, 113, 130n96
Issik Qaghan 120
Istami Khagan 93

Jade Chapters (Gu Yewang) 17
Jia Baoyu 281
Jia Dan 135; Entering the Western Territories through Anxi Protectorate 2
Jiaqing (Emperor) 302
Jiasha 56, 110
Jin dynasty 24
Jin Liangwang 201
Jin Nong 151
Jin Tianmin 333n50
jinzhe 18
Jistuzo, Kuwabara: *Studies on Pu Shougeng* 185
Jottings from the Life-Long Learning Hut (Lu You) 46, 180, 192
Jottings from the Thatch Hut of Subtle Views (Ji Xiaolan) 201
Journey to the West 148

Kachins 92
Kaiyuan era of Tang period 12, 17, 24, 27n19, 41, 46, 54, 118, 129n80, 165
Kang Alanyan 56
Kang Ayiqu 36, 37, 131n109
Kang Gecha 35
Kang Jieshifen 55
Kang Kunlun 81
Kang Mobi 35
Kang Moliang 34
Kang Tuoyan 55
Kang Wupoyan 3, 55
Kang Xian 36, 37
Kang Yijin 56
Kangguo wozi (pugs from Samarkand) 14
Karlgren, Bernhard 55, 157
Karm-Khwāra 50
Kashkarii, Mahmud 140
Kendrick, John: *Lady Washington* 230
Khshathra Vairya 69
Kiachta exchange market 200, 204, 221
Kiachta tea market 221–222
Kiachta Trade Agreement 200
Kintsius, Pieter 285
Kirghiz 91, 110, 111, 135, 177
Kirilov, Porphyrii Yevdokimovich 255–257
Kiselev, Sergei Vladimirovich 107–108
Kong Guangren 209
Kong Shangren 169
Korobitsyn, Nikolai Ivanovich 246
Krusenstern, Adam Johann von 234–236, 238, 241–243, 245, 246, 250n22
ku li 311
Kul Tigin Monument 96, 109, 113, 128n38, 128n48
Külüg Tarkhan 114
"A Kunlun Lad" (Zhang Ji) 193
Kunlun slaves in Buddhist books 185–186; civilization 188–190; *A Forest of Pearls from the Dharma Garden* (Shi Daoshi) 190–191; *Sound and Meaning of All Sutras* (Shi Huilin) 186–188; in Zen talks 191–194
Kuwabara Jitsuzo 53
Kuwayama Shoshin 173n28

Labor Service Register 54, 55
Lady Washington (Kendrick) 230
Laufer, Berthold 156
Le Coq, Albert von 43
Le Jun 272, 282
The Legend of Emperor Mu (Guo Pu) 160
Leontiev, Aleksei 259–260

Li (Prince) 255, 258n7
Li Bai 46; "Writing as a Guest" 16
Li Changfu 333n41
Li Changji: "The South Garden" 22–23
Li Deyu 191
Li Dongyang 159
Li Dou 167, 273
Li Hao zhuan: A Biography of Li Hao 41
Li He: Song of the Palace Maids 19
Li Hongzhang 208, 264–266
Li Shangyin: Willow (Liu) 21
Li Shen: "Lament for the Maestro" 81
Li Shengzhen: Bamboo Ballads for Acrobatics 149
Li Shimin 136
Li Shizhen 158; Compendium of Materia Medica 16, 19, 140
Li Tingyu 177, 180
Li Yanyu 228, 238–241, 247
Li Yu 160; Twelve Towers 281–282
Li Zhi 146
Li Zhongjue 332n23; A Description of Singapore 310, 313
Li Zhu'er 140
Liang dynasty 22, 165, 189
Liang Jiabin 201
Liang Yabao 312
Liang Zhangju 161
likin tax (lijin) 207, 208, 211, 223n38
Lin Dachuan 317
Lin Lanchi 151
Lin Shichang 177
Linghai 295, 306n17
Linyi 186
lions in China 156; eyes of ancient Chinese 159–163; in folklore 167–171; lion's roar 171–172; sinicized lion image 163–167; from Western regions 156–159
The Lion's Roar (Chen Tianhua) 172
Lipovtsov, Stepan Vasilevich 245
Lisianski, Yuri Fedorovich 234
Literaturnaya Gazeta 260
The Little Bean Arbor (Zeng Yandong) 287n23
Liu Bingquan 300
Liu Hu Zhou 135
Liu Kunyi 208
Liu Ruoyu 148
Liu Shengmu 212
Liu Shixin 285
Liu Xun 188
Liu Yi Rebellion 329–330
Liu Yongfu 329, 330, 335n93
Liu Yu 160
Liu Yuxi: "An Improvisational Outpouring of Emotions upon the Visit by Mr. Linghu from Bianzhou" 21; "For my Ophthalmologist – A Brahman Monk" 21; "Listen to the Former Palace Singer Mu Singing a Song" 81
Liu Zhengyan 43
Livshits, Vladimir Aronovich 37, 55
Local Chronicle of Macau (Yin Guangren and Zhang Rulin) 152
local products of Turks 134; horses 135–137; iron 134–135; Turkish medicine 140; Turkish sparrow 137–139; Turkish wine 139–140; Turkish yurt 140–141
Lu Guanheng 228, 242
Lu Kai 141
Lu Rong 158
Lu Xu 145
Lu You 182; Jottings from the Life-Long Learning Hut 46, 180, 192
Luchendun 232–235
Luo Changpei 156
Luo Teqin 56
Luo Zhenyu 185
Lv Haihuan 324, 329, 333n51
Lyangusov, Spiridon Yakovlevich 200

Ma Changshou 110, 128n48
Ma Duanlin 49
Ma Huan 160, 162
Ma Mingda 70
Ma Shenwu 264
Ma Shou 265
Macartney mission 293
Mai Jun 312
Malyshev, Ivan 245
Manichaean funeral rites 181
Manichaeism 55, 84, 176–183
Manuscript of My Mission to Russia (Wang Zhichun) 213
Maria Feodorovna (Empress) 236
maritime market of Canton 280
marriage, Sogdian society and culture in Middle Ages 36–37
Marx, Karl 105, 109, 198, 204, 309; The History of the Polish Question 260; Revolution in China and in Europe 229
Master Hulu (Ulug) 176, 178, 181, 182
Mazda, Ahura 69

Memoir of the Pilgrimage to the Five Kingdoms of India (Huichao) 37, 44, 117
Meng Hanqing 147
Meng Yuanlao 169
Mi Jifen 37, 55
Miao Yousun 213, 217–218, 259; *Compilation of Travel Diaries in Russia* 215
Miller, Gerard Fridrikh 198
minerals, tributes from the Nine Surnames 17–19
Ming dynasty 17, 25, 84, 138, 146, 148, 158–159, 161, 162, 169, 183, 194, 201, 281
Miscellaneous Chants of the Tea Market (Zhonggan) 202
Miscellaneous Notes of the Bamboo Leaves Pavilion (Yao Yuanzhi) 203, 206
Miscellaneous Poems about the Capital (Yang Jingting) 257
Miscellaneous Records by Yishan (Li Yishan) 82
"Miscellaneous Records of Emperor Ming: Additions" (Zheng Chuhui) 14
Miscellaneous Records of the Social Customs of the Ming Dynasty (Tian Yiheng) 148, 162
Miscellaneous Records of the Western Capital (Zhao Feiyan) 45
Mochuo Qaghan 122, 124, 131n109
The Moheluo Doll (Meng Hanqing) 147
moluojiali 19
Mongol era 110
Monk Daoyan 191
Monk Shouchu 194
Mordvinov, Mikhail Ivanovich 236
Mouru in *Khordeh Avesta* 74
Mu Boxi 78
Mu Daoling 82–83
Mu Gougou 79
Mu, Nine Surnames of the Sogdians in Tang period 74–75; old records and new evidence 75–77; people in Tang dynasty 77–83; State of Mu 84–85
Mu Shancai 80–81
Mu Sha'nuo 79
Mu Shishi 79
Mu Simi 83
Mu Xiang 80
Mu Yu 80
Mu Zhaosi 82
Muqan Qaghan 104, 109, 111, 120–122

Mysterious Strange Record 145

NanēBandak 54
Napoleonic Wars of 1812 199, 231, 249
Neck, Jacob Corneliszoon van 270
Nestorian temples 76
Nestorianism 55, 84, 85
Neva 232–236, 238–240, 246, 248
New Book of Tang: Account of Rites and Music 34, 39, 55, 79, 93, 98, 114, 167
New Book of Tang: Record of Samarkand 13, 26, 44, 47, 49
New Book of Tang: Records of Persia 40, 67
New book of Tang: Records of the Western Regions 18
New History of the South (Qian Yi) 83
New Poems for Today 149
Ni Yue 159
Nikitin, Gavrila Romanovich 200
Nine Surnames of the Sogdians in Tang period: rituals and customs of (*see* rituals and customs, Nine Surnames of the Sogdians in Tang period); seven as venerated number (*see* seven as venerated number, Nine Surnames of the Sogdians in Tang period); state of Mu (*see* Mu, Nine Surnames of the Sogdians in Tang period)
Nine Surnames of the Sogdians in the Tang dynasty and the Turkic Culture (Cai Hongsheng) 75
Nine Tribes of Zhaowu *see* Nine Surnames of the Sogdians in Tang period
1911 Revolution 172, 218, 330
Ningningfen (nnyprn/Ningfen) 56
The Nirvana Sutra 163
Niu Shangshi 158
Notes of Wang Rangqing (Wang Kangnian) 171
Notes on Pingzhou (Zhu Yu) 187, 190
Notes to Herbal Medicine (Tao Hongjing) 23

Ode to Crystal (Wei Yingwu g) 22
"Ode to the Sogdian Bed: A Reply Poem" (Yu Jianwu) 22
Odds and Ends about Guangdong (Liu Shixin) 285
Old Book of Tang: Biography of Zheng Yuanshu 25, 36, 41, 107, 113, 114, 122, 124, 125, 130n99, 135, 138, 140, 145, 157

Old Book of Tang: Records of Persia 45
Old Book of Tang: Records of the Turks 122
Ongin Inscription 107, 127n17
Opium War 199, 204, 219, 222, 245, 249, 255, 262, 309, 317
Origin of Chinese Characters (Luo Changpei) 156
Orkhon inscriptions 104, 110, 125
Orkhon-Yenisei inscriptions 105
The Overall Survey of the Ocean's Shores (Ma Huan) 160, 162
Overview of Overseas Chinese from Qiongzhou in Singapore (Yun Yumin) 333n46

A Palace History of the Ming (Liu Ruoyu) 148
"Palace Lyrics" 17, 21
Pan Changyao 241
Pan Qiguan 242
Pan Youdu 228, 247, 282
"Panic in My Heart" 319
Panshan Baoji 193
Pascal, Blaise 178
The Pearl Boat (Hu Shi) 161
Pearl River 272, 273, 277, 300, 302
Pei Huaigu 124
Pei Xing 194
Pei Xingjian 2, 19
Pekingese 144
Pelliot, Paul 20, 139, 156, 176
penalties 123–125, 248
Penjikent 42, 43, 46
Peregrinations in the North (He Qiutao) 201, 205, 229, 244, 254
Persia 1, 9, 17, 20, 22, 25, 26, 40, 41, 44, 45, 74, 75, 79; law 68; lion worship in 157; theology 69, 71; Zoroastrianism 68
Persian-style theological structure 69
Petitpierre-Boy, C. H. 304
Peyrefitte, Alain 280
Phoenicians of Inner Asia 1
Pierre Frapperie 254
pig trade 311–321
pipa 49, 52, 53, 78
plants, tributes from the Nine Surnames 15–17
"A Play on Snow Lions: A Quatrain" (Zhang Wenqian) 169
"Poem of Declining the Tribute Lion" (Li Dongyang) 159
Portlock, Nathaniel 230

Prime Tortoise of the Record Bureau (Wang Qinruo) 3–4, 11, 15, 16, 33, 36, 47, 79
Privy Council of Russia 219, 228, 235, 237, 245, 247, 248
pugs 144–149, **154**; Beijing 149–151; Canton 152–154; Yangzhou 151–152
pugs of Samarkand 14–15, 40

Qapaghan Qaghan 96, 135
Qi dynasty 20, 78, 86
Qianlong (Emperor) 149, 201, 232–244, 272–285, 290–305
Qin Huan 254–257
Qing dynasty 45, 95, 144, 148, 149, 151–153, 154n2, 158, 164, 166, 168–170, 185, 198–202, 208, 209, 211–213, 218, 220–222, 228, 233, 237, 240, 245, 254, 257, 258n2, 258n6, 259, 262–264, 267, 270, 271, 277, 280, 281, 284, 286, 290, 292, 295, 300, 304, 305n2, 305n5, 332n23
Qingyuan prefecture 176
Qu Dajun: *A New Encyclopedia of Guangdong* 152, 294; "Sea-conquering Tower" 270
Qu Wentai (King) 3, 145
Quanzhou 176–182, 314
Qushuzhi (King) 36, 93, 110
Qutayba Ibn Muslim 9
Qutlugh Qaghan 105, 108, 122

Recorded Sayings of the Ancient Worthies (Zezangzhu) 191–192
A Record of Buddhist Monasteries in Luoyang (Yang Xuanzhi) 160
A Record of Buddhist Practices Sent Home from the South China Sea (Shi Yijing) 186, 188, 189
Record of Strange Things of the Far South (Liu Xun) 188
Record of the Imperial Court and Beyond (Zhang Zhuo) 51
Record of the Jade Hall (Yang Shicong) 138
Record of the Western Minorities (Wei Jie) 34, 40, 42, 47–48, 64–65
Record of the Xuan Chamber 69
Record of Travels (Du Huan) 21, 23, 37, 42, 45, 47, 75–77, 84
Record on the Investigation of the Divine (Xu Xuan) 178

Records after the Guests Have Left (Zhao Yushi) 43
Records of Antiquities (Xu Hao) 80
Records of Discontinuing Farming in Nan Village (Tao Zongyi) 147, 160, 161
Records of Diverse Matters (Zhang Hua) 24
Records of Mysterious Manifestations (Wang Yan) 45
"Records of Samarkand" 2, 13, 23, 26, 44, 47, 49, 93
"Records of the Arab Empire" 157
Records of the Expedition to the West (Liu Yu) 160
Records of the Grand Historian: An Arrayed Account of the Xiongnu (Sima Qian) 95, 105
Records of the Imperial Music (Cui Lingqin) 116–118, 129n78
Records of the Three Kingdoms (Chen Shou) 20
Records of the Yangzhou Barges (Li Dou) 167, 273
"Records of Yanqi" 2
Regulations about Chinese Tea 219
Religion of Light 176–183
religious colors, with Sogdian personal names 55–56
Representative Answers from the Region beyond the Mountains (Zhou Qufei) 20
Revised Land Trade Regulations 205, 266
Rezanov, Nikolai Petrovich 236
Rin Shihei 295
Rites of Zhou (*Zhouli*) 16, 28n43
rituals and customs, Nine Surnames of the Sogdians in Tang period 32–33; business 50–53; calendar 47–48; diet 46–47; dress 43–46; dwelling 42–43; family 33–36; festivals 48–50; funeral and burial 38–42; marriage 36–37; Sogdian nomenclature 53–56
Roberts, John 228
Romanov dynasty 236
Rong (Prince of) 255
Rong Quanzu 210
Rossokhin, Larion 259
Rouran 105, 119, 121, 134
royal marriage, Sogdian society and culture in Middle Ages 36–37
Ruan Yuan 229, 283, 284; *General Chorography of Guangdong* 300
Ruizong (Emperor) 39

Rules and Cases of the Court of Colonial Affairs 245
Rumyantsev, Nikolay Petrovich 236
Russia: caravan tea 198; case in Tianjin Missionary Incident 262–268; diplomatic archives 207; Privy Council 219; Russian hotel in Beijing 243–245; *Three Character Classic* 259–261

Salm ibn Ziyad 9
Sasanian ornamentation 45
Sassanid dynasty (Empire) 21, 50, 76, 77, 79, 84, 85, 91
Scherenberg, R. 280–281
seasonal worship 96
Sequel to Chang Chu Zhai (Liu Shengmu) 212
seven as venerated number, Nine Surnames of the Sogdians in Tang period 63–64; cosmological structure of Zoroastrianism (*see* cosmological structure of Zoroastrianism); historical evidence of 64–68; Seven Holy Immortals 69–71
seven holy immortals 63, 69, 70, 71
Seven Sacred Knives 70, 71
seven stages of creation 68–69
Shad, Aoshe 122
Shad, Axian 118–119
Shad, Ilteber 122
Shad, Nibu 122
Shang Kexi (King) 152
Shang Zhixin 152
Shanxi Consortium 201
Shanxi Tea Merchants, trading activities of 201–205
Sha Wujing 168, 192; *Journey to the West* 148
Shelikhov, Grigory Ivanovich 231
Shen Muqin 273
Shevelev, Mikhail Grigoryevich 214–216
Shi Bodifen 55
Shi Chongjun 55
Shi Haiping 192
Shi Huilin 38, 43, 158; *Sound and Meaning of All Sutras* 21, 44, 46, 50, 65, 77, 137, 186–187, 191
Shi Jicheng 191
Shi Jun 86
Shi Liaoyan 55
Shi Mochuo 36
Shi Ning 109, 111

Shi Ningfen 55
Shi Pantuo 53, 54
Shi Potuo 35
Shi Puji 191
Shi Shifen 55
Shi Wupoyan 55
Shi Xilin 18
Shi Yanfen 55
Shi Yijing 186, 188, 189
Shibi Qaghan 115, 122
Shihei Hayashi 295
Shishpin (King) 36
Siam 295, 296
Siavash (King) 36
Silk Road 18, 86n6
silver peaches 14–15
Simocatta, Theophylact: *History* 90
Singapore 308, 312–316, 318–321, 329, 335n98
single-tipped cannon 9–10
Sinicized Russian 222
Sino-Russian Land Trade Regulations 265
Sino-Tartars Glossary 95
The Six Statutes of the Tang Dynasty 162
Skachkov, Konstantin Adrianovich 220, 263–268
Sky God 90, 95, 96, 97
Sogdian legal documents 34
Sogdian personal names 53–54; commonly used last word in 55; religious colors with 55–56; Turkic elements in 56
Sogdiana 3, 9, 11, 13, 15, 20–26, 37, 39, 42, 46, 49, 67, 84, 85, 93, 117, 134
Song Bai 146
Song dynasty 15, 20, 43, 46, 63, 69–71, 83, 145, 146, 151, 153, 166–169, 176, 179–182, 187, 190, 191–193, 274
Song Jingang 130n99
Song Yun 39
Songs for an Exhausted Stallion (Qiao Zhizhi) 13
Sources to the History of Foreign Relations during the Qing Period (Wang Yanwei) 322, 324
Spenta Armaiti 69
spirited dogs (*junquan*) 40
The Spring and Autumn Annals of the Ten Kingdoms (Sun Guangxian) 83
Stalkov, Vassily 200
Statistical Description of the Chinese Empire (Bichurin) 219
Staunton, George Leonard 302; *An Authentic Account of an Embassy from the King of Great Britain to the Emperor of China* 279–280
Stein, Marc Aurel 140
stone honey 22–23
The Story of Embroidered Ru (Xu Lin) 148
Straits Settlements 308, 318
Studies on Pu Shougeng (Kuwabara Jistuzo) 185
A Study of Turkic Official Titles (Han Rulin) 139
Sugar Law 308
Sui dynasty 2, 26n1, 36, 50, 74, 78, 84, 86, 107, 109, 111, 159, 190
sumozhe 65–66
Sun Guangxian 83; *Trivial Tales from North of Meng* 82
Sun Wanrong 131n101
Sun Yat-sen 330
Sun Yuting 243, 247, 248
Supplement to Sound and Meaning of All Sutras (Shi Xilin) 18
Sutra of the Original Endeavour of the Prince in Accordance with All Good Omens 157
Suyab 2, 13, 26n6, 90, 158
S. W. Litvinoff & Co. 214, 215, 263, 265, 266
Sy Yabghu Qaghan 90
Syr Tarduš 106, 109

Tactics in a Series 147
tadeng 19–20
Taiping Heavenly Kingdom 209
Taiping Rebellion 210, 321
Taizong (Emperor) 24, 39, 107, 111, 136
A Tale of the Fisherman and the Woodcutter 147
Tang dynasty 3, 7, 21, 26n1, 33–39, 41, 45–47, 50, 52–56, 63, 74, 75, 79, 84–86, 94, 95, 106, 109, 111, 135, 156, 164, 177, 260, 274
Tao Hongjing 23
Tao Xian 191
Tao Zongyi 147, 160, 161
Tardu Qaghan 91, 97, 105
Tardush Shad 116
Tarkhun (King) 10, 36
Taspar Qaghan 120
tax (collection) 3, 56, 108, 110, 208, 211, 216, 223n34
Tea Room Notes (Yu Yue) 148
Tengri Qaghan 10
Tengrism 95–97

Tengri worship 96
textiles, tributes from the Nine Surnames 19–21
Thatched Hut 183
The Theory of the Leisure Class (Thorstein Veblen) 153
thirteen hongs (Thirteen Hongs) 152, 205, 228, 230, 237–239, 242, 249, 272–275, 282–286, 290, 300, 302
A Thorough Explanation of Qu and Ci of the Song, Jin, Yuan, Ming and Qing Dynasties (Wang Xueqi) 147
three-bladed whistling arrows 135
Three Character Classic, in Russia 259–261
Three Dots Society 312, 329
Three Hundred Songs of the Hanjiang River (Lin Lanchi) 151
Tian Er 263
Tian Shenglan 201
Tian Yiheng 148, 162
Tianfang 84
Tianjin Missionary Incident 262, 268
Tianjin tea port 265–267
Timurid era 99
Titsingh, Isaac 278, 293
Tokugawa Mitsukuni 293
Tong Yabghu Qaghan 36, 56, 90, 106, 110, 116, 121
Tongzhi (Emperor) 206
Topical Compendium of the Buddhist Clergy (Zanning) 177
Transoxiana 2, 7, 9, 11, 24, 25, 37
"Treatise on Officialdom" 11
Treaty of Kiachta in 1727 259
Treaty of Nerchinsk 200
tribute letters: from Geluopulu 10–12; from Qutayba Ibn Muslim 9–10; from Tughshada 8–9; from Yina Tudun Qule 10
tributes, Nine Surnames of the Sogdians in Tang period 1; categories and interpretations 12–26; letters, analysis of (*see* tribute letters); route and frequency 1–4, **4–7**, 7
Tsar Alexander I 236
Tsar diplomacy 267–268
Tsar Paul I 231
Tughshada (King) 8–12, 47, 84
Turkic Khaganate 99, 104–105; criminal law 123–125; family and marriage 112–118; throne succession 118–123; Turkic law 105–112

Turkic law 105; delimited lands and livestock marks 105–109; slave and courtier 109–112
Turks (*Tujue*)/Turkish people 63; ancestors 134; belief system 91; clan system 112; criminal law 123–125; cultural relics 105; elements, in Sogdian personal names 56; era 94, 112; horses 135–137; iron 134–135; legal system 104; medicine 140; nomadic society 112; sorcerer 97–99; sparrow 137–139; tribes 136; wine 139–140; yurt 140–141
Tuyuhun Xie 114

utensils, tributes from the Nine Surnames 21–22

Van Braam Houckgeest, Andreas Everardus 277–280, 292, 296; *An Authentic Account of the Embassy of the Dutch East-India Company, to the Court of the Emperor of China, in the Years 1794 and 1795* 279
Veblen, Thorstein 153
Verses of Chu 17
Vlangali, Alexander Georgievich 264
Vohu Manah 69
Voyzekhovsky, Joe Pa 255

A Wanderer's Talk (Liang Zhangju) 161
Wang Bangwei 188
Wang Dayu 201
Wang Dengku 201
Wang Fangyi 2
Wang Jian 21
Wang Jingzhu 147
Wang Jun 152
Wang Junyu 190
Wang Juzheng 179
Wang Kangnian 171
Wang Qi 19
Wang Renyu 145
Wang Shiji 304
Wang Shizhen 59n95
Wang Shoutong 256, 257, 258n2
Wang Wei 167
Wang Wengao 278; *Collected Poems from Yunshan Hall* 290–292, 295, 304; gold leaf memorial 296–298
Wang Xianqian 205, 265
Wang Xueqi 147
Wang Ya 145

Wang Yan 153
Wang Yinzhi 258n2
Wang Youguan 162
Wang Zhichun 213
Wanyan Linqing 173n29
Watters, Thomas 156
Wei dynasty 12, 19, 54, 134, 164
Wei Jie 40, 47, 48, 64
Wei Yuan 198, 286
Wei Zheng: *Book of Sui: Records of Persia* 45; *Book of Sui: Records of the Ryukyu* 139; *Book of Sui: Records of the Turks* 17, 18, 20, 33, 36, 41, 42, 49, 71, 74, 97–99, 119, 120, 123, 134, 139, 157
Wen Tingshi 95, 158, 186, 195n4
Wen Yanbo 124
Western Merchants, of caravan tea 209–213
Western Turkic Khaganate 2, 19, 36, 44, 93, 100n24, 104, 109, 118, 134
Whampoa (Huangpu) 230, 294
White Tartars 38
William (King of Holland) 296, 297
witch doctor 67–68
wozi *see* pugs
Wu Bolun 37
Wu Chongyao 302
Wu Dacheng 221; purchase and shipping of black tea 213–216
Wu Dunyuan 229
Wu Jiabin 203
Wu Pinghu 302
Wu Shu 189
Wu Tian 318
Wu Xiongguang 228, 235, 240, 242, 243, 245, 247–248
Wu Yuanhua 302
Wu Yuanwei 302
Wu Zetian (Empress) 13, 15, 80, 164, 173n27
Wude era 13; Wude Emperor 145; Wude reign 101n37
Wuzong (Emperor) 18, 177

Хара–Бурра 10
Xi He 288n44
Xiang Da 46, 53, 75, 129n80
Xianggong 152
Xiang Wu 263
Xiao Dan 165
Xiao Jing 165
Xiaoge 152
Xiaozong 159

"Xiayi Tower" 282
Xicheng Hang 238–240, 246, 247
Xie Dengke 314
Xie Tongqin 314
Xie Tongzhu 314
Xie Yudi 313
Xie Yurou 313
Xindian 214
xin ke 311
Xu Beihong 172
Xu Chenglie 152, 284
Xu Guangqi 148
Xu Hao 80
Xu Qinming 96
Xu Tongshen 332n34
Xu Xuan 178
Xuanhe (Emperor) 181
Xuanzang 39, 46, 51, 52, 76, 94, 192; *A Biography of the Tripitaka Master of the Great Ci'en Monastery* 90; *Great Tang Records on the Western Regions* 7, 15, 17, 32, 42, 44, 84, 106, 129n77
Xuanzong (Emperor) 13, 14–15, 19, 24, 79, 84, 113, 136, 137; *Great Tang Records on the Western Regions* 15
Xue Tao 145
Xunzhi 75

Yabgh Chuluohou 120, 121
Yabghu Qaghan 109
Yami Qaghan 115
Yanfeng 228, 232, 233, 245, 246, 248
Yan Shigu 106
Yan Suihou 165
Yang Baolin 285
Yanghang, Sabaoshi 267
Yang Jingting 257
Yang Long 183
Yang Ru 216–217
Yang Shicong 142n14; *Record of the Jade Hall* 138
Yang Su 97
Yang Xiu 81
Yang Xuanzhi 160
Yang Zhong 189
Yangzhou 151–152
Yangzhou Art Gallery Records (Wang Jun) 151–152
Yangzhuang black tea 211
Yanqi 51
Yao Runeng 98
Yao Shu 13, 158

Yao Weiyuan 53
Yao Yuanzhi 203
Ye Huanbin 212
Yehu kehan 36
'Yellow Pit' (*huang keng*) 41–42
Yelv Chucai 15
Yicheng (Princess) 113, 115
Yihui (Prince) 254, 255, 257
Yina Tudun Qule (King) 8, 10, 47, 84
Yizhi Nishidu 91
Yu Jieqing 212
Yu Pengyun 209
Yu Shinan 13, 166; Rhapsody on the Lion 160
Yu Xin 183
Yu Yue 148
Yuan dynasty 15, 24, 147, 148, 164, 180
Yuan Mei 152, 273
Yuan Zhen (Minister of Court of State Ceremonial) 114
Yuan Zhen (Poet): "A Merchant's Pleasure" 18
yuenuo fabric 20
Yue Shi: *Universal Geography of the Taiping Era* (*Taiping huanyu ji*) 56, 130n98, 135, 139; *The Unofficial Biography of Yang Taizhen* (*Yang Taizhen wai zhuan*) 144, 145
Yun Yumin: *Overview of Overseas Chinese from Qiongzhou in Singapore* 333n46
Yun Zuyi 214
Yuri Alexandrovich Golovkin 237

Zabulistan 18–19
Zanning 177
Zarathustra 68
Zen Buddhism 41, 191–194
Zeng Guofan 262, 264
Zeng Qiru 152, 275, 281, 282, 284
Zezangzhu 191, 192
Zhai Pantuo 54, 65
Zhai Tang 201
Zhang Guoshun 263
Zhang Hua 24
Zhang Jiuyue 272, 273, 281, 287n13
Zhang Shuo 66; "Songs of Dancing Horses" 14
Zhang Tingyu 161
Zhang Wen'an 281
Zhang Wenqian 169
Zhang Xintai 168, 173n35
Zhang Yichun 76
Zhang Yongcheng 304
Zhang Yu 274
Zhang Zhidong 214, 216, 217, 221, 312, 314, 321
Zhang Zhuo 51
Zhangjiakou 201–209, 217, 220, 221, 265, 266
Zhao Delin 169
Zhao Feiyan 45
Zhao Hongwen 304
Zhao Kuangyin 146
Zhao Yi 294
Zhao Yushi 43
Zhaozong 82, 83
Zheng Guangzu 147
Zheng Ji 153, 166
Zheng Qi 7
Zheng Shiliu 329
Zheng Shiwu 329
Zhenguan period (reign) 34, 50, 51, 54
Zhi Facun 20
zhicheng 45
Zhou dynasty 86, 109
Zhou Fang 145
Zhou Han 191
Zhu Changlin 212
Zhu Pu 82
Zhu Yu 187, 190
Zhu Yuanzhang 148
Zhu Yutian 212
Zhu Zigui 211
Zhuang Chuo 181
Zhuang Dukan 314, 315
Zoroastrian calendar 47, 48
Zoroastrian God and Turks 93–95
Zoroastrian God-inviting ritual 65
Zoroastrianism 25, 40, 41, 85
Zoroastrian Practice 71
Zou Yan 288n43
Zuo's Commentary on Spring and Autumn Annals 255
Zuo Zongtang 210–212